Praise for THE PRINCE OF DARKNESS

"Fascinating . . . An enlightening field guide to the politicians and journalists." —*New York Times Book Review*

"Highly readable account of a remarkable journalistic career . . . A meaty book, full of delicious anecdotes." —*Wall Street Journal*

"Anyone interested in politics, journalism, and the course of public events over the last fifty years who does not buy and read *The Prince of Darkness* is denying himself one of the pleasures that life on this earth very seldom offers." —**Michael Barone,** *Weekly Standard*

"You won't be able to put this book down." —*American Spectator*

"A remarkable account of a remarkable career." —**Charlie Rose**

"Sprawling, candid, informative, nostalgic, and entertaining . . . [Novak] turns his gimlet eye as readily on himself as on those he covers." —*National Review*

"Novak should be celebrated for his brutal honesty." —*Christian Science Monitor*

"An extraordinary inside look at life in Washington over the last fifty years." —**Tim Russert**

"Arguably the best journalist in Washington in the last half century . . . Both a brutally candid and important book, as well as a riveting read." —**Patrick J. Buchanan, syndicated columnist**

"This is history as it happened, without spin or an agenda. . . . While older people with much experience in life may be better able to appreciate this outstanding book, it should be especially valuable to the young in presenting a realistic and three-dimensional picture of the world." —**Thomas Sowell, syndicated columnist**

"[Novak is] a Washington institution who paints himself, convincingly, as churlish, brave, resilient, petty, and indefatigable. I got it as soon as it came out and found it entertaining, human, and frank." —**Peggy Noonan,** *Wall Street Journal*

"A book that anyone interested in politics or journalism ought to read. . . . This is a book to savor." —*Human Events*

"Hard to put down. It's both engaging and engrossing, filled with compelling stories. . . . A book likely to be mined by historians for years to come for its insights into people and events that helped shape American life." —*Columbia Journalism Review*

"Page-turning and very readable . . . So informative is the book, and so rich its story of Washington, D.C., over the past half century, that many readers no doubt will long for more. . . . Far richer than a host of other Washington memoirs." —*Washington Times*

"Bob's book is to be savored, with the only drawback that, with 638 pages, it is just a bit too short." —*Claremont Review of Books*

"One of the rare true journalists of our age, whose new book, *The Prince of Darkness*, is a must-read. . . . Terrific." —**Rush Limbaugh**

"A thick bundle of historical sweep, brutal self-assessment, sharp insights into the reporter's trade and ways of Washington, and defiant candor about who in town he considers to have been good guys and phonies. . . . This book is indispensable. Seldom do so many pages fly by so delightfully." —*The American Conservative*

"Every now and then a book comes along that everyone interested in politics should read. The new memoir by veteran journalist Robert D. Novak, I think, is one of those books." —**Deal W. Hudson, former publisher of *Crisis* magazine**

"Novak's insider perspective, vitriolic pen, and damn-the-torpedoes frankness make it a lively and eye-opening account of big-foot journalism." —*Publishers Weekly*

"Great reporters like Robert Novak can write great memoirs. . . . A fascinating and instructive read . . . As a reporter, columnist, and television pundit, Mr. Novak illuminates the territory with a bright and often garish light. It's not pretty, but it's real." —**Suzanne Fields, *Washington Times***

"The controversial conservative columnist bares all. . . . Novak's memoir offers a rich self-assessment of his work. Sure to be popular reading inside the Beltway, and worthy of an audience far beyond it as well." —*Kirkus Reviews* (**starred review**)

THE
PRINCE OF DARKNESS

50 YEARS REPORTING IN WASHINGTON

Robert D. Novak

THREE RIVERS PRESS
NEW YORK

Published in the United States by Three Rivers Press,
an imprint of the Crown Publishing Group,
a division of Random House, Inc., New York.
www.crownpublishing.com

Three Rivers Press and the Tugboat design are registered
trademarks of Random House, Inc.

Originally published in hardcover in the United States by
Crown Forum, an imprint of the Crown Publishing
Group, a division of Random House, Inc.,
New York, in 2007.

Library of Congress Cataloging-in-Publication Data

Novak, Robert D.
The Prince of darkness : 50 years reporting in Washington /
Robert D. Novak.—1st ed.
    p.   cm.
1. Novak, Robert D. 2. Journalists—United States—
Biography. I. Title.
PN4874.N68A3 2007
070.92—dc22
[B]   2007001345

ISBN 978-1-4000-5200-4

Printed in the United States of America
Design by Robert Olsson

10 9 8 7 6 5 4 3 2 1

First Paperback Edition

To Geraldine Williams Novak,
my intrepid and loving partner.

CONTENTS

THE PRINCE OF DARKNESS

CHAPTER I

The Plame Affair

On sunday morning, July 6, 2003, I drove from my downtown apartment to the studios in far northwest Washington to appear on NBC's *Meet the Press* for the 236th time. As I came to the door of the green room, where guests are parked before going on the air, I encountered a sight that, because of events that followed, is emblazoned on my memory forever.

Seated at the far end of the green room was a man I knew I had seen somewhere. What now made him extraordinary was his conduct. The NBC green room always had been quiet, almost hushed. Roundtable participants like me read the thick file from the Sunday newspapers and the weekly newsmagazines prepared for them by the *Meet the Press* staff. Conversation among guests and their aides was usually limited to small talk and avoided confrontational debate.

But this unknown gentleman was speaking in stentorian tones, as if delivering a speech to his silent companions in the green room. Because most of the seats were taken, I remained standing at the end of the room. Having come in the middle of his harangue, I could barely get the gist of it. He kept saying *"We"* did this" and *"We"* did that." The "we," I soon surmised, consisted of the National Security Council staff in the departed Clinton administration. He was making clear that "we" handled affairs better than "they"—the Bush NSC—did now. In view of what followed, I hope I can be excused for the vulgarism that crossed my mind: "What an asshole!"

After a few minutes of this, I was summoned to makeup. I then learned the identity of the green room orator. He was Joseph C. Wilson IV, a retired Foreign Service officer who had been chargé d'affaires in Baghdad in 1990 for the run-up to the Gulf War. His face was vaguely familiar to me because I had lately seen him being interviewed on television without paying close attention to exactly what he was saying.

But he had just made news, which is why the *Meet* producers had called the night before to book him as the lead guest, bumping two senators. Wilson had written an op-ed that morning in the *New York Times.* Sitting in the makeup room, I read it.

His big news went back to sixteen words in President George W. Bush's State of the Union address on January 28, 2003, which were included as part of the justification for military intervention in Iraq that would come six weeks later: "The British government has learned that Saddam Hussein recently sought significant quantities of uranium in Africa."

On June 12 the veteran *Washington Post* investigative reporter Walter Pincus reported that an unnamed retired diplomat a year earlier had returned from a CIA-sponsored fact-finding trip to Africa with a negative report on the alleged uranium shopping by Iraq. The next day, June 13, Nicholas Kristof, a *New York Times* columnist with a decided anti-Bush slant, said an unnamed former ambassador had come back from Niger with intelligence that nearly a year earlier had contradicted Bush's sixteen words. Wilson next went public by offering the *New York Times* what he said would be the full story in his op-ed piece.

A reader of the famous op-ed years later would find no trace of the flamboyant Joe Wilson the world soon came to know—throwing around the word "liar" and making unsupported accusations. Instead, Wilson used the language of diplomacy, carefully avoiding direct indictment of the president. He gave no hint that he was a fierce opponent of Bush, anxious to join the next Democratic administration.

Wilson affected to write more in sadness than in anger: "I have little choice but to conclude that some of the intelligence related to Iraq's nuclear weapons program was twisted to exaggerate the Iraqi threat." He related that the CIA had asked him to go to Niger to investigate Iraq's alleged quest for yellow cake uranium used in nuclear weapons development. He gave this memorable exposition of how he functioned:

> I spent the next eight days drinking sweet mint tea and meeting with dozens of people: current government officials, former government officials, people associated with the country's uranium business. It did not take long to conclude that it was highly doubtful that any such transaction had ever taken place.

He disclosed he had never filed a written report. He added there "should be at least four documents" in government files based on his oral briefing, none of which he had ever seen. He was still the careful diplomat in the op-ed's two-paragraph conclusion:

I was convinced before the war that the threat of weapons of mass destruction in the hands of Saddam Hussein required a vigorous and sustained international response to disarm him. Iraq possessed and had used chemical weapons; it had an active biological weapons program and quite possibly a nuclear research program—all of which were in violation of United Nations resolutions. Having encountered Mr. Hussein and his thugs in the run-up to the Persian Gulf War of 1991, I was only too aware of the dangers he posed.

But were these dangers the same ones the Administration told us about? We have to find out. America's foreign policy depends on the sanctity of its information. For this reason, questioning the selective use of intelligence to justify the war in Iraq is neither idle sniping nor "revisionist history," as Mr. Bush has suggested. The act of war is the last option of a democracy, taken when there is a grave threat to our national security. More than 200 American soldiers have lost their lives in Iraq already. We have a duty to ensure that their sacrifice came for the right reasons.

By the time I had finished my makeup, hastily read the op-ed, and entered the green room, Wilson had left to be interviewed by NBC's Andrea Mitchell (subbing for Tim Russert) in the opening *Meet the Press* segment. We did not meet that day.

WHEN I WENT to my office the next day, Monday, July 7, Joe Wilson was not in the forefront of my mind. Frances Fragos Townsend was. She had just been named deputy national security adviser at the White House though her background was in liberal Democratic politics, including Attorney General Janet Reno's inner circle during the Clinton administration. Her appointment was a political mystery of the kind I had been exploring for forty years in my column. While I was placing calls to wrap up the story on Monday, I asked the same sources—including administration officials—what they thought about the dispute concerning uranium in Africa. Everybody seemed to concede a mistake had been made in using the sixteen words in the State of the Union, a view that they said apparently was shared by the president. None of my sources attacked Joe Wilson. Nobody had much to say about him at all.

I wrote the Townsend column Tuesday morning because I had a busy schedule the rest of the day, including a 3 p.m. appointment with Richard Armitage, deputy secretary of state. I had no idea what a big event it would turn out to be.

Armitage was then fifty-eight years old and had spent much of his life in public service following graduation from the U.S. Naval Academy. During the Reagan administration, he held the important post of assistant secretary of defense for international security affairs.

When George W. Bush's administration began in 2001, the new secretary of state, Armitage's close friend Colin Powell, had sought to place Armitage at the Defense Department as deputy secretary. But he was blocked by the new secretary of defense, Donald Rumsfeld, who felt one department under General Powell's control was enough. Instead, Armitage became Powell's deputy at State, where the two officials were described to me as joined at the hip—two men operating as one.

I asked to see Armitage early in their administration and repeated my request after the terrorist attack of September 11, 2001. Powell and Armitage were widely perceived as being out of step with the rest of the administration about military intervention in Iraq. I had ready access to Powell, in person and over the telephone, but he was circumspect in what he said to me, while Armitage had a reputation for being less guarded in conversations with journalists. Armitage rebuffed me, not with the customary evasion of claiming an overly full schedule but by his secretary making clear that he simply did not want to see me. I assumed that Armitage bracketed me, a notoriously conservative columnist, with the Iraqi war hawks who were unsympathetic toward his views. If so, he had somehow missed my written and spoken criticism of the Iraqi intervention.

Then, in the last week of June 2003, Armitage's office called to agree unexpectedly to my request and set up the appointment for July 8. No reason was given then or subsequently for this change of heart. However, he apparently was following the recommendation of his political adviser, Washington lobbyist Ken Duberstein, a longtime source of mine. It is important to note that Armitage reached out to me *before* Joe Wilson went public on the *New York Times* op-ed page and on *Meet the Press.*

I was ushered into Armitage's big State Department inner office promptly at 3 p.m. Since we had no personal relationship and never before had had a conversation, I was surprised that no press aide sat in on our meeting. I carried no tape recorder for the session, and, as frequently was my practice, did not take notes. Armitage seemed relaxed and our hour together was more conversation than interview—precisely the kind of session I preferred. Nuggets of news are more likely to get dropped in an informal setting.

Neither of us set ground rules for my visit. I assumed, however, that what Armitage said would not be attributed to him but would not be off the record. That is, I could write about information he gave me but would not identify him by name. How could I be so precise about the ground rules if we never discussed them? During a long career, I had come to appreciate that sort of thing in countless interviews without putting it into so many words. I viewed what Armitage told me to be just as privileged as if he had made me swear a blood oath.

Armitage was giving me high-level insider gossip, unusual in a first meeting. About halfway through our session, I brought up Bush's sixteen words. What Armitage told me generally confirmed what I had learned from sources the previous day while I was reporting for the Fran Townsend column. At that point, I had pretty well decided to write a column for the next Monday's papers about the Niger uranium issue, which Wilson had turned into a big story.

I then asked Armitage a question that had been puzzling me but, for the sake of my future peace of mind, would better have been left unasked. Why would the CIA send Joseph Wilson, not an expert in nuclear proliferation and with no intelligence experience, on the mission to Niger? "Well," Armitage replied, "you know his wife works at CIA, and she suggested that he be sent to Niger." "His wife works at CIA?" I asked. "Yeah, in counterproliferation."

He mentioned her first name, Valerie. Armitage smiled and said: "That's real Evans and Novak, isn't it?" I believe he meant that was the kind of inside information that my late partner, Rowland Evans, and I had featured in our column for so long. I interpreted that as meaning Armitage expected to see the item published in my column.

The exchange about Wilson's wife lasted no more than sixty seconds. Armitage offered no interpretation of Wilson's conduct and said nothing negative about him or his wife. I am sure it was not a planned leak but came out as an offhand observation.

I never spoke to Armitage again about Wilson. But he acknowledged to me nearly three months later through Duberstein that he was indeed the primary source for my information about Wilson's wife. Shortly thereafter, he secretly revealed his role to federal authorities investigating the leak of Mrs. Wilson's name but did not inform White House officials, apparently including the president.

After Patrick Fitzgerald, the U.S. attorney in Chicago named as a special prosecutor in the case, indicated to me he knew Armitage was my source, I cooperated fully with him. At the special prosecutor's request and on my lawyers' advice, I kept silent about this—a silence that subjected me to much abuse. I was urged by several friends, including some journalists, to give up my source's name. But I felt bound by the journalist's code to protect his identity.

Later that Tuesday while I was walking up 19th Street on the way back to my office from the State Department, I engaged in a bizarre episode that later made me wonder whether I had lost my good sense at age seventy-two. A nondescript little man without tie or jacket approached and began walking alongside me. He said he had seen me on *Meet the Press* Sunday and wanted to ask me if I did not think Bush was in big trouble for taking the country to war on the basis of false information. He struck me as one of the liberal news junkies who infest Washington. I should have asked him to leave me alone. Instead, I let him walk with me and engaged him in conversation for a couple of minutes.

In answer to his question about the sixteen words, I suggested that the administration had not handled this issue well but that too much was being made of it. The man then goaded me with the criticism that I was soft on Bush, and argued that Ambassador Wilson "really had nailed the president on *Meet the Press*." He then asked what I thought of Wilson. "I think he's an asshole," I said, using the same inelegant description that had crossed my mind when I saw him lecturing in the NBC green room two days earlier. The man responded that Wilson had gone to Africa on a CIA mission and discovered intelligence that the president ignored. I blurted out the information I had just learned, telling him Wilson was no intelligence expert but had been sent on the mission to Niger by his wife, who worked on counterproliferation at the CIA.

I then broke away from the man and went on my way—as I should have done two minutes earlier. I knew, of course, that I had done something stupid by revealing the information about Wilson's wife to a perfect stranger. I wondered whether it was old age, the fatigue of a busy day, or walking around in Washington's midsummer heat in a heavy three-piece pinstripe suit (as I always did). But, I rationalized, it really did not make much difference. I was planning to include the nugget about Mrs. Wilson in my column for the following Monday. Then, everybody would know about it. Anyway, I did not consider it earth-shattering news.

I wanted to question Karl Rove about the story. I had known Rove since he was a young Republican political consultant in Austin, Texas, almost twenty years before. Now he was one of the most powerful men in the world. He was President Bush's political adviser and architect of all his campaigns dating back to his run for governor of Texas in 1994. But he was much more. He was the effective leader of the Republican Party, and involved in all manner of policy throughout the U.S. government.

Karl and I had grown close since he began plotting Bush's path to the presidency as early as 1995. In four decades of talking to presidential aides, I never had enjoyed such a good source inside the White House. Rove obviously thought I was useful for his purposes, too. Such symbiotic relationships, built on self-interest, are the rule in high-level Washington journalism, though journalists seldom are as candid about them as I will be throughout this book.

There were limits to our relationship. While I don't believe Rove ever lied to me, he did not of course tell me everything. Nor did he ever give me any information that would hurt the president. He knew I was in sympathy with Bush's conservative principles, and strongly supportive of his tax cuts. He also knew I opposed the president on his education and prescription drug programs and was deeply concerned about his military intervention in Iraq.

Rove returned my call late that Tuesday afternoon. I had several items to bring up, most of which I still consider confidential. Wilson's wife came up at the end of our conversation. I relate this part of the talk because Rove himself broke the confidence, through his attorney.

I mentioned that I had heard that Wilson's wife worked at the CIA in the counterproliferation section and that she had suggested Wilson be sent to Niger. I distinctly remember Rove's reply: "Oh, you know that, too." Rove and I also discussed other aspects of Wilson's mission, but since he never has disclosed them publicly, neither have I.

At seven o'clock the next morning, I got a telephone call from Sam Feist, the young executive producer of CNN's *Crossfire,* where I was a regular co-host. Sam had never called me that early. He told me he had an urgent message. Eason Jordan, CNN's chief news executive, had called Sam at 6 a.m. He had asked Sam to call me at home immediately, to inform me that Joe Wilson desperately wanted to get in touch with me. "What's going on?" Feist asked me. "You'll find out in due course," I replied.

I had been on CNN since it began in the summer of 1980. But I was a well-paid independent contractor for the network, never a CNN employee. No CNN executive had ever attempted to supervise my non-CNN journalistic activity.

I telephoned Wilson when I got to my office, but he was not in. I next called Bill Harlow, chief of public information at the CIA. I had worked with Harlow periodically over the last year and a half, amiably but not intimately. He was sophisticated and clever, an accomplished novelist and an old hand at government press relations. I am sure he gave me only what his boss—George Tenet, director of Central Intelligence—wanted to give me.

When I got Harlow on the phone Wednesday, I asked him to confirm that Mrs. Wilson worked for the CIA and that she had suggested the mission to Niger for her husband. Harlow did not react immediately to my question but said he would get back to me. I was sure he was checking with higher authority, probably Tenet himself.

Wilson and I did not make telephone contact until the following morning, when I called him again. It was the first conversation ever between us, and he started it by revealing something that shocked me. The little man who had stopped me on the street Tuesday afternoon happened to be a friend of Wilson's. Immediately after my imprudent comments, Wilson told me, his friend walked over to the office the former ambassador kept. The man then filled in Wilson on what I had said. Wilson was clearly reading from notes in relating my comments to the man. It was a pretty accurate account of my profane description of Wilson and my disclosure of his wife's employment, but it omitted his friend's goading.

After telling me he knew about Tuesday's encounter on the street, Wilson apologized profusely in behalf of his friend. He told me that it was very poor behavior for a stranger to accost a well-known person to draw him into a debate and said that he had admonished his friend. Nevertheless, Wilson continued, he could not imagine what I was thinking when I blurted out the information about his wife to a perfect stranger. I said I agreed with him, and I apologized for my behavior. (His 2004 memoir *The Politics of Truth* reports my apology but not his.)

I then told Wilson I had heard about his wife's CIA employment, and asked if he would confirm that she worked there. My distinct impression is that he reacted without anger. "I will not answer any question about my wife," Wilson said, adding: "The story was never me. It was always the statement in his [Bush's] speech." He told me that once the White House admitted error in the sixteen words on July 6, he had declined all requests for television and radio interviews and would remain silent. (Wilson omits that statement from his memoir's account of the conversation. The omission was prudent, considering that he would be omnipresent on television and radio, talking about his wife, in the coming years.)

Wilson next read to me this 1990 newspaper excerpt from Baghdad:

> The chief American diplomat, Joe Wilson, shepherds his flock of some
> 800 known Americans like a village priest. At 4:30 Sunday morning,
> he was helping 55 wives and children of U.S. diplomats from Kuwait

load themselves and their few remaining possessions on transport for the long haul to Jordan. He shows the stuff of heroism.

I suspected Wilson had something up his sleeve. He informed me that this excerpt was taken from an Evans & Novak column, written by my partner (and forgotten by me). Wilson told me sarcastically that I might well check my own column's files before writing about him. He added that the description of him by Evans & Novak was treasured by his mother, yet another comment omitted from his memoir.

Finally, Wilson offered to send me everything he had written in the last year so that I could see he was not antiwar ("just anti-dumb war," he recalled in his memoir, though I don't remember his using those words). I did not take him up on his offer, but my staff did a search of all his writings. Oddly, he had not become really critical of Bush publicly until the day following his *Meet the Press* appearance, only *after* the White House admitted its mistake in Bush's sixteen words. On that Monday, he suggested for the first time that the president had "misrepresented" facts and "lied."

I closed the conversation by apologizing again for my encounter with his friend, and my recollection is that he apologized again for his friend's behavior. It had not been exactly a convivial conversation, but it had been civil—and hardly a foretaste of the unpleasantness to come.

What did Joe Wilson have in mind when he called me? Was he trying to pressure me into not revealing his wife's employment to my friends, much less total strangers on the street? He certainly did not ask me to refrain from putting this information in my column, or even express the worry that I might do so.

The CIA's Bill Harlow telephoned me that afternoon. By now he obviously had been briefed on Wilson's mission to Niger, and we had a relatively long conversation about it. In my previous contacts with Harlow, his comments implicitly had been not for attribution (a ground rule I had followed with official CIA spokesmen since the 1960s). Because Harlow later identified himself to the news media as my official CIA source on Mrs. Wilson's CIA employment, I am relieved of keeping it confidential.

Harlow confirmed that Wilson's wife was indeed employed in the CIA's Counterproliferation Division. That gave me a third source. But he contradicted one aspect of Armitage's version of the story that Rove had seemed to confirm. Harlow denied that she had inspired Wilson's selection for the African mission but said she had been delegated by her colleagues to contact her husband.

Harlow next asked me to keep Mrs. Wilson's CIA connection out of my column. He said she probably never would be given another foreign assignment but added that revelation of her name might cause unspecified "difficulties" if she traveled abroad (not specifying traveling abroad on a government mission as he later claimed). He did not press the point and did not warn me that Mrs. Wilson's or anybody else's safety would be endangered if I used her name. I had had enough experience with CIA jargon to infer from what Harlow told me that Mrs. Wilson at one time had been engaged in covert activities abroad but was not now and never would be again. (I learned much later that Mrs. Wilson had been "outed" years earlier by the traitor and Soviet agent Aldrich Ames, which had ended her career as a covert agent long before I wrote about her.)

What troubled me on Thursday afternoon was not the prospect of revealing Mrs. Wilson's CIA identity but the difference between Armitage and Harlow on whether she had suggested her husband's mission or had just been a go-between. Much later I would learn from a public Senate Intelligence Committee report of a CIA memo showing that Mrs. Wilson had indeed suggested the assignment for her husband. I don't believe Bill Harlow was lying to me. I think the officials who briefed him had lied to him. George W. Bush had lots of enemies in the bowels of the Agency.

I NORMALLY WROTE and e-mailed to Creators Syndicate in Los Angeles on Friday my column for Monday's newspapers. On July 11, 2003, I got into my office at seven thirty a.m., and even though my afternoon schedule was filled from twelve fifteen on, I still had four and one half hours (more than twice as much time as I usually needed) to write a 690-word column that was a few notches above routine. I never dreamed that it would become the most personally fateful column I ever would write.

On Friday morning, I checked the current edition of *Who's Who in America*. Joseph Wilson was listed, and his wife was identified as Valerie Plame. I used that name in the column, and that gave the ensuing controversy a label. Valerie Plame somehow sounded more exotic than Valerie Wilson, and the story became the "Plame Affair." I was later told that in her covert days in Europe, she had used the name Valerie Plame. If that is so, Wilson's putting that name in *Who's Who* was either an act of recklessness or a sign that his wife was not now engaged in covert operations. I am sure the latter was the case.

As I sat down at my office computer that Friday morning, Valerie Plame Wilson was not my major concern. The real story for me then was the background of Joe Wilson's mission that had not yet been revealed. By doing my regular style of reporting, I thought I could put the situation in perspective. I titled my column "Mission to Niger" and began it:

The CIA's decision to send retired diplomat Joseph C. Wilson to Africa in February 2002 to investigate possible Iraqi purchases of uranium was made routinely at a low level without Director George Tenet's knowledge. Remarkably, this produced a political firestorm that has not yet subsided.

Wilson's report that an Iraqi purchase of uranium yellowcake from Niger was highly unlikely was regarded by the CIA as less than definitive, and it is doubtful Tenet ever saw it. Certainly, President Bush did not prior to his 2003 State of the Union address, when he attributed reports of attempted purchases to the British government. That the British relied on forged documents made Wilson's mission, nearly a year earlier, the basis of furious Democratic accusations of burying intelligence though the report was forgotten by the time the President spoke.

Reluctance at the White House to admit a mistake has led Democrats ever closer to saying the President lied the country into war. Even after a belated admission of error last Monday, finger-pointing between Bush Administration agencies continued. Messages between Washington and the Presidential entourage traveling in Africa hashed over the mission to Niger.

Wilson's mission was created after an early 2002 report by the Italian intelligence service about attempted uranium purchases from Niger, derived from forged documents prepared by what the CIA calls a "con man." This misinformation peddled by Italian journalists, spread through the U.S. government. The White House, State Department and Pentagon, not just Vice President Dick Cheney, asked the CIA to look into it.

With Wilson assigned the mission to Niger, I provided a little background about him at this point in the column. I quoted from the favorable 1990 report from Baghdad by Rowland Evans that Wilson had cited to me. I noted that President George H. W. Bush had named Wilson as ambassador to Gabon in 1991 and that President Bill Clinton in 1993 had put him in charge of African affairs at the National Security Council.

Then came the column's fateful sixth paragraph:

Wilson never worked for the CIA, but his wife, Valerie Plame, is an Agency operative on weapons of mass destruction. Two senior Administration officials told me Wilson's wife suggested sending him to Niger to investigate the Italian report. The CIA says its counter-proliferation officials selected Wilson and asked his wife to contact him.

I next described Wilson's oral report on his mission as saying an Iraqi uranium purchase was "highly unlikely," though I said he "mentioned in passing that a 1988 Iraqi delegation tried to establish commercial relations" with Niger. I quoted CIA officials as not regarding "Wilson's intelligence as definitive, being based primarily on what the Niger officials told him and probably would have claimed under any circumstances."

Wilson obviously wanted me to take into consideration his overall outlook on Iraq. I think I did so:

During the run-up to the invasion of Iraq, Wilson had taken a measured public position—viewing weapons of mass destruction as a danger but considering military action as a last resort. He has seemed much more critical of the Administration since revealing his role in Niger. In the Washington Post July 6, he talked about the Bush team "misrepresenting the facts," asking: "What else are they lying about?"

In the last paragraph, I quoted Wilson's remark to me that "the story" was not about him, and then I concluded the column this way:

The story, actually, is whether the Administration deliberately ignored Wilson's advice, and that requires scrutinizing the CIA summary of what their envoy reported. The Agency never before has declassified that kind of information, but the White House would like it to do just that now—in its and in the public's interest.

I defy anyone to read my column and agree with the claims by Wilson and his wife that I had defamed and ridiculed him and his wife or the subsequent assertion of their supporters that I was a slavish voice of the Bush administration.

IN THE YEARS since, I have been asked two questions repeatedly:

The first is: "Why did you reveal Valerie Plame Wilson's CIA employment?" The answer is simple. One puzzle of Joe Wilson's mission is why the CIA would choose for an African fact-finding mission a former Clinton White House aide with no track record in intelligence and with no experience in Niger since being posted there as a very junior Foreign Service officer in 1976–78. The answer that Wilson was suggested by his wife, a CIA employee, shows how peculiar events at a high governmental level in Washington can be. I reported this fact in my column without comment.

But I thought it showed at the least incompetence within the CIA and at the most a poisonous hostility there to George W. Bush.

The second question: "If you had it to do over, would you still reveal her CIA employment?" The answer depends on whether I judge the case on its merits or from my personal interest.

Judging it on the merits, I would still write the story. There never was any question about its news value or its accuracy. I broke no law and endangered no intelligence operation. Mrs. Wilson was not a covert operative in 2003 but a desk-bound CIA analyst at Langley, Virginia. Her secret CIA identity had been outed long ago, and what I wrote was no danger to her or to anybody else. If Bill Harlow had told me that disclosure of Valerie Wilson's employment would endanger her or anyone, I would not have mentioned her in the column. He did not tell me that because there was no such danger. If George Tenet had personally intervened to ask me not to identify her, I would have agreed. He did not do so because, I believe, he did not consider this a serious matter until Bush's enemies in the Agency made it a cause célèbre.

Judging by personal interests, I probably should have ignored what Armitage told me about Mrs. Wilson. I am amused by people who described me as delighted by being in the spotlight, by being a newsmaker instead of a news chronicler. Those three little sentences resulted in a series of negative consequences for me. They eventually undermined my twenty-five-year relationship with CNN and kept me off *Meet the Press* for over two years. I had to pay substantial legal fees. I came under constant abuse from journalistic ethics critics, from some colleagues, and especially from bloggers. I have written many, many more important columns, but the one on the CIA leak case will forever be part of my public identity.

As a columnist for more than forty years, I often had to make quick decisions whether to report secret information with the advice only (for most of that time) of my partner Rowland Evans.

It is not a good idea for me to second-guess what I have decided. It is possible I might well have gone ahead with divulging the fact about Valerie Wilson even if I knew of the negative personal consequences that would follow. Those consequences were all material ones. They mean less to me as I near the end of my career and my life. I have not really suffered personally from the difficulties of 2003 and 2004 because they are less important than the love of my wife, my children, and my grandchildren. My conversion to the Catholic faith has put in perspective any petty personal difficulties. There is not really that much that can be done to me at this stage of my life. As the long-hidden details of the "Plame Affair" were disclosed, I felt a sense of vindication.

I am proud of my journalistic philosophy—to tell the world things people do not want me to reveal, to advocate limited government, economic freedom, and a strong, prudent America—and to have fun doing it. For the sober-sided younger generations of journalists, having fun may seem unserious. But it was the kind of journalism that prevailed when I started. I had a terrific time fulfilling all my youthful dreams and at the same time making life miserable for hypocritical, posturing politicians and, I hope, performing a service for my country.

CHAPTER 2

Political Beginnings

ON A WARM Sunday morning, May 12, 1957, I packed most of my worldly belongings in my yellow '56 Ford convertible and set off, top down, from Indianapolis, to Washington, D.C. At no time in my life, before or after, have I felt so exhilarated. I was twenty-six, with a little more than two-and-one-half-years as a newsman for the Associated Press under my belt. The AP had just transferred me to the nation's capital, an assignment that in those days went only to people with a lot more experience. That I had reached it early was attributable to the combination of hard work and very good fortune.

I arrived Sunday evening with no living arrangements. I tried to book a room down Pennsylvania Avenue from the White House at the then run-down Willard, where Abraham Lincoln and Ulysses S. Grant had once stayed. The desk clerk gave me an "Are you kidding?" stare and said they were filled up. I walked to the even shabbier Hotel Washington but it too was filled. So I headed out of town, down Route 50 into Virginia, seeking the first motel without a "no vacancy" sign.

Lack of housing arrangements matched my absence of an ideological agenda. I was a registered Republican, moderate on domestic policy and hard-line on the cold war. In college I had preferred Dwight D. Eisenhower over Robert A. Taft for the 1952 Republican nomination but had been disappointed by his presidency. I had no crusade to launch. I wanted to do what I had tried to do in two state capitals: to break stories nobody else had and explain what was really happening behind the scenes.

AS A SMALL boy, I never heard a good word about FDR over the dinner table. But on October 14, 1936, when I was five, President Roosevelt came to my hometown of Joliet, Illinois. My mother took me to see him. "I thought we hated Roosevelt," I protested. "He's *the president*," my mother replied.

Reading a transcript of his remarks nearly seventy years later reminded me of the millions of words of claptrap that I have heard and written about over the years. Speaking from a train car in an elevated rail station, the president told the assembled Jolietans that "people are living better than they were four years ago." You could have fooled them. There were no jobs to be had. The city's three steel mills closed in 1929, never to reopen. The city's unemployment rate was frozen above 25 percent, the same percentage of my classmates whose parents were on "relief." I spent my childhood playing in half-built homes and excavations abandoned at the onset of the Depression. When I was growing up, my father never earned more than fifty dollars a week as superintendent of a gas production plant, but that went a long way in Depression-era Joliet. The pot roast special at the Crescent City restaurant downtown cost thirty-five cents, beverage and dessert included. My mother hired a uniformed maid at seventy-five cents a day, and my father drove a company car.

That same year, 1936, my father noticed me looking at a picture in the *Chicago Tribune*. It showed Alf Landon, the Republican governor of Kansas, wearing a sunflower—his state's official flower and the symbol of his presidential campaign. "Bobby," my father told me, "that's the next president of the United States." Landon would carry only Maine and Vermont.

My father—Maurice Pall Novak—was anti–New Deal. He thought FDR was meddling with the system that had permitted him, the son of poor immigrants, to achieve middle-class respectability as a low-level corporate executive and a respected officer of local civic organizations. This made him a rare Republican Novak.

MY IMMIGRANT GRANDFATHER was a passionate Democrat, displaying a picture of FDR in the front window of his second-floor walk-up apartment overlooking Sacramento Boulevard on Chicago's West Side. Ben Novak was a secular Jew (none of his four sons were bar mitzvahed), a heavy drinker (he began every day with a schnapps at breakfast), and an inflexible authoritarian. (That may explain why my father was a Republican, at least a nominally observant Jew whose only son was a bar mitzvah boy, a light drinker, and a relatively permissive father and husband.)

Ben Novak was proud of his quick fists (he would die of a heart attack after getting in a fight in a West Side tavern in 1946) and that he had been a soldier in the Imperial Russian army. Only long after his death did I realize that the czar's conscripts were in for twenty-four years—a virtual life sentence. So, Ben must have deserted, fleeing to England with his bride.

In 1902, they moved on to New York City, where immigration officials arbitrarily changed the family name from Novikov to Novik. That year, twin boys—my father and his brother Julius—were born. The John Deere Company was recruiting workers for its plow production line in Moline, Illinois, and Ben's family was soon on a westbound train. (The family name somehow became Novak, common among factory workers in Illinois.) After ten years, Ben borrowed a hundred dollars to purchase a little store in the West Side slums of Chicago where he eked out a living selling goods damaged by flood, fire, or other catastrophe. My father had exchanged growing up poor in a small town for poor in the inner city.

Ben Novak boasted that he spoke five languages—English most poorly. But he ordained English would be the only language spoken in their home. His twin boys, only sixteen when they graduated from Medill High in Chicago, enrolled in the University of Illinois, more than a hundred miles to the south in farm country.

With hardly a penny in their pockets, the twins had to work their way through college (my father was a waiter in a sorority for four years). They were wonderful students. Julius left after two years for medical school in Chicago (on his way to becoming one of the nation's leading tuberculosis specialists). My father graduated with honors in chemical engineering. Their two younger brothers followed them to Champaign-Urbana, Sidney becoming a legendary high school basketball coach in Chicago and Leonard a businessman (following World War II combat in Africa and Italy). The University of Illinois unlocked the door to the middle class for them.

After graduation, my father became an expert in gas production for Western United Gas & Electric Company and was assigned to the Lockport plant outside Joliet. He soon became assistant superintendent and later superintendent, still so young that the older workers—many of them Eastern European immigrants—could not quite call him "Mr. Novak" and settled on "Mr. Maurice."

Visiting a Joliet radio station one night, my father met and not long thereafter married a forceful and attractive young woman—Jane Sanders—who was playing the piano to fill airtime in those primitive days of broadcasting. Her family owned the station but soon gave it up as a waste of time and money. Their real business was a tire and appliance store.

Jane's father was Jacob Sander, a Lithuanian Jew who had come to America two decades before Ben Novak. Jacob went to Philadelphia and became a peddler, carrying his pack of wares on his back through Pennsylvania and did well enough to buy himself a horse. He followed relatives to Chicago and finally went to Joliet, where he opened a grocery store called Sander's. The apostrophe somehow got lost, and the family name became Sanders.

The Sanderses were Republicans. But like many Republican Jews, they abandoned the GOP and turned to FDR in protest over Republican failure to cope with the Depression. Maurice Novak and his loyal wife were the only anti–New Dealers on either side of my family. In 1940, my father became a small cog in the national network of public utility executives supporting Wall Street utility mogul Wendell Willkie for president.

And he was a news junkie. We subscribed daily to the *Chicago Tribune* and the *Joliet Herald-News* and on Sunday to the *Chicago Sun,* when it began publication in 1941. My father listened regularly to radio commentators H. V. Kaltenborn and Gabriel Heatter and sometimes Raymond Gram Swing. He subscribed to *BusinessWeek;* when the European war began in September 1939, we added *Newsweek.*

Before my ninth birthday the next year, I had become addicted to politics. Seated on the living-room floor and listening to the 1940 Republican convention in Philadelphia, I kept track of the delegate count. Willkie started in sixth place, took the lead on the fourth ballot, and was nominated on the sixth, at one o'clock in the morning on June 28, midnight Joliet time. It was the first time my parents had let me stay up that late.

On November 5, Willkie won the support of twenty-two million Americans, but FDR had twenty-seven million. In the Electoral College, it was Roosevelt, 449 to 82—just as the New York Yankees had earned my perpetual hatred two years earlier by annihilating our beloved Cubs in the World Series, four games to none. In politics as in sports, I learned, disappointment is routine.

WHEN I ENTERED the University of Illinois in September 1948, I was required to take the English proficiency examination that included writing an impromptu essay. I wrote how Governor Thomas E. Dewey of New York would be elected president. Despite my foggy crystal ball, the faculty board gave me three hours of credit for passing freshman English without taking the course.

In 1952, Dwight D. Eisenhower was a war hero, the most popular man in America—and the University of Illinois was no academic isle of resistance. Even my overwhelmingly Democratic Jewish fraternity, Alpha Epsilon Pi, included several Ike supporters. It was hard to find any backers on campus of Senator Robert A. Taft, Eisenhower's conservative opponent for the nomination. In the spring of 1952, Taft spoke at midday outside the venerable Lincoln Hall, in the heart of the Illinois campus. He was interrupted by sarcastic-sounding laughter from the students. "Turn around, Senator!" somebody shouted. Taft turned and observed a "WE LIKE IKE!" poster unfurled from the top story of Lincoln Hall. Taft turned to his grinning audience, without the trace of a smile, paused for a moment, and then plowed back into his prepared speech. Taft died of cancer a year later, but his pain that day in front of Lincoln Hall was not physical.

Bob Taft had spent his entire life in Republican politics, fighting for limited government, lower taxes, and the Grand Old Party. Tom Dewey had lost in 1948 when he turned his back on the many accomplishments of the Taft-led Republican 80th Congress. Now, in 1952, Taft's golden moment was about to be taken away by a victorious general who knew nothing of what Republicans should stand for and probably had never voted.

Whenever I pass the carillon erected in Taft's memory on Capitol Hill—a monument today that probably puzzles both Washingtonians and tourists— I am reminded that on that spring day in 1952, I was on the wrong side.

I CAST MY first vote for president, for Dwight D. Eisenhower, by absentee ballot in November 1952 as a second lieutenant on active duty with the U.S. Army at Fort Devens, Massachusetts. When I enrolled in the University of Illinois in 1948, two years of "Military Science" were still mandated at all land-grant colleges. To my surprise, I enjoyed the military and joined the Pershing Rifles drill team. I signed up for the optional third and fourth years of Reserve Officers Training Corps, completion of which would give me a reserve officer's commission in Army Security (the communications intelligence branch) and the likelihood of being called up for active duty if war came.

It came. On June 25, 1950, North Korean Communist troops invaded South Korea, and President Truman immediately intervened with ill-equipped, unprepared U.S. forces. After finishing college in 1952, I was sent to Fort Devens as a second lieutenant in the Army Security Agency (ASA). I did not go to Korea. On July 27, 1953, six months into the Eisenhower administration, negotiators at Panmunjom signed a truce with a demarcation line between North and South Korea, about where the opposing American and Chinese armies had dug in two years earlier. The war was over, and the U.S. Army had no real use any longer for most of its young reserve officers. The army being the army, however, my colleagues and I spent another year in uniform—a year in which I did some serious reading (and drinking as well).

The greatest spur to my thinking was a book I read when I still stood to go to war in Korea. It was Whittaker Chambers's *Witness,* the 1952 autobiography of a disenchanted Communist, culminating in his bearing witness against Alger Hiss as a Soviet agent. In a preface for a 1987 reissue, I wrote that reading *Witness:*

> . . . changed my worldview, my philosophical perceptions, and, without exaggeration, my life. I am not alone. From time to time in after-dinner conversation with politicians on the campaign circuit over the years, I find a common bond with other people—some a generation younger—who have been alarmed, entranced, and always inspired by *Witness.*

It came at a time for me when Harry Truman's mismanagement of Korea had led me to wonder whether the cold war was just a squandering of blood and treasure. *Witness* showed that the struggle against international communism was a defense of our values, transcending the foolishness and weakness of Western political leaders.

Beyond the struggle with communism, *Witness* led me to think about my spiritual void. I had grown up in a Jewish household that was only nominally observant. We attended services during the High Holy Days, but not otherwise. My religious education was cursory, and my interest in Judaism waned after my bar mitzvah. By the time I went to college, I considered myself an agnostic. It was an illusion. As an army officer who might be sent into combat, I found myself praying for the first time in years—not praying to keep from going to war, but praying that I would perform bravely and that I would survive.

That was my spiritual state when I read Chambers's description of communism posing "the most revolutionary question in history: God or man? If man's mind is the decisive force in the world, what need is there for God?" Calling the twentieth century the first in which man "has deliberately rejected God," Chambers described an "irrepressible" conflict between and within nations, with the combatants "those who reject and those who worship God."

What side had I chosen? I did not want to be on the side of those who reject God, but I knew I did not really worship God.

CHAPTER 3

Cub Reporter

Being a journalist has been my only life's ambition. Early on I wanted to be a sportswriter.

My father and most of my uncles, on both sides of the family, were excellent athletes. I was not, even though I attempted—and failed at—every sport imaginable. In my sophomore year at Joliet Township High School, I became a manager on the varsity track team and Don Kienlen, the track coach, had me submit the meet results to the *Spectator,* a local weekly. I did more than that. I submitted newspaper-style accounts. The *Spectator* was a shopper's paper that didn't even have a sports section, but it welcomed my stories. At age fifteen I was a regularly published writer (of overblown prose).

In my junior year, I became sports editor of the student weekly *J-Hi Journal,* and now was submitting my track reports to the daily *Joliet Herald-News.* In my senior year, I became the newspaper's first Joliet Township all-sports stringer, at ten cents a column inch. My boss at the *Herald-News* was its newly hired sports editor, Robert Bigelow Laraway, the first of many professional mentors I would have the luck to learn from. Bob Laraway was a brilliant underachiever. He had writing skills, imagination, and charisma—everything except a dedication to work and an ability to stay away from strong drink. He was only twenty-five but already had been a sportswriter on the prestigious *Champaign News-Gazette.* That made him a commanding figure in my eyes.

Laraway delegated a lot to me, and at age sixteen I became a regular by-lined writer ("By Bob Novak"). Soon Laraway asked me to come in on Saturdays to help with the rush of sports news for the weekend papers. Until then, my mother (who had been a private secretary) had typed up my long-hand reports. Now I was forced to type under deadline pressure. I improvised a hunt-and-peck system that I still am using as I type these words.

In the summer of 1948 after my senior year, the *Herald-News* hired me (at $42.50 a week) as a full-time staffer. Every summer for the next few years, I worked on the sports page and anything that came after the ten a.m. sports deadline. The *Herald-News* was my school of journalism. I learned the formula for writing obituaries, how to lay out a page and write headlines, how to cover police news without getting sued for libel. I learned to bluff when I didn't know much about the subject, covered a gangland slaying, and when the woman who usually wrote such things was having a baby, I did a weekly home furnishings feature.

The *Herald-News* avoided controversy. It ran canned anodyne editorials and only one syndicated columnist, Drew Pearson. One summer I came up with the idea of listing, by actual addresses, all the many illegal bookies in Joliet. John Lux, the paper's publisher, called me into his big private office—the only time I set foot there. "Bob," he told me, "we think you're the best young reporter we've seen in a long time. You remind me of myself when I was your age. But let me give you some advice. It's always better to be a 'builder-upper' than a 'tearer-downer.' " John Lux was very kind to me, but I never dreamed of taking that advice.

IN DECEMBER 1947, I was covering a holiday high school basketball tournament at Centralia in southern Illinois for the *Herald-News,* when I met Jack Prowell. He was not yet thirty but already a legendary figure in Illinois sports and newspaper circles: the *Champaign News-Gazette* sportswriter who personally selected the high school football and basketball all-state teams and whose column ("Prowling Around with Jack Prowell") was read all over Illinois by coaches and sports editors. I was drinking beer in the hotel bar with other sportswriters (though I was only sixteen), and Prowell took a liking to me. A few months later, he offered me a job for that coming fall when I would be a University of Illinois student. I was elated—but not for long. My father absolutely forbade it.

He considered me, quite accurately, immature even for my sixteen years. He prophesied, also accurately, I would have a tough enough time as a spoiled only child away from home and mother for the first time without having to shoulder a full-time job.

At Illinois, I was the beneficiary of a splendid education in the liberal arts. Instead of taking journalism and relearning the craft taught me at the *Joliet Herald-News,* I majored in English to open a new world—especially poetry. I most enjoyed Milton, John Donne, Shakespeare, Yeats, and, in particular, T. S. Eliot and Ezra Pound. My studies in modern American literature deepened my love for Hemingway and Fitzgerald and excited unwarranted ambitions to be a novelist. After all, didn't Hemingway start as a newspaperman?

Those ambitions were dampened by my friendship with Stanley Elkin, a moody, witty classmate from Chicago who would become one of America's great novelists in the second half of the twentieth century. We took many classes together, including some in creative writing, where it was clear Stan was so far superior to me that I had better concentrate on newspapering.

A liberal education lets the mind roam to distant places. Reading Dante's *Inferno,* I was intrigued by Bertrans de Born—a medieval nobleman who raised hell in the south of France, raiding and burning down castles and making a general nuisance of himself. Dante consigned him, in death, to stand sentry at the gates of Purgatory with his severed head in his hand, because "in life, he was a stirrer up of strife." His fate intrigued Ezra Pound, who depicted de Born in his *Cantos.* Stirring up strife seemed to me a proper role for a journalist.

AS SOON AS my father vetoed my working for the *News-Gazette,* I turned up at the student newspaper—the *Daily Illini*—and presented myself to the sports editor. I was no mere high school neophyte, I made clear, but an experienced professional journalist. I had a letter from the *Herald-News* to prove it.

By my sophomore year, I was covering the varsity track team and spending one night a week in the sports "slot" (copy desk)—assignments that usually went to seniors or at least juniors. By my junior year, I was heir apparent to sports editor Al Shrader, whom I helped cover varsity football and basketball.

Getting to be sports editor was no minor matter at Illinois. Two *Daily Illini* staffers—editor and sports editor—were routinely tapped for MaWanDa, the select men's society that included the class president, Inter-Fraternity Council president, and major sport captains. I had excellent grades, including straight As in the first semester of my junior year, and was scheduled to graduate with honors. I envisioned my yearbook entry: MaWanDa, sports editor, honors graduate.

There was no other junior even competing to be sports editor. Then I learned that Morris Beschloss, a senior who had covered gymnastics for the past two years and was isolated from mainstream sports at the university, was planning to take a fifth year in college for the purpose of becoming sports editor. Morrie was a pleasant small town boy from Taylorville in southern Illinois who had no enemies and no particular writing or editing talent.

Beschloss was said to be lobbying members of the faculty-student committee that selected the sports editor. I had not approached them because I knew I had the job in the bag, The committee always took the advice of the outgoing sports editor. That was my friend Al Shrader. We had been guests in each other's homes and the closest of collaborators in putting out the sports section. Over the last year, I had been his stand-in.

In my long life, I never have had a shock to compare with the news that the board had selected Beschloss as sports editor. I thought I would die. A half century later, I cannot recall it without feeling the pain afresh. For years to come, I was tormented by puzzlement over how the publications board could reject Al Shrader's recommendation. Illinois coaches (with the exception of the gymnastics coach) were stunned, So, I believe, was every staffer on the *Daily Illini*. The bookie who ran the illegal parlay cards and bookmaking operations in the college town stopped me on the street. "Bob, who is this guy?" he asked. "What can I do to turn this around?" He had close connections to the mob. I thanked him for the thought.

Outside my small circle of friends, there were few tears shed for me at my own fraternity house. Although I would have been the first AEPi to make MaWanDa since before World War II, there was private rejoicing that I got what I deserved for my arrogance. The younger members detested me. One brother whom I had mercilessly taunted for his lack of sophistication could not wipe the smile off his face for days.

The Beschloss editorship was, just as I suspected it would be, undistinguished, free of mistakes, and equally free of successes. His column was pedestrian, and I think he wanted the job as a matter of campus politics rather than getting ahead in journalism. I never thought he would be a professional newspaperman, and in fact he became a rich and successful businessman by running the factory he took over from the man whose daughter he married. To the greater world, he is best known as father of the brilliant historian Michael Beschloss.

Al Shrader and I were reunited in the 1970s in Washington, when Al took over promotions for the *Evening Star*. We always had a good time together, enjoying each other's company. Then, one night over drinks after dinner at Shrader's home in the Virginia suburbs, he told me something he thought I should know. He had recommended Morrie Beschloss to the board twenty years earlier.

"Why?" I asked, astounded by the news. "Because," Shrader replied, "I thought Morrie would get along with the young reporters, and I worried that you would have trouble, would be too demanding. I was wrong. It was one of the biggest mistakes I ever made. You would have made one of the great sports editors ever. I'm sorry."

This incident changed my life. It taught me that politics for me was a lot like sports. I was a lot better reporting it than practicing it. I am not a person who is easy for a lot of people to like. No stirrer-up of strife is ever very popular. For the short term, my reaction to this disappointment brought disastrous consequences.

WHEN I LOST the *Daily Illini* editorship, I immediately telephoned Bert Bertine, sports editor of the *Champaign-Urbana Courier.* (I felt I had grown too close to Jack Prowell to work for him at the *News-Gazette.*) With a combined population of sixty thousand, the twin college towns of Champaign and Urbana had two competing afternoon papers. And did they ever compete—especially in sports. Each had a four-man sports staff, and they were intent on getting exclusives.

Bertine knew me from covering events the past couple of years, and hired me in a second when I called—to start when the next school year began in September. It would be a magical time, helping Bert cover varsity sports in the most successful year ever (1951–52) for the University of Illinois.

The high point was taking a student train to Los Angeles to cover the Illinois-Stanford Rose Bowl game. Train porters complained in wonderment that they ran out of booze for the first time ever on a Chicago-LA run. I helped Bertine with pregame feature stories, took a train up to San Francisco to cover the East-West Shrine Game, and on Rose Bowl day covered the dressing room of the badly beaten Stanford team (where players I interviewed included fullback Bob Mathias, the defending Gold Medal Olympian in the Decathlon and future Republican congressman from California).

It was heady stuff but strange thoughts about covering sports started to enter my head. I worried about the Korean War, about the coming presidential election, about where the country was going. Isn't that what I ought to be reporting and writing about?

WHEN I ENTERED the *Courier* city room one morning in the spring of 1952, Bertine gave me a quizzical stare, then commented: "Well, if it isn't the *ex*-student." His sources inside the university had informed him that I was about to be expelled on charges of flagrant nonattendance of classes and illegal harboring of an automobile (which was prohibited for students). He had the word before I did.

I quit attending most classes my senior year, and skipped just about all class assignments. I was working well over forty hours a week for the *Courier* ($1.25 an hour, with time and a half for overtime), but it wasn't just the burden of time. When I felt betrayed by the university on the *Daily*

Illini, I lost interest in the university (though I maintained perfect attendance in Military Science classes, to protect my army commission).

My heavy class schedule for my first three years meant I needed only ten credit hours a semester my senior year to graduate, far below the norm of fifteen hours. I performed well enough in taking exams to actually get an A in Modern Drama and Bs in Modern European History and Municipal Government my senior year, even while skipping classes and doing no assigned work.

I did not write a single line for my long-anticipated honors thesis and hardly started what I was supposed to hand in for advanced creative writing, flunking both.

My problem was English Literature from 1789 to 1837, taught by Professor Paul Landis, one of the most beloved figures on campus. I had loved Landis's famous Shakespeare course taken my second semester in school (he gave me an A). Although I attended few of his lectures my senior year, I was sure I could ace his final exam. But Landis's toughness was belied by his cherubic demeanor. Since I did not attend enough of his classes, he ruled, I could not take the exam. He flunked me, and I fell one hour short of the 120 needed for graduation.

Far from being an honors graduate, I wasn't even going to graduate. That was certain. The question was whether I would be expelled, taking away the hours I did earn my last semester, and making sure I would never graduate. Significantly, expulsion would prevent me from getting my second lieutenant's commission in the U.S. Army Reserve as scheduled.

I was summoned to appear before a student-faculty disciplinary committee, and I tried my best to display the contrition I genuinely felt. I was told, however, that the student members thought I was arrogant and voted to expel me. All that saved me was a faculty member of the committee: wrestling coach emeritus H. E. (Hek) Kenney, a venerated figure. Coach Kenney knew me a little bit, argued that I was a good guy who got mixed up in his senior year after an exemplary three-year record and should be cut some slack. Not for the first or last time had I benefited from the patronage of an older man. I was not expelled, I was commissioned as an army officer, and I was only one hour short of graduation.

WITH THE KOREAN War ended, the army was clearing out its excess officers—including me. Jobless, my army career ended, I returned to Joliet to my parents' home. I went job-seeking in Chicago (including a visit to the *Sun-Times*) without success. Al Orton, the Chicago bureau chief for the Associated Press, said he would love to hire me if a position opened up anywhere. I was skeptical. I did have one newspaper offer—from the *Joliet Herald-News*. But I did not want to settle down in my hometown. I still hoped something would turn up but stopped actively looking for it. Weeks rolled by. My routine was to sleep late, watch the Cubs on television in the afternoon, and then go out drinking. I was flat broke and living off my parents.

At the end of August, I got a phone call from Al Orton. The Omaha Associated Press bureau needed a vacation replacement for just twelve weeks. Would I be willing to take it? *Would* I!

CHAPTER 4

From Omaha to 'Naptown

Thanks to credit for eighteen months of full-time experience at the *Joliet Herald-News* and the *Champaign-Urbana Courier,* my AP salary was $68 a week ($512 in equivalent 2007 buying power)—substantially less than I had earned as a first lieutenant. That did not go far even in Omaha. But I was tipped off to American Legion Post No. 1 in downtown Omaha, where, as a veteran, I could rent a maid-service room for forty-seven dollars a month—and with the added benefit of a bar that was often frequented by unattached ladies.

I never made any real friends in Omaha, except for a couple of bartenders, the local bookie, and Ross Lorello, who ran the best steak house in a city renowned for steak houses. I ate at Ross's as often as I could, which was not often. What I could afford was reading library books, including Arnold Toynbee's multivolume study of civilizations. It kept my brain active at a time when my main work on the night shift consisted of rewriting state and regional news for Nebraska radio and television stations. With no more than two news staffers in the bureau at one time, I also was expected to help write stories phoned in by stringers. I was particularly busy every evening after Randall Blake took over as night editor. He was a delightful character who had seen much better days at the AP and now, waiting for retirement, was dedicated to doing as little work as possible.

Blake took two weeks' vacation every year to attend the World Series, and in 1954 asked me to write his Nebraska high school football predictions during his absence. "Randy," I said, "I know nothing about Nebraska high school football." "Kid," he replied, "do you think *I* do?" Following his instructions I lifted the expert predictions from the *Omaha World-Herald* galley proofs and made a few changes so that it would look kosher.

Early in December, I was offered another temporary assignment as a full-time reporter—in the Lincoln bureau to cover the biennial session of the unicameral Nebraska legislature that convened in January 1955. The Lincoln bureau had only two permanent staffers. Odell Hanson, the "Correspondent," was a brilliant wire service writer but preferred to stay in the downtown bureau rather than cover the legislators. That duty was supposed to be handled mainly by an old AP hand, but, luckily for me, he was having personal problems, and I ended up doing the heavy lifting. Given a weekly columnlike legislative feature, I changed my byline from "Bob" to "Robert D."

The pressing issue of the legislative session was finding money for Nebraska's depleted highway system. The construction lobby was attempting to pass a "ton-mile tax" on trucks that was vigorously opposed by the truckers lobby. The truckers seemed to have more money and put on a nightly buffet and open bar that attracted plenty of senators—and me. Living in the basement apartment of a private home in a lower-income suburb, cooking my own meals, I was delighted to freeload off lobbyists as often as I could. The truckers won the battle and killed the ton-mile tax.

The newly elected Republican governor of Nebraska, Victor E. Anderson, was neutral on this as on most issues. He was considerably less impressive than the athletic coaches who up until then had been my most intimate news sources. But so were nearly all the legislators. This first impression of the political class did not change appreciably in a half century of sustained contact.

Anderson was almost totally inarticulate. He seemed uninterested in public policy and had no ideology except a vague desire to stand pat. He held no news conferences out of fear that he would commit horrendous bloopers that newsmen would accurately report. When we needed to quote him, however, he was always available for quick interviews. His staff apparently figured that, one-on-one, the reporters would clean up his syntax. I did, and so did everybody else.

I had followed politics since I was nine, but government was something different, and now, at age twenty-four, I was learning how to cover it. It took more elbow grease and chicanery than cerebral brilliance. The other legislative reporters went home every night, but I had no desire to be in my basement apartment. I hung out at night with legislators and lobbyists as much as I could. I also learned it paid to be good friends with low-level staffers. Flirting with the female secretary at the Nebraska Supreme Court provided me with a few minutes' lead in getting the court's opinions—important in beating out the United Press, the dominant wire service in Nebraska.

I wrote the AP wrap-up of the 1955 legislative session that ran on the front pages of many Nebraska daily newspapers. For somebody who knew nothing about the state less than a year earlier, I was willing to offer authoritative judgments. I deplored the "striking lack of important legislation" that came out of the five-and-a-half-month session. Looking back after five decades, I would say it was a pretty good session.

I also wrote profiles of legislators. One I remember was of a retired farmer named William Purdy, serving his first and only two-year term as the representative from Norfolk. I think I was the only reporter to interview him. Purdy was a cipher, but he was a cipher on purpose. He had campaigned for the unicameral on these pledges: to serve only one term, to make no speeches on the floor, to introduce no bills, to vote against each and every bill to increase taxes or expand government. He faithfully kept all these promises.

My profile of the old farmer was as snide and dismissive as AP style would allow. Over the years, however, Bill Purdy has become one of my heroes.

I WAS ON borrowed time. I assumed the AP would put me out of my job when the unicameral finally adjourned. I scoured the *Editor & Publisher* want ads. *Congressional Quarterly* rejected me for a political reporter's job in Washington. Thankfully the English-language *Beirut Star* turned me down for a subeditor's job in Lebanon.

Then I got a reprieve—a new four-month vacation relief assignment in Omaha. That four months was almost up when Omaha "Correspondent" Ed Makiesky called me into his little office to tell me I had hit pay dirt in Indianapolis, assigned there permanently as the bureau's second-ranking political reporter.

GOING FROM THE AP in Nebraska to the AP in Indiana was like going from Double-A to Triple-A in baseball. That is no comparison of cities. Indianapolis in 1955 was down-at-the-heels compared to Omaha (in Illinois, we referred to it as 'Naptown). But the Indianapolis AP bureau was twice as large. It had a "Chief of Bureau" rather than a mere "Correspondent," a full-time political reporter, a full-time sportswriter, a photographer, and a bureau secretary. And in Indiana, AP was the dominant wire service.

There was also an active Indianapolis Press Club, where I spent some rollicking evenings and where I would meet my first wife (then working for the Republican State Central Committee). Sometimes a liquor-laden crowd would close the press club and reconvene at my second-floor walk-up apartment in the city's "burglar belt" to scramble some eggs and do some more drinking.

· · · ·

INTRIGUE AND FACTIONALISM were nonstop in both Indiana parties. In 1955, three years had not healed the deep cleavage between the Indiana Republican Party's Taft and Eisenhower wings. I had been unduly influenced by an adoring 1955 *Time* cover story on Governor George North Craig, a former national commander of the American Legion in his first political office. Calling him a "swift-footed, swashbuckling lawyer-politician," the magazine cast him as the great hope of Eisenhower's "New Republicans" aligned against the state's reactionary Taft wing headed by the McCarthyite senator William Ezra Jenner.

Things were not nearly so simple. The Indianapolis press corps despised Craig as a corrupt and arrogant bully. Jenner at least had some ideals, even if they were not as acceptable in the Republican Party then as they would be a generation later: limited government, low taxes, and "home rule" (a euphemism for states' rights).

But ideals were not what the factional battle was about. Indiana was one of the last patronage states. Some sixty thousand jobs were in the hands of the governor. A closed-door meeting of the Republican State Central Committee in the spring of 1956 demonstrated Craig's way of wielding power. The governor's forces pressured a committeeman, a coal mine owner in private life, by warning him that his coal contract with the state government was in jeopardy if he did not give Governor Craig his vote. I heard this with my own ears, and so did the other reporters on the political beat. Journalists usually are not accorded this view of the political world's dirty underside. But in this case, the conversation in the room drifted through the Claypool Hotel's ventilating system, and we all eavesdropped.

The Craig versus Jenner showdown came during the party convention at the Indiana State Fairgrounds Coliseum on June 29, 1956. At issue was the nomination for governor to succeed Craig. Massively unpopular at his party's grass roots, Craig was booed by delegates chanting, "We want Jenner!" Jenner stayed in seclusion, pulling convention strings behind the scenes.

The convention nominated Lieutenant Governor Harold W. Handley, Jenner's choice and the only one of five Republican candidates deemed "unacceptable" by Craig. The lame duck governor was finished. Never shy about speculating, I wrote in my account for AP's national wire: "It was possible that Craig, highly regarded by the Eisenhower Administration, might have lost his chance for a high federal appointment." The story was carried by the *New York Times*.

IN MAY 1956, I had a brief encounter that wound up changing my life. Douglas B. Cornell, the AP's top political writer out of Washington, arrived in Indianapolis to write the national wire stories on Indiana's Democratic presidential primacy. Handsome and self-assured, he was a figure of awe for us provincials. I was assigned to be his "caddy"—to brief him on the intricacies of Indiana politics from the depth of my six months' experience. Cornell had been brought in not to just report raw primary results but to assess the political situation, and he peppered me with questions.

On Tuesday night, Cornell did stories for the morning newspapers and then wrote for the afternoon ones. He came into the bureau briefly early Wednesday before catching the plane back to Washington. He instructed me to write a new lead for late afternoon editions over his byline.

Before he left, Doug asked: "How would you like to come to Washington?" I allowed that I could imagine nothing better but did not think that it seemed likely. "Don't be too sure," he said.

To SAY THAT I was born and bred antiunion would be an exaggeration, but not much of one. My father detested labor negotiations, his antipathy to unions becoming personal when a union organized the workers at his Lockport plant just after World War II.

Now that I was a permanent AP employee in Indianapolis, I was pressured to join the American Newspaper Guild. Night editor Leonard Pearson, a soft-spoken gentleman nearing retirement age, was the de facto shop steward for the guild and a stickler for union privileges. Just before I arrived in Indianapolis, he had suffered a massive heart attack and spent many weeks in convalescence. When he returned to work, his doctors limited him to three nights a week indefinitely.

I had been in Indianapolis only for a few months when the bureau chief, Peter McDonald, called me into his office. McDonald had taken a liking to me. Now, in confidence, he showed me Pearson's applications for time-and-a-half overtime payments for several nights when he had stayed on an extra ten or fifteen minutes to file late high school basketball scores.

"Can you believe this guy?" McDonald asked me, as he threw Pearson's reports on his desk. "We give him every break, pay him full time for three days' work when it's not required by the contract, and he wants ten minutes' overtime. Novak, if I ever see you do something like this, I'll clobber you. That's why I'm showing you this."

Shortly after his return, Pearson approached me and expressed surprise that I did not belong to the guild. This broke the previous unanimous membership in the Indianapolis bureau. He urged me to join and suggested that my stay in Indianapolis would be "more fulfilling" if I did. After talking it over with a couple of the bureau's younger staffers (each more than ten years older than I), I decided that joining was the better part of valor.

Several months later in the fall of 1956, I noted that Secretary of the Treasury George Humphrey, strongman of the Eisenhower cabinet, was coming to the Claypool Hotel the following week to speak at a hundred-dollar-a-plate Republican fund-raiser. Our top political reporter was off that day. McDonald agreed to let me cover it.

Len Pearson kept an eagle eye out for "illegal" schedule changes. He quickly told me that my change had been posted less than the two weeks minimum notice required by the union contract. I told him that it was my fault for not having informed McDonald earlier. "Doesn't matter, Bob," Len responded calmly. "It's management's responsibility." He said I must demand time-and-a-half overtime for the entire day. I told him I had no intention of doing that and walked away, thinking the issue was resolved.

It wasn't. What followed convinced me of the value of right-to-work legislation, which guarantees employees the right to join—or not join—a union. Pearson went to McDonald and demanded I be paid time and a half. McDonald refused. Then, said Len, the guild unit would submit a formal grievance to go through adjudication.

I told Pearson that if he submitted the grievance, I would resign from the guild, never to rejoin. I walked away before he could reply. No grievance was filed.

The sequel to this story came at the 1957 session of the Indiana legislature, which passed a state right-to-work law. Len Pearson and his counterpart on the day shift, Herman Olsen (also an ardent union man nearing retirement), insisted on putting "so-called" in front of right-to-work as well as quotes around the title. Using both so-called and quotes, I told Len and Herman, constituted an editorial comment by the AP. They ignored me. I went to Pete McDonald, who agreed with me and instructed the deskmen to take out the so-called. They did, but these two faithful old servitors of the AP were icy toward me for the rest of my time in Indianapolis.

THE NOVEMBER 1956 election produced a massive Republican landslide in Indiana—and a stupidly juvenile act by me. When my absentee ballot from Illinois arrived, I voted for Eisenhower. But I had also registered in Indiana, and on Election Day voted again for Eisenhower. Double voting for Ike reflected my smart-aleck streak more than enthusiasm for the president.

During the campaign, Eisenhower did not lift a finger as Soviet troops invaded Hungary and put down the freedom fighters. Adlai Stevenson would have done no better. But was this all that could be expected from the Republicans?

IN JANUARY 1957 when the General Assembly convened, I was assigned to the House of Representatives, and I had an advantage. All my competitors were married men with families. I was a bachelor whose girlfriend had gone to Peru, Indiana, as a cub reporter on the daily newspaper there. So every night I could go to lobbyist parties or hang out at the bar of the Indianapolis Press Club, across the street from the statehouse, to harvest tidbits from legislators and lobbyists.

I did not find Governor Handley much more impressive than Vic Anderson in Nebraska. Nor were Hoosier lawmakers above the level of the Nebraskans. I was especially unimpressed by the very green House minority leader, at age twenty-nine the youngest floor leader in state legislative history: a lawyer and second-term representative from Terre Haute named Birch Bayh. He was pushed around on the floor by his Republican counterpart and not given much help by the Democratic caucus chairman, the much more experienced Otto Pozgay of South Bend. In my weekly column-type feature, I wrote this appraisal of the young Democratic leader:

> . . . Bayh has appeared to be second best. Inexperience in the floor leader's role has caused him to make some parliamentary errors, and a divided delegation on the gas tax issue hasn't helped his prestige.
>
> Pozgay, by limiting his action on the floor and showing a more conservative side than in previous sessions, may have gained some strength.

Actually, I thought Bayh was superficial and ineffective, a good-looking glad-hander who might not even be returned to the leadership in the next session. Instead, he became Speaker of the House when the Democrats took control in 1959, was elected to the U.S. Senate in 1962, was a national figure in the party by 1970, and ran for president in 1976 at age forty-eight. I thought Pozgay was a powerful figure with an unlimited future. Instead, he ended up losing a local race for township trustee.

THE 1957 SESSION of the Indiana General Assembly ran two days over the sixty-day statutory limit, and the legislators were awake and working most of those last forty-eight hours. So was I. Unlike the lawmakers, I was paid for it. While totally exhausted, I had never been so rich. The last two-week check I received for the legislative session, instead of the usual take-home pay of around two hundred dollars, with time-and-a-half for over-time totaled over eight hundred dollars.

Besides being extraordinarily flush, I felt more settled than at any time in my adult life. I liked Indianapolis, I loved my job and the girl working on the *Peru Tribune,* whom I planned to marry in the fall.

In my contented mood shortly after the session ended, I attended a black-tie dinner at the Indianapolis Press Club with my girlfriend. I was just digging into a blood-rare steak when Pete McDonald approached our table. "I got some news for you," the bureau chief told me, "that you'll like better than I do. [Pause] You're going to Washington." Doug Cornell was not kidding.

CHAPTER 5

Advice from Ezra Pound

THE WASHINGTON I entered on Sunday evening, May 12, 1957, did not look much like the nation's capital of the early twenty-first century. It was shabbier and less pretentious.

The cliché is that World War II transformed Washington from a sleepy southern town into a busy eastern metropolis. In truth, Washington in 1957 was still a city with southern efficiency and northern charm. Pennsylvania Avenue, intended by the capital's designer Pierre L'Enfant to be America's avenue, was disfigured from Georgetown to Capitol Hill by old two- and three-story buildings with tacky stores and cafés on the ground floors. Between the White House and the Capitol, 9th Street was a sex zone with a burlesque theater, peep shows, and porn shops. No New York–style posh restaurants were to be found.

If the city was a little down at the heels, it was better run on a "colonial" system than it would be under the home rule that followed. The president of the United States appointed three District of Columbia commissioners, with one of them mandated by law to be a major general in the U.S. Army Corps of Engineers in charge of public works. In contrast to what followed, there were no potholes and snow was cleared expeditiously.

For a twenty-six-year-old newspaperman with no relatives or friends in Washington, there was one place to go: the National Press Club. Every night, the magnificent wood-paneled stand-up Members Bar on the top floor of the National Press Building (all male, as was the club itself) was packed with journalists and lobbyists. It was a place where a nobody like me could meet and listen to the wit and wisdom of such big-time Washington correspondents as Merriman Smith of United Press. After fifty-cent highballs, you could eat well in the Members Bar by ordering the NPC (National Press Club) Steak, at $1.25.

Otherwise, Washington was expensive for me though my AP salary had now reached \$125 a week (\$929 in 2007 purchasing power). My difficulty in finding a decent furnished apartment I could afford was solved by Tom Nelson, a House reporter for United Press and a fellow Illinoisan. He lived with four other bachelors in a big, elegant house in Georgetown that was the Washington residence of Robert Woodward, a senior career diplomat who then was U.S. ambassador to Costa Rica. Woodward rented it furnished for five hundred dollars a month. One of the bachelors had gotten married, leaving a vacancy. Tom offered it to me, and I jumped at the chance.

Bill Sunderland, another UP reporter, was a third newsman in the house. The identity of the other two occupants illustrates how remote the Washington of 1957 was from what exists today. Charlie Stockton worked for the CIA, and Doug Bonner described himself as a Foreign Service officer, though he really was an undercover CIA man. The idea of journalists and CIA operatives living together is unthinkable today.

Also unthinkable today is a government where spending is under control, as it was in 1957. The federal government had not grown organically since New Deal days and would not until President Lyndon Johnson's Great Society eight years later. During the week that I arrived in Washington, President Eisenhower went on national television pleading for public support against congressional budget cutters. "Ike Fights to Save Budget" headlined the *Washington Post*. Eisenhower faced a Democratic-controlled Congress seeking to reduce his \$71.8 billion budget—about \$517 billion in 2007 money (compared with President George W. Bush's 2007 budget of \$2.77 trillion).

THE SIZE OF the government was not on my mind on Monday morning, May 13, 1957, when I drove back up Highway 50 from my motel in Virginia to the antique *Evening Star* building on the corner of 11th and Pennsylvania in downtown Washington. The Associated Press took up a whole floor, with a newsroom looking like a large metropolitan paper—telephones ringing and phone conversations droning amid the clatter of typewriters and teletype machines, punctuated by ringing teletype bells.

This was a far cry from the vest pocket AP bureaus that I had known, with more than one hundred staffers (overwhelmingly male). I was the only AP newsman in Washington less than thirty years old, and there were precious few under forty.

It was my fourth AP bureau, the first where the bureau chief did not greet me as a new employee, and the first boss with whom I never established a personal relationship. Nevertheless, William L. Beale's attitude would exert a major influence in my life. Beale was reclusive, communicating through short, cryptic notes scrawled in orange crayon. Many were poisonous, but his infrequent missives to me were all complimentary. The poison was administered in our only two private talks, both lying more than a year ahead.

I was one of the bureau's twenty-two regional staffers who supplied state and local news out of Washington. A story divulging new rivers and harbors projects could make newspaper front pages whereas serious developments from the State Department or the Treasury might not.

I was assigned Illinois, Michigan, and Indiana. What a delight to get a reporting job covering something I knew about, including a Senate investigation of the Indiana state highway scandal. However, a close look at the regional staff made me wonder whether my fortune was all that good. The average age of these men (and one woman) was higher than that of the bureau as a whole, which was plenty old. Many regional reporters once held important AP jobs but had failed to make it to the top and now were nearing retirement. Of the regional reporters when I arrived in Washington, only one ever advanced to the bureau's general staff.

A few regional reporters worked their beats hard, but most mailed it in. They were professionals who could handle this without half trying by relying on handouts and an occasional phone call. A disproportionate number of card players in the congressional Press Galleries worked on the AP's regional staff.

I pondered a puzzle. I had been brought to Washington at an unusually early age with unusually little experience because Doug Cornell spotted me as a talent to be brought along quickly. Why then assign me to a graveyard rather than insert me as a junior reporter covering Congress, the State Department, or Pentagon? Because the veteran reporter covering the Illinois-Michigan-Indiana beat was leaving the AP to take a higher-paying job as an Illinois congressman's administrative assistant, creating a vacancy. At the same time, the Indiana legislative session was ending, making me available. It all fit together.

AS A REGIONAL reporter in Washington, I tried the same techniques of shoe-leather reporting I had used in Lincoln and Indianapolis. I immediately found it more difficult in the nation's capital.

I was assigned to cover a hearing by the Senate Internal Security Subcommittee, which preceded the McCarthy Committee in Red hunting. The subject was a Communist-infested outlaw local of the United Auto Workers in Detroit, which made it a Michigan regional story for the AP.

Presiding over a one-man hearing was a familiar face from Indiana: Senator William E. Jenner. The death of Joe McCarthy two weeks earlier had made Jenner the senator most detested by the Left. Seated beside Jenner on the raised dais was the subcommittee's staff director, Judge Robert Morris, a prominent conservative Republican from New Jersey. Since the Senate was controlled by Democrats, how was it possible for two right-wing Republicans to conduct this hearing? Things were less partisan then, particularly on the Internal Security Subcommittee, where party was less important than anti-Communist credentials.

Still more peculiar was the gentleman seated on the other side of Senator Jenner. He was in late middle age, plump with a jolly pink face, and smoking a cigar. When I asked, the reporter seated next to me at the press table told me it was Willard Edwards of the *Chicago Tribune,* whose reports from Washington I had read for years in Illinois. "How come a reporter sits on the dais?" I asked in wonderment. "He's no reporter," my companion answered sourly. Willard, who was to become my mentor, was actually a superb reporter but also a diehard right-wing Republican who was part of the Red-hunting establishment.

The other reporters at the press table—from the other two wire services and the three Detroit newspapers—seemed bored by the hearing, but I found fascinating the exposure of Communist penetration in the UAW local. After two hours, Judge Morris announced a final day of hearings on the subject the next day. Trained to try to put fresh material in rewrites for the next day's afternoon papers, I approached Morris to ask what was ahead. He seemed surprised, but filled me in—with more detail than I expected.

As I entered the hearing room the next day, the United Press reporter approached me. He and the reporter for International News Service had received "rockets" from their New York news desks with the message: "How Pls AP?" Translated: How come the Associated Press has stuff about this investigation that we don't have? Reporters for two afternoon Detroit newspapers were similarly questioned about why their desks had to use AP copy for the first edition. None had interviewed Morris.

The UP reporter, twenty-five years my senior, had been delegated to instruct the green kid from the AP about life in Washington. "With Internal Security," he told me, "we never write anything except what happens in open hearing. We never, ever interview Morris."

"Why?" I asked.

"Because nothing they do deserves it," he responded.

It was censorship by a self-created news cartel. As the most junior reporter in Washington, I could do nothing about it.

. . .

THE KIND OF story that won front-page play and kudos from Mr. Beale, written in orange crayon, was advance word on appropriations for air force bases in Michigan. The major regional stories that I covered included Senator Albert Gore's investigation of those Indiana highway scandals, House Democratic probing of conflict of interest charges against the U.S. attorney in Chicago, and Chicago's perpetual quest for congressional approval to divert water from Lake Michigan.

A source on this beat was Representative August E. Johansen, an Old Guard Taft Republican from Battle Creek, Michigan, whose dull conservative orations I occasionally reported for Michigan newspapers. He appreciated it.

On April 18, 1958, Johansen telephoned me in the House Press Gallery. "Novak," he said, "I got a scoop for you if you come right over." I was in his congressional office within ten minutes. Seated in his inner office was an elderly man, in wrinkled jacket and slacks, with his sports shirt hanging out, and his gray hair and beard uncombed. "Robert Novak," the Congressman said, "meet Ezra Pound."

Ezra Pound? The idol of my college poetry-reading days?

I loved Pound's poetry, particularly the *Cantos*. His fascist, anticapitalist, and anti-Semitic ideology seldom was reflected in his poems. An expatriate in Italy since 1914, Pound began broadcasting for Mussolini when World War II began. Allied troops, occupying Italy, interned him in May 1945. He could either be tried for treason or committed as insane. The latter appeared to be the better way to handle a great poet, and he was sent to St. Elizabeth's mental hospital in Washington.

Twelve years in an insane asylum seemed enough for Ezra Pound in the opinion of prominent friends led by poet Robert Frost and including Gus Johansen. Pound's wife called him "incurably insane." The government agreed that he was incapable of standing trial for treason and at age seventy-two posed no threat to the community. The chief district judge dismissed fifteen-year-old treason charges and pronounced him a free man.

Congressman Johansen did not deliver the "scoop" he promised. A few hours earlier Pound had appeared in open court, where the charges were dropped. But he gave me an exclusive interview, which ran on the AP's national wire. Pound did not have much to say other than expressing pleasure at seeing Washington's famous buildings for the first time and his desire to return to Italy.

As I left, the poet asked me: "Young man, do you intend to spend your entire life in journalism?" I replied that I did. "Well, then," Ezra Pound told me, "in that case, I have a piece of advice for you. Above all, avoid too much accuracy."

As I related that advice to colleagues, they said it validated Pound's insanity. He could have meant the truth would get me in the kind of trouble he had faced. But I thought he was saying I should not let a plethora of little facts get in the way of the greater truth. That difficult injunction for a journalist is one that I have tried to follow, not always successfully.

I DID NOT find the caliber of politicians in Washington generally any higher than what I had encountered in Indianapolis and Lincoln. Within the three-state limits of my beat, however, I found interesting national figures. The two senators from Illinois, Democrat Paul Douglas and Republican Everett Dirksen, were fascinating personalities, though Douglas was less effective and Dirksen was deeper than I had thought. Representative Charles Halleck of Indiana, a leader of the state party's Eisenhower wing and a power in the House, came over as an old-fashioned politician who was very crotchety. Representative Gerald Ford of Michigan, a handsome ex-football star seen as a moderate Republican voice for the future, was nice to a young wire service reporter but seemed to me a little shallow.

Then there was William Ezra Jenner of Indiana. When I got to know Jenner, I was surprised how easy it was to deal with a man described as unapproachable by my colleagues. Jenner was a genuine conservative who antagonized other members of the Indiana delegation by trying to limit pork for the state. In private conversation, he was intelligent and well informed.

On December 2, 1957, Jenner announced he would not seek a third term. He was only forty-nine years old, at the height of his power as Indiana's dominant Republican. His retirement was unexpected, but the reasons were no mystery for anybody who knew him. Jenner detested moderate Republicanism and what he perceived as the nation's leftward drift at home and abroad, which he considered himself powerless to stop. He felt alone in the Senate after the death of his friend Joe McCarthy.

Jenner thought himself the last of a defeated breed. He never dreamed Barry Goldwater would be nominated for president in six years and Ronald Reagan elected president sixteen years after that. Jenner was around for the advent of the Reagan Revolution but never saw it coming.

CHAPTER 6

Joining the Journal

M Y FRUSTRATIONS AS a regional reporter were eased because the general desk in the AP's Washington bureau co-opted reporters from the regional desk as "tail gunners" on major hearings. When the main AP reporter left the hearing room to phone in a new lead, the tail gunner would take notes and then either give them to his colleague or phone in an insert himself.

It was considered menial duty by the regional staff's old-timers. Such chores, they grumbled, cut into time devoted to their regional beats (though I suspected they were really complaining about cutting into their card-playing time). If they hated being co-opted, I loved it.

During my first month in Washington, the general desk assigned me as tail gunner for a week of hearings by the Senate Select Committee on Improper Activities in the Labor-Management Field (shortened by the press to the Senate Rackets Committee)—the first of many assignments there. That was my ticket to a broader new world. I ended up talking to John F. Kennedy, Robert F. Kennedy, Barry Goldwater, Edward Bennett Williams, Kenneth O'Donnell, and Pierre Salinger. That was something for a twenty-six-year-old reporter new to Washington.

Jack Kennedy, running for president in 1960, understood that liberalism was no longer enough to win in America. Republicans were dismantling the New Deal coalition by cutting away ethnics, Catholics, blue-collar workers, and southerners. Kennedy's answer was to pose as a fearless investigator of ties between organized labor and organized crime. The trick was to concentrate on the mob-infested Teamsters, who were leaning toward the Republicans anyway. Labor leaders feared the investigation would spread beyond the Teamsters and lead to corrective legislation that would adversely affect the nation's labor-management balance. If it did, Kennedy—and his presidential candidacy—would be held responsible.

Kennedy, walking a political tightrope, was relying on his little brother, Robert Francis Kennedy, his chief political strategist, to keep him upright. Bobby controlled the Rackets Committee as its chief counsel, and brought in the Kennedy first team to run the investigation. Committee chairman John L. McClellan of Arkansas, a conservative Democrat and a segregationist, was deftly manipulated by Bobby.

The committee's conservative Republicans also were playing a delicate game. Not wanting to seem soft on crime or corruption, they joined Democratic senators in berating the Teamsters and James R. Hoffa. At the same time, they prodded the Kennedys to investigate violence by the United Auto Workers of Walter Reuther, who had become a huge power in the Democratic Party.

Arizona's Barry Goldwater, elected to the Senate for the first time in 1952 along with Jack Kennedy and now emerging as a dynamic leader of the Republican Party's conservative wing, was the committee's most visible counterweight to the Kennedys. But often he seemed erratic and unable to pursue a consistent course.

WHEN THE AP'S general desk discovered I was possibly a more capable and certainly a more enthusiastic tail gunner for Rackets Committee hearings than older regional staffers, I was co-opted frequently and given broader duties—often writing the national wire overnight story that would be published in the first edition of the then more numerous afternoon newspapers until new developments produced a new lead. Newspaper editors often picked which wire service they would use through the day based on the first few paragraphs of the overnight story, and it was important for the AP to win that competition.

By August 1958, I had become an old hand at this sort of thing. Bobby Kennedy, to prove his point that Jimmy Hoffa could not clean up the Teamsters because it was under mob control, was calling as witnesses a collection of bizarre hoodlums—such as three-hundred-pound ex-convict Barney Baker, a prototypical labor goon. For the overnight report of Thursday, August 21, when Baker was scheduled to testify before the Rackets Committee, my competitor with the UP (now United Press International after its merger with Hearst's International News Service) led his story with a report that Baker long ago had killed vaudeville comedian Joe Penner's famous duck. I took a different approach:

WASHINGTON, Aug. 21 (AP)—Senate investigators sought today to discover how Robert (Barney) Baker, $125-a-week Teamsters Union

organizer, managed to lavish thousands of dollars on a blonde convicted slayer.

Baker was called back by the Senate Rackets Committee to answer
questions about testimony that he enabled blonde Mrs. Ruth Brougher
to live in plush Miami surroundings in 1955 while she awaited the outcome of an appeal from a manslaughter conviction.

Mrs. Brougher, brought here from a Florida prison to testify, swore
Wednesday she had no idea where the money came from. Chairman
John L. McClellan (D-Ark.) had asked whether it was from Baker's
own funds, the Teamster treasury, or stolen or kidnap money.

The AP killed UPI competitively on that story. A blond killer would
trump Joe Penner's duck any day.

Information about both the blonde and the duck came from Bobby
Kennedy's daily briefing to reporters regularly covering the hearing. That
was where I got to know him a little and dislike him a lot. It was a stacked
deck against Bobby's enemies. He would deal out a preview for the next
day's newspapers, with rebuttal witnesses denied coverage because their
comments would be immediately overtaken by a new story line.

Determined as Kennedy was to snare Jimmy Hoffa, he was no less fixed
on shielding Walter Reuther. To protect his brother's presidential nomination, he had to prevent conservative Republicans from drawing equivalency
between Teamsters corruption and United Auto Workers violence.

Senator Goldwater was the committee's most visible Republican face. I
found him charming, eager to help me, and always committed to the conservative cause, without Bill Jenner's overriding hopelessness. But I also
found him far less focused than the Kennedys and tending not to follow
through on what he had told me and other reporters he planned to do. It
was an uneven contest. Two feckless Republican staff investigators, constantly harassed by Bobby, were aligned against Kennedy's seventy-two
staffers. As a witness, the voluble Reuther talked down the committee.

I THOUGHT I discovered an entry to the AP's general staff: a new beat created to cover atomic energy. I had written a national wire analysis on a
Michigan dispute over a proposed nuclear power plant that I had covered
closely for the regional staff. The AP did not have anybody specifically covering this important field (as the *New York Times* and the *Washington Post*
did). I wrote a detailed two-page memo to Beale, proposing an atomic energy beat and adding that I was eager to cover that beat. Jim Marlow, the

AP's venerable national columnist who was a mentor to me and other young AP reporters, thought the memo was cogent, and Beale's secretary (who liked me) thought her boss would buy it.

She was wrong, as was shown in the first of two face-to-face meetings with my bureau chief. William L. Beale, very thin with a long face and a crimson complexion, seldom smiled. Having read my memo, Beale ascertained, correctly, that I was a lot more interested in getting off the regional staff than I was in atomic energy. He made clear he had no intention of creating a new beat and strongly implied there was no prospect for me joining the general staff in any capacity.

A few weeks later, in late August 1958, I was approached in the House Press Gallery by Alan Otten, senior congressional correspondent of the *Wall Street Journal.* I had briefed him on Indiana politics earlier that year in preparation for his reporting trip to Indianapolis. Now Otten asked me whether I would be interested in interviewing for a job with the *Journal* covering the Senate.

ALBERT CLARK, BUREAU chief of the *Wall Street Journal,* took me to dinner at the Ambassador Hotel, across the street from the newspaper's offices on 14th Street in midtown Washington. After perusing my AP clippings and interviewing me over dinner, Clark offered me a job covering the Senate and politics all over the country.

That might seem a dream job that a frustrated regional reporter would snap up. In fact, it was not that easy for me. By 1958, its genius publisher, Bernard Kilgore, had made the *Journal* America's first national newspaper through simultaneous publication in five regional publishing plants, but its 536,000 circulation was far from the two million level it would reach. Nobody I knew read what was then still wrongly considered a stock market tip sheet. The *WSJ* had yet to become must reading in the political community, and I never read it myself.

The AP exerted a powerful tug on me after four years, if only I were given some hope of getting off the regional staff. So I requested another meeting with William Beale to tell him I was considering a job offer from the *Wall Street Journal.* My second meeting was no more productive than my first. I asked bluntly whether I had any chance in the foreseeable future to get on the AP's general staff covering Congress or anything else. Beale replied bleakly that he saw no likelihood of that. Not once did he ask me to stay.

Considering Doug Cornell's role in getting me to Washington, I felt constrained to tell him I might be leaving the AP. After hearing about my meeting with Beale, Doug thought I should snap up the *WSJ* offer. So did Jim Marlow. Unlike Beale, both expressed regret that the AP did not find a place for me.

I accepted the *Journal*'s $160-a-week salary, offered me on a take-it-or-leave-it basis after I said I would not take the job if I was not paid more than the $150 the AP was paying me then.

EVEN AFTER I gave notice to the AP, I kept trying to develop exclusive regional stories. I dropped into the National Republican Senatorial Committee (NRSC), which ran the party's Senate campaigns. They told me that a Republican senator on my beat, Charles Potter, was dead meat for reelection in Michigan. That assessment was not surprising, but the fact NRSC managers would speak so frankly was news.

On September 26, 1958, my AP account ran throughout Michigan. ("GOP Is Aware Potter May Be Defeated," headlined the *Adrian Daily Telegram*'s front page):

WASHINGTON (AP)—Republican campaign strategists here now agree with their Democratic counterparts that only a political miracle can save Sen. Charles E. Potter (R-Mich) from defeat in November.

A check of national-level party officials shows bipartisan agreement that all signs point to a win for the Democratic Senate candidate, Lt. Gov. Philip A. Hart. . . .

GOP campaign planners . . . say Potter has less chance than any other incumbent Republican Senator. And they concede the Republicans will lose some seats this year.

Potter went down to the defeat, as predicted, by 170,000 votes.

My report contained too much truth for Republican politicians and some small-town newspapers in Michigan. Potter's handlers were enraged, and talked Republican publishers of several newspapers that had run my story into writing a letter of protest to the AP. A friend of mine who worked for Potter showed me a copy of William L. Beale's reply to the publishers. Beale agreed the story never should have been written and then provided this kicker: Mr. Novak is no longer with the Associated Press. The implication that I had been fired was unprofessional mendacity.

(In 1978 I was taken into the Gridiron Club, an organization of senior Washington-based journalists that included the retired Bill Beale as one of its elders. In years to come, I avoided any contact with him at the club's annual white-tie dinner.)

It is unfortunate to conclude my account of four years with the Associated Press on such an ugly note. The AP provided a twenty-three-year-old neophyte journalist fresh out of the army with amazing opportunities that became the foundation of my career. I am profoundly grateful, and shall always consider myself an AP man.

CHAPTER 7

Emperor of the Senate

THE MONDAY MORNING in October 1958 when I changed jobs began unchanged from my previous routine. I drove my Ford convertible from our three-room apartment in Georgetown, dropped my wife (my Indiana girlfriend whom I married in September 1957) at the *Washington Evening Star* where she was a reporter-trainee, then went up to the news media parking area off the Capitol's east front.

Nothing was really the same, however. While there were dozens of AP reporters covering Congress, the *Wall Street Journal* then assigned only three reporters to Capitol Hill: Al Otten, to take an overview and cover the Senate Finance and House Ways and Means committees, and one man each for everything else in the Senate (that was me) and the House (my former AP colleague and future national television star Paul Duke).

First, I had to cover business-oriented news in greater detail than any other general publication or wire service. There was no time to *write* these stories for the newspaper. They had to be dictated off the cuff while standing up in the *Journal*'s closetlike booth in the Senate Press Gallery. I also had to dictate breaking business news to the Dow-Jones news ticker. Second, I was expected to get plenty of exclusives, ahead of everybody else. Third, I was supposed to produce "leaders" (long, comprehensive reporting stories for page one) and perhaps "editpagers" (editorial page analytic features).

On a beat as busy as the Senate, there was no time to write leaders and editpagers during the workday, so they had to be taken home for nighttime and weekend attention. I loved it. This was the caviar to compensate for the mashed potatoes of business-news coverage. I wrote more than my share of leaders. But where I excelled was the editorial page. I wrote more editpagers than any of the paper's reporters before, since, or ever. (Since then an iron wall has separated the editorial page and the news sections.) Freed from circumscribed regional news, I now saw the world as my oyster. I could write an editpager about anything, national or international, political or ideological, economics or foreign policy—anything I could sell to the editorial page.

I made a sale my first week on the job: an editpager on Everett Dirksen, about to become Senate Republican leader succeeding William Knowland. Until I came to Washington, my lasting impression of Dirksen was the bombastic Old Guard Republican I had watched on television at the 1952 Republican National Convention in Chicago. Dirksen stuck with Bob Taft to the bitter end, insisting that Thomas E. Dewey was leading the party to defeat a third time, this time with Eisenhower. Now, five years later, Dirksen was much subtler. He was also more of an Eisenhower man than Knowland, who had backed Ike in Chicago.

After making calls to Senate contacts I had developed over the last year and a half, I turned in this copy to Bureau Chief Clark:

> Senate Republicans, badly outmaneuvered by a slim Democratic majority during the past four years, will exchange the bludgeon for the rapier in the next Congress. The wielder of the new weapon: Everett McKinley Dirksen, the velvet-voiced Senator from Illinois.
>
> G.O.P. Senators long have looked with grudging admiration on the ability of Democratic Leader Lyndon B. Johnson to effect compromises. . . . Now, in Mr. Dirksen, they will have a leader bound to borrow more than one page from the Johnson book. . . .
>
> To the tourist watching the Senate, Mr. Dirksen, 64, is the prototype of a Senator. Tall, with white, curly hair, he is one of the Senate's last exponents of old-fashioned oratory. Mr. Dirksen employs hand gestures, alliteration, polysyllabic words and a mellifluous voice in a style that has led critics to dub him, "the wizard of ooze."
>
> Behind this façade, however, is a toughness that may be deeper than the famed Knowland severity.

Al Clark called me in, and said this was really an excellent piece, much more sophisticated than my AP work. "Bob," he asked, "did you write that entirely by yourself, or did somebody help you?" Clark was less than adroit in personal relations.

Al Clark was unpopular in his own bureau, for which he would pay sooner than he could imagine. He was a rural southern conservative in a bureau filled with urban northern liberals. Reporters in the bureau, feeling superior to Clark, made fun behind his back of his stilted language and awkward behavior. I think he saw me as not quite a kindred spirit but somebody a little more conservative than the other reporters and somebody who might give him respect. I quickly concluded he was an excellent newspaperman in the wrong place at the wrong time.

Clark forwarded the Dirksen piece to the editorial page in New York, which published it without significant change.

Dirksen would treat me differently as the *Wall Street Journal* Senate correspondent than he had as an AP regional reporter. He became easy to get on the phone and easy to see. After the new session of Congress opened in 1959 with Dirksen the Senate minority leader, he invited me to one of his cocktail hours with intimates in late afternoon that in those days were staples of senior members of Congress.

Dirksen hosted these small sessions in his ornate suite on the Capitol's second floor. Everybody drank whiskey, Scotch or bourbon. Two Republican senators from opposite ends of the party's ideological spectrum—the very liberal Thomas Kuchel of California and the very conservative Roman Hruska of Nebraska—were intimates of Dirksen and were always present. A little later, a third regular appeared: Senator James Pearson of Kansas, who ideologically was equidistant between Kuchel and Hruska. Another Republican senator sometimes completed the invitation list.

When four decades later I told Senate Republican Leader Trent Lott about the Dirksen gatherings, he expressed astonishment that I had been invited and said a reporter could not possibly be present today. The first time I appeared at Dirksen's invitation, I perceived the other senators lifting eyebrows and wondering what a twenty-seven-year-old newspaper reporter was doing here. After it became apparent I would neither report nor gossip about what I heard there, I was accepted as an occasional guest.

When I first entered the inner sanctum and saw Tommy Kuchel and Roman Hruska, I anticipated a spirited debate over the Republican future. It was nothing of the kind. Dirksen engaged in a soliloquy, starting with old anecdotes appropriate to the news of the day—like the Iranian diplomat asking Dirksen to procure prostitutes to service the regent of Iran on a visit to America.

After the stories, Dirksen would get down to what was going on in Washington—especially the Senate. Nobody, I believe, has ever matched his encyclopedic knowledge of the Senate's current progress: what bills had been voted out of committee and, remarkably, what was in the bills. Dirksen himself, not a staffer, prepared a one-page precis of every bill reported by committee. At Dirksen's gatherings, the other senators seldom spoke unless spoken to, and I almost never did. Although I could not print most of what I learned, these sessions provided incomparable intelligence for a rookie Senate correspondent.

TIDBITS FROM EVERETT Dirksen expanded my knowledge of what was happening behind the scenes and built my reputation as a reporter, but my first responsibility for the *Wall Street Journal* was detailed reporting of complicated business-related stories. And a lot of what I was covering now was beyond me. Lost in the complexities of the balance of payments problem, I bought a book by the economist Robert Triffin but was appalled by pages of calculus equations. In college, I had learned about the metaphysical poetry of John Donne but no calculus. I needed sources who could explain these mysteries. Most were staffers, but there were a few helpful senators such as Russell B. Long of Louisiana.

When I met Russell Long in 1959, he had been a senator for ten years but was still only forty years old. He was the son of the assassinated Kingfish, Huey Long, populist, power mad, and dictatorial liege lord of Louisiana in the thirties. Russell, physically the spitting image of Huey, was his father writ small: populist, but on the best of terms with big business; a power politician, but limited to insuring his own political survival rather than ruling Louisiana, much less the United States.

By the time I met him, Russell Long had become a superb legislator. Later, the breakup of his marriage and a struggle with alcohol led to a decline in the sixties and the loss of the Senate Majority Whip's post to Senator Edward M. Kennedy after the 1968 elections. He once showed up dead drunk at noon for a private luncheon with me in his Capitol hideaway. Living alone in an apartment without window blinds, he would be awakened by the sun after dawn and—hungover or still half-drunk—he sometimes telephoned me to complain about something I had written for that morning's paper. A second marriage revived Long, dried him out, rehabilitated his career, and launched the longest tenure ever as chairman of the Senate Finance Committee. For twenty-eight years, he was my indispensable source.

It began in 1959 during my early months on the Senate beat when the Finance Committee was marking up an insurance tax revision—an area so hideously complicated that it is a mystery to many people who claim to understand it, which I did not. All committee markups then were conducted behind closed doors, and official briefings for the press, barely sufficient for wire services and general newspapers, did not begin to supply the information I needed. Filling in for an absent Al Otten on the insurance tax bill, I was panicky.

Senator Long came to my rescue. He understood the legislation, kept notes on everything that took place and patiently explained it to me. Much of the committee's activity consisted of rejecting Long's amendments requested by the insurance industry. I finally asked the senator whether he felt frustrated by this process. Long chuckled: "Oh, no, it's not like that at all. I don't expect any of these amendments to get adopted. But I get a campaign contribution for every one of these I introduce. This is my fund-raising season. I love it."

Russell Long was telling me that the system was no more on the level in Washington than it had been in Lincoln and Indianapolis.

IN MID-APRIL 1959, my wife and I separated permanently after nineteen and one-half months of marriage. Neither of us was unfaithful to the other, but we proved incompatible. She was an Indianapolis debutante and provisional member of the Junior League, from a different social, cultural, and religious background than I had known. I realized that at age twenty-eight I was a spoiled only child, very difficult to live with, and perhaps was not meant to be married.

I took it hard. After only six months on the *Journal*'s Senate beat, I had to take off several weeks. Washington entailed memories of my short but difficult marriage, and I thought a change of scenery might help, perhaps as a regional political reporter working out of the San Francisco or Dallas bureau. Al Clark told me he would rather keep me in Washington but would do what he could to find me a new venue. But Al Otten, who was becoming a mentor, urged me to suck it up and stick it out in Washington, where he thought my future lay. I took his advice, for which I shall always be grateful.

BY THE TIME I returned to the Senate beat, the labor chickens had come home to roost for the Kennedys on their risky attempt to fight union corruption without alienating Big Labor. While they were able to limit the Senate Rackets Committee investigation to Teamsters-bashing, "labor reform" legislation was getting out of hand—just as AFL-CIO leaders had warned the Kennedys it would.

Jack Kennedy's innocuous bill was supposed to sail through the Senate. But the conservative Democratic senator John McClellan, freed from his role as a Kennedy satellite with the end of the hearings, unexpectedly pushed a labor "bill of rights" guaranteeing rank-and-file union members the right to speak out, sue the union, and inspect its records, with criminal penalties imposed for violating those rights. This was the interference in their business that the union chiefs dreaded. The old Republican–Southern Democratic coalition revived to pass the McClellan amendment, forty-seven to forty-six, in a night session of April 22, 1959.

I dictated this big story off the cuff on deadline, describing it as a major defeat for Senator Kennedy and organized labor. My Press Gallery booth's direct-line telephone to the *Journal*'s Washington bureau rang. It was Al Clark. "Bob," he said in his deep North Carolina drawl, "you did a good job, but you're missing the real story. This is a high-level exercise in presidential politics." He pointed out that Senator Kennedy, Senate Majority Leader Lyndon Johnson, and Vice President Richard Nixon, all presidential candidates, were playing high-stakes legislative poker. Clark was belittled behind his back by his bureau's liberal reporters as a redneck, but in fact he was a shrewd political analyst.

I took Clark's advice. Using his very words in the lead paragraph ("a high-level exercise in presidential politics"), I went on:

> Vice President Nixon, who has been recently emphasizing his con-servative tendencies, voted with the coalition to break a tie. In doing so, he not only took sides with the conservatives and against the union "bosses" but, also, dealt at least a temporary setback to Sen. Kennedy. . . .
>
> The severe defeat he [Kennedy] suffered last night was considered at least a temporary setback to his political prestige.
>
> Senate Majority Leader Johnson . . . made no discernible effort to corral Democrats to support Mr. Kennedy's position, though he voted for it himself.

The *Wall Street Journal* was the only newspaper in America to cast the story that way, and I got credit as an astute political reporter. But it was Al Clark's doing.

The antilabor genie was out of the bottle. The Landrum-Griffin bill, the House version of labor reform, blunted such union weapons as picketing and secondary boycotts. It passed the overwhelmingly Democratic House by twenty-eight votes. When the bill returned to the Senate, I was in my closest contact yet with Jack Kennedy. He was the most attractive political personality that I have met, before or since: handsome, witty, charismatic, and very nice to me. I thought he was much more likable but not nearly as tough as Bobby.

Jack faced an agonizing decision. Now that his reform had become a union-buster, should he try to kill the whole bill? It would not be easy, with no certainty that LBJ would be any more helpful than he had been on the McClellan bill of rights.

Instead, JFK tried to neutralize Landrum-Griffin by removing or softening its antiunion provisions. I covered the Senate-House conference closely, and he lost on every issue. That killed his dreams of going into the presidential campaign with a Kennedy Labor Reform Act. He told me he did not want the final legislative product called the Kennedy-Landrum-Griffin Act, as was offered him. It became law as the Landrum-Griffin Act, and the Kennedys prayed that organized labor would not retaliate against them in the presidential contest ahead.

Jack Kennedy wanted to come over as a hard, relentless Irishman, but he lost the labor fight and finessed the after-battle strategy—a foretaste of his presidency.

IN THE COURSE of the labor legislation fight, I learned more about Barry Goldwater. Next to Dirksen, Goldwater was my closest Senate source. He frequently sent me letters praising my stories and, when was I covering Senate Labor Committee hearings, sometimes would send notes down to me, seated at the press table, to fill me in on his intentions.

On one occasion when I was in the Press Gallery seats watching Senate floor action, Barry motioned me to come down to see him off the floor. He told me of plans to turn the Senate inside out on the Kennedy labor reform bill. He said he had prepared one hundred amendments, giving the Senate a choice: accept his key amendments and improve what business interests considered a sham bill, or defeat every amendment and suffer death by a thousand cuts. It amounted to filibuster by amendment. Goldwater said he hoped I would print just that. I did, in a big story on the back page of the *Journal* (a choice spot in the newspaper).

It took three days to dispose of the first two Goldwater amendments, and he then declared he had made his point and would offer no other amendments. *Made his point?* I rushed down from the Gallery to call Goldwater off the Senate floor. I told him he had embarrassed the *Wall Street Journal* and me by selling me a story that turned out to be pure hokum. Always solicitous, Goldwater told me he was sorry he had embarrassed me and should not have gone overboard. It was a rerun of his Rackets Committee performance when he reneged on promises to dig deep into United Auto Workers violence. Charming though Goldwater was, was he serious?

Even more irritated than I by Goldwater's performance was the man who drafted the hundred amendments. Michael Bernstein worked for

Goldwater as chief counsel of the Republican minority on the Senate Labor Committee and as his resident intellectual on Capitol Hill.

In making the rounds on my Senate beat, I found myself lingering in Bernstein's office but not to talk labor legislation. I received a tutorial from Mike. He introduced me to Hannah Arendt, Joseph Schumpeter, and much more. He attacked my belief that the country was better off if the two major parties were close in ideology. Since liberals were fighting to take command of the Republicans as well as the Democrats, he argued, conservatives better try to take control of just one party.

FROM MY FIRST day as the *Journal*'s Senate correspondent, I entered a special, difficult environment controlled by Senator Lyndon Baines Johnson of Texas. He was no mere majority leader but a dominating presence, the unprecedented emperor of the Senate.

The sense of impending change in Washington heightened when the Democrats gained sixteen Senate seats in their 1958 landslide. That replaced six years of an evenly contested Senate with a sixty-four to thirty-two Democratic majority. Did this mean the postwar gridlock had been broken? On the contrary, it spelled trouble for Lyndon Johnson.

Only two reporters on the Senate beat those last two years of Johnson's leadership suggested that LBJ had lost his leverage amid so many Democrats. One was Sam Shaffer, the veteran chief congressional correspondent for *Newsweek*. Garrulous and generous, he was the only old hand in the Senate Press Gallery who offered a helping hand to the *Wall Street Journal*'s new correspondent.

Shaffer was a World War II Marine Corps combat correspondent in the Pacific and not intimidated by Lyndon Johnson. But LBJ was nobody to take lightly. That was underlined to me one afternoon in 1960 when I was in the outer office of the Taj Mahal (Johnson's lavishly redecorated new majority leader's suite in the Capitol) waiting for a scheduled appointment with him. He never was on time for such meetings, but this wait was unusually long. After an hour, a man barged out of the inner office, his face a mask of anger. It was Kenneth Crawford, *Newsweek*'s Washington bureau manager.

In the inner office, I found the majority leader no less upset than Crawford. He was never communicative in any interview that I had requested, but this time he was sphinxlike. I did notice something strange. On a table next to Johnson's desk were two piles of *Newsweek*, with tabs sticking out of magazines.

What was going on later reached me via the Senate Press Gallery grapevine. LBJ had called in Ken Crawford to ask him to take Sam Shaffer off the Senate beat because he was so "anti-Johnson." The stacked magazines tabbed Shaffer-written stories that the majority leader considered "anti-Johnson" because they revealed that the emperor had no clothes. Crawford asserted that Shaffer was a damn fine reporter who was going to continue covering the Senate.

The only other Senate reporter to report the ebbing of Johnson's authority was I, the most junior correspondent in the Gallery. Through 1959, I was pecking away at the press's conventional wisdom that Johnson was as masterful as ever. On January 21, 1960, I brought my contrarian views to the *Journal*'s editorial page, describing LBJ, seeking the presidential nomination, as unable to control Democratic liberals. The "immediate political impact" of the liberal Senate revolt, I wrote, "has been to chop away at Mr. Johnson's stature" as a masterful Senate leader.

Why would Johnson demand Sam Shaffer's scalp while he ignored me? Partly because he considered *Newsweek* more important than the *Wall Street Journal*, which then was not yet a powerful force. Partly because Shaffer was a much more formidable figure than I.

But LBJ knew what I was writing about him, as indicated in a bizarre incident two months after my liberal revolt column. Late in the evening of March 31, 1960, I was drinking in the Members Bar of the Press Club with my good friend Bob Jensen of the *Buffalo Evening News* (as I often did after my marriage collapsed). Somebody burst into the bar to say LBJ was in the club's ballroom, "drunk as a loon." Jensen and I went to check

The report was not exaggerated. Johnson was attending the seventieth birthday celebration of Bascom Timmons, a famous Texas journalist who headed his own Washington news bureau. To my surprise, I found the majority leader without aides or limo. LBJ, who until then had shown little interest in me and absolutely no affection, spotted me and wrapped one of his long arms around me. "Bob, I like ("lahk" was the Texas pronunciation) you," he drawled drunkenly, "but you don't like me." He chanted it over and over, embracing me and swirling me in a little dance.

Celebrants at the Timmons birthday party, mostly Texans, were as drunk as Johnson and uninterested in saving the majority leader from embarrassment. So, Bob Jensen and I guided the much taller man to the elevator, down to the National Press Building's 14th Street lobby, and out into a taxi to be taken home.

The next day, a cool, immaculately groomed Senator Johnson was seated, as usual, in the majority leader's chair on the Senate floor prior to the noon convening time. That was the only time reporters were permitted on the floor, huddled around Johnson's chair for five minutes of questions and answers. Johnson often, as he did on this occasion, kept his eyes down reading what was in front of him and then looked up suddenly, registering seeming surprise at seeing himself surrounded by reporters. When he did that this time, he stared at me, exclaiming: "Well, Novak, saw you at the Press Club last night. Got a little drunk out, didn't it?" The other reporters chuckled appreciatively, thinking it was I who had been "a little drunk," as LBJ intended.

Johnson's credo was to reward allies and punish adversaries, applying it to journalists as well as politicians. I was not one of his friends, as he sometimes demonstrated with petty behavior. In 1959, Johnson was delaying confirmation of the Philadelphia banker Thomas Gates as secretary of defense. I had been pestering the majority leader for his plans. Near the end of a mini-press conference on the floor, I asked again whether he had plans to confirm Gates. "None at all," muttered Johnson, without looking up. As I entered the Press Gallery one floor up a few moments later, one of the Gallery's attendants who knew I was tracking the Gates nomination told me that the Senate had just confirmed him. Johnson had hardly waited for the opening prayer to end before calling up Gates's nomination and confirming him with no debate and no roll call.

Why, I asked myself, would Johnson engage in juvenile duplicity when it would have cost him nothing and given me no useful news to have told me he was about to confirm Gates? I now understand he wanted to show the cocky young reporter from the *Wall Street Journal* that Lyndon B. Johnson, and nobody else, was in charge.

Whenever I wanted to see him, seeking some small piece of information, it was difficult to get an appointment and impossible to see him without a long wait. When he initiated a meeting, it frequently came in early evening when I was on deadline or late for a dinner date—as if he were reading my mind.

No reporter, certainly not I, ever rejected such an "invitation." When I would enter his office, very stiff (at least double strength) Scotch and water drinks would be poured for me as he pressed me to keep up with him, drink for drink. Only years later would I learn that Johnson's Scotches were watered down so much they were barely alcoholic. He usually called me in to pump me about something he thought I might know, but occasionally would tell me something—not to help me but to help himself. LBJ was a taker, not a giver.

CHAPTER 8

Driving with Kennedy

O N   A   T U E S D A Y in early December 1959, I spent the night in the Travelers Hotel outside New York's LaGuardia Airport to depart on New York governor Nelson Rockefeller's chartered Eastern Airlines jet early the next morning for South Bend, Indiana, beginning a trip to explore his chances for the 1960 Republican presidential nomination. I was so excited I could hardly sleep, anticipating my first travel with a presidential campaigner. I had to act cool, however, as though I were an old hand on the political trail—befitting a reporter for the *Wall Street Journal.*

The plane was filled with some thirty people from the news media, including a few big-timers but mostly reporters from Albany and New York accustomed to covering the governor. They all were male and even more liberal than the White House reporters covering President Dwight D. Eisenhower but unlike them were in love with the politician they covered. "Rocky," as he was now called for the first time in his fifty-one years, was accessible to any reporter who wanted to talk to him, and in addition held two news conferences every morning (the real one for print reporters and then a shorter one for TV cameras, whose presence was objectionable to the dominant print media).

It would be hard for today's ultraserious journalists to imagine what fun it was on the campaign circuit then. A poker game most nights, and drinking around the clock. Everybody started the morning with a Bloody Mary. Near the end of the trip when Eastern Airlines ran out of vodka, reporters nearly rioted. Flight attendants solved the problem by mixing the Bloody Marys with gin. Nobody complained.

A ringleader in fun making was the New York City bureau chief of the Gannett newspapers: short, rotund, balding, with a cigarette between his lips and a drink in his hand. It was Jack Germond. He was only three years my senior, and we both enjoyed tobacco, alcohol, and politics. It began a friendship spanning more than forty years. Germond worked hard, and so did I. Besides my daily coverage of Rockefeller, I published one front-page leader and two editpagers in ten days—considered phenomenal at the *Journal.*

Rockefeller's message to party regulars: He was "a card-carrying Republican," who got his start after college with a job on the local health board given him by the Westchester County party "boss." While Vice President Richard Nixon at that point never strayed from the Eisenhower line, Rockefeller took positions to the *right* of Eisenhower and Nixon—advocating resumed underground testing of nuclear weapons and compulsory arbitration to settle crippling strikes.

After ten days, Rockefeller's staff expressed satisfaction that the trip had gone well and predicted their chief would announce his candidacy within thirty days (as I reported in the *Wall Street Journal*). Then just before Christmas, Nelson Rockefeller, not for the last time, surprised the political world. He announced he would not seek the presidential nomination, publicly complaining that party regulars had sewed it up for Nixon.

I believe Rockefeller could have won the nomination. Party regulars told me all during the December trip that if the governor could beat Nixon in just one primary, they would take a close look at him. Rockefeller could have won New Hampshire and, if he had, Wisconsin was tailor-made for an upset. Nixon's base in Wisconsin relied on Catholics, who were determined to cross into the Democratic primary that year to vote for Kennedy.

Rockefeller as the Republican nominee, I am convinced, would have beaten Kennedy by carrying New York, Pennsylvania, and Michigan, all states that Nixon lost. Rockefeller's administration would have been hardly less liberal than Kennedy's but much more orderly, particularly in foreign affairs. I cannot believe Rockefeller would have wandered into war in Vietnam without a plan for winning it or that he would have been buffaloed by Nikita Khrushchev. On the other hand, Rockefeller as president would have forced a long postponement of the desirable realignment into conservative Republican and liberal Democratic parties. This might have eliminated a Goldwater candidacy and a Reagan presidency. Big government would have gotten even bigger, without the mitigation of Kennedy and Reagan tax cuts.

Personally, I was devastated by Rockefeller's decision. I was then a one-issue voter attracted to which candidate was the toughest cold warrior, and Rockefeller fit that description. In truth, though, I was most upset by not being able to cover a slam-bang intraparty slugfest between Rockefeller and Nixon. Nor did having to focus on Nixon for the campaign year ahead appeal to me. Our relationship started poorly in the 1960 election cycle, and did not get better during the next three decades.

THE FIRST TIME Richard Nixon took notice of me resulted from a leader in the *Wall Street Journal* on March 31, 1960, co-authored by Al Otten and me. In bygone days before the *Journal* hired high-priced pollsters, its reporters would accost people at random in shopping centers and on street corners. Otten and I over the course of a week questioned hundreds of Wisconsin voters about that state's hot Democratic presidential primary between John F. Kennedy and Hubert H. Humphrey. We found Kennedy ahead, which is the way the primary turned out. But comparing notes, we also discovered many Wisconsin voters who said they had voted for Eisenhower in 1956 and would under no conditions vote for Nixon in 1960.

The resulting Otten-Novak story declared that Nixon "appears to be in serious political trouble," with the front-page headline blaring that "He Faces Uphill Fight for Presidency." Veteran *Washington Post* reporter Carroll Kilpatrick picked up the story and ran a page-one piece on it. Otten's unknown collaborator was incorrectly identified by the *Post* as "Robert O. Novak," but I was still thrilled. Richard Nixon was not so thrilled, I was told by his aides. He ranted about reporters drawing these conclusions from an amateurish, unscientific poll. He was right. Nixon won Wisconsin in November.

Nixon was even hotter when he picked up the *Journal* of April 25 to read my leader reporting that presidential candidates now "judiciously leaked" the polls they commissioned "to sway the course of politics." I was evenhanded in exposing this chicanery on a bipartisan basis, but Nixon was only interested in what I wrote about his campaign: I revealed "the latest of a series of private polls leaked by the Nixon camp to counteract his falling rating in public polls."

A furious Nixon complained to the *Journal*—not to me, not to the Washington bureau chief, but right to the top. He called Bernard Kilgore, president of Dow-Jones and publisher of the *Wall Street Journal,* and complained that Novak was anti-Nixon. Kilgore said merely he would pass this on to Warren Phillips, the paper's managing editor. I was walking into my little Georgetown apartment when the phone rang with Phillips on the line to relay Nixon's complaint. "What should I do?" I asked. "Nothing," Phillips replied. That was the joy of working for the *Wall Street Journal.*

IN THE EARLY autumn of 1959, I was invited along with the other sixteen reporters in the *Wall Street Journal*'s Washington bureau for dinner with Barney Kilgore at a suite in Washington's Sheraton Park Hotel. I was surprised to see that Al Clark was not present. Kilgore started by saying that he wanted to find out what was good and what was bad about the way the bureau was run, adding that everything said would be strictly off the record. From whom? Clark obviously. As deftly guided by Kilgore, the conversation turned into an auto-da-fé against the unpopular bureau chief. I remember only two staffers present who defended Clark, and I—the bureau's newest member—was one of them. Kilgore had decided to replace Clark, and wanted evidence that he had lost control of the bureau.

But the publisher's real complaint against Clark was that he was not Scotty Reston. Barney Kilgore was building a great national newspaper and wanted his man in Washington to be as much a presence in the capital as James Reston of the *New York Times* and his predecessor, Arthur Krock. Hardly anybody in Washington knew Al Clark. He was replaced by Henry Gemmill, a golden boy of the *Wall Street Journal* who had been the paper's managing editor at age thirty-one and was now a roving reporter. Keeping his managing editor's salary of $50,000 (in 2007 dollars, $342,000), he was in 1960 the highest paid reporter in America. Gemmill knew far less about government and politics than Clark and never showed interest in educating himself, but he was a superb packager of the news.

Gemmill displayed that talent soon after arriving in Washington when Rowland Evans, ace congressional reporter for the *New York Herald-Tribune,* and I separately got hold of the same Democratic memo warning that continued attacks on Nixon could boomerang by making him the object of sympathy. I wrote it as an interesting but not earth-shaking story, and the new bureau chief called me into his office. Gemmill told me he thought we had a leader if we punched up the prose. The memorandum should be described as "prepared secretly, circulated privately and now given the closest attention by key party figures." I wrote this, word for word. My story appeared in the left column of the *Journal*'s page one, while Evans's was buried inside a Saturday edition of the *Herald-Tribune.* Rowly had been beaten, and he would remember it.

Gemmill became the first *Journal* staffer since Kilgore to be taken into the Washington Gridiron Club and the paper's first Washington bureau member ever to appear on a Sunday television interview show. But he never became another Arthur Krock or Scotty Reston. No *WSJ* bureau chief was a major Washington figure until Albert Hunt many years later.

Al Clark's heart was broken, and he turned down offers to become a reporter-at-large for the newspaper and finished out his career at *U.S. News & World Report* with largely administrative duties. I had been given another illustration of the dangers of being a corporate employee.

. . .

AT EIGHT THIRTY on a Friday morning early in February 1960, I took a call in the Senate Press Gallery. It was Senator John F. Kennedy complaining about an item in the "Washington Wire" weekly column that morning in the *Wall Street Journal* reporting that his campaign for the presidential nomination was losing momentum. "Bob," he said, "how can you say that when we haven't even had a primary yet? Why don't you come out to Wisconsin and see what's really happening?"

The Wisconsin primary on April 5 was the first test for Kennedy's strategy of winning the nomination by entering every possible primary. Fear of nominating the first Roman Catholic since the Al Smith disaster of 1928 had to be overcome by Kennedy demonstrating his electability in the primaries. Only Senator Hubert H. Humphrey of Minnesota was also entering the primaries, but one primary loss could be fatal for Kennedy. Waiting to seize that opportunity were two serious candidates: Lyndon B. Johnson and Senator Stuart Symington of Missouri. Or would "non-candidate" Adlai E. Stevenson slide in as the party's nominee for the third straight election?

With his customary generosity to a junior colleague, Al Otten opened the way for me to go to Wisconsin in early March. Although Kennedy and Humphrey were both liberals who disagreed on little, their contest was bitterly divisive for Wisconsin Democrats. One night I went to dinner at a Madison steak house with the state's pro-Kennedy Democratic state chairman Patrick Lucey (a future governor) and his fiery Greek-American wife, Jean. She spotted two young former Lucey aides who had gone over to the Humphrey campaign and started shouting: "You little sons of bitches! You traitors!" All the while, Pat was remonstrating: "Jean, please, please."

I hit the hat trick again during my first week in Wisconsin—a leader and two editpagers. On the March 10 editorial page, I tried to describe vivid differences in the two campaigns.

He [Kennedy] makes the ordeal of campaigning as painless as possible: Saving time by flitting about the state in his twin-engine plane, keeping about as close as any campaigner ever can to his schedule, finding time each evening for two hours of rest and privacy in his hotel room. . . .

Mr. Humphrey, on the other hand, maintains a frenetic pace, fighting against time by racing across the countryside in a chartered bus but making a shambles of his schedule before his 18-hour day is over. . . .

Whatever inward tension he might feel, Senator Kennedy sprawls in an airplane seat between stops, reading or quietly talking politics with aides and reporters. Bone weary as his bus tries vainly to reach the next town on time, Senator Humphrey nevertheless conferences excitedly with a campaign planner or delivers animated lectures to reporters on the Soviet menace and the need to preserve the family farm.

After this column was published, a young Kennedy supporter named Harris Wofford (a future U.S. senator from Pennsylvania) wrote me a letter complimenting me on describing the difference between a liberal "whose spring has sprung" and one whose future was before him. I had tried to be fair, but perhaps my preference for JFK showed. He was great fun to cover, while being with HHH was an ordeal.

After my March visit to Wisconsin, Kennedy gave me a ride back to Washington in his plane, the *Caroline.* When we got to National Airport, Kennedy asked me where I lived. When I said Georgetown, he said he lived there too and would give me a lift home. It was a wild ride, with the senator driving his convertible at breakneck speed and looking at me out of the corner of his eye to see how frightened I was.

On April 5, Kennedy won the Wisconsin primary. The last real chance to stop him was in the West Virginia primary on May 7.

LESS THAN A week before the West Virginia primary, LBJ's aide George Reedy entered the Senate Press Gallery with an invitation. Senate Majority Leader Lyndon Johnson, who had been bragging he was "keeping the store" in Washington while Kennedy and Humphrey campaigned, was going to step out that Friday and Saturday on a three-state tour of Pennsylvania, Ohio, and West Virginia. He was inviting the regular Senate press corps to come along. Restricting the traveling news media entourage to his faithful Senate claque would guarantee more favorable coverage. Unfortunately for Johnson, however, I was among the Senate regulars.

The three stops were carefully selected. East Liverpool, Ohio, was the constituency of the mercurial Congressman Wayne Hays, who had defected from Kennedy after endorsing him and now backed Johnson. Then on to Pittsburgh, where Mayor Joseph Barr was making signs that he would break Kennedy's hammerlock on Pennsylvania by supporting Johnson. Finally, the windup in Clarksburg, West Virginia, a state where LBJ had many supporters who wanted to kill the JFK candidacy by backing Humphrey in the upcoming primary.

Reporters traveling with Johnson expected that, following a Saturday Democratic fund-raising dinner in Clarksburg, the majority leader's personal plane would go back to Washington. Not so. Reedy informed us belatedly that Johnson was headed for the LBJ ranch in Texas to finish out the weekend and would not return to Washington until Monday. We were all invited as guests at the ranch. The alternative was to somehow find our way home from rural West Virginia. We all went to Texas.

On Sunday, the ranch was inundated by Texas politicians (including a future speaker of the House, Jim Wright), all singing the praises of their host to the non-Texas reporters. It was a nonstop eatathon, drinkathon Sunday starting with a huge breakfast of thick bacon and deer sausage, followed by an immense barbecue lunch, and, before all that could be digested, a sit-down steak dinner. Johnson had never been so nice to me, personally driving me on a tour of his ranch in his Lincoln convertible.

This era of good feelings between the majority leader and me ended abruptly Monday morning when Johnson's plane, returning to Washington, stopped for refueling in Nashville. At the airport somebody bought a copy of that day's *Wall Street Journal* and gave it to Lyndon, who I was told was infuriated by the headline: "Sen. Johnson Gaining Little Support Among Northern Politicians in Bid for Nomination." What followed in my report was even more stunning:

> He can bedazzle convention delegates with his Texas charm, impress them with his self-assurance, surprise them with his little-known talents as a stump speaker. But despite the onslaught, Northern delegates continue to express the same lingering doubt:
>
> "I'm afraid he might hurt the ticket in this state." . . .
>
> There is no question that the Texan is opening Northern eyes to his skills as a campaigner. But it seems doubtful that he has opened them nearly enough to turn to him as their choice for president.

I exposed in detail how flimsy were LBJ's hopes. In Ohio, Congressman Hays could not even control the delegates in his own district. In Pennsylvania, Mayor Barr's admiration for Johnson as "a leader of men" did not translate into delegates. In West Virginia, Johnson had to depend on Humphrey to break JFK's lock on the nomination.

At the Nashville stop, a Johnson aide asked me whether I had dictated the story Sunday from a telephone at the ranch. I said that I had. "Well," I was told, "the senator considers this a distinct violation of his hospitality." I asked how I was supposed to transmit my story. I was told that I should not have written that kind of story at the ranch. That was LBJ's attitude toward the press: bring them into your warm inner circle, and expect—indeed, demand—a quid pro quo.

ON THE DAY after my unfavorable report on his travels, Lyndon Johnson had a lot more than me to worry about. On May 10, Jack Kennedy trounced Hubert Humphrey in West Virginia, three-to-two.

To keep open the prospect of a brokered convention, Johnson's agents had done everything possible behind the scenes for Humphrey. But Joe Kennedy bought the presidential nomination for his son in West Virginia. Howard Norton, reporting from Charleston, wrote in the May 11 *Baltimore Sun:* "Votes were being bought and sold openly in the streets of this city today."

To my knowledge, the *Wall Street Journal* was the only news organization that tried to find why all those West Virginia Protestants voted for Jack Kennedy. Two of the paper's best reporters, Joe Guilfoyle from New York and Roscoe Born from Washington, were sent to West Virginia for five weeks. We were all sworn to secrecy, and this effort did not become known for forty-six years (in Seymour Hersh's *The Dark Side of Camelot*).

Born wrote a carefully documented report of how a presidential nomination was purchased in West Virginia through illegal, clandestine payoffs to sheriffs who controlled the voting process. The story was killed by the newspaper's high command in New York. The official internal explanation was the refusal of sources to sign affidavits, but the real problem was the story's predictable impact just before the Democratic convention in Los Angeles. The word inside the newspaper was that Barney Kilgore ordained it was not the place of the *Wall Street Journal* to decide the presidential nominee of the Democratic Party.

KENNEDY'S "SMASHING UPSET victory" in West Virginia, Otten and I wrote on May 12, "all but clinches" the nomination. Even so, a Johnson-for-President office was set up in midtown Washington at the Ambassador Hotel. I found the bejeweled wives of Texas congressmen stuffing envelopes and answering telephones. I met John Connally, brought up from Houston to run the campaign, and found him urbane and charming—nothing like his political patron, LBJ. In hand-to-hand combat with Bobby Kennedy for delegates, Connally lost most of them but was preparing a coup for the biggest prize in the west.

Jack Kennedy had gone seven-for-seven in primary elections but passed up certain victory in California, the last scheduled primary with the rich reward of eighty-one delegates. State Democratic Chairman William Munnell, majority leader of the State Assembly, pleaded with the Kennedys not to provoke a contested primary against favorite son Governor Pat Brown that would open deep rifts in the California party. In a secret meeting in Carmel, the Kennedys agreed to stay out in return for a commitment from Munnell to hand over the delegation once Brown won the primary.

Was California really Kennedy's, ending any doubt about the nomination? On my first reporting trip to the Golden State for a big Democratic dinner attended by all the candidates, less than six weeks before the national convention, I found the delegation in play, with LBJ's operatives working hard to keep JFK from cashing in on the Carmel commitment.

One source for my analysis was Joe Cerrell, Munnell's young executive director of the State Democratic Committee. I had dinner in Los Angeles at Trader Vic's in the Beverly Hilton Hotel with Cerrell and his pretty blond girlfriend (and future wife), Lee Bullock, who also was a political operative. As I consumed one mai tai after another without taking a note, Joe and Lee never dreamed that anything they said would appear in the *Wall Street Journal* of June 3, 1960.

It did. I reported that "talks with scores of party leaders and convention delegates discloses a fragmented delegation with substantial backing" for Stevenson and "lesser support" for Johnson and Symington. The unwillingness of the newly desirable California Democrats to commit themselves to Kennedy was reflected in my story by this quote from Cerrell: "California Democrats are something like a girl who has just got rid of her teeth braces and thrown away her glasses; she doesn't say yes to the first suitor."

After we both returned to Washington, Senator Kennedy telephoned me with a complaint. "Bob, you really got this one wrong," he told me. "We have California all wrapped up. If we don't, I'll eat your story."

LOS ANGELES IN 1960 was the first convention I covered. Arriving in Los Angeles the week before the convention, I wrote on the editorial page of July 7 that Kennedy "is tantalizingly close" to the nomination despite "eleventh-hour anti-Kennedy outbursts," which I proceeded to analyze. Arriving in LA a day after me, Al Otten expressed to me his resentment that I had rushed in to write the very piece he said he had planned himself.

During my two years with the *Journal,* Otten had shared political coverage with me and been kind in other ways. When I was suffering from the breakup of my marriage, Al and his wife, Jane, provided advice and consolation. With my Ford convertible in temporary possession of my estranged wife, the Ottens loaned me their Volkswagen Bug to drive up to Cape Cod (a kindness I repaid by burning a cigarette hole in the front seat). His complaint in Los Angeles was the first sign that this *Journal* veteran might resent his pushy young colleague—a factor in a major decision in my life two years later.

The July 7 piece was the first of three editpagers I wrote from the Los Angeles convention. The second two would be processed by Vermont C. Royster, the illustrious editor of the *Wall Street Journal,* once he arrived in Los Angeles. Short and stocky with a thick North Carolina accent, Vermont Connecticut Royster was a formidable character. He ended World War II as the captain of a destroyer escort, and thereafter conveyed the image of being on the quarterdeck of a warship.

My editorial page contributions had been handled in New York by Royster aides who seldom changed them. In LA, I was to get very different treatment from Royster. The first piece I gave Royster commented on the lack of passion among convention Democrats as they prepared to nominate Kennedy. When I entered the *WSJ* workspace in the Biltmore Hotel the next morning, Royster handed me an "edited" version of the column. "I made a few changes heah and theah," he drawled. In fact, he had completely rewritten the first six paragraphs in his lyrical style that could not have been more different from my matter-of-fact prose.

"Roy, I would like to make one more change," I said. I took out a pencil, crossed out "By Robert D. Novak" at the top and replaced it with "By Vermont C. Royster." He stared at me without smiling, and I was scared to death. Would the old naval commander chew out this insolent staffer? Would he send me back to Washington? Would he fire me? "Well," he finally said softly, "let's see if we can have a meeting of minds." We worked together on a third version that retained my prose with a few Roysterish touches. The final editpager I wrote from LA was processed by Royster with minimal changes. I had done the right thing to impress Vermont Royster, and henceforth he was my staunchest advocate in the *Journal*'s executive hierarchy.

In addition to my editorial page contributions, I was assigned a front-page leader on John F. Kennedy and daily news stories. There was not much time in Los Angeles for horsing around, but I slipped away late one night to the Cinegrill Bar of the Roosevelt Hotel in Hollywood, a notorious pickup place. I never had been good at this, but I made contact with a cute English girl working as a nanny in Beverly Hills. She showed little interest in me, until I revealed I was covering the convention. "Oh," she squealed in her working-class British accent, "do you think I could meet Jack Kennedy?" It was clear to me that if I was going to have any fun with her, the answer had better be yes.

Kennedy was doing the rounds of state delegations, and I brought along my English friend to one such reception. Kennedy rewarded each delegate with a handshake and grin, accompanied by a brief word before moving on. But Jack Kennedy was a sucker for pretty girls. He lingered with us a few moments as they talked about what part of England was her home. Then he asked us: "Where did you meet?" I broke an awkward silence when I said: "In a bar." Kennedy laughed delightedly. I was afraid she would be offended, but she was walking on air after her conversation with John F. Kennedy.

The Sunday before the convention, the big, boisterous California delegation caucused at the cavernous NBC studios. State Democratic Chairman Munnell had welshed on his Carmel commitment to Kennedy. While he now publicly endorsed Stevenson, he was plotting with Connally behind the scenes as a crypto LBJ man. Joe Cerrell, Munnell's aide, told me that when his boss reached the senator in the receiving line at NBC, Kennedy declined to shake his hand. A roll call of California's 162 delegates showed an edge for Stevenson, with Kennedy in second place.

The California caucus proved the high-water mark of the Johnson-Stevenson collaboration. Kennedy was nominated on the first ballot Wednesday night, and all that remained was picking a vice president.

That presented a problem for the *Wall Street Journal.* I had already written the JFK profile as the right-hand column leader in Thursday's paper, and it was locked in early Wednesday. We also needed a profile on the vice presidential nominee, whose identity would not be revealed until late Wednesday afternoon, with the deadline approaching for our nationally published newspaper.

We had asked JFK campaign manager Bobby Kennedy for help. Strictly for guidance and not to be published, would he give us the names of *all* possibilities as his brother's running mate? We would then write a profile on each, and at the last minute slip in the story on the one selected. He gave us three names: Senator W. Stuart Symington of Missouri, Senator Henry M. (Scoop) Jackson of Washington, and Governor Orville Freeman of Minnesota. We all thought it odd for the little-known Freeman to be in that company.

I don't believe Bobby intentionally misled us. I came to believe Freeman already had been chosen, and Bobby put up the two senators as decoys. Bobby knew about the selection of LBJ only a few hours before we did.

As the staffer who knew Johnson best, I was assigned the rush job. With no time to write this story, I dictated off the cuff to the New York desk. "This attempt to win the election by adding strength to the ticket in Southern, Border and some Western states," I said, "involves the calculated risk of losing Negro and labor voters in the North." What I did not write (because I did not appreciate it) was that Kennedy could not have possibly been elected president without Johnson on the ticket.

On Friday morning, the newly nominated John F. Kennedy was proceeding through the Biltmore's lobby on his way to a Democratic National Committee meeting to exert his new power by purging the anti-LBJ Paul Butler as national chairman and replacing him with Scoop Jackson. Followed by reporters and television cameras, Kennedy motioned me over. I congratulated him on his nomination, and he responded by recalling my prediction of troubles in California: "You were right. If you have a little mustard, I'll eat it right now." I can't imagine any other presidential nominee recalling a foolish statement at the moment of his greatest political triumph. That was the style that personally endeared Jack Kennedy to people who harbored doubts about his capacity.

CHAPTER 9

New Frontier

On the saturday following the 1960 Democratic National Convention, I was off to Nashville to cover Tennessee's Senate Democratic primary campaign. Senator Estes Kefauver, the nation's best known Democrat next to John Kennedy and Adlai Stevenson, was being challenged by a segregationist named Tip Taylor.

I phoned the state's junior senator, Albert Gore, to ask him about his senior colleague, with whom he was not friendly. Since I had not been close to Gore during two years of covering the Senate, I was surprised when he insisted that I join him for a family supper at his home in Carthage, not far from Nashville. Gore, his charming wife, Pauline, his two attractive children, and I enjoyed a fried chicken dinner, with the senator and me drinking Budweiser from the can. His polite twelve-year-old son (introduced to me as "Little Al") took in every word.

Gore was candid with me as he never had been in Washington (nor would be when we returned to the capital). He felt Kefauver was running a poor campaign and was washed up politically in Tennessee, as he was nationally. Nevertheless, Gore predicted accurately, Kefauver would win the Senate primary more easily than expected. Segregationist Democrats like Tip Taylor, he said, were finished. What Gore did not see coming was the Republican tide that would inundate him a decade later.

After dinner, we turned to the coming presidential election. I don't think Albert Gore was much of a drinker, and two cans of beer may have loosened his tongue. He suddenly stared at me and said in his deep baritone: "Bob, you were at Los Angeles last week. Tell me. Why would the Democratic Party pick Jack Kennedy when they could have had me?" I could not imagine how to answer, but Pauline Gore saved me by intervening. "Albert!" she yelled. "Now, you stop that."

Prior to that chicken dinner in Carthage, I did not realize how deeply

Gore harbored presidential dreams. How much was Little Al pressed into a political career by his father's disappointment, making the son intent on surpassing the father's accomplishments? When I related this anecdote to the younger Gore during his first campaign for president in 1988, he smiled weakly and changed the subject.

MY NEXT ASSIGNMENT took me to Cape Cod, Massachusetts, to cover Kennedy. On my first morning there, the nominee was himself briefing the press. I was wearing khaki shorts that had seen better days and a faded T-shirt with the stigmata of a coffee spill. "Well, Bob, welcome to Cape Cod" said a beaming Jack Kennedy. "But you really haven't improved the dress code around here, have you?"

The principal news story of my week at Hyannis Port was the arrival Friday, July 29, of Lyndon Johnson. I ran into a sexy LBJ secretary I had been flirting with for a year. But the woman I really wanted to take out was Geraldine Williams, LBJ aide George Reedy's younger, elegant-looking secretary, who was standing nearby. Al Spivak of UPI, a bachelor in his thirties, was also at hand, and I suggested that all four of us go out that night for dinner and do the nightspots of Hyannis. I hoped to get to know Geraldine better.

But it never happened because of *Time* correspondent Hugh Sidey. Late in the afternoon, Sidey told me he was going to camp outside JFK's house in the family compound, where Kennedy, Johnson, and their campaign staffs were meeting that night. Sidey, only a few years older than I, was sure the old guard reporters never would cover this, and we would have the story to ourselves. I could not resist this opportunity, and paid my regrets to the Johnson secretaries. Geraldine would have to wait.

It soon appeared I had bought into a fiasco. Sidey and I stood in the country lane outside JFK's house for three and one-half hours, as Johnson read from a bag full of memos specially prepared for the meeting, though Hugh and I could make out nothing of what he was saying.

Finally, at one a.m. Saturday, Senator Johnson left the modest clapboard house, accompanied—peculiarly, I thought—by Kennedy press secretary Pierre Salinger. Sidey whispered to me: "Let's follow them."

We did, in Sidey's rental car, to the Yachtsman Hotel, where Johnson was staying. We stationed ourselves in a stairwell above Johnson's suite. While we could not hear everything, Sidey and I both were experienced eavesdroppers and picked up a lot.

It soon became apparent why Johnson brought along Salinger. Johnson could never figure out why Kennedy was so much more popular than he was and at this point had concluded it was due to Pierre Salinger. An investigative reporter for *Collier's* magazine whose probes of labor corruption gained Bobby Kennedy's attention and an investigator's job on the Senate Rackets Committee, Salinger had become Senator Kennedy's presidential campaign press secretary. Insiders laughed at the notion that Pierre was responsible for Jack Kennedy's popularity.

At the Yachtsman, amid the sound of ice cubes clinking in highballs, I heard LBJ declare that what he really needed was his own Pierre Salinger. George Reedy was in the room, and I could imagine Johnson's long-suffering press aide with his sad face, sitting silently as his efforts were disdained.

Johnson was preoccupied by the need to sell himself to the American people. We heard him quote what he said Palmer Hoyt, publisher of the *Denver Post,* had told him but what sounded more like Lyndon Johnson: "You got a little maturity and all that, but what makes people holler when you walk by is your six-foot-three inches, good looking, broad shouldered Texan. You ought to capitalize on that. Matt Dillon [the town marshal who was the hero in the TV western *Gunsmoke*] ain't popular for nothing."

They drank and talked until nearly three a.m. The next day, I buttonholed enough people to put together a good story for Monday's paper on what was decided at Senator Kennedy's house—how they would campaign and what they would do in the postconvention session of Congress. My story included, and was most remembered for, the Matt Dillon quote.

MY FIRST CAMPAIGN was 1960, and the last when I would be on the road continuously from before Labor Day to election day, beginning in California to report on the contest for that state's big bag of electoral votes. I concluded and wrote in the *Journal* that Nixon had the edge (he did win California narrowly). My most memorable interview during a week's reporting there, however, contributed nothing to my story. I was told the youngest Kennedy brother, whom I had never met, had been assigned to Los Angeles as western states coordinator for Jack's campaign. I got an appointment to meet Teddy in a newly rented office on Wilshire Boulevard, furnished with leased metal furniture and free from the clutter of a real working office.

Edward M. Kennedy was then twenty-eight years old, a year younger than I. He was robust, trim, and good-looking. When I asked him about the tense battle for California, he floored me by telling me this state was not included in his domain as western coordinator. That meant he was in charge of thinly populated states with few electoral votes that Nixon was going to win anyway. I wasn't much interested, but asked about his states to be polite. He replied he was brand-new on the job and didn't know anything about them. Teddy was neither charming Jack nor ferocious Bobby. He had the reputation of a playboy but also seemed a lightweight.

I next flew to Indianapolis to pick up Richard Nixon on the first day of a whirlwind dash across the country in the first campaign using jet aircraft. Freezing in early September on the Great Plains, I bought my first three-piece suit in Sioux Falls, South Dakota—where Nixon and Johnson appeared at the national plowing contest—and put it on the *Wall Street Journal* expense account, where it went through without question as everything always did. From there, I picked up Kennedy and traveled with him for a week. For ten weeks, I spent a total of three nights at my Georgetown apartment. Neglecting to pay my utility bills caused telephones, heat, and water to be turned off.

In mid-October, I was traveling with Kennedy when he stopped in Minneapolis one Saturday where I was greeted by Joe Alsop. "My deah boy," he gushed, in his quasi-English accent. "You *must* tell me how Kennedy is doing." Joseph W. Alsop, one of America's leading syndicated columnists, introduced himself to me one day in 1959 in the Senate Press Gallery. He told me he really liked my editorial page commentaries in the *Wall Street Journal* and started the first of many conversations (though I cannot remember ever getting to say much as Joe held forth).

We sat together in the press section for the Minnesota rally. Alsop and I had heard Kennedy's cool presentation many times, but Joe got excited and started cheering at every applause line. When the speech ended, he jumped on the press table and began chanting: "Jack! Jack! Jack!" Alsop was a life-long registered Republican and a cousin of Theodore Roosevelt's children.

Joe was more ostentatious than other journalists, but the press corps was solidly for Kennedy. Traveling with Nixon the last week of the campaign, I was having drinks with other reporters in a hotel bar. Somebody mentioned to star reporter William Lawrence of the *New York Times* that it was tough duty on the Nixon tour. "No," Bill said, "I think I can do Jack more good when I'm with Nixon."

Even reporters not committed to Kennedy felt more comfortable with him than with Nixon. Ideology aside, reporters switching from the Nixon plane to the Kennedy plane felt they were leaving a cold orphanage and entering a warm home. The only consistently accessible staffer to me on the Nixon plane was Peter Kaye, a young *San Diego Union* reporter brought along by *Union* editor and Nixon press secretary Herb Klein as a press aide. Pete was helpful but not all that knowledgeable. In contrast, all senior

Kennedy staffers were eager to talk to me, and I usually could get a few words with the candidate himself.

This was a presidential campaign where both candidates anchored themselves in the middle of the road, minimizing policy disagreements as they underlined personal and character distinctions. The Kennedy campaign was fun, with large, boisterous crowds sometimes waiting hours for the senator to entrance them with a twenty-minute speech. The Nixon campaign was drudgery, with large, orderly crowds rewarded by an on-time vice president who delivered a long, stilted address.

The unique characteristic of the 1960 campaign had nothing to do with issues. That John F. Kennedy was a Roman Catholic had vast meaning for millions of Americans. Driving a rental car on Sunday morning in southern Illinois, I switched from one radio station to another and on nearly every one, I could hear fundamentalist preachers call Kennedy the pawn of Rome.

Roman Catholics, who had been slowly drawing away from traditional attachment to Democrats, were returning to vote for Kennedy. Riding in the Kennedy press bus, I observed something older colleagues had never seen before and I would never see again: Roman Catholic nuns in full habit holding hands and leaping in the air, their faces filled with joy as they gazed on the handsome young defender of their faith.

IN LATE OCTOBER, I covered Nelson A. Rockefeller for a couple of days in upstate New York. He knew Nixon would lose New York and was pretty sure he would lose the election. Rockefeller was campaigning so he could make the point in 1964 or future years when he was running for president himself that he had not abandoned the party's nominee in 1960.

That Saturday night, October 21, flying down to New York City in his private plane from campaign stops in Dutchess County, Rockefeller asked me up front for a drink. This is what he told me (as recorded in my first book, *The Agony of the GOP, 1964*):

It looks very much as though Nixon is going to lose the election for failing to pick up enough electoral votes in the big industrialized states. He's losing the big industrialized states, because he's chasing a will-o'-the wisp trying to capture Southern states. No matter how hard he tries, Nixon can't win the South. But he can alienate the North, which is attainable—and absolutely necessary.

On the Saturday before the election, I phoned Barry Goldwater at his home in Phoenix (where he had stayed for much of the campaign). He had emerged as Mr. Conservative at the Republican National Convention in Chicago, quelling a right-wing delegate revolt against Nixon. Goldwater now agreed with Rockefeller that Nixon was going to lose, but that was his only agreement with the governor. This is what Goldwater told me (as recorded in my book):

> Nixon made his basic mistake by moving to the left to woo an urban Democratic vote and particularly a Negro vote that was irrevocably Democratic. . . . Nixon's gestures toward the left . . . had not only lost Nixon his golden opportunity to become the first Republican in a generation to bring out the full conservative vote but also had botched up the chance to sweep all or most of the segregationist South.

I thought then that Rockefeller was correct and Goldwater wrong. I realize now it was much more complicated. Rockefeller was an exceptional candidate who could have defeated Kennedy by amassing industrialized states, which Nixon—or any mainstream Republican—could not have done. Whether Nixon could have won by following Goldwater's southern strategy cannot be determined, but there is no doubt that Goldwater was correct in seeing the future of the Republican Party as distinctly southern.

Dick Nixon, who had trouble figuring out who he was, took a little of Rockefeller and a little of Goldwater. Nixon did things that antagonized Goldwater such as bowing to Rockefeller on the party platform and picking the liberal Republican Henry Cabot Lodge as his running mate. At the same time, Nixon campaigned in the South as no Republican ever had since the party's first campaign 104 years earlier.

On the week after Labor Day, Nixon visited Lafayette, Louisiana, and Jackson, Mississippi—becoming his party's first presidential candidate ever to campaign in those states. It was my first visit to the Deep South. I felt I was in a foreign country, as bands played a campaign ditty especially prepared for the occasion ("Dixie Is No Longer in the Bag"). The heavy black population in the two states was nowhere to be seen.

Nixon ended his campaign by going to Los Angeles for a Saturday night rally three days before the election, determined to carry his home state (which he did). Supporters in pivotal states pleaded with Nixon to visit them Sunday and perhaps push them over the top. Instead, he left Los Angeles late Sunday afternoon to go to Alaska.

Alaska? Why would Nixon take a time-consuming journey to spend an hour speaking at a rally in a Fairbanks high school gym in a state whose three electoral votes were guaranteed for him? Because he had pledged the previous summer to be the first presidential candidate to visit all fifty states. He got Hawaii out of the way early, but never fit in Alaska—until the final weekend.

Nixon next went to Detroit for a Monday afternoon "telethon." Carefully screened telephone callers from around the country would question him on live television. Pool reporters would represent the daily press inside the television studio, rotating in fifteen-minute shifts. By luck of the draw, I was the daily press pool reporter for the first segment and was permitted in the studio a half hour before the telethon began.

The vice president entered the studio fifteen minutes before airtime, looking like a man who had not slept much. The set had not been arranged the way he wanted, and Nixon erupted. "God damn it!" he yelled. "Can't you stupid bastards do anything right?" Nixon continued his profanity-laced rant up to airtime, but not a word appeared in print or on the air. The wire service, radio-television, and periodical press pool reporters did not report his conduct. Neither did I as the daily press pool reporter. That's the way journalism was in those days.

After the telethon, Nixon went to Chicago to tape his election eve message to America from the CBS downtown studios. My father drove up from Joliet to pick me up to spend the night with my parents. I did not get my Illinois absentee ballot in time, and I would vote in Joliet Tuesday morning and then head back to Washington to cover the election.

As he drove the thirty-seven miles from Chicago, my father asked me whom I would vote for. I told him Kennedy. He expressed a little surprise but said he also would vote Democratic for only the second time in his life "because I think Nixon will be a bad president." When he asked why I was voting for Kennedy, I told him I thought the struggle for survival against the Soviet Union was the only issue that mattered and that I believed Nixon was weak and that Kennedy could be strong.

The events of the next decade showed I was right about Nixon and wrong about Kennedy. I really believed Kennedy at the Mormon Tabernacle in Salt Lake City when he declared "a struggle for supremacy between two conflicting ideologies: freedom under God versus ruthless, godless tyranny." His presidency was to suggest that this was mostly posturing.

I sometimes wonder whether I cast my vote based too much on my personal reporter's contact with candidates, leading me to like Kennedy and dislike Nixon. If I were as committed then as I am today to conservative economic policies, would I have voted for Nixon? Hardly. Nixon's conservatism was mainly rhetorical. Nobody can claim he was less committed to big government than Kennedy, who had the saving grace of being a tax-cutter—a quality that eluded Nixon.

NOBODY GOT MUCH sleep on election night 1960 as we waited to learn that John F. Kennedy would be the next president. Kennedy's victory was tenuous. The change in the tone and the very nature of our national government that everybody had awaited since I arrived in Washington would be more stylistic than substantive. The New Frontier would have more to do with tone than policy. Nevertheless, it would bring immense change for me, professionally and personally.

CHAPTER 10

LBJ Hosts a Wedding Reception

MY NEARLY SLEEPLESS election night followed a year of frantic activity. When I wrapped up my postelection coverage on Wednesday evening, November 9, 1960, I confronted five weeks of leisure—two weeks of vacation and three weeks of compensating time off in lieu of overtime. A colleague told me that in Puerto Rico, the San Juan Hotel near the airport offered bargain-basement rates for mainland reporters. I was off to San Juan Saturday morning.

Checking into the hotel, I paid my first visit to a casino. I hit an incredible streak of luck at the roulette table with a "system" I made up on the spot. I won over $1,200 at one point, and as my system began to fail, I walked away from the table with $980 ($6,700 in 2007 dollars). I quickly lost twenty dollars at the roulette wheel each of the next two nights, and stayed away from the gaming tables the rest of my vacation. I was flush for my long stay in Puerto Rico.

Democratic State Chairman John Bailey of Connecticut, a Kennedy insider resting in Puerto Rico, spotted me playing roulette that first lucky night. The next day at the swimming pool, Bailey called me over and whispered: "Bob, could you let me in on the system you use?" I said it was secret. When I encountered John Bailey in future years as he rose to become Democratic National Chairman, he seldom neglected to ask about my roulette system.

I got an invitation for a cocktail party on the roof of La Fortaleza—the 450-year-old governor's palace. I collared Governor Luis Munoz Marin to discuss Puerto Rico's status that he had designed to make the island a self-governing "commonwealth" of the United States. The result when I returned to Washington was a *Wall Street Journal* editpager ("Status Mania") that enabled me to charge off as expenses to the newspaper my round-trip airfare plus a week's lodging and meals. A poor reporter has to make the best of the cruel, hard world.

I FINALLY RETURNED to Washington the week before Christmas and immediately heard the unexpected. The president-elect had named his thirty-five-year-old brother Bobby attorney general of the United States. I asked Bureau Chief Henry Gemmill if I could send a "Brother Bobby" editpager up to New York.

A few hours later after I had submitted copy, a smiling Gemmill beckoned me into his office. "It is a little harsh, isn't it, Bob?" asked Henry. "We need a rewrite to tone it down." He had already used his copy pencil to add balancing phrases to my criticisms, and he wanted a lot more of that. I loudly declared that Henry was ruining my piece. I had become the king of edit-pagers and was accustomed to seeing them in print without modification.

However, I did not go so far as saying what I felt was Gemmill's real motivation. Henry was shy on strongly held views on any serious subject. I was sure he envisioned getting the *WSJ* off on the right foot with the new administration and did not want the bureau's number one trouble-maker to create tension by attacking the new regime's second most powerful figure.

A vexed but still smiling Gemmill suggested "we calm down" and compromise. I had no choice but to rewrite the piece with Gemmill's modifications. It was filled with Henry's balances that I detested. Bobby as AG could be "an unqualified disaster," but he also could achieve "a mammoth record of accomplishment." My documentation of his shortcomings as a lawyer was balanced by assertions of his administrative talents. While describing his ability to offend everybody in sight as his brother's campaign manager, he "showed signs of maturing." However, I insisted on keeping one largely unbalanced paragraph that summed up what worried me most.

> The real basis for the liberals' concern about Bobby stems from what they consider his contempt for civil liberties displayed as chief counsel for the rackets committee. He showed an impatience with the cumbersome apparatus of Anglo-Saxon justice in his zeal to put [Teamsters Union president James] Hoffa and associates behind bars. Liberals saw the specter of the hated Senator McCarthy in his badgering of witnesses, his use of hearsay testimony by police officers, his frequent practice of making a case against a witness without giving him a chance to reply the same day.

Gemmill insisted that I add to the end of the paragraph these words: "practices long fairly common in varying degrees among congressional investigators." That and the other balancers did not mollify the Kennedys—especially father Joe. I was told that when Joseph P. Kennedy raved about "that bum Novak, whoever he is" after reading my modified piece, he was most upset by my saying Bobby's outlook was closer to his father's than his brother's.

BACK IN WASHINGTON, I started my first working day with breakfast at the press table of the Senate restaurant in the Capitol. Seated there were Vice President–elect Johnson's press aide, George Reedy, and Reedy's lovely young secretary from Texas, Geraldine Williams. I did not know Geraldine very well and had not seen her since the plowing contest at Sioux Falls, South Dakota, in September, but I was anxious to know her better. When I saw Geraldine next, early in the new year at the restaurant press table, I asked her to the Inaugural concert the evening of January 19 at Constitution Hall—the night before the Inauguration.

Our first date coincided with the great Inaugural blizzard of 1961. I changed into a tuxedo at the *Wall Street Journal* bureau and set off to find a taxi to pick up Geraldine where she lived on Capitol Hill. The historic twenty-four-hour snowstorm, leaving more than eight inches of snow in the capital, made it very difficult to get cabs in a city jammed with visitors.

I finally arrived at the house Geraldine shared with other government girls an hour later than I planned. The blizzard was worsening, and it seemed silly to try to inch ahead through heavy traffic to get to Constitution Hall to hear considerably less than half the concert.

Instead, we got out of the taxi on Pennsylvania Avenue and walked a couple of blocks through the snow to the National Press Building. It was too late for dinner, so we went up to the Press Club and into a small cocktail lounge where women were permitted. We both drank Scotch and smoked cigarettes until midnight when the club closed. We then walked several blocks to the Mayflower Hotel, where we got a snack and kept drinking and smoking until the bar closed down at two a.m.

Geraldine reminded me of a younger Lauren Bacall, only much prettier. Her elegance made her seem to have grown up in a garden. Unlike the chirpy twang of other Texas girls, her faint southern accent and perfect grammar seemed like products of a finishing school up North. None of that was true.

I learned from her that night that she grew up not in a garden but on a farm thirty miles from Waco, where she was picking cotton before she could read or write. She was born in Willie Nelson's dilapidated hometown of Abbott and went to high school in the small, alcohol-free town of Hillsboro, which surely was no finishing school. Her Texas accent had been nearly totally extinguished by sheer willpower during one year in Washington. She had celebrated her twenty-fourth birthday one night before, and she indicated to me she wanted to get back to Texas soon to get the college education she thought she needed.

By the time I got Geraldine home to Capitol Hill and took a taxi cross town to my apartment in Georgetown, it was four a.m., and I had to sleep fast. Covering John F. Kennedy on Inauguration Day, I walked through the snow in Georgetown from one side of Wisconsin Avenue to the other to be at the president-elect's home by eight a.m. The day's activities began a few blocks away with mass at Holy Trinity Church. It was my first exposure to the Latin liturgy.

It was also my first presidential inauguration, and I was fortunate to spend the hours between mass and the end of the parade, nine hours later, as a pool reporter a few feet from the new president. The snow had stopped, but the winds howled and it was bitterly cold. John Fitzgerald Kennedy, the youngest man (at age forty-three) and the first Roman Catholic elected president, delivered a magnificent inaugural address whose bold affirmation of American purpose in the cold war eased my nagging doubts about my vote against Nixon the previous November. No inaugural address I heard in the following four decades approached Kennedy's. It was in a class with Lincoln's second and FDR's first.

At bleachers erected for parade watching in front of the White House, Bobby Kennedy gave me a gruff thank-you when I congratulated him. Stanley Tretick, a UPI photographer close to the Kennedys, said to him: "Bobby! What are we supposed to call you now? General? Mr. Kennedy? Your Excellency?" He replied: "Just call me son-of-a-bitch, like everybody else is going to."

IN THE SPRING of 1961, I received a call from a young man with a peculiar accent. It was Daniel Patrick Moynihan, a thirty-four-year-old new assistant secretary of labor. He and his wife were living in the splendid caretaker's quarters at Tregaron, the vast Joseph Davies estate in northwest Washington. Moynihan invited me to a stag cookout there.

About twenty men were there, and I recognized some from Capitol Hill. I had no idea why I was invited until, after dinner, Pat Moynihan rose to speak. He said all of us (Moynihan excepted) had Illinois connections. His boss, Secretary of Labor Arthur Goldberg, was a native Chicagoan and had been a labor lawyer there. Now, Moynihan asked confidentially, what would we think of Arthur being the Democratic candidate for governor of Illinois in 1964?

As each gave his views, I heard nothing but praise for Goldberg's erudition and character. By the time my turn came, I had drunk more than my share. I said I had shaken hands with Arthur Goldberg only once and never engaged him in conversation (the only man there to admit he did not know Arthur). But, I went on, I had heard him testify before Congress many times, and I thought he was pedantic and boring, his voice was too thin, and he was physically unattractive—a terrible candidate all around. My screed was followed by shocked silence. Then the laudatory comments of the others resumed, with mine ignored as though they never had been uttered.

(Arthur Goldberg never ran for governor of Illinois. After serving briefly on the Supreme Court and later as U.S. ambassador to the United Nations, he stayed in New York City and ran for governor of New York in 1970. He was just as bad a candidate as I predicted, and he was crushed by Nelson Rockefeller.)

Pat Moynihan became a cherished friend and one of my favorite politicians. But after that spring evening in 1961, he never again asked my advice.

I WAS TAKING out three women early in 1961, but the one I liked best was Geraldine Williams. We especially enjoyed the Jockey Club, the fancy new Manhattan-style restaurant on Embassy Row. But sometimes we would have hamburgers and drinks at Harrigan's, a saloon in old Southwest Washington (soon to be leveled by urban renewal). One night in March, I asked Geraldine to bring to Harrigan's her Texas absentee ballot for an election created by the megalomania of her boss, Lyndon B. Johnson.

With Johnson up for the 1960 Senate reelection in Texas, the customary procedure would have been for him to drop out of the Senate race when he was nominated for vice president. Instead, LBJ ran for both vice president and senator in 1960 and won both contests. He then resigned from the Senate, forcing a special Senate election.

The ballot in the April 4 nonparty election was bedsheet-size, containing the names of seventy-two candidates. In Texas, you then voted by crossing out the names of the candidates for whom you were not voting—in this case, seventy-one of them. So while drinking and smoking at Harrigan's, Geraldine and I had a little fun. She crossed out one rejected candidate after another, until she was left with one: Representative Jim Wright, the future speaker of the House and an LBJ protégé backed by Johnson's political apparatus.

But Wright had to compete with three other moderate-to-liberal candidates. That left two other serious candidates, both conservatives. One was the sixty-three-year-old multimillionaire William Blakley, former owner of Braniff Airlines and an old-style Tory Democrat appointed to fill Johnson's seat temporarily. The other was an unknown thirty-five-year-old college professor named John Tower, the only Republican in the field.

The outcome could not have been worse for LBJ. Blakley finished first with Tower second, forcing a runoff between two anti–New Frontier conservatives. The vice president did not care for Cowboy Bill Blakley, a Dallas business tycoon who affected Western garb. But as a Democrat, Blakley was infinitely preferable over Tower, a five-foot-five-and-a-half-inch right-wing Republican intellectual who proclaimed himself an acolyte of Barry Goldwater.

Johnson bestowed his political assets on Blakley in the runoff, but nobody thought they would be needed. Texas was still a one-party state with only one Republican in the congressional delegation and one Republican in the legislature.

I talked Henry Gemmill into sending me to Texas for a week, and I soon found this was no cut-and-dried election as was thought in Washington. Blakley was a terrible candidate, and Tower was not half bad. Lifelong Democrats were defecting—from the left because they hated Blakley, from the right because they liked Tower. Nevertheless, the conventional wisdom drummed into me on this my first reporting trip to Texas was that a Republican could not win statewide. I was about to write a bet-hedging analysis. Geraldine Williams saved me.

Geraldine never leaked a word to me of what went on in Lyndon Johnson's office and had no inside information for me about the 1961 special election. What she supplied was an invaluable introduction to her cousin Jody. He was Joe James, a forty-something lobbyist for West Texas Utilities. James and his girlfriend, Joyce, had befriended Geraldine during her one year in Austin (when she worked first for her state senator and then for LBJ). Both Jody and Joyce loved her, and made clear I was lucky if she deigned to have anything to do with me.

They hosted me for drinks and dinner in the private club at Austin's Commodore Hotel, which was packed with legislators drinking and the lobbyists who paid for their drinks. James introduced me to everybody, and all gave me the conventional wisdom of Blakley winning. Then, near the end of a bibulous night, Jody set me straight: "Let me tell you something, Novak. John Tower is going to win this election. I guarantee it. Write it in your newspaper. The good ol' boys around here don't appreciate what's happening. The Bill Blakleys are finished. They are going to be extinct."

On the front page of the May 25 *Wall Street Journal,* I wrote: "Democratic Texas may be about to take a giant step toward establishment of a two-party system, giving the Republican Party an important foothold in the South." Tentative though it was, my story was the only prediction anywhere of a Tower victory. When Tower won what was everywhere recorded as a stunning upset, my reputation as a political savant swelled.

My postelection editpager of May 31 is actually a more impressive analysis. I said flat out that two-party politics had arrived in Texas, and predicted that "what is happening in Texas today may well be repeated through the rest of the old Confederacy in the decades to come."

To BEGIN 1962, Les Tanzer, the White House correspondent of the *Wall Street Journal,* left the paper to join Kiplinger's *Changing Times* magazine. It was a frequent case of a crack *Journal* reporter going lower down the journalistic food chain for a higher salary.

Al Otten moved over to the White House beat, and (after a little more than three years with the paper) I became its senior correspondent on what was now a Capitol Hill staff of five reporters. That meant me doing big congressional overviews, but my daily beat was the House Ways and Means and Senate Finance committees—covering taxes, international trade, and Social Security.

On this beat, I became acquainted with three memorable political personalities: Wilbur D. Mills, Harry F. Byrd Sr., and Robert S. Kerr. There has not been anybody like them in Congress for some time. Even then they seemed anachronistic, certainly out of tune with the New Frontier. These three personalities provided a congressional counterpoint to John F. Kennedy's cultural transformation of Washington.

AL OTTEN SUGGESTED I kick off my new assignment with a leader on the Ways and Means Committee, the most important committee in Congress where all tax and trade legislation is constitutionally mandated to originate. In "Ways and Means Woe," I described the committee's "resistance to any kind of controversial action, whether desired by the Administration or business." Its powerful chairman, Democratic representative Wilbur D. Mills of Arkansas, had "an apparent capacity for indecision and inaction that maddens" his critics on the committee.

Mills, a Harvard law graduate, had been elected to Congress in 1938 at age twenty-nine and now at fifty-three was at the peak of his prestige. He was considered the smartest man in Congress (as I noted in my leader), and to suggest that the chairman had no clothes was scandalous. A conservative Republican congressman approached Mills on the House floor the day my story ran to chide him. "Well, everybody knows that Novak is a notorious leftist," Mills replied.

It was mutually disadvantageous for the Ways and Means chairman and the *Wall Street Journal* lead reporter to be at odds. I routinely asked to see him, and he accommodated me. He was a marvelous source, with encyclopedic knowledge of the bills he handled, and was willing to share much of his plans. After our rocky start, my relationship with the chairman became so close during the next dozen years that I was condemned for serving as Wilbur Mills's mouthpiece in return for his news tips.

Mills wanted confiscatory tax rates lowered drastically as the incentive for getting rid of tax deductions, exclusions, and credits. This was essentially what President Kennedy proposed, but business interests decided tax reform was too high a price to pay for tax reduction. Kennedy became convinced that high tax rates so stifled the economy that they must be lowered—with or without tax reform. That was where Kennedy lost Mills, who dogmatically declared no reform, no tax cut. Simultaneously the chairman was blocking Medicare (medical care for the aged), which he correctly prophesied would impose an ever-heavier burden on the federal government. The smartest man in Congress meant mostly pain and suffering for the New Frontier.

Mills's political career ended in 1974 with the exposure of a drunken affair with a striptease dancer. Nothing could have been a bigger shock to me or others who thought they knew him. Nobody on Capitol Hill had ever observed the sixty-five-year-old man who now declared himself an alcoholic even taking a drink. He once declined an invitation to dinner at my home on grounds he and his wife never went out at night.

WHEN I WENT on my new beat in 1962, I never thought about a similar exposé of the Senate Finance Committee, a leaderless backwater under the chairmanship of Senator Harry F. Byrd Sr. of Virginia. In 1962, he was seventy-five years old, and whatever fires burned within him long ago had been banked.

Harry Flood Byrd was Virginia's dominant political figure for four decades. The Byrd Organization controlled the state's public offices from top to bottom. Virginia was not only a one-party state but a state without competition in that one party. Byrd entered the U.S. Senate in 1933 at age forty-six after a term as governor, but did not become Finance Committee chairman for twenty-two years. Never deeply involved in the committee's complicated issues, he was committed to legislation only when it touched on controlling the growth of government, protection of the textile industry, and states rights (headed by the preservation of racial segregation).

He was perhaps the most reactionary member of Congress. He had long since separated himself from national Democratic candidates, observing "golden silence" in endorsing nobody for president in 1952, 1956, and 1960 (as Republicans carried Virginia). But with his nominal Democratic affiliation making him part of the Democratic Senate majority, he never entertained becoming a Republican.

Reporters on the tax beat in Congress ignored Byrd. He did not know that much, and did not reveal much of what he did know. However, he was totally accessible to anybody from the *Wall Street Journal*. I never got much help from the senator in covering my beat, but I enjoyed our conversations. I remember especially two of them.

Byrd was opposing Senate ratification of a multinational treaty governing exploration of Antarctica. I asked him why he cared. "I'm worried about what Richard might think of this," he replied. "Richard" was Admiral Richard Evelyn Byrd, the great American aviator and explorer of the Antarctic, who planted American flags in that vast frozen waste. He was the senator's beloved, late younger brother. I told him, truthfully, that Admiral Byrd had been one of my boyhood heroes. The old man was touched, and it strengthened our relationship.

The second conversation took place after Byrd had publicly broken with Virginia's Governor Albertis Harrison, a rare rupture inside the Byrd Organization. Harrison ended Virginia's "massive resistance" to school desegregation by reopening Prince Edward County's schools that had been closed to evade court-ordered racial integration. I had become close enough to Byrd to ask: "Senator, don't you think that in the end you are bound to lose the fight over school segregation?" "Of course, Bob, of course," he said softly. "That's just the point. When that great son of Virginia, Robert E. Lee, was beaten at Gettysburg, the war was over. But the fact he kept fighting for the state's freedom for another two years has made him the hero of Virginians for a hundred years. Albertis Harrison was duty bound to follow the course of Robert E. Lee, but he didn't." In Byrd's view, massive resistance was the lineal successor to the South's "Lost Cause" of secession.

Committed to a free American hand in Antarctica and adherence to dying white supremacy, Byrd was a reactionary romantic who dedicated his public career to a world that had disappeared long ago.

In poor health, Byrd resigned from the Senate in 1965, the year before his death. Harry Flood Byrd Jr. replaced him for the next seventeen years but never matched his father as a famous figure of the Right. Virginia was leading the South into a political realignment of majority conservative Republicans and minority liberal Democrats. Unable to win the Democratic nomination and unwilling to become a Republican, "Young Harry" became an Independent for his last thirteen years as a senator.

EARLY IN 1962, I was chatting with Senator Byrd in a hallway of the New (now the Dirksen) Senate Office Building outside the Finance Committee offices when a look of terror came over the chairman's face. "Excuse me," he mumbled as he ducked into the committee room. I turned around and saw an apparition. Lumbering down the hall was a sixty-six-year-old man, standing six-foot-three and weighing over 230 pounds. He wore a baggy, cheap-looking double-breasted suit, a "feedsack blue" shirt, and old-fashioned galluses. It was Senator Robert Samuel Kerr, Democrat of Oklahoma, the richest man in the Senate.

I was not sure whether Harry Byrd darted away from me because he did not want to talk to Bob Kerr, did not want Kerr to see him talking to me, or both. The word among Senate insiders was that Byrd was a little afraid of Kerr, who was the second-ranking Democrat below Byrd on Finance but was the committee's dominant member.

Born in a log cabin in Indian Territory, Kerr got into oil production and untold riches as chairman of Kerr-McGee Oil Industries, Inc. While visiting in his office in 1962, I asked Kerr for his estimated net worth. He sighed heavily (as he often did) and then said he would give me one guess only and he would then tell me whether I was high or low. I figured to go high, and guessed sixty million (which was about four hundred million in 2007 dollars)—an unimaginable figure in my eyes. Kerr guffawed. "You're low," he said. "Way low."

Mixing private and public business was habitual with Bob Kerr. He had brains, money, ambition, dynamism, courage, and determination—everything but moderation in advancing his personal fortune. Brazenly inserted in the lapel of his baggy suit jacket was a gold Kerr-McGee button, leading him to be called the senator from Kerr-McGee.

Kerr's most spectacular abuse of power was confided by him to me during an off-the-record chat in 1962. I reminded him that when I arrived in

Washington in 1957, he was conducting confrontational hearings on Eisenhower administration economic policy with Treasury Secretary George Humphrey in the dock as the defendant. Then the hearings recessed, never to be resumed. "What happened?" I asked. The senator sighed heavily, then replied slowly: "Well, my company had some problems with the IRS [Internal Revenue Service]. They went away—and so did my hearings."

Kerr, unhappy with the Kennedy-Johnson ticket, sat on his hands for most of the 1960 general campaign as Nixon carried Oklahoma. With his ally Johnson kicked upstairs to the vice presidency, Kerr feared his own power in the Senate would be diminished. In fact, the opposite occurred. LBJ's successor as majority leader, Montana's Mike Mansfield, abhorred power and the resulting vacuum was filled by Big Bob Kerr. After two years, liberal Senator Paul Douglas of Illinois, one of Kerr's many enemies, was calling him "the uncrowned king of the Senate."

Kerr was such a forbidding presence that few reporters sought him out. They missed a lot. Whereas I explored tax policy with Wilbur Mills and talked philosophy with Harry Byrd, I received a tutorial in deal making from Bob Kerr. He explained to me the deal he cut on December 26, 1960, with President-elect Kennedy at the Kennedy mansion in Palm Beach, Florida. Kerr would carry Kennedy's tax and tariff bills. Kennedy, in response, would give Kerr pork barrel spending for Oklahoma, tax and trade concessions for oil and gas, and just about anything else the senator wanted. But Kerr, with Mills, opposed Medicare to the end.

I was looking forward to a day of football bowl watching on January 1, 1963, when I received an early telephone call. Robert Kerr had died of heart failure that morning at Doctors Hospital in Washington, where he was recuperating from a mild heart attack. Called in to do a leader for the *Journal,* I wrote:

> Perhaps Mr. Kerr's greatest asset as a Senate manipulator was his undoctrinaire approach. As it suited his purpose, he was a budget balancer or a tax cutter, a free spender or an economy advocate, a neo-populist or a hard money man, a protectionist or a free trader.

AT TIMES, I felt as out of touch with the New Frontier as Bob Kerr, Wilbur Mills, or even Harry Byrd. The winter of my discontent began shortly after the high of the Kennedy inauguration. I had talked myself into believing I had to achieve something significant by the time I reached age thirty. I had a premonition I would die on the battlefields of Korea. When I wasn't sent there, I still felt I would have a short life. I drank too much, I drove too fast, and often I combined them by driving under the influence. I was a four-pack-a-day cigarette smoker, which provoked recurrent asthma attacks that had periodically afflicted me since my second year in college. I often missed meals and was a little underweight. I fainted while drinking one night with Bob Jensen at the standup Members Bar at the National Press Club. Jensen insisted I see a doctor, who advised me to drink less, stop smoking, and start eating chocolate sundaes. I ignored the first two recommendations, and followed the third only for a short time.

With apparently little time left, I awaited my thirtieth birthday on February 26, 1961, with the grim recognition that I was only a hack journalist. Nobody planned a birthday party. I had taken out Geraldine Williams several times since our Inaugural eve date, and I asked her to dinner for my birthday. In a black mood, I told her I thought my career had been disappointing up to this point, and then I lapsed into silence. We spent the evening smoking and drinking Scotch without saying anything. Geraldine was the first girl I had ever dated who did not interrupt my dark reveries, and that was probably a mistake for her.

About two months later, Henry Gemmill took me to dinner at Rive Gauche, a fancy French restaurant in Georgetown. My boss said he realized things had gotten dull for me after the excitement of the 1960 campaign, that I was bogged down in what Henry called the "scut work" of covering legislation and that I felt a little left out of the New Frontier.

True, but what was Henry going to do about it? I hoped he would relieve me of some scut work. Instead, he told me that, effective immediately, my pay was going from $170 a week to $200. That meant for the first time I was a five-figure annual income earner ($10,400 or about $70,000 in 2007 dollars). I never dreamed I would make that much money in journalism. But as a bachelor I had bucks to burn and was going to pay cash in buying a new Corvette for $5,000. That my neurotic discontent had nothing to do with money was something Henry Gemmill did not understand.

About a year later, Vermont Royster called from New York and asked me to dinner the next night. "By the way, Bob," he told me, "I'm not going to have time to stop by the bureau on this trip, so don't say anything to Henry." Although Royster had the title of editor, his responsibility was limited to the editorial page. He had no authority over Gemmill. So whatever he was up to, he was going behind my bureau chief's back.

Royster picked Napoleon's, a shabby little French restaurant on Connecticut Avenue that was a favorite of his dating back to pre–World War II days. He quickly came to the point, asking: "Are you a little bogged down with all the details of what you have to cover?" Yes, indeed, I said. I would like to get rid of covering in excruciating detail very complicated decisions made behind closed doors. "Then," Roy said triumphantly, "come up to New York."

He asked me to become an editorial writer for the *Wall Street Journal.* I would write unsigned editorials on any subject that a) interested me and b) fit the paper's line. I could write as many signed editpagers as I wanted, with no requirement for compatibility with the *Journal*'s opinion. To report and research for this, I would have an unlimited expense account to report anywhere in the world.

Then came his kicker. He would be retiring before too long. A transitional figure would replace him, but the paper had to develop a younger person for the long haul. Nothing was guaranteed, of course, but there was a real possibility for me. Robert D. Novak as editor of the *Wall Street Journal*! It teased the ego, even though that was nothing I had craved.

I cited two reasons to Royster for saying no. First, I thought I was not conservative enough to write *Wall Street Journal* editorials. Second, I did not want to leave Washington. An accomplished debater and logician, Royster demolished both arguments. What I did not say was that my experience being rejected as sports editor of the *Daily Illini* suggested I was no good at office politics. And the way Al Clark was purged as Washington Bureau Chief indicated it was risky mounting the *Journal*'s slippery pole.

Two years later, Roy found his man in Robert Bartley, a young reporter in the *Journal*'s Chicago bureau who later became the most influential editorial page editor in America. I know I could not have matched Bartley's accomplishments, and I question seriously whether I ever really could have been named editor. I know I took the right path at Napoleon's, even though sometimes I wonder what might have been.

BY THE SUMMER of 1962, Lyndon Johnson apparently had become resigned to my relationship with Geraldine, who had left George Reedy's office to work directly for the vice president. We both were invited to dinner at The Elms, the mansion in far northwest Washington where Democratic socialite and, briefly, ambassador to Luxembourg Pearl Mesta once entertained lavishly (celebrated as "The Hostess with the Mostest" in the hit musical *Call Me Madam*). The place had just been purchased by LBJ in the absence then of an official vice presidential residence.

After a Texas-style cookout, LBJ reclined, nearly prone, by the swimming pool. It was just the two of us drinking Scotch, and he spoke with a candor he never bestowed on me before or after. He felt the Kennedy administration was in serious trouble, losing the cold war to the Soviet Union and losing the legislative war to conservatives in Congress. He said he had done everything the Kennedys wanted, including foreign missions that only guaranteed him bad publicity.

He was repaid with insults and humiliation, especially from the attorney general. Johnson was sure Bobby Kennedy was plotting to dump him in 1964. "But I'm going to fool them," he said. "I'm going to pack it in after the term ends and go home to Texas." That would have been a huge scoop, but I knew Johnson was just blowing off steam.

As for going back to Texas, the political environment there was hardly more congenial for LBJ than it was in Washington. Johnson's protégé, John B. Connally, had just won the Democratic nomination for governor of Texas, which still all but guaranteed election in Texas. As secretary of the navy, Connally had been the highest Kennedy administration official bearing the LBJ brand.

But campaigning for governor, Connally removed the brand. With JFK and LBJ both unpopular in Texas, Connally ran against the administration he had just left, and won. Talking about Big John that summer evening in 1962 led Johnson into self-pity. "John has turned my picture to the wall," LBJ told me. "You know I never would turn *his* picture to the wall."

Later that summer, I made a decision I long had been pondering. I had known for months that I loved Geraldine, and I hoped she loved me. The question was whether it was wise for me to try marriage three and one-half years after failure on my first attempt. Geraldine and I were drinking Scotch at the cocktail hour on the roof of the Hotel Washington on 15th Street overlooking the Treasury when I proposed to her. She had no quick response, being a deliberate person under any condition and especially deliberate when faced with a dangerous proposition. Two weeks later, she said yes.

It was taken for granted in that era that she could not work for the vice president and be married to me at the same time. When she told Johnson, he immediately offered to host our wedding reception at The Elms. I thought that a bad idea, and Geraldine so informed her boss. He responded that he planned to hold the reception whether Geraldine and Robert came or not. It was classic LBJ, and it worked.

Johnson sent his private plane to Texas to pick up Geraldine's family and bring them to Washington. At the small rehearsal dinner hosted by my parents at the Sheraton-Park Hotel the night before the wedding, the vice president stopped by and thrilled my mother by kissing her on the lips. The reception at The Elms the next night was a great success with Johnson presiding over the toasts.

When Johnson insisted on the wedding reception, I told Geraldine: "He must think a lot of you." "No," she replied. "It's you he thinks a lot of." What she implied was confirmed after we returned from our honeymoon by Frank Erwin, a very rich, very conservative lawyer from Texas who had been installed as state Democratic chairman by Governor Connally. Erwin was one of the Texas right-wingers who did not go over to the Republicans (and is immortalized by the Frank C. Erwin Jr. Special Events Center, home of the University of Texas basketball team). Erwin told Geraldine that he had heard about the wedding reception and now he expected "better" stories from Novak. I'm sure he got that straight from Johnson. That bothered me, but I figured it really didn't matter. After all, how important is a vice president who stands no realistic chance of ever being president?

THE WEDDING WAS held the first Saturday after the 1962 mid-term elections, when Democrats captured big majorities in both houses of Congress for the third straight election.

A $13,000-a-year salary ($87,000 in 2007 dollars) went a long way in 1962. We purchased (with a big mortgage) a tiny $17,000 row house ("the doll house," my mother called it) behind the U.S. Supreme Court on Capitol Hill. My election year-ending compensating time off from the *Wall Street Journal* gave us a five-week honeymoon—beginning with a week sailing first-class on the *Constitution* for a four-week tour of Spain. With liberal Americans and Europeans leery of visiting Franco's dictatorship, it was the best bargain in Europe. We ended up in a suite at Madrid's Fenix Hotel for $7.50 a night.

When I returned to the Washington bureau of the *Wall Street Journal*, I found a dozen telephone messages on my typewriter from somebody I barely knew: Rowland Evans Jr. of the *New York Herald-Tribune*'s Washington bureau. Al Otten, whose desk faced mine, noted that "Rowly Evans sure is anxious to get hold of you. He's been calling nearly every day." Reporters by nature are curious, and Otten wanted to know the source of Evans's sudden interest in me. So did I.

CHAPTER II

The Odd Couple

I PHONED ROWLY EVANS the day of my return to Washington—December 17, 1962—and he said we must have lunch that day, adding that I should say nothing about it to anybody. He picked Blackie's House of Beef, an inexpensive steak house frequented by government workers. For one of Washington's upscale journalists to pick such a downscale place suggested he did not want us to be seen by anybody he knew.

After we ordered hamburgers and beer, Evans asked me to join him as a full partner in a jointly written political column nationally syndicated by the *Herald-Tribune*. I was stunned. Until this moment, I doubt we had exchanged a hundred words.

My first recollection of Evans comes from the last night of the 1957 congressional session. As an Associated Press regional reporter, I was in the first row of the Senate Press Gallery covering the Lake Michigan water diversion bill. Rowly came up to the Senate beat reporters seated beside me and said, "Let's all go down and say good-bye to Bill." That was the Senate Republican leader, William F. Knowland, who was leaving the Senate to make an unsuccessful run for governor of California that finished him in politics.

Rowly seemed incredibly preppy, and I was amused to hear a reporter on a first-name basis with the ponderous, unfriendly Knowland. But Rowly Evans then called everybody by his first name. Even the austere Senator Richard B. Russell of Georgia was "Dick." Evans was lunching in the Senators Dining Room one day with his friend, Senator John F. Kennedy, when Senator Harry F. Byrd Sr. passed by. "Harry, how are you?" asked Rowly. After Byrd left, JFK said: "You call him, 'Harry'? I've never heard anybody call him by his first name." (As he entered his sixties and seventies, Evans reversed himself and addressed the most obscure political figures by their honorifics as "Congressman" or "Mr. Secretary.")

The longest time Evans and I had been alone was fifteen minutes. In

1962, after we both covered a political event downtown, I gave him a ride home to Georgetown and dropped him off in front of his elegant house on O Street. He did not invite me in for the drink I could have used. Jules Witcover, a political reporter with a mordant wit, said I never would have seen the inside of Rowly's house had I not become his partner.

No two Washington reporters could have come from more starkly different backgrounds. Evans was a social friend of Jack Kennedy and a regular on the dinner party circuit that I then only faintly perceived and was never asked to join. Blond and slim, Rowly seemed elegant even when sprawled on a hard Capitol Hill floor with other reporters waiting for a committee meeting to break. I remember one such occasion late on a Friday when he was complaining he had to catch a plane to Florida "for a little tennis, a little bridge." I knew he wasn't going to Miami Beach.

When Nikita Khrushchev visited Washington in 1959, one of the Soviet leader's English-speaking aides asked American reporters who would be "the next Walter Lippmann." The Russian had a nominee: Rowland Evans. The story spread through the Senate Press Gallery as a source of amusement. Rowly had a reputation as an amiable lightweight who relied more on social connections than journalistic skills. Ideologically, he was regarded as a Dewey Republican who became a Kennedyite through friendship. They were wrong on all counts.

The Evanses did not come over on the *Mayflower*, but it wasn't long after that they arrived—in Pennsylvania late in the seventeenth century as Quakers from Wales. A Civil War–era Rowland Evans was so ardent a Democrat and Copperhead (Confederate sympathizer) that he was thrown out of Philadelphia's Union League Club. Rowly's father—another Rowland Evans—idolized Franklin D. Roosevelt and may have been the only New Deal Democrat riding the Main Line to downtown Philadelphia (site of Evans's insurance business).

The Evanses, though not fabulously rich, were "very comfortable." Rowly grew up with a governess and then was boarded at the exclusive Kent School in Connecticut. He was the family cutup. After his death, his widow found a "bad boy" file chronicling youthful misbehavior.

Rowly, held in check by boarding school discipline, experienced real freedom when, like the previous two generations of Evanses, he entered Yale in the autumn of 1940. Spending weeknights playing bridge and weekends partying in New York, he flunked out before Christmas. Rowland Evans Sr. sent him to Chicago to a clerical job at the railroad yards and a room at the downtown YMCA.

Evans tried again at Yale in the autumn of 1941 and stuck to the books this time. For how long nobody ever will know because the Japanese bombed Pearl Harbor on December 7. On the morning of Monday, December 8, a long line of patriotic Yalies snaked around the corner in New Haven waiting to enlist in the U.S. Marine Corps. Rowly Evans was among them.

He survived the fierce combat of the Solomon Islands campaigns in the Pacific, earned his sergeant's chevrons, contracted malaria, and returned home with a medical discharge in the autumn of 1944. Rowly Sr. prevailed on him to make a campaign speech for Franklin Roosevelt's reelection, dressed in his marine uniform with combat ribbons.

Although his father expected him to make a third stab at Yale, life as a twenty-three-year-old freshman did not appeal to Rowly. Instead, he got a job as a copy boy on the *Philadelphia Bulletin*. In 1945, he received a call from a boyhood pal from the Main Line, a fellow Yalie and marine, Phil Geyelin, in Washington. Geyelin was a low-level copy editor at the Associated Press bureau, and they had a place for Rowly, too, if he would come down quick. Before long, the two young marine vets were ghostwriting an AP advice to veterans column published in hundreds of newspapers.

Evans was inquisitive and charming, invaluable assets for a reporter. Defying the AP's usual glacial rate of advancement, he soon was on the coveted U.S. Senate staff, where he made such an impression that the *Herald-Tribune* picked him off.

Rowly set his sights early on being a syndicated columnist who would mix hard news with opinion in the style of his friends, Joseph and Stewart Alsop, in their influential column. Evans lobbied for a column, and the opportunity came when James Bellows became editor of the *Herald-Tribune*. Bellows wanted a dynamic new *Trib* to come out of the debilitating New York City newspaper strike of 1962–63, envisioning a Washington column with the vigor to match the New Frontier's.

I doubt Bellows even knew who I was when he asked Evans to write a 650-word column, six days a week, Sunday through Friday, that would be heavier on news than opinion. Rowly protested he could not possibly accomplish that by himself. Then get a partner, said Bellows.

Evans chose me, nearly a total stranger. Why not his old friend Phil Geyelin, at that time my colleague on the *Wall Street Journal*? Because, said Rowly, they were too much alike. He said they were both interested mainly in foreign policy, but he might have added they were both upper-class boys from the Main Line.

Ideologically, Evans was neither his father's son nor his wife's husband. Katherine Evans, a vivacious redhead, was a fine journalist who later edited the *Washington Journalism Review*. She shared the liberalism of her father, David Winton, who, as owner of vast timber resources in the Pacific Northwest, was a pillar of Minnesota's Democratic-Farmer-Labor Party and a staunch supporter of Hubert Humphrey. When young Kay Winton told her father about Rowly, she gushed: "And, Daddy, he's a liberal!"

Or was he? In long conversations I now had with Rowly, I became convinced that he was more interested in a good story than in saving the world. Nor did he seem totally committed to the Kennedy family as I grew to think Kay was.

At the *Journal*, I was accustomed to collaborating in double byline stories with Al Otten and Paul Duke. It was just as easy working with Rowly as we prepared five sample, nonideological columns for Jim Bellows. He liked them and accepted me as Evans's partner.

This took us to April 1963 when Rowly and I rode the Eastern Airlines shuttle to New York to hear Bellows's offer: a seventeen thousand dollar salary for each of us ($71,000 in 2007 money) to pay for appearing on the newspaper's editorial page and leading off the *Herald-Tribune* wire service six days a week, plus a 50 percent share of sales of the column individually sold to newspapers not signed up for the wire service. We were to be independent contractors rather than employees of the paper, but the *Trib* would supply us with office space and secretarial service.

Jim Bellows was different from the buttoned-down news executives I had known at the Associated Press and *Wall Street Journal*. Handsome and charismatic, he spoke softly as if pursuing a hidden agenda. He was innovative and imaginative as the "last editor" in succession at the *New York Herald-Tribune,* the *Washington Evening Star,* and the *Los Angeles Herald-Examiner,* trying to save these newspapers but failing in each instance— the operation being a great success but the patient dying.

This was my first visit to the *Herald-Tribune* building in Manhattan on West 41st Street. While I was impressed by the large lobby photographs of Walter Lippmann and other famous *Trib* luminaries, the facilities could be called run-down—particularly when compared with the sleek *WSJ* building downtown. I felt I was leaving a winner for a loser.

Still, how could I turn down a column syndicated nationally by a famous newspaper? I told Bellows I owed it to the *Journal* to alert them about what was going on before I irrevocably committed myself.

I THOUGHT HENRY Gemmill was not a big fan of mine and would not make a serious effort to keep me. My bureau chief asked how much the *Tribune* was offering. When I told him, he said that was not a problem and that the *Journal* would pay me $20,000 (in 2007 money, about $132,000)—a whopping 54 percent pay hike over my *WSJ* salary of $13,000.

That surprised me. I mumbled my thanks but added that this wasn't really about money. Asked what it really was about, I said I had had enough of the tedium of legislative reporting and would like to spread my wings a little by covering national security questions and going to diplomatic conferences. "Sure, I can understand that," Gemmill said understandingly. "And you *should* go to Europe on assignment—and take your wife," he added. He promised he soon would take me off the legislative beat and give me an extended general assignment.

The issue was now no longer so cut and dried, and it soon became more complicated. Gemmill told New York what was happening, and Vermont Connecticut Royster came down to see me. It was dinner at Napoleon's again, only this time with Geraldine present at his request.

Roy declared it would be ridiculous to leave an expanding newspaper for a dying one. Then he got down to business. Effective as soon as the paper's congressional staff could be reshuffled, I would be given a regular column on the editorial page of the *Wall Street Journal,* with an unlimited franchise to travel any place, any time I wanted. Furthermore I would report directly to Royster. In effect, I would be on the editorial page staff working in Washington. Now I was truly stunned.

I called Evans the next morning to say that I did not think I could refuse this offer. Rowly was distraught. The *Herald-Tribune* wanted to start the new column in May. It was too late to find a new partner. Rowly's inclination was to hire an assistant, but that would not be easy either.

Assuming Royster had filled in Gemmill on his proposal, I went to the bureau chief's office the next day to see how soon it would be before I was relieved of my congressional reporting duties. But this was all news to Henry, who told me he had some appointments to keep before we could talk. A few hours later, Gemmill called me into what I called his lavish "ceremonial" office.

"Bob, I am very, very disappointed in you," he began. He accused me of making new demands and trying to leverage the *Herald-Tribune* offer into an ever-fatter deal with the *Wall Street Journal.* Beyond his disappointment, he went on, he worried about me as a human being. He asked whether I belonged to any religious denomination. When I said I did not, he recommended that I join one. Henry Gemmill was no angel, and I resented him preaching to me. But I held my tongue and waited for him to come to the point.

The point was sharp. His generous salary increase still held, but everything else was off the table. My duties would remain exactly as now. The expanded writ was indefinitely postponed. "I don't suppose that you'll want to stay with us now, Bob," he said, "but if you do, we can consider broader duties in the future. It will be a test of your patience." He was showing me the door, but I asked him to put in writing what the newspaper really wanted.

The next day, I received from Gemmill a five-and-one-half page, double-spaced memo that he had typed himself. In the piquant style Henry often affected, the salutation was "Friend Robt:" and the signoff "Love, Henry." It amounted to still another proposal, stressing that the higher salary was in place and making a new promise: "I want you to produce a new editorial page product, which will in essence be a columnist-sort-of-thing" with "a standing head and probably regularity of printing."

Henry's memo next turned to something he had not mentioned in our last unpleasant meeting. He feared the influence of Vermont Royster, while not mentioning Royster's name:

> I have one demand concerning this product. It must embody your own best insight. I would want you to undertake it only if you feel satisfied you could and would preserve this integrity, and would sturdily resist any NY pressure—overt or more likely subtle, conscious or more likely unconscious—to parrot an editorial line.
>
> Because of my concern about this point, at this moment, I do not offer you the right to write *exclusively* for the edit page. I would require that you retain some spot news responsibilities. . . . You are not to be agent of the edit-page crew stationed in Washington. You are to be a member of the Washn buro. . . .

As a supreme office politician, Henry was worried about Royster putting one of his own subordinates in the Washington bureau. He went into mumbo-jumbo to clothe his power struggle with Royster.

"I shove you over into the realm of the spiritual," he wrote, demanding "a personal concern" from me "for the well-being of the entire shop." He said he would not "execute" the shift in my status at least until Congress completed action on tax legislation, and then explained why: "I have demanded that you undertake any new function in this bureau in saintly spirit." Henry called the delay "this symbolic test, this exercise, this Lenten sacrifice—before you can so much as begin getting at the gravy."

The implicit message to me from Gemmill: you are on probation—albeit at a higher salary—while I see who you're working for; if you're working for me, the sky is the limit.

Sitting down with Geraldine that night, I listed my options. On the one hand was a guaranteed columnist's job on America's fast-growing, only national newspaper, but I would be working every day in a hostile environment presided over by a ferocious bureaucratic in-fighter. On the other hand was collaboration with a partner whom I hardly knew and whose professional reputation was dubious and working for a declining newspaper with a limited life expectancy, but I would be free of corporate supervision and with a chance to be printed in every major city.

Now I sought advice from my *WSJ* colleague Alan Otten, who had brought me into the paper, who had been my mentor, and who had become my badly needed friend. The conversation did not last long. Otten was the senior correspondent in the bureau and for years had been seeking a column. To give me a column after four and one-half years on the paper, he said, would insult and humiliate him. He was angry. I thanked him for his comments and terminated our conversation. (It did not terminate our friendship. Al was to sponsor me for the Gridiron Club. To this day, we have never mentioned this subject to each other.)

Otten settled a close question. If he were to join Gemmill in hostility to my new status, my life as a Washington-based *Wall Street Journal* columnist would be truly intolerable. Also, ambitious as I was, I could not slip a knife into the back of someone who had been my indispensable supporter. I called Rowly that night to tell him to stop looking for an assistant.

I owed the *Wall Street Journal* so much that I tried to forget the tensions of my last days there. I had not reconstructed the negotiations leading to my departure until it came time to write this memoir. Alan Otten taught me much about reporting politics and government. I am still thrilled when I think of the confidence placed in me by Vermont Royster's offer.

NOT LONG AFTER my decision, I went into the George Washington University Hospital in the middle of the night suffering from my worst asthma attack ever and stayed there for two days.

I believe asthma is essentially psychosomatic. My attacks started in college when I was under tension, were absent during two serene years as an army officer and returned when I went to work for the *Wall Street Journal,* peaking during my negotiations about whether to stay or leave the paper. Whether or not my asthma was psychosomatic, I thought my physician had something when he told me chain-smoking nonfiltered Kools cigarettes exacerbated my illness. Doctors had been telling me this for years, but this last attack was so severe I listened for the first time. I always felt I would be unable to write without a cigarette in hand. But now I had a full week, between leaving the *Journal* and beginning my column, with nothing to write. I told my fellow Kools smoker, Geraldine, I was quitting cold turkey and asked her to join me. She did, though she sneaked cigarettes behind my back for a while.

The asthma disappeared by the end of the summer of 1963, and I never smoked another cigarette. That's why I am writing my memoirs as a septuagenarian.

THE *HERALD-TRIBUNE* LAUNCHED a publicity barrage never since approached for me personally. In a takeoff on the "I found my job in the *New York Times*" advertisements that showed people doing jobs secured through the newspaper's want ads, Rowly and I were photographed drinking at the National Press Club, with the caption: "We found our jobs in the *New York Herald-Tribune.*" This poster was put in New York subway and commuter railroad stations, making my forehead a favorite target for obscene graffiti.

Bellows rented for us a dingy little office in the National Press Building, one floor below the *Herald-Tribune* bureau. In July 1964, the *Herald-Tribune* moved its Washington bureau five blocks to the top floor of a shiny new office building at 1750 Pennsylvania Avenue, one block from the White House. We were given a two-room suite down the hall from the *Trib's* newsroom, with a desk in the outer office for a secretary. Eventually, we doubled our space by renting the office next door and knocking out the wall, and had as many as four paid employees.

However, we hardly varied the routine established in our little Press Building office. After we decided each day which of us had the better story, the winner would try to finish the column by four p.m. The other partner then would pencil in his changes. Art Buchwald, the humor columnist who had an office across the hall from us at 1750 Pennsylvania, claimed one of us would type a column and then the other one would cross out all the typing and pencil in a new column. He wasn't far from wrong sometimes.

Next, the column's original writer cut the word count to 650 to fit the inflexible space reserved at the bottom of the *Herald-Tribune* editorial page. After the column was teletyped to the *Herald-Tribune,* the originating writer would talk to the editor in New York about recommended changes in the column. The whole process was never finished before six p.m. and often would go to seven or even seven thirty. Since both of us tried to schedule separate eight a.m. breakfasts with news sources, this meant an eleven-hour day was routine (not counting coverage of nighttime political events or dinners with news sources).

During a planning lunch at the Metropolitan Club, Rowly and I agreed that the column would be ideology free and avoid public policy goals—with one exception. We would not be neutral on civil rights and were unequivocally opposed to racial segregation. Considering what followed, this determination is steeped in irony.

A column's name was used by newspapers much more then than now, and it was descriptive of its content ("Matter of Fact" by the Alsops, "Today and Tomorrow" by Walter Lippmann). We decided on "Inside Report," and this may have been the title shaping the column. It evoked our decision to make sure every column included exclusive information not previously published—whether a scoop or a tidbit. It was a standard that mandated constant reporting.

The nation's most prestigious newspapers received the Evans & Novak column free as subscribers to the *Herald-Tribune* wire service. As a result, the column was used on a regular or semiregular basis by the *Los Angeles Times, Boston Globe, Philadelphia Inquirer, Miami Herald,* and many other big papers—a fortuitous sendoff for a new column.

The biggest question was the *Washington Post,* which subscribed to the *Herald-Tribune* service. It was crucial for any new Washington column to be read by newsmakers, and few read the *Herald-Tribune.* The *Post*'s decision was up to the managing editor Al Friendly. Rowly knew him socially (as he knew just about everybody in town), and lobbied him personally. Bellows wrote Friendly urging him to publish the column.

Friendly gave us no indication whether he would use our first column on May 15, 1963. I had trouble getting to sleep the night of May 14. At six a.m., the *Post* arrived at the front door of our dollhouse, and I was supremely relieved to find that the column had run—in the news section of the paper but printed as a column, not a news story.

Subsequently, Friendly ran the column every day, but it was several weeks before he moved it to the op-ed page—a signal that our probationary period had ended. Through the next four decades, the *Post*—under several editors—faithfully published the column, though in the years to come its position on key issues would diametrically oppose the newspaper's editorial stance. My gratitude was and is immeasurable.

AS ROWLY'S PARTNER I was given a seat at his table and also was invited by hostesses who previously had not known of my existence. Katherine Graham, publisher of the *Washington Post,* asked Geraldine and me to a lovely al fresco sit-down dinner party that first summer of 1963 at her Georgetown mansion. But the invitations (other than Rowly's) soon ceased because the Novaks were not equipped to host return dinners at their dollhouse. In the summer of 1964, we purchased and moved into a three-story, seven-room Victorian house in an unfashionable section of Capitol Hill, but it too was unsuitable for multitable dinner parties.

The invitations also dried up because I was not a dinner table raconteur in the style of an Arthur Krock, a Joe Alsop, or a Rowly Evans. I had a grim-visaged demeanor that led a friend, John J. Lindsay of the *Washington Post* and later *Newsweek,* to label me "The Prince of Darkness"—not because I was then a hard conservative but because of my unsmiling pessimism about the prospects for America and Western civilization.

ON A TRIP to New York City to clean up details before the column was launched, Evans suggested we visit the city's newest important resident: Richard M. Nixon. Following his disastrous campaign for governor of California, he came east in May 1963 to practice law in New York City. Rowly thought we should pay the former vice president a visit and tell him about our column. That was vintage Rowly Evans, nothing I ever would have contemplated.

Neither Evans nor I was high on Nixon's hit parade. But perhaps because he was lonesome in the big city, he told us to come into his downtown offices. The former vice president congratulated us on our new column, then executed a Nixonian turn. "I know you fellows have terrific contacts with the Democrats," he said, "but let me give you a little friendly advice. Don't do a one-party column. Give the Republicans a little break now and then. Believe me, it will help you in the long run."

If Nixon read our six-a-week column when it started, he would have seen no pro-Kennedy, no pro-Democratic, and no liberal bias. In fact, there was no bias for anything or anybody. That does not mean "Inside Report" began bland. Readers expressed delight over a daily political column without pretensions to heavy thinking. Dwight McDonald, a leading left-wing essayist, wrote how much he enjoyed what he called the Evans & Novak "political gossip." When McDonald said the column read as though dashed off in the backseat of a lurching taxi, I took it as a compliment. Within a few months, *Esquire* listed us among Washington's top fifty journalists.

Reading our columns of the first six months (from the beginning until John F. Kennedy's assassination), a twenty-first-century critic might wonder why this new column won such favorable attention. There was little depth and no overview. Each column contained at least one exclusive kernel as promised, but they have not withstood the test of time.

Nevertheless, six mornings a week, in a world without cable television,

Hotline, and the Internet, we exposed a little of what really went on in Washington.

THE LAST SIX months of John F. Kennedy's life (and the first six months of the Evans & Novak column) marked the low point of his presidency. His legislative program, including tax reduction, seemed hopelessly stalled. The civil rights revolution was moving toward racial warfare. The campaign to oust Fidel Castro had failed. The United States was getting stuck in Indochina. The Soviet Union was on the offensive worldwide.

The Evans & Novak column never conveyed the sense that the president was in trouble. Evans and I never discussed this deficiency, and nobody took us to task for it. If somebody had, we would have said we were too busy prospecting for little scoops to spin out sophisticated analysis. But we had precious few scoops about what was happening behind closed doors at the Kennedy White House—nothing like the backroom gossip we would dispense about future presidents.

Rowland Evans was a great reporter, more tenacious than I. But his tenacity failed in reporting on President Kennedy. It is not easy to report on a president who has been a guest in your home and who invites you to be a guest in his.

Many aspects of America were worse after the assassination. While John F. Kennedy was a failed president, Lyndon B. Johnson was a disaster. One of the few things that improved was the Evans & Novak column. On that terrible Friday afternoon in November, we wrote about "the great test" facing America after Kennedy's assassination:

> For the last six months, the country has been torn apart on the civil rights issue. The Republican Party has been torn apart by a conservative revolt. . . . The party of President Johnson is also split down the middle along similar liberal-conservative lines. This is the underlying reason for the legislative stalemate in the 88th Congress. To break this stalemate now becomes the new President's high responsibility.

Readers of Evans & Novak had not previously seen such an analysis. This column marked the first time we had taken an overview and written about big ideas. It was the first of many such columns. We did not hesitate to scrutinize Lyndon B. Johnson's presidency and combine shoe leather reporting with broad assessments—as the Alsops had done. Our tone changed markedly after November 22, 1963. It became more abrasive, more argumentative, and more serious.

CHAPTER 12

The Goldwater Revolution

IN 1962, I signed a contract with the Macmillan Company for my first book, an account of the 1964 GOP presidential race for an advance of $2,500 (in 2007 money, $17,000), with the working title of *Republicans Four.*

All four were candidates for governor in 1962: Nelson A. Rockefeller, running for a second term in New York; George W. Romney, head of American Motors, making his political debut in Michigan; William W. Scranton, a first-term congressman, running in Pennsylvania; and Richard M. Nixon, the former vice president and near-miss presidential candidate in 1960, trying to deprive California Democratic governor Edmund G. (Pat) Brown of a second term.

Nixon lost by nearly 300,000 votes, eliminating the only center-right candidate for president. It was now "Republicans Three." Rockefeller, Romney, and Scranton—all center-left and all winning impressive victories in Democratic-dominated states in 1962 during the third consecutive general election resulting in overwhelming Democratic control of Congress.

What about Barry Goldwater, the hero of the party's conservative foot soldiers?

THROUGHOUT 1961 and 1962, Goldwater told me he had no intention of being a candidate. During the midterm election campaign of 1962, he said, he would make no more than nine speaking appearances outside Arizona though he was the Senate Republican campaign chairman. In all of 1963, he went on, he would accept only ten out-of-state engagements, compared with more than 225 in 1961. "I believe I deserve a letup," Goldwater explained. "Boost for Rocky Seen as Goldwater Curtails Nationwide Politicking," declared the headline over my story in the September 14, 1962,

Wall Street Journal. Goldwater was signaling he really was bowing out of the presidential race.

In the spring of 1963, Goldwater disclosed to me a series of secret breakfast meetings with Rockefeller at the governor's Washington mansion on Foxhall Road. This was the basis of the first Evans & Novak column published on May 15, 1963 ("The Rocky-Barry Axis").

Nelson Rockefeller was a master courtier who had risen in the dissimilar administrations of Franklin D. Roosevelt and Dwight D. Eisenhower. I think so much personal attention from this leader of one of America's most famous families flattered Goldwater. Rockefeller also cleverly convinced Goldwater that they were in the same boat, as I wrote in the first E&N column:

[T]he strange fusion of the leaders of the party's Left and Right wings is directed against the Presidential boomlet for Michigan's Gov. George Romney. But in a deeper sense the Rockefeller-Goldwater alliance is trying to block both former President Eisenhower and Richard M. Nixon from playing a kingmaker's role behind the scenes.

For more than a year, Rockefeller and Goldwater have been convinced that the Eisenhower-Nixon forces are maneuvering to engineer the nomination for Romney.

At the end of April 1963, two weeks before Evans and I launched our column, Rockefeller's position for the nomination seemed impregnable. Nixon appeared eliminated. Romney and Scranton were kept busy as rookie governors. That left Goldwater, who not only trailed Rockefeller in the polls but seemed neutralized by him.

All that changed on Saturday, May 4, 1963, when Rockefeller telephoned Barry Goldwater in one of his few personal calls to any politician that day and three hours in advance of the public announcement that forever would change the Republican Party and American politics. That afternoon at the Rockefeller family's baronial estate in Pocantico Hills, New York, he married Mrs. Margaretta Fitler (Happy) Murphy. At age thirty-six, she was twenty-one years her new husband's junior and the mother of four small children. Her divorce from Dr. James S. Murphy, a Philadelphia physician, had been finalized one month earlier.

When I talked to Goldwater to complete the reporting for our first column of May 15, he remained enamored of Rockefeller and expressed the view that the governor still led for the presidential nomination. I suggested to Goldwater that, for the first time, he really had a chance to be nominated because of Rockefeller's remarriage. Goldwater seemed genuinely distressed. "Don't say that," he told me. "Please don't say that."

In our inaugural column, I wrote, inconclusively, "Rockefeller's remarriage has clipped the wings of his once high-flying candidacy." In fact, he had crashed and burned.

Before the remarriage, the national Gallup Poll of Republicans showed 43 percent for Rockefeller and 26 percent for Goldwater. In Gallup's first survey after the remarriage, the outcome flipped: 40 percent for Goldwater, 29 percent for Rockefeller. As the weeks went by, the margin widened.

WITH GOLDWATER NOW the front-runner, an organization calling itself the Draft Goldwater Committee announced a Fourth of July rally at the non-air-conditioned National Guard Armory in a black neighborhood in southeast Washington. I asked the opinion of Vic Johnston, a political old pro who worked for Goldwater at the Senate Republican campaign committee. "Oh," he replied, "that's really stupid. It's being put on by a guy named Clif White. Strictly a PR type from New York. Not a politician."

Although noncandidate Goldwater would have nothing to do with it, more than 9,000 people crowded their way into the 6,500-seat armory before the fire marshal locked the doors. I was impressed, and in early July I asked Clif White out to lunch. Vic Johnston was wrong. White was one of the most effective politicians of his time.

F. Clifton White, as a World War II veteran teaching at Cornell University and dabbling in Young Republican politics, attracted the attention of Governor Thomas E. Dewey's well-oiled political machine. White headed "Youth for Dewey" in the governor's 1948 race for president and became Tom Dewey's muscleman in Young Republican politics. As a loyal Deweyite, he backed Dwight D. Eisenhower against the conservative Robert A. Taft for president in 1952. Still, White never was a liberal. After he started his own public relations firm in New York, he told me, he came to believe big government was stifling individual freedom and opportunity and that Republicans like Nelson Rockefeller were part of the problem.

For a year prior to the 1964 Republican national convention, I met with White—usually for a meal—once a week and talked to him on the telephone more frequently. He made available to me (for use in my book) secret memos dating back to 1961. They detailed a covert operation unknown to national political reporters, including me, until the 1963 Fourth of July rally. By the autumn of 1961, White had established a secret organization dedicated to the nomination of an unnamed conservative—who, of course, was Barry Goldwater. They were plotting a revolution in the Republican Party.

CLIF WHITE WAS developing the cadre for a mass movement whose members were unaware of his efforts. In our column of June 13, 1963, I wrote:

> Unlike the carefully constructed Kennedy campaign organization of 1960, the Goldwater boom is the closest thing to a spontaneous mass movement in modern American politics.
>
> It is a poorly organized rank-and-file movement of Republicans who recognize Goldwater as their savior and await his Presidency as their salvation.

A week later, I was in Denver for a Republican National Committee meeting and observed "a little-understood transformation in the party's power structure" that was widely ignored by political reporters. In our June 24 column from Denver, I wrote:

> This transformation . . . is nothing less than a quiet revolt. The aggressive post-war club of conservative young Republicans from the small states of the West and South are seizing power, displacing the Eastern party chiefs who have dictated Republican policy and candidates for a generation.

On July 14, 1963, Governor Rockefeller declared war against the conservative wing of the Republican Party. His statement contended "that the vociferous and well-drilled extremist elements boring within the party utterly reject" the party's traditional principles. He cited the recent Young Republicans national convention in San Francisco as proof of "extremist groups" taking over the Republican Party with "tactics of totalitarianism." Specifically, he condemned the bid for southern support as a plan "to erect political power on the outlawed and immoral base of segregation."

Goldwater was stunned and disillusioned. He concluded Rockefeller was interested in personal friendship and party unity only when he was ahead in the polls. The Declaration of July 14 removed any doubt that Goldwater would do what he so often had pledged never to do: run for president. It was just delayed by Kennedy's assassination. On January 3, 1964, Goldwater announced from his hilltop home near Phoenix. Because of Rockefeller's attack and the assassination, Goldwater had lost his big public opinion lead among Republicans. Gallup's January poll showed non-candidate Nixon (29 percent) ahead of Goldwater (27 percent), with Rockefeller falling fast (12 percent). But in declaring his candidacy, Goldwater did not reach out: "I will not change my beliefs to win votes. I will offer a choice, not an echo."

Goldwater disbanded the Draft Goldwater Committee and brought close social and political friends east from Phoenix to take over. I believe I was the first to designate them as the Arizona Mafia. Most had no experience in big-time politics.

On January 5, Clif White telephoned me in high anxiety. In the five months I had known him, I had been impressed by his calm in a world filled with hysterics. Now his aplomb was gone. He had spent three years building an organizational superstructure on top of a mass movement and trying to connect with an aloof leader who did not want to lead. Now, White told me, he and his colleagues had been sent packing and replaced by Arizona amateurs.

White told me he was not going to hang around as a flunky. I was thirteen years younger than White, but I urged him to calm down and think things over.

White stayed. Goldwater's politically inexperienced campaign director, his Phoenix crony Denison Kitchel, was ready to get rid of him, but the Arizona Mafia member sent to replace White, Richard Kleindienst, intervened. Having served as Arizona Republican state chairman, Kleindienst knew enough about politics to realize the Arizona Mafia were unqualified to run a national presidential campaign and that he needed a pro. White's management of the campaign for delegates was one of the most impressive political performances I ever covered.

MEMBERS OF THE eastern Republican establishment were beside themselves. Although Goldwater had dropped in the polls, he was the only viable runner on the track. Rockefeller, his only announced opponent, looked like a dead man walking. The easterners had no interest in Nixon. Romney's early attraction had faded. Who could stop the dreaded Goldwater?

If I had any doubts about the identity of the presumed Goldwater-slayer, they were dispelled when Rowly and I lunched at the Metropolitan Club shortly after Kennedy's assassination with Walter Thayer, a suave Manhattan lawyer who as president of the *New York Herald-Tribune* was a major player in establishment Republican politics. He made clear that the *Trib,* unofficial house organ of eastern Republicanism, had made its choice: William Warren Scranton of Scranton, Pennsylvania, who had only three years' experience in the political arena and had been elected governor of Pennsylvania just a year earlier.

The rich, aristocratic Scrantons, giving their name to their hometown, had helped finance the Republican Party in Pennsylvania since Lincoln's time. But Bill had nothing to do with politics until 1960, when at age forty-three he was elected to Congress. In 1962, he was elected governor. In Congress, Scranton gave President Kennedy his vote on key issues. Once installed as governor, he concentrated on mobilizing Republican legislators in favor of a huge tax increase.

Why would the *Herald-Tribune* want Scranton for president? I tipped it off in our column of December 5, 1963 ("The Scranton Boomlet"), after our lunch with Thayer. With Kennedy's death, I wrote, "influential Republican leaders" now argued that a candidate different from Goldwater was needed against Johnson (though these leaders did not really want Goldwater against Kennedy either). "To combat the homespun Johnson," I continued, "many Republican professionals want another Kennedy-type candidate— patrician, youthful, Ivy-league. Scranton, boyish with graying hair, fits that formula."

I was among many Washington-based political reporters who traveled to Harrisburg, where we were wined, dined, and lobbied by Scranton's ardent aides. They assured us that, when the time was ripe, Scranton would run. After rebuffing out-of-state speaking bids, Scranton started accepting them in early 1964. He agreed to a fund-raising speaking engagement for January 29 on the Indiana Roof in downtown Indianapolis. Scranton's expedition into Goldwater country attracted reporters from major newspapers and television networks.

My January 31 column from Indianapolis described Scranton as "a poised and attractive political star" who "is the hottest piece of merchandise in his party today." I mentioned only in passing the governor's wife, Mary. She would have been called plain had she not been rich, aristocratic, elegantly turned out, and evoking an aura of authority that eclipsed everyone in her presence, including Bill Scranton.

Mary Scranton did her duty, table-hopping with Bill on the Indiana Roof to shake every hand possible. But I got a clue something was amiss when I traveled in the governor's limousine away from the postdinner reception. As Bill Keisling, Scranton's chief of staff and enthusiastic advocate for president, entered the car, Mrs. Scranton said, with a cutting edge in her voice: "Now be sure to close the door, Bill. We wouldn't want to lose you. Or *would* we?" I later learned Mary hated the trip to Indiana, which she blamed on Keisling. She wanted no more of this. Governor Scranton turned down pending political invitations precisely when he should have been accepting them to build his base for a presidential run. After Indianapolis, he became (in *Newsweek's* description) "the Hamlet of Harrisburg."

AS 1964 BEGAN, Clif White had a two-part strategy. First, he had perfected a nationwide grassroots organization to swamp anti-Goldwaterites in competition for delegates in nonprimary states. Second, Goldwater would sweep through the 1964 primaries as Kennedy had in 1960, instantly returning to the top of the polls.

Although I had found Goldwater an ineffective senator, Jack Kennedy was not much of a senator either and proved a terrific campaigner. I assumed that Goldwater, as a conservative evangelist, was tailor-made to sweep Republican primaries. Was I ever wrong.

Before he became an official candidate and was (in his own phrase) "just pooping around," Goldwater on the campaign trail replicated his free and easy style in the Senate. Rockefeller traveled on his private plane with one press secretary for himself and one for his wife, a radio-television adviser, a speechwriter, an advance man, a stenotypist, and a New York State Police bodyguard. Goldwater traveled on commercial airliners like a salesman, either with one aide or none at all.

There was none at all when I picked him up the second week of September 1963 at the WBKB-TV studios in the Chicago Loop where he was taping a segment of *Chicago Sun-Times* columnist Irv Kupcinet's Saturday night talk show. It was a foreign policy debate with the University of Chicago political science professor Hans Morgenthau, a liberal who had been a member of the Democratic National Committee's disbanded Advisory Council. I don't believe Goldwater had advance knowledge of what he was getting into, and he was waxed by Morgenthau. The senator seemed oblivious.

Goldwater next informed me he had made no arrangements for his next stop: the national convention of the National Federation of Republican Women. Drive time from WBKB to the Conrad Hilton Hotel was normally ten minutes. But at rush hour in the rain, Barry and I could not get a cab. Very late for his speech, he just looked at me and shrugged. Luckily, a young man driving home from work stopped his car, saying: "I don't know where you're going, Senator, but I'm for you, and I'll take you there."

His travel plans tightened once Goldwater became a formal candidate, but his mind seemed more disorganized. On January 5, 1964, on NBC's *Meet the Press,* he made one mistake after another. He defended his opposition to the nuclear test ban treaty because "just the other day, Dr. Hans Morgenthau, one of the great physicists in the world, backed my position up." I had been in the WBKB studio three and one-half months earlier to hear Morgenthau, no scientist and certainly no foe of the test ban treaty, debate foreign policy with Goldwater.

REPORTING ON THE Goldwater versus Rockefeller battle in New Hampshire one Friday in early February, I was approached by an aide to Rockefeller, who said the governor was flying to New York City that night and offered me a ride. After we agreed the conversation would not be for quotation, Rockefeller opened up.

He said he considered Goldwater a lightweight at best, a menace to the Republican Party at worst. Rockefeller described himself threatened by two powerful elements. The first was the merciless personal assault he was undergoing every day in William Loeb's *Manchester Union-Leader*, the state's most powerful newspaper. The second was a write-in campaign in the Republican primary for Henry Cabot Lodge, who was on the other side of the world and barred from political activity as the Democratic administration's U.S. ambassador to South Vietnam.

Rockefeller presumed Lodge could not win the primary but as a New Englander from neighboring Massachusetts could take enough votes away from him to permit Goldwater to finish first. Rockefeller angrily told me Lodge had turned a deaf ear to entreaties to turn off his young acolytes in New Hampshire. It was not for himself that Rockefeller said he worried, but for the Republican Party—and the country. I was turned off by the implicit claims of entitlement by one of the richest men in the world. I believe he wanted to sound tough, but it came across to me more like whining.

I soon received a bill for $63 for the plane ride from Manchester to New York ($412 in 2007 money and well above the prevailing commercial rate) payable to Rockefeller-for-President. Instead, I made it out to Nelson A. Rockefeller. I thought my mother would enjoy hearing about her son writing a check to a Rockefeller, and she did.

GOLDWATER TURNED OFF New Hampshire Republicans, but these voters could not swallow Rockefeller after his remarriage. A well-organized write-in campaign gave Lodge a landslide on March 10 with 35 percent to 22 percent for Goldwater, 21 percent for Rockefeller, and 17 percent for a slapdash Nixon write-in.

Clif White's dream of a Kennedy-like romp through the primaries was dead, and Goldwater's descent in the Gallup continued—down to

14 percent nationally with the absentee Lodge suddenly transcendent at 42 percent. Lodge was not a New England phenomenon. Rank-and-file Republicans were rejecting Mr. Conservative. His performance in the Illinois, Indiana, and Nebraska primaries was indifferent. His prospects in the coming Oregon primary on May 15 were so poor that he stopped campaigning there.

The eastern Republican establishment and its allies in the news media sighed in relief. They knew not who would fill the void, but Goldwater was surely dead. Or was he?

On April 9, 1964, the Evans & Novak column ("Reassessing Goldwater") defied the conventional wisdom by calling him "the victim of premature burial," adding:

> Goldwater never really has been stopped. To the contrary, he is still very much the man to beat. . . . Goldwater's foes today have no clearcut plan for stopping him. . . . [I]f Goldwater beats Rockefeller in the June 2 California Primary, as now seems likely, Rockefeller is finished. Goldwater could enter the convention with perhaps 550 votes (only 100 less than is necessary for the nomination) and nobody else even a close second.

I had been doing the Evans & Novak reporting and writing about Republican politics, but this column was Rowly's idea. He had breakfast April 7 with Nixon political aide Charlie McWhorter, who while advising Nixon kept close watch on local delegate contests. McWhorter's Goldwater delegate count had reached 550, and he passed his research on to Evans. I told Rowly that confirmed what Republican politicians had been telling me and said we should go ahead with the column.

This meant Goldwater would be nominated, without sweeping the primaries and without leading opinion polls, by beating the Republican establishment, delegate by delegate, in the trenches. Clif White agreed with me that this state of affairs made the need to pacify the defeated liberal Republicans all-important.

ALTHOUGH POLLS SHOWED the absent Henry Cabot Lodge (still in Saigon) substantially ahead in the May 15 Oregon primary, Nelson Rockefeller, the only candidate to campaign actively in Oregon, pulled ahead at the end. Rockefeller won his first important primary with 33 percent to Lodge's 27 per cent and Goldwater's 18 percent.

Goldwater's California lead immediately vanished in the polls. Lou Har-

ris gave Rockefeller a ten-point lead there, and Mervin Field made it thirteen points. A week later I haunted the halls at the Marriott Twin Bridges
Motel across the Potomac from Washington in Arlington, Virginia, where
the Republican National Committee was meeting May 24–26. All but the
most diehard Goldwaterites had abandoned the senator, sure Rockefeller
would win in California June 2. Bill Scranton would be nominated, and the
revolution would be over.

Then at four fifteen p.m. on May 30, three days before California voted,
a seven-pound, ten-ounce Nelson Rockefeller Jr. was born in New York
Hospital. The Harris Poll showed Rockefeller's California lead dropping
precipitately from nine percentage points on May 30 to two points on June
1. On June 2, Goldwater won the California primary with 51.3 percent to
Rockefeller's 48.7 percent—a difference of 59,000 votes out of more than
two million cast.

That clinched Goldwater's nomination and a changing of the guard in
the Republican Party, but the fratricidal bloodshed had barely begun.

CHAPTER 13

The Agony of the GOP

LATE IN JUNE 1964, I walked into the Senate Press Gallery, and Willard Edwards of the *Chicago Tribune* motioned me over to his desk. The veteran political reporter had been my friend and mentor (even after my new column began running in the rival *Chicago Sun-Times*). Willard, an integral part of the conservative movement, often knew more than he was permitted to write. He told me now that Senator Everett McKinley Dirksen had agreed to deliver the nominating speech for Goldwater at the Republican National Convention. Constrained from running the story himself, Edwards was giving it to me if I could confirm the information independently.

I made two calls—to Clif White and to Everett Dirksen. They both confirmed the story, but asked me not to write it until it was formally announced. I ignored this common admonition by news sources, as I often would similar pleas over the years. It was a stunning development. Dirksen, an old-fashioned Taft conservative, had not yet endorsed Goldwater and, prior to the remarriage, had been considered a likely Rockefeller supporter. When I talked to Dirksen after getting my tip, he told me that there was no way to stop Goldwater in the Illinois delegation and he might as well join the parade. Goldwater later told me: "The old boy's got an antenna three feet long. He knows where the winner is."

The *Herald-Tribune* put the Evans & Novak column ("Barry Captures Dirksen") on page one: "Dirksen's decision . . . destroys the fragile hopes of Gov. William Scranton. Support from Dirksen might have cracked Goldwater's strength in the Illinois delegation and started a national breakthrough."

It was a major exclusive at a fortuitous time. *Newsweek* was planning a press section article on Evans and Novak, and the Dirksen scoop provided a good lead. Titled "Insiders," it ran in the July 27 convention issue with a *Newsweek* staff photo of Dirksen, Evans, and me on the floor of the convention at the Cow Palace in San Francisco.

Newsweek's flattering profile cited the Dirksen column and my exclusive a week later pinning down Goldwater's selection as his vice presidential running mate of Republican National Chairman William Miller. "Evans and Novak," said the magazine, "make up the hottest political-reporting team since the Alsop brothers split up." It should be revealed that that story was written by *Newsweek* staffer Michael Janeway, a close friend of Geraldine's and mine. Little in Washington is on the level.

A problem with the *Newsweek* piece developed just before it went to press. In the week prior to the convention, I was covering platform proceedings at San Francisco's St. Francis Hotel. A young man with an angry expression came up to me. It was a Young Republicans delegate from California I had quoted as expressing racist remarks in my column at the YR national convention a year earlier. He ranted at me for misquoting him and/or quoting his off-the-record comments, ending by calling me "a slimy bastard." Hungover from carousing with press pals, I took a swing and hit him in the face.

My father and his father were quick with their temper and their fists, and I inherited both qualities. The difference was that they could handle themselves in a brawl and I could not. I'm sure I did no damage to my young anatogonist, and because bystanders immediately intervened, I suffered no damage.

I quickly told Rowly about it for fear he would hear a distorted version. He thought it hilarious, but I told him to keep it mum. He promised. Always the life of any party, however, he entertained friends that night over dinner with a suitably embellished story of my pugilism. At the table was the famous *San Francisco Chronicle* columnist Herb Caen, who put the story in the next morning's paper.

Mike Janeway called me to say his editors at *Newsweek* had read Caen's column item and instructed Janeway to put a couple of lines about it in our story. I was appalled. Whom could I see to avert this? Mike said either Evans or I should go to Ben Bradlee, *Newsweek*'s Washington bureau chief. Rowly was a social friend of Bradlee's on the Georgetown party circuit, but he had no interest in this matter and said I should intervene myself if I were that upset.

So I went to see Bradlee at *Newsweek*'s convention workspace. I told him my inexcusable loss of self-control was really out of character, was not reflective of what the article said about our column, and certainly was unfair to Rowly. Benjamin Crowninshield Bradlee stared at me, evoking the essence of upper-class WASP superiority, then said quietly: "Bob, your points are well-taken, but we're going to use the story [about the punch] anyway."

After describing Evans as "sleek and sandy-haired, a well-dressed Philadelphia patrician," *Newsweek* reported that "Bob Novak, 33, is a 'Front Page' type from Joliet, Ill., and the University of Illinois, whose clashing clothes and muricated manner give the team its one-two punch. Punch two became a reality in San Francisco when Novak, angered by a budding politician who called him a vulgar name, bopped the heckler and won the press-room title Killer ('I am the Greatest') Novak."

TWO DAYS AFTER winning the California primary, Goldwater dictated a letter to me disputing my column's assertion that he was unhappy about the selection of Oregon governor Mark Hatfield, a liberal close to Rockefeller, as the convention's keynote speaker. He conceded he had preferred Bill Miller as keynoter because "he is more of a stump speaker than Mark," but added:

> While Mark and I do not agree 100% philosophically, I'm a great admirer of his and feel that he has a definite place in the future of the Republican Party.
>
> You and Roland [sic] are continuing to do a great job, so keep it up and if you ever feel the need of a personal contact, give a whistle—I'm usually around.

The letter demonstrated two things about Goldwater at that point. First, Goldwater wanted to lead the full array of Republicans, including liberals like Mark Hatfield. Second, playing his Lauren Bacall to my Humphrey Bogart in asking me to just whistle, he wanted to repair his longtime relationship with me, which had become frayed because of my criticism of Goldwater the campaigner.

Goldwater signaled after California that he preferred Scranton as his running mate, but the idea of a Goldwater-led unified party was intolerable to the eastern Republican establishment that continued to pressure Scranton for a late presidential run. Following the California primary Scranton nearly announced his candidacy during the National Governors Conference in Cleveland but backed out. It was too late at Cleveland, and it was far too late *after* Cleveland. But at this tardy juncture, Mary Scranton decided her husband was being humiliated by his vacillating performance. According to quotes supplied to the *New York Times* by the Scrantons, she told her husband: "Bill, I think you better run." He did.

On Saturday night, July 13, two days before the convention started, Bill Keisling banged out an insulting letter from Scranton to Goldwater demanding a debate. Charging "ill-advised efforts to make us stand for Gold-waterism instead of Republicanism," it was sent to Goldwater without Scranton seeing or signing it. That ended whatever chances remained for a Goldwater-Scranton ticket, and won Scranton no delegates.

I was one of the few reporters admitted to the Goldwater campaign's inner sanctum on the top floor of the Mark Hopkins Hotel the week before the convention. But when Goldwater arrived in town, the atmosphere grew colder for me. I later learned that the Arizona Mafia felt my columns had been unfriendly and cut me off. As Goldwater suggested in his June 4 letter to me, I gave him "a whistle." In San Francisco, I asked him for a meeting or at least a telephone conversation. He never whistled back.

On the day after the convention, July 17, 1964, I had a going-away drink at the Mark Hopkins bar with Clif White. Goldwater had just named a member of the Arizona Mafia—Dean Burch, a state capital lobbyist in Arizona and former administrative assistant in Goldwater's Senate office—to the job White wanted: Republican National Chairman. Goldwater had not even contacted White. That signaled that the senator still was uncomfortable reaching out beyond the Phoenix country club set and, after the Scranton letter, had lost interest in closing the yawning divide within the Republican Party.

AFTER MY DRINK with Clif White, I left with Geraldine for a weekend on the Pacific Ocean at Carmel. It was not all leisure. On my Olympia portable typewriter I started work on the final three chapters of my book about the campaign for the 1964 Republican nomination.

Since the original working title of *Republicans Four* had been overtaken by events and my substitute working title of *The Road to San Francisco* was too bland, Macmillan senior editor Peter V. Ritner decided on *The Agony of the G.O.P., 1964.* That, I thought, implied a New York liberal judgment that the Goldwater revolution was a disaster.

The book itself was Ritner's idea, and so was the plan to rush it into print during the autumn general election campaign to describe how Goldwater won, or lost, the Republican nomination. By June 1964, he wanted chapters covering "the last stretch" to the convention, and then the remainder of the book "a few days after the convention itself," with publication "in about six weeks" (or early in September). "You must observe deadlines to the day," he told me. I thought he was exaggerating. He wasn't.

When I first signed my contract with Macmillan in early 1962, I never dreamed I would be collaborating on a six-day-a-week newspaper column with a partner who played no part in my book project.

Late on Saturday night, August 22, in Washington, I finished the last chapter. Geraldine typed the final version and mailed it Special Delivery to Ritner in New York. I was less than a month behind Ritner's deadlines, which I thought made possible publication at the beginning of October. I was sure *The Agony* would come out in the heart of the campaign, as planned.

I flew on Sunday, August 23, to Atlantic City, New Jersey, where the Democratic National Convention would begin Monday. When I entered the work area of the *New York Herald-Tribune* at the Atlantic City Convention Hall Monday morning, I telephoned Ritner's office in New York. I was informed that Peter and his family were incommunicado, vacationing on the tiny French island of Saint-Barthélemy in the Caribbean, had been there for a couple of weeks and would not return until mid-September. He had not seen my final chapters (including those sent before he left weeks earlier) and they had not been edited. That meant no plans to publish the book before the November election.

My co-workers in the *Herald-Tribune* workspace that morning must have been shocked when they heard me profanely abusing first a secretary and then an executive at Macmillan's. I felt I had lost my chance to make *The Agony* a best seller by not publishing during the campaign.

"I understand you were upset to find that I sometimes go on vacation," Ritner wrote me on September 16 after reappearing in Manhattan. Why had he never contacted me with a warning about what was happening? "Before deciding on the correct publishing strategy (like everybody else, we have our little pomposities) it was necessary to get the book entirely in hand. It was not desirable to harass you on the telephone every day or so."

Not until the first week of March 1965 was the book published.

AFTER FOUR YEARS of Republican upheaval with unpredictable turns, the election outcome of 1964 was preordained. The split in the Grand Old Party was in some ways worse than the great schism of 1912. Liberal colleagues in Washington journalism have teased me by telling me that as junior high school students, they enjoyed the "liberal" Evans & Novak column because it mercilessly trashed Goldwater in 1964. The truth is more complicated, as I can attest after rereading the full Evans & Novak product. Our columns hardly ever dealt with the candidate's positions but took issue with his failure to reach out to the rest of the party.

Reading old columns, I find a litany that Goldwater was bringing down Republican candidates all over the country. Traveling to Connecticut, New York, Pennsylvania, Virginia, Ohio, Michigan, Illinois, Kansas, Oklahoma,

Texas, Wyoming, Nevada, and California, I reported Republicans terrified by the Goldwater impact. For example, in Nevada, I found Lieutenant Governor Paul Laxalt, at age forty-two one of the brightest young political figures in the West, being dragged down by Goldwater in his bid for the U.S. Senate. I worried about Goldwater's political impact, not his ideology.

STILL TRAVELING ABOUT 80 percent of the time after Labor Day, I saw little of Clif White, who was stuck in the capital as national director of Citizens for Goldwater-Miller. The political virtuoso who had engineered Goldwater's revolutionary climb to the nomination was condemned to a campaign backwater.

While he recognized the inevitability of Lyndon Johnson's election, White wanted to avoid a landslide that might prevent the nomination of a conservative in his lifetime. To this end, he proposed a filmed television speech on Goldwater's behalf delivered by Ronald Reagan, a fifty-three-year-old former Hollywood actor hosting *Death Valley Days* on television. Goldwater intimates William Baroody and Denison Kitchel, controlling the senator's campaign, told him that Reagan's comments were "unscholarly" and politically dangerous. But White mobilized California money interests to pressure Goldwater into putting the speech on television six days before the election.

Ronald Reagan, Clif told me, was the candidate that Barry Goldwater was not and could never be: committed, intelligent, and intensely ambitious. Reagan, said Clif, was the hope for a conservative future. I knew Reagan only from watching him in the second movie of Princess Theater double features in Joliet (though we all pronounced his name *Ree*gin, not *Ray*gin). I wondered how this aging B movie actor, who had just changed his party registration from Democrat to Republican and never served one minute in public office, could lead the Grand Old Party.

BILL SCRANTON, NOT Reagan, looked to me like the future of the GOP, and I so wrote in two columns that fall. Just before the election, the Pennsylvania governor's office telephoned to say that Bill and Mary Scranton were inviting me and Geraldine to spend election night as their overnight guests at Marworth, the Scranton family estate outside the city of Scranton. I had a cordial professional relationship with the Scrantons, but nothing personal. The inviter merely said the governor and Mrs. Scranton thought it would be nice to be with me that night.

The invitation made me uncomfortable, and I wanted to turn it down. Rowly, more accustomed than I to being a guest of the mighty, thought it a wonderful chance to get inside dope from the man likely to lead the Republican Party back to "normalcy." I bowed to my partner's wisdom.

Before flying to Scranton on November 2, 1964, I voted in the District of Columbia, which was casting votes for president for the first time. Unlike 1960 when I voted for Kennedy with misgivings, I had decided weeks earlier I had no alternative other than casting my second straight presidential vote for a Democrat. Millions of other Republicans joined me in abandoning the GOP. I had no more favorable opinion of LBJ than ever, but I felt Goldwater was too disorganized and unfocused to be president. I also had bought into the liberal propaganda about Goldwater's extremism (though I would have been hard-pressed to say where exactly I disagreed with him other than his opposition to the voting rights bill).

A small group assembled for an early supper at Marworth on election night, and its composition made me all the more uneasy about being there. Except for Geraldine and me, all the guests were close friends or important supporters of Scranton. It was an evening short on either celebration or gallows humor as the Republican Party suffered one of the worst defeats in 104 years of contesting presidential elections.

Johnson won a record 61.3 percent of the vote and all but five states. Democrats picked up forty seats in the House, giving them a two-to-one advantage in both houses of Congress. Many state legislatures changed to Democratic domination, including New York and Michigan. Fallen Republicans included presumed Republican stars of the future—Chuck Percy in Illinois, Bob Taft Jr. in Ohio, and Bud Wilkinson in Oklahoma.

The pall cast at Marworth by the election returns was broken momentarily when Barry Goldwater appeared on TV emerging from an Arizona polling place. Asked how he had voted, Barry replied that he had never voted a straight party ticket and was not about to start now. That generated sarcastic laughter from Scranton's friends, but not the Scrantons themselves. Bill Scranton, who had been pleading with Republicans around the country to hold their noses and vote for Goldwater, muttered: "That's Barry for you." Mary Scranton's face was a study in contempt.

Geraldine and I flew back to Washington from Scranton at the crack of dawn on Wednesday, so that Evans and I could get out two columns on the election for the Thursday and Friday newspapers. I wrote the Thursday column ("Return to GOP Normalcy"). Revealing plans by "Republican party leaders and office holders" to oust Dean Burch as Republican National Chairman, I wrote: "Putting first things first, the party's realists want to bury the reminders and vestiges of Goldwaterism. Unlike Goldwater himself, they read the word repudiation in the wreckage of Nov. 3."

Having been ahead of the journalistic pack in foreseeing the rise of Goldwaterism and understanding the revolutionary nature of its takeover of the Republican Party, I now retreated to the protective warmth of the conventional wisdom. I missed the reality that the Republican Party and American politics had been changed profoundly even though it would take another sixteen years before its full impact was felt. (Burch was jettisoned when his mentor and former boss Goldwater would not lift a finger to save him. Barry was interested in calming turbulent party waters that he had roiled so he could return to his beloved Senate in the 1966 election instead of consolidating the ideological takeover of the Republican Party.)

IN THE LATE winter of 1965 at the Statler Hilton in Washington, I attended a reception that screened the film version of Theodore White's new best-selling book, *The Making of the President 1964.*

Now, at the 1965 reception, White complimented me on *The Agony of the G.O.P., 1964* and said he had enjoyed reading it. "I guess we have the same problem," he told me. "How do we invest all the money that's pouring in?" Teddy was not being snotty but terminally naive.

My book advance, my share of newspaper serialization (led off by the *Herald-Tribune*), and book club selections by the Literary Guild, the Mid-Century Book Club, and the Kiplinger Book Club amounted to income for me of $7,825 (about $50,000 in 2007 dollars). Not bad for me, though hardly comparable to Teddy White's take. I thought Peter Ritner did a good job of advertising the book and pushing for newspaper syndication and book clubs, but I had to remind him to send me the thousand dollars due on final submission of the manuscript.

THE AGONY'S SALES were modest, but reviews were flattering. My ego was bloated by reviewers comparing me with Theodore White. James Perry, one of the nation's top political reporters, said of me in a *National Observer* review: "He has written a big, important book filled with insights and illuminations." William Henry Chamberlin, the conservative columnist for the *Wall Street Journal* wrote: "On the basis of first-hand experience as reporter and commentator, Mr. Novak has created an enduring record."

There were published critiques of my book by liberal Republicans— plus unpublished criticism from one of my favorite sources of the 1964 campaign. Covering the California primary, I had grown close to pro-Rockefeller liberal Republican members of the State Assembly, including Houston I. Flournoy, a thirty-four-year-old political science professor. On March 31, 1965, Flournoy wrote me praising *The Agony* as a "superb account" of 1964. But like published liberal critics, he took exception to my closing analysis, in which I concluded: "In the final analysis, then, Rockefeller and Scranton lost because they had nothing to offer the people but themselves. Goldwater had a moral philosophy that stirred enough people to the heights of enthusiasm so that the nomination was his."

The Goldwater movement's ability to arouse dedication in its followers, Flournoy said, is "precisely this element in American politics which is foolhardy and self-defeating." To ask the GOP's liberal wing to imitate the party's Right "is merely to ask that it curtail its electoral appeal." That, Flournoy told me, would assure the Republicans were sure losers in future elections. One year later in 1966, a landslide of California's voters elected as governor Goldwater's ideological heir Ronald Reagan. Houston Flournoy rode Reagan's coattails to squeak in as state controller, holding that office for eight years before becoming the party's losing nominee for governor in 1974.

On March 19, 1965, Bob Snodgrass, an old-fashioned southern liberal who had been purged as Republican National Committeeman from Georgia by the ascendant Goldwaterites, wrote me about my book. He saw the right-wingers dominating his party in the South and leading it to destruction: "It is my estimate that as long as the Republican Party in Georgia follows this type of leadership, there is no hope for it long-range-wise, and it will be heading down a dead end street, getting fewer and fewer votes in the years ahead." In fact, following that type of leadership, Republicans came to dominate Georgia and the South.

One final critic of my book who neither published a review nor sent me a letter was Mary Scranton. The governor's aides told me she was upset about the criticism of both Scrantons in *The Agony* and considered it a betrayal after I had been a guest at Marworth on election night. Of course, all the criticism of the Scrantons was in Macmillan's hands long before I entered their home. Nevertheless, it was a mistake for Mary Scranton to invite me, it was a mistake for me to accept her invitation, and it was a mistake I vowed not to make again. Bill Scranton, barred by law from reelection as governor, made no effort at the 1968 presidential nomination. He never again sought elective office, refused all offers of full-time federal appointive office, and left politics forever after a career that spanned six years.

CHAPTER 14

The Great Society: In Ascent

IN EARLY DECEMBER 1963, less than two weeks after John F. Kennedy was buried, presidential press secretary Pierre Salinger placed a telephone call to Rowland Evans. "Rowly," he said, "you should know that things have changed, and you better get used it. You used to have a pipeline over here, but you don't anymore."

That was not the good-natured "Lucky Pierre" whom Rowly and I knew as a Kennedy aide. Salinger later confirmed our assumption that his call was on orders of President Johnson, who had retained Salinger as his press secretary. Salinger sounded so stilted that Rowly was sure Pierre was reading from a script (in future years called "talking points").

Salinger complained in his own name, not Johnson's, about the Evans & Novak column of December 6 in which I reported "a typically Johnsonian attempt to embrace all of President Kennedy's liberal economic programs while maintaining an exterior conservative enough to keep the business community happy."

Johnson had assured liberal economist Walter Heller, the column continued, that he not only would be retained as chairman of the President's Council of Economic Advisers but that LBJ would push Heller's brainchild, the massive Kennedy across-the-board tax cut. (In those days slashing income taxes was considered liberal rather than conservative.) I also wrote that Johnson had told Heller and the rest of the JFK economic team that "he never had been afraid of high federal spending for a good cause."

We reported less than we knew. Heller gave Rowly what the economic adviser called "highly confidential notes" of his meeting with Johnson at the White House on Saturday night, November 23, the night after the assassination. The notes quoted the new president as saying:

I want to say something about all this talk that I'm a conservative who is likely to go back to the Eisenhower ways or give in to the economy bloc in Congress. It's not so, and I want you to tell your friends—[Arthur] Schlesinger, [John Kenneth] Galbraith and other liberals that it is not so. . . . If you looked at my record, you would know that. I am a Roosevelt New Dealer. As a matter of fact, to tell the truth, John F. Kennedy was a little too conservative to suit my taste.

A few days later, Johnson met with his old friend, Wall Street financier and fellow Texan Robert Anderson. In the column, I described Anderson as "the high priest of balanced budgets and hard money" while serving as Secretary of the Treasury during Eisenhower's second term. Anderson spread the word around town that Johnson had told him the free-and-easy spending days of the liberal Kennedy gang were over.

Which was the authentic LBJ, the Walter Heller liberal or the Bob Anderson conservative? Both, I think.

Read forty years later, my column does not seem particularly tough on Johnson. But Salinger later told us Johnson was infuriated. LBJ detested this kind of analysis, and complained that Evans & Novak never had taken Jack Kennedy through this wringer (and, indeed, we had not).

I think Johnson's misuse of Salinger—and not just in this case—may have stemmed from his desire to push around Kennedy aides who he felt had treated him with disrespect when he was vice president. I am sure that the telephone call to Rowly had less to do with the substance of the offending column than the delight in having a Kennedy aide tell a Kennedy intimate that his day at the White House was done.

WHEN THE Evans & Novak column started in May 1963, Rowly asked the vice president's office whether Johnson could see us. We got no response. Then, late on a Friday afternoon in September, Rowly was called at about five o'clock by one of the vice president's secretaries to tell him he would see us immediately. "He's waiting for you," we were told.

That resulted in a poor decision on our part. We were running late that Friday on two columns due for Monday and Tuesday, and a predictable long session with Johnson would make us hours late. So Rowly called the vice president's office to say, politely of course, that we were on deadline and, very sorry, but we just could not get up to the Hill right now, adding we sure would like a rain check (that never came). We learned Lyndon regarded our performance as a coldly calculated snub. In truth, it betrayed stupidity and, yes, a little arrogance by us.

Two weeks before the assassination, I wrote a rare column about the vice president—one that did not make him happy. It came about because of a conversation I had with a Texas pal of Geraldine's, Larry L. King, the future playwright and novelist.

King was a liberal and no Johnson fan. But he had to make a living and was working as an aide to the LBJ protégé Congressman Jim Wright. King told me Johnson was secretly imploring Wright to run against liberal senator Ralph Yarborough in the 1964 Texas Democratic primary and promised him all-out money support. That displeased President Kennedy, who did not want an attempted purge of the one senator from the old Confederacy who solidly supported New Frontier legislation.

It was a terrific story, but King was worried that the Wright angle— which was its big exclusive nugget—would be traced to him. Larry asked whether I could get to Texas any time soon and write the column with a Texas dateline so that it would seem my sources were there. By coincidence, Geraldine and I were ending my three-week reporting trip to Latin America in October 1963 by visiting her parents in Hillsboro, Texas. King was delighted and soon presented me with an "Evans & Novak column" entitled "Johnson vs. Kennedy" and carrying a Hillsboro dateline.

I informed Larry that we did not use ghostwritten columns, but thanked him for the help. I did borrow heavily from King's draft while rewriting it, retaining the "Johnson vs. Kennedy" title and changing the dateline from Hillsboro to Dallas, where our plane from Mexico City would land. The column, published November 8, described "a blood feud between Johnson and Yarborough that transcends ideology." LBJ hated publication of intraparty feuds involving him, but what really antagonized him was publication of his secret overture to Wright. The messy political situation in Texas prompted Kennedy's late November visit to Texas. (Once he became president, Johnson shifted completely and successfully prevented any primary challenge of Yarborough.)

BY THE TIME Lyndon Johnson entered the White House, his relations with Rowly and me had reached a low. Robert Kintner, the former NBC News president, was an old friend of Johnson's who came into the White House to advise him on news media relations. Kintner advised the president that there was no point feuding with Evans & Novak. He talked Johnson into inviting Evans (not me) into the Oval Office for a chat.

It was just Johnson, Evans, and Kintner—no aides, no stenographer— for an unhurried conversation. It failed. Rowly told me Lyndon was in his "Ah-ain't-gonna-tell-you-nothin' mood," and as arrogant as he could be.

The meeting was not repeated. Neither Evans nor I ever sat down with Lyndon again during the five years of his presidency.

I did experience one social contact with him when I received an invitation for Geraldine and me from the White House for a black-tie state dinner on June 30, 1964, honoring Costa Rica's President Francisco Orlich. Johnson kept a pretty close tab on who got such favors, but I don't think he was courting me. I guessed some of Geraldine's old pals on the president's secretarial staff decided she ought to get a taste of the high life.

As usual, I had a little too much to drink, and as a nondancer joked and gossiped with Congressman Charles Weltner of Georgia, who was exiting from elective politics in his state by supporting Johnson's civil rights bill (and going on to a long career on the Georgia Supreme Court). Weltner and I, both fortified by drink, thought it hilarious that the president's younger daughter, then seventeen years old, had just changed the spelling of her name from Lucy to Luci. We both decided the way to pronounce her new name was Loo-*si,* with a ridiculously heavy emphasis on the second syllable.

As a cocky thirty-three-year-old nationally syndicated columnist, I thought this would be the first of many White House state dinners that I would attend. It wasn't. It was the last.

President Johnson did not like the critically analytical tone of our columns, but his real problem with us was Rowly's intimacy with LBJ's archenemy Robert F. Kennedy. Not until more than three decades later when Bobby's papers were unsealed and Lyndon's surreptitious White House tapes were released was it realized how much these two strongmen despised each other.

Johnson envisioned a cabal of socially prominent journalists aligned with Bobby Kennedy trying to sink his presidency from the start, and he regarded Evans as a co-conspirator. I was only Rowly's accomplice. I did not realize how adamantly Johnson viewed us as foot soldiers in Bobby's army and did not realize how close Rowly was to the attorney general. I did not know Rowly was part of the "Hickory Hill Gang": administration officials, politicians, and journalists, plus their wives, who gathered at Hickory Hill, Bobby's estate across the Potomac in Virginia. I did not even know such a gang existed.

Rowly's oral histories reveal tidbits about Bobby that did not find their way into our column and that he never confided to me. However, Evans & Novak columns, under careful inspection today, betray no bias in the LBJ versus RFK death struggle.

EVANS DID NOT need the Johnson-inspired telephone call from Pierre Salinger to understand that his White House connections would soon be gone, because the tenure there of his old Kennedy friends would be short. Rowly took it as a challenge to penetrate the Johnson inner circle. He had a candidate: Bill D. Moyers. In the week after the assassination, he invited Moyers and his wife, Judith, to "supper" on Friday night, November 29, at the elegant Evans home in Georgetown, with the Novaks the only other guests.

Moyers arrived in Washington early in 1960 as a twenty-five-year-old Baptist minister and new staffer for Majority Leader Johnson. By the time of the Democratic National Convention in Los Angeles that summer, Moyers was indispensable to LBJ. After the election, Moyers became deputy director of the only significant Kennedy addition to government, the Peace Corps. Moyers happened to be in Texas on November 22, 1963, and returned with Johnson to the White House—to stay there as a senior aide, never returning to the Peace Corps.

Rowly considered Moyers as more approachable than Horace Busby, Jack Valenti, and the even more stereotypical Texans who soon joined Johnson. Behind his boyish appearance, Billy Don Moyers was fiercely ambitious, shrewd, and occasionally duplicitous. He was our best LBJ source, and I believe the best LBJ source for many other reporters.

Rowly began predinner cocktails by asking Bill and Judith where they lived. When he learned their home was in an unfashionable Virginia suburb, he told them that "you must move to town." By "town," Rowly did not mean Capitol Hill, where Geraldine and I lived, but one of the socially upscale neighborhoods, such as Georgetown. "It makes it so much easier to get around," Rowly explained. What he meant was that it would be easier for Moyers to get on the dinner circuit that Evans traveled.

I sat in admiring silence at Rowly's audacity. The purpose of the dinner party was to inject Evans (and me) into a new White House power structure where we had no foothold. Now Rowly had turned this on its head by offering Moyers and his wife entrée into Washington's special social circle. He made it appear that he was doing Bill a favor, instead of the other way around.

Moyers carried his own agenda to O Street. He could not wait to enter the Evans dining room for the meal before he sent his message. When he did, Rowly and I exchanged excited glances. The rest of the evening was informative and entertaining, but I was anxious for Moyers to leave so that Rowly and I could exchange notes on what he had told us.

We had already written and teletyped to New York our columns for Monday and Tuesday. That Friday night we decided that Moyers's information was so important that we had better come into the National Press Building Saturday morning to write a new Monday column. I wrote the first draft, and Evans did the rewriting and heavy editing. The title for the new December 2 column was "Shriver for V.P.":

> The leading prospect for the Vice-Presidential nomination in President Johnson's own mind is Sargent Shriver, President Kennedy's brother-in-law and Director at the Peace Corps. . . .
>
> [A]t this early date, Shriver is the President's first choice. . . .
>
> As a relative but not a blood-relative of the murdered President, Shriver would bring the Kennedy glamour and vote appeal to the ticket without opening the way to charges of dynasty building.

Evans and I were certain Moyers would not dare accept Rowly's dinner invitation without Johnson's approval. We were equally certain the Shriver message came straight from Lyndon. If our column seems recklessly unequivocal in identifying "the President's first choice," it was because his messenger to us was so unequivocal.

We interpreted this as a trial balloon by Johnson, and we were willing to hoist it without caveats about the defects of a Johnson-Shriver ticket (as we surely would have done in the years to come). Our balloon was promptly shot down by Chicago Mayor Richard J. Daley. Robert Sargent Shriver had been conscripted into the family business when he married Eunice Kennedy and was sent to Chicago to run Joe Kennedy's Merchandise Mart. He was not part of the Daley Machine, and the mayor was not going to tolerate a non-Daley Chicagoan on the national ticket.

So why did Johnson authorize Moyers to inform Evans and Novak, as I am sure he did, that Shriver was his "first choice" when surely he had Senator Hubert Humphrey in mind from the start? Partly to provoke Bobby, using both his brother-in-law and a personal friend, Rowly, to do so. But I also am convinced that the ersatz Shriver trial balloon was intended to send Robert F. Kennedy a clear message: Under no conditions will *you* be my running mate. Although that was Johnson's clear determination, Kennedy did not fully grasp its finality for months to come.

ON THE SECOND day of the 1964 Democratic National Convention at Atlantic City, the Evans & Novak column of August 25 was titled: "The South in Space." Under an Atlantic City dateline, it began:

> As Lyndon Johnson's Southern loyalists gather here for the Democratic National Convention, they have one lethal weapon to save

Dixie from Barry Goldwater: the old Federal pork barrel, with some space-age trimmings.

One shrewd Southern Democrat puts it this way:

"These bright young Republican boys think they can shout nigger, nigger, nigger and run all over us. Well, they're going to learn there are other things the South cares about."

The "other things" are goodies from Uncle Sam, including some particularly valuable Federal pork from the moon shot program. Southern voters will be told incessantly from now to Nov. 3 that a vote for a budget-balancing, penny-pinching Goldwater administration would shut off the Federal spigots.

Noting that the South "swallowed the lion's share" of federal expenditures for the Kennedy-Johnson program to put a man on the moon, the column itemized space spending in Texas, Louisiana, Mississippi, Alabama, and Florida. The conclusion was that "the fight for the South boils down to this question: What are Southerners most interested in, segregation or pork?" The way I wrote the column implied that the answer was "pork."

For students of Washington cryptology, the "shrewd Southern Democrat" quoted in the column's second paragraph was identified in the fourteenth paragraph. I wrote that space program dollars in the South "are going to be driven home with regularity this fall by Rep. Hale Boggs of New Orleans, House majority whip and a leading Southern loyalist."

Thomas Hale Boggs Sr., then fifty years old, was a leading congressional power broker. In 1964, he already had spent twenty years in the House, had been elected to the third-ranking party position of majority whip at the early age of forty-eight, would move up a notch to become majority leader in 1971, and appeared certain to become Speaker of the House. (While Boggs campaigned for a colleague in Alaska in the autumn of 1972, the four-passenger plane carrying him was lost in that state's trackless wastes.)

Boggs was the archetypal Southern Democratic "loyalist" of that era, still voting against civil rights legislation but dedicated to preserving the Solid South for the Democrats—preservation essential to the party's perpetual majority in Congress. That was Boggs's real goal on August 19, 1964, when he invited Rowly and me for a typical Capitol Hill luncheon of that era (whiskey highballs followed by steak and red wine). He handed us memos and tables showing how federal pork would throttle Goldwater in the Deep South. Boggs was close to LBJ and made clear he was giving us the president's views.

Looking back I consider this column important in debunking the myth that Lyndon Johnson committed a noble sacrifice by passing major civil rights bills and assuring the right to vote to southern blacks at the cost of southern domination by Democrats. In truth Johnson and the southern Democratic establishment felt the end of segregation actually would liberate their region and their party from racial demagogues while remaining solidly Democratic because, as Boggs bluntly informed us, southerners were addicted to federal pork. Just as LBJ thought he could fight communism in Vietnam while building the Great Society at home, he envisioned civil rights attained without political upheaval.

SOON AFTER LBJ was elected in November 1964, I left with Geraldine on a four-week reporting survey to the Southern Cone of South America. The trip got off to a bad start on the Pan American Clipper's famous overnight flight from New York to Rio de Janeiro. Geraldine became deathly ill, and lost her breakfast before we landed. Geraldine blamed her malady on eggs served by Pan Am, but she experienced continued nausea throughout our ten days in Brazil.

When we arrived in Buenos Aires, the aroma of the justly famous Argentine beef cooked on outdoor grills wafted through the air of the southern hemisphere summer as we rode to our hotel from the airport. I loved it, but it made Geraldine sick to her stomach. When we ordered steak in a Buenos Aires restaurant, Geraldine—normally an enthusiastic meateater—barely touched hers.

Geraldine finally told me she suspected she might be pregnant, which was promptly confirmed by a visit to an Argentine clinic. We were 5,218 miles from Washington at the most distant point of our month-long journey. Geraldine's first pregnancy had ended in a miscarriage the previous year, and it seemed prudent for us to return home forthwith. But I had two weeks of scheduled appointments in three countries. Geraldine said we should stick it out on the road.

On the evening of the day we learned of the pregnancy, we had dinner with a friend of Geraldine's from her days in Austin: Frank Manitzas, an Associated Press reporter in Texas who now worked in the AP's Buenos Aires bureau. Manitzas had to cover a demonstration *(manifestation)* by a Peronista labor union in the Buenos Aires working-class district of Avellaneda. Often, he said, such demonstrations ended in violence—a sign of Argentina's internal conflict that might be useful for me to observe as a columnist. I suggested to Geraldine that I go alone. She said she would rather go with us.

I chatted with several workers at Avellaneda. They detested their employers and their government, yearning for the return of exiled strongman Juan Domingo Peron. A hero to his country's working class (the "Shirtless Ones"), Peron had forced extravagant wage increases that fueled Argentina's economic miseries.

Shirtless Ones hoisting banners prepared to march that beautiful December evening when suddenly khaki-clad, well-armed police, some mounted, appeared a block away. In Caucasian Argentina, these police were of Indian stock and contrasted vividly with the all-white demonstrators. The demonstrators started marching. The police told them to halt. The demonstrators kept marching. The police opened fire with tear gas canisters—fired at point-blank range to do bodily damage. The demonstrators heaved large stones at the police. The police retaliated with water cannons. When the demonstrators threw more stones, saber-wielding mounted police launched a ragged cavalry charge. Geraldine and I were in the cross fire between tear gas and stones, pinned against a building. Was that any way to treat a pregnant lady? The little war was over in less than ten minutes.

In our next stop in Chile, Geraldine experienced morning sickness and a dinner hosted by local journalists at a Santiago restaurant proved too much for her. I ordered a Chilean mixed grill with goat's meat, a pig's innards, and other unspeakable items producing a heady aroma that sent Geraldine racing to the ladies' room, never to return to the table.

The last South American country on our trip was Bolivia, the poorest on the continent, where Andean altitudes posed health challenges even for nonpregnant North Americans. La Paz, with an altitude of 11,913 feet is the world's highest capital. U.S. embassy staffers met us at the airport with an oxygen tank, but could not prevent Geraldine from becoming sicker than at any previous stop.

The Bolivian doctor who came to our hotel room was a young, fair-skinned Caucasian (in the continent's most heavily Indian country) who spoke flawless English and informed us he was a graduate of Harvard Medical School. He told us this was no place for a pregnant woman and Mrs. Novak had better leave La Paz on the next flight to save her baby. I told him I had important meetings here. Well then, he said, send Mrs. Novak down to the Peruvian capital of Lima immediately so that she could be near sea level while Mr. Novak finished his business in the mountains.

"Doctor," I said, "I notice a lot of Bolivians in Bolivia. That means women are able to have babies in this country at this altitude." "Mr. Novak," he replied, "perhaps you also noticed the way our Indian women in Bolivia are built—all torso, very short legs—caused by natural selection during centuries in the Andes and enabling them to breathe in this thin air." He glanced at my long-legged, willowy wife. "Obviously, Mrs. Novak is not built that way."

I had a breakfast appointment two mornings later with the president of Bolivia, my only scheduled visit with a head of a state during the four-week trip. Air Force Major General Rene Barrientos had just seized power in a military coup, the familiar Latin American process that President Kennedy had labeled unacceptable. I was anxious to hear the new Bolivian military dictator's views.

We had three options. First, cancel the appointment and leave immediately. Second, send Geraldine to Lima while I kept my date. Third, keep our schedule and pray no harm came to Geraldine and our unborn baby. I suggested the second option, but Geraldine insisted on staying with me in La Paz. Not for the first or last time, she was self-sacrificing and I was selfish.

Our first child, Zelda Jane Novak, was born August 2, 1965. She enjoyed a short but successful career as a political aide and journalist before becoming a wife and fabulous mother of four. She is a beautiful, intelligent, and feisty woman, whose personality I like to think was influenced by her prenatal travels through South America, a riot in Buenos Aires, and the thin air of the Bolivian Andes.

LYNDON JOHNSON WAS blessed with the biggest congressional majorities since 1936–37 thanks to the 1964 Goldwater election disaster. The president was intent on legislating the "Great Society" that he had promised during the campaign. In January 1965, Johnson called middle-level officials he had appointed into the Fish Room at the White House for a lecture. They included John Sweeney, federal co-chairman of the Appalachian Regional Commission, a Democratic political operative from Michigan who was my longtime friend. He kept careful notes that he gave to me but not for use in our column. LBJ began:

> I have watched Congress from either the inside or the outside, man and boy, for forty years, and I've never seen a Congress that didn't eventually take the measure of the President it was dealing with. . . . I was just elected President by the biggest popular margin in the history of the country, fifteen million votes. Just by the natural way people think and because Barry Goldwater scared hell out of them, I have already lost about two of these fifteen and am probably getting down to thirteen. If I get in any fight with Congress, I will lose another couple

of million, and if I have to send any more of our boys into Vietnam, I may be down to eight million by the end of this summer.

So what should he do with his Great Society program? The LBJ answer: Pass it all *now,* before he lost all his public support.

At first, Johnson's success dwarfed even FDR's New Deal thirty years earlier, easily passing measures that had eluded Democrats for the two decades since the end of World War II: Medicare, federal aid to schools, black voting rights, and much more.

Bryce Harlow, the Republican wise man who had served in the Eisenhower White House and would be a Nixon aide, told me that Johnson was "stockpiling adversity" in cramming so much legislation down the throat of Congress. The "adversity" began September 29, 1965, when the House defeated home rule for the District of Columbia—just to repudiate LBJ. There was much worse ahead for Johnson, as racial turmoil and Vietnam loomed.

CHAPTER 15

The Great Society: In Descent

IN AUGUST 1965, I lunched at Washington's historic Occidental Restaurant with Daniel Patrick Moynihan. He was resigning as an assistant secretary of Labor to seek the Democratic nomination for city council president of New York (his first attempt at elective office and the only election he ever lost). Moynihan brought a going-away present: a seventy-eight page Labor Department report. This was the soon-to-be famous—or infamous— "Moynihan Report" (as I labeled it for the first time). It would place unfairly a racist tag on the Evans & Novak column and permanently alienate Pat Moynihan from the Democratic Party's liberal wing that had been his home.

Thanks to me, the column had taken a turn increasingly hostile to the new, more radical black leadership. An early example was the December 2, 1964, column in which I viewed with alarm young leaders of the Student Non-Violent Coordinating Committee (SNCC) who were "moving faster than most politicians realize, and in a frightening direction." I reported that Robert Moses, a future legend of the civil rights movement, and John Lewis, a future congressman from Georgia, had visited Guinea where they conferred at length with President Sekou Toure, a leftist tyrant and Soviet fellow traveler. I noted, too, that Moses "was a speaker last week in New York at the annual dinner of the National Guardian, a publication widely regarded as the most flamboyant exponent of the Chinese Communist line in this country."

Many columns of this nature written by me brought accusations of "Red-baiting" (with the novelist Joseph Heller attacking us in a letter to the *New York Herald-Tribune*). Conservatives expressed delight (with *National Review* reporting that "even the liberals Evans and Novak" were alert to what was happening).

The column resulting from lunch with Moynihan addressed a problem deeper than leftist penetration. Passing one civil rights bill after another, I wrote, would not resolve America's race question. Northern racial riots of the long, hot summer of 1964 led Moynihan to ask questions that no government official ever had posed. I reported them in our column of August 17, 1965:

> He [Moynihan] wondered, for instance, why in a time of decreasing unemployment, the plight of the urban Negro was getting worse—not better. His answer: a 78-page report (based largely on unexciting Census Bureau statistics) revealing the breakdown of the Negro family. He showed that broken homes, illegitimacy, and female-oriented homes were central to big-city Negro problems.

Moynihan's boss, Secretary of Labor Willard Wirtz (a Kennedy holdover) felt this was too much truth to handle and would feed racist prejudices. Wirtz thwarted Moynihan's desire to release the report, but it leaked to several media outlets. Although my column was far from the first disclosure of Moynihan's report, it intensified the debate because I did not soften racial implications—especially when I repeated what Moynihan had been indiscreet enough to tell me at the Occidental.

> Moynihan believes the public erroneously compares the Negro minority to the Jewish minority. When discriminatory bars were lowered, Jews were ready to move. But the implicit message of the Moynihan Report is that ending discrimination is not nearly enough for the Negro. But what is enough?
> The phrase "preferential treatment" implies a solution far afield from the American dream. The white majority would never accept it. . . .
> Yet, the Moynihan Report inevitably leads to posing the question.

I had opened the door to a national debate over affirmative action and racial quotas that would still be raging forty years later. Civil rights legislation did not solve the problem of race as Lyndon Johnson, the quintessential legislator, believed it would.

THE CONTEMPT Lyndon B. Johnson and Robert F. Kennedy had for each other focused on Vietnam. Kennedy, elected to the U.S. Senate from New York in 1964, gradually drew away from the intervention his brother had instituted, as Democrats divided between these two strong-willed men.

On Saturday, February 19, 1966, Bobby Kennedy burned his bridges. "Viet Coalition Rule Urged by Kennedy," was the headline on page one of

Sunday's *Washington Post*. "Negotiated Settlement Must Include Reds as Concession, He Says." Senator Kennedy told a Washington news conference that "military victory" in Vietnam "was at best uncertain, and at worst unattainable." He proposed a "middle way" between a "widening war" that might bring in China and the Soviet Union and unilateral U.S. withdrawal: a "compromise government" with cabinet posts for the Communist National Liberation Front (NLF).

It is difficult to replicate the shock in Washington that winter weekend. I was on the telephone Sunday and Monday for political reaction. While no expert on Vietnam, I considered myself a good political reporter and this was a political story. That's what I told Rowly in the office Monday morning.

I had written exactly one column dealing with Vietnam at that point, while Evans had written dozens. Still, I insisted this was a political column that I should write. Rowly seemed in physical pain late that afternoon when he read my draft. He questioned whether this wasn't "a little too rough on Bobby." I asked for his specific disagreements. There were no major ones, he said, and then revealed his problem.

He had lunched with Kennedy at the Sans Souci restaurant near our office on Saturday before the senator's news conference. Bobby had shown him his prepared statement. Rowly told me he had made a few suggestions, but said to Kennedy that it was okay. ("The thrust of it, as I read it very fast, seemed okay," Evans said in a Kennedy Library oral history interview on July 30, 1970.)

"Rowly," I said, "it was a coalition government proposal. We've been against it all along. How could you say it was okay?" "You don't understand," he replied. "Bobby was waiting for me to finish, waiting for my verdict. It was a terrible situation." In the oral history interview, Rowly said: "I just kind of glanced through it very quickly. . . . He knew how I felt on Vietnam. I was on the hawkish side." While Kennedy had become a dove, Rowly had "this ambivalence in my own mind as to how much of it [Kennedy's opposition] was pure, raw politics—anti-Johnson politics."

What I did not know until I read the oral history forty years later in researching this book was that Kennedy called Evans from New York that Monday morning. "I told him we were writing a column," Evans said in the 1970 interview, adding Kennedy wanted "to make sure that I understood certain nuances. I said, 'I understand that.'" So Rowly had been personally briefed by Bobby about how to write the column after he had been given an advance look at and an opportunity to critique his statement.

Nevertheless, Rowly agreed to my column after a few edits toning down criticism of Kennedy. (In the oral history interview, Evans said: "It was a difficult column for me to write because of my relationship with Bobby. It was, in terms of an accurate political [assessment], 100 percent . . . It was a tough column, it was a rough column.")

The column (to run Wednesday, February 23) began by saying that Kennedy "is now aligned on the extreme edge of the Senate peace bloc," adding:

> Kennedy and his friends failed to realize that his pro-coalition stand was more extreme than the public position of peace Senators. . . .
>
> [B]itter words are being said by old friends in Washington. He is privately accused of seeking headlines, undermining U.S. foreign policy, and dividing his party. . . .
>
> [I]t points up a political fact about Kennedy: his need to play the role of critic, when it serves no apparent political purpose.

Tuesday was George Washington's birthday, and I remember Rowly coming into the office without a tie, wearing a sweater and a very long face. I never had seen this vivacious, upbeat man so morose. He told me he regretted the column that would run the next day, which he was sure would prove enormously embarrassing to him when Bobby read it.

We had to change our procedure, he said. Henceforth, he went on, we must have the option of single bylines when we disagreed with each other. I told him that was not possible after three years of double-byline columns. It would, I said, lead to rival Evans & Novak columns dueling on consecutive days over Kennedy and Vietnam. "Then, perhaps," I remember Rowly saying, "this is the end of the column."

How could it be that Rowly had so readily acquiesced to my column on Monday but the next day, after it had been transmitted to newspaper clients and already was in type in some papers, was ready to dissolve our partnership? I don't know, because we never discussed it in the years that followed. I speculated silently that perhaps on Monday night Rowly talked about it with his wife, Katherine Evans, an intimate friend of Bobby's wife, Ethel, and even closer to the Kennedys than Rowly was.

After suggesting the imminent end of our partnership, Rowly admitted to me that his friendship with Bobby Kennedy was incompatible with being an independent journalist. "I never again will have that kind of relationship with a politician," he said. "Never again." Four years later, he told the oral history interviewer: "Without question, the closest and probably the last close friend that I'll ever have in the area of politics is Bobby. It was much more difficult with him than anybody else. I mean

George McGovern, Fritz Mondale, or Chuck Percy are acquaintances. They're not friends."

After the column was published Wednesday morning, Rowly talked with Bobby on the phone. He never told me about that conversation, which I learned from the oral history. "Listen," Evans said he told Kennedy, "you know I really hated to write that column, Bobby, and I wouldn't blame you for being really, really furious, and I understand all that." According to Rowly, Bobby replied: "Don't give it another thought. I know what you're going to have to do. This doesn't make any difference. Don't worry about it."

I learned forty years later from the oral history that Rowly went out to Hickory Hill for breakfast on Thursday with the senator. Rowly quoted himself as telling Kennedy: "Well, you know Bobby, when two people are writing a column, sometimes it doesn't come out to fit wholly the views of either one of them. Compromises, you know. Having a partner isn't the easiest thing in the world." While driving back to Washington from McLean after breakfast, Rowly told the Kennedy Library interviewer, "Bobby said: 'I've spent my life with a partner'—meaning Jack. He understood. He was very understanding about that." After that breakfast with Bobby, Rowly never again brought up single-bylines, much less termination of our partnership.

Oddly, for the twenty-seven subsequent years of that partnership, we never mentioned this incident that almost killed it. In the remaining two years of his life, Robert F. Kennedy grew ever more dovish on Vietnam while Evans & Novak remained hawkish, though increasingly critical of the way Lyndon Johnson conducted the war. Bobby made no effort to influence our course, apparently resolved not to risk his friendship with Rowly.

Read forty years later, the column that caused us so much anguish seems less "rough" than Rowly claimed. The criticism could have been harsher if we had addressed the substance of Kennedy's position and not just the politics. Despite his reputation as a tough pragmatist, Bobby shared the liberal illusions of the sixties. He did not realize that the Communists were determined to achieve a unified Communist Vietnam and the NLF was an appendage of Hanoi. His fear of Chinese or Soviet intervention had no basis in reality.

ON SUNDAY, APRIL 24, 1966, the *New York Herald-Tribune*, the voice of the Republican establishment on the East Coast, closed its doors forever. Its last editor, Jim Bellows, had turned the *Trib* into one of America's most readable newspapers but had not made it solvent. The paper's proprietor, John Hay Whitney, would not indefinitely pour his fortune into this money-loser unless a break-even point was visible, and it never was.

Field Enterprises, which owned both the *Chicago Sun-Times* and Publishers Newspaper Syndicate (which distributed our column), decreed that the *Sun-Times* would be our home newspaper.

Undetermined was our New York City newspaper outlet. The *New York Journal-American* (the city's last Hearst paper) and the Scripps-Howard *New York World-Telegram and Sun* ended their independent lives and combined with the *Herald-Tribune* to form the new *World Journal Tribune*. The new hybrid, though managed by Hearst, would be honeycombed with *Herald-Tribune* editors and writers (including most of its columnists). Rowly and I saw it as the *Herald-Trib* reincarnated, and assumed the new paper would run our column.

However, the syndicate informed us that Dorothy Schiff, proprietor of the *New York Post*, wanted Evans & Novak and would pay a lot more for us than would the *WJT*. The syndicate advised us to take the money. Rowly was noncommittal, but I protested vociferously. The *Post* was a left-wing tabloid whose views I abhorred. Its columnists ran from liberal to far left, and I could not imagine what Dolly Schiff—a grande dame of the New York Left—wanted with a middle-of-the-road reporting column straying rightward.

The syndicate's salesmen had other products they wanted to sell the *Post* and did not want to offend Mrs. Schiff. Sales manager Bob Cowles reluctantly agreed to refuse to sell her Evans & Novak only if she was told that it was the authors of the column—not Publishers Newspaper Syndicate—who preferred to be in the *WJT*. We agreed, and were kept out of the *Post*'s leftist clutches.

The *WJT* was a wretched concoction that died a deserved death a year and a half after its birth. Its demise reduced New York City's daily newspapers to three—the *Times*, the *Daily News*, and the *Post*. Of these, only the *Post* was a potential purchaser of our column. The left-wing tabloid that was so abhorrent to me eighteen months earlier was now our necessary window in New York.

I thought we were cooked. But Mrs. Schiff told Cowles she would buy the column—with one caveat. Evans or Novak would have to call personally and tell her they *really wanted* to be published in the *New York Post*. Since I had been so adamant in resisting, Rowly said I would have to shoulder this onerous duty.

I called Mrs. Schiff, fearing the worst. But, belying her ferocious reputation, she graciously did not bring up my previous rudeness. That began a treasured relationship (now approaching four decades) with the *Post* through multiple changes in ownership and ideology at the paper. Dolly

Schiff, an ardent supporter of Israel, staved off demands to drop the column from Jewish subscribers and advertisers who objected to our columns on the Middle East, when other newspapers succumbed to such pressure.

After the death of the *Herald-Tribune*, and its news service, some fifty newspapers were quickly signed up by Publishers Newspaper Syndicate as their salesmen launched a lightning offensive for Evans & Novak clients. They included thirty-three of the thirty-five subscribers to the *Herald-Tribune* News Service, keeping the column in every large American city. For the first time, we were a genuine syndicated column. We shared half of all royalties, giving each of us $22,000 a year ($143,000 in 2007 dollars)—more money than I ever imagined making when I became a newspaperman.

Executives of the *Chicago Sun-Times*, our new home newspaper, gave me the impression they felt that Field Enterprises had forced them into a morganatic marriage. The *Sun-Times* had hitherto published us sporadically, and for several years even after 1966 did not run every column. But as in other arranged marriages, Evans & Novak and the *Sun-Times* learned to love each other. Rowly and I developed a more intimate relationship with the Chicago newspaper over forty years than we had in our three years with the *Herald-Tribune*, writing special pieces for the *Sun-Times* (a practice I continue today).

The *Washington Post*, our column's most important outlet, remained just a client—subject to cancellation. Its managing editor in 1966, Ben Bradlee, wanted to take us aboard and syndicate us, and so did we. But Field convinced us we had an unbreakable contract. For some time, Evans & Novak has been the *Post*'s only regularly published column not produced by its writers, and that has been an immeasurable blessing for me.

I HAVE ALREADY mentioned luncheon at Sans Souci, where Rowly and I conducted business for more than a decade. Located a five-minute walk from the White House, it seated no more than forty people for lunch (making it economically vulnerable even in its heyday). It was not all that expensive. My diary for 1966, which shows me eating at "San Sook" (as Art Buchwald called it) about every other day when I was in Washington, reflects an average bill of ten dollars for two diners (about sixty-two dollars in 2007 dollars). That included a premeal drink apiece, usually a Scotch or bourbon highball or a gin martini.

Alcohol was then a way of life in Washington. A Nixon subcabinet officer as my guest at Sans Souci on one occasion downed three double bourbons on the rocks before lunch and sipped a single bourbon during the meal, telling me nothing unintended in the process. I regarded as a wimp the rare news source who would order campari and soda or kir. I cannot remember anybody ordering iced tea (today's preluncheon beverage of choice for power lunchers, including me).

Sans Souci's menu was so-so, and there were several better French restaurants in Washington, but nobody went there for the food. It was for seeing and being seen. San Souci operated commercially for evening meals, with a stranger getting a booking if there was a vacancy. But for lunch, San Sook was a virtual club. If you were a regular (as Rowly and I were), you could *always* be seated. If you weren't, you *never* got a table even if you called months in advance.

Art Buchwald lunched there every day he was in Washington, often with the other two members of his nameless "club"—Ben Bradlee and Edward Bennett Williams—with a metal plaque marking his banquette. Sometimes, I would be startled to see First Lady Pat Nixon coming in with a couple of lady friends for a late lunch.

So pleasant an institution was bound to go under, as life in the capital was hardened by Vietnam and Watergate. San Souci declared bankruptcy in 1981 and closed. Its space now is occupied by a McDonald's. When I occasionally enter to buy a Big Mac, I always note how small it is, even for fast food.

IN JANUARY 1965, Evans and I signed with McGraw-Hill to write *Lyndon B. Johnson: The Exercise of Power*, a full-scale biography of the new president. Our editor was Robert A. Gutwillig, who would play a major role in my life over the next three decades. He was a published novelist, editor, journalist, political operative, businessman, salesman—and lover (as certified by three marriages and many girlfriends).

I still am unsure how we pulled off this book, while taking off no time from writing a six-day-a-week reporting column. In addition to drawing on our personal experiences covering LBJ, we conducted over two hundred interviews. Rowly and I divided the chapters, setting strict deadlines for submitting chapters to each other for editing. All-nighters were common for me, even though they were followed by a full day's work on the column.

Rowly and I took to Gutwillig as a shrewd editor and delightful companion. Consequently, Rowly and I were devastated to learn early in 1965 that he was leaving McGraw-Hill for a better job at New American Library. Our contract was with the company and not the editor, but we were having none of it. We informed McGraw-Hill that we would not write the book for them and wanted to give back our advance to be free to sign with NAL so that Gutwillig could edit the book. We pulled off this shift of publishers, and Gutwillig became close to a third collaborator who mediated noisy late-night disputes between Rowly and me.

A COUPLE OF weeks before the 1966 election, I received a telephone call from a man who identified himself as Ed Turner, news director of WTTG, Channel 5 in Washington. He was to become our principal television guru for a quarter of a century.

Turner asked us to be commentators on Channel 5 for the 1966 midterm elections. Relying on old movies and syndicated programming, WTTG previously had gotten by with no news staff. Turner, a professional broadcast journalist, was hired by Metromedia to change all that. He put together an excellent staff for a full hour of news at ten p.m., one hour ahead of other Washington stations. For the national midterm elections, while the networks were preempting their regular schedules Turner decided to show the movie classic *Casablanca*. He would break into the movie for ten minutes every hour with election returns, relying on the Associated Press wire plus comments from Evans and Novak.

Ed Turner was a rare conservative Republican among broadcast news executives, and he thought Evans and Novak in 1966 were the least liberal political columnists he could find.

Evans had been appearing for years on network Sunday interview shows, but I did not get my first chance until late 1963 after our column started when I questioned guests on CBS's *Face the Nation* and then the next year on NBC's *Meet the Press.* Lawrence A. Spivak, the originator, producer, and absolute boss of *Meet the Press,* was the toughest interrogator in television, and I tried to copy him.

I became one of Spivak's favorite guest questioners, and once filled in for him—when he was stranded in New York by a blizzard on Saturday, January 29, 1966. The *Meet the Press* guest was Julian Bond, a twenty-six-year-old firebrand civil rights leader from the Student Non-Violent Coordinating Committee (SNCC). He had just been denied a seat in the all-white, segregationist Georgia House of Representatives that he had won in a landslide the previous November. I cited SNCC's statement that the U.S. government "squashes liberation movements":

Novak: Do you mean this is not the Viet Cong we are fighting in Vietnam? Are we fighting someone else besides the Viet Cong?

Bond: There are a lot of differences of opinion about who is fighting.

Novak: You don't think it is a Communist-led operation, the Viet Cong?

Bond: I don't know if it is.

After the program, Bond asked me for a ride back to Capitol Hill, where the SNCC headquarters was located not far from my house. Bond and his two associates squeezed into Geraldine's new Mustang, and we made slow progress through snow-covered streets until, going up Constitution Avenue just beyond the Capitol, the car got stuck. At that point, the three black men left the car to push their white tormentor out of the snow and up the hill. It was a bizarre tableau, but there was nobody to witness it.

Even when sitting in Larry Spivak's seat on that one occasion, I was still a guest. The 1966 election night bit on Channel 5 in Washington marked my debut as a professional television performer. While the movie played, Rowly and I telephoned sources around the country for our hourly commentaries. Thanks to *Casablanca,* we beat the network stations in the ratings, and Rowly and I became regulars on Channel 5.

ON TV THAT night we reported a disaster for Lyndon Johnson and the Democratic Party—a startling change from the Democrat-LBJ landslide two years earlier that had led to instant analysis that the Republican Party was dead. Everybody—Evans and Novak included—was taken aback by Republicans gaining a net of forty-seven seats in the House of Representatives, though Democrats still maintained big margins in both houses of Congress. As Rowly and I worked the phones at Channel 5, we reported Democrats blaming LBJ for losses. I wrote it more carefully in the Evans & Novak column of Thursday, November 10, 1966 ("Johnson in Trouble").

In the early morning hours yesterday after their Election Day debacle, Democratic leaders of Michigan were whispering that Lyndon Johnson must be removed from the top of the ticket in 1968 to avert another disaster two years hence. . . .

The widely shared belief among key Democrats across the country is that if President Johnson had been on the ballot Tuesday, he would have been beaten and beaten badly.

IMMEDIATELY AFTER President Johnson's humiliation in the 1966 midterm elections, *Lyndon B. Johnson: The Exercise of Power* by Rowland Evans and Robert Novak was published. It began with serialization in four issues of the *Saturday Evening Post* and newspaper syndication in fifteen parts (with the *Washington Post* trumpeting its publication of "this widely acclaimed political biography" in full-page advertisements). Deals were made for publication in Britain and West Germany and for paperback publication in the United States.

The hardcover book was the main selection of the Literary Guild. Trade publications heralded a major printing by New American Library. I appeared on NBC's *Today* program. Evans and I were guests at book and author luncheons (I was thrilled to be seated next to John Dos Passos at one event, but could not bring myself to tell him that he was an idol of mine when I was studying modern American literature in college).

William Henry Chamberlin in the *Wall Street Journal* called it "an uncommonly interesting book, a full, objective survey of Johnson's political life." *Newsweek*'s Kenneth Crawford, for the *Washington Post*'s daily review, wrote: "The facts are permitted to speak for themselves through scores of meticulously researched episodes." The Sunday *New York Times* review by John Pomfret praised "a masterly job of analytical and retrospective reporting." The *Times* daily reviewer Eliot Fremont-Smith, apparently not expecting much, called the book a "fascinating, detailed and surprisingly perceptive political biography." Arthur Schlesinger Jr., in the cover review for the *Washington Post*'s Sunday book section, wrote:

> [Evans and Novak] have at last produced the first serious political biography of the 36th American President. But they have done a good deal more than fill a gap in the literature; they have written a book impressive in its own right for its research, its objectivity, its astute understanding of American politics, and its dramatic and often poignant evocation of an incredibly complicated man caught in the turbulent rush of national and world affairs.

By the time *The Exercise of Power* was published, the Evans & Novak column—originally thought by Nixon and other Republicans to be a mouthpiece for the Kennedy Democrats—was regarded as Republican and moderately conservative. Consequently, many reviewers expressed surprise at our objectivity, fairness, and even sympathy in dealing with LBJ.

(The most authoritative review in my eyes was not written until 2002 and consisted of one sentence: "For Robert Novak, whose own book on Lyndon Johnson has enriched mine in more ways than I can ever count. With thanks, Robert A. Caro." He wrote that in a copy he gave me of *The Years of Lyndon Johnson: Master of the Senate*, the brilliant third volume of his LBJ biography. *The Exercise* was cited by Caro fifty-six times in foot-notes with forty-one mentions in the index, high praise for a thirty-six-year-old book that long had been out of print coming from the esteemed biographer who had made Lyndon Johnson much of his life's work.)

The United States Information Agency (USIA) let it be known that it would not purchase *any* copies of *The Exercise* for U.S. libraries around the world. (The USIA previously had purchased an extraordinary 214,000 copies of *The Lyndon Johnson Story,* a panegyric by longtime LBJ aide Booth Mooney.) Reviewing our book in the *New Republic,* Larry L. King noted the USIA's censorship and commented: "This is a shame. No more defini-tive biography of Lyndon B. Johnson exists."

The Exercise never made the best-seller list, but did sell more than 75,000 hardcover copies, better than any Johnson book did for a genera-tion. A paperback edition, ordered by many college professors as the best available description for political science classes of how the U.S. Senate works, provided us modest royalties for twenty years. But Evans and I never thought of this book as a money machine. We did come to regard it as the best we could do in our chosen trade.

IN 1967, THE American Society of Newspaper Editors was meeting in Washington, and Publishers Syndicate executives suggested that Rowly and I entertain editors who purchased our column when it had gone on the open market following the *New York Herald-Tribune*'s demise a year earlier. Rowly arranged a dinner party at his home.

It was the only time we ever did anything like that—because of the way things turned out. We invited the editors of ten of our most important newspapers and three prominent officials including Robert S. McNamara, the secretary of defense, who managed the increasingly unpopular Vietnam War. Editors from the *Washington Post, Los Angeles Times, Boston Globe,* and other major papers were there, but the most imposing figure on our guest list was John S. Knight, publisher and editor in chief of his large and grow-ing newspaper chain (including the *Miami Herald* and *Detroit Free Press*).

Jack Knight, seventy-two years old, arrived a little late—but quickly stepped up his drinking and was into his cups by the time of the men's post-dinner conversation over brandy and cigars.

Knight blamed President Johnson for persecuting American business while leading the nation into a disastrous war. Everybody else present wanted to avoid a debate with a tipsy press lord—everybody but Bob McNamara. He declared he was not going to sit there and permit some-body to defame a president defending the free world against the Communist tide. "I really am exasperated with businessmen like you," McNamara told Knight, "not appreciating that President Johnson gave you a tax cut you never got from the Republicans, and I say that as a Republican." Knight, not accustomed to being contradicted in public by a man thirty years his junior, exploded with a shouting denunciation of the Democratic war policy. The defense secretary responded with a didactic exposition of how well he was running the war. Only with difficulty did Rowly break up the debate.

If an establishment figure like Jack Knight was denouncing the Vietnam War with passion, LBJ was paying the price for failing to build public support. For the first time, I appreciated that Bob McNamara was humorless and authoritarian, unwilling to see that anyone had a contrary opinion worth entertaining. I saw hard going ahead for the Great Society.

IN 1967, Katherine Graham, president of the Washington Post Company, invited Rowly and me to lunch at the newspaper. Rowly knew Mrs. Graham well from the Georgetown social circuit, but this was the first time he had ever received an invitation of this kind (and it certainly was new to me).

I awaited the luncheon with apprehension. Kay Graham, age fifty in 1967, had become one of the most powerful women in journalism. I admired her, but never felt comfortable in her presence. She was a shy woman, and her shyness seemed to deepen when she was around me— causing me to be more uncomfortable.

J. Russell Wiggins, the *Post*'s editor and vice president, made it four for lunch in the newspaper's private dining room. He shaped an editorial policy making the *Post* the nation's strongest liberal newspaper voice supporting LBJ's prosecution of the Vietnam War. Wiggins and Mrs. Graham were staunch Johnson backers—especially Wiggins. (In 1968, Wiggins would retire from the paper at age sixty-five and be named by Johnson as the U.S. ambassador to the United Nations).

The purpose of the luncheon emerged. President Johnson had urged Mrs. Graham to get Evans and me to ease up on him. Of course, she could not dictate even to her own columnists, much less the two of us who were not on her payroll though printed regularly by her paper. Yet, because the president of the United States had pressed her to do this, she obviously felt obliged to put in a few good words for him.

"Lyndon is really doing such a good job under such difficult conditions, coming in after the assassination," she told us, "and he is trying so hard to take a prudent course in Vietnam. I hope you can try to look at the problems he faces through his eyes." She was embarrassed, as was everybody at lunch. Only Rowly's charm enabled us to survive this difficult encounter.

Several weeks later, on Monday, October 9, 1967, I received a phone call from my good friend Andrew J. Glass that led to a much more serious confrontation with Mrs. Graham. Andy, our former *Herald-Tribune* colleague, now on the *Washington Post*'s national staff covering Congress, told me he wanted to come over to show me something important.

Glass was at my office within a half hour with a thirteen-page, double-spaced memorandum. It was a detailed, nearly verbatim account of an off-the-record session with Secretary of State Dean Rusk over lunch on September 27 at *Newsweek*'s Manhattan headquarters with executives of the magazine and its sister publication, the *Washington Post,* including company president Katherine Graham. It was dynamite.

Andy told me that what Rusk had to say revealed so much about him and the Johnson administration's attitude toward the war that it had to be published. But neither *Newsweek* nor the *Post* was going to reveal what was said. Since Rusk had spoken under cover of an off-the-record agreement, Glass knew his leak could cost him his job. So he gave me the memo under the caveat that if anybody from the *Post* should ask where I received the information, I would say it came from somebody at the State Department. I agreed to lie.

On this day, Rowly was beginning the final week of a monthlong round-the-world reporting trip. I have no idea whether Rowly would have heard alarm bells in my writing this column, to which I seemed oblivious. All I could think was that an unknown number of copies of a thirteen-page document might be floating around town, and I did not want to be beaten on a story already two weeks old. My desire to be first prevailed over prudence.

My only concern was whether what Rusk said in New York was an aberration. I called my only good high-level source at the State Department, Assistant Secretary Bill Bundy, read him Rusk's comments, and asked, strictly off-the-record, if he could tell me if he had ever heard the secretary of state say anything like that. Indeed he had several times, Bundy replied. That was enough for me to write the column for publication two days later. I omitted the fact that the executives Rusk addressed in New York were from the Washington Post Company. I am not sure what purpose this little deception served other than to indicate that I sensed I was entering dangerous territory.

My column of Wednesday, October 13, 1967, published as usual in the *Washington Post,* began by saying the soft-spoken Georgian, secretary of state throughout the Kennedy-Johnson years, revealed the "embitterment and alienation" of that administration caused by Vietnam. He "shed the public image of long-suffering serenity" and "bitterly lashed out at 'pseudo-intellectual' critics of the war." Much of the opposition, he said:

. . . resulted from Communist influence. FBI infiltrators in the Communist apparatus, he said, tipped him to the exact wording of a peace telegram from an "innocent" peace group weeks before he officially received the same message. . . .

Communist influence, Rusk continued, helped build rabid anti-Vietnam sentiment among college students. But he placed a greater responsibility on what the students learn from their professors—Rusk's "pseudo-intellectuals": . . .

"Have you ever noticed how these people react against a Southern accent?" the Secretary asked his luncheon hosts. "Almost any other—British, New England, Hungarian, French—is acceptable to them. But not Southern."

. . . he told how one of his cousins in Georgia, when asked by a reporter why the United States was in Vietnam, replied: "We promised 'em we would, didn't we?" Rusk's comment: "There was a great deal of profundity there. Compare it with the gossamer threads spun by Arthur Schlesinger."

Rusk expressed his contempt for his fellow former New Frontiersmen who had left the administration and turned against Vietnam policy, such as Schlesinger and former Assistant Secretary of State Roger Hilsman. My column continued:

The Schlesingers and Hilsmans, according to Rusk, only deepen the unpopularity of the war with a naturally isolationist American public. He believes the public's attitude, in turn, augments Hanoi's conviction that the American people will not support the war over the long haul.

The *Washington Post* copy editors who processed my column were unaware of the identity of the "select group of New York executives" that I mentioned in the lead paragraph. But Kay Graham was well aware.

She phoned me Wednesday morning at the start of the business day. It was the first call she had ever placed to me. Gone was the shy and halting manner I had associated with her. She did not raise her voice, but her upper-class accent was covered with frost. She told me that I had caused her *personal* humiliation. Dean Rusk had been promised that nothing he said would be published, and he unburdened himself to editors of a newspaper that supported him and his policy. It was intolerable for a near verbatim account of his remarks to be published in that newspaper and probably crippled the *Post's* future efforts to talk to news sources on a confidential basis.

She concluded by telling me: "Our personal relationship is now at an end." With that, she terminated our one-sided conversation.

In truth, I was not aware I had much of a personal relationship with Kay Graham. What terrified me was that our *professional* relationship was endangered—that the column's position in the most important newspaper running it was at risk.

I immediately sat down at my Royal office typewriter and wrote a five-hundred-word letter to Mrs. Graham on the Western Union copy paper we used. Fulfilling my promise to Andy Glass to protect him, I lied that I had received the memo from a State Department official. "We have tried to shed light on public affairs by revealing what public officials say and do in private," I wrote. "I felt the Rusk luncheon minutes fit that category and did cast light on the Administration's position toward the most difficult problem facing it."

I took the position that there would have been no question that I would have used the memo without thinking had Rusk made such comments in a government meeting and that it "would have been back-scratching inside the journalism fraternity" if I spiked the story because of its venue. I then used a lame but familiar excuse: ". . . if the meeting's minutes were slipped to me, they would be given to somebody else if I didn't write it." I concluded by shamelessly throwing myself on Mrs. Graham's mercy:

> Finally, and most important, I did not for a moment consider all this in relationship with you and with the *Washington Post*. In retrospect, I am afraid this was a grievous error in judgment. . . . I have greatly admired you and the job you have done to turn the *Post* into a great paper, and I have been proud of your kind words for our column. Had I viewed this column as a personal affront or embarrassment to you, I can assure you I would not have written it and, consequently, now regret doing so. At this stage, however, all I can offer is my sincere apologies.

I had our assistant, Mary Jo Pyles, type the letter on my personal (not office) stationery and *mailed* it Special Delivery to Mrs. Graham at the *Post*'s offices about six blocks away. (In 1967, there were no faxes, e-mails were far in the future, and I did not use messengers to carry letters.)

Rusk was asked about the column the next day at his Thursday press conference. While declining comment "on third-hand reports," the secretary took an on-the-record whack at anti-Vietnam intellectuals. The *New York Times* and *Los Angeles Times* ran stories crediting the Evans & Novak column, which were distributed nationwide on their wire services. The *New*

York Times account went beyond my column to identify the mysterious executives in New York as coming from *Newsweek* and the *Washington Post.*

Rowly and his wife, Katherine, were returning Saturday. Not wanting him to hear about Mrs. Graham's rage before I could warn him, I drove to Dulles International Airport to break the news. I was in a bad state of nerves. Arriving early at the airport, I went into a bar for a double Scotch. The Evanses knew something was up when they saw me (the only time I ever welcomed him home). After hearing the bad news, Rowly displayed his normal WASP cool and said he doubted there was anything to worry about.

On that Saturday, Katherine Graham wrote me a two-page handwritten letter—mailed, of course—that reached me Monday. "I think I owe *you* an apology," she began. "My temper about this episode can only be described as shrewish." She added, "I also agree with you that there is too much back-scratching within the journalistic fraternity, including too much non-reporting of news when it concerns ourselves." But she wasn't happy:

> Having said all that—of course I still feel it hurt us very much as a news gathering entity to have an off-the-record interview with Rusk appear verbatim—and I don't suppose it will help future interviews of this kind.

She concluded that "your letter was awfully nice and I appreciate it," but I feel the incident cooled my future relations with a woman I greatly admired. We never again mentioned what happened, and I shall never know how much it seriously endangered the column's relationship with the *Post.*

Nor did I discuss the incident with Andy Glass until March 2004 when I brought it up in connection with this book. Andy told me he was not at the New York meeting and that he had been given the verbatim account by someone who was: Walter Lippmann, whose column had been syndicated by the *Washington Post.* Glass had just written a sympathetic front-page interview with Lippmann on the occasion of his retirement and return to New York City from Washington in a state of bitterness over Lyndon Johnson and Vietnam. America's most prestigious liberal voice was appalled by Rusk's remarks, wanted them published, and gave a copy to Glass for that purpose.

LBJ's Era of Good Feeling II had led to a Washington where such dignified establishmentarians as Dean Rusk and Walter Lippmann were at each other's throats. Washington had lost its civility and never would regain it. And the bitter, angry election campaign of 1968 was just ahead.

CHAPTER 16

Clean Gene, Bobby, and LBJ

T HE YEAR 1968 began with a personal step that took the Novak family away from danger. Geraldine never really liked our old Victorian house on Capitol Hill that looked like it was out of a Charles Addams cartoon. I loved its eccentric design with ten-sided rooms, but then I did not have to cope with its tiny kitchen and antiquated features. What really bothered Geraldine was the neighborhood, years away from gentrification.

Our daughter, Zelda, would celebrate her third birthday in August, the month when our second child was due. D.C. public schools were wretched, meaning our children would have to get up early every morning to catch the bus to a pricey private school miles away. The sound of police sirens signified nightly danger. But as the year began, we never dreamed that black rioters a few months hence would attack the 1000 block of Mass Avenue where we lived. The deciding factor for us to move was a murdered man dumped in a parked car on our very street.

We bought a new split-level, four-bedroom house in the then distant Maryland suburbs, just outside the Washington Beltway, with a $64,000 price tag ($373,000 in 2007 money) that stretched our finances. It was a white bread house in a white bread neighborhood. "Well, you finally got yourself a decent house," my father told me on his first visit.

Suburban Washington in 1967 was not densely settled. I could drive to my office in thirty minutes, less than half the time it would take in years to come. On the way, I passed a working farm with cows grazing on ground that would become the headquarters of Marriott International.

Geraldine, who kept the family books and had assumed all other onerous chores in our marriage, handled the move while I went about my daily pursuits. On moving day, Rowly and I were late getting out the column, and I made one or two wrong turns on the unfamiliar journey to suburbia. I rushed into the new house minutes before the eight p.m. telecast of President

Johnson's State of the Union Address. I headed for a TV set, muttering my regrets to a next-door-neighbor couple who had come to welcome us to the neighborhood. That set the tone for twenty-four years in Rockville's Luxmanor neighborhood. I was *in* the suburbs but not *of* the suburbs.

Compared to these shiny new suburban houses, our Capitol Hill neighborhood was shabby. But our neighbors there included congressional members and staffers, federal officials and journalists. Luxmanor's population was upper-middle income, predominantly Jewish, with lots of doctors, lawyers, and merchants not connected with the government. All I had in common with our neighbors was physical proximity. We never held the get-acquainted party that Geraldine thought would be a good idea, and I never made friends in the neighborhood. But Geraldine did, and so did our children. Luxmanor was filled with kids who attended public elementary, middle, and high schools all within walking distance. It was a great place to grow up.

THE 1968 CAMPAIGN actually began for me Saturday, October 29, 1966, in southern Indiana. I was following Richard M. Nixon on his remarkable comeback trail. He had spent the entire autumn traveling America campaigning for Republican congressional candidates, with a dual mission: to get as many Republicans elected as possible and to rehabilitate himself.

October 29 started in Evansville, Indiana, with a rally for congressional candidate Roger Zion, a forty-five-year-old businessman making his first attempt at public office. Nixon ignored Vietnam and racial unrest but had a lot to say about "Roger Zion's opponent," without mentioning his name. He was seventy-year-old Winfield K. Denton, a World War I U.S. Army Air Corps pilot serving his seventh term in Congress. Nixon, as he had done in other congressional districts, tied Denton to the increasingly unpopular LBJ: "If you believe Congress should be the servant of Lyndon Johnson, then vote for Roger Zion's opponent." Zion was one of the many Republican candidates Nixon visited in 1966 who were elected.

Nixon traveled lean on the campaign circuit, accompanied that day by a single aide—a tall, tough-looking young man. I did not bother to introduce myself to somebody I figured was another of Nixon's temporary coat holders. He was Patrick J. Buchanan, who at age twenty-six had lashed himself to Nixon's seemingly shaky mast by leaving the *St. Louis Globe-Democrat,* where three years earlier he had been hired out of the Columbia University Graduate School of Journalism as the nation's youngest editorial writer for a major newspaper.

Years later after I had become Buchanan's friend, he recalled that day in a high school gym in Evansville. He and Nixon were backstage waiting for the rally to begin and were sneaking a peek through the stage curtain at the audience. The former vice president pointed to me in the front-row press section and told Pat: "Look at him. That's Bob Novak. That's the enemy."

The Evans & Novak column actually was on a slow journey to the Right, criticizing Lyndon Johnson, attacking black radicalism, and insisting on a war-winning strategy in Vietnam. How could we be Nixon's "enemy"? Because Nixon was supremely nonideological. All politics was personal to him, and he saw me as his personal enemy no matter what my position on issues.

PRIOR TO GOING to Indiana in October 1966, I asked Nixon's office whether I might talk to him there for a few minutes. The answer was no. It continued to be no throughout his long life. My relations with Nixon had been cool beginning with the 1960 campaign, and the temperature dropped still lower in the aftermath of the 1964 election.

After Nixon declared his own political career at an end when he lost for governor of California in 1962 and relocated as a big-time lawyer in Manhattan, he plotted a clandestine campaign for the 1964 presidential nomination. His presumption was that opposition to Barry Goldwater was so extensive that a deadlock was inevitable. Nixon figured he would resolve it as the compromise candidate. When the deadlock did not develop naturally, Nixon sought to create it artificially by launching an eleventh hour effort to stop Goldwater. It was the worst political performance of his career, which I described in the November 1964 *Esquire* in an article titled (the idea of the magazine's editors) "The Unmaking of a President."

The article documented Nixon's backstage maneuvers in intricate detail: "Each one of his carefully calculated moves in 1964—most of them shrouded from public view—was followed only by his own further political deterioration. When it all ended at the Cow Palace, he was a fallen idol." I was told that what really infuriated Nixon was something not of my making. *Esquire*'s editors used this headnote by the nineteenth-century English painter and poet Dante Gabriel Rossetti: "Look in my face; my name is Might-have-been;/I am also called No-more, Too-late, Farewell."

I don't think Geraldine liked politicians much, but the Nixon lieutenant Charlie McWhorter, an AT&T lawyer, was an exception. We entertained Charlie in our home, and he reciprocated at his Manhattan bachelor's apartment. So it was with my regret that a third party passed the word from McWhorter that he wanted no further contact with me. It was not a personal decision by Charlie, who in fact had been a major confidential source for the offending *Esquire* article. I suspected he was following Nixon's orders to break relations with me—a hunch confirmed in due time.

My subsequent reporting on Nixon leading up to the 1968 nomination did not improve our relationship—specifically my reporting a typically Nixonian maneuver. He wanted support from the party's Goldwater right-wing while convincing the party's centrist and liberal wings that he was no Barry. I reported in the Evans & Novak column of October 14, 1965, that, in a recent off-the-record interview with reporters (one of whom passed it on to me), "Nixon described the Buckleyites as a threat to the Republican Party even more menacing than the Birchers."

William Rusher, publisher of William F. Buckley's *National Review,* was his magazine's resident skeptic about Nixon. He read my column in the *New York Herald-Tribune* that morning, and immediately wrote Nixon demanding to know whether he really said that. No reply (because, of course, he did say it). Rusher renewed his request in another letter to Nixon on November 2, asserting that "it is important to know" the accuracy of the "bitterly hostile words attributed to you by Mr. Novak. Quite frankly, I cannot believe that you uttered those words." (I suspect Bill was disingenuous, that he could all too easily believe Nixon uttered those words.) Still, no reply.

Only after yet another letter from Rusher on January 2 and a March 8 editorial in the *National Review* insisting on an answer did Nixon's young aide Pat Buchanan respond with a letter that Rusher later described as "a masterpiece of broken-field running." Buchanan said only that Nixon "invariably" responded to press queries during William Buckley's 1965 campaign for mayor of New York by saying Buckley "made himself a much stronger candidate" by denouncing the John Birch Society.

Nearly two years later, the Evans & Novak column of July 24, 1967, reported how Nixon's aides had rebuffed support from New York City maverick conservative Vincent Leibell. I wrote: "They are willing to cede Leibell-type mavericks and doctrinaire conservatives to Reagan, or as one Nixon insider put it to us: 'Let Ronnie have the kooks.' "

The last thing Nixon wanted was a quarrel with Ronald Reagan, just finishing his first year as governor of California and even then eyeing the White House. Not until the publication in 2003 of *Reagan: A Life in Letters* was an August 4, 1967, letter from Nixon to Reagan made public. Nixon wrote: "Like many other columns on Richard Nixon by Evans and Novak, this one is fabricated from whole cloth. Neither I nor my personal staff have had anything to do with the brace of them for the past two years." That cutoff coincided with the 1965 publication of the *Esquire* article, when Charlie McWhorter and other Nixon supporters were told not to talk to Rowly and me.

In his 1967 letter to Reagan, Nixon said that his then national campaign chairman, Dr. Gaylord Parkinson, "denies that he has talked to [Evans and

Novak], and has no idea who the 'Nixon insider' could be." In fact, it was Parkinson's deputy, Bob Walker, a professional politician who later left the Nixon campaign to join the brief Reagan-for-president campaign in 1968.

While not really that popular among Republicans, Nixon enjoyed immense advantages in seeking the 1968 nomination for president. The logical successor to Barry Goldwater in leading the conservative movement was Reagan, but he could not immediately launch a presidential campaign as a first-year governor. The candidate of the moderates and leader in the national polls was Governor George Romney of Michigan, whose bombast did not wear well, who claimed that he had been "brainwashed" in Vietnam, and whose candidacy was dead by December 1967.

THE CONTEST FOR the Republican nomination paled in intensity compared to the spectacle of the Democratic Party ripping itself to pieces. Personal animosity between Lyndon Johnson and Bobby Kennedy now seemed secondary to national upheaval over Vietnam. The nation's majority party was fractured on multiple fault lines: young versus old, reformers versus regulars, liberals versus conservatives, and above all hawks versus doves.

Although he despised Johnson, Kennedy resisted challenging him in a struggle he feared would destroy the party. Hostility to Johnson and his war policy among Democrats was such that it was necessary to find a sacrificial candidate. It turned out to be somebody that nobody expected: Gene McCarthy.

In 1968, Eugene Joseph McCarthy of Minnesota was fifty-two years old and had served ten years in the Senate after ten years in the House. He had arrived in Washington as a left-wing Catholic intellectual but by the time I met him as a first-year senator in 1959, he was well on his way to becoming a complete cynic. That cynicism, plus his good company and propensity for leaking news, endeared him to reporters—especially me.

McCarthy had entered the Senate in the oversize Democratic class of 1958, seemingly another liberal predisposed against Majority Leader Johnson. Instead, he soon was drawn into the LBJ orbit. I think he saw Johnson as the instrument to prevent Jack Kennedy becoming the nation's first Catholic president. In my private conversations with McCarthy, he described JFK as controlled by his reactionary father and a Catholic in name only.

Although McCarthy delivered the greatest national convention speech I ever heard in placing Adlai Stevenson's name in nomination for president in 1960 at Los Angeles, Gene's support of the "draft Stevenson" movement was intended to stop Kennedy and nominate Johnson. The Kennedy assassination opened new possibilities for McCarthy. Johnson led McCarthy to believe he was about to become the Catholic on his ticket as the vice-presidential nominee. So long as McCarthy was deluded in that belief, he was far from joining the peace bloc.

It was not until the Democrats already had convened at the National Convention at Atlantic City in 1964 that McCarthy acknowledged the obvious. Johnson long ago had selected Humphrey, and McCarthy was merely a prop to effect an artificial element of suspense at the convention. Distraught at being played for the fool, McCarthy retreated into political isolation for four years—until he agreed to be Al Lowenstein's sacrificial candidate.

Allard K. Lowenstein was thirty-eight years old when his moment in history arrived, but he was well known as a leader of the nation's antiwar youth. McCarthy, the cool Catholic intellectual, and Lowenstein, the emotional Jewish activist, had contempt for each other but fulfilled each other's needs. Lowenstein needed a candidate, and McCarthy needed a political role.

NEW HAMPSHIRE'S PRIMARY election was the first in the nation, March 12, 1968. McCarthy was the only listed major Democratic candidate, but nobody doubted Johnson would overwhelm McCarthy with a write-in vote, orchestrated by what I initially described as "well-oiled" statewide precinct organization "wholly new" to the state.

By the first week of March, however, it was apparent that the LBJ write-in organization that I had hyped earlier was under-funded, unable to overcome Johnson's unpopularity and, as I wrote in March, "may be a paper tiger." I added that "contrary to early boasts by the Democratic regulars here that McCarthy would be held to 10 percent, his total is likely to exceed 25 percent and conceivably could climb to 40 percent." That, I predicted, "should cause deep concern at the White House next Tuesday evening."

In those days before frequent polling, I was out on a limb. In fact, I underestimated the anti-LBJ tide, though I was closer than my startled colleagues. McCarthy won 42.4 percent of the actual vote to Johnson's 49.5 percent. So low were expectations for McCarthy that this was widely interpreted as a "victory."

AT EIGHT A.M. on January 30, 1968, I was seated directly across from Bobby Kennedy at a long table in the narrow President's Room of the National Press Club. Godfrey Sperling, a political reporter for the *Christian Science Monitor*, had invited fourteen journalists to question Kennedy. ("Breakfast with Godfrey" was in its infancy.) While saying nothing positive about Johnson, Kennedy declared he would not run for president under "any conceivable circumstances."

On Sunday, March 17, five days after McCarthy's stunning showing and the day after Kennedy announced his candidacy, Bobby was the guest on *Meet the Press.* He plain out lied when I asked him whether he was "hoping" that McCarthy would drop out.

> Kennedy: No, no. I would hope that we are going to be working in tandem and that we will make a common effort.
>
> Novak: A lot of people don't understand . . . how you can work together when you are both getting your votes from the same people who are opposed to President Johnson and the war.
>
> Kennedy: . . . I think together we establish the opposition to the present policy. As I said, I think one of us can do that—two of us can do that better than one of us. I think that is important. . . .
>
> Novak: . . . You are a very practical politician, and I still don't see the arithmetic on how the anti-Johnson forces are not divided by you in states such as Oregon and California.

I could see that Bobby was irritated by me, his discomfort aggravated by the fact that he viewed McCarthy as corrupt and lazy but for tactical reasons could not offend Gene's followers. He would be further irritated the next day when the Evans & Novak column I wrote proclaimed that "the last few days have seen Bobby Kennedy at his worst as a politician" who did not "let McCarthy savor the aroma of his New Hampshire victory." I concluded that "Kennedy has fewer friends and more enemies than he did a week ago and the image of the bad Bobby is overshadowing the good Bobby."

In the same column, I reported that Kennedy brother-in-law and family campaign manager Steve Smith just before the New Hampshire primary had completed a study and found Johnson with "well over" the 1,312 delegates needed to be nominated. That meant Kennedy had the awesome task of wresting party regulars away from LBJ by defeating both Johnson and McCarthy in the primaries.

Bobby knew that this column was written by me and not Rowly because Evans was on a monthlong reporting trip to the Middle East. On Monday morning, March 18, Kennedy's secretary asked whether I could drop by for a little chat with the senator in his Capitol Hill office, the only time I received a summons from him.

He closed the door of his private office with no staffers present, and told me our "conversation" would be "strictly off-the-record." With another senator we probably would be seated in a couch and easy chair, while coffee was brought in. Not with Bobby. Shirt-sleeved as usual, he planted himself behind his big desk and seated me in a straight-back chair, eye to eye with him. There was no coffee and no mistaking who was in command.

I expected complaints about my column's references to the "bad Bobby." Instead, he said, he was concerned by repeated references in the column about "party regulars" supporting Johnson.

"I'm sure you appreciate, Bob, how weak the regulars are," he told me. "My brother and I found out in 'sixty how weak they were. We rolled them. Now, I don't want you to write this, but we're not worried about the party regulars this year. They showed how weak they were in New Hampshire when they couldn't even beat Gene McCarthy. That's not our concern. We can crush them."

When Rowly returned from the Middle East and I had filled him in on my visit, Evans told me: "I really hope you get to know Bobby better and learn to like him"—ignoring that I had been dealing with him from my first month in Washington. Rowly neglected to tell me then that he already had been in touch with Bobby after his return to the United States. I learned about it in 2004 when I read Evans's 1970 oral history interview. When Rowly and Katherine had dinner with Bobby and Ethel, Kennedy "complained bitterly" about my questioning of him on *Meet the Press*. Evans said he replied: "Well, Senator, take it up with Novak. Don't take it up with me."

CONTRARY TO HIS dissembling on *Meet the Press*, Kennedy from the moment he announced his candidacy did everything he could to convince McCarthy to get out of the race to create a straight LBJ versus RFK contest. He failed.

Bobby was only a spectator in the primary following New Hampshire, in Wisconsin on April 2, where he had missed the filing deadline. Johnson still would not campaign himself. But surrogates, headed by Vice President Humphrey and four cabinet members, poured into Wisconsin. Unlike New Hampshire, Johnson's name was on the Wisconsin ballot.

I thought I'd better get to Wisconsin for a couple of days' reporting in the state. I started with a dinner date at Milwaukee's Pfister Hotel on Wednesday, April 27, with the Johnson campaign Wisconsin executive director: a twenty-nine-year-old member of Defense Secretary Robert McNamara's Whiz Kids with a PhD from MIT but scant political background. He was Les Aspin, a future congressman from Wisconsin, chairman of the House Armed Services Committee, and secretary of defense (incorrectly identified in my column from Milwaukee as "Dr. Les *Aspen*").

Aspin talked with amazing candor to a columnist he had just met, making clear how unhappy he was to be there. He explained he had been drafted to run the campaign because he was from Wisconsin and, as a Pentagon official, could be counted on to back Johnson on Vietnam (though Les expressed to me his misgivings about the war). He then laid out the president's problems in Wisconsin, which I recorded in my column: "a dilapidated Party organization, growing unpopularity of the Vietnam War, lack of deep personal commitment by the President's supporters, a pathetically late start."

Aspin was blunt. Bobby Kennedy on the Wisconsin ballot would beat Johnson in a landslide. Gene McCarthy won't do that, he said, but will win. He urged me to accept that as absolutely certain. The president's man on the spot did not seem broken up by the sad prospects for April 2. Les Aspin gave me the impression of being a nonpolitical egghead eager to get back to numbers-crunching at the Pentagon. He did not reveal to me his intent to run for Congress from Wisconsin in 1970, beginning a twenty-two-year career in the House that ended only when President Bill Clinton tapped him for his cabinet.

My column for Monday, the day before the primary, predicted defeat in Wisconsin for the president. On Sunday night, Geraldine and I watched Johnson address the nation on television from our new suburban home. Like everybody else in Washington, I was amazed when LBJ followed his announced pause in the bombing of North Vietnam by declaring: "I shall not seek, and I will not accept, the nomination of my party for another term as your president."

WITH JOHNSON GONE, the new candidate of the Democratic regulars was Vice President Hubert H. Humphrey. He had been a good source for me, particularly during his tenure as Senate Majority Whip (1961–65). But as both a thinker and leader, he struck me as well meaning and weak.

Humphrey was much stronger in the Democratic Party outside the South than Johnson. While April was late to begin a presidential campaign, Humphrey inherited Johnson's support among party regulars plus old-fashioned liberals and labor leaders who were estranged from LBJ. Deadlines for nearly all primaries had passed, and he would not have to run against peace candidates Kennedy and McCarthy in Oregon and California. This was the last year when so many convention delegates were picked outside the primary process that a candidate could be nominated without running in the primaries.

I was in the huge press contingent following the vice president to Pittsburgh on Thursday, April 4, four days after LBJ's dropout, to address the Pennsylvania AFL-CIO convention. Humphrey's trip was cut short by news from Memphis that Martin Luther King had been assassinated. I booked an early evening flight from Pittsburgh to Washington, and stopped by the bar at the Pittsburgh Hilton for a couple of drinks before I went to the airport. The bartender was in his late fifties, white, unsmiling. I asked him whether he had heard the news. "He [MLK] asked for it, and he got it," the bartender said softly. "I'd say he got what he deserved, stirring up all that trouble. Good riddance."

Here is the white backlash, I thought. At the moment of Dr. King's death, he was no biracial icon. Although this bartender was a bigot, all of King's critics were not. I long resisted immortalizing him with a national holiday. I was no more than fifty feet from MLK at the March on Washington in the summer of 1963, where he delivered his "I Have a Dream" speech, and I thought it one of the greatest orations I ever had heard. But I came to think of him as an exceptional orator who was badly organized in thought and deed and incapable of leading a great national movement. The Evans & Novak column upbraided him for neglecting the civil rights agenda and concentrating on anti-Vietnam agitation in collaboration with unsavory leftist activists.

I must admit I also was influenced by King's well-documented personal lechery. FBI Director J. Edgar Hoover had bugged King's hotel rooms in hope of finding conspiracy with Communists and instead stumbled on multiple assignations. I received a copy of pornographic bedroom conversations in FBI verbatim transcripts. Like other journalist recipients, I did nothing with them.

When my plane from Pittsburgh arrived over Washington, I saw smoke rising from the nation's capital. Before federal troops dispersed the rioters, unimpeded burning and looting closed Washington businesses with largely black clienteles. The People's drugstore at the corner of Massachusetts and 11th Street N.E., one block from our former residence on Capitol Hill, was cleaned out and never reopened.

Edward Banfield, the conservative professor of sociology at Harvard, contended that there was no political purpose behind these disturbances and originated this memorable aphorism: "They riot for fun and profit." Friday morning's *Washington Post,* the edition that reported the King assassination, carried pictures of Washington blacks overburdened with clothing and television sets they had stolen from stores in their neighborhoods.

Yet it was wrong for me to discount King's impact on African-Americans, as I should have known from a 1965 incident during one of my frequent trips to the Deep South to report on civil rights. I was dining at the Patio Club in Jackson, Mississippi, with segregationist politicians—including one of my best sources in the state, Frank Barber, a political lieutenant of Mississippi's most powerful figure, the arch-segregationist Senator James O. Eastland. Well fortified by liquor, we engaged in a spirited discussion about Martin Luther King. While asserting I was no great fan of MLK, I argued his appeal to ordinary blacks. "I know the colored, Bob," Barber insisted, "and they have no use for King. He's an invention of the northern press. Here, let me prove it to you."

Barber called over the Patio Club's longtime waiter, a tall, heavyset, extremely deferential African-American in his early fifties, and asked his opinion of King. I implored Barber not to embarrass the man, but Frank persisted. The waiter looked to the floor, as the eyes of the white men seated at the table fastened on him. "Well, gentlemens," he finally said, "I consider him a great man." Barber broke the ensuing silence by saying, "Thank you, we appreciate your honesty"—though, of course, he did not.

Well into the 1970s and beyond as I pondered this incident, I saw it as helping me understand that Martin Luther King was a mythic figure for blacks. His professional, political, and personal shortcomings were subsumed in his ascension as symbolic leader of African-Americans, who demanded and deserved a national holiday for him. The people who opposed it, including me, were wrong.

ON THE DAY of King's murder, Bobby Kennedy was in Indiana to begin his first state primary campaign against Gene McCarthy. I arrived in Indiana a week later and found that Kennedy family political retainers Ted Sorensen and Pierre Salinger had spread the word there was no way for Bobby to win the May 7 primary against the patronage-driven regular state Democratic organization headed by popular Governor Roger D. Branigin. Originally intended to be a stand-in candidate for President Johnson, Branigin now was running in the presidential primary as a "favorite son."

I suspected Bobby's agents were playing games. Knowing Indiana from my days as political reporter there, I was doubtful voters would waste their votes on a noncandidate who was a covert stand-in for Humphrey.

How to validate that theory? As a columnist, I had continued the nonscientific interviewing of voters I had practiced as a *Wall Street Journal* reporter, but I had lost confidence in their reliability. Rowly and I decided we needed help from a professional and went to New York–based Oliver Quayle, the country's hottest private political pollster whose clients included President Johnson. He agreed to write a special one-page questionnaire for us, select areas for polling, and send his local polltaker to accompany Rowly or me on door-to-door interviews. Ollie did it for reimbursement of out-of-pocket costs—and the publicity.

The result was a column, published April 19, that put Evans & Novak ahead of the competition on Indiana. Datelined Anderson, Indiana, it began: "Obscured by his own poor-mouthing and monolithic opposition from the state's regular party organization is the tremendous popularity Sen. Robert F. Kennedy begins with among Indiana's Democratic masses." I continued:

The key ingredient in Kennedy's popularity is neither his Vietnam nor domestic policies—neither of which have been keenly perceived—but his family identification. Many volunteered that they were voting for Kennedy to bring back what they regard as the John F. Kennedy golden era.

These Democrats, including Bobby's supporters, were surprisingly hawkish and "seemed unaware of Kennedy's well-publicized dovishness, some of his supporters actually supposing he would escalate the war if elected." Some Kennedy backers said they thought that as president, he would use the iron fist against black rioters. We found "a vast majority of those interviewed dismissed charges that he is too political, tough and ruthless, opportunistic, or not to be trusted." Not the profile painted by friends or foes, it was what ordinary voters thought.

Bobby Kennedy won Indiana by eleven percentage points over Branigin and fifteen over McCarthy. The downside for Kennedy, I wrote, was "his miserable showing among middle class, white collar voters." McCarthy, while running a poor third statewide, "showed his appeal for the very middle-class voters that Democrats find it so difficult to attract." Even as Kennedy ran first in the northern Indiana industrial communities of Gary and South Bend, McCarthy carried all the suburban townships in those areas.

That spelled trouble for Bobby in the next primary test on May 28: Oregon, a state described by worried Kennedy aides as "one big suburb." I went across the continent and got a few private minutes with Bobby in Portland. In the eleven years I had covered him, I never had seen Kennedy so unsure and so pessimistic. He was derisive toward Nixon but much harsher in his private denunciation of McCarthy as a corrupt man without a real purpose.

Bobby lost by six percentage points to a better-organized McCarthy in Oregon, the first time a Kennedy had ever lost an election. His remote chance of overcoming the huge advantage in delegates collected, first for Johnson and then for Humphrey, had depended on winning every one of the four primary elections remaining after Indiana to build an image of electoral invincibility that would pry committed delegates away from Humphrey.

While Oregon stamped Kennedy as a limited candidate who could not appeal to a broad range of Americans, I believed there was no way Bobby could lose to McCarthy a week later in diverse California, supported by blacks, Hispanics, and Jews. I was surprised at how close the vote in California turned out, with Kennedy's winning margin over McCarthy less than five percentage points. Most important, my calculations showed such delegate strength for Humphrey that a Kennedy win in California almost surely could not produce enough momentum to nominate him

On election night, I was three thousand miles away in Washington. My wife and our two-and-one-half-year-old daughter that night were at the little oceanfront house we had built in 1966 at York Beach in Delaware. I was in a room at the Hay Adams Hotel rented by Bob Gutwillig, who now was a one-third partner in the *Evans-Novak Political Report* (our biweekly newsletter we launched in 1967). I was getting information from California that night and writing memoranda to Gutwillig, who then put it in final form for the newsletter.

I had gone to bed when Gutwillig awakened me with the news that Bobby had been shot. Any small doubts that Hubert Humphrey would be the nominee were now gone. Early Wednesday morning, I was in our office, where Evans joined me to write a substitute column for the next morning's paper. I cannot remember exactly who wrote what. I do know that we fully agreed on an analysis that was unfashionable and controversial at the time.

> As political reporters, we have noticed the change insidiously picking up momentum across the country. The passion of political hatred against a Lyndon Johnson or a Bobby Kennedy passes old bounds. The political dialogue, public and private, becomes more rancorous. The dissenters—particularly the Negro poor and the war protesters— turn to "direct action" and most un-civil disobedience.
>
> What this adds up to is nothing less than a rejection of conventional forms of political action. From this, it is one step to the burning and looting of the Negro ghetto and another step to a plot to kill Martin Luther King or a lunatic impulse to destroy Robert Kennedy.

Bobby Kennedy had grown closer to Rowly than his brother Jack had ever been. Evans was a pallbearer and accompanied the body on the slow train trip Saturday from New York to Washington. But Evans exhibited WASP sangfroid in not exhibiting grief.

By the time he ran for president, Bobby's position on Vietnam had moved from his unrealistic call the previous year for a negotiated settlement and a coalition government in Saigon to unilateral U.S. troop withdrawal.

Kennedy made no public declaration but confided this change to close friends—including Rowland Evans. He told Rowly: "We've got to get out of Vietnam. We've got to get out of that war. It's destroying this country." That ran counter to what Rowly and I held to be most vital to the national interest. For Robert Kennedy to run for president and not reveal his real views on Vietnam put him in the same category as Richard Nixon—and, for that matter, as Hubert Humphrey.

(Rowly never mentioned to me Bobby's comments, as he never mentioned any of his conversations with Bobby, though they were central to our coverage of Kennedy. I did not learn about what he was told until I read it in 1978 in *Robert Kennedy and His Times* by Arthur M. Schlesinger Jr., who drew it from Rowly's oral history interview of 1970 for the Kennedy Library. I was a little annoyed, but Bobby had been dead for ten years and the Vietnam War had ended four years earlier. Why cause a fuss with my partner? I did not obtain the transcript of Rowly's oral interview until 2004 in researching this book.)

Robert F. Kennedy left no plan to achieve his proclaimed goals of eliminating poverty and achieving racial justice. The Vietnam War continued for six years after his death. His biggest impact was to guarantee the presidency of Richard M. Nixon by helping divide the Democratic Party.

FRIDAY, JUNE 28, 1968, found me at Manhattan's Commodore Hotel, for the delegate-picking meeting of the State Democratic Committee of New York. This would be the last time that Democratic Party functionaries would determine how New York's delegation to the national convention would vote.

Hubert Humphrey, who had announced his candidacy by extolling "the politics of joy," was being carried to the nomination by the party's least savory elements—county leaders who were not comfortable appealing to a broader public beyond the Democratic neighborhood clubhouse. Implacable hostility was exhibited at the Commodore between regulars (Humphrey) and reformers (McCarthy). When the pro-Humphrey state chairman declared a heavy majority of delegates for the vice president, the reformers pointed to the regulars and chanted, "Hack! Hack! Hack!"—and then walked out en masse. The regulars rose, waved their handkerchiefs at their departing comrades, and cheered.

The great Democratic coalition, seemingly invincible in the 1964 landslide, was disintegrating before my eyes. It was not much clearer to me than to other journalists, but this was part of a complicated realignment of American politics that had begun with the Goldwater debacle.

CHAPTER 17

Realignment 1968

Tedium gripped the convention from the clack of the opening gavel," Theodore H. White wrote of the Miami Beach Republican convention in *The Making of the President 1968*. He continued: "No convention in history had been as dull as this except, perhaps, Eisenhower's renomination in San Francisco in 1956."

He was wrong. The fight for the nomination at Miami Beach in 1968 was one of the most fascinating, closely contested convention struggles I ever covered. White's chapter on Miami Beach was subtitled: "Rockefeller Versus Nixon." But Rockefeller never had a chance. The real struggle was between *Reagan* and Nixon.

After Rockefeller announced on March 21 that he was not running, his aides told me the governor had concluded that if the Republican Party felt it needed him to save its soul, it would come to him without him being required to enter the primaries. By the time Rockefeller bowed to the entreaties of the eastern Republican establishment and belatedly announced his candidacy on April 30, it was too late. Rockefeller could not come within 200 delegates of the 660 needed to be nominated. Rockefeller's rationale for contesting the nomination at Miami Beach was based on the eleventh-hour candidacy of Ronald Reagan creating a convention deadlock.

I had first met Reagan the year after the Goldwater debacle on June 9, 1965, when he addressed a Republican fund-raiser at the Cincinnati Gardens. The Evans & Novak column of June 14, datelined Cincinnati, dubbed Reagan "the new messiah of the Goldwater movement." I wrote that "his carefully polished basic speech" had followed "the JFK system of spewing out a profusion of statistics, wit and literary allusions (including one quote from Hilaire Belloc)." (*Washington Evening Star* columnist Mary McGrory, who revered Jack Kennedy's memory, called me that morning to assail me for daring to compare a great president with a washed-up B-movie actor.)

F. Clifton White saw Reagan as the candidate he had hoped Goldwater would become but never did. He was ready to reassemble his nationwide team that had won the nomination for Goldwater. As Clif related it to me, however, he had a major problem: Californians did not like their governors running for president while still in office. If Reagan openly sought the presidential nomination soon after arriving in Sacramento in 1967, his governorship would be dead on arrival. His California supporters, who had worked hard to get him into office, told Reagan he could not let that happen.

White detailed for me an intricate minuet. A few emissaries under cover would try prying delegates from Nixon even though Reagan was not a candidate. A few weeks before the convention, according to White's plan, Reagan would declare himself "California's favorite son" candidate and make trips in search of delegates even though he would swear he was not an active candidate. When his name was placed in nomination on the convention floor at Miami Beach by the California delegation, he then would become an active—though theoretically reluctant—candidate. That's almost exactly how it worked out.

Late in July 1968, Clif White called me to report that Reagan, who had announced as a favorite son, finally was going on the road. The big event would be in Birmingham, Alabama, with ninety delegates and alternates from all over the Deep South flown in by private plane. The date was Wednesday, July 23, with the convention just ten days away. These southerners had been quietly wooed by Bob Walker, Nixon's former deputy campaign chairman who was hired by the California convention delegation under the guise of arranging its physical arrangements at Miami Beach. But when the southerners entered the ballroom at Birmingham's Tutwiler Hotel to meet Reagan, I heard Walker announced as "Governor Reagan's southern campaign chairman." Clif White, also hired by the California delegation and not the noncandidate, was at Reagan's side throughout the talks with delegates. Ronald Reagan was a candidate in everything but name.

At Birmingham, I was told by some southern delegates that they so distrusted Nixon that they were desperate for any alternative. But many others complained it was too late. If Reagan had come to them earlier, they said, they would have endorsed him but now they had an unbreakable commitment to Nixon. Several added to me, however, that if there were a second ballot, they would bolt to Reagan.

When I arrived in Miami Beach, I found Clif White had reassembled his 1964 Goldwater team (including his lieutenant, Frank Whetstone of Cut Bank, Montana) at the Deauville Hotel.

Clif White talked Reagan into going on a Sunday interview program on

August 4, the day before the convention opened, to show delegates that he really was a candidate now. It was CBS's *Face the Nation,* and I was on the three-man panel as the non-CBS journalist. His answer to my first question passed Reagan over his Rubicon.

> Novak: Governor Reagan, how do you square the fact that you have not and say you're not going to announce for President, and yet you have a highly competent, highly professional staff working out of your hotel here in Miami Beach on a full-scale delegate basis?
>
> Reagan: Well, you say that I have a staff of that kind. This has been, I'll admit, a very unusual situation. I didn't set out to be a favorite son. I was asked to be by the party. There were people throughout the country that started these movements in my behalf, and some in California. I was aware of them. I couldn't help but be aware of them. I told these people in advance they were doing this with no help from me. I also, however, told them that I would be entered into nomination—placed in nomination by the California delegation at the convention. Now, these people have continued to work, and are working, and there is no question about it. Once I'm placed in nomination, I am a candidate, if the delegates choose to consider me along with those who have been campaigning, this they are free to do. And so this effort now has reached the convention stage, when these people—there's no question about it—are openly and actively working, because of their belief that I should be the nominee of the party.

Ronald Reagan had just become a candidate for president, employing the tortuous formula laid out for me by Clif White.

Nixon's southern flank was about to come unhinged. Rowly and I both had excellent sources throughout the southern delegations that Teddy White lacked. I had a permanent floor pass and roamed the southern delegations every night. There was no question that rank-and-file delegates wanted to bolt to Reagan, depriving Nixon of a nomination he thought was wrapped up.

One man saved Nixon: Senator J. Strom Thurmond of South Carolina, a hoary veteran of southern politics still fighting a rearguard action against ending racial segregation. Clif White told me that former Democrat Thurmond confessed to him he would have preferred Reagan over Nixon, but did not want to be marginalized in his new party as he had in the old one as an undependable bolter. He almost single-handedly put down the southern rebellion after the *New York Times* reported that Nixon was considering the liberal Republicans Nelson Rockefeller, John Lindsay, and Charles Percy to be his running mate.

I did not help Nixon's cause on Wednesday, the day of balloting for the nomination. An Evans & Novak column reported that Nixon had requested and received the previous week a report that there was no constitutional impediment to Mayor Lindsay as a vice presidential nominee even though at that time both he and Nixon were residents of New York City. "Nixon Appears to Be Reaching Toward the Left For Running Mate Despite Southern Hostility," said the *Washington Post* headline on the column, which the Reagan campaign distributed to southern delegates. This story contributed to a crisis in the Florida delegation that almost changed the course of American history by flipping it to Reagan under the winner-take-all unit rule. "The Reagan delegate hunters, led by F. Clifton White, were simply out-gunned in a majority of Southern states by Thurmond's massive authority," I wrote in Friday's Evans & Novak column. The spectacle of Strom Thurmond determining the nominee of the Republican Party showed how far political realignment in America had progressed.

Save for Thurmond, I believe Reagan would have been nominated and would have been elected, by a bigger margin than Nixon. I also reject the Republican cliché that it was fortunate Reagan was not elected for another twelve years, by which time his ideological framework was better refined. While Reagan had not yet embraced supply-side tax cuts in 1968, his election that year would have averted Watergate and its dreadful consequences for the Republican Party, for conservatism, and for America.

THE WAY RICHARD Nixon won his second nomination for president left him with an incalculable debt to Strom Thurmond, carrying consequences—beginning with the selection of a vice-presidential running mate. Thurmond ruled out as too liberal John Lindsay (who was being supported by Charlie McWhorter). He also blackballed Senator Mark Hatfield of Oregon (who was backed in a memo prepared for Nixon by conservative advisers Dick Whalen and Martin Anderson and signed by several other aides).

Still, plenty of progressive young Republicans passed the Thurmond test—including Senator Howard Baker of Tennessee and Congressman George Bush of Texas. The selection instead of Maryland governor Spiro T. Agnew represented the folly of picking a vice president at the convention under deadline pressure in the dead of night.

It also signified the dark side of Richard M. Nixon. What appealed most to Nixon was Agnew at his public worst—administering a demagogic public tongue-lashing to black leaders in Baltimore after the riots following the death of Martin Luther King. In the absence of any vetting process, nobody suspected that Agnew was one of the most crooked politicians in America.

The Nixon campaign staff moved across the continent from Miami Beach's Hilton-Plaza to the Mission Bay Inn, a California resort outside San Diego. My friend, the young conservative journalist Richard J. Whalen, who had been working for Nixon, had been downgraded along with other young campaign staffers—forbidden even to leave the premises without permission. It was too much for Whalen. He left Mission Bay to return home to Fort Sumner, Maryland, near Washington, without making a public fuss. He was accidentally discovered by me, as he reported in his 1972 book, *Catch the Falling Flag.*

> By chance, I threw a scare into the high command, for I picked up the telephone at home and Bob Novak, who was making a social call to a campaign widow, showed his keen reporter's instinct. "What the hell are you doing there, Dick?" he asked. I explained that my daughter was ill and that I had taken a furlough from the campaign. Novak laughed. The next day, the Evans-Novak column bore the headline: NIXON WHIZ KID WALKS OUT.

I reported in the column: "Whalen was not alone. Most of Nixon's younger aides left Miami Beach in a blue funk over the Agnew selection."

I HAD LEFT our home in Rockville, Maryland, on Sunday, July 28, for two weeks in Miami Beach, expecting Geraldine would give birth to our second child any day. I called daily from Florida, but the summons to return home never came. Our baby son was born at the most convenient time for me—on August 14 during the single week's interval in 1968 between my coming home from the Republican convention and leaving for the Democratic convention.

I wanted to name him Alexander Augustus Williams Novak, and Geraldine agreed. Alexander was the greatest conqueror and Augustus the greatest ruler of the ancient world (Williams was Geraldine's maiden name). It was pretentious, and so was my mailing Alexander's birth announcement to politicians around the country who were news sources rather than personal friends.

Most responded with polite acknowledgments, but the irrepressible Governor Roger Branigin of Indiana went further. He named Alexander a Sagamore of the Wabash, the Indiana equivalent of a Kentucky colonel, and sent us a fancy certificate of his rank. This was an honor accorded only to the most prestigious Hoosiers, and bestowing it on a non-Hoosier infant typified Roger Branigin's sense of humor.

(Twenty years later, when my daughter Zelda was working in the political office of Vice President Dan Quayle, one senior aide—like Quayle, a Hoosier—had just been named a Sagamore of the Wabash and proudly brandished his certificate. "Oh," Zelda said in fake innocence, "my brother got one of those when he was a baby. We kept it on his dresser.")

EVEN BEFORE THE first gavel in Chicago, I was writing that 1968 promised to be the Democrats' worst convention since the 102-ballot New York City disaster of 1924. It was an extraordinary event that a journalist could cover as a police reporter from the riot-torn streets or as a political reporter from the chaotic convention.

Antiwar demonstrators, a rough lot who looked nothing like the young "Clean for Gene" McCarthy idealists, poured into town the weekend before the convention. I knew the Chicago cops well enough to be sure some skulls would be cracked. The demonstrators came looking for trouble and got what they wanted.

Rowly and I concentrated on Hubert Humphrey's Vietnam dilemma. While desperate to soften his stand on the war, the vice president could not move without President Johnson's approval. LBJ controlled enough delegates—including the Texas delegation headed by Governor John B. Connally—to deny Humphrey the nomination.

On the Sunday afternoon before the convention, I was hanging around the *Chicago Sun-Times* workspace at the Conrad Hilton when I was approached by an extremely well dressed couple. The man asked (in a Texas accent) if I knew the whereabouts of Rowland Evans. When I replied that I did not, he introduced himself and his wife as Bob and Helen Strauss of Dallas, Texas. He had met Evans, and he had a "big story" to give him. But since Rowly was not around, he would give it to me. Thus began my thirty-six-year relationship with Robert S. Strauss.

Strauss told me he was the Democratic National Committeeman from Texas and a close associate of Connally. Strauss tried to give the impression he was telling me his darkest secrets when, in truth, he was—to use a phrase of the future—spinning me. Strauss said he had been sent to Chicago early by Connally, because the governor worried that things were getting out of control. Specifically, Humphrey was "fishtailing" (a phrase I used in our column) on the Vietnam plank in the party platform. If Humphrey dared retreat on Vietnam, said Strauss, Johnson would fly to

Chicago to announce his candidacy and end Humphrey's chances to be president.

(In 2004, over lunch in his Washington law office in the DuPont Plaza building that bears his name, I asked Strauss whether he had been in direct contact with Johnson. He replied his information came from Marvin Watson, a right-wing Texas steel executive who had become LBJ's chief political henchman. Strauss said he thought Johnson really wanted to be nominated and elected to a second term. I still think he was trying to control Humphrey by frightening him.)

NIXON'S CAMPAIGN GOT going Labor Day weekend. I caught up with him in San Francisco, where the Republican candidate's strategy became obvious: Sit on your huge lead and do nothing to jeopardize it. Rowly and I dropped into the Nixon road show occasionally that autumn, but he was running out the clock until the very end. In contrast, there was plenty of news to report traveling with Humphrey—all of it bad.

After the disastrous Chicago convention, Humphrey was exhausted, his campaign treasury depleted, and the whole operation unready for a general election campaign. The traditional starting date of Labor Day could not be met and slipped to a week later on Monday, September 9.

I joined Humphrey on September 12 as he left Washington in a motorcade heading north. The first stop was the dedication of a new span of the Delaware Memorial Bridge, connecting the states of Delaware and New Jersey. The crowd was pathetically small, and the candidate's political speech inappropriate for a bridge dedication.

From the Delaware Bridge, the motorcade went to Sea Girt, New Jersey, where Humphrey was to address a state Democratic fund-raising dinner. In the pressroom with tongues loosened by an open bar, my liberal Democratic media colleagues expressed contempt for Humphrey's toadying to LBJ at Chicago and vowed they never would vote for him.

When I entered the huge tent where the dinner would be held, I immediately feared the worst for Hubert. The assembled Democrats were party hacks with flashy ties and pinkie rings. Each table was loaded down with booze, and the boys were there for a good time. Humphrey was preceded by a long program of corny vaudeville acts highlighted by a fire-eater who evoked thunderous cheers from the well-oiled audience.

It was after ten o'clock before a beaming presidential candidate arrived. I think Hubert always imagined freshly scrubbed liberal activists from Minnesota's Democratic Farmer Labor Party seated before him, eager to share

his wisdom. Facing drunken hacks who wanted no more than fifteen minutes of shouted party slogans, Hubert waded into forty-five minutes of programmatic liberalism. The table talk rose in volume, until halfway through
his talk, Humphrey could hardly be heard. He seemed oblivious.

Humphrey's next scheduled event was a speech to party workers in Pittsburgh's William Penn Hotel on Friday night. He appealed to party loyalty
and trashed Nixon in his law-and-order mode as "Fearless Fosdick," the
comic strip detective. Humphrey's audience was left cold. Hubert did not
finish speaking until after eleven o'clock, after which he went up to his
hotel suite to meet local Democratic personages. On hand was a longtime
Humphrey ally in western Pennsylvania, Meyer Berger, the national treasurer of the liberal Americans for Democratic Action (ADA). I knew Berger
slightly, and ran into him Saturday. Berger obviously wanted to tell somebody how he had complained to his old friend that he had said nothing
about Vietnam in his speech that night. For Hubert to have any chance to
carry Pennsylvania, Berger went on, he must publicly split with LBJ on the
war. What came next I wrote in an Evans & Novak column, datelined
Pittsburgh.

Humphrey glumly replied he simply could not in good conscience
break with the Administration. . . .

Revealing that in Administration councils he had opposed every
Vietnamese troop buildup, Humphrey complained he could not now
move a step leftward without being stymied by the President. "You
know," he confessed, "I have about as much power as you in the
White House."

He next exhibited an uncharacteristic fatalism, musing that perhaps the American electorate "has to learn a lesson" every so often. He
wondered, however, why antiwar protesters ignored Richard M.
Nixon while they hounded him by chanting—and Humphrey here
imitated that chant—"Dump the Hump. Dump the Hump. Dump
the Hump." And there was, he added, non-support from the ranks of
organized labor who were forsaking the Democratic Party now that
their "bellies were full." . . .

. . . [T]he Vice President has begun his campaign not only far behind but with two crushing liabilities: no strategy for regaining dissidents and an irrational schedule which wears him out without
accomplishing anything. Understandably, even Humphrey the con-
genital optimist must confess a note of cold depression, as in those
mournful early morning hours in Pittsburgh.

Actually Humphrey had two hopes. One was that Lyndon Johnson would sue for peace in Vietnam before the election. The other was that George Corley Wallace would siphon off sufficient votes from Nixon to elect Humphrey.

THE HOPE THAT George Wallace would save Hubert Humphrey collapsed three weeks later in Pittsburgh. On Thursday, October 3, the great bomber commander General Curtis E. LeMay was unveiled as Wallace's vice presidential running mate on the ticket of the American Independence Party. On that morning, the Gallup Poll showed Nixon at 43 percent, Humphrey 30 percent, Wallace 24 percent.

Curt LeMay, standing behind Wallace in a ballroom at the Pittsburgh Hilton, looked ponderous and older than his sixty-two years. A brilliant air war tactician, he was named U.S. Air Force chief of staff by the newly elected President Kennedy in 1961 to begin an unhappy relationship marked by constant disagreement. LeMay was reputedly the model for General Jack D. Ripper in the 1964 antiwar movie, *Dr. Strangelove.*

What transpired in Pittsburgh after the LeMay announcement produced one of the most bizarre moments in my half century of covering politics. When the general was asked about "your policy in the employment of nuclear weapons," he was off and running.

Now, nuclear war would be horrible. To me any war is horrible. It doesn't make much difference to me if I have to go to war and get killed in the jungles of Vietnam with a Russian knife or get killed with a nuclear weapon. As a matter of fact if I had the choice, I'd lean towards the nuclear weapon.

That was incredible, but LeMay was not finished. He launched into discussing what he purported to be a government study of animal life on Bikini Atoll in the Pacific after extensive testing of nuclear weapons there, with the good news that "the rats out there are bigger, fatter and healthier than they were ever before."

It really did sound like General Jack D. Ripper. I had my eyes fixed on Wallace, his expression betraying astonishment and despair. *Los Angeles Times* reporter Jack Nelson, a relentless critic of Wallace, asked LeMay about the nuclear bomb: "If you found it necessary to end the [Vietnam] war, you'd use it, wouldn't you?" LeMay replied: "If I found it necessary, I would use anything that we could dream up, including nuclear weapons."

That was enough for Wallace, who interrupted his running mate.

LeMay, said Wallace, "prefers to negotiate" rather than use any weapon and "hasn't said anything about the use of nuclear weapons."

Reporters did not disguise their appetite for feasting on LeMay over the coming month. That night at a Wallace rally in Toledo, LeMay was silent. When reporters approached him for questions, they were kept far away by Secret Service agents who surrounded the vice presidential candidate.

I wanted to talk to Wallace, but it was not easy to even make contact with him. Disgusted with hostile reporters, Wallace had abolished the office of campaign press secretary. At the Toledo rally, I managed to get to Wallace political aide Bill Jones and asked to see the governor for a few minutes to talk about LeMay.

At about eight o'clock the next morning in Toledo, I got a phone call in my hotel room from Jones telling me that if I wanted a word with Wallace I better hustle to his suite. Since the campaign motorcade was supposed to leave for the airport at eight thirty, I figured it would be few words indeed. When I arrived, I found Wallace—still in his bathrobe—seated at a table with a bacon-and-eggs breakfast for two. He invited me to join him for the meal, with this admonition: "Now, *Mister* Novak, this is *strictly* off-the-record. I mean *strictly*. Got that?"

Wallace told me he had wanted as his running mate Albert B. (Happy) Chandler—former governor of Kentucky, former U.S. senator, former commissioner of baseball. Chandler was seventy years old and eager to get back into politics on the Wallace ticket. "But mah' money men"—he didn't name them—"vetoed Happy." Chandler was too liberal on economics and race. He had not been forgiven for his role in breaking baseball's color bar with Jackie Robinson.

The "money men" were intent on LeMay, Wallace went on. "I said yes against my better judgment, and I never should have. He's an *absolute* disaster. Did you *hear* him yesterday? But that's the last you will ever hear from him. Nothing more! Not a word!"

Wallace felt he was just starting to break into the northern white workingman's vote. "When's the last time you heard me say *conservative*?" He was praising Bobby Kennedy, opposing "right to work" laws, taking Alabama labor union leaders with him on his trips north, opposing tax exemptions for giant foundations, urging tax cuts for the workingman, and promising to get out of Vietnam if the war could not be won with *conventional* weapons.

It was now well past the scheduled departure time of eight thirty, and I nervously glanced at my wristwatch. "Now, Novak," Wallace scolded, "don't you worry 'bout that. Ah'm the candidate, and we ain't goin' *nowhere* 'til Ah'm good and ready."

Wallace resumed the monologue. He still felt he could get enough votes in the Electoral College to keep Nixon from a majority. If Nixon would not deal with him for electors (as Nixon said he would not), so much the better. He would deal in the House of Representatives with one vote per state. By that time, Wallace figured, Nixon would be ready to give him concessions. Maybe it would be cabinet posts, maybe policy positions. That's as definite as Wallace would be with me.

After the LeMay meltdown, electoral votes in the South and voters all over the country that were lost to Humphrey now were lost to Wallace and went to Nixon. Curtis LeMay for the remaining twenty-two years of his long life must have pondered his performance during his fifteen minutes of fame in Pittsburgh.

THE YEAR THE DREAM DIED was the title of an account of the 1968 campaign by Jules Witcover published in 1997. It was a terrible time for liberals like Witcover and a pretty bad year for a lot of nonliberals as well, but it was a terrific year for Evans and Novak. We had perfected our reportorial nonideological style. We were at the peak of our game and the apex of our prestige.

Our status was reflected in the cover article ("The Evans and Novak Story" by Julius Duscha) on October 6 in *Potomac,* the Sunday magazine of the *Washington Post.* The cover by caricaturist David Levine showed Rowly and me smirking while eating slices out of the capitol building. Washington was one big piece of cake for us.

Duscha, a former *Washington Post* political reporter, played on the usual physical contrasts between Rowly and me. Evans: "suave, sandy-haired, handsome, trim." Novak: "dark, brooding, unkempt, overweight." Julius took at face value our ideological self-descriptions—Novak as a "moderate conservative and registered Republican" and Rowly as a "moderate liberal and independent politically."

In researching his long article, Duscha found no ideological or political bias in the column. On the contrary, we were depicted as giving everybody a hard time. "Evans and Novak would make conflict in heaven," Hubert Humphrey was quoted as saying.

Duscha described our many activities and put a price tag on some: a syndicated column purchased by 179 newspapers at from $5 to $200 a week, regular commentaries for Channel 5 WTTG in Washington and other Metromedia stations, lectures at $1,000 per columnist, the Evans-Novak Political Report at $50 a year, a newly published paperback version of *Lyndon B. Johnson: The Exercise of Power*. While dropping hints about how all this had "paid off handsomely" for us, Julius did not attempt to estimate our income.

All this put together meant less money than many people guessed. My income for 1968 at age thirty-seven was just short of $70,000 (around $407,000 in 2007 dollars). With big mortgages on our Maryland home and our Delaware beach house, I was not saving a dime. At age thirty-seven, I had become famous but not rich.

THE EVANS & Novak column of Monday, October 28, reported that Congressman Mel Laird, a great Evans & Novak source who had entered Nixon's inner circle, was pushing the candidate away from John Mitchell's super-cautious, stay-off-TV counsel. On Laird's advice, Nixon agreed to go on nationally televised interviews the last two Sundays of the campaign—including *Meet the Press* on November 3, two days before the election. Laird knew more about politics than Mitchell ever imagined and saw the peace liberals returning home to Humphrey after a highly publicized Salt Lake City speech in which the Democratic nominee made a special appeal to antiwar voters.

On Thursday, October 31, Johnson called a halt to the bombing of North Vietnam and announced "prompt, productive, serious and intensive negotiations" in Paris. The return of peace Democrats to Humphrey was accelerated. The euphoria experienced by peace advocates and by Humphrey diminished sharply the next day when General Nguyen Van Thieu, the South Vietnamese president, announced that his government would not attend the Paris talks. The rumor immediately spread that Nixon was keeping Thieu away from Paris.

Nixon's *Meet the Press* appearance took on special importance, and I felt responsibility as a panel member. Why then, did I not ask Nixon straight out whether he had interfered with Saigon to derail the peace plan? Perhaps I should have, but I had only rumors on which to base any questions. There was so much going on that the reporters sitting opposite Richard Nixon in Los Angeles did not know.

Anna Chan Chennault was a Chinese beauty who was the widow of a celebrated World War II hero, Brigadier General Claire Chennault, commander of the Flying Tigers in China. Now a naturalized American, she was a strong Nixon supporter with ties to the Thieu regime. Wiretaps ordered by the FBI and passed on to President Johnson overheard her pleading for Saigon's boycott of the Paris talks. There is no question she was manipulated by John Mitchell and Spiro Agnew. Nixon had deniability, but I hardly think it conceivable that Mitchell and Agnew would have acted without Nixon's knowledge.

To this day, I suspect that Dick Nixon got away with the most successful dirty trick of his career. It hardened the mind-set that led to the many-sided catastrophe of Watergate.

Dick Whalen had it right in *Catch the Falling Flag* published four years later: "[T]he politicians continued to the very end to deal with the overriding issue of Vietnam on the same petty level as they had throughout the campaign."

DURING THE LAST week of the 1968 campaign, I went out to dinner in Washington with Ann Dowling. I had dated Ann when she was a secretary at the *National Observer,* sister publication of the *Wall Street Journal.* She had remained a friend and become a source as a political operative, now employed by the Democratic National Committee.

DNC headquarters were located at the Watergate, a new building on the Potomac River. Ann suggested we end the evening with drinks at the Watergate cocktail lounge. Seated near us was Robert C. McCandless, a twenty-nine-year-old Washington lawyer who ran Humphrey's national campaign for president, drinking with several young aides.

"So you're the famous Bob McCandless!" I said when Ann introduced me. That sarcastic greeting triggered a debate over the outcome of the election less than a week away. We all had ingested a lot of alcohol, and I challenged McCandless with a bet: ten dollars for each electoral vote. It was a sucker bet. Even if the popular vote was close; Nixon threatened to win in an electoral vote landslide. The best Humphrey could do in a stunning upset was a narrow electoral vote margin. McCandless knew as well how lousy that bet was, but he later told me he could not let me show him up in front of his young staffers.

I next brought up the U.S. Senate race in McCandless's home state of Oklahoma. Veteran Democratic senator Mike Monroney had a formidable Republican challenger in Henry Bellmon, a former governor. I offered to bet a case of Chivas Regal Scotch whiskey (my brand was Cutty Sark, but Chivas was more expensive) that Bellmon would win. McCandless agreed, but he clearly was not happy with me.

ALL MY LIFE I had heard tales about the Chicago Democratic machine's skullduggery in the city's African-American precincts. In 1968, with Illinois a closely contested state, I wanted to observe firsthand whether these reports were exaggerated. The result was one of my favorite Evans & Novak columns.

I contacted Operation Eagle Eye, an organization of Illinois Republican activists looking for vote theft and asked for Republican poll watcher's credentials for election day, November 5. I was told the Democratic machine would permit only one outside Republican in one voting place at any time. I would be on my own.

Two men from Operation Eagle Eye picked me up at dawn at the Drake Hotel and drove me to the West Side, where my father had been a teenager when it was a Jewish ghetto. Now it was poorer than ever and totally black. The car dropped me at the James Johnson School, polling place for the 45th precinct in the 24th ward. No reporter was permitted in such a polling place, but I gained admission on my poll watcher's credential. I was the only white person I saw there, or at any other precinct I visited.

In an Evans & Novak column, I wrote that "lurid Republican charges leveled for years have not been exaggerated."

> [V]oter registration was meaningless. A nod from the Democratic precinct captain allowed an unregistered voter to vote by merely signing an affidavit. Whether he might vote in another precinct as well would be impossible to determine. . . .
>
> Without asking whether the voter wanted help, the election judge . . . entered the booth with every voter and instructed him to pull the Democratic straight-party lever, breaking the state law.
>
> Once the curtain had closed and the voter was alone inside the booth, the judge would hover just outside so that the vote was anything but secret.

Voters were supposed to be given up to four minutes inside the booth. If a voter in the 45th precinct stayed inside for more than thirty seconds and consequently appeared to be splitting his vote, the Democratic precinct captain would tap him on the shoulder or even enter the voting booth. When one woman persisted by refusing to get out of the booth after a full minute, I heard the captain say: "Come on, get her out of there."

Time magazine's issue of November 22 carried a flattering account of my reporting, concluding: "This was the kind of performance that has come to be expected of the Evans-Novak team, which avoids pontificating and concentrates [on] examining the inner machinery of politics." Nobody accused me of carrying water for the Republican Party or trying to intimidate African-Americans. We were indeed at the peak of our prestige.

WHEN I RETURNED late in the afternoon on election day from my clandestine poll watching in Chicago, I voted in Montgomery County, Maryland, for the first time. I had not voted for a Republican presidential candidate since Eisenhower in 1956 even though I had grown ideologically much closer to the Republicans than the Democrats. I had decided some time ago to vote for Nixon, but not with pleasure. I thought both Humphrey and Nixon were weak leaders but that Nixon was better able to deal with the Soviet Union—in retrospect, probably misplaced confidence.

BOB MCCANDLESS HAD lost his sucker bet with me. Nixon beat Humphrey by 110 electoral votes. At $10 a vote that added up to $1,100 (a considerable sum then, $6,395 in 2007 dollars). I was accustomed to getting stiffed on political bets and had never collected on one that size. McCandless, though his financial condition was now reduced by being shown the way out by both his law firm and his heiress wife after the election, immediately mailed me a check for $1,100.

As for the Oklahoma Senate race where Republican Bellmon defeated Democrat Monroney, McCandless dropped me a note saying the case of Chivas Regal constituted one bet too many. He could not cough up the money immediately, he said, but would send by messenger a fifth of Chivas at the first of every month for the next twelve months. Geraldine really missed it after twelve months when the monthly bottle of Chivas did not arrive, but she retained a warm feeling about McCandless.

CHAPTER 18

Den of Vipers

A MONTH AFTER the 1968 election, I attended the Republican governors' conference in Palm Springs, California. In those days, I was a regular at such events, along with Jack Germond, Jules Witcover, David Broder, and a few other national reporters. Nothing much in the way of news ever happened, but the meetings provided a chance to gossip with politicians while relaxing with more than a few drinks.

The conference ended Saturday, December 7, 1968, but I stayed in Palm Springs that night to have dinner with Pat Hillings, one of my favorite California politicians. In 1950, Patrick J. Hillings at age twenty-seven had won the congressional seat vacated by Nixon when he ran for the Senate. For the next eight years, Hillings was Nixon's man in the House of Representatives. He ran for attorney general of California in 1958 but was defeated in the Republican primary by Caspar Weinberger. I took it for granted that Nixon's election meant that Hillings, only forty-five in 1969, would be a top White House aide. Consequently, over dinner that Saturday night, I was surprised when Hillings informed me he would not be joining the Nixon administration.

"Not a chance!" Pat told me. "Those teetotaling Christian Scientists don't want any part of me, and I don't want any part of them." "*What* Christian Scientists?" I asked. "Haldeman and Ehrlichman," he said, referring to two Nixon aides who had eclipsed him. I wasn't aware of Bob Haldeman's religion. I was barely aware of John Ehrlichman's existence.

Hillings's subsequent remarks are emblazoned in memory. "I don't trust a man who never takes a drink. It's worse than that. I know Dick Nixon about as well as anybody in politics, and I know his weaknesses. The Christian Scientists will bring out the worst in him."

This seemed to me more than the complaint of somebody who had lost out in the power game, but I never dreamed how prescient Pat Hillings would prove.

ON SUNDAY, December 8, 1968, the day after my dinner in Palm Springs with Pat Hillings, I entered my room at the Dunes Hotel in Las Vegas and looked for the first time at the message I had picked up when I checked in at the front desk. It was from Bob Ellsworth, who said it was imperative to call him immediately.

I was in Las Vegas for a few days' leisure time with my friend Joe Cerrell, now a Democratic consultant from Los Angeles, his wife, Lee, and some of their friends. The daily routine would be sleep late, eat a big breakfast, get a massage from the Dunes masseur, hit the craps and blackjack tables, go out to a lavish dinner with the Cerrell party, catch a big room headliner (Frank Sinatra) or a lounge act (Buddy Hackett), and return to the gaming tables until the early morning hours. While I pursued this sybaritic interlude, Geraldine was back in Maryland taking care of our infant son and three-year-old daughter.

But why was Bob Ellsworth calling? Robert F. Ellsworth had been a news source for me since his election to Congress in 1960, at age thirty-four, from the Kansas suburban area across the Missouri River from Kansas City, Missouri. He was a liberal Republican, a type in much greater supply then than today. Ellsworth combined his progressive agenda with a well-informed, muscular anticommunism in world affairs that especially appealed to me.

Bob was extremely well informed, and—to my delight as a reporter—extraordinarily candid. After an unsuccessful Senate bid in 1966, he joined fellow liberal Republicans Ray Price and Bill Safire on Richard Nixon's staff, and became his campaign chairman. Ellsworth fell victim to the intrigue constantly swirling around Nixon, as the candidate's law partner John Mitchell took command. But Ellsworth stayed on in a lesser position.

Now, one month after the 1968 election, Bob Ellsworth had learned my whereabouts from Geraldine and left word for me at the Dunes. When I reached him, Bob told me he had a big story for me. Mel Laird was going to be named secretary of defense. "Not Melvie!" I said, in shock. "Is this a trial balloon?" "No, it is hard. The decision has been made." Laird had agreed on Friday night, Ellsworth related, and it would be announced Wednesday.

It is difficult for anyone who never has been a reporter to appreciate the adrenaline rush I felt when I heard this news. The consensus in Washington had been that Senator Henry M. (Scoop) Jackson of Washington state would take the Pentagon post as the high-profile Democrat that Nixon craved for his cabinet.

Congressman Melvin R. Laird of Wisconsin loved power, exercised from the inner recesses of the congressional hierarchy. There had been no mention of Laird for any Nixon administration post, much less the critically important Defense portfolio. At age forty-five he had no managerial or administrative experience, only legislative.

Melvie was notorious for dispensing poison pills about his adversaries, and for a time I was on the receiving end. After I wrote about him in a mildly critical way, he spread the word in the Republican cloakroom that Novak was a hard-bitten liberal Democrat. But mutual acquaintances on Capitol Hill conjectured that Laird and Novak constituted a marriage made in heaven. And so it was.

He may have been my best congressional source ever. I relished private luncheons in his Capitol leadership office—a highball ("Let's have a little shooter," he would say), followed by the customary steak. Laird would dispense delicious political gossip, inside tips, and grand strategy. That provoked wisecracks on Capitol Hill about how amazing it was that Mel Laird found the time to write the Evans & Novak column.

My first impulse was to call Laird for details. But Ellsworth admonished me not to check the story with *anybody*—particularly not Mel, who would quickly inform Nixon to make it clear that he was not the source. Nixon was obsessive about leaks and might well announce Laird's selection then and there. I would have to trust Ellsworth as a longtime reliable source.

Our next regularly scheduled column was Wednesday when Ellsworth said Nixon would announce Laird. But Nixon could speed up the announcement or the news could leak before then. I called Rowly in Washington, and he said we had to write a special column now for the next morning's papers. An editor was called into the Publishers-Hall Syndicate offices in Manhattan, and our client newspapers were alerted that a major exclusive was on the way.

The column, a rush job with no chance for the interviewing that Rowly and I normally would do, stands up after four decades. Apart from breaking the news, the most important element in the column was a nuance that eluded many straight news reports on Laird's selection. I wrote that Laird would be "a strong force for a quickly negotiated settlement of the Vietnam War." From my many conversations with Mel, I knew he regarded the war as unwinnable. The importance of ending U.S. involvement is why, I think, he gave up a job he loved that would have stretched twenty years or more into the future for a thankless assignment that would not last more than four years.

Based mainly on what Ellsworth told me, I explained in the column what had happened to Scoop Jackson as defense secretary.

> . . . [M]uch to the surprise of Nixon insiders, Jackson last week rejected the offer—thereby heeding the pleas of several Democratic Senators who warned him Nixon would use him as the scapegoat for reduced domestic spending. Whether Jackson agreed with that view or not, he did feel—and so informed Nixon aides—that liberal Democrats in the Senate would make his life miserable as Secretary of Defense.

Wire services reports credited the Evans & Novak column as the sole source of the Laird appointment. Many purchasers of our column, including the *Chicago Sun-Times* and the *Boston Globe,* ran our story on page one. The *Washington Post* started the column on page one until its reporting staff got its own news story, slipping our column back to the op-ed page. It was probably our clearest, cleanest scoop ever on a big story.

Celebrated as a mighty reporter, I would not have learned about the Laird appointment if Ellsworth had not called me in Las Vegas. So why do leakers leak? It can be to promote an idea or to prevent something from happening, for self-glorification or defamation of an enemy, or to curry favor with the reporter. In the case of Bob Ellsworth's leak, it was none of the above. When I telephoned Bob in 2004 to ask permission to reveal him as the leaker after thirty-six years, he said he was just trying to help out a friend.

Laird got hold of me Monday to complain—obliquely, as was his style. He said I had nearly killed his aged mother when she learned the news without being alerted by her son. He tried to be jocular, but he was upset and our relationship cooled a little. Exclusive stories often cost the reporter.

THE TRANSITION FROM Johnson to Nixon was the second handover of power from one party to another that I had covered. The mood in Washington bore no resemblance to the transition from Eisenhower to Kennedy eight years earlier. The arrival of the New Frontier had been a time of high excitement and anticipation. While there was widespread relief in 1969 that LBJ was leaving, not even Republicans were excited about what was ahead. Inaugural week parties seemed pedestrian compared to Kennedy's in

1961 or even the LBJ parties of 1965. I had attended a spectacular 1965 party hosted by the *Washington Post* publisher Katherine Graham at a huge tent on the grounds of her Georgetown mansion. In 1969 Mrs. Graham gave no party, but she did attend one that Geraldine and I hosted at our modest suburban home.

It was our first inaugural party, beginning an annual event that continues into the twenty-first century. The onslaught of chauffeur-driven limos created a stir in our middle-class neighborhood. Among senior Nixon aides, Bob Haldeman, John Mitchell, and Chuck Colson were not invited; Bob Finch, Mel Laird, and Bryce Harlow were invited, and attended. I thought it was the best party of inaugural week, but that assessment may have derived from more consumption of Scotch than was fitting for a host.

ROWLY AND I had been performing in a variety of roles for Channel 5 WTTG, the Metromedia station in Washington, ever since Ed Turner tapped us for election night commentary in 1966. To begin 1969 and the Nixon administration, Turner crafted a new half-hour weekend program for us, *The Evans-Novak Report*, with us interviewing a major newsmaker. Turner, the WTTG news director, talked Metromedia into running the program on its other stations (in New York, Los Angeles, Kansas City, and Chicago) and sold its usage at a nominal fee to independent stations. That constituted a neat little jerry-built network of eighteen stations, just for Evans and Novak.

Turner would go on to be a big-time news executive, but there was nothing big-time about Metromedia in 1969 except for top-drawer guests that Rowly and I talked into coming on our show. Our program was taped early every Wednesday evening in the WTTG studios in northwest Washington to leave enough time for tapes to be airmailed to subscribing stations for broadcast on Saturday or Sunday. Our four-day-old tapes were competing with *Meet the Press* and other network interview programs that were broadcast live. Maybe news moved more slowly then, but I cannot remember being beaten or overtaken by events.

I have found television executives to be among the least imaginative people, but Ed Turner was a notable exception. Only thirty-three years old, he grafted onto *The Evans-Novak Report* the first innovation in TV news interview programs since Lawrence Spivak had produced the basic format a quarter of a century earlier. Ed noted that all these programs failed to explain to viewers what the guest had said or failed to say.

Time led the "Television" section of its February 28, 1969, issue with a review of our program called "The Empty Chair Approach." The show contains, said *Time,* "one new wrinkle," which it went on to describe.

> . . . [D]uring the last 2½ minutes of the half-hour interview, the guest is excused, and the two inquisitors tear apart what he has said—and not said.
>
> The format calls for subject to leave the set during the last commercial break. Then the camera pans past his empty chair and the two interviewers sum up whatever news they may have coaxed from him and expose any equivocations. Robert Finch, Secretary of Health, Education and Welfare, was on his way out but still within earshot when Evans commented on the subject of federal welfare standards, "we got a lot of gobbledygook."
>
> Novak (the saturnine-looking one) observed that Democratic National Chairman Fred Harris was "trying to carry water on both shoulders" in discussing whether the old-line politicians or the new black groups should represent the party in Georgia.

After cataloging other insults to guests, the magazine concluded:

> The empty chair approach offers an obvious advantage to the interviewers, who can demolish a guest for inconsistencies, evasions or even outright untruths, without having to do it to his face. If it seems rather unfair, the fact is that TV's panel interviewers only occasionally offer that sort of candid criticism while the guest is still around to fight back.

Rowly and I were delighted to have our own TV program, but we regretted that this would end our appearances on *Meet the Press.* Rowly thought we should give Larry Spivak advance notice, and we ended up as luncheon guests of the *Meet the Press* creator at his apartment in the Sheraton Park Hotel.

Spivak came across on television as hard-boiled, but he was really a warm gentleman of sixty-eight years. He told us how much he would miss Rowly and me on his program but said he would welcome us back when we returned. He added: "It won't be that long. Metromedia is not the kind of organization that will stick to a program like this."

He was right. If a Metromedia program did not bring in money, it was off to the slaughterhouse. The *Evans-Novak Report* simply did not produce enough cash. Ed Turner fought hard to save his and our creation, but the gods of Metromedia killed the program early in 1970 after one year.

ON APRIL 21, 1969, Nixon nominated Congressman Donald Rumsfeld of Illinois as director of the Office of Economic Opportunity (OEO)—the antipoverty program that was the heart of LBJ's Great Society and had been attacked by Nixon and other Republicans in the 1968 campaign. But the OEO was retained under the "Moynihan Doctrine." Democrat Pat Moynihan, brought into the Nixon White House as a Cabinet-level counselor, had convinced Nixon to follow British practice of a conservative government retaining the social initiatives of its liberal predecessor.

When he resigned from Congress, Don Rumsfeld was thirty-six years old, a protégé of Minority Leader Jerry Ford, and seen as his eventual successor. But the congressional Old Guard detested Rumsfeld as an arrogant know-it-all. An ambitious Rumsfeld felt he had run out of string on Capitol Hill after four terms, though he required the upgrading of the OEO post to cabinet status to come on board.

"Stay in touch," Rumsfeld wrote me November 4, 1968, after a favorable column by me. I paid Rummy a visit in his new office in the Executive Office Building next door to the White House. He greeted me in the outer office and introduced me to his new assistant, a pleasant-faced young man of twenty-seven. It was Dick Cheney. I recall few of the hundreds of assistants I have met through their bosses, but I remembered this one—and also what Rumsfeld told me. He would, in effect, follow the Moynihan Doctrine, not only retaining the Great Society's antipoverty program but keeping it largely as the Democrats had conceived it. He would shock former colleagues on the Hill, fighting a veto for governors on poverty proposals. He was influenced by Paul O'Neill, a brainy civil servant inherited from the Kennedy-Johnson administration (and denounced by the conservative weekly *Human Events* as a liberal intruder in the Republican administration).

ONE SENIOR NIXON aide who paid no attention to the president's prohibition on contacts with Evans and Novak was National Security Adviser Henry A. Kissinger. Immediately after the 1968 election, Rowly began cultivating Kissinger (and his illustrious young staff that included Al Haig and John Negroponte) as major sources for our column. I don't recall Rowly ever writing a word critical of Kissinger. Negative comments in the column (increasing as the years passed) about Kissinger's détente policy all came from me. I assumed that Rowly blamed the criticism on me when he talked to Henry, but I did not realize until more than thirty years later that he could attribute to me a column that I had not even seen.

The Evans & Novak column published on April 5, 1973, reported that former NSC staff members of Kissinger's, who was now secretary of state, were being blackballed by Chief of Staff H. R. Haldeman at the White House in their quest for high State Department positions. There was nothing in the account critical of Kissinger, but he did not want his relations roiled with the powerful Haldeman. On the morning the column ran, Kissinger called Evans from California to protest, as I learned in the summer of 2006 from a surreptitiously recorded White House telephone tape.

"Why don't you check your columns with me?" Kissinger demanded. Instead of defending his column, Rowly took the Novak default position. "That was a product of my partner's reporting exercise," he replied. "Yes," Kissinger replied, "but why not check it? Good grief, you call me often enough." Later in their conversation, Evans pressed home his point: "Well, listen, I'm telling you the truth that my partner did most of the work on this, and he is now in Japan. And if it is not a fair portrayal, I'd like to correct it. And I'm sorry."

But Rowly was not "telling you the truth." Not only did I not do "most of the work" on the column, I had not even seen it at the moment Kissinger and Evans were talking about it. When either Rowly or I was abroad, the traveling partner did not see in advance the columns written in Washington by the other partner. The April 5 column was written while I was in Tokyo on an Asian reporting trip.

Rowly never mentioned to me his conversation with Kissinger. I wonder how often he used this ploy?

ROWLY AND I had no contact at all with the two most powerful Nixon advisers: Attorney General John Mitchell and Chief of Staff H. R. Haldeman. Neither had any interest in talking to reporters or returning their calls. Perhaps Haldeman as an advertising agency account executive hawking Black Flag insecticide never learned that avoiding the press did not guarantee safety from press exposure. But some of Haldeman's colleagues, especially Bob Ellsworth, were eager to talk about what was happening at the White House. On April 2, 1969, the Evans & Novak column reported:

> . . . [S]ome of Haldeman's critics felt he and his young crew-cut lieutenants, termed the Beaver Patrol behind their backs because of Boy Scout tendencies, had emphasized petty intraoffice efficiencies while neglecting vital policy coordination between government departments.

The major point of the column, however, was to reveal the emergence of "an obscure aide named John Ehrlichman, purposefully assuming direction of domestic policy." I wrote that Ehrlichman was eclipsing Haldeman by seizing the policy reins. That was wrong. I was only as accurate as my sources, and my sources were inaccurate in this case. Ehrlichman and Haldeman were not competitors but more like Hindenburg and Ludendorff governing Germany at the end of World War I. Nevertheless, this was the first journalistic effort to come close to who was really running the government under Richard Nixon.

Haldeman wrote in his diary on April 7:

> Press trying to build up idea of internal feud: E[hrlichman] vs. me. Hard to sell, but Evans and Novak giving it a try, to great glee of some White House staff. [Ellsworth?] . . .
>
> Long session tonight with Larry [Higby, Haldeman's deputy] and [Dwight] Chapin [Nixon's appointments secretary] about Haldeman image. They're concerned by Evans and Novak and other adverse publicity, feel we need to get our line out, and that I have to move more into public eye. Problem is to define first the exact view we want to project. They had some good ideas, had put in a lot of time and thought. Also [speechwriter] Bill Safire working on general suggestions. Probably do need to do something to avoid letting the "von Haldeman" concept become firmly entrenched.

This entry reflects the perpetual meandering talk about public relations in the Nixon White House, exposed by the invaluable, posthumously published *The Haldeman Diaries*. Little was done about the "Haldeman image." He made no appearances in 1969 on any Sunday television program. The only instance of putting him "more in the public eye" that I can find was his appearance as a guest on April 23 on *Breakfast with Godfrey* (where I was present). He said and accomplished nothing.

I am amused to think of Haldeman spending a whole evening with two "Beaver Patrol" members, Chapin and Higby, vainly seeking a way to counter the Evans & Novak column. They probably never considered the simple expedient of Haldeman answering one of my phone calls and maybe inviting one of us to lunch in his West Wing office.

Am I suggesting a news source could buy off Novak with a hamburger in the White House? No government official or politician can secure immunity from a reporter by helping him out. Even my most important sources—such as Mel Laird and Wilbur Mills—were not immune from an occasional dig. Still, Bob Haldeman was treated more harshly because he refused any connection with me. He made himself more of a target than he had to be by refusing to be a source.

MEL LAIRD INVITED Rowly and me over to the Pentagon for lunch on March 20, 1969. He flashed the same crooked grin familiar from simpler days on Capitol Hill. Henry Kissinger, the new national security adviser, in private conversations with colleagues had already called Laird "devious" (which fit the old saw of being called ugly by a frog). I learned over the next hour just how devious Laird could be. He had dispensed political morsels to me in our Capitol luncheons. But now at the Pentagon, he provided a whole feast.

Laird laid out his plan for removing U.S. troops from Vietnam. The clumsy old phrase "de-Americanization" was changed to "Vietnamization," but in fact the whole concept was changed. Nixon's original plan had been to prepare South Vietnam's Army of the Republic of Vietnam (ARVN) to take over military duties from the Americans *after* ongoing talks in Paris, orchestrated by Kissinger, had agreed on mutual withdrawal of U.S. and North Vietnamese regular troops.

Now, Laird revealed to us, the Americans were being replaced by suitably equipped and trained ARVN forces no matter what Kissinger accomplished in Paris. Ready or not, here we go! Laird indicated Kissinger did not like it and the generals were deeply apprehensive, but it was going to happen anyway.

On an easel in Laird's office was a large chart hidden from view by a cover. Cautioning us that this was *really* off the record, the secretary briefly removed the cover before hiding it again. I got a glimpse of a detailed plan to replace, unit by unit, U.S. with ARVN troops.

Laird ignored the Paris peace talks. Mel appreciated that the Communists would agree to nothing less than a unitary Vietnamese state under one-party Communist rule. Thus, Laird understood—and tried to get Nixon to understand—that his primary mission was to end not the Vietnam War but U.S. participation under the most favorable conditions for the anticommunist Vietnamese.

What Laird revealed to Rowly and me did not resemble the new administration's public statements. On March 19, Laird told the Senate Armed Services Committee that the United States planned no troop pullout "at the present time." Five days later, under a *Washington Post* headline of "Secret Laird Plan Will Allow Early Troop Pullouts," our column began:

Working behind an essential curtain of secrecy, the new Administration has now developed an anti-war strategy which is all but certain to start significant withdrawals of U.S. forces from Vietnam within six months. . . .

Laird now talks about equipping the South Vietnamese to handle both the Vietcong and North Vietnamese regulars, with steadily declining combat aid from the U.S.

Administration spokesmen declared there was not a shred of truth to our column, but it was Evans & Novak at our best. The first troop withdrawals were announced officially in June, giving us a six-week beat. Thanks to Laird, we also were proved correct on longer-range predictions. We wrote that "save for heavy equipment, logistical support, and Green Beret troops—most U.S. combat forces could be withdrawn by the summer of 1970." When I arrived in Saigon in April 1970, most were gone

ROWLY AND I, heeding the advice of columnist Joe Alsop, Rowly's friend and mentor, each took at least one foreign reporting trip annually (more for Rowly). My 1969 trip was for three weeks to seek signs of the Soviet empire unraveling by reporting from Eastern Europe.

Rowly, who had superb intelligence contacts, made available to me a special service the CIA then provided select journalists. Prior to every overseas trip, I would go to Langley, be ushered into an antiseptic room, and briefed on the countries I was visiting. Although this service gave me useful detail, I sometimes found the CIA's findings contradicted by subsequent reporting.

Such was the case with Czechoslovakia in 1969. The CIA's analysts insisted to me that the Soviet intervention of 1968 would fail in a short time and Moscow would release its hold. I stopped in Munich on the way to Prague for a briefing by Radio Free Europe's analysts, and they took seriously the Brezhnev Doctrine, with Soviet president Leonid Brezhnev declaring the Kremlin's determination that no nation could throw off the yoke of communism.

The pessimists were correct. The sources I had met on my first visit to Prague in 1967 seemed personally diminished in 1969 by the Soviet intervention. They felt that they had lost the fight for freedom, with no hope for a foreseeable reversal.

Dan Morgan, a young correspondent for the *Washington Post,* was responsible for the most memorable moment of my 1969 visit to Prague. He introduced me to Emil Zatopek, symbol of the triumph and the suppression of the human spirit in Czechoslovakia in the 1960s. I am a hero worshiper who, in my line of work, has found few heroes to worship. Zatopek, the greatest distance runner of all time, was a global sports icon and a national Czech hero. He had been promoted to colonel in the Czech army by 1968 and lived a comfortable life coddled by the Communist state. When the moment of truth came in the Prague Spring, he chose freedom and abandoned security to support the anticommunist revolt and oppose Soviet intervention. Zatopek was cashiered from the army, expelled from the Communist Party, and faced criminal punishment when I met him in 1969.

When Dan Morgan led me into a basement café in Prague to meet Zatopek, I was thrilled to meet this paragon of sports and patriotism—age forty-six but looking much older. Would he, I asked, consider leaving Czechoslovakia? I quoted him in an Evans & Novak column from Prague: "My place is here to the bitter end." That led me to conclude the column with this final paragraph:

> That end will be bitter, indeed, in the opinion of the liberals until the day, far off if it ever comes, of a liberalization of the Soviet regime itself. A former commentator for Radio Prague, prohibited now from writing or broadcasting, told us with typical Czech irony: "I see the Russians relenting—about 20 years from now." It was the most optimistic prophecy we heard in Prague.

My radio commentator's accuracy was uncanny. It was twenty-one years before freedom came to Czechoslovakia when Communist rule ended with the Soviet Union's breakdown and the bloodless "Velvet Revolution" in Prague. Emil Zatopek paid dearly, forced into six years at hard labor in the country's uranium mines that produced raw material for the Soviet nuclear weapons program. He was a true hero.

WHEN NIXON HAD been in office for eight months, issue 59 of the *Evans-Novak Political Report,* published on September 10, 1969, offered this analysis:

> We continue to note a strange contrast between the President's apparent state of euphoria and specific difficult problems—Vietnam, the economy, the tax bill—that are piling up. We find increasing sentiment among Republicans that Mr. Nixon must devote far more personal attention to the details of specific issues.

The newsletter went on to relate how Nixon had backed away from his announced firm stand against inflation, then added this paragraph (underlined so that our readers could not miss the significance):

> We continue to feel that Nixon's ambivalence on this subject (as well as Vietnam, desegregation, etc.) is giving his Administration a blurred image at best, raising doubts about the Government's direction, intentions and, most damaging, competence.

Three days later, September 13, President Nixon was not happy with what he read in his morning news summary, which included a report on the September 10 edition of our little newsletter. The White House summarizer called it "some of the most negative comment on the Administration to date." Thanks to William Safire's account of the pre-Watergate Nixon administration *(Before the Fall)*, we know that the president fired off written instructions to White House communications chief Herb Klein: "1. Get some tough letters to these guys from subscribers. 2. Be sure they are cut off [from contact with the White House]."

"Klein did neither," Safire wrote. "His routine refusal to carry out these ukases are why Old Hand Klein was not in close, and why he emerged from the ruins with his reputation intact." Indeed, while colleagues went to prison, Klein returned to a senior executive position with the *San Diego Union,* where he remained into the twenty-first century.

Bob Ellsworth and John Sears, two Nixon aides who were prime sources for me, both left the White House in 1969. Just as Klein forfeited being "in close" with Nixon by refusing to carry out Nixon's madcap schemes, Ellsworth and Sears did not help themselves by being on good terms with journalists.

Sears told me Ellsworth had gotten in the doghouse with Haldeman and Mitchell, dating back to the 1968 campaign when Mitchell replaced Ellsworth as campaign manager. It continued into the White House, Sears continued to me:

> Those kind of things never get any better. The longer people are together in a situation suspicious of each other, people tend to get more and more suspicious of each other and then they forget why they started to get suspicious of each other. . . . It was easy for them [Haldeman and Mitchell] to come around [and] say, "Hell, Bob, we don't have an awful lot for you to do. 'X' is doing this, 'Y' is doing that. Where do *you* fit in here?"

The men on Nixon's dark side were about to run out of the government one of the president's most able supporters after only a few months in 1969. Kissinger came to the rescue. He arranged for Nixon, who never liked to fire anyone, to send Ellsworth to Brussels as the U.S. ambassador to NATO in April—removing him from this den of vipers for one of the best jobs in government.

John Sears stayed on at the White House six months longer than Ellsworth, but was not so fortunate. Mitchell was determined to be done with his brilliant young former law partner, complaining that Sears drank too much and talked too much to the press. What I think really bothered him was that Sears was not afraid of John Mitchell.

By the early summer of 1969, Sears later informed me, "I felt I didn't have any effectiveness. I had outlived my usefulness." He was never fired but in October left voluntarily—not dreaming at age twenty-nine that a man of his intelligence, charm, and ambition never again would be on a government payroll. I asked whether he saw the president before he left. "No, he was embarrassed. I did ask to see him once when I had decided to go. I was refused the opportunity. I am sure he was embarrassed."

Could Richard Nixon not bear to face a valuable young lieutenant who had resigned? Sears later sat in the small conference room in our expanded little suite of offices on Pennsylvania Avenue, eating a sandwich lunch with me, and talking about Nixon:

> He can be a very tough guy as long as he doesn't have to see the other guy. In personal relationships, he has a good bit of cowardice because he can't do things they can do. He can't make small talk. He can't talk and derive a result that's satisfactory. He doesn't want to get involved in confrontations with people.
>
> He's supposed to be [a] hard, tough politician, and he can't take what another politician is saying about him. He'll sit there and act really strong, hard, tough. He's not. He's saying all those things to convince himself, also to convince the people [in the room], because that's part of convincing himself. That's part of the reason he doesn't like to see a whole lot of people.

These words, never published until now, are a corrective to the White House tapes and the Haldeman diaries, pored over by historians who conclude that Nixon was a tyrant in embryo. Based on Sears's assessment, Nixon was a fraud—a make-believe tough guy.

CHAPTER 19

Vietnam

T URNING AGE THIRTY-NINE in 1970, I was a Korean War–era veteran who never had heard a shot fired in anger and a major Washington correspondent who had never covered a war. The time was past due for me to go to Vietnam, but I was in no hurry. My rationalization was that Rowly, the old marine combat veteran, was covering Indochina for us with annual trips starting in 1965.

However, suddenly and inexplicably, my partner early in 1970 told me he would travel to Vietnam no more. "That opens the way for you to go to Vietnam, Bob," Evans told me. "I really envy you." If he envied me so much, I wondered, why didn't he keep going himself?

I arranged a four-week trip to Southeast Asia in April 1970, mostly in Vietnam with a few days in the secondary battleground of Laos. I didn't plan to go to Cambodia, where nothing much was happening under the "neutralist" (mainly procommunist) Prince Norodom Sihanouk, and where it was difficult for a Western journalist to get an entry visa.

THE HIGH POINT of my first trip to Vietnam was getting acquainted with one of the most remarkable figures I have encountered in a lifetime of meeting strong personalities: John Paul Vann, then the senior U.S. government official in the Mekong Delta. He had been lionized in the American press by such disparate journalists as the dove David Halberstam and the hawk Joseph Alsop.

Vann was forty-six years old, a small, wiry man whose humble appearance belied the reality that he was one of the world's great antiguerrilla tacticians. While many U.S. Foreign Service officers assigned to Vietnam's pacification program went "cowboy" with slouch campaign hats and M-16 rifles slung over their back or .45 pistols at their belt, Vann dressed in nondescript civilian clothes and carried no weapons.

Neil Sheehan, David Halberstam, and Malcolm Browne were young reporters who worked closely with Lieutenant Colonel Vann in 1963 in telling
the world about the foolish conduct of the war. By 1970, his old reporter
friends thought Vann had changed. He thought they did not understand
that conditions in Vietnam had changed. Actually, their goals had always
differed. The journalists, who in 1963 joined Vann in denouncing the way
the war was being conducted, never shared Vann's determination to prevent
a Communist takeover in Vietnam.

I had been in country four days when I met Vann at IV Corps headquarters in Cantho in the Mekong Delta. He told me he had been ordered by
"Abe" (General Creighton Abrams, the U.S. commander) to take me along
for the next three days, and Vann was not particularly happy about that.

"This won't be a pleasure trip," he told me. "I'll be moving fast, and
right into 'Indian Country.' Or you can make your own schedule. I'll get
you a chopper and an officer escort and you can go anywhere you want in
IV Corps." Despite Vann's reputation for risk-taking, I could not pass up a
three-day tutorial from the leading American expert on Vietnam.

The Mekong Delta, the rice bowl of Indochina and birthplace of the
Vietcong insurgency, had changed radically since 1963 when Vann was a
principal source for Halberstam, Sheehan, and Browne. American heavy
infantrymen then were destroying the delta in their futile quest of sleek,
motivated Communist guerrillas. Seven years later IV Corps was more Viet-
namized than anywhere else, with the Vietcong on the ropes.

Those three days were routine for Vann, but high adventure for me.
Vann traveled through IV Corps from dawn to dusk in a U.S. Army helicopter (often taking the controls himself). South Vietnamese district
officials were not alerted in advance of Vann swooping down to interro-
gate, chastise, and exhort them. As promised, he took me into "Indian
Country"—such as Kienthahn District, where a fragile government presence had just been established and where, Vann told me, the Vietcong still
ruled the night.

After our frosty beginning, Vann reverted to his normally garrulous
self. I took an immediate liking to him, and I think he may have reciprocated. Vann was famous for getting by on four hours of sleep a night, and
I had trained myself in college to make do with five or six hours. In
overnight talk sessions, one night in sleeping bags under the stars, I was instructed by John Vann.

From the start, Vann told me, U.S. authorities had told the Vietnamese
to step out of the way while we Americans won this war—quickly. He said
General William Westmoreland, Abrams's predecessor, was a disaster with

no appreciation of Vietnamese nationalism and dreams of parlaying the war into the American presidency. Lyndon Johnson, supporting Westmoreland all the way, was hopeless, Vann added. Not until recently, Vann told me, had Washington permitted ARVN units to be given M-16 automatic rifles in place of obsolete World War II–vintage M-1s. Now, he wanted regional militiamen to get M-16s as well. He said Vietnamization was the only hope for a non-Communist Vietnam to survive.

Had I, he asked, noted the differences between the districts we visited? Kienthanh, where we found militiamen gambling in filthy barracks in the middle of the day, was ready to be overrun by the enemy. A few kilometers away, Kienhen district's militiamen were in high morale, going out on all-night patrols (a rarity for ARVN forces). "The soldier in South Vietnam," Vann told me, "is as good as the American, really better because he is harder. After all, he comes from the same stock as the VC. The problem is the officers. Most of them are terrible." To survive, he said, South Vietnam must develop a better officer corps that did not rely on American air power.

That was the biggest lesson of my first visit to Vietnam. The dozens of ARVN officers I talked to all over the country were products of the French colonial system who had fought against their country's independence. They opposed departure of the American troops and told me they could not survive without U.S. helicopters and bombers, assets they could not count on forever.

A MONTH BEFORE I left for Southeast Asia in 1970, an unexpected event in Cambodia in which the United States played no part significantly altered the region's political climate. Prince Norodom Sihanouk, Cambodia's saxophone-playing, playboy chief of state, had tried to keep his country out of war by appeasing North Vietnam. He permitted fifty thousand NVA and Vietcong troops to use Cambodia as a supply base and refuge in the Vietnamese war. By early 1970, however, Sihanouk protested to Hanoi that it had violated his hospitality by continued infiltration of forces into his country. In March, he went to Moscow to implore the Soviets to intervene with Ho Chi Minh. Lieutenant General Lon Nol, the Cambodian premier and army supreme commander, took advantage of the prince's absence to lead a right-wing coup deposing Sihanouk. The new government immediately demanded withdrawal of all Vietnamese troops.

My CIA briefers in Langley said the Agency had nothing to do with the Cambodian coup, and I believed them. They also admitted they did not know exactly what was going on in Cambodia. They advised me to stay out of Cambodia, asserting what I could learn there would not justify the danger of entering such an unstable situation. (Seventeen Western journalists, three of them Americans, would be seized in Cambodia by Communist forces in 1970, many never to return.)

When I arrived in Saigon, my plans changed. I encountered a former colleague from the *Wall Street Journal,* Jim Wallace, a professional foreign correspondent now working for *U.S. News & World Report.* His wife, Haya, went everywhere with him, and they now made their home in a single room at the Caravelle Hotel in Saigon. But Jim told me the action was in Cambodia, and they soon would be leaving for Phnom Penh.

So was much of the Saigon press corps. It was impossible to get an entry visa for Cambodia with the country's consular service in disarray after the coup, so reporters were just showing up in Phnom Penh. I rearranged my schedule to go to Phnom Penh—without documents or appointments there—and I entered a French colonial town that was pure Graham Greene. Phnom Penh until then had been untouched by war and was bereft of American influence. There were few automobiles and Southeast Asia's most beautiful women gracefully pedaled their bicycles through city streets. A large opium den operated openly in a city lacking reliable means of communication with the outside world. The Hotel Royale, where everybody stayed, was run-down but betrayed a former elegance.

The Wallaces had been there a week when I checked in. Something was happening in Cambodia, but nobody could be sure what. This was not Vietnam or Laos where U.S. authorities did their best to make life easy for me. The daily briefing at the Defense Ministry reported great battles with Cambodian forces devastating the NVA. The briefer was named Am Rong—appropriate as he dispensed pure fiction.

There were no U.S. aircraft to take me where the action was. American reporters, usually in groups of two or three, would hire a car with driver and interpreter at a daily rate of ten dollars in town and twenty-five dollars in the countryside (with a premium of one hundred dollars if shot at). All the air-conditioned Mercedes sedans had been taken by the time Wallace got to town, and he managed only a timeworn four-door Chevrolet Impala, with a two-man crew that was a little slow on the uptake.

Daniel Southerland, a young reporter for the *Christian Science Monitor,* joined Wallace and me to split costs three ways and we set off early one morning to find the war. When we reached the Neak Leung ferry station on the Mekong an hour out of Phnom Penh, there was a line of Mercedes sedans carrying reporters, immobilized by what they saw. I had never seen anything like it, and neither had reporters with extensive experience of war. We saw an endless procession of dead bodies—thousands of them—

floating down the river. We thus learned of a genocidal slaughter in process. The dead were ethnic Vietnamese, not invading troops but civilian residents, some of whom had lived in Cambodia for generations and now had been slaughtered by their fellow Cambodians, ethnic Khmer, and dumped in the river. We were close enough and the river was moving slowly enough so that we could see facial wounds and death mask expressions.

The Lon Nol government had been exhorting the populace to patriotic fervor against intruding Communist Vietnamese troops. The populace reacted by turning on their harder-working Vietnamese neighbors, whose economic success they envied.

Late in the afternoon, we located the headquarters of the Cambodian Army brigade holding the provincial capital of Svayriengville. We were told the colonel commanding the brigade was just finishing his daily siesta(!), but if we could wait ten or fifteen minutes, he would be more than happy to see us. The fifteen minutes stretched closer to forty-five, but we had put in so much time we figured we had best wait it out.

We found the colonel wearing a silk dressing gown and offering us cognac. He proceeded with an extended monologue in what sounded to me like pretty good French. Two decades earlier, he said, he was a lieutenant in the French colonial army, which he said always administered a beating to the Communist Vietminh (neglecting to mention that the Vietminh won that war). It was the colonel's fancy that the Communist commanders he faced now were the young officers he claimed to have defeated in the 1950s. "We know these Vietcong as we know our household dogs," he told us. Surrounded on three sides by these "dogs" and facing encirclement as he sipped cognac, the colonel was a fool.

Wallace, Southerland, and I were in nearly as much danger as the colonel. We had wasted so much time at brigade headquarters that night was falling with a lot of ground for us to cover before reaching the Neak Leung ferry.

It was pitch-dark as we traveled down a lonely country road and heard a burst of automatic rifle fire. The driver slammed on the brakes. "You idiot!" shouted Wallace. "Accelerate, accelerate! Don't stop" The driver could not understand a word of English, but the interpreter relayed Jim's instructions and we sped out of danger.

When we arrived at Neak Leung, we found it deserted. The ferryboat was tied to its moorings, and the ferryman was nowhere to be seen. The only person around was a teenaged boy who told us the ferryman had gone home for the night and that he had no idea where the ferryman lived. The boy then took off running into the darkness, whether to stay away from possible trouble or to alert Communist troops we did not know.

Smart enough to appreciate our situation, the driver began to sob. "Shut up!" Wallace yelled. But I felt like sobbing myself. We faced a night without lodging in the Cambodian countryside filled with hostile guerrillas, who by now probably were aware of our whereabouts. Then, out of the night, we heard truck engines. Guerrillas don't travel by truck. It was a Cambodian Army company, with the ferryman in tow. It might as well have been the U.S. Cavalry to the rescue as they carried us across the Mekong.

When we finally got to the Hotel Royale in Phnom Penh, we found Jim's wife, Haya, beside herself. In these pre–cell phone days, we had no way of informing her that we were safe. Late as it was, eight of us went to a Chinese restaurant to celebrate our narrow escape. Peking duck never tasted so good.

I FLEW TO Honolulu to join Geraldine for a week's vacation in the outer Hawaiian islands. Upon arriving in Honolulu, I had a morning appointment on April 30, 1970, with the Commander in Chief, U.S. Forces in the Pacific (CINCPAC), who had nominal authority over the Asian wars. I didn't expect to learn much from him, but I scheduled the meeting anyway because I knew and liked the current CINCPAC, Admiral John S. McCain Jr.

Admiral McCain had been chief of Naval Information at the Pentagon during the first year of the Evans & Novak column and had been helpful to me. We found we were neighbors on Capitol Hill, and we saw each other occasionally at social events. His father, John S. Sr., was an admiral who commanded a World War II task force in the Pacific. His son, the future senator John S. III, was a naval aviator who was a North Vietnamese prisoner of war while his father was CINCPAC.

In the Honolulu office where Geraldine joined us, the admiral gave me the standard Vietnam briefing, charts and all. I told him of my experience in Cambodia and suggested the military situation there was so bad that the country would become more of a sanctuary for the NVA than ever before. McCain tensed up, a surprise because he always had been open with me. When I pressed him with more questions about Cambodia, he waved me off and said: "Bob, I just can't talk anymore about this. All I can say is watch the president's speech tonight."

Actually, it was afternoon time in Hawaii when Nixon addressed the nation and the world. Geraldine and I watched from our Honolulu hotel room as the president announced a joint incursion of U.S. and South Vietnamese forces into largely unpopulated areas of Cambodia to remove it as a sanctuary for the NVA. In a month of intense reporting in Indochina, I had not heard a whisper of this. What shocked me was Nixon's rhetoric.

> We will not be humiliated. We will not be defeated. If when the chips are down the U.S. acts like a pitiful helpless giant, the forces of totalitarianism and anarchy will threaten free nations and free institutions throughout the world. It is not our power but our will that is being tested tonight. . . .

This attempt at Churchillian prose or at least Eisenhower's D-Day declaration was exaggerated for an eight-week border raid. It was to be in and out, with no attempt to stabilize the Lon Nol regime's rule. Laird wanted only South Vietnamese troops used in Cambodia, arguing this was the opportunity to show that the ARVN could stand up to NVA regulars. General Abrams wanted a combined U.S.–ARVN operation, because he felt the South Vietnamese could not perform the mission by themselves. Abrams won the argument. We analyzed what had happened in a column where Rowly and I pooled our information:

> . . . [O]ne high-ranking civilian official told us in Vietnam: "Abe just doesn't understand Vietnamization." He and other civilians feel Abrams and the uniformed military are missing an essential point of Vietnamization—that South Vietnamese troops must take over from the Americans not when they are ready, but ready or not. Otherwise, the South Vietnamese never will be ready.

The "high-ranking civilian official" was John Paul Vann. When I saw him in Vietnam the next year, Vann told me he feared the failure to make the Cambodian incursion an all-ARVN operation reduced the confidence of the South Vietnamese high command with dire implications for the future. The excellent performance of South Vietnamese troops inside Cambodia showed that Laird and Vann were correct and Abrams and the other generals were wrong. The cost of using American troops was, as Laird had predicted, a regeneration of the antiwar movement in the United States and a decline in support for the war that would have tragic consequences four years hence.

CHAPTER 20

The Frustration of Power

WHILE NIXON WAS struggling in the second year of his presidency, I spent an evening of diversion that would affect the rest of my life.

I had decided in 1952 against a career of sportswriting, but I never stopped being a sports fan. Geraldine and I had a partial season ticket plan for the Washington Senators baseball team. (Walking to the games from our home on Capitol Hill fulfilled my lifelong desire to live that close to Major League Baseball.) In 1966, Geraldine dropped into the Washington Redskins downtown ticket office and purchased two season tickets—the last year it was possible to do that before all tickets were sold.

Still, my great love was basketball, especially college basketball. The Washington area had no big-time basketball when I arrived in 1957, but I attended NCAA tournament games at the University of Maryland (a few miles from the District of Columbia line), including the famous 1966 title game when all-black Texas Western changed the face of college basketball by upsetting all-white Kentucky. I also saw the 1969 regional championship at Maryland when North Carolina, coached by Dean Smith, edged little Davidson College, coached by Lefty Driesell, on a last-second shot to go to the Final Four. Immediately thereafter, Maryland hired Lefty away from Davidson, and I knew that big-time college basketball had come to Washington.

I went to my first game to see Maryland with Driesell as coach on January 28, 1970, when his unranked team played nineteenth-ranked Duke. The 12,000 fans (short of the 14,500 capacity that regularly would be filled in years to come) were described by the *Washington Post* as "the largest Maryland basketball crowd in years." Lefty's prize recruits, whose successes would make Maryland a national power, had to sit out their freshman year under the rules then in effect. So he faced powerful Duke with leftovers from the previous year's losing team. My parents were visiting from Illinois, and I picked up a couple of excellent tickets at three dollars apiece(!) for my father and me.

Driesell slowed down the game to neutralize the odds against the vastly superior Dukies and keep the score close until the end, when anything could happen. The "anything" was a shot from near half court that gave Maryland a stunning 52 to 50 victory. When I entered the arena that night, I was not even sure which team I wanted to win. But then and there I became a Maryland fan. The Driesell Era had begun, and I was hooked on college basketball again.

I asked Geraldine to drive over to the college and buy season tickets for the next year. The man in the ticket office suggested, and Geraldine purchased, a $500-a-year ($2,600 in 2007 money) membership in the Terrapin Club, the booster organization, in return for free tickets for both basketball and football. (As this is written, it takes a $10,000 membership for the right to even buy tickets at $33 apiece per game.) Geraldine did not realize she had opened the door to a lifelong obsessive relationship for me.

THE EARLY CONSENSUS among Republicans was that Nixon's penchant for novelty and his quest to look "hard" had led him to a disastrously bad decision at Miami Beach in 1968 when he picked Spiro T. Agnew for vice president. Digging out Agnew's foibles as vice president became a cottage industry for the Evans & Novak column.

The talk in Republican circles midway through 1969 was that Agnew surely would be dumped from the ticket in 1972. But Agnew rehabilitated himself. The vice president did much of his own writing, as he launched a fierce rhetorical attack on his critics, especially those in the news media. Delighted by the enthusiastic reaction, Nixon assigned Pat Buchanan to help Agnew's speechwriting. Overnight Spiro T. Agnew became hero of the Right, supplanting a Ronald Reagan bogged down in California state government.

I traveled to Minnesota on February 20, 1970, to hear Agnew address the fund-raising dinner of the state's liberal-leaning Republican Party. Arriving in Minneapolis in midafternoon, Agnew answered just two questions from reporters and then hurried to more than six hours of seclusion in his Sheraton-Ritz Hotel suite. He failed to appear, as promised, at the reception of the Minnesota Elephants Club (five hundred dollars a ticket), claiming a "tight schedule." He was an hour late for the hundred-dollar-a-plate dinner at the St. Paul Auditorium, disdaining the banquet cuisine and eating in his hotel suite's solitary splendor.

Minnesota party leaders were incensed, but not the unprecedented capacity audience of nine thousand at the auditorium. Ignoring the state party leaders' admonitions to soften his rhetoric for the bland Minnesotans, Agnew attacked left-wing radicals as "societal misfits" and accused Democrats of harboring "a weird desire to suck up the political support of organized dissidents."

ON THE MORNING of September 8, 1970, Nixon gave instructions to four of his most valuable aides. Bryce Harlow, Pat Buchanan, Bill Safire, and Martin Anderson were assigned to accompany Agnew on cross-country campaigning beginning the next day. In a Buchanan-written speech that Nixon liked, Agnew coined the term "radiclib"—for radical-liberal. Nixon's plan was to use Agnew's presumed popularity to nationalize the midterm elections.

Agnew turned out to be tendentious, unattractive, and ultimately uncontrollable. By October, the tides were turning for the Democrats. The Republican law-and-order, anti-student-demonstrator theme was growing tiresome. Nixon felt a change was needed—not of the message, but of the messenger. Nixon would take over Agnew's duties and theme with a twenty-three-state presidential tour between October and the November 2 election day.

Nixon's attempt to nationalize the midterm elections failed. Republicans lost a net of eleven governors, and Democrats maintained big majorities in Congress (by a seventy-five-seat margin in the House and ten seats in the Senate). Republicans made no net progress in the South, losing statewide contests in Texas, Florida, Arkansas, and South Carolina.

Two vignettes from the 1970 campaign are noteworthy because they involve two Republicans who would climb to the summit of political power: Donald Rumsfeld and the senior George Bush.

In 1968, the peace activist Allard K. Lowenstein had won a seat in Congress from a district on then Republican-dominated Long Island. Lowenstein did not even rent temporary quarters for a Tuesday-through-Thursday residence when Congress was in session but crashed on the living room sofa of his good friend Don Rumsfeld.

Al and Rummy were both college wrestlers and had kept wrestling as a hobby. They met on the mats when they were both unknown young men driven by ambition and ideals. This political odd couple soon discovered they were innovative politicians dissatisfied with the leadership of their respective parties. Each told me how much he liked the other as a public figure and friend. Rumsfeld publicly issued virtual endorsements of Lowenstein in his House races.

The Republican bosses of Long Island could not tolerate Lowenstein representing one of their districts in Congress, and recruited an excellent 1970 opponent in State Senator Norman Lent (at thirty-nine, two years Lowenstein's junior). Nor could they tolerate a Nixon cabinet member supporting Lowenstein, and made this clear to the White House. Word was relayed to Rumsfeld that the president insisted Rummy publicly endorse Lent. Rumsfeld didn't like that but followed orders and abandoned his friend.

The 1970 campaign drove Allard Lowenstein out of Congress after one term and dissolved a cherished friendship. I think losing Rummy as a friend bothered Al more for the rest of his short life (he was assassinated in 1980 by a mentally deranged former protégé) than losing his House seat. I knew Rumsfeld well enough to ask whether ditching Lowenstein bothered him. "Sure," he replied, "but that's politics." It was the first time that I fully appreciated Rumsfeld's genuine hardness.

Once George H. W. Bush failed in an improbable bid for the 1968 vice-presidential nomination, he determined—after only two terms in the House—to try a second time for the Senate in 1970. Senator Ralph Yarborough was much too liberal for Texas and at age sixty-seven was ready to be beaten by Bush. But Bush never got the chance. The Tory Democrats, who had ruled Texas for more than a century but now were being realigned out of power, made their last play with Lloyd Bentsen, then a conservative, aristocratic financier from South Texas. Bentsen crushed Yarborough in the Democratic primary.

I traveled with Bush less than two weeks before the general election. I then had a warm relationship with the senior Bush, and he spoke to me frankly about the campaign. Although his polls showed him ahead of Bentsen, he felt the outcome was far less certain than it would have been against Yarborough. Still, he told me, he welcomed running to the Left of a Democrat (the last time that would be the case for a Texas Republican).

My two days on the Bush campaign included his joint appearance with President Nixon at Longview in East Texas, a segregationist hotbed of backing for George Wallace and, therefore, for Lloyd Bentsen. Nixon, at the Bush campaign's request, excoriated school busing and campus disorders. But Bush in Longview stuck to his campaign theme of reaching out to rebellious youth ("You shouldn't write off an entire generation."). Bush was not just running for the Senate, but for president. In our column the Sunday before the election titled "The GOP's Southern Star," I wrote:

... Bush—young (46), handsome, a Connecticut Yankee turned Houston oilman—is a glittering exponent of the "modern" school of Southern Republicans as contrasted with the "primitives."

... H[e] will be the South's foremost prospect for the national ticket—if not in 1972, then later—providing he defeats Bentsen.

If that sounds like I had gone overboard for Bush, a column by the prudent David Broder at the same time also heralded Bush as the Republican presidential hope for the future. To me Bush was a welcome relief from the coarseness of Nixon and Agnew. But for the last time the old-line Texas Democrats put together agricultural and corporate interests, rural whites, Mexican-Americans, and African-Americans to elect Bentsen.

I thought Al Lowenstein probably would find another congressional seat and, even if he didn't, would remain a major force in the Democratic Party. In fact, he lost four subsequent elections for Congress, and faded from public view before his untimely death.

I thought George H. W. Bush as a two-time loser for the Senate was finished in elective politics and certainly his presidential hopes were gone. I badly underestimated his tenacity.

A further footnote to the 1970 campaign: The Senate contest in Rhode Island attracted no national attention. Longtime Democratic senator John Pastore was so invulnerable that anybody could have had the Republican nomination to oppose him for the asking. The anybody who asked was a nobody—a Jesuit priest new to politics and known as a liberal who wrote movie reviews and lectured about sex. He ran as an antiwar candidate well to the left of Pastore, who was one of the diminishing breed of Democratic lawmakers holding firm on Vietnam.

Pastore was reelected in a landslide with 67.5 percent of the vote. In 1971, I was amazed to read the conservative *Human Events* predicting, with horror, that the priest was in line to enter the White House as a speechwriter. I learned that my old *Herald-Tribune* colleague, Nixon's most liberal speechwriter Ray Price, was sponsoring the priest. I wrote this in the lead item for our Sunday column of June 13, 1971:

A few weeks ago, it was all but determined that Father John McLaughlin, a 43-year-old Jesuit . . . would join President Nixon's writing stable. A former editor of America, the Jesuit publication, he was counted on to liven up Mr. Nixon's generally drab prose style.

Then came the anti-McLaughlin campaign. Some conservatives in the White House . . . argued that McLaughlin's philosophy was much too far to the left of the President's.

I concluded in the column that this opposition "has just about killed the idea." In fact, McLaughlin was resurrected and hired by Nixon. Perhaps the president thought that anybody condemned by Evans and Novak could not be all bad. Once in the White House McLaughlin turned sharply Right. The good Father really did not believe in much more than Nixon did, which perhaps explained why he was the last White House staffer who wanted to go down fighting when the end came in 1974.

IN 1971, Evans and I were in the midst of our second book collaboration, an account of the Nixon administration thus far. Random House gave us a handsome advance of $37,500 ($188,000 in 2007 money) to be divided by us. They also agreed to our request that Bob Gutwillig, our editor for the Johnson book and our partner in the *Evans-Novak Political Report*, edit the book as a freelancer.

Writing a full-fledged biography of Lyndon Johnson four years earlier was far less difficult because LBJ was easier to understand and portray than the inscrutable Nixon. Still, we encountered little or no reluctance by people connected with Nixon, conducting more than fifty interviews of past and current administration officials.

One interview deserves special mention. As he had always planned, Pat Moynihan returned to Harvard at the end of 1970 to preserve his tenure. I arranged a seven p.m. dinner for February 10, 1971, at Locke Ober, my favorite Boston restaurant dating back to my army days at Fort Devens.

Spending an evening with Professor Moynihan always meant a lot of drinking. I was a pretty fair country drinker, but Pat was a big Irishman who could drink me under the table. After predinner cocktails and dinner wine, we moved into postdinner high gear. Moynihan that night was drinking gimlets (gin and Rose's lime juice), while I was sticking with my usual Cutty Sark and water. After first trying to keep up with Pat, at the end of four hours I was having trouble downing one drink to his two. The price for dinner (which I picked up, of course) was $58.65 ($294.70 in 2007 money). When we left Locke Ober at eleven p.m., I could hardly walk. Even though he had a lot more to drink, Pat was in better shape than I and guided me down Tremont Street and across Boston Common to the Ritz-Carlton Hotel, where I was staying.

The next morning I telephoned Rowly in Washington. He was eager to learn what Moynihan had told me. "Not much, I'm afraid," I replied.

"How could that be?" Rowly persisted. "He just didn't have much for us." "Well, that's a real disappointment." The truth, which I did not reveal to my partner, was that I could not remember anything said by either of us amid the haze of alcohol at Locke Ober.

But I had four one-hour tapes recording our entire evening at the restaurant. When I returned to Washington that night, I played the tapes and was pleasantly surprised. For the first three hours, Moynihan was cogent and revealing about what happened inside the White House. I doubt any other single interview provided nearly as much copy for our book. Thank goodness for tape recorders! As for the tape of the fourth hour, the gimlets and Scotches had taken their toll. Nobody shall ever hear that hour of Moynihan and Novak in drunken dialogue.

Nixon in the White House: The Frustration of Power was published the first week of October 1971. Comparing the Nixon book with *Lyndon B. Johnson: The Exercise of Power,* James A. Perry in the *National Observer* called us "the best reporting combination in Washington" who "proved it again last week with the publication of a second superb book. . . . It is just as revealing, just as exciting as their first book." Edwin M. Yoder Jr., editorial page editor of the *Greensboro Daily News* in North Carolina, was even more flattering in a front-page review in the *Washington Post*'s *Book Week:* "Incisive, rich in fascinating detail, fair-minded, commanding in its grasp of the problems of the presidency, it is by all odds the best study to date of Mr. Nixon and his men."

In contrast, critical reviews were written by the reporters covering the White House beat for the *New York Times* and the *Washington Post.* Writing in the *New York Times Book Review,* Robert Semple said that "my own view as a White House reporter, is that some things are not (or were not) as simple as the authors make them out to be." Don Oberdorfer, writing the *Post*'s daily review, was harsher:

> Analyzing supposedly "inside stories" in the Evans-Novak columns and in this book, the reader is forever tempted to cry out to the authors: how do you know? How can you be so sure of your version? There is rarely any attribution or indication of sources, though some are childishly easy to guess. This form of inside journalism, it seems, has to be taken on faith or not at all.

Was it "the reader" or "the White House reporter" who was forever questioning our reporting which he had not obtained himself? It was about this time that the liberal Washington media establishment began to turn on

Evans and Novak. I don't believe I ever exchanged a harsh word with Don Oberdorfer or Bob Semple, but they were members of the liberal establishment and it was becoming clear that we were not.

NOT LONG AFTER the publication of our book, on September 30, 1971, William C. Sullivan was fired by J. Edgar Hoover as the number three official in the Federal Bureau of Investigation. That cut off the best source I ever had inside the FBI.

I met Bill Sullivan in 1969, when we both were addressing a business group. I had heard about Sullivan as the "resident liberal Democrat" in the FBI who was widely regarded as a good influence on Hoover. He introduced himself to me, said he liked our column, suggested we have lunch some day, and followed up on the telephone. I suggested Sans Souci, my restaurant of choice. He said he preferred the Hotel Washington.

The Washington was a little seedy when I tried and failed to get a room there upon my arrival in the capital in May 1957 and it had gone downhill since. Sullivan did not say so, but he did not want to be seen in a place where we would be recognized. With the hotel's dining room frequented by tourists and anonymous bureaucrats, I never saw anyone whom I knew during two years of frequent lunches there with Sullivan.

Bill wore the Hoover-prescribed FBI uniform (dark suit, white shirt, dark tie), but was far from the Bureau's stereotype. He was a short, squat, tough-looking Massachusetts Irish farm boy. He was also a fascinating conversationalist, well read and far-reaching in his thoughts. I found him no liberal and hardly a party-line Democrat. While declaring himself a civil rights advocate, he had doubts about Martin Luther King and detested black extremist groups. He had nothing but contempt for the war resisters and described himself as an admirer of Richard Nixon and John Mitchell.

For our second luncheon, Sullivan had two instructions for me: meet him before lunch in the Hotel Washington men's room and carry a small briefcase. In the men's room, he gave me a document to put in my briefcase. It was an FBI report on the Black Panthers. The Bureau had penetrated the extremist organization, and the report produced a good column. That began a steady flow of FBI secret information about subversive organizations, most of it leading to columns. Sullivan was the creator of COINTELPRO, highly effective spying on domestic subversives that would later come under so much criticism from civil libertarians.

By the time of our third lunch, Bill had come to trust me enough to talk about more than subversives. He gave me my first intimate picture of life inside the FBI, and it was not pretty. I had grown up following the much-publicized exploits of G-men mowing down gangsters in the 1930s, and J. Edgar Hoover was a hero. He was attacked by the Left when he changed his principal focus from crime to communism, which did not diminish him in my eyes.

So I was not prepared for what Sullivan told me about J. Edgar that was worse than any liberal criticism. As Bill described it, the FBI had degenerated into a giant public relations machine for Hoover's aggrandizement. He was a megalomaniac and petty tyrant who micromanaged everything. He strictly prohibited the exchange of information with local law enforcement and the CIA, creating a climate that would bear bitter fruit thirty years hence. This was an eye-opener from the third ranking official in the Bureau.

One day over lunch in 1970, an angry Sullivan told me that Hoover had ordered an end to FBI "bag jobs" on foreign embassies, in which agents became burglars to open diplomats' safes and copy documents for a valuable flow of intelligence. Sullivan ran the whole program. The frustrating element of my relationship with Bill Sullivan was that he put all this inside information about the Bureau absolutely off the record—not to be published. However, by the middle of 1971, he had become so frustrated that he handed me an explosive memo from Attorney General Mitchell to Hoover and gave me permission to paraphrase it, though not quote it directly.

In view of recent political bombings in California (particularly against the Bank of America), Mitchell warned, the FBI's operations had to be improved or it might be replaced by another federal agency (a warning that Sullivan felt led to the creation of the Plumbers and to Nixon's ruin). I reported this in an Evans & Novak column of June 2, 1971, as a signal from the Justice Department that the Nixon administration was unhappy with the seventy-six-year-old FBI director, who now was being told he must take orders. I added:

> . . . [T]he FBI's esteem as a great law enforcement agency, built by Hoover, is now slipping under Hoover. In short, the longer he stays in power the faster his luster as No. 1 G-man—and the luster of the FBI—dims.

On June 3, Hoover wrote me an incendiary, menacing letter, in which he said my column set "a new low" in "accuracy" and was "filled with malicious and venomous innuendo." Sullivan told me J. Edgar was furious. While Hoover had cautiously refrained from illegal wiretaps along with embassy bag jobs, Sullivan told me that the director had ordered the Bureau's Washington field office to put taps on my office and home telephone lines. Sullivan said he quietly countermanded the order.

Sullivan told me how close he was to Mitchell and how much he admired Nixon, but said he wondered whether the president could stand up to Hoover. In the end, he didn't. It was Sullivan who left the FBI, not Hoover. The old director struck back. Based on Sullivan's information, I revealed on October 11, 1971, what nobody else had written about what was going on inside the FBI:

> With the ruthless self-preservation born of 48 years as grand vizier of the FBI, Hoover has lashed back against in-house critics. The result, hidden from public view, has been a reign of terror. Some respected FBI officials have been demoted or summarily transferred, others reduced to nervous prostration in wholly realistic fear of surveillance by Hoover agents.
>
> Enough of this is known at the White House and Justice Department to redouble the private conviction there that Hoover, 76, should go and go soon. But concern about further undermining of President Nixon's standing on the right has mesmerized the administration.

Hoover died in his bed the next May, triumphant to the end over frightened politicians. Sullivan came to our house in the Maryland suburbs in June 1972 for lunch and a long conversation about my plans for a biography of Hoover (a project I abandoned as just too ambitious an undertaking). Before he left, Bill told me I probably would read about his death in some kind of accident but not to believe it. It would be murder.

On November 9, 1977, twenty minutes before sunrise, sixty-five-year-old William C. Sullivan, was walking through the woods near his retirement home in Sugar Hill, New Hampshire, on the way to meet hunting companions. Another hunter, a twenty-two-year-old man using a telescopic sight on a .30 caliber rifle, said he mistook Sullivan for a deer, shot him in the neck, and killed him instantly. Tass, the Soviet news agency, was accustomed to staged accidents and claimed Sullivan had died in an FBI/CIA plot. The authorities called it an accident, fining the shooter (the son of a state policeman) five hundred dollars and taking away his hunting license for ten years. Sullivan's collaborator on his memoir, the television news writer Bill Brown, wrote that he and Sullivan's family were "convinced" that the death was "accidental."

Sullivan's death did not prevent publication of the memoir, telling all about the disgrace of J. Edgar Hoover and the FBI. After Watergate, with all the principals dead or out of office, it received little attention.

LATE IN 1971, I attended the annual black-tie dinner at the Washington Hilton Hotel in Washington of the White House Correspondents Association. I started attending these events in 1959 and had gone just about every year by 1971. I'm not sure why I enjoyed these events that I now find unendurable, except that in those days I would welcome a night of marathon drinking.

In 1971, I was the guest of my friend and office neighbor, Martin Nolan of the *Boston Globe*. Another guest of Marty's was twenty-seven-year-old John F. Kerry, who had made a stir that year as a war protester and leader of the radical Vietnam Veterans Against the War (VVAW). He had testified to Congress wearing combat decorations on his battle fatigues (against regulations), was filmed throwing away what was thought to be his decorations, and appeared on *Meet the Press* accusing the U.S. government of war crimes. I thought then it was a disgraceful performance.

Meeting Kerry for the first time, I thought him arrogant and pretentious. Toward the end of the evening, Kerry approached me. "Bob," he said, "I'm going to run for Congress next year, and I'd be privileged to feel free to call on you for advice now and then." I replied: "John, what makes you think I'm for you?" Kerry did not call on me and was defeated for Congress. I did not see him again until thirteen years later when he ran for the Senate.

CHAPTER 21

"Amnesty, Abortion and Acid"

I N 1954, Maine for the last time held its election two months before the rest of the country. That election put the national spotlight on a new governor, Ed Muskie. He was tall, young (forty), and handsome in a rugged way. He was a Roman Catholic, the son of Polish immigrants, and a Democrat in a state where previous officeholders had all been Protestant, Yankee, and Republican. His victory signaled the coming political realignment that would end upper New England as a Republican preserve.

After four years as governor, Muskie was elected to the U.S. Senate in 1958. His Down East accent and apparent dignity helped make him the most celebrated member of the oversize Democratic Senate class of 1958. As he quickly separated himself from Majority Leader Lyndon B. Johnson, however, it seemed to me Muskie was just another reflexive liberal who would not amount to much in the midcentury Senate.

Nobody would have marked Muskie for national leadership until Hubert Humphrey in 1968 picked him as his vice presidential running mate for the old-fashioned reason of ticket balancing. His actual campaigning was undistinguished, but a powerful, nationally televised speech on the eve of the 1970 midterm elections transformed Muskie into the front-runner for the 1972 presidential nomination and the Democrat shown by polls as the man who could beat Nixon.

Muskie's appeal was as the cool New Englander, calm when all about him were in tumult. Nothing could have been further from the truth. He was an erratic personality with an uncontrollable temper and soon was detested by many of the top Democratic operatives who had hurried to his standard. He also was dull and devoid of ideas.

Early in 1971, Muskie invited me to a one-on-one lunch in his Capitol hideaway. The customary heavy luncheon fare of that era included prelunch drinks, shrimp cocktail, steak and French fries, red wine, and apple pie with ice cream. The session was a monologue, with Muskie droning on about his agenda for America. The pedestrian rhetoric, accompanied by the cuisine, nearly put me to sleep.

Finally, the senator asked for *my* views on the world. I usually hate it when a politician does that, but this time I welcomed the respite from Muskie's soliloquy. I was no more than a minute into my recital, however, when the prospective presidential candidate did fall asleep—a deep slumber with snoring. I stopped speaking, but that had no effect on the sleeping senator. At last, I cleared my throat loudly. Muskie awoke with a start, and I said: "And those are my views, Senator." "Very interesting, Bob," he said.

In May 1971, I experienced firsthand the Muskie temper. He was campaigning in Wisconsin as the undisputed favorite to win that state's important primary election ten and one-half months later. I planned to spend Sunday, May 16, covering him and asked for a few minutes with the senator. I was told I could interview him on a private flight that morning from Milwaukee to Wausau.

By the time we boarded the plane, Muskie was steaming. His Sunday morning in Milwaukee began by breakfasting with labor leaders. In introducing him, an old-time union boss commented: "We're familiar with muskies here in Wisconsin. I caught one fishing just the other day." The labor skates laughed uproariously, but I noticed the senator was not amused. That was followed by an aimless one-hour conversation with disengaged students. Muskie was rushed from there to the small plane taking him to Wausau, where he would hurry to play a round of golf with one of that city's favorite sons, Tony Kubek, a famous New York Yankee who then was the expert commentator on NBC's baseball *Game of the Week*. The last straw in a terribly crowded morning for Muskie, I believe, was having to spend an hour with a columnist who had been increasingly critical of him. Politics aside, I was told he did not like me personally.

The plane's door had hardly closed when Muskie turned on his advance man. The senator raged at him, ignoring me (the only other passenger in the small aircraft). "Are you crazy?" Muskie snarled. "Don't you have any regard for me? Do you realize that your schedule doesn't leave me any time to go to mass today? That's just outrageous!" When Muskie subsided, I gingerly asked him a question (certainly not about his complaint to the advance man). His answer was curt and uninformative, his manner indicating how unhappy he was to be with me. He then turned again to the advance man with another diatribe, even angrier than before. So it went all the way to Wausau, worthless answers to me alternating with loud recriminations against his aide.

I concluded my column from Milwaukee by noting "irrational scheduling, uncoordinated speechwriting and tardy organization" had not prevented Muskie from being the front-runner in a weak field. I didn't write about his Sunday morning temper tantrum. Reporters permitted close access to candidates did not reveal such incidents in those days. Nor did I write about whether a person with a hair-trigger temper was the right man to be president.

IN MID-APRIL 1971 I received a call from Nixon's speechwriter Bill Safire. We had been talking about far leftist elements taking over the anti-Vietnam War movement, and now Bill advised me he had interesting documents for me. The White House was one block from our office, and he walked over the papers. We met behind my building on G Street, with Safire handing me a large unmarked envelope. The envelope contained domestic intelligence reports on the National Peace Action Coalition (NPAC), sponsors of a giant antiwar demonstration planned for Saturday, April 24. They disclosed that NPAC was dominated by the Socialist Workers Party (SWP) and the party's youth arm, the Young Socialist Alliance (YSA). The SWP and YSA together comprised the Trotskyist Communist movement in America. The papers listed by name prominent Trotskyites who were running NPAC and the peace demonstrations.

Trotskyites? That was something out of the past. Leon Trotsky was a Bolshevik leader who lost out to Stalin in a struggle for power and went into exile. He led a global movement to the Left of Stalinism in advocating immediate worldwide revolution—until Stalin in 1940 had him murdered in Mexico City.

I called my source at the FBI, Assistant Director William C. Sullivan, and confirmed the facts in Safire's documents. The YSA was now the most important radical organization on college campuses, and the reborn Trotskyist Communists were the most dynamic, effective organization on the American far Left.

The relevance for Safire was Edmund S. Muskie's endorsement of the April 24 antiwar demonstration. I called the senator, and asked whether he had checked the background of NPAC leaders before endorsing their event. He replied: "There is no way for us to inquire into the ideological beliefs of anybody in this organization." That quote was a building block for the Evans & Novak column of April 19, 1971. Titled "Muskie and the Trotskyites," it proved one of the most heavily criticized columns I ever wrote:

In their rising antiwar sentiment, Muskie and other prominent Democrats are determined to back *any* non-violent peace demonstration.

. . . [H]e has aligned himself with left revolutionary forces who do not merely oppose the U.S. participation in the war but openly advocate a Communist victory. . . .

Growing antiwar passion has shielded these realities from the liberals. Well-organized and purposeful, the Trotskyists take the trouble to plan nationwide demonstrations, and liberals such as Muskie feel compelled to cooperate. The result is what would have been unimaginable a few short years ago: Hundreds of thousands of Americans marching in their capital under Trotskyist command.

The outrage this column generated was typified by the reaction, face-to-face, of Muskie's national political director Mark Shields. We and our wives were guests at a Saturday night dinner in late April hosted by Bob McCandless and his wife at their Northwest Washington home.

I first met Mark Shields after the 1968 election when I went to Capitol Hill to report on Teddy Kennedy ousting Russell Long as Senate Democratic Whip. Mark identified himself to me as a former aide to Senator Bill Proxmire of Wisconsin and a presidential campaign operative for Bobby Kennedy. He had a tip for me concerning Teddy's successful race for whip. In the intervening two years plus, Shields supplied me with a few more news morsels (usually involving his clients as a campaign consultant).

Until the McCandless dinner, we never had exchanged a harsh word. The problem that night was that Shields and I were nonstop drinkers. I put down one Scotch and water after another. Shields could consume as much beer at one sitting as anybody I ever encountered. We were both pretty drunk sitting in the living room after dinner, when Shields started abusing me—at the top of his voice—for "Muskie and the Trotskyites." He called it a McCarthyite slandering of a fine American and derided me for being so foolish as to think that the followers of Leon Trotsky were a menace in the year 1971. I responded stupidly with an ad hominem response, asserting that Mark was in the Muskie campaign only because he wanted to ride in limos and enjoy other perquisites of political power. He shouted back that this constituted an assault on his integrity, and I shouted back that I intended it as such. We were both on our feet now, and McCandless—fearing that words would not settle our dispute—stepped in to break it up.

MANY DEMOCRATIC activists remembered that Muskie never joined the peace bloc until after the Humphrey-Muskie ticket was defeated. So

Muskie's strategists considered it prudent politics to endorse peace rallies, no matter how unsavory their sponsors might be. But Muskie was also tugged in the opposite direction—personified by Ben Barnes, the thirty-one-year-old lieutenant governor of Texas.

Barnes was a shooting star who had become speaker of the Texas House at age twenty-eight. A charismatic and immensely likable redhead, Barnes had been adopted as the Democratic hope of the future by Lyndon Johnson, Bob Strauss, and (before he moved over to the Republicans) John Connally. Strauss thought that the 1972 election for governor would be a way station for Barnes to the presidency (maybe in 1980). I agreed with Strauss.

I had grown close to Strauss since meeting him in 1968. In 1971, he became treasurer of the Democratic National Committee and the preservator of the party's fading establishment. Since his election to the party post required his frequent presence in Washington, he started a branch of his big Dallas-based law firm, Akin Gump, and brought a young lawyer north to open a small office. Akin Gump would become one of the largest Washington lobbying firms, with hundreds of lawyers (more than in the Dallas home office) now working out of the Robert Strauss building on DuPont Circle.

By 1971, people were noting there was never a critical word about Strauss in our column. I started betting with Bob, a hundred dollars a game, between my Washington Redskins and his Dallas Cowboys. One night that autumn, Strauss and I scheduled a dinner with our wives at the Jockey Club. As we entered the restaurant, he suddenly pulled out a hundred-dollar bill to pay me for losing our last bet. His motive instantly became clear. Standing nearby was former California governor Pat Brown. Before greeting Brown, Strauss said to me in a loud voice as he handed me the c-note: "Bob, that last column was excellent! Thanks very much!" Brown's eyes widened at the sight. Strauss loved the stunt, and was still retelling it more than thirty years later.

(Strauss was involved in my last personal contact with Lyndon Johnson. Bob invited Geraldine and me to the January 1, 1971, Cotton Bowl game at Dallas in which Notre Dame and quarterback Joe Theisman upset heavily favored Texas. LBJ was seated not far from us on the fifty-yard line, and I shook hands with him during a pregame reception. He seemed frosty toward me and proved it when he got Strauss aside. "Just keep hanging around with Novak," Strauss later informed me that the former president told him, "and he'll stab you in the back just like he did me." In fact, my friendship with Strauss has more than survived my occasional public criticism of him over the years.)

In 1971, Strauss was committed to a centrist Democratic Party, and

Barnes seemed to him the man to lead it. I then thought it in the best interests of the country if the two political parties resembled each other (a view I later came to reject). My favorite Republicans then looked a little like Democrats (for example, Nelson Rockefeller) and my favorite Democrats looked a little like Republicans (mistakenly I put Ben Barnes in that category).

In retrospect, I don't think Barnes was conservative at all but made himself look that way trying to survive in a Texas inexorably going Republican. After his political career imploded unexpectedly in 1972, he became a conventional Democrat. (In his sixties in the new century, Barnes was describing himself, in jest, as the last white Democrat in Texas and had become the fund-raiser for the state's liberal Democrats.) He was to be part of the attack on George W. Bush in the 2004 presidential campaign, claiming credit for favoritism toward Bush in getting him a Texas Air National Guard Commission.

Barnes gave me lots of news tidbits, but mostly I just enjoyed drinking and having fun with him. On one occasion when Geraldine and I were making our annual Christmas visit to her family in Texas, Ben sent a plane to pick us up in Hillsboro and take us to his luxurious new home in Brownwood for a steak dinner and an overnight stay. Geraldine and I once hosted a dinner for Barnes (attended by Strauss and other Washington notables) at our suburban Maryland home. I was embarrassed when a couple of Washington correspondents for Texas newspapers showed up to "cover" the event.

Barnes's name appeared in the Evans & Novak column so often it became a laughing matter among my press buddies. As I reviewed my Ben Barnes columns for this book, I was surprised by how many of them concerned his efforts to pull Muskie—as the presumptive presidential nominee—to the political center. They failed. Muskie and his team felt a genuine kinship to the war protesters and other radicals.

FOR MORE THAN two years, Bill Safire had been a source for Rowly and me in violation of Nixon's poorly enforced ban on contacts with us. But Safire's transmission to me in April 1971 of the material linking Muskie to the Trotskyites was an authorized leak. It soon became clear to me that Haldeman or perhaps Nixon himself had decided a better strategy than boycotting Evans and Novak would be to use the column. In hindsight, I preferred boycott.

I did not become aware of one egregious attempt to use us for about three years. In late 1971, I received in the mail a half-dozen Muskie campaign memos. I authenticated through my own sources inside the campaign that they were the real thing. I was delighted to open a flow of secret Muskie information, but there was one serious drawback. As news, the memos were worthless.

I did not want to turn off a source who I thought eventually might come up with something valuable. So to encourage her (I deduced from the tone of the brief covering letters that my source was a disillusioned woman volunteer at the Muskie campaign), I cited two of the missives in our Sunday Evans & Novak item columns. My first use of the material was a secondary item in the column of Sunday, December 12, 1971, which described Muskie as interfering in a California tax initiative. A couple of weeks later a secondary Sunday item was based on a memo listing Muskie's left-wing foreign policy advisers. This was thin gruel. When I received no more anonymous documents, I assumed my source was discouraged by the skimpy use I made of the material.

I did not learn the truth until 1974 when former White House aide Jeb Magruder, awaiting federal prison time in the Watergate scandal, published his memoir *An American Life*. Magruder, who in 1971 had left the White House to become deputy chairman of the Committee to Re-elect the President (CREEP), revealed that CREEP chairman John Mitchell was under pressure to collect "intelligence" from the Muskie campaign. Mitchell assigned that task to Magruder, who placed "a retired taxi driver" as a volunteer driver for Muskie at the price of $1,000 a month ($4,840 in 2007 money). No disaffected woman, this was my source.

While my two Sunday items were the only fruit of Magruder's initiative, his memoir left the false impression that the Nixon operation was giving me a steady flow of information about the Muskie campaign. Magruder claimed not to recall whether he personally gave me the pilfered documents or (as was the case) mailed them to me anonymously.

Not until early 1972 did Magruder contact me (on orders of his superiors), asking for a lunch meeting. This was the first overt gesture toward me from Nixon's dark (Haldeman-Mitchell) side, and I took Magruder to lunch at Sans Souci three times. (Years later, one of Mitchell's aides told me how irritated CREEP bean counters were by the pricey expense accounts submitted by Magruder for our Sans Souci lunches. This aide was surprised when I informed him that I had paid for all of Magruder's meals.)

Jeb Stuart Magruder came from old but recently impoverished American stock. (General John B. Magruder, one of the less-competent Confederate commanders, was an ancestor.) After face-to-face contact, I sized up Magruder as a slick operator who could not be trusted. Magruder was carefully programmed as to what he could tell me and would not engage in the gossipy trivia that I treasured.

Magruder did give me one story, however, that at the time I considered a scoop. The Evans & Novak column of April 19, 1972, reported that Nixon's staff had issued this ultimatum to the city of San Diego:

> Become more cooperative or, even at this late date, we shall move the 1972 Republican National Convention to another city.
>
> The Nixon men carefully avoid public statements. But private negotiations in San Diego indicate their patience is gone. Specifically at issue is whether the San Diego Arena can be ready by the Aug. 21 convention opening. Beyond that, Mr. Nixon's agents are fed up with what they regard as price-gouging obstructionism and lethargy in San Diego. . . .
>
> That habitually secretive Nixon men would purposely expose dirty linen testifies to the seriousness of the situation. Unless they get satisfaction this week from the hitherto intractable arena owners, they warn, immediately steps will be taken toward a new convention site—most likely Miami Beach, where the Democrats will meet in July.

At Sans Souci, Magruder showed me an internal memo that detailed the problems with San Diego I wrote about. Everything in the column was completely accurate and the convention did move to Miami Beach, but I did not learn the *whole* truth until Magruder's *An American Life* in 1974.

The main reason for moving the convention, Magruder wrote, was something he never mentioned to me: fear of "massive demonstrations during the convention" that "would turn our convention into a nightmare like the 1968 Democratic Convention in Chicago." He cited an estimate of 250,000 demonstrators by G. Gordon Liddy, who as CREEP's general counsel would help plan the Watergate break-in.

"How did we leave San Diego," Magruder asked in his book, "without admitting the embarrassing fact that we'd been forced out by the threat of antiwar demonstrations?" So the Nixon campaign concocted "a cover story," accurate but incomplete, that was given to me. Magruder explained in his memoir:

> My talk with Novak resulted in a column that said exactly what we'd hoped it would say. . . .
>
> A good leak must go to a writer who had both credibility and mass circulation, and Novak had both. I might have leaked the story to a

wire-service reporter, but a wire story ("Republicans Ponder Convention Switch") would probably have gotten less attention than an Evans-Novak column, with its aura of inside information.

I had been used. Nixon's change in attitude toward Rowly and me was confirmed in 1994 by *The Haldeman Diaries.* On November 8, 1972, the day after Nixon's reelection landslide, Haldeman said the president told him "to tell Henry [Kissinger] that it's OK to talk to Evans and Novak, but not to the other people."

Nixon had cracked the code on Evans and Novak. We were so ravenous for exclusive news that we were susceptible to manipulation by leaks, compromising our credibility. I am surprised other politicians did not use this technique and surprised Nixon used it so seldom.

I FIRST HAD covered George McGovern in his unsuccessful 1960 run for the Senate from South Dakota. He was then thirty-eight years old, a college professor elected to Congress four years earlier. McGovern had been a college debater, but he was blown out of the water in the debate I watched between him and incumbent senator Karl Mundt, the tough Old Guard Republican. McGovern came back two years later, in 1962, to win election to the Senate and become a leader of the peace bloc harassing President Johnson.

Now he was campaigning for the Democratic presidential nomination, a Great Plains radical droning on with outrageous formulations in his nasal regional monotone. I traveled with him in New Hampshire less than two weeks before the March 7 primary. Only a handful of reporters and no television crews were covering McGovern one night, and a young female reporter asked me what I—a widely syndicated columnist—was doing there. Muskie, I told her, was a sure winner in New Hampshire and I was there just to get a New Hampshire dateline on my column. What I learned from my sources in the state I reported in the Evans & Novak column of February 28 (datelined "Manchester, N.H.")

To Muskie managers here, McGovern's onslaught [attacking Muskie's '68 Vietnam position] in this lackluster campaign could reduce the Muskie total, once 70 per cent in polls, to around 50 per cent. Even so, a Muskie win is inevitable. At best, McGovern cannot hope for much more than 25 per cent, a poor second in a drab field.

That reeked of overconfidence, born of too much success in fourteen years of national political forecasting. It was also an embarrassing example of being overtaken by events. I wrote the column on Friday, February 25, for publication in Monday's papers. I was home in Rockville, Maryland, for the weekend, and missed one of the bizarre events in American politics that occurred Saturday, February 26.

That was my forty-first birthday, and I was quietly celebrating it with my family. But Ed Muskie that night permitted his temper to destroy his candidacy. He could no longer tolerate the assault on him by William Loeb's *Manchester Union Leader.* Attacking Loeb in a speech delivered in front of the *Union Leader* building in downtown Manchester, Muskie's voice broke and he appeared to be crying.

I phoned sources in New Hampshire Saturday night, but they shrugged off the incident. I decided, in error, there was no need to change the Monday column. On March 7, Muskie won 46.4 percent of the vote to McGovern's 37.2 percent. In terms of expectations and momentum, Muskie was through,

One week after New Hampshire, on March 14, George Wallace parlayed a campaign based on opposition to school busing into a Florida landslide of 42 percent. Hubert Humphrey was far behind in second place with 18.6 percent. Muskie was fourth with 8.9 percent.

Muskie went on national television from Miami to ascribe to the 42 percent of Florida Democrats who voted for Wallace "some of the worst instincts of which human beings are capable." Nixon White House staffer Dick Cook telephoned me Wednesday morning, March 15, in a state of euphoria. "Muskie was attacking Archie Bunker," Cook said. I used Cook's quote (attributed to a "delighted Nixon aide") in an Evans & Novak column of March 17. I reported a "panicky depression" inside the Democratic Party that Muskie was driving the Archie Bunkers into the arms of George Wallace and Richard Nixon.

NOT LONG AFTER the Florida primary, I went to the campus of Kenyon College in Gambier, Ohio, for a three-day seminar on "The Mass Media and Modern Democracy" sponsored by the Public Affairs Conference Center (PACC). This was the eighth closed-door PACC conference I had attended, first at the University of Chicago and later at Kenyon in rural central Ohio. It was the first such conference for which I submitted a paper. And it was this paper on the mass media that signaled my ideological orientation had changed from center to right. "The New Journalism" argued:

. . . [T]he press corps has been ideologized into a part of the liberal establishment. More and more, the members of the Washington press share in total the worldview taken by the dominant liberals who control the Democratic Party. More and more they share axioms that profoundly influence their coverage of day-to-day events in the worlds of politics and government.

I listed seven "axioms" that were "shared by the Washington press corps of 1973": anti–Vietnam War, reduction of defense spending, environmental protection rather than economic growth, total war against "white racism" using such weapons as forced school busing, protection of civil liberties against President Nixon, greater federal funding for "social rebuilding," and redistribution of wealth through the tax system and fiscal policy.

> [I]ncreasingly a rigid conformity has emerged among the Washington press corps, which reflects in part conformity in the colleges producing the new journalists. But beyond this, the young journalist who violates these axioms can scarcely expect a rapid rise up the ladder of advancement. . . .
>
> The result is a gap of widening proportions between the national journalist and the mass of Americans, paralleling a gap between liberal politicians and the masses, specifically the white workingman.

Next, I addressed the transformation of journalists into advocates—not TV commentators, editorial writers, columnists or writers in opinion journals, but supposedly straight reporters. I concluded that the news media's necessary function of "watchdog critic" in a free society cannot be performed if it has "lost credibility." I called for "the return of the media to a goal of objectivity."

This might seem tame in light of how the media has been attacked since then, but these words were incendiary in 1972. My first sign of that came at the Kenyon seminar, with my main antagonist being Geraldine's old boss in Lyndon Johnson's office, George Reedy. It had been a long time since George was a United Press reporter, but he still considered himself a newspaperman and was now dean of Marquette University's College of Journalism.

What Reedy said was the pure denial I have heard endlessly from my liberal colleagues. First, he argued "no newspaperman in Washington would accept all seven axioms—certainly not in the form in which they are written—let alone a substantial number." Second, most of Washington's news comes from nonelite journalists "who do *not* eat at the Sans Souci." Third, there is no liberal domination of the news media. ("I am still unclear as to the precise nature of Mr. Novak's definition of liberalism.")

Papers from previous PACC sessions had attracted no attention. Their exposure was limited to publication, about two years after each conference, in books nobody reviewed. The twenty-five participants invited to PACC sessions were senior public officials, corporate executives, leading academics, and prominent journalists—and, this year, a thirty-one-year-old Senate aide, George F. Will.

As the most junior person at the Kenyon conference, George kept his remarks pithy, in agreement with my paper. He brought my paper back to Washington and gave it to his boss, Senator Gordon Allott, to insert in the *Congressional Record* (where it was printed in agate type).

President Nixon's news summarizers spotted my paper there and put it on the distribution list for senior staffers. I was unaware of the White House attention until Sunday morning, May 7, when I watched Nixon domestic policy chief John Ehrlichman interviewed on *Meet the Press.* Hugh Sidey of *Time* suggested that Nixon was leading an orchestrated attack on the news media. Ehrlichman's answer surprised me:

> There is no orchestration as far as I know in the Administration on this subject. I see, around the country, important members of the journalism community also raising questions about the objectivity and the reliability of the media. I don't know if you have seen the speech and the paper that Robert Novak of Evans and Novak delivered in the Midwest the other day, but I think it is a very important and useful paper on the problems of the media and their objectivity. It ran in the *Congressional Record* on the first of May, and it seems to me that ought to be required reading not only for every journalist, for everybody who watches the news or picks up a newspaper. It talks about advocacy journalism and the dedication of journalists today to salting away in their reporting on facts their own personal points of view of what should or should not be done. . . .
>
> If the nature of fact reporting in the media has changed in that, and I think every journalist has to be alert to it, and he has to figure out whether that is really the direction in which he wants to see his profession run.

With no idea what Ehrlichman was talking about, Sidey and the other *Meet the Press* panelists did not respond. Ehrlichman's comments signified that the Nixon White House had moved away from Spiro Agnew's primitive media bashing to a more sophisticated message. What chilled me was that I had supplied the gospel text for the sermon.

In Sacramento, Governor Ronald Reagan, always alert to ideological nuances, at his weekly press conference also recommended that assembled reporters read my paper. He even rhapsodized that Bob Novak was undergoing the same conversion to conservatism that Ronald Reagan had experienced twenty years earlier. I told friends then that this was sheer nonsense, but Reagan actually was close to the truth. When I wrote a critical column about the governor on an unrelated subject, Reagan told another press conference that I was in denial about my transformation. That, too, was closer to the truth than I would admit.

Thanks to Ehrlichman and Reagan, my heretical views were now exposed to the journalism fraternity. Ben H. Bagdikian, a veteran newspaperman and media critic who was filling the new rotating post of ombudsman for the *Washington Post,* reacted much as George Reedy had. He did so in a full-page rebuttal in the Outlook section of Sunday's *Washington Post* on July 16, 1972. That was an extraordinary allocation of valuable newspaper space to rebut a report that to this day never has been reprinted in the *Post* or any newspaper.

I believe the Kenyon report and the reaction marked my departure from the mainstream of Washington journalism. I had broken a tribal taboo in publicly criticizing colleagues. Rowly, of course, had no part in this. We talked about issues endlessly but never about this little paper that proved decisive in the public perception of us. He was a loyal partner and never criticized me for it, but I am sure he was not happy about what I did.

ON APRIL 25 George McGovern captured the Massachusetts primary by a mind-boggling thirty-one percentage points. The next day I phoned Democratic politicians around the country who agreed with my assessment that blue-collar workers voting for McGovern did not understand what he really stood for. What one of these politicians said would have far-reaching consequences for me. He was quoted in the fourth paragraph of the Evans & Novak column of April 27 that reported the seemingly comatose candidacy of Hubert Humphrey had been revived by fear of McGovern:

> The reason is given by one liberal Senator, whose voting record differs little from McGovern's. He feels McGovern's surging popularity depends on public ignorance of his acknowledged public positions. "The people don't know McGovern is for amnesty, abortion and legalization of pot," he told us. "Once middle America—Catholic Middle America, in particular—find this out, he's dead."

With that, McGovern was the "Triple-A" candidate who supported "Amnesty, Abortion and Acid." It became Humphrey's battle cry to stop McGovern—especially in the Nebraska primary on May 9. McGovern backed away from his past positions on all three issues (even amnesty for Vietnam draft evaders), and he beat Humphrey in Nebraska by six percentage points. But the Triple A label was to haunt McGovern into the autumn campaign against Nixon.

The column was correctly attributed to me rather than Rowly. The liberal establishment—including journalistic colleagues—never forgave me. This finally put me beyond redemption, and the issue did not die with the 1972 campaign.

In 1973, Timothy Crouse, a contributing editor for the left-wing *Rolling Stone* magazine, published a book about press coverage of the 1972 campaign, *The Boys on the Bus,* that became a bible for Washington journalists. In it, Crouse said my Triple-A characterization of McGovern was "simply wrong" and "the lowest blow of all" to the senator's campaign. He quoted Dick Dougherty, McGovern's press secretary, as saying of Rowly and me: "Well, those guys have to write five columns every week, so I guess sometimes they sort of soup things up to get a good story." Was Dougherty suggesting that we would make up a quote just to "soup things up"?

Confrontational language was out of character for Richard Dougherty, our colleague in the last days of the *New York Herald-Tribune* as national political correspondent for the 1964 campaign. Because our personal relationship always had been cordial, I did not expect what Dougherty wrote about the Triple-A column in his 1973 memoir of the McGovern campaign *(Goodbye Mr. Christian)*, published after Crouse's book:

> I've known Bob Novak and Rowley [sic] Evans for years and I like them, although they're mean as hell and somewhat to the right of McKinley. But I don't believe for a minute that any *liberal* senator, at least a Democratic liberal, told them McGovern was for abortion and the legalization of marijuana. . . .
>
> Still, the rascals printed it, and it did enormous damage around the country. It sounded like a fact even though it was attributed to an unnamed, and possibly nonexistent, source. . . .
>
> It was pointless to get a retraction out of Evans and Novak.

Dick did not call us with this complaint when the column ran or in the preparation of his book. After the book's publication, we never spoke again.

To rebut this slander, however, I thought we had to get the source (whom I shall call "Senator X") to permit me to identify him by name. I made a lunch date with him, and got Rowly—much better than I in applying soft soap—to come along.

At Sans Souci, the very liberal Senator X did not disavow his quote (as I feared he might). Indeed, he told us the calamitous Nixon landslide against McGovern substantiated his—and our—warning of what McGovern's nomination would entail. Nevertheless Senator X said he was going to run for reelection, and he feared terrible retribution from the McGovernites in his state if he were identified as an author of their hero's destruction. That ended what had been a mutually beneficial relationship between me and Senator X, in which we had been dinner guests in each other's home.

I had not been in touch with Senator X for thirty years, when I began working on these memoirs in 2003. I wrote him—now *Mr.* X, retired from the Senate and from public life—asking whether I could identify him. After all, I said, there is no longer fear of retribution from McGovernites. His answer was swift and succinct: "Dear Bob, what I told you—or was it, Rowly?—it was off the record, and I still consider it that way."

Four years later, on Sunday morning, March 4, 2007, Mr. X died of heart failure at the age of seventy-seven—relieving me of the need to conceal his identity. It was Thomas F. Eagleton, who at the time he delivered his Triple A quote was forty-two years old and in his fourth year as a U.S. senator. Neither of us dreamed, when we talked on the phone April 26, 1972, that two and one-half months later McGovern would select Eagleton as his vice presidential running mate. Only eighteen days after that, Eagleton would be forced off the ticket for failing to inform McGovern that in the 1960s he had been hospitalized and undergone shock treatment for a nervous disorder. He was to serve for thirteen more years in the Senate.

The ironic source of the Triple A quote was kept secret for thirty-six years. Eagleton shared McGovern's opposition to the Vietnam intervention but was an antiabortion Catholic who favored a constitutional amendment to overturn *Roe v. Wade*. He never repudiated what he said about McGovern while concealing the fact that he said it.

ON SATURDAY, May 6, my friend Ben Barnes's career in elective politics ended in Texas's gubernatorial primary. Tarnished by purported involvement in a state political scandal and overwhelmed by the McGovernite tide, he placed third. The linear successor to Lyndon B. Johnson and John B. Connally was finished, and so were the Tory Democrats of Texas.

On the Friday night before the primary, I sat drinking with Lieutenant Governor Barnes and his closest friends in his State Capitol quarters in Austin. The mood was eat, drink, and be merry, for tomorrow we lose. We left the Capitol late that evening to drink margaritas and eat tacos in a Tex-Mex restaurant. Everybody was a little drunk when the loud Texas talk and laughter subsided for a moment, and Barnes looked at me. "Novak," he said. "I am going to get my ass beat tomorrow. Are you still for me?" I replied: "Yes I am, Barnes. But I'm also still for the South Vietnamese Army." Everybody roared, and I was complimented for gallows humor as a promising political career was being extinguished.

THIS WAS THE third presidential campaign for Hubert Humphrey, at age sixty-one facing the last chance for his life's ambition. The "white knight of civil rights," who provoked a walkout of Deep South delegates at the 1948 Democratic delegation, had become the candidate of the Democratic Party's dying remnants: southerners, old-line labor leaders, and big city bosses, plus pragmatists who perceived in George McGovern the embodiment of defeat and decline for the party.

Humphrey was all that stood between the Democratic Party and McGovernism. Humphrey won four straight primaries that brought him to a showdown with McGovern in the California primary on June 6. The winner there would be nominated. I spent two weeks working out of the Century Plaza Hotel in Los Angeles. (Rowly was in Moscow at the same time, covering the Nixon-Brezhnev summit, our dateline alternating between California and Moscow.) I was delighted when Larry Spivak selected me for the panel in a weeknight *Meet the Press* debate between Humphrey and McGovern from Los Angeles on May 30, one week before the primary.

I was standing alone in the cavernous NBC studio in Burbank prior to the debate, thinking over my questions when I came under intense observation by twenty-five-year-old Tim Crouse as he collected material for *The Boys on the Bus.* Crouse was a clever writer with an impressive lineage as the son of playwright Russel Crouse and brother of actress Lindsay Crouse. Beneath its congenial style, *The Boys* was a left-wing screed assailing the news media for mistreatment of McGovern.

Crouse's portrait of me began with his impression from the NBC debate, comparing me with the other hundred or so reporters at the Burbank sound stage:

. . . [T]hey were making a party of it—waving, backslapping, telling stories, laughing. But Novak was standing off to himself. He was short and squat, with swarthy skin, dark gray hair, a slightly rumpled suit, and an apparently permanent scowl. He kept his hands in his pockets and looked at the floor. Some of the other reporters pointed him out and whispered about him almost as if he were a cop come to shush up a good party.

"Novak looks evil," said a gentle, middle-aged *Times*man. "He can't help it, poor fellow." . . .

"There's a real tight coil of bitterness in the guy," said a magazine writer. "So much of what he writes and talks about in private tends to reinforce one impression: he's against anything good-looking, anything fashionable, anything slick—and liberalism is slick in the circles he travels in. I think that's why he's down on it."

Crouse was three years out of college with his journalistic experience largely limited to pop music criticism. *The Boys on the Bus* is full of errors, but I shall mention only those affecting Evans and me. I never served in Korea. I went to college before, not after, my military service. I never was "a great friend of Lyndon Johnson's." Rowly was selected to write a column for the *Herald-Tribune* by Jim Bellows, not by Jock Whitney. Rowly never was a "Dewey Republican." And he always spelled his name "Rowly," not "Rowley."

In *The Boys,* Crouse credited me for hitting both McGovern and Humphrey with "tough questions" in the debate. I noted that separate studies had independently calculated that McGovern's welfare plan would mean higher federal income taxes for anybody making over $12,000 a year ($59,982 in 2007 equivalents). McGovern's answer was not reassuring: "It is very difficult, Mr. Novak, for the Senate staff committee, or for a newspaper writer, or for George McGovern or anyone else to put an exact cost factor on this program." Humphrey, the Vietnam hawk of 1968, now was claiming no difference between him and McGovern in supporting an immediate end to all U.S. aid to South Vietnam. In view of the North Vietnamese invasion then under way, I asked Humphrey, whether "considering your past positions, if you would be willing to cut them off flat?" His reply was chilling: "Yes, I would, because I believe that it is no longer in our interest to be there."

Reflecting the overall California campaign, McGovern was shrugging off implications of his radical left-wing agenda and Humphrey was poaching on McGovern's signature issue of Vietnam. Advantage McGovern. Indeed, McGovern would narrowly defeat Humphrey to clinch the nomination—with fateful consequences.

. . .

FIVE DAYS AFTER McGovern's victory in California, on June 11, 1972, a U.S. military helicopter carrying John Paul Vann crashed in the Central Highlands of South Vietnam. He was killed instantly. I had spent no more than a combined six or seven days with Vann during my reporting trips to Vietnam in 1970 and 1971. But we were together continuously during that short time and had been in touch with each other the past two years with John contacting me on his visits to Washington. I felt his death was a devastating blow to the diminishing chances to save Vietnam from communism.

As Rowly or I had made a protracted reporting trip to Vietnam for each of the last seven years, we thought we could give Vietnam a rest for the election year of 1972. It was a mistake. On March 31, North Vietnamese Army (NVA) regular divisions poured across the Demilitarized Zone into a South Vietnam stripped of U.S. infantry and relying on the Army of the Republic of Vietnam (ARVN). The ARVN repelled the invading troops. Devastating U.S. saturation bombing was one reason for beating back the communist offensive. The other was John Paul Vann. When I learned of John's death, I wondered who would take his place to avert eventual communist victory.

I was invited as a guest to John's military funeral on June 16, 1972, at Arlington National Cemetery. I was struck by the ironic "prominence" at the funeral, I wrote in an Evans & Novak column, "of Cabinet members and four-star generals, symbolizing the very establishmentarians, whose bungling in Indochina he [Vann] battled for a decade."

> He despised the armchair generals in their air conditioned officers clubs and loathed those Foreign Service officers assigned to the pacification program who valiantly tried never to hear a shot fired in anger.

The column ran Thursday, June 22, and I had hardly arrived in my office that morning when Bob Komer was on the phone for me. Robert W. Komer was Rowly's source, not mine. Originally a career CIA official, he was closely tied to the Democratic Party and a major Vietnam adviser for President Johnson. Vann, who didn't think much of LBJ, despised Komer for currying Johnson's favor with unrealistically good war news. (Shown the door when Nixon became president. Komer would return to government as Jimmy Carter's under secretary of defense.).

"You only sully the reputation of John Vann!" Komer shouted over the telephone. "How dare you degrade those brave Foreign Service officers! Just who the hell are you talking about?"

I did not tell Komer that in my mind's eye one was John Gunther Dean, a distinguished Foreign Service officer who was the pacification director for I Corps when I met him in 1970, seated in his air-conditioned office in Danang, immaculate in tropical suit, tie, and French cuffs. When I asked whether I might travel with him if he was going out into I Corps, he told me it was not his mission to go into the field. He went on to a successful diplomatic career as ambassador to Cambodia, Denmark, Lebanon, Thailand, and India. John Vann, who did go into the field, was dead.

An occurrence six days after the death of John Vann would have an even more disastrous impact on Vietnam. In the early morning of June 17, 1972, a break-in was discovered at the Democratic National Committee offices in the Watergate building.

THE REPUBLICANS HAD begun to realize that in the age of television, orderly conventions were essential. But even with a virtually unopposed incumbent president, the Republican leaders, gathering in Miami Beach, could not prevent a long and messy floor fight in 1972 over future distribution of delegates. This was the kind of factional fight that I loved at conventions. Clarke Reed, the Mississippi party leader, was determined to pass a delegate formula to give the South a larger share of delegates. I reported that Nixon campaign chairman Clark MacGregor on Tuesday morning offered a compromise. Reed and the southerners turned him down flat. The southerners had the votes, and the once mighty eastern establishment led by Nelson Rockefeller did not—another sign of change in the party's balance of power.

One interesting side issue was that a thirty-seven-year-old first-term congressman from upstate New York not only sided with the southerners against Governor Rockefeller but went on the convention floor to speak during the debate. It was Jack Kemp, who had gone straight from quarterbacking the Buffalo Bills professional football team to election in 1970 from a suburban Buffalo district.

I first met Kemp earlier in the year when I was in Los Angeles covering the Humphrey-McGovern primary race. I was in the sunken lobby cocktail lounge of the Century Plaza Hotel drinking with Democratic sources when Jack approached me, introduced himself, and gave me a handout proclaiming his sponsorship of a tax reduction bill. I was not then all that interested in tax policy, and thought Kemp was a little pushy. I did not dream this would begin one of the closest relationships I ever had with a politician.

More than three months later, reporters noting Kemp's defiance of state Republican Party discipline in opposing Rockefeller at Miami Beach, commented to me that this football player was a right-wing ideologue who did not seem to care for his political future in the Empire State. He didn't. Jack Kemp's interest was national.

THE NIXON LANDSLIDE campaign of 1972 was even duller than the LBJ landslide campaign of 1964. I spent little time traveling with the candidates, but in the process uttered words permanently associated with me. The version that haunted me appeared in Timothy Crouse's *The Boys on the Bus,* with McGovern campaign director Frank Mankiewicz the obvious source:

> In September, Novak showed up to follow the campaign for a couple of days, and Mankiewicz insisted on banishing him from the Senator's plane, on which all the reporters from the big papers rode and putting him on the Zoo Plane, with the foreign reporters and TV technicians. Novak did not take this well. At the first stop, he went up to Mankiewicz and protested vociferously. Mankiewicz was implacable. It was the Zoo Plane or nothing.
>
> "OK," said Novak, in his one endearing comment of the campaign. "No more Mr. Nice Guy."

The only thing accurate about the story was my quote. Mankiewicz, the son of the legendary Hollywood scriptwriter Herman Mankiewicz, loved show business and dramatized events. Mankiewicz did not make the assignment putting me in the Zoo plane, and was not present when I said "No more Mr. Nice Guy." I will let McGovern press secretary Dick Dougherty relate the true story, as recorded in *Goodbye Mr. Christian:*

> Robert Novak provided a memory to be cherished. As I think I said earlier, I've known and liked Novak and Rowland Evans for a long time, and I continued to do so even though they were vicious in their treatment of McGovern, I'm specially fond of Novak, who is an earthy, elemental man. He makes you feel that if you were drowning he'd try to save you, something I wouldn't say of Rowley [sic], although he, one could depend on it, would be properly outraged at the absence of the lifeguard.
>
> In any case Novak joined us for a couple of days the first week out on the trail and, on the day he did so, there was in truth no seat available on the *Dakota Queen,* I put him on the Zoo plane. Throughout the day he offered no complaint about this profoundly *infra dig* situation. But that evening—in Dallas I think—as, he, [McGovern aide

Fred] Dutton and I were having a drink, he looked at me with his huge, round, ageless dark eyes and said: "I get it, Dougherty."

"You get what, Robert?" I said.

"Never mind," he said, nodding gravely. "I get the message and I'm telling you: from now on no more Mr. Nice Guy."

As Mankiewicz made it up, I was an angry fool. As Dougherty correctly told it, I was trying to be ironic. Regrettably, Mankiewicz's fiction has been copied in dozens of accounts, while Dougherty's truth has been ignored.

I did get on the *Dakota Queen* late in the campaign and discovered that the boys on the bus were so deeply in love with McGovern that they had taken leave of their better judgment. Several told me McGovern was going to win.

As expected by everyone but a liberal boy on the bus, McGovern suffered one of the worst repudiations in American political history. He carried only Massachusetts and the District of Columbia, losing by nearly eighteen million votes—the largest margin of defeat ever.

Yet Republicans gained only twelve seats in the House and actually lost two seats in the Senate, so that Democrats controlled the Senate by fourteen seats and the House by fifty-one. The explanation lies in the South. Nixon's biggest margins, exceeding 70 percent, were in southern states. But in the eleven states of the old Confederacy, the Democratic margin was nine in the Senate and forty-six in the House. For the rest of the country, the congressional balance was about even.

Nixon really did not really campaign in 1972, and did little or nothing for southern Republicans. I traveled with the Nixon campaign toward the end of the campaign, and found him saying nothing. He was relying on voter revulsion with McGovern as a leftist outside the political consensus, but that did not help Republican candidates. It delayed the impact of realignment, but a bigger threat was the specter of Watergate.

CHAPTER 22

Watergate

RICHARD NIXON'S personal satisfaction from his forty-nine-state landslide in 1972 was diminished by the threat of Watergate. Inside the White House, Nixon and his closest aides continuously improvised tactics. One impromptu scenario involved me. On Friday morning, February 9, 1973, Nixon discussed it with Chief of Staff H. R. Haldeman, as recorded in *The Haldeman Diaries.*

> [Nixon] wants to get our people to put out that foreign or Communist money came in support of the demonstrations in the campaign, tie all the '72 demonstrations to McGovern and thus the Democrats as part of the peace movement. Broaden the investigation to include the peace movement and its leaders, McGovern and Teddy Kennedy. To what extent they were responsible for the demonstrations that led to the violence and disruption. We ran a clean campaign compared to their campaign of libel and slander. . . . Maybe let Evans and Novak put it out and then we'll be asked about it. Can say that we knew, that the P[resident] ordered that it not be used under any circumstance.

Nothing could be more Nixonian. The president was proposing that material be leaked to Evans and Novak, indicating foreign/communist sponsorship of the peace movement and the McGovern campaign. When we would write a column and the White House would be asked about it by reporters, they would be told that Nixon knew about it but had ordered nothing be said of it—in contrast to Democrats leaking information about Watergate.

Haldeman does not comment in his diary about this harebrained scheme. The first I knew of it was reading Haldeman's book in 1994. In fact, there was no documentary evidence of the foreign/communist connection beyond the Trotskyist material given me two years earlier.

I believe Nixon knew he could never get Rowly and me to write a sweeping Watergate defense of him as Joe Alsop and some conservative columnists did. Nevertheless, he knew we were suckers for exclusive news, and that was how we could be manipulated. This had been demonstrated two weeks earlier by Chuck Colson, the Nixon aide whose mind-set most closely fit Nixon's.

CHARLES COLSON, the same age as I, was a high-priced Washington lawyer before and after entering Nixon's service. He was smart and ruthless, as he demonstrated Wednesday, January 24, 1973, four days after the beginning of Nixon's second term when Colson's secretary asked me to see him at the White House. He was hot about a story in the previous week's issue of *Time* based on an alleged conversation between the four Watergate burglars and their controller, E. Howard Hunt: "When Hunt recruited them into the Watergate conspiracy, he grandly told them: 'It's got to be done. My friend Colson wants it.' " The magazine reported the guilty plea by the four Watergate defendants "staved off" their courtroom testimony that they had been told Colson approved the crime. What Colson next said to me was the basis for a long lead item in our Sunday column of January 28. It began:

> Charles Colson, President Nixon's top political strategist, has threatened Time magazine with a multi-million-dollar libel suit unless the issue out tomorrow says it regrets not publishing his denials of any link to the conspiracy to bug Democratic National Headquarters at the Watergate.
>
> On advice of counsel, Colson declined to talk to us. But based on our conversations with his associates in and out of the White House, Colson seems deadly serious about seeking at least $2 million in punitive damages unless Time prints a statement of regret. At this writing, lawyers for Colson and Time are still negotiating Colson's demands.
>
> Colson leaves the White House around March 1 to resume private law practice in Washington but even then is expected to maintain immense influence at the White House. For anybody that close to the President to threaten a libel suit against a major national publication is without precedent in contemporary politics. It can be regarded as part of the administration's hard-line campaign against the media, attempting in this instance to forcibly remind newsmen of the libel laws.

I thought it was a terrific exclusive, but it turned out to be a terrible story for me. *Time* issued no apology, and Colson did not sue for libel. He had gotten what he wanted: the Evans & Novak column advertising his unhappiness with *Time*. I was used, in a much more serious way than the convention transfer from San Diego to Miami Beach.

This was just about the worst column I wrote during four decades, exposing a weakness in my reporting technique. I was such a sucker for an exclusive story that I sometimes committed errors indefensible even for a cub reporter. Not revealing a source is acceptable, but falsely denying a source is not. I lied when I said that "Colson declined to talk to us." He had made that a condition of giving me the story. My bigger sin was reporting a libel *threat,* rather than a libel suit. It is not done even when the purported plaintiff is trustworthy, which Colson was not.

Within days of that column, I realized I had been duped, and vowed to stay out of Colson's way. Outside of one last face-to-face contact with him on CBS's *Face the Nation* on July 1, 1973, the next time I would see Colson was after he had served seven months in a federal penitentiary and had become a Christian and truly a different man.

MY EMBARRASSING ITEM about Chuck Colson threatening to sue *Time* marked a rare reference to Watergate in our column. The next time was March 21, when I wrote criticizing President Nixon's extraordinary stretching of executive privilege by refusing to permit aides to testify before Congress about Watergate. (Even Republican politicians were "wondering whether the President is really covering up White House involvement in political espionage.") Our neglect could not be defended, but we were not alone in the Washington press corps.

Lack of news media interest led Nixon to think he had contained Watergate to the January trial where the five burglars and their two handlers were convicted without going higher up the president's chain of command. That illusion collapsed March 20 when James W. McCord Jr., the Nixon campaign security chief who was the lead Watergate burglar, wrote Federal Judge John Sirica that John Mitchell and other Nixon principals had suborned perjury.

I realized Watergate had become a transcendent news story, and it could not have come at a worse time for me. I planned to leave Washington on Saturday, March 31, for a six-week around-the-world reporting trip—beginning with a week in Japan, the next three weeks in Indochina, followed by reporting in Europe and ending with a week's vacation with Geraldine on the French Riviera.

Could I be out of the country as Watergate broke? My travel plans included appointments with heads of government, and neither Rowly nor I had been to Vietnam for two years. Besides, Geraldine was looking forward to a week's vacation. Rowly and I decided that I should go.

I had time for only one serious Watergate column following the McCord revelation before leaving Washington. I broke the news in a March 28 column that "six new legal and public affairs aides to deal with Watergate" had been added to the payroll of CREEP (Committee to Re-elect the President), kept alive after the president was reelected because of the scandal. I concluded that "the White House has decided to brazen it out—a decision that Mr. Nixon may come to deeply regret."

In January, Henry Kissinger and his North Vietnamese counterpart, Le Duc Tho, had come to terms in Paris to "end" the Vietnam War. I did not fully appreciate until I got to Saigon that the communists were flagrantly violating the peace treaty and conducting the war as if Le Duc Tho had signed nothing.

A senior U.S. Embassy official made available to me a U.S. Army helicopter to transport me into the countryside. Over the Central Highlands not far from where John Paul Vann crashed a year earlier, I saw a blur shoot past our chopper. "What was that?" I asked. The warrant officer pilot told me it was a Soviet-supplied SAM missile now in common use by the NVA (North Vietnamese Army). Just as I was reassuring myself this was business as usual, the pilot sighed: "Boy, was that ever close."

I missed John Paul Vann, but not nearly as much as the South Vietnamese did. The best officers in the ARVN (Army of Vietnam) were morose. At Fire Base Truong Son Nam near the north-south border, I heard Communist artillery booming. I wrote about "habitual cease-fire violations" by the enemy while the South Vietnamese obeyed the rules. I quoted highly regarded Brigadier General Nguyen Diu Hinh, commander of the 3rd ARVN Division: "The cease-fire is good for you Americans. You have gone home. But it is bad for us." I concluded the column by describing:

> . . . a mood of grim foreboding in these northern provinces. Forced to accept a disadvantageous cease-fire because President Nixon wanted it, and required to obey it scrupulously lest the U.S. Congress halt vital aid, South Vietnam must watch the Communist buildup and hope the United States, ultimately, will not permit catastrophe.

In Laos, G. McMurtrie Godley, the U.S. ambassador, invited me to a departure ceremony at Long Tieng, the secret CIA fortress barred to most other journalists. After four years in Laos, Godley had been named assistant secretary of state for Far Eastern affairs.

At the ceremony, he promised that U.S. bombers would respond to "flagrant and violent" Communist violations of the cease-fire in Laos ordered by the Paris peace pact. I wrote in the column "the assembled Lao generals and politicians heard [Godley] promise continued U.S. protection with smiles on their lips but fear in their hearts." (Mac Godley was a throwback to Foreign Service cold warriors of two decades earlier. His day was done. Looking at his record fighting what liberals called the "secret war," the Senate denied him confirmation.) I concluded my final column from Laos:

> Even CIA-advised irregulars, Thai troops and U.S. airpower may be unable to stop North Vietnamese regulars, heavy artillery and antiaircraft rockets. Without such help, however, this sleepy, misty little country will surely lose its independence, unmourned by the rest of the World.

I left Indochina certain of the total communization of Vietnam, Laos, and Cambodia.

ON APRIL 19, I was flown by U.S. Army helicopter from Long Tieng to Vientiane, where I picked up a three-day-old English-language *Bangkok Post*. I was stunned when I read a two-paragraph Reuters dispatch, quoting the *Washington Post* reporting the prospective resignations of H. R. Haldeman and John Ehrlichman. The U.S. government was in crisis, and here I was in the backwaters of Southeast Asia. When I made contact with Rowly via telex, he advised me to finish my trip as planned.

GERALDINE AND I returned from Europe to Washington on Saturday, May 12, 1973. Getting on top of Watergate began Monday morning with a phone call from Alexander Lankler, whom I had met in 1964 when he was working on Nelson Rockefeller's campaign. He told me he had bought a piece of the new Washington franchise of the Palm restaurant and wanted to show it off to me that day.

Over lunch, I asked Lankler how the president would try to save himself, by getting to the bottom of the break-in or stonewalling all the way?

Sandy gave me a baffled glance, then replied: "Bob, You're really out of touch to ask that question. It doesn't matter what Nixon does. He's gone. Dead. Finished. Everybody knows it." Lankler was a liberal Republican with no use for Nixon, but he did not make rash statements.

Next, Rowly imparted the information that Bob McCandless, my adversary-cum-friend, was now one of disenchanted former White House counsel John Dean's lawyers. McCandless and Dean had been married to daughters of the late Democratic senator Tom Hennings and remained friends after both marriages were dissolved. I asked Bob to lunch the next day, Tuesday, at the old Roger Smith Hotel across the street from my office on Pennsylvania Avenue.

McCandless said candidly that he had entered a line of work not taught in law school: media manipulation. His new principal occupation was to feed the major media with pro-Dean, anti-Nixon information. I now joined colleagues partaking from the McCandless conveyor belt.

On the next day, Wednesday, I took Nixon's new Watergate mouthpiece to lunch at Sans Souci. Ken Clawson, thirty-seven, who had just gone from the *Washington Post*'s national reporting staff to the Nixon White House's communications office, was clever and filled with ambition. That Wednesday, we had a couple of Scotches each before lunch and then a couple of Heinekens. Alcohol aside, Ken was thoroughly programmed, with two messages for me. First, Nixon silence on Watergate was over. Second, John Dean was a liar and backstabber who was betraying the president to stay out of prison.

My fourth lunch that week, on Thursday, was with William D. Ruckelshaus. He was somebody I knew well, but now held a position I never dreamed he could fill. L. Patrick Gray, a former career naval officer and faithful Nixon servitor, had been named FBI director on the death of J. Edgar Hoover in 1972. In the chaos of April 1973, Gray was forced to resign after burning Watergate-related documents. Nixon needed an incorruptible FBI director he trusted. Nobody filled that description better than Bill Ruckelshaus, despite the absence of law-enforcement experience. But I could imagine no greater miscasting than inserting this buoyant man into the pestilential waters of the FBI.

Elected to the Indiana state legislature in 1966 at age thirty-four, he was elected house majority leader his first day there. Badly beaten in 1968 by Democratic Senator Birch Bayh, Ruckelshaus was given a humdrum Nixon administration job: assistant attorney general running the Civil Division in John Mitchell's Justice Department and then a thankless promotion as first administrator of the Environmental Protection Agency (EPA). Ruckelshaus was anxious to get back to Indiana to try again for elective office. But with the government coming apart, Nixon wanted his skills of management and conciliation at the FBI.

When I sat down with Ruckelshaus at Provençal on May 18, 1973, it was his nineteenth day as acting FBI director. He had picked an obscure French restaurant where nobody would recognize the head of the FBI lunching with a columnist. Ruck's usual high spirits were tempered with bleak realism. He described a dreadful situation at the FBI. Hoover had cleaned out all the Bureau's independent thinkers (such as my old source Bill Sullivan). The Hooverites had run the show during the short tenure of Pat Gray, who sought only White House approbation. Now Ruckelshaus was confronted with a poisonous atmosphere at the FBI that impeded effective investigation of Watergate-related scandals.

I learned in the next two weeks of a White House plot to pin the blame for the Watergate burglary on the CIA and full responsibility for this alleged CIA cover-up on John Dean. But nobody believed the thirty-four-year-old midlevel aide could possibly have undertaken this on his own. I wrote in the column of May 25, 1973: "Senate investigators will be trying to find whether Dean sought to implicate the CIA on the orders of Ehrlichman and Haldeman or of Mr. Nixon himself. Some of the President's old Senate supporters strongly suspect the worst." I was referring to Senator Henry M. Jackson, Nixon's favorite Democrat. Scoop, who had fabulous CIA contacts, told me the boys at Langley were sure Nixon was trying to saddle them with Watergate.

One week after this column ran, I met with George Bush, like Ruckelshaus, one of the squeaky clean, good guys Nixon was adding to his team to cope with Watergate. After his second defeat for the U.S. Senate in 1970, Bush was written off for future elective politics. But like Ruckelshaus, Bush was admired by Nixon as a high-principled, aristocratic, attractive politician of a type the president could never be. In 1971, Nixon named Bush U.S. Ambassador to the United Nations, but to start 1973 asked Bush to become chairman of the Republican National Committee.

I lunched with Bush on June 1, 1973, at Sans Souci. We had known each other for seven years, we were on good terms, and I had never written or said a critical word about him. So I expected Bush to be as candid with me as Ruckelshaus had been.

Bush began by saying Democrats must be desperate if they were harping on Watergate. I asked: "George, what's your plan for protecting the

Republican Party in 1974 if the president is impeached?" Bush looked stricken. *"Impeachment?* What are you talking about, Bob? There's not going to be any impeachment." "I'll bet that, one way or another, Nixon will be gone by the '74 elections." "That's just ridiculous," Bush replied.

I did not think Bush was trying to deceive but wondered for the first time whether he had difficulty perceiving reality.

WHATEVER HOPE THERE was that Nixon might yet save himself ended in June when Senate hearings on Watergate became a long-running television feature. Not since the Army-McCarthy hearings nineteen years earlier had Americans been so enthralled by a glimpse into the seamy side of Washington.

I never attended a session. The previous year I had talked my reluctant partner into buying a small black-and-white TV set for the little conference room in our suite, and now I had it brought into the back office where Rowly and I had our desks. It was easier to keep track of the hearings on TV, and use the telephone to get the inside story from sources.

I had plenty of sources, including one interesting new face: Fred Thompson, the Republican counsel for the Senate Watergate committee who had been brought to Washington by his fellow Tennessean, Senator Howard Baker, the committee's top Republican. I met Thompson when he joined friends at The Exchange, the ground floor bar in the office building next to ours where I usually had my after-work drinks. Thompson stood six-feet-seven, was only thirty-one years old, and, with a deep southern voice, exuded a commanding presence.

Thompson was a stalwart defender of the Republican Party and his patron, Howard Baker, but not Richard Nixon. The deck was stacked against the president on the Watergate committee—Democrats out to nail him, Republicans out to look good themselves.

The committee's climax came June 25, when John Dean took the witness stand. This was the moment the White House awaited, with Ken Clawson telling me that now Dean would be shown up as a liar and cheat. It didn't happen. Dean was not likable but was believable. Baker and Thompson, while subjecting him to tough cross-examination, did not launch the auto-da-fé the White House desired. In the Evans & Novak column of June 28, I reported that Republican House members installed a portable TV set in their cloakroom and, "ignoring the debate on the floor, hung on every word" of "Dean's gripping testimony." After two days, I wrote, these Republicans "reluctantly gave Dean high marks as a witness." My assessment of Dean's testimony:

. . . Mr. Nixon may now be crippled as President of the United States. All over Washington this week, the offices of senior administration officials have been closed to routine business, their telephones turned off for all but emergency calls and their office television sets turned on. The reason: morbid fascination with Dean's testimony and the efforts of the President's dwindling defenders to prove Dean a liar and crack his credibility.

. . . Dean's testimony may have finally broken the self-confidence of the Nixon Administration. If that has happened, the President's painful choice lies between resignation or a presidency crippled far into the future.

INCLUDED IN BUSHELS of White House documents John Dean turned over to Senate Watergate investigators in the summer of 1973 was a list of 148 government officials, politicians, academics, writers, show business personalities, and journalists who were designated as Richard Nixon's opponents. Generated by Chuck Colson, this was the infamous "Enemies List." Inclusion was a matter of pride, as Nixon's descent accelerated.

Rowland Evans Jr. was on the list. Robert D. Novak was not, which was a little embarrassing to me. I had assumed Rowly was listed because of his connection with the Georgetown set and friendship with the Kennedys. But in retrospect, I believe Colson thought I should be kept off the Enemies List because I could be manipulated. I think I proved that was no longer the case when I returned from Europe in May 1973 and started reporting on Watergate in earnest.

In late summer 1974, after Nixon's fall, an Enemies List party was held at Jimmy's in Manhattan. The "enemies" were honored guests, but Rowly had no interest in going. At that point in my life I liked having fun in New York, and went as my partner's surrogate. It was quite a party, but I became disaffected with liberal Nixon-haters surrounding me as the alcohol took hold.

My disaffection peaked in the early morning hours, when I found myself at P.J. Clarke's for hamburgers and a nightcap. At the table was the former head of the Federal National Mortgage Association who had resisted his removal from that post by Nixon and so was listed by Colson. He told us, with pride, how his son avoided service in Vietnam by fleeing to Canada, comparing that with his father avoiding conscription in the czarist army by fleeing to America. Quite drunk, I commented: "I guess it runs in the family's blood, and the color is yellow." There was shocked silence around the table, but somebody changed the subject. These were not the kind of people who started a fistfight over an insult, but I decided I better be more selective in my drinking companions.

WHEN THE SENATE Watergate investigation recessed in early August, Bob McCandless asked whether I would like to talk to John Dean, not-for-quotation. Although the Evans & Novak column had defended Dean's testimony as credible, I had disliked him from a distance and liked him even less as I now met him for the first time. He seemed to typify the Nixon "Beaver Patrol"—not just short on principles but smug and arrogant, odd for an informer who had turned against his own president and was on his way to prison. (After his release, Dean turned to writing fiercely anti-Republican books. He stiffed McCandless for legal fees charged for services rendered that had caused severe damage to Bob's legal career.) Dean was of little or no help to me.

In the Evans & Novak column of August 13, 1973, on my own I pieced together bits of information for a story previously not told in full: Assistant Attorney General Henry Petersen, a career civil servant heading the Justice Department's Criminal Division, on April 15 told Nixon that Haldeman and Ehrlichman faced criminal prosecution and should be fired but that Dean should not because he was cooperating with the prosecutors. After Petersen's warning, Nixon fired neither Haldeman nor Ehrlichman. Instead, just hours later, he gave Haldeman surreptitious tape recordings of the March 21 meeting in which Dean told Nixon there was "a cancer growing on the presidency"—evidence Petersen did not know existed. Nixon asked Haldeman to review the tapes. On the next day, April 16, Nixon demanded Dean's written resignation, further defying Petersen's admonition.

I gave readers two possible explanations for Nixon's behavior. One was "abominable judgment by the President but scarcely an impeachable offense." The other: "The President and Haldeman were involved in some dark arrangement which made a mockery of Petersen's recommendations."

This was the kind of reporting and analysis I produced in 124 Watergate columns between my return from Europe and Nixon's resignation a year later. I don't think any other columnist performed such acute surgery on Nixon's Watergate performance. I make such an immodest statement because of the widespread impression in the liberal establishment that Evans and Novak were apologists for Nixon.

One summer afternoon in 1975, long after Nixon was gone, I went down to The Exchange for a late lunch of a hamburger and a beer. Whom did I see at the bar but the columnist Jimmy Breslin, down from New York and roaring drunk. Breslin and I had been in the same stable of new columnists assembled by *Herald-Tribune* editor Jim Bellows in the spring of 1963. We once were friendly and had good times drinking together. But I perceived coolness toward me by Jimmy as I moved rightward ideologically, particularly after the McGovern campaign.

"Were you happy defending Nixon right up to the end?" Breslin asked. I had learned it made no sense to argue with a drunk, particularly if I was sober. Breslin was echoing many liberal journalists. If I had savaged George McGovern, it naturally followed that I would protect Richard Nixon.

It was lose-lose for me. If my fastidious reporting of Watergate won no plaudits from liberal colleagues, it generated wrath from conservatives—including the editors of my most recently acquired client newspapers.

ONE PROMINENT COLUMNIST whom Nixon could have counted on to support him unconditionally on Watergate was David Lawrence. But he died on February 11, 1973, at age eighty-four—before the scandal developed. Lawrence's column ran in over three hundred dailies, mostly small town afternoon papers. Reading it in the *Washington Evening Star,* I thought the column conveyed a stodgy conservatism favored by many newspaper editors of that day. His column lasted fifty-seven years, a record for longevity. (The two longest-running columns at this writing are William F. Buckley's and mine, both started in 1963.)

Publishers Newspaper Syndicate acquired David Lawrence in 1967 when it merged with the Hall Syndicate. He had more newspapers than any other political columnist in the Publishers-Hall stable, but how long could an octogenarian last? Bob Cowles at the syndicate was seeking a successor.

I had a candidate: my young friend George F. Will. After the 1972 election and the defeat of his boss, Senator Allott, Will picked journalism over government service and became Washington editor of *National Review.* George wrote four or five sample columns for me to give Publishers-Hall, with a higher caliber of prose than was customary for op-ed pages.

Cowles was a working-class guy who had spent years on the road as a syndicate salesman. I always thought Bob was more comfortable hawking comics, crossword puzzles, and astrology features than dealing with self-important Washington columnists. Cowles phoned me to say he had rejected Will: "The words are too long, the sentences are too long, the paragraphs are too long, the whole damn columns are too long. Bob, it's not a *newspaper* column." I replied: "Bob, you've just made the biggest mistake in your life."

When David Lawrence died without a designated successor, Cowles tried to sell his three-hundred-plus newspapers other Publishers-Hall columns—especially Evans & Novak. More than one hundred of Lawrence's papers already bought our column, and Cowles's salesman got more than seventy-five of his small newspapers to take Evans & Novak. That raised our total clientele to close to three hundred.

Just as the former Lawrence clients began receiving our product, my tough Watergate reporting kicked in. This certainly was not David Lawrence! We quickly lost almost all our new papers, and some old ones as well. In our tenth year, the Evans & Novak column was squeezed—too anti-McGovern to be accepted by the liberal establishment, too anti-Nixon to be accepted by conservatives.

George Will was even tougher on Watergate than we were, and I think he would have had trouble keeping those three hundred David Lawrence newspapers if Bob Cowles's judgment had been more astute. Instead, the *Washington Post* began syndicating Will's column in 1974. Before long, he had 460 newspapers and a Pulitzer Prize—achievements never attained by Evans & Novak.

ON APRIL 30, when Haldeman, Ehrlichman, and Dean were cut loose, Richard Kleindienst also was sacked as attorney general (a post he had held since succeeding John Mitchell in 1970). Kleindienst, who would be convicted of perjury, was conservative, cynical, and confrontational—the "hard" man Nixon tried to be, To replace Kleindienst, Nixon took the squeaky-clean route and picked Elliott Richardson, who had been secretary of defense for only three months after being moved over from secretary of health, education and welfare. Richardson was liberal, high-minded, and the caricature of the upper-class Yankee. At Justice, he was a cocked pistol pointed at Nixon.

Richardson bowed to Democratic demands for a special prosecutor and then, without consulting Nixon, selected sixty-one-year-old Archibald Cox, Richardson's Harvard Law School professor. Cox filled his staff with fervent liberal lawyers and a non-attorney more important than all the lawyers: *Washington Evening Star* reporter James Doyle, as his press secretary.

My relationship with future special prosecutors tended toward the clandestine, but Doyle arranged for me to have breakfast with Professor Cox on June 13, 1973, less than a month on the job, at the Hay Adams dining room—one of Washington's most visible places and a favorite of White House aides. I lunched on July 11 with Doyle, who picked Paul Young's restaurant, a hangout for lobbyists, who are notorious gossips. On the evening of July 31, Jimmy invited a dozen columnists and bureau chiefs to his home in the close-in Maryland suburbs for a session with Cox. On August 23, I lunched with Doyle at Paul Young's. On September 27, I had breakfast with Doyle and Cox at the Hay Adams.

Cox and Doyle put everything off the record, but I got a good idea about what was going on. I concluded that Cox and his eager lawyers were intent on investigating the White House Plumbers unit that committed crimes under the guise of plugging news leaks. Most important, Cox would not agree to receiving an edited or truncated version of Nixon's secret White House tapes.

On Saturday evening, October 20, 1973, Geraldine and I were at Cole Field House on the University of Maryland campus attending a preseason basketball exhibition. When I got in the car and turned on the radio a little after ten o'clock, I learned for the first time of the Saturday Night Massacre, eliminating Archie Cox and then Elliott Richardson and Bill Ruckelshaus (who had left the FBI to become deputy attorney general) for refusing to fire Cox.

Orchestrating the Saturday Night Massacre was his new chief of staff, General Alexander Haig, who had bowed to Nixon's plea to leave the army and replace Haldeman. Haig demonstrated his political deaf ear by sending FBI agents to Cox's office to seal his files. This created an aura of fear, amid much wild talk of a coup d'etat. I worked the phones on Sunday and got most of my information from Ken Clawson and Jim Doyle. On Monday morning, I wrote a column for the next morning's newspapers:

> . . . [T]he President miscalculated in his lightning thrusts last week-end. Well aware of Congressional reluctance to impeach a President, he felt he could get rid of Cox and the White House tapes controversy in one move with impunity. Instead, Mr. Nixon not only was forced to bow to the federal court order yesterday but finds the Watergate scandal spotlighted more than ever with new demands for an independent prosecutor. . . .
>
> Mr. Nixon clearly expected Cox's dismissal would be followed by resignation of his top staff. Instead, White House aides were stunned Sunday afternoon when Cox's press spokesman, James Doyle, announced the Cox operation was staying intact to bring Watergate's wrongdoers to Justice.

Four years later when Doyle published his excellent account of the Watergate special prosecutors *(Not Above the Law)*, I learned my Tuesday column brightened the mood of Cox's forlorn staff. Doyle explained:

The younger lawyers passed the column around. The junior staff was coming together, beginning to sense that there might be great advantage in remaining at their posts and showing a united front.

CONGRESS INSISTED ON a new special prosecutor. Haig needed one with a reputation for integrity and with legal credentials to suit Acting Attorney General Robert Bork (who turned down several Haig suggestions) but also with a deeper respect for the presidency than Archie Cox had.

Leon Jaworski, a millionaire Houston corporate lawyer who was part of the fading Tory Democratic establishment in Texas, met all qualifications. Clawson told me Haig was sure he had found a faithful Lyndon Johnson supporter who would not make life miserable for any president of the United States. I checked it out with Bob Strauss, who ran in the same Texas political circles as Jaworski. Strauss gave me a quote I attributed to a "prominent Texas Democrat" in the column: "Leon is impressed by power. I would think he will be terribly impressed by Mr. President in the Oval Office." Other Texas friends of Jaworski did not think he ever would take Nixon into court to force the release of documents or would press investigations that would personally embarrass the president.

Perhaps to insure myself, I wrote in the Evans & Novak column of November 5 (which was Jaworski's first day on the job) that "there is another aspect to Jaworski," adding this last paragraph:

He is a man of considerable ego, fellow lawyers in Houston report, proud of his many civic endeavors. At age 68, he will be sensitive to accusations of cover-up and could conceivably come around to the investigative course taken by Cox. If so, the White House will then have irrevocably lost all control of the Watergate prosecution.

This last paragraph was the most prophetic part of the column, as the White House immediately pressured the new prosecutor. Disappointed that Cox's staff did not resign when he was axed, Nixon now wanted Jaworski to fire them. "Jaworski sure as hell has the right to bring his own team on," Clawson told me (a quote attributed in my November 5 column to a "presidential aide").

It was all a pipe dream. Jaworski gave full support to the inherited staff. I reported on November 18 that "the last lingering doubts" about Jaworski by the holdover Cox lawyers ended when the new special prosecutor filed a court brief arguing that not even the president has the right to break the law in the name of national security.

The Evans & Novak column of November 26 contained one of my most important Watergate exclusives. I broke the story of how Nixon lawyer J. Fred Buzhardt, on the previous Wednesday, requested and was granted a meeting with Jaworski. That marked the first time any Nixon attorney had entered the special prosecutor's offices (located on the ninth floor of a commercial office building near the White House). The prosecutors guessed Buzhardt was about to bring them long-denied documents, but they were spectacularly wrong.

Buzhardt, accompanied by White House counsel Leonard Garment, had an extraordinary revelation and an even more extraordinary request. The revelation: eighteen minutes had been erased from the critically important tape recording of Nixon's conversation with Haldeman on June 20, 1972, the first working day after the Watergate burglary. The request: please give us a few days to get our ducks in a row before going to Judge John Sirica with this information that would shock the nation. I wrote:

> Had Jaworski granted the delay, he would have committed a heinous offense, particularly in the eyes of zealous deputy prosecutors inherited from Cox—would, indeed, have endangered his relationship with them. Instead, Jaworski said no.

> The prosecutors immediately notified Sirica, who scheduled a hearing for the next Monday where, I wrote melodramatically, Nixon's "presidency may hang in the balance."

> That Jaworski flatly turned down the appeal powerfully reinforces his status as independent prosecutor. But far more important, the fact that the White House actually asked for a delay shows how ominously this latest fiasco looms in the wary eyes of President Nixon's lawyers.

In his book, Jim Doyle did not speculate how I so quickly obtained all this inside information. He certainly did not finger himself as the source, and—from the distance of thirty years—neither shall I. In the interest of full disclosure, however, I find that my 1973 expense account record shows that on Friday, November 23, I lunched with Jim Doyle at Sans Souci. My records show lunch that day cost me $18.19 ($82.88 in 2007 dollars). The total indicated that Jimmy and I enjoyed more than one drink apiece. I then could shake off a couple of Scotches and a beer to write cogent copy. I left Sans Souci at about two p.m. to walk across the street and write a column containing my scoop.

· · ·

WHILE RICHARD NIXON was sweeping forty-nine out of fifty states in the 1972 election, a future nemesis was elected to his first term in the U.S. House of Representatives from the state of Maine. It was liberal Republican William S. Cohen, the thirty-two-year-old mayor of Bangor.

Cohen was assigned to the House Judiciary Committee, which before long would be considering impeachment of the president. Cohen publicly declared that Nixon's conduct met the constitutional test of high crimes and misdemeanors required for impeachment. I did too and telephoned Cohen to get acquainted. From May 2 to July 22 of 1974, we had lunch or breakfast five times. As the impeachment struggle climaxed, I talked to Bill on the phone nearly every day.

A Unitarian who was the son of a Jewish father and Irish mother, Cohen was a poet, athlete, and idealist. As I drifted to the Right, I still preferred to associate with liberal Republicans. Much as I enjoyed Cohen's company, what I really appreciated was his steady flow of information. Cohen and I agreed that Nixon would be impeached and convicted if he did not resign, and Bill felt the president would resign if enough Republicans turned against him.

During a July 9 lunch with Cohen at the Members Dining Room, we were in deep conversation when Congressman Trent Lott approached our table. Like Cohen, Lott was a freshman Republican House member (at age thirty one year younger than Bill) and a lawyer assigned to Judiciary. But they were different in every other possible way. Lott had spent the previous five years as an aide to Representative William Colmer of Mississippi, a Deep South segregationist Democrat, and ran for his seat as a Republican in 1972 when Colmer retired. Lott went on Judiciary as an unequivocal supporter of Nixon.

"Well," Lott drawled, "so this is how the liberals hang out." After Cohen introduced me, Lott continued: "Now I know where those anti-Nixon columns come from." After he left, Cohen and I agreed Lott was a jerk. I could not imagine I was in the presence of both a future Republican Senate majority leader and a secretary of defense in a Democratic administration. Even less imaginable was the prospect that Trent Lott would become as good a source of mine as Bill Cohen.

White House Chief of Staff Alexander Haig was a good source for Rowly dating back to his days as a Kissinger aide and saw a lot of my partner in his new role. Because Rowly was out of the country when an Evans & Novak column suggested Nixon's desperate plight in the impeachment fight, Haig knew I was the author. I obeyed his summons to his West Wing office (my first such meeting with a presidential chief of staff during seventeen years in Washington).

"Bob," Haig began, "I always have thought of you as a patriot who puts the national interest first." His volume rose as he told how Watergate was undermining U.S. interests, threatening Vietnam, and making us vulnerable to the Soviet Union. He reached a high-pitched climax, punctuated by smashing his big West Point class ring on his desk and asking: "How can you defy your commander in chief?"

Haig had used this ring-banging routine on several Republicans in Congress who described it to me. So, if Haig pulled it on me, I had prepared an answer: "General, President Nixon is commander in chief of the U.S. armed services, not of the American people. I have not been an active duty army officer since 1954 and have not been a reserve officer since 1962. Therefore, President Nixon is not *my* commander in chief." Unfortunately, however, with Haig shouting and pounding his desk, I went mute.

Senator William Emerson Brock III of Tennessee was a forty-three-year-old regular Republican with a seemingly boundless future. Brock, a member of the Chattanooga aristocracy, was handsome, rich, and conservative. A three-term congressman, he had endeared himself to Nixon in the otherwise disappointing 1970 elections by defeating the despised liberal Democratic senator Albert Gore.

Consequently, I was told, Nixon was outraged at the end of October 1973 when Brock wrote him recommending disclosure of all tapes and documents. I was interested in this position by so staunch a Nixonite, and called Brock, though I did not know him well, for a lunch date. We got together at Sans Souci on Tuesday, November 6, and that afternoon I wrote a column for Thursday reporting:

> One influential (and pro-Nixon) Republican Senator feels Mr. Nixon cannot survive unless like Henry II, the 12th Century King of England who atoned for the murder of Thomas à Becket by being publicly scourged, he makes public penance.

The "influential" senator was not identified, but Brock's letter was mentioned four paragraphs later and it was easy to figure out that he was the source. Nixon aides were incensed. Clawson asked me: "Are we going to go out crawling on our bellies or are we going to go out swinging?"

BY THE SUMMER of 1974, Rowly and I had spent eight years as commentators for Channel 5 WTTG, Metromedia in Washington. But our status there was at low ebb. While we started with a daily fifteen-minute feature and once had a half-hour weekend show, by 1974 we were down to one two-minute weekly commentary for each of us on the ten p.m. news ($55 per commentary, or $226 in 2007 money). Ed Turner, our patron at WTTG, had moved on, and his liberal successors were not fans of Evans & Novak.

However, Channel 5 had one last big use for me when it became clear I was advocating Nixon's impeachment. The House Judiciary Committee began impeachment consideration the week of July 22, 1974. The producers proposed a nightly five-minute impeachment "debate" on the ten o'clock news. I would support impeachment. Opposing impeachment would be a White House speechwriter who had become Nixon's most uncompromising public defender: the Reverend John McLaughlin, the forty-seven-year-old Roman Catholic priest.

Although McLaughlin had campaigned for the Senate in Rhode Island in 1970 as an anti-Vietnam War Republican, inside the White House he became rabid in backing the president. I learned over the years that John did not believe in much of anything, theologically or politically. While still a priest as a Nixon aide, he abandoned the Roman collar, wore expensive suits, and lived in a pricey apartment at the Watergate. Rumors abounded that he had abandoned his priestly vows of poverty and chastity. I learned from White House sources that he wasn't much of a speechwriter, but he appeared ever more frequently on television as Nixon's fierce defender—leading to the WTTG debate proposal.

My first reaction was that it was not a good idea for me to debate a presidential aide on television. But I wanted to strengthen my tenuous relationship with Channel 5, I could use the money (five hundred dollars in all), and the prospect of public combat excited me.

I first met McLaughlin shortly before our initial debate July 22. He was taller than I expected, blond, ruddy-complexioned, an unsmiling presence glowering at me. But I was not prepared for the nature of the debate. While I had anticipated a cool, Jesuitical logician, McLaughlin—his eyes bugging out—shouted at me. I just shouted back.

While I wanted to discuss details of Nixon's high crimes, McLaughlin argued the nation could not stand a trial of its president in the midst of cold and hot wars. It delighted producers at Channel 5 because the nightly debate generated high ratings.

In the first debate, I addressed McLaughlin as "Father." After we finished that night, he asked me to call him "Dr. McLaughlin." (He had earned a secular PhD from Columbia University.) When I persisted in calling him "Father" for the second debate, the producers virtually ordered me to knock it off. I did, but I did not call him "Doctor"—or anything else.

Late in the second and final week of our debates, McLaughlin asked if we could have drinks after the program that night. I told him I thought five minutes on the air arguing about impeachment was about all I could stand. He assured me this was about something entirely different, and impeachment would not even be mentioned.

Over drinks at a big Italian restaurant across Wisconsin Avenue from the WTTG studios, McLaughlin told me he wanted to create and moderate a conservative version of television's Agronsky and Company. The only conservative on Martin Agronsky's five-man panel then was syndicated columnist James Jackson Kilpatrick. McLaughlin told me he wanted me as a conservative on his panel and, furthermore, would name a third conservative to outnumber two liberals. Since I knew Washington journalism, he asked me to help pick the other three panel members.

It was surprising he came to me, whom he had known only in a bitter adversarial relationship. But the real shocker was the overall idea. Agronsky was an experienced television journalist who had worked for all three broadcast networks. McLaughlin was a third-string presidential speechwriter whose journalistic experience was with a Jesuit publication.

I had been approached often by people with television proposals that rarely reached the pilot stage. McLaughlin's looked less promising than most. But I gave him the same answer I gave everybody else: I'll be happy to talk with you if you find backing for your project. I never expected to hear from him again, and when he did contact me nearly eight years later, I had forgotten about our late-night conversation in the Italian restaurant.

ON MONDAY AUGUST 5, 1974, my parents concluded a stay at our beach house in Delaware. Geraldine at midday was driving my mother and the kids to Washington, where my parents would take a plane back to Illinois. I had to leave the shore at seven a.m. to make a morning appointment in Washington, and my father wanted to ride with me to experience the joy of speeding through Delaware and Maryland country roads in an open Corvette.

The news came over the car radio. The transcript of the tape-recorded conversation on June 23, 1972, between Nixon and Haldeman, finally released, was the "smoking gun." It showed that six days after the Watergate burglary, Nixon was attempting to stop the FBI from investigating the case on grounds it would stir up unspecified details about the CIA and the Bay of Pigs. In other words, Nixon was trying to pin Watergate on the CIA as I had told George Bush at Sans Souci on June 1, 1973, and as I had implied in a column shortly before that.

"It's over," I told my father, as I drove toward Washington. "How can you tell?" he asked. "Believe me," I replied. "The June 23 tape has always had the answer. He will be gone before the week is over."

The seventeen House Judiciary Committee Republicans who had voted against all counts of impeachment switched their positions—even Trent Lott, to make it unanimous in the committee.

CHAPTER 23

The Ford Interlude

O N OCTOBER 10, 1973, Spiro T. Agnew resigned as vice president of the United States—the first vice president since John C. Calhoun to do so, and not, like Calhoun, because he felt the job was not big enough for him. Envelopes passed to Agnew, each with as much as twenty thousand dollars in cash, were kickbacks from Maryland contractors. I reacted to the news of Agnew's resignation by going up to Capitol Hill. In the Speaker's Lobby off the floor of the House of Representatives, I ran into Barber Conable of New York, a member of the House Republican leadership.

"Bob, I shouldn't tell you this, but I just can't keep it to myself," Conable said. Gerald R. Ford, the Republican leader of the House and a close ally of Conable, had approached him an hour earlier in the GOP cloakroom. Ford informed Conable that President Nixon was about to disclose an appointment for vice president under the new Twenty-fifth Amendment to the Constitution, and asked Conable whether he planned to attend the White House ceremony. Conable replied that he had not planned to go, but Ford said softly to him, "Barber, I really would like you to be there." Conable concluded to me: "I can't guarantee it, Bob, but I'm pretty sure that Nixon's going to name Jerry vice president." Conable's tone was one of wonder. In an Evans-Novak profile of Vice President Ford in the *Atlantic Monthly* the next year, I wrote, "at 60, Ford simply was not considered among the front rank of Republicans." But thanks to Conable, I had an exclusive that I reported on Channel 5 WTTG.

When Agnew fell, Nixon was sure he could survive and was not necessarily looking for the best qualified presidential successor. Nixon wanted no part of either Rockefeller or Reagan, neither of whom he trusted. His choice was John B. Connally. Mel Laird gave Rowly and me the story of how he dissuaded Nixon from picking Connally. Laird had resigned as secretary of defense at the beginning of Nixon's second term but was back in the White House with Haig six months later for a Watergate rescue operation replacing Haldeman and Ehrlichman. Haig took charge, but Laird's advice and personality were found uncongenial by Nixon, and he was ignored—except in this case, as I wrote in the *Atlantic:*

> Connally, Laird told the President, simply would not do. He had come too recently into the Republican fold; whatever his qualifications, he would never be confirmed by Congress. Democrats feared his ability and scorned him as an apostate. Republicans were not about to turn over to an acolyte of Lyndon Johnson the fortunes of the Grand Old Party for the next decade. Having warned Nixon for more than an hour that he had damn well better consider his party and not just himself, Laird then guaranteed that the Democratic Congress would confirm Ford as Vice President "within two weeks."

Laird convinced Nixon to name Ford, but he was wrong about two weeks. The Saturday Night Massacre poisoned the atmosphere on Capitol Hill and delayed Ford's confirmation for seven weeks.

I DID NOT worry about Ford being another Nixon. What concerned me was my interview with Ford in his Executive Office Building office for the *Atlantic* piece. When I asked whether he felt expanded power had endangered the presidency as an institution, I recorded in the article what happened next:

> Ford went to his desk and picked up a copy of *The Twilight of the Presidency* by George Reedy, Lyndon Johnson's onetime press secretary, given to him the week before by reporter Marjorie Hunter of the *New York Times*. In a gloomy pre-Watergate view of presidential decline, Reedy indicts the remoteness of the kingly presidency in the last third of the twentieth century.
>
> Yes, Ford said, no doubt about it—and he wasn't singling out Richard Nixon. What has happened, Ford said, is that "Presidents develop this aura of infallibility. They all sort of operate the same way—even Eisenhower [Ford's favorite president]. Anybody that's hired over there [at the White House] ought to read this book," because what it describes is "avoidable." . . .
>
> "I'm simply saying that I think Presidents and their staffs have to have a somewhat different attitude to the Congress and to the job."

I did not comment in the article on this remarkable position by the president-in-waiting, but I thought it strange. While other presidents prepared to enter the Oval Office intent on maximizing their power, Ford was concerned with minimizing his. Of the ten presidents I have covered, only Ford was a believer in congressional supremacy.

I thought the *Atlantic* profile offered a sophisticated analysis of Ford, but one reader was not impressed—my father. I had discerned that Maurice P. Novak, an unreconstructed liberal Republican, was distressed by my rightward drift. But he never had criticized me until he read the Ford profile (making sure these remarks were made out of earshot of my adoring mother). "I thought you were too soft on Ford," my father told me. "He's a political hack. Nixon is a crook, but he is a man of substance. Ford will be a disaster as president. Wait and see." My father did not live in the world of politics, but his political assessments were consistently prescient.

ON SEPTEMBER 6, 1974, in the fourth week of the new presidency, I was called by Robert T. Hartmann, a former newspaperman who was Ford's political adviser and chief speechwriter and now a counselor with cabinet status. He said he had to see me immediately. I scheduled lunch with him that day at Sans Souci.

Bob Hartmann was not my buddy. A member of Stanford's class of 1938 and a World War II Navy veteran, in 1974 he was fifty-seven years old— part of an older generation. When I arrived in Washington in 1957, he was chief of the tiny *Los Angeles Times* bureau. The *LA Times* was then still a virtual component part of the California Republican Party, and Hartmann was part of a tough-talking band of Republican-oriented Washington bureau chiefs from just such newspapers. In 1964, Hartmann was hired by Mel Laird and five years later went to work for Ford when Laird left for the Pentagon. Since I had ready access to both Laird and Ford, I had no contact with Hartmann until Ford became vice president. I then took him to lunch once at Sans Souci without getting much out of him.

The September 6 lunch was entirely different. Hartmann was on a mission, and it began even before we ordered prelunch drinks. He started with one of the truly classic quotes I ever recorded: "The White House staff run by Haig is still functioning in the interest of Richard Nixon and the walking wounded of a lost war." He gave me a second delicious quote after asserting that Al Haig must leave as chief of staff: "Until that happens, the President will be the Prisoner of Zenda in his own house." These quotes were buttressed by a wealth of detail.

It was two fifteen p.m. when I returned to our office a half block away. This was Thursday, the deadline for our Sunday column, which already had been teletyped to Chicago (headquarters for the renamed Field Syndicate). But the material given me by Hartmann was so hot that Rowly and I agreed we could not wait until Monday to publish it, and I would write this story as a new Sunday column superseding the old one. The column was Evans & Novak at its best or worst, depending upon the outlook. It began:

An urgent feeling by President Ford's closest aides that Gen. Alexander Haig must be removed as chief of staff soon—perhaps immediately— hit fever pitch in two backstage developments last Thursday.

Development No. 1: Haig entered the Oval Office with a commission for Mr. Ford to sign nominating Pat Buchanan, Richard M. Nixon's longtime political adviser and speechwriter, as ambassador to South Africa. Despite Haig's fervent arguments, the President delayed his decision.

Development No. 2: The General Services Administration was instructed by Haig deputy Jerry Jones to move furniture into two Executive Office Building suites next door to the White House for two ex-Nixon aides now in San Clemente [Nixon's California home]: Room 352 for ex-press secretary Ron Ziegler; Room 348 for ex-appointments secretary Steve Bull.

Describing Ford's "own aides" (meaning Hartmann) as "thunderstruck," I went on to label Buchanan as "the symbol of bloody-nose Nixon politics" and Ziegler as "the bad old days incarnate." I then cataloged Haig's efforts to manipulate the Ford presidency, from opposing his amnesty plans for Vietnam War draft evaders to blocking his new White House portraits of his favorite presidents (Lincoln and Truman) in place of Nixon's (Teddy Roosevelt and Wilson).

Although Hartmann talked to me off the record, I slipped in both those beautiful Hartmann quotes (attributing the first to "one Ford man" and the second to "one aide"). Hartmann's name was not mentioned until the next to last paragraph of a fifteen-paragraph column: "Hartmann and a handful of Ford men simply cannot compete with the Haig system. Thus, they feel President Ford must cut loose Al Haig." Even if the Washington gossip circuit had not reported Novak and Hartmann lunching at Sans Souci two days before the column appeared, it would not be difficult to ascertain its source.

The *Washington Post* played the column at the top of the Sunday op-ed page with a four-column headline: "Mr. Ford's Advisers: Gen. Haig Must Go." I was enjoying this in my office off the family room, when Geraldine knocked on the door a little after seven a.m. to tell me the general was on the phone.

Haig apparently had read his *Post* and immediately called me without giving it much thought. He was shouting: "Novak, this is full of lies, all lies. You have libeled me, and you, my friend, are going to pay for it. I am going to sue you for five million dollars." "Al," I protested, "you're out of luck. I don't have five million dollars." Haig shouted something unintelligible, then hung up.

Of course, Haig never sued me. Nor did he ever mention this incident to me again in the course of many contacts in ensuing years. This column, however, was often mentioned years later by Pat Buchanan, after we had become friends. Pat often noted that I had cost him the privilege of representing our country in Pretoria.

Less than three weeks after the "Haig Must Go" column, the general was, in effect, replaced by Don Rumsfeld. Soon Buchanan, Ziegler, Bull, and the other prominent Nixonites were gone too.

THE VOLCANIC TELEPHONE call from Al Haig did not end my adventures that memorable Sunday, September 8, 1974. At the suggestion of Senator William E. Brock, we had breakfast at the Hay Adams before his appearance on *Face the Nation,* where I would be the non-CBS questioner. The guests were the chairmen of the Senate Republican and Democratic campaign committees, Senators Brock and Lloyd Bentsen. In our off-the-record breakfast talk, Brock and I shared our disappointment with the first month of the Ford presidency, particularly its muddled economic policy.

We were nearly finished, when one of the senator's aides approached our table with news. He informed us that President Ford had just issued a complete and total pardon for Richard M. Nixon. Brock shook his head in disbelief. While the pardon in time would be praised for saving the nation from a painful experience, on September 8, 1974, it seemed a Republican disaster.

The stunning news obviously changed the direction of that day's *Face the Nation.* Noting Nixon's just-released statement from San Clemente—"I can see now that I was wrong in not acting more decisively and more forthrightly in dealing with Watergate."—and remembering that Brock had been the unattributed author of the Henry II analogy, I asked on the air whether Nixon should say more in expiation of his sins. "I don't see that it would add much to the process," Brock now said on national television. "I don't want to see President Nixon abject himself in an effort to achieve penance." So much for scourging.

THE REPUBLICAN PARTY was staring into a midterm election abyss on Thursday, October 31, when Ford touched down in Sioux City, Iowa, a late stopping point in a twenty-one-state tour. I was covering the president there and on his next stops in California.

Ford was in Sioux City to promote the candidacy of the Republican district's congressman, Wiley Mayne, a stodgy standpatter who, on the Judiciary Committee, voted against all Nixon impeachment counts. My Iowa political sources considered Mayne dead, less because of his stubborn loyalty to Nixon than the faltering farm economy for which farmers blamed the administration's agricultural policy. Ford supported Mayne at the Sioux City rally by defending his farm program, causing local Republicans to wince. I wrote in a column published the day before the election: "How anyone was helped by the President's Sioux City speech defending that policy defies the imagination."

The presidential campaign went on to California for a five-hundred-dollar-a-plate party fund-raising dinner Thursday night at the Century Plaza Hotel in Los Angeles. I had telephoned Maureen Reagan, the governor's daughter, in advance to see whether we could get together for a drink. I had met Maureen while covering California politics the previous spring, and found her excellent company and an inexhaustible source of political intelligence. She was thirty-three, a stunning blonde (in between overweight periods), irreverent, and frightening to most politicians. Because I was not a politician and she didn't frighten me, we got along.

Maureen got me into the VIP reception at the Century Plaza prior to the black-tie dinner. (The White House press pool reporter wrote disdainfully: "Novak managed to get on the inside of the reception ropes with the rest of the Republicans.") "I've got *so* much to tell you," Maureen said with her trademark giggle and arching of her eyebrows, "but it will have to wait." We arranged to meet for drinks at midnight at a small bar in the hotel.

The dinner was another mini-disaster for Jerry Ford, who was supposed to boost Houston Flournoy's uphill campaign for governor against Democrat Jerry Brown. Ford's thirty-five-minute speech, I wrote in the Monday preelection column, "was dull, overly long and badly delivered (following Bob Hope and Reagan, two brilliant platform performers)."

I shook hands with Flournoy at the reception, and he invited me to his hotel suite for a postdinner drink. Flournoy was the youngest of the liberal Republican state assemblymen to whom I had grown close a decade earlier during the 1964 California presidential primary when they were supporting Rockefeller against Goldwater, and I had enjoyed drinking and talking with him on both coasts.

Immediately after the dinner, I found Flournoy relaxing in his hotel suite, a drink in his hand and his tuxedo jacket and tie removed. I told him what he had not heard: Ford would visit his seriously ill predecessor the next morning. Flournoy could only utter a four-letter expletive.

In my midnight drink with Maureen Reagan, I asked what she thought of Ford's speech. "He's still a turkey," she replied, adding: "Compared to this guy, even Flournoy [who was a notoriously dull speaker] is William Jennings Bryan." Both those quotes found their way, attributed to a "Reagan insider," into my Monday column.

Then Maureen dispensed the inside dope she had for me. On Thursday evening when Air Force One landed at Los Angeles International Airport, secretly waiting in the presidential limousine was Governor Reagan. The thirty-minute drive to the hotel enabled Ford and Reagan to have their first confidential chat. That represented an abrupt change in attitude by Ford and Bob Hartmann, who had wanted no part of Reagan in August when everybody and his brother (including me) was being ushered in to see the new president. Hartmann had not disguised his view that Reagan was a used-up relic. Everything was changed by Ford's precipitous postpardon drop in the polls and leaks from Sacramento that Reagan would run for president.

Maureen told me the secret Ford-Reagan "summit" continued another thirty minutes in the Century Plaza presidential suite. Ford, she said, did his best to ingratiate himself with her father. The president sought his advice on specific personnel and policy decisions and told Reagan he would continue to do so even after he left the governor's office on January 6, 1975.

However, Maureen advised me not to be misled by this or by anything I might be told by Reagan's aides or by Reagan himself. She guaranteed me that Ronald Reagan would challenge Gerald Ford for president in 1976.

Ford did visit Nixon in his Los Angeles hospital room the next morning, Friday, November 1, depressing Republican prospects three days before the election. After his politically foolhardy sick call, Ford resumed his disastrous campaign to help struggling Republican candidates. The next stop on Friday: Fresno in California's Central Valley, where Bob Mathias was seeking reelection to Congress.

Like Mayne in Iowa, Mathias was burdened not only by Watergate but the rotten farm economy in a Central Valley district that was eighty percent agricultural. Mathias had been the world's greatest athlete, only seventeen years old when he won the gold medal in the Decathlon in the 1948 Olympics and then again in 1952. I had interviewed Mathias on January 1, 1952, in the locker room of the defeated Stanford football team at the Rose Bowl in Pasadena, California. As a student journalist, I was struck how inarticulate Mathias was for an international celebrity. As I listened to Mathias address the Fresno rally, his eloquence did not seem to have advanced much in the intervening twenty-two years. Ford's speech was even drearier.

On election day, November 5, Houston Flournoy lost in California, Bob Mathias lost in Fresno, and Wiley Mayne lost in Sioux City. Democrats picked up forty-nine House seats to increase their margin over the Republicans to an overwhelming 145 seats. A gain of four Senate seats gave the Democrats a sixty-one to thirty-nine majority. The Democrats gained four more governorships, giving them thirty-six out of fifty. This was the political legacy of Richard M. Nixon.

WE NEVER MENTIONED Israel or the Middle East until three years after Evans & Novak was launched. The notion is sheer fantasy that Evans started the column with a prearranged agenda he had plotted with his Arabist pals at the State Department. He became fascinated by the Israeli question during a reporting trip to the region shortly after the Six Day War of 1967. During the next twenty-one years, Rowly wrote hundreds of columns from Washington and on the spot in the Middle East with the theme that Israeli intransigence sowed the seeds of war.

I wrote no columns about Israel during those twenty-one years, but my name appeared on every one of them and I agreed with my partner. The issue just was not at the top of my priority list, then or now. After Rowly's retirement in 1992, I wrote a handful of columns about Israel that all followed the Evans line.

Amid hundreds of critical letters about Israel sent to the column, perhaps a dozen signed by people with Jewish surnames were addressed personally to me. They asked how I as a Jew could be critical of Israel. One was from a University of Illinois fraternity brother who became a rabbi, and sent me a postcard expressing his disappointment in me.

Another was from Morrie Beschloss, who in college beat me out as sports editor of the student daily. I had heard that the mild-mannered campus politician had been transformed, now that he was a rich industrialist, into somebody unpleasantly dogmatic who tolerated no ideas differing from his own. The letter was shrill, comparing me to Jewish trusties in Nazi concentration camps who collaborated in the extermination of their brothers and sisters. Of all the venomous letters (now e-mails) I have received over the years, this was the first from somebody I knew.

(A few years later, Morrie Beschloss wrote me again without any reference to his earlier attack on me. He told me his son Michael, a historian, was coming to Washington and asked me whether—for old-times' sake—I could help him. Michael Beschloss turned out to be not only a brilliant historian, but a warm and engaging personality who became a good friend of Rowly's and an amiable acquaintance of mine. He reminded me a little of the way his father was in college, only smarter and more talented.)

One day in the summer of 1975, an editor from the *Newark Star-Ledger* was in town and asked to have lunch. I took him to Sans Souci, and we had a jolly time during which we talked politics and he told me how much he liked the column. Finally, he came to the point. Advertisers were not happy with our "anti-Israel" columns. He asked: Could you ease up on this subject? It would make life a lot easier, he added. I gave an evasive answer about watching our language.

Within the year, the *Star-Ledger* cancelled our column. It was one of about a hundred newspapers that we lost in a surprisingly short period of time. Whatever the reason—and I had my suspicions—we never built back our base.

IN REVIEWING Evans & Novak columns during the brief Ford presidency, I am surprised in two ways. First, the columns are unrelenting in criticizing Ford. No wonder my seventeen-year relationship with him did not survive after he entered the Oval Office. Second, palace politics—to use Bob Hartmann's phrase—was unremitting. More than under any other president, struggles for power were leaked to reporters (including Rowly and me) in abundant detail.

Jerry Ford, the nicest person to be president during my career, was ill equipped for the job. He was a quintessential product of the House and of the minority Republicans, suffering from a pernicious side effect of perpetual minority status: lack of a clear ideology guaranteeing the absence of a clear agenda.

WHEN I RETURNED in early July 1975, from a three-week, eight-nation reporting trip in Asia, I found Ford drifting into conduct that would cause him incalculable difficulty. He had declined an invitation to attend an AFL-CIO dinner in Washington on June 30 honoring the Russian novelist

Alexander Solzhenitsyn, recently awarded the Nobel Prize for literature and a heroic figure in the eyes of anticommunists.

My reporting produced a July 17 Evans & Novak column in which an "unimpeachable" source described in detail a "personal memorandum" to Ford from Henry A. Kissinger, simultaneously serving as secretary of state and national security adviser. My source would not let me quote it verbatim but supplied enough details so that I could write that Kissinger used "his often dogmatic concept of détente" to inform the president that it would be "politically inadvisable" to attend the AFL-CIO banquet.

The memorandum added, however, it would be acceptable for Mr. Ford to meet the great anti-Communist novelist at some White House reception. The converse, by implication: a private Ford-Solzhenitsyn meeting would not be acceptable.

I went on to report that neither Secretary of Defense James Schlesinger nor White House Chief of Staff Donald Rumsfeld, both of whom would have recommended that Ford see Solzhenitsyn, was consulted. Nor was the issue brought before the NSC. I wrote that the incident reflected qualities "more typical" of Nixon than Ford: "lack of informed political consultation, gross insensitivity, equivocal explanations, just plain bad manners."

While the State Department had barred its officials from attending the AFL-CIO dinner, other administration officials did show up: Secretary of Defense Schlesinger, Secretary of Labor John Dunlop, UN Ambassador Daniel Patrick Moynihan, and John Lehman, deputy director of the Arms Control and Disarmament Agency. If someone guessed that the "unimpeachable" source of the Kissinger memo was on that dinner list, he would be correct. It was Pat Moynihan.

Two weeks after the dinner, on July 13, after nearly daily consultation with his aides, Ford issued a press release saying he would see Solzhenitsyn if the Russian asked for it. Appearing the next day on *Meet the Press*, Solzhenitsyn said he did not come to America to see government officials. I wrote that Ford's "belated, backhanded invitation" was "rejected with deserved contempt."

A follow-up column on July 20 was written by Evans using details provided by AFL-CIO Secretary-Treasurer (and future president) Lane Kirkland, who played poker regularly in the same group with Rowly. Evans reported that Kirkland on July 14 hosted an intimate, unpublicized dinner party in his home honoring Solzhenitsyn and attended by Vice President Nelson Rockefeller. Shortly before the evening ended at eleven thirty p.m.,

Rockefeller informed Solzhenitsyn that Kissinger greatly admired him and his writing and would like to meet him—in private, of course, without publicity. No private meetings, Solzhenitsyn replied curtly. Two days later, on July 16, Kissinger publicly denounced Solzhenitsyn as a threat to world peace. Rowly was too much of a reporter not to write this about his friend Henry (though he added the implausible caveat, over my objection, it was "unclear" whether the Russian's counter-snub had led to the secretary of state's outburst).

SHORTLY AFTER THE Solzhenitsyn snub in the summer of 1975, Geraldine and I were invited to dinner at the middle-class suburban home in Bethesda, Maryland, of Fred Ikle, who as director of ACDA was head of disarmament for the Ford administration. I hardly knew Ikle, and I knew personally only one other person there. It was John Lehman, Ikle's deputy director at ACDA. Richard Perle, Senator Scoop Jackson's national security aide who was then a close friend and future business partner of Lehman (a partnership that destroyed the friendship), introduced us late in 1974. Perle sold me on doing a column late in 1974 on the efforts of liberal staffers on Capitol Hill to block Lehman's confirmation as ACDA deputy. Lehman was on Kissinger's NSC staff, but the Democratic Senate staffers had it right. He was a hard-liner on Soviet policy, as was Ikle. The column about Lehman's confirmation was the last one I wrote mentioning his name while he was at ACDA. Like Perle, Lehman became a covert source for me.

Everybody at Ikle's dinner party, whether government officials or people from think tanks and educational institutions, was connected with arms control. All were alarmed by the U.S. march toward another arms agreement with the Soviets being driven by Kissinger. During predinner cocktails, I was introduced to Lieutenant General Edward Rowny, the Pentagon's representative at arms control negotiations. "Well, Ed," somebody greeted him, "I hear you just got back from Moscow." "Yeah," he replied. "One of these days, I hope we'll go there and not concede all the bargaining points as soon as we see the towers of the Kremlin." Rowny, a tough-looking career army officer, glanced at me, as if to make sure I was taking this in.

I had been poaching on Rowly's coverage of international affairs to write about arms control. I think Ikle invited me to dinner that night because I had not bought into the news media's euphoria over arms control and particularly the Vladivostok agreement of 1974. Ford had painted the agreement as a miraculous breakthrough, which was so reported by the press. Based mainly on information from Perle, I reported on November 28 that the agreement gave the Soviets a major advantage in permitting multiple warheads on their huge missiles.

After the Ikle dinner, my reporting on arms control became more frequent and more trenchant. On July 24, I reported that Kissinger's "negotiating posture dangerously omits power, size and accuracy of nuclear weapons while concentrating on numbers."

On August 14, I reported "informed opinion high in the government that Kissinger will endanger a SALT agreement by not sticking to the Pentagon position on critical questions affecting long-range security of the United States."

My criticisms reflected not only an ongoing tutorial on arms control conducted for me separately by Perle and Lehman but also occasional conversations with Secretary Schlesinger in his Pentagon office. Schlesinger was on a collision course with Henry Kissinger.

Kissinger explained to Rowly that it was necessary to cut arms control deals with the Kremlin because he did not believe the overwhelmingly Democratic Congress would spend enough to keep up with the Russians. Having since then read everything Henry has written, I believe he also doubted the West's moral fiber. Schlesinger was more straightforward, pressing for caution on arms deals and aggressiveness on defense spending.

When on September 20, 1974, I wrote about the "pipe-smoking, donnish" Schlesinger's "professorial style of exposition" turning off Ford, Schlesinger angrily telephoned me to complain that his hard-line policies ought to please me. They did, I replied, but he simply was not "Churchillian."

A month later, the office of the secretary of defense called me with a virtual order to accompany Schlesinger to Jacksonville, Florida, on Friday, November 8. This was the weekend of the annual football game between the universities of Florida and Georgia ("the world's largest outdoor cocktail party"), its nonstop drinking and frivolity each year broken at a Friday luncheon featuring a major speaker. Schlesinger was the 1974 speaker and insisted that I accompany him on his Air Force executive jet so that I could be there firsthand to hear him deliver a saber rattler avowing the American will to prevail in the cold war. "Was that Churchillian enough for you?" Schlesinger asked me as we flew back to Washington.

It did not help Schlesinger with Ford to play Churchill. Nothing helped. He was only forty-four years old when he became secretary, but seemed a much older man. He was sarcastic, caustic, and politically incorrect—not the House of Representatives style. I wrote in my column of July 24, 1975: "On a subject so puzzling as SALT, there has been no contest between the immensely persuasive Kissinger seeing Mr. Ford for one hour every morning, and the slow-talking Schlesinger, visiting the Oval Office occasionally."

On Monday, November 3, 1975, Ford pulled the trigger for what would be known as the Halloween Massacre. Vice President Rockefeller was bumped from the 1976 ticket; Schlesinger was fired and replaced at the Pentagon by Rockefeller's archenemy, Don Rumsfeld (who was replaced as White House chief of staff by his thirty-four-year-old deputy, Dick Cheney); CIA professional William Colby was fired as DCI (and replaced by George Bush). The conventional wisdom was that Rumsfeld at the Pentagon would acquiesce in Kissinger's plans. Like much else in the Ford interlude, this was a massive miscalculation.

The Evans & Novak column of December 6 reported that the Kissinger-led national security bureaucracy was drafting major concessions to the Soviet Union in the quest for a SALT II agreement. I quoted "one outraged Administration official" as saying: "I think it's a disaster." That official was ACDA Deputy Director John Lehman.

Lehman was then thirty-three years old and could be described as dashing, combining scholarship with bravado. An upper-class Catholic from Philadelphia, he had earned his PhD from the University of Pennsylvania, was a U.S. Naval Reserve aviator (who would go on to a spectacular tenure as secretary of the navy just six years in the future), and flew his private plane to his place on the Jersey shore.

Neither Lehman nor I thought he was being disloyal to Ford but was trying to deflect the president from a disastrous course for the nation plotted by Kissinger. I considered him a patriot of great courage. We decided we could not be seen together in public or go to each other's offices. John picked a place where we were sure nobody we knew ever went—the Café de Paris, a one-room dump on Georgetown's M Street—for breakfasts starting at seven thirty a.m. Two odd stories about my meetings with Lehman at the Café de Paris:

One morning just before eight a.m., a senior Washington journalist entered the restaurant. Lehman flinched, but not as much as the journalist did. Accompanying him was a sexy young lady who was perhaps a third the reporter's age. He obviously would recognize John, and I had known the reporter well. He quickly avoided my gaze and headed for an opposite corner of the single room, confirming my judgment that he had just spent the night with the young lady, who was not, of course, his wife. None of us there that morning had anything to fear because of mutually feared destruction.

Geraldine learned from me that my very early trips from our home in the Maryland suburbs, starting at six forty-five, were to the Café de Paris. That sounded pretty exotic. So when our friend Lee Cerrell from Los Angeles visited Washington, Geraldine invited her to lunch at the Café de Paris. They were stunned to discover a crummy place with a crummier clientele.

Lehman told me he thought Rumsfeld would in the end prove a bigger problem for Kissinger than Schlesinger because he was more clever, would keep his cards shielded, and would stay on good terms with Ford. The final paragraph of my December 5 column read:

> Donald Rumsfeld, Schlesinger's successor, was the silent new boy Nov. 28 on the Verification Panel [setting U.S. SALT policy] and, even when settled in his new job, will surely reserve his advice for the President's ears only. The advice, if any, Rumsfeld gives next week may decide SALT II and influence the future of this country.

On January 26, 1976, the Evans & Novak column reported that in two months as Secretary of Defense, Rumsfeld had "won few admirers and fewer friends but has convinced the Pentagon that he has plenty of what his better-loved predecessor grievously lacked: sufficient influence at the White House to challenge . . . Kissinger on arms control." I recounted with obvious admiration how Rumsfeld had deftly interfered with Kissinger's SALT plans while quietly restoring defense budget cuts that Schlesinger had been powerless to stave off. I concluded that while Rumsfeld lacked the expertise to become a "great" Secretary of Defense, "he so clearly exceeds his predecessors in influence that he could surpass them in shaping the course of history."

Working beneath the radar, Rumsfeld was instrumental in the death of SALT II. Schlesinger became a resource for anybody, Republican or Democrat, who was running for president against Ford and wound up in the cabinet of the next Democratic president. Like much else he attempted, the Halloween Massacre did not work out for Jerry Ford.

AS 1975 ENDED, Ford made a presidential decision that enhanced my view that he had no public purpose and that extended his negative impact decades beyond his presidency.

Justice William Douglas, a left-wing Democrat who had served on the Supreme Court for a record thirty-six years, suffered a debilitating stroke at the age of seventy-seven and resigned on November 12, 1975. Ford had the opportunity to nominate a young person who was Douglas's antithesis as an advocate of judicial restraint, limited government, and free markets. The ideal choice would have been Solicitor General Robert Bork. But lacking a public purpose, Ford was interested only in finding a nominee who would easily be confirmed by the Democratic Senate. Bork did not meet that test.

John Paul Stevens did. He had been named five years earlier to the U.S. Court of Appeals in Chicago, where he had served without distinction or controversy. The fifty-five-year-old Stevens belonged to a rich Republican Chicago family that had built the massive Stevens Hotel on Michigan Avenue (later bought by Hilton and renamed the Conrad Hilton). After the tumult created over the preceding decade by the Supreme Court nominees of Lyndon Johnson and Richard Nixon, everybody seemed ready to acquiesce in so pedestrian a choice as Stevens—which was exactly Ford's intention.

Everybody but me. The Evans & Novak column of December 4, 1975, contended that in "seeking the best qualified nominee likely to win confirmation," Ford "furthered a trend toward capture of the nation's highest court by the organized legal profession that could convert it into a body of legal mechanics rather than law givers." I accused Ford of "a timid inability to seize the challenge and opportunity of a coveted court vacancy. The end product comes over as the politics of blandness." By accepting the credo of the American Bar Association president Lawrence E. Walsh (about whom much more would be heard in years to come) that previous judicial experience was required for a Supreme Court nominee, I wrote that Ford eliminated academicians such as the University of Chicago's Philip Kurland and congressmen such as California's Charles Wiggins. He also, the column continued, would have blackballed past justices John Marshall, Roger Taney, Louis Brandeis, Felix Frankfurter, Charles Evans Hughes, and Earl Warren, and current justices Lewis Powell and William Rehnquist.

For his first decade on the court, Stevens performed as expected: a swing vote whose positions could not be classified ideologically. However, as the Reagan administration raised basic questions before the high court in the 1980s, Stevens increasingly became identified with liberal causes. By the 1990s he was lionized by leftists as a savior.

John Paul Stevens was the only lasting legacy of the Ford interlude, an immutable vote on the Supreme Court against everything Republicans hold dear. I am not sure that Jerry Ford in retirement realized this, or cared much if he did.

CHAPTER 24

Reagan's Rebellion

T HE DEVASTATING SWEEP by Democrats in the 1974 midterm elections was a humiliating rejection of Gerald R. Ford. As the first nonelected president, he seemed vulnerable to a challenge by Ronald Reagan for the 1976 Republican presidential nomination. When Ford announced on November 5, 1974, that he definitely would be a candidate for president, I was off to Sacramento to look into Reagan's intentions.

The afternoon of November 21 I was given a half hour with Reagan. In the many times I had seen him over eight years, he was invariably charming but told me very, very little. This time was an exception, as spelled out in the Evans & Novak column of November 25:

> . . . [W]ith Reagan's philosophy that his final political fate is in divine hands, beyond his own control, Reagan tells friends [in this case, me] the Ford presidency may take three possible directions: successful, leading to Mr. Ford's election; middling, leading to Mr. Ford's nomination and defeat; poor, leading to Mr. Ford's not running. Only in the latter case would Reagan run, and today he is against direct action to bring about that condition.

So I began the column by stating flatly that with Reagan's "recent notions of leading a new political party crushed by vital financial backers," he "has abandoned even shrouded plans for challenging" Ford "either inside or outside the Republican Party."

My conclusion was based on accurate reporting: conversations with Reagan's advisers and Reagan himself. But less than a month earlier, Maureen Reagan had told me over midnight cocktails not to pay any attention to what Reagan's men or even Reagan himself told me. Her father was going to run, she said. The worst part of it was that, intuitively, I thought Reagan probably would run.

IT WAS NOT until April 30, 1975, as I sat beside Ronald Reagan on a small, slow two-engine plane wending its way through ferocious thunderstorms on the way to Florida from Mississippi that I became convinced he would challenge Ford.

Ever since my ill-conceived column the previous November when I all but ruled out a Reagan challenge to Ford, I had been reporting signs from the West Coast to the contrary. The bright young theoretician Jeff Bell had moved from Governor Reagan's staff to Citizen Reagan's. Political aide Bob Walker became a vice president of the Coors brewing company, then a virtual adjunct of the Republican Party, and was spending a lot of time with Reagan. So was Reagan's longtime press aide and political adviser Lyn Nofziger.

And one new addition appeared in the spring of 1975. It was John Sears, the brilliant young lawyer who had been driven out of the Nixon White House and had been hungering for a new candidate. Even before Nixon's 1972 reelection campaign, Sears was manager-in-waiting for Spiro T. Agnew's 1976 campaign for president. Over drinks in January 1971, Sears confirmed to me his Agnew connection. While I then had no idea of the vice president's bribe-taking, I had a low opinion of Agnew and expressed my surprise to Sears about his new connection. "I'm a jockey looking for a horse," Sears told me. "Agnew is the best horse around."

When that horse fell and had to be destroyed in 1974, Sears looked upon Reagan as the best available substitute. Sears could be a very smooth operator when he tried and in 1974 turned on the charm to influence Nancy and Ron. Sears was not much of a conservative, but that did not bother the Reagans. After all, in Ron's first campaign (for governor in 1966), he gave full power to political consultants Bill Roberts and Stu Spencer, who were much more liberal than Sears.

On April 30, I joined Reagan in Jackson, Mississippi. Clarke Reed, finishing ten years as Mississippi Republican chairman and about to become the state's Republican national committeeman, and his sidekick, state party finance chief Billy Mounger, were guiding Reagan through a crowded Republican fund-raising reception. "This is Reagan Country," Reed assured me.

Reagan never mentioned Gerald Ford's name—or Henry Kissinger's. But in the peroration of his speech to the Mississippi Republicans, he attacked the Ford-Kissinger détente policy: "If the Communists get the prestige and material aid they want without having to change any of their own policies, the seeds of future conflict will be continually nourished, ready to sprout anew with little or no warning." Reagan had first uttered those words in London two weeks earlier, and now he was repeating them across America. They drew cheers in Mississippi, as they did everywhere.

I had made arrangements to fly with Reagan that night from Jackson to Boca Raton, Florida, where he would address a pharmaceutical industry convention the next day in a paid speech (standard fee: $5,000, or $19,000 in 2007 dollars, plus expenses). Besides the pilot and co-pilot, there were four passengers: Reagan, an aide, a bodyguard, and me. I anticipated a rare long, uninterrupted conversation. It was that and more. Fierce thunder-showers more than doubled the length of the journey to over four hours. It was the most time I would ever have alone with Ronald Reagan.

In previous visits with Reagan, I had the impression the old actor was reading from a script. This plane ride was different. I did not get far with questions relating to his possible confrontation with Ford. Reagan did not like to talk politics with anybody. Instead, he started telling jokes—Irish, Italian, and mostly Jewish dialect jokes. His Jewish dialect was hilarious. "My staff won't let me tell these stories in public anymore," he told me.

From there, he told Hollywood anecdotes—about Jack Warner, Sam Goldwyn, Errol Flynn. I had seen Reagan's movies, and we talked about *The Santa Fe Trail, King's Row, The Spirit of Notre Dame,* and even *Bedtime for Bonzo.*

Then Reagan got personal, which he seldom did. He talked about the troubles in his first marriage, to actress Jane Wyman (Maureen's mother). "After the marriage broke up," he said, "I tried to go to bed with every star-let in Hollywood [pause and smile]. And I damn near succeeded. That was before I met Nancy."

We arrived late in Boca Raton to end a twenty-hour day. Reagan was up early to deliver his bread-and-butter speech. Next we were on to Atlanta, where he spent the afternoon in private sessions with Republican politicians. That evening he gave a town-and-gown lecture at Georgia Tech, in which he disobeyed President Ford's admonition against "recriminations" over the loss of Vietnam. The Democratic-controlled Congress lost Vietnam, said Reagan, by acting "more irresponsibly than any Congress in our history" and now has "blood on their hands."

I had covered Reagan for ten years, and I had never seen him work that hard, resulting in my column analysis:

> . . . A determined eight-hour sleeper with regular daytime rest periods as Governor, Reagan demanded light campaign schedules in Califor-

nia. . . . What he agreed to put himself through this week would have stunned old Reagan operatives.

Reagan steadily lost sleep through interminable days of speaking and handshaking aggravated by slow, small private planes. . . . Most startling to longtime Reagan watchers, he did not even complain.

I described "an unprecedentedly tousled and wrinkled Reagan" who looked "every day of his 64 years," and asked why he punished himself so hard. My answer: "Having convinced himself Mr. Ford is not up to the presidency, Reagan must also convince himself he could stand a frantic national campaign."

It took three more months for everybody to recognize that Reagan was running. The unmistakable signal was his syndicated newspaper column of July 15. In it, Reagan criticized Ford in print by name for the first time. Noting that Ford press secretary Ron Nessen defended the president's snub of Alexander Solzhenitsyn because he insisted on "substance" in any scheduled meeting, Reagan wrote: "For substance, the President has met recently with the Strawberry Queen of West Virginia and the Maid of Cotton."

SHORTLY BEFORE REAGAN announced his candidacy on November 20, 1975, I sat down for drinks with John Sears to hear his plan for replacing the incumbent Republican in the White House. Sears liked to tell the story of how Gettysburg was not specifically chosen by Robert E. Lee as the site for a climactic battle; the armies arrived accidentally because Lee was seeking shoes for his troops. Ford might not want his fate settled in New Hampshire, but that little state tucked away in remote upper New England held the nation's first presidential primary. That was Ford's misfortune, in Sears's opinion.

Reagan was supported in New Hampshire by William Loeb's *Manchester Union-Leader* and Governor Meldrim Thomson. Vigorously backed by Loeb, Thomson had defeated liberal governor Walter Peterson in the 1972 Republican primary. Sears was counting on the same forces to defeat Ford there on February 24, 1976, with the momentum carrying Reagan into another victory in conservative Florida on March 9. Ford would lose for the third time the following week on March 16 in Illinois, Reagan's birthplace and where he spent his youth and young manhood. This third primary defeat would finish the president. "Illinois would be his Waterloo," I told Sears. "Yes, Waterloo," Sears replied.

Dick Cheney, Ford's thirty-four-year-old, politically inexperienced chief of staff, asked former Reagan campaign strategist Stu Spencer to supply professional campaign expertise to the President Ford Committee (PFC).

When I learned that Spencer was going to work for Ford, I phoned him in Los Angeles. He said Ford was in bad shape in New Hampshire, where a defeat could send him down a road of successive defeats.

But Spencer described Reagan as a lazy, undisciplined candidate who would commit grievous errors unless guided carefully. He was implying Reagan without Spencer was a loser. Spencer then hinted he already had caught Reagan in a serious error, and that indeed was the case.

ON SEPTEMBER 26, 1975, two months before he formally announced his candidacy, Reagan addressed the Chicago Executives Club and delivered a speech called "Let the People Rule" containing a Jeff Bell proposal: "Nothing less than a systematic transfer of authority and resources to the states." Reagan suggested "welfare, education, housing, food stamps, Medicaid, community regional development, and revenue sharing to name a few." This would "reduce the outlay of the federal government by more than $90 billion [$339 billion in 2007 dollars]."

Only two reporters attended the speech, and only one put Bell's proposal in his story. Joel Weisman, the Chicago stringer for the *Washington Post*, buried the "$90 billion plan" deep in his report, which in turn was buried deep in the newspaper. It was a bad idea—unworkable, politically dangerous, and typical of old-fashioned conservatism. I didn't even notice the plan, and hardly anybody else did except the sharp-eyed Stu Spencer.

Spencer immediately perceived the opportunity as it related to New Hampshire. If $90 billion in spending were to be transferred from Washington to the states, wouldn't that mean higher state taxes? Peter Kaye, a *San Diego Union* reporter who was the young number three press secretary in the 1960 Nixon campaign, was brought into the Ford campaign. Kaye shared with most of the California press corps a low opinion of Reagan and was eager to cut him down. Between them, Spencer and Kaye knew every political reporter in the country, and they put out the word. They wanted Reagan challenged on the ninety-billion-dollar scheme, especially over TV, expecting he would mess up an answer.

They got their wish when Reagan appeared on ABC's *Issues and Answers* Sunday interview program on November 30, ten days after he announced his candidacy. Bob Clark of ABC News asked a question that fit Spencer's purposes perfectly:

> Clark: In candor, wouldn't you have to tell the people of New Hampshire that you are going to have to increase your [New Hampshire] tax burden and that probably as a sales tax or a state income tax?

Reagan: But isn't this a proper decision for the people of the state to make?

I can imagine Spencer gloating and Sears groaning over Reagan's answer that threatened New Hampshire's cherished freedom from both income and sales taxation. Jeff Bell later told me he had briefed Reagan to explain that the tax burden would not be shifted from the federal to the state government, but the candidate had not done so.

I spent the next three days reporting the reaction to the Reagan proposal and wrote an Evans & Novak column warning that it "threatens to be an albatross around his neck. . . . The Reagan campaign embraced, needlessly, in hindsight, a proposal bearing high political risks. . . . Reagan must begin his campaign partly on the defensive—losing the challenger's greatest advantage."

The conservative Craig Shirley, in his 2005 account of the 1976 Reagan campaign, *Reagan's Revolution: The Untold Story of the Campaign that Started It All*, wrote that "the issue faded" until my column of December 9 breathed new life into it. That apparently reflected the view of Reagan campaign survivors, but it is nonsense. Spencer was ready to ram the ninety-billion-dollar issue down Reagan's throat no matter what appeared in Evans & Novak.

BY THE END of January, I wrote from Concord, New Hampshire, "the $90 billion monster was a shadow of its former self"—proposing only the transfer of a few selected programs. But the spellbinder whose 1964 televised speech had transformed a faded movie actor into a leading Republican seemed uneasy with the anodyne campaign theme ordered by Sears. My January 31 column from Concord concluded: "In his basic new speech lasting 35 minutes, Reagan devotes 30 seconds to foreign policy—rejecting détente as 'a one-way street' for the Soviet Union. Invariably, it gets more applause than anything else."

Sears had not wanted criticism of the Ford-Kissinger foreign policy to alienate the Republican establishment and cripple Reagan for the general election. But in a new speech delivered for the first time at Exeter, New Hampshire, Reagan accused Ford of "acting as if we expect the Soviets to inherit the earth." I wrote in a February 12 column from Concord (less than two weeks before the primary) that Reagan "has shifted from the nitpicked intricacies of governmental accounting for the broad sweep of global strategy."

Reagan climbed back to lead in the polls, but he was banging against the iron wall of incumbency. On election day, Reagan finished second with

48 percent of a heavy vote to Ford's 49.4 percent—losing by 1,587 votes out of 110,190 cast. Two weeks later on March 9, Ford defeated Reagan decisively in Florida. One week after that on March 16, Ford routed Reagan in his native Illinois. Ford also clobbered Reagan in Vermont and Massachusetts, making Reagan's won-lost record zero and five. Nobody I talked to gave Reagan the most remote prospect against Ford, and I certainly did not.

Rogers Morton, who had just resigned as secretary of commerce to become Ford's campaign chairman, began secret talks with Sears on how to end Reagan's candidacy. Morton, Cheney, and Spencer stressed to me the need for haste, to end the drain of campaign funds devoted to beating back Reagan and to begin the long planned sidestep to the Left to defeat the Democrats. They had an unexpected ally in Nancy Reagan, who wanted Ronnie out to spare him the humiliation of more primary defeats.

Reagan wanted to stay on for one last primary—in North Carolina. On March 23, one week after the Illinois debacle, Ronald Reagan would have been a footnote in history save for a tough fifty-five-year-old trial lawyer from Raleigh, North Carolina, named Tom Ellis.

TOM ELLIS EMERGED in politics in 1972, managing the election to the U.S. Senate of the right-wing local television commentator Jesse Helms. With North Carolina's middle of the road Republican organization appalled by Helms, Ellis created an alternative party structure—the Congressional Club.

On Tuesday night, March 23, 1976, I was at the Channel 5 WTTG studios in Washington to tape a commentary when I heard the stunning news that Reagan had won the North Carolina primary by six percentage points. In my column, I attributed the "wholly unexpected" outcome in North Carolina to "a Reagan campaign more highly ideological and more geared to national security than previous efforts." It was Tom Ellis's doing.

I met Ellis shortly after the North Carolina primary, and found him intractable when he took a position, as well as being a well-informed conservative ideologue. Ellis and Sears had met in Washington for the first time two weeks before the New Hampshire primary and took an instant dislike to each other. As Ellis later related it to me, he told Sears that the national campaign's ads were insipid, and he demanded something to put on the air portraying Reagan's qualities and hitting hard against détente and the looming surrender of the Panama Canal. Sears chuckled (a tendency that antagonized people who disagreed with him) and said victory in New Hampshire would take care of that.

When Reagan lost in New Hampshire, Ellis intensified his demand that the undiluted Reagan be put on TV. Sears refused. The Reagan campaign finally gave Ellis a tape of a half-hour Reagan speech for a single Florida station. Poor though its quality was, it contained the essential Reagan that Sears tried to hide ("To continue on the present course is to recognize the inevitability of a Socialist America"). Fifteen of North Carolina's seventeen television stations showed it on prime time.

The Republican establishment was apoplectic about North Carolina, realizing that Reagan's campaign had been revitalized. What nobody (not even true believers like Tom Ellis) realized was that North Carolina had saved not only Ronald Reagan's 1976 campaign but also his and the conservative movement's future in America.

BY THE LATE winter of 1976, I had known Richard Perle for four years as an invaluable source and a pleasant companion. We had a lot in common, but not our attitude toward spectator sports. I loved them. Richard could not care less. In 1976, however, he was dating his future wife, Leslie Barr, who was a fervent basketball fan.

I was in my second year as a season ticket holder of the Washington Bullets basketball team. On Sunday, March 7, 1976, the Bullets were playing the New York Knicks at the Capital Centre in Landover, Maryland. My close friend, the journalist Fred Barnes, whose two season tickets were next to mine, was not attending the game and I invited Richard and Leslie to use them, joining Geraldine and me. I could hardly imagine that this social occasion would yield perhaps the most influential column I ever wrote.

As we sipped cocktails at the arena's Capital Club prior to the game, Perle pulled some papers out of his inside jacket pocket and handed them to me. "A little payment for your hospitality," he said, with a wry smile. It was a copy of a seven-page State Department cable reporting on a mid-December 1975 closed-door briefing in London of U.S. ambassadors to European capitals by Helmut Sonnenfeldt, counselor of the State Department. I had read only a few paragraphs when I told Perle: "Wow, this is something." Richard smiled his slow, conspiratorial grin. "I thought you would like it," he said.

"I don't really see that it amounts to much," Evans told me after reading the Sonnenfeldt speech. Rowly's normally acute news sense sometimes failed when a valued source was at risk. Hal Sonnenfeldt, called Kissinger's Kissinger, was Rowly's frequent lunch companion. But I believe the source Rowly wanted to protect was Sonnenfeldt's boss, Secretary of State Kissinger. With some shouting, I talked Rowly into my doing the column. We engaged in a little bargaining to agree on mutually acceptable language, to soften the blow on Kissinger rather than Sonnenfeldt.

The tone of the Evans & Novak column that ran Monday, March 22, 1976, was more subdued than most of our efforts. When you have a great story, there's no need to shout. It began:

> Intense debate was set off within the Ford Administration three months ago when Secretary of State Henry Kissinger's right-hand man declared in a secret briefing that permanent "organic" union between the Soviet Union and Eastern Europe is necessary to avoid World War III.
>
> That policy, going well beyond any public position of the U.S. Government, was enunciated in mid-December by State Department Counselor Helmut Sonnenfeldt. He told a London meeting of U.S. ambassadors to European nations that the "inorganic, unnatural relationship" between Moscow and Eastern Europe based on Soviet military prowess threatens world peace. "So," he concluded, "it must be our policy to strive for an evolution that makes the relationship between the Eastern Europeans and the Soviet Union an organic one."
>
> When transcripts of Sonnenfeldt's remarks hit Washington, some officials complained that this amounted to U.S. underwriting of Soviet dominion over Eastern Europe. As such, these critics contended, the Sonnenfeldt Doctrine never had been U.S. policy and should not be now.

The column went on to quote Sonnenfeldt telling the ambassadors that Soviet "inability to acquire loyalty in Eastern Europe is an unfortunate historical failure" because of Moscow's "natural interest" in the region. He added that the "inorganic, unnatural relationship is a far greater danger to world peace than the conflict between East and West."

All this was damaging enough for Ford, but the "Sonnenfeldt Doctrine" hit bottom when we reported the State Department counselor praising Poland as a good example for submitting to Soviet domination: "The Poles have been able to overcome their romantic political institutions which led to their disasters in the past." No language could be more carefully calculated to antagonize the large, fiercely anti-Soviet Polish-American population.

The first reaction came from outraged leaders of nationality groups and their agents in Congress—especially Congressman Edward J. Derwinski, a Republican from Chicago's unfashionable south suburbs. An early Goldwater backer for 1964, Derwinski was one of Ford's most important conservative supporters and a Polish-American leader. He had been complaining privately about the Ford-Kissinger pursuit of détente and was devastated when he read our Sonnenfeldt Doctrine column. It threatened Derwinski's efforts to keep ethnic Americans away from Reagan.

For two years, conservative Republican House members who called themselves the Study Committee had sought a meeting with Kissinger to grill him on détente. After our Sonnenfeldt column ran on March 22, 1976, Derwinski virtually ordered the secretary of state to appear. Three days later, Kissinger sat down with the Study Committee, unannounced to the public, over breakfast in a private room on the first floor of the Capitol. The full results of the meeting leaked to me and appeared in the Evans & Novak column of March 30.

Derwinski opened the meeting by describing how unhappy he was that Kissinger at a recent diplomatic conference in Helsinki had acquiesced in Soviet control of the Baltic states. Now, Derwinski continued, Sonnenfeldt's briefing in London was "the straw that broke the camel's back." Kissinger claimed the Evans & Novak column was based on inaccurate State Department cables caused by sloppy note-taking in London. "Henry's answer did not satisfy me, or I suppose, any of the others," Derwinski told me.

After this column was published, Sonnenfeldt on the same day visited Derwinski's office. When Sonnenfeldt claimed his remarks had been distorted, Derwinski asked to see the official State Department account of the London briefing. Sonnenfeldt refused and invoked executive privilege (which can be invoked only by the president) on a document whose many copies now were bouncing all around Washington. Derwinski told me he was "astonished."

On March 31 Ronald Reagan—fighting to stay alive in his endangered challenge of Ford—in a national television address declared that the Sonnenfeldt Doctrine meant "slaves should accept their fate."

The authentic State Department response came two days later on April 2 in the form of an op-ed column by *Washington Post* editorial writer Stephen S. Rosenfeld. He denied there was any Sonnenfeldt Doctrine, asserting: "My point is not that the policy is beyond criticism but that it's old hat." The State Department defense was that Sonnenfeldt was merely reiterating old policy. That did not please Ed Derwinski and the ethnic vote.

LATE ON THURSDAY afternoon, April 22, 1976, I boarded the press plane at Andrews Air Force Base to accompany Air Force One and Gerald R.

Ford to Indiana, where he would campaign for that state's May 4 primary. What worried Stu Spencer was a cluster of three southern primaries— Texas on May 1 and Alabama and Georgia on May 4. He recognized the possibility of Reagan doing in those states what he did in North Carolina. So it was essential for Ford to pin down Indiana, where he was a heavy favorite in that state's May 4 primary. I referred in a column to "a deepening sense of foreboding" in the Ford camp.

In Indianapolis, Ford recited his mantra that Kissinger "can stay as Secretary of State as long as I am President of the United States." Ford looked surprised to hear booing from his friendly Hoosier audience. His arrival in Indiana was preceded by Reagan radio commercials attacking the Ford-Kissinger foreign policy.

On May 1, Reagan crushed Ford in Texas, winning one hundred out of one hundred delegates. Three days later, he swept Alabama and Georgia with 71 percent and 68 percent respectively. The real shocker was Indiana, a state where early polls gave Ford a twenty-point lead and where he expected to ride to an easy victory on the shoulders of Governor Doc Bowen's patronage machine. Reagan won the popular vote narrowly and captured forty-five of fifty-four delegates.

Four Reagan primary victories, I wrote in the May 5 issue of the *Evans-Novak Political Report,* "opens the *distinct possibility that President Gerald R. Ford may not win the Republican Presidential nomination* [underlined in the newsletter]." It was the kind of fight for the Republican nomination I had awaited for more than sixteen years, not out of ideological fervor but from a reporter's lust for a bloody political battle.

ONE OF THE primary states where Ford had a clear advantage (and where he actually won comfortably May 18) was Maryland, the state where I lived.

I registered as a Republican in Maryland when we moved there in 1967, and I had voted in Republican primaries since I was old enough to vote. I was my father's son, and I always voted for the more liberal Republican in a primary contest.

As much as I had liked Jerry Ford as a congressman, I believe he had proved a disorganized, incoherent, and incompetent president. I had come to believe Reagan was smarter and better qualified. Nevertheless, I was inclined to vote for Ford as the representative of the centrist Republican Party I had favored all my life.

But Ford failed on the one issue that I personally cared about: the epochal struggle between freedom and Communism. I felt his snub of Solzhenitsyn, his weak posture in negotiating with the Soviets, and his failure to repudiate the Sonnenfeldt Doctrine suggested he was in thrall to Dr. Kissinger. That meant he failed to appreciate that the life of the West and its democratic institutions depended on the struggle against the Soviet Union. Reagan understood.

I voted for Reagan.

JUNE 12 FOUND President Ford in Springfield, Missouri, where the final nineteen (out of the state's forty-nine) national convention delegates were to be picked by the Republican state convention. The president was there out of fear he would be shut out despite support from everybody important in the Missouri Republican Party. If Reagan were to sweep at-large delegates in a state that in press accounts had been conceded to Ford, it could be a bad signal for the remainder of the delegate chase.

Ford was given four hours to meet with the 1,440 state convention delegates and try to turn around Reagan supporters (Reagan was allotted only one hour for delegate chats). The president repeated what delegates heard in preconvention delegate phone calls from the two young stars of the Missouri Republican Party: Governor Kit Bond, thirty-seven, and State Attorney General John Danforth, forty. Both had tough contests coming up in November—Bond for reelection as governor, Danforth for the U.S. Senate—and told delegates: If you want *me* to win, do not nominate Reagan because he would guarantee my defeat. The effort, I wrote in a pre-Springfield convention column, was "to frighten grass-roots conservative diehards into ignoring their hearts and following their appointed President."

In what I described as a "humiliating rebuff" to Ford, Reagan won eighteen out of the nineteen delegates. The nineteenth delegate was given to Ford by the grace of Sears, so that Governor Bond could be a delegate at the national convention. (That did not prevent the anti-Reagan Bond's defeat for reelection, though he later became a U.S. senator who enthusiastically supported Reagan programs. The anti-Reagan Danforth was elected to the Senate and in 2004, as an Episcopal priest, presided at Ronald Reagan's funeral and delivered the principal eulogy.)

TWO WEEKS BEFORE the national convention, John Sears was running out of time and contested delegates. The *Evans-Novak Political Report* count gave Ford a lead of only forty-six delegates with fifty-seven still uncommitted. But Ford's total of 1,124 put him a mere six delegates short of the number needed to clinch the nomination.

I talked to Sears frequently, sometimes taking him to an alcoholic lunch at San Souci. In mid-July, with all delegates selected, I told John, that I could see no way that Reagan could be nominated. He hinted that he had hidden away forty or fifty covert Reagan delegates in the big organization-controlled eastern delegations—New York, Pennsylvania, and New Jersey. He said they were pledged to Ford but at the proper moment would switch. Sears was close to businessman-politician Drew Lewis, the chairman of the Pennsylvania delegation.

I thought Sears was covering up his own strategic error. As part of his original plan to force Ford out of the race in mid-March by winning the New Hampshire, Florida, and Illinois primaries, Sears felt the eastern delegates would fall like ripe fruit to a Reagan who had not antagonized the party establishment. But when Sears's early primary strategy failed, it was too late to contest for primaries in New York, Pennsylvania, and New Jersey—outraging conservative activists from those states. Out of 324 delegates elected from the three states, Reagan had only 33.

Sears was an inventive political strategist and came up with a solution: to pick a vice presidential running mate from one of the three eastern states in advance of the convention to pry loose delegates. The name of the liberal Republican chosen by Sears for vice president was so unfamiliar to most conservatives that outrage was limited. The fifty-year-old Senator Richard S. Schweiker had not attracted much attention since being elected from Pennsylvania to the House in 1960 and the Senate in 1968. He was a type of Republican then common in big industrial states, a self-described party loyalist who voted the straight liberal-labor line in Congress. Schweiker had a one-hundred-percent AFL-CIO voting record, was weak on national security questions, belonged to the liberal Republican Wednesday Club, and was an enthusiastic Ford-for-president advocate as an elected national convention delegate. I considered him an "ultra-liberal" and so labeled him in the column about his selection.

As for Reagan's agreement to this arrangement, I'm sure he had no idea who Dick Schweiker was. The old actor was submitting to his director. Reagan was inflexible on principles, flexible on details—a pattern that would prove both a strength and weakness in years to come.

A jubilant Sears phoned me July 26, the day the Schweiker ploy was formally announced, to say the number of Ford delegates defecting as a result of Schweiker being selected by Reagan could reach sixty. Drew Lewis could switch a substantial chunk of Pennsylvania's 103 delegates. That, in turn, could affect other delegations.

I phoned around to check eastern state defections predicted by Sears. Nothing, except for three or four Pennsylvanians tied to Schweiker. The big question was how many Reagan delegates had been lost. I made contact with Senator Helms, who told me Reagan phoned him at 9:05 p.m. Sunday. He said he noted the precise time because "I wanted to record for posterity the exact time I received the shock of my life." As a senator he knew how liberal Schweiker was. Nevertheless, Helms was the good soldier, standing by Schweiker's side Monday as Reagan made the announcement. Other Reagan stalwarts I telephoned, while not happy, also were sticking with their candidate.

THE REPUBLICAN CONVENTION opening on Monday, August 16, 1976, at the Kemper Arena in Kansas City has been described as the last national political convention—and the first since the conventions of both parties in 1952—where the nominee's identity was not known. That is not really the case, however. In the column I wrote from Kansas City a week before the convention began I said Ford "almost certainly will be nominated." Our delegate count showed Ford about eighty delegates ahead of Reagan with only about eighty uncommitted delegates left.

The balloting late Wednesday night at Kemper ended with Ford just fifty-seven delegates (out of 2,259) over the minimum needed for nomination. Ford was better than usual Thursday night in his acceptance speech, but it could not compare with what Reagan said after being coaxed to the podium to deliver impromptu remarks. Reagan did not mention Ford by name, referred to his nomination only in passing, and stressed the convention's adoption of a platform that was not to the president's liking. It was, he said proudly "a banner of bold, unmistakable colors with no pastel shades."

As I listened to Reagan's stirring words, I thought the plight of the Republican Party was desperate. It had just rejected its most compelling personality, who would be sixty-nine years old at the time of the next election and surely too old to try again. The Democrats, by nominating somebody from the Deep South, seemingly had dashed Republican hopes for party realignment. Jerry Ford trailed Jimmy Carter in every southern state, but that was hardly the extent of the party's problems.

The Republican national convention issue of the *Evans-Novak Political Report* on August 20 published a state-by-state rundown of the presidential race that showed that if the election were held that day, Carter would have 517 electoral votes to 21 for Ford (Idaho, Kansas, North Dakota, Utah, and Wyoming).

CHAPTER 25

Jimmy Who?

THE 1972 DEMOCRATIC disaster of George McGovern's candidacy had not expelled the virus of "reform" that spawned the party's unprecedented midterm national convention in Kansas City on December 5–7, 1974. It featured efforts by National Chairman Robert Strauss to bring Democrats back to moderation against the radical elements that had nominated McGovern.

Organized labor's delegates, a majority of them supporting Strauss, were holding a closed-door caucus as the convention began Friday night. I noticed labor delegates entering a large meeting room with only cursory attention paid to who walked in. In those days before I was a regular television performer, I was not recognized and did not pay attention to my personal appearance. Wearing a wrinkled sports jacket with no tie and needing a haircut, I at age forty-five could pass for a labor skate. With close to three hundred people in the room, I unobtrusively took a seat in the rear.

A commotion at the door halted proceedings that had just begun. Arguing with labor officials (one with a firm grip on his arm) was Christopher Lydon, a reporter for the *New York Times*. Very tall and preppy looking, Chris was wearing a tweed jacket with a colorful ascot, a press pass around his neck. A union official grasped him firmly, ejecting him from the meeting. Suddenly, he was pointing at me, showing the union officials that one reporter already was there. I was quickly given the bum's rush out of the caucus.

"You son of a bitch!" I shouted at Lydon in the hallway outside the room. "What good did it do you to get me kicked out?" Lydon shrugged and flashed a supercilious grin. That did it, and I took a swing at his jaw. But with Chris half a foot taller than I, my feeble punch landed on his chest and fellow journalists grabbed us before anything more serious transpired.

Unfortunately, a brief account of the incident appeared on the front page of Sunday's *Kansas City Star,* enhancing my reputation as a madman.

The convention itself involved a struggle over racial quotas where Strauss, by giving ground, averted a walkout by black delegates. But I missed the real story taking place at the Holiday Inn where small groups of delegates trooped into a small room to be pitched by a little man with a deep southern accent. It was Jimmy Carter, in his last days as governor of Georgia. I did not even know he was in Kansas City until 1977, when I read about it in Jules Witcover's account of the 1976 campaign, *Marathon: The Pursuit of the Presidency.* On December 12, Carter announced his candidacy, an event so widely ignored that I was not aware he was running for president until five months later.

ON AN UNSEASONABLY warm Manhattan early evening in April 1975, I was unable to find a taxi and set out for a sweaty twelve-block walk from the St. Regis Hotel, where I was staying, to the Century Club, where I was scheduled for cocktails with Daniel Patrick Moynihan (then President Ford's U.S. ambassador to the United Nations).

I was walking rapidly when a long black limousine pulled up. A rear window went down, and a voice, in a nasal New York accent, called out: "Novak! Get in the car! We'll take you wherever you want to go!" I couldn't see inside the limo, but the voice belonged to Eliot Janeway, the economic analyst, investor, and would-be political kingmaker.

When I entered the car, I was surprised to see Jimmy Carter. "You know Governor Carter, don't you?" Janeway said. "We're on our way to see Ted Sorensen [Jack Kennedy's aide and speechwriter] to talk about the campaign. [pause] The governor is running for president." I responded "Really?" Carter said nothing, but fixed a manic grin on his face.

I thought my friend Eliot had picked another lemon. Janeway envisioned himself as part Bernard Baruch (counselor to the great) and part James Farley (political maestro). He was an early booster of Lyndon Johnson, but Janeway despised the Kennedys and broke with LBJ after he went on the 1960 ticket with JFK. He tried to pump up presidential support for House Ways and Means Chairman Wilbur Mills and Senator Vance Hartke of Indiana, but their unlikely candidacies fell flat. Carter seemed to me to be in the same category.

THE FIRST TIME I ever really took Carter seriously for president was a few weeks after I saw him in Eliot Janeway's limo. I was lunching at San

Souci with Alan Baron, one of the truly unique characters I have known in politics.

Alan was a Democratic activist from Sioux City, Iowa, who was very liberal, very Jewish, obese, and a cocaine user and homosexual. He was loud in an accent more Yiddish than Iowan, and exhibited atrocious table manners, sometimes emitting a fine spray of food while talking. And did he ever talk. I can't think of anybody with whom I would rather talk politics than Alan. We disagreed ideologically on everything, but we never talked ideology. Baron loved political gossip and passed it on to me for column-writing purposes. He also made brilliant interpretations of voting results to draw fascinating conclusions.

At lunch late in August 1975, Alan and I agreed President Ford was in such bad shape that any Democrat could win. There was no favorite in the large field of serious Democrats: Scoop Jackson, Birch Bayh, George Wallace, Morris Udall, Sargent Shriver, Jerry Brown, Fred Harris, Lloyd Bentsen, Terry Sanford, Milton Shapp, Frank Church, Dale Bumpers, and Jimmy Carter. When I asked Baron whom he thought would win, I was shocked when he chose Carter, who was dead last in the polls.

Alan was on the left wing of the Democratic spectrum (at that time on Senator George McGovern's staff) and feared Carter would sell out the liberal cause. (In 1976, McGovern fired Baron for attacking Carter, by that time, the all but certain nominee.) Baron regarded Carter as untrustworthy and of poor character, who would hurt the Democratic Party if nominated and hurt the United States if elected. He would, Alan said, do everything he could to stop Carter.

Yet, Baron told me, he sensed in Carter the same determination possessed by McGovern in 1972. Forget the polls, he advised. But how, I asked, could the former governor of Georgia survive the New Hampshire primary? "New Hampshire is no longer first," Baron replied. "The Iowa caucuses are first." But nobody paid attention to them. Not anymore, Baron told me. He kept in touch with his home state, and Carter was working it hard. The other candidates—like sheep led to the slaughter—were being sucked into Iowa to cut off Carter. That suddenly made Iowa important. If Carter won there, he could roar into New Hampshire and win it with momentum from Iowa and then capture Florida by convincing liberal candidates he would be their surrogate there to stop Wallace. Little Jimmy would then be the frontrunner.

ON SUNDAY, NOVEMBER 30, 1975, Jimmy Carter was the guest on CBS's *Face the Nation*. By then, he and the Iowa caucuses were no longer a secret known only to Alan Baron. The scenario that Baron laid out for me in August was well under way.

On *Face the Nation,* Carter was asked whether he favored the 1974 post-Watergate campaign finance reform (putting limits on contributions). Carter began: "I favor the law. I've been a member of Common Cause for a long time, and participated in the evolution of the ideas that led to that law."

As I sat in the family room of our suburban Maryland home that Sunday, alarm bells went off in my head. I had covered campaign finance reform legislation and never caught a whiff of Jimmy Carter. And the governor of Georgia, a member of Common Cause, a liberal do-gooder organization?

On Monday, November 31, I checked my sources in campaign finance reform. Yesterday, they said, was the first they ever heard from him. I then called Common Cause. Just as I suspected, Jimmy Carter was not now and never had been a member (though his wife, Roslyn, had joined).

So I had caught Carter in two little untruths. Coming from the presidential candidate who at every campaign stop said, "I'll never lie to you," that was not trivial. But it was not all. The first question to Carter on *Face the Nation* was why he was running against Scoop Jackson after making his nominating speech at the 1972 Democratic convention. Carter replied: "I certainly wouldn't disavow a long-standing friendship [with Jackson]. I've known Scoop since I was working under Admiral [Hyman] Rickover on the atomic submarine program and he was a junior member of Congress involved with atomic energy."

That, too, rang false to me. I got in touch with people who had worked with Rickover in the nuclear program. They thought it impossible that Carter as a navy lieutenant would have had serious contact with Jackson, a member of the powerful Joint Congressional Committee on Atomic Energy (or with Rickover himself, for that matter). I then called Senator Jackson. Scoop told me he was sure he did not know Carter when he was in the navy and did not meet him until he ran for governor of Georgia in 1970. Two more untruths.

Carter was questioned by Godfrey Sperling's group of reporters over breakfast at the Sheraton Carlton Hotel on Thursday, December 2, five days after the *Face the Nation* broadcast. Sitting across the long narrow table from the smiling candidate, I brought up these discrepancies. He blandly admitted he never had joined Common Cause but considered Roslyn's membership ("She writes the checks") as his own. As for what Jackson told me, he recalled reminiscing about "the old days with Scoop" when he breakfasted with the late Senator Richard B. Russell of Georgia. That entailed a check by me with one of Russell's former aides, who angrily told me that Carter's talk about chummy breakfasts "greatly exaggerated" his relationship with the southern patriarch.

Carter's December 2 breakfast produced more varnishing of the truth that I checked out. The worst was his claim to have "worked hard" on Atlanta's voluntary school busing plan. I placed calls to several school board and NAACP members in Atlanta, and none could recall Carter working on the busing compromise. As governor he did sit in on a lone negotiating session between the school board and the NAACP, where his only contribution was to state his objection to school busing.

Carter also told the reporters on December 2 that he always had favored federal revenue sharing going to local governments and not the states, taking that position even when he was governor of Georgia. I checked high and low, but could find no public record or personal recollection of such an unselfish position by Carter. I did find a 1971 statement to Congress by Governor Carter: "I support the concept of sharing additional federal revenues with state and local governments." There was no mention of cutting off the states.

Finally, on December 2, among those listed by Carter as policy experts with whom he consulted were Wilbur Cohen, former secretary of health, education and welfare, and George Ball, former under secretary of state. That sounded fishy to me, and I called both men (whom I knew well). Cohen told me he spent a day with Governor Carter in Atlanta in 1973 and had not seen him since. Ball said he had breakfasted with Carter once the previous autumn—and had never seen him again.

It took me a month to follow all these leads and make sure there was no evidence to support Carter's claims. Finally, in the Evans & Novak column of January 6, 1976, within the span of 650 words, I documented nine separate untruths uttered by Carter in his *Face the Nation* and Sperling breakfast appearances. I quoted a black leader from Atlanta who was a leader in negotiating the school busing compromise as saying: "For him [Carter] to claim that he did anything to help a settlement is an outright lie." Then I added my view:

Actually, "fibbing" better describes falsely claiming credit—common among candidates, who usually have more than a little Baron Munchhausen in them. But Carter is the anti-Washington, anti-government, anti-lawyer candidate telling audiences "I'll never lie to you" and setting post-Watergate standards of honesty. Against that pledge, old enemies in Georgia use the words "lie" and "liar" with disturbing frequency to describe him.

I FOLLOWED Alan Baron's admonition to get to Iowa early, and found in the autumn of 1975 that Carter was planting deep roots in the state. By the time I returned to Iowa the second week of January 1976, everybody recognized the state's importance and knew Carter was leading there. I was one of six reporters who showed up to follow Carter on a motorcade through rural northwest Iowa.

Carter's press secretary Jody Powell greeted me in Sioux City on Monday, January 12, where the trip started. My "Carter Lies" column had run a few days earlier, and Powell informed me that he and the governor considered *me* the liar. He handed me a point-by-point rebuttal that was more than twice as long as the column.

Assuming all the reporters wanted private time with the candidate, Powell said each of us could ride with Carter in his auto on a leg of the daylong trip. Jody said we would rotate in order of seniority, which would be determined by the reporters. Johnny Apple of the *New York Times* looked us over, and said Novak was the most senior and that he, Apple, was second. So with foreboding, I got in the backseat with Carter that cold January morning.

"Bob," Carter said, "you have done me a grave injustice and you may well have damaged my candidacy. But that's not what bothers me. I'm just sorry that you have such a low opinion of me. That really hurts me." Then he smiled and directed his innocent gaze toward me. "Well," I said, "I'm sorry you feel that way, Governor." "Let's just forget about this, Bob," Carter said, holding his own rebuttal to my column in his hand, "and have a good candid conversation." Candid, hardly! After that, Carter gave unresponsive answers to my uninspired questions.

It was a long, boring day, and at the end of it, Kevin Horrigan, a young *Kansas City Star* reporter, approached me. As the most junior correspondent, he had traveled the last leg with Carter. He had many questions for the candidate about the Evans & Novak column, but he said Carter told him that matter had been taken care of that morning. "Bob Novak apologized to me," said Carter. "He said he was sorry he wrote the column."

"Did you really apologize to him?" Horrigan asked me. "No," I replied, "I said I was sorry he felt that way about me." After the Iowa incident, I became convinced I was too soft in my column by talking about "fibbing." Jimmy Carter was a habitual liar who modified the truth to suit his purposes.

A week later, as voters assembled for the Iowa caucuses, Carter led all candidates in the crowded field with 27.6 percent. Indiana's Senator Birch Bayh was a poor second at 13.1 percent.

IOWA PROPELLED CARTER into New Hampshire with momentum. Still, this upper New England state did not seem hospitable to a little-known ex-governor from the Deep South. What I did not realize was that Carter for the past year had been methodically preparing the soil in New Hampshire just as he had in Iowa.

Besides being good, Carter was lucky. Inexplicably, Scoop Jackson and George Wallace skipped New Hampshire. As I reported in a column from Manchester one week before the primary, "Carter clearly has the center right road all to himself."

On February 24, Carter won New Hampshire with 30 percent of the vote, as his liberal opponents divided their vote: Udall, 24 percent; Bayh, 16 percent (ending Bayh's once promising candidacy); Harris, 11 percent; Shriver, 9 percent.

CARTER AGAIN SHOWED his tactical genius in the Florida primary on March 9. He convinced what was left of the liberal pack—Udall, Harris, and Shriver, before Brown and Church began their late-blooming campaigns—to stay out of Florida to prevent a victory there by the dreaded George Wallace. They gave Carter a clear field as the liberal(!) candidate, and an easy win against Wallace and Jackson.

That left the Illinois primary on March 16 as the last real chance to stop Carter (though Udall, Brown, and Church would continue into June). Covering Carter in Chicago, I was given time to chat with the candidate and was seated beside him on a campaign bus ride on Friday, March 12.

Jimmy ended our interview with something strange and Carteresque: "You know, we really don't know each other very well, Bob. I think we should really try to know each other better, so we could understand each other. Could you come down to Plains for a day or two, to spend some quiet time together away from the campaign? Could you do that?" I decided to play along. "Governor," I replied, "I can't think of anything I would enjoy more. It would be really helpful to me." Carter said he would call my office to set it up. I never expected the call would be made, and it never was.

Two days later, on March 14, we faced each other in CBS's Washington studios for *Face the Nation*. I wanted to flush Carter out on his declaration that he would reduce nineteen hundred federal agencies down to two hundred without revealing what agencies would be eliminated. Ed Rabel of CBS News apparently had the same idea and preceded me at the beginning of the program by asking which of those agencies would be closed. Carter responded with a typical evasion: "There is no way I can take off from campaigning, do a complete and definite study of what the federal government is and what it's going to be three or four years in the future."

I followed up sarcastically: "Governor, I'll give you a question you don't have to take time off from campaigning to answer." Noting that state spending in Georgia actually increased while he was eliminating agencies, I asked: "Would you reduce the federal payroll, and if so, by how much, forgetting about how many agencies you eliminate?" Carter replied: "I can't say that I would."

I seized on something that typified Carter's demagogic style. I had done some research on it, and sprung the trap:

Novak: Governor, when you were asked on the campaign trail about foreign policy, I noticed that you always make a criticism and get a good deal of applause for it: that one of the things wrong with our foreign policy is whenever you run into an embassy and see quote "a fat, bloated, ignorant, rich, major contributor to Nixon who can't even speak the language of the country in which he serves." You think that's part of what's wrong with our foreign policy. Governor, can you name one such fat, ignorant, bloated ambassador who can't speak the language?

Carter: No, I wouldn't want to name any.

Novak: Well, *can* you name one, though? You make the accusation all over. There are only four ambassadors, Governor, who gave contributions to Mr. Nixon. Are any of them that fit that category?

Carter: Well, I wouldn't want to name names. But the point I'm making is, and I don't do it every time I make a foreign policy speech—

Novak: Pretty nearly.

Carter: Every now and then I do, but not often. . . .

Novak: Governor, your credibility has been challenged by your critics and by some people in the press. And there are only four people who are now serving as ambassadors who gave money to Nixon. Three of them know the language of the country that they work in, and one of them is taking language training. Isn't that bordering on demagoguery when you make a flat statement about these kind of quote "fat, bloated, ignorant ambassadors"?

> Carter: Well, I don't believe so. I think it illustrates a point very clearly. . . .
>
> Novak: Are you going to continue to use that formulation and get applause from it?
>
> Carter: I may or may not.

In fact, Carter did not. But on *Face the Nation,* he was furious and dropped his smile for once. I had a final shot at Carter—and I took what I learned Carter felt was a cheap shot—as the last question of the broadcast.

> Novak: Governor, when you are ever asked about your desire to cut the defense budget 7 or 8 billion dollars, you always mention how many generals or admirals there are. Do you know, either in percentages or in flat amounts, what the cost of salaries of the generals and admirals is?
>
> Carter: No, I don't.
>
> Novak: It's four one-hundredths of one percent, or 41 million dollars. Don't you think that also borders on exaggeration in making that a major issue?
>
> Carter: No, it doesn't, because the actual number of admirals and generals is mirrored all the way down the ranks.

I had made Carter look like a fool. There was no smile in his cold eyes, as he said to me after the program ended: "Bob, you're very tough and very good." "Thank you, Governor," I said. "*You're* very good." I lied. I thought it was a very poor performance by Carter and one of my most effective efforts as a television interrogator. Other people apparently did not agree.

My first appearance on national network television came in 1963 on *Face the Nation.* The program's format then had one print journalist joining two CBS correspondents on the panel each week. In the intervening fourteen years, I was asked to be the outside questioner more than anybody else—and usually with a prime guest, such as Jimmy Carter. But after that Carter program on March 14, 1976, now more than thirty years ago, *Face the Nation* never again asked me to be a questioner. Nobody at CBS ever told me why, and I did not ask. I learned that a Carter aide had complained to CBS that I was biased, and I assume that the network wanted a less aggressive questioner.

Two days later, on March 16, Carter won the Illinois primary in a landslide. I could see there was no way to stop him from a nomination to oppose an unelected Republican president who looked like a sure loser.

. . .

GERALD R. FORD was so battered by his struggle for the Republican nomination that he began the general election campaign trailing Jimmy Carter by 30 percentage points in the popular vote and 496 votes in the Electoral College, according to my rundown.

Because the Republican convention was so late in 1976, Ford's kickoff did not come until nine days after Labor Day on Wednesday, September 15. The venue also was unusual to start a Republican presidential campaign: Ann Arbor, Michigan, home of the leftist-dominated University of Michigan and a liberal Democratic stronghold.

But this university was Ford's alma mater. His strategists waited so long to start because they wanted him fully prepared for a carefully honed speech delivered in an academic setting.

I was a pool reporter when the president joined the Michigan football team for dinner at their training table. It was an uncomfortable meeting for the '76 Wolverines and the old grad (Class of '35) former football captain. Bo Shembechler, Michigan's uptight coach, was displeased with this distraction, and the players seemed uninterested in dining with the president of the United States. Although he was a big man, the players dwarfed him. Ford, seeming ill at ease, made no attempt to break the ice with the players. I could not have imagined Ronald Reagan similarly disengaged from the young men.

The real difficulty with this kickoff was epitomized by the lead paragraph of the Evans & Novak column of September 19, 1976, datelined Ann Arbor:

> The presence of a Washington super-bureaucrat aboard Air Force One when it arrived in Michigan for the Ford campaign kickoff suggested the clinical nature, and hence the limitations, of the President's vision of America's future.

The "super-bureaucrat" was Paul O'Neill, the career civil servant who was deputy director of the Office of Management and Budget. Don Rumsfeld and Dick Cheney, as President Ford's successive chiefs of staff, worked closely with him at OMB. (In 2001 Cheney brought O'Neill, then CEO of Alcoa, back to government for an ill-fated two years as secretary of the treasury.) O'Neill was in Ann Arbor to explain to reporters accompanying the president the details of Ford's proposals on housing, employment, and education. I wrote that "the new 'vision for America' that White House press agents had predicted would emerge from Ann Arbor is essentially the vision of a Washington bureaucrat."

Ford's speech was delivered to an audience of fourteen thousand—predominantly students and preponderantly friendly. They were, I wrote, "anesthetized by Mr. Ford's recitation of programs concocted for him by the federal bureaucracy." Bad as this was, the worst at Ann Arbor came when Ford thought it necessary to laud Henry Kissinger and his new peacemaking mission for southern Africa:

> At my direction, Secretary Kissinger [booing begins] is now engaged in an intensive effort [prolonged, accelerated booing, forcing the President to stop temporarily] to help all the parties, black and white, involved in the mounting crisis in southern Africa, to find a peaceful and just solution [continued booing].

I wondered how Jerry Ford, tethered to the bureaucracy and Henry Kissinger, could possibly come back against even a flawed opponent.

WITH PRESIDENTIAL DEBATES scheduled for the first time since 1960, Carter looked ill at ease and ineffective in the opening debate. On September 29, I wrote this in the *Evans-Novak Political Report:*

> The election is rapidly boiling down to this: *Will the public decide that Jimmy Carter is so weird and unreliable* that the gap in key industrial states, already narrowing, closes entirely and tips the election to Ford?
> *The answer may depend, in large part, on Debate No. 2* next Wednesday evening on foreign policy and national security, subjects in which we do not believe the supposed Ford advantage is as great as generally perceived. *If Carter takes a hard line,* he might regain his lost momentum.

Seldom have I proved so prophetic. Never have I played such a personal role in fulfilling my own prophecy.

STILL BELIEVING THAT the best way to cover a debate was watch it on TV from a remote location, I attended none of the 1976 debates. But Rowly was at the Palace of Fine Arts Theater in San Francisco for the second debate of October 6, 1976. I wish I had been there, for this was probably the only debate that ever, by itself, has determined the outcome of a presidential election—an influence that could be traced to me, however unintentionally.

The drama occurred midway when Max Frankel of the *New York Times* asked Ford whether he was too soft on the Soviet Union. Frankel's drawn-out question contained this sentence, which got Ford's attention: "We've virtually signed, in Helsinki, an agreement that the Russians have dominance in Eastern Europe." Ford stumbled through a verbose answer but would have been all right had he stopped before he uttered this fateful final sentence: "There is no Soviet domination of Eastern Europe and there never will be under a Ford Administration."

I could not believe my ears, and neither could veteran diplomatic correspondent Frankel, who jumped in with a follow-up question, starting an extraordinary colloquy that may have changed the course of history:

> Frankel: I'm sorry. Could I just follow? Did I understand you to say, sir, that the Russians are not using Eastern Europe as their own sphere of influence in occupying most of the countries there and in, and making sure with their troops that it's a Communist zone? Whereas, on our side of the line, the Italians and the French are still flirting with the possibility of Communism?
>
> Ford: I don't believe, Mr. Frankel, that the Yugoslavians consider themselves dominated by the Soviet Union. I don't believe that the Romanians consider themselves dominated by the Soviet Union. I don't believe that the Poles consider themselves dominated by the Soviet Union. Each of those countries is independent, autonomous. It has its own territorial integrity and the United States does not concede that those countries are under the domination of the Soviet Union.

This was not merely a candidate making one incredible mistake. Ford had repeated the same mistake four times. I knew immediately that I was to blame. Ever since my March 22 column on the Sonnenfeldt Doctrine accepting Soviet domination of Eastern Europe, Ford had been under pressure from conservative Republican and ethnic nationality groups to reject any such policy. Ford stubbornly refused, out of fear it would be interpreted as a disavowal of Kissinger and détente.

But now, with the election a month away, he went into the San Francisco debate determined to put this issue to rest if somebody raised it. He intended to say simply that the United States did not recognize the permanent organic union of the Soviet Union and its satellites. Instead he said there is no Soviet control over Eastern Europe, a policy Spoonerism of which only Jerry Ford was capable. Nothing could be better calculated to upset conservatives and antagonize ethnics (especially Polish-Americans).

Carter instantly recognized the rich prize dropped in his lap. He accused Ford of failing to enforce the Helsinki agreements and then took dead aim:

We've also seen a very serious problem with the so-called Sonnenfeldt document [sic], which apparently Mr. Ford has just endorsed, which said that there's an organic linkage between the Eastern European countries and the Soviet Union. . . . He's also shown a weakness in yielding to pressure. The Soviet Union, for instance, put pressure on Mr. Ford and he refused to see a symbol of human freedom, recognized around the world, Alexander Solzhenitsyn.

Rowly and I immediately recognized the scope of Ford's blunder. Writing from San Francisco on deadline after the debate, Rowly referred to Ford "freeing Poland with the slip of a tongue" and questioned how the president "could so confuse reality to forget about four Soviet army divisions permanently stationed in Poland." I put the political spin on what happened in the *Evans-Novak Political Report* of October 13:

Those contemplating the damage done to Ford's ethnic hopes by the Polish blooper miss the point: the problem is what the gaffe did, to ethnic and non-ethnic alike, in painting the picture of somebody who really does not know what he is talking about.

General Brent Scowcroft, who had succeeded Secretary of State Kissinger as national security adviser, watched the debate in an adjoining room and was described by Stu Spencer as "turning white" when he heard Ford's words. But he was alone among Ford staffers, according to a candid account of the Ford inner circle's reaction from Bob Hartmann in his memoir *Palace Politics*. "Only Scowcroft caught the slip," Hartmann wrote.

It took four days for Ford to issue a non-apology apology that claimed a misunderstanding. That slowed Ford's comeback, which had brought him within two percentage points of Carter in the Gallup Poll taken just before the second debate.

JAMES A. BAKER III had taken over the Ford general election campaign. I had met Baker during the great delegate chase, and saw he was unlike politicians to whom I had grown accustomed. He was handsome, well groomed, and exceedingly smooth. He replaced Ford's meandering style on the stump with a two-item agenda: middle-class tax cuts ("The best tax reform that I know is tax reduction") and defense preparedness ("I have a deep personal commitment to a strong national defense program"). Under Baker's direction, Ford had ceased his personal attacks on Carter that made him look unpresidential. A special preelection edition of the *Evans-Novak*

Political Report showed Ford had closed the gap so much that he was only fifty electoral votes behind Carter going into the election. The switch of one big state could elect Ford.

Yet, there was something too slick, too gimmicky and inauthentic in Ford's new campaign style, as often was true of enterprises controlled by Jimmy Baker. But Carter seemed even less authentic to me—the presidential candidate in my experience who had the most difficulty telling the truth.

Actually, Carter was the last Democrat for whom I seriously considered voting. How could that be when I considered him a liar and charlatan? Because much of his rhetoric on *my* issue, the cold war, when he talked about Solzhenitsyn or the Sonnenfeldt Doctrine, was better than Ford's. The problem was that it was just rhetoric. I did not think Ford was any better than Carter as a cold warrior. But I hoped he would use in his first full term people who would be a counterweight to Henry Kissinger détente: Fred Ikle, John Lehman, and the enigmatic Don Rumsfeld. So, with misgivings, in mid-October I made a private decision to vote for Ford.

IN SEPTEMBER, Ford's campaign chairman Rogers Morton publicly conceded the entire South to Carter. Jerry Ford was the last old-fashioned Republican candidate for president. Swamped in the South, Ford lost the country by two percentage points in the popular vote and by fifty-six electoral votes (six more than the *ENPR* forecast). Democrats increased, by one seat in each House, their huge congressional majorities that had been bloated by the 1974 Watergate elections. Republican Senate and House candidates made no gains in the South. Bill Brock, one of the Republican Party's shining stars in the Senate, was defeated for reelection in Tennessee. In New York, Pat Moynihan ousted conservative James Buckley in a landslide. It was a dismal election night for Republicans. I was not perceptive enough to see there would be a renaissance ahead after Americans had four years of Jimmy Carter in the Oval Office.

CHAPTER 26

The Snopes Clan in the White House

Just before the 1976 election, the Australian press lord Rupert Murdoch shocked the newspaper world by purchasing the financially strapped *New York Post* from Dorothy Schiff for $30 million ($106.7 million in 2007 dollars). Murdoch was despised by the Left, which viewed him as a predatory businessman, a yellow journalist, and a political conservative who was building a global news empire. For him to replace Mrs. Schiff, a doyenne of Manhattan liberalism, was almost too much to bear.

In 1976, you surely would not hear Rowly or me say anything negative about Dolly Schiff. She was Jewish and a staunch supporter of Israel, but for nineteen years had fought off demands by Jewish friends—including badly needed advertisers—to remove Evans & Novak from her newspaper. We were sorry Mrs. Schiff had to sell the newspaper she loved. But selfishly, we guessed the future of the *Post* was more secure as part of the Murdoch empire and our column was more securely anchored in the *Post* under a conservative proprietor.

But after the 1976 election, we got bad news from a friend's telephone call. Rupert Murdoch had given an interview to the *Village Voice,* a far-Left tabloid that ran advertisements by prostitutes, revealing his plans for the *Post.* My "friend," a little too eagerly I thought, told me Murdoch said he could not stand the Evans & Novak column and planned to replace it with liberal Mary McGrory.

Quickly obtaining a copy of the *Voice,* I found Murdoch had been interviewed by the leftist journalist Alexander Cockburn. The pertinent portion of the wide-ranging interview follows:

> [T]here really are too many columns in the bloody paper. Eight columns a day. They seem to be there because they're available, rather than for any quality—a cheap way of filling the paper. . . .

I'm growing irritated by Evans and Novak. It doesn't represent my point of view, but I like [William] Buckley. I tend to read him. I get cross about it, but his column is articulate. Evans and Novak tend to be sucking up to the political establishment in Washington, because Kissinger is leaking to them, or someone is. But I shouldn't knock them too much. They often break a story. Carl Rowan I can't read . . . I like [James] Wechsler's column.

It was not as bad as I had been told. Murdoch's alleged yearning for Mary McGrory was a figment of somebody's imagination. He did not say he was going to cancel Evans & Novak and even expressed grudging admiration for our reporting. Nevertheless, it was less than a vote of confidence by the new proprietor of our outlet in the nation's largest city.

Murdoch now was based in Manhattan, and it was no trouble making an appointment for Rowly and me to see him in December 1976 at his unpretentious office in the old *Post* building along the East River. Rupert was forty-five years old, exactly my age, ten years younger than Rowly, and much more congenial than I had expected.

I told Murdoch that Rowly and I were concerned about his assessment of our column contained in the *Village Voice*. I had not completed the thought when Murdoch interrupted me with a dismissive wave of his arm. "Oh," he said in his Australian accent, "don't pay any attention to that." He said he liked our column and considered it one of the *Post*'s assets.

In fact, said Murdoch, he had something else he would like us to consider. Murdoch informed us he owned the *National Star* (soon shortened to *The Star*), a supermarket tabloid competing with the *National Enquirer* for circulation and the most sensational stories. Syndicated columnist Jack Anderson had been supplying the *Star* with a Washington gossip column, but Murdoch complained that Anderson "is just giving us what amounts to his regular column and not tailoring it for us." So would Evans and Novak be willing to replace Anderson as Washington columnist for the *Star*?

Rowly and I were not anxious to be writing for a supermarket tabloid. Murdoch also had implied we could not phone it in and had to exert more effort than Anderson. We would have to find time to produce one more original column in addition to our regular five columns, plus our biweekly newsletter.

But we could not say no. We had taken the shuttle to New York, hats in hand, to plead for a stay of execution from Rupert. He had pardoned us, but we owed him a service we could hardly refuse.

The editors of the *Star* told us most of the paper's readers were women.

With that in mind, we began ten years of writing for the *Star*. Our gossip column (called "The Washington Grapevine") included paragraph items with such information as Betty Ford telling husband Jerry not to run for president again because she liked life in the California desert. On alternating weeks, we wrote profiles of such people as Phyllis George, the former Miss America who was now the First Lady of Kentucky.

ROWLY AND I had talked White House Press Secretary Jody Powell into cocktails at the Metropolitan Club at seven p.m. on March 28, 1977. He was not forthcoming with us, and our session broke up in under an hour. Jody then announced he was off to the Class Reunion, a journalists' hangout several doors down the block, to watch the NCAA championship basketball game between Marquette and North Carolina—and have another drink or two.

The presence of news sources was not enough to attract me to the Class Reunion in 1977. I spent countless hours in the press clubs of Indianapolis and Washington during my twenties and thirties but by 1977 preferred to get away from my journalistic colleagues.

It was not that I no longer enjoyed drinking. Nearly every day I was in Washington, I had lunch with a news source, and I *always* started with one or two Scotches, often followed by a bottle of beer with the meal. I usually wrote my column after such an alcoholic lunch without taking a nap, a feat I regard with awe a quarter of a century later. Rowly and I usually put the column to bed around seven p.m., and I invariably headed to The Exchange, a bar located on the ground floor of the building next to ours on Pennsylvania Avenue. It was frequented mostly by lawyers, and I typically was the only journalist present. Spending an hour at The Exchange, I would drink two Cutty Sarks and water. I seldom picked up any news there. The argumentative conversation usually was about sports rather than politics and was mostly civil. (An exception occurred one night when a union organizer for the American Newspaper Guild, influenced by too many drinks, wandered in and started calling me a scab. I initiated a scuffle, consisting of pushing, that was quickly broken up by lawyers at the bar.)

Following my session at The Exchange, I would head home to the Maryland suburbs. When I arrived at Luxmanor around eight to eight thirty, Geraldine and I would have our own cocktail hour with a Cutty and water for each of us. (That was the only time during a weekday when I spent any time with Zelda and Alexander, ages twelve and nine in 1977.) At dinner, Geraldine and I would have wine.

That adds up to around eight alcoholic drinks for me during a normal workday. That's a lot of booze, but there was considerably more intake for me on any day that I attended a dinner party or reception or was on the road, as frequently was the case. And there were occasions when I, a forty-something, would go on a collegiate-style drinking binge.

On one late summer Saturday, I drove 130 miles to Carlisle, Pennsylvania, to watch a Washington Redskins intrasquad scrimmage. I was accompanied by Mike Posner, an usher at my wedding to Geraldine who was a reporter for Reuters. Mike and I had been drinking companions at the old Members Bar of the National Press Club when we both were single, and our expedition to Carlisle looked like an attempt to relive old times.

On the way to the game, we stopped at a roadside store and bought fried chicken and several bottles of cheap wine, which we consumed during the scrimmage. Mike and I then concocted a mad scheme of stopping on the way home at every tavern, where each of us would consume a shot of Wild Turkey bourbon, chased down by a glass of beer. Geraldine and I were invited that night to a dinner party at the Northwest Washington home of Ellie and Andy Glass. I was not only very late but also dead drunk. I disguised my condition with uncharacteristic silence. But by intermittently dozing off, I must have excited suspicion.

Not even such behavior prompted me to question whether I might have a drinking problem, as any reasonable person would conclude. I observed that I did not have the warning signs of alcoholism: inability to adhere to work schedules, imbibing in the morning, withdrawal symptoms if deprived of hard drink. Thus reassured, I went on consuming vast amounts of alcohol. In retrospect, I know I had a major drinking problem that would carry grave consequences if not confronted and corrected.

IN EARLY FEBRUARY 1977, I sat in Hamilton Jordan's big office in the West Wing of the White House. It had taken plenty of nagging to get him to see me. Jordan was a thirty-one-year-old Georgian who had spent the past eight years as Carter's political aide and now would be doing everything for the president from trying to kindle warmer relations with the Democratic old guard on Capitol Hill to handling the current military strongman in Panama.

Although the Carter team had been in the White House a couple of weeks, it looked as though Jordan had just moved in. Cartons with books and file folders remained unpacked. Jordan was without a necktie and generally disheveled. As a reader of Faulkner, I felt the white trash Snopes clan had taken over a mansion of the aristocratic Sartoris family. Jordan was neither helpful nor pleasant with me, and another one-on-one meeting between us never happened.

Jordan was an easy target rather than a source for me. Indiscretions extended to what Jordan said, which provided us with column material—such as this item in our Sunday column of October 16, 1977:

Relations between the White House staff and the Cabinet took another downward step when top presidential aide Hamilton Jordan let it be known that—with two exceptions—he does not think much of President Carter's Cabinet.

Jordan's remarks came in a private White House session with top assistants of Senators. Only two Cabinet members, he said, are worth much—Interior Secretary Cecil Andrus and Agriculture Secretary Bob Bergland.

If Andrus and Bergland are the best, one Senate aide asked, who are the worst? A smiling Jordan quickly replied—he could not single anybody out because one is about as bad as another is.

I had double-sourced the story and I was absolutely sure that was what Jordan had said. But I made a stupid mistake. In a letter to the editor that the Field Newspaper Syndicate distributed to our newspapers, Jordan denied making those comments and wrote: "While I have become accustomed to Evans and Novak columns being erroneous, my tolerance for their casual regard for the facts will not allow me to remain silent after reading their recent column. . . . I can state categorically that I have never met at the White House in any private sessions with top assistants of Senators. About a month ago, I did attend a breakfast meeting for Senate staff members in the Senate Office Building." I had gotten the wrong impression about the site of the meeting. I checked several more Senate aides, who confirmed that I was accurate in quoting Jordan. But Jordan, while lying about what he said, emphasized the error I had made about one detail. It was a clever means of undermining our credibility.

Later in the year, Jody Powell asked Rowly and me to see him at six o'clock one evening—the first time he had reached out to us. We were ushered into Powell's West Wing office but were told he was busy and we should sit tight for a bit. The bit lasted more than twenty-five minutes. When Powell showed up, he had Hamilton Jordan in tow.

Powell and Jordan had a menacing message: The Evans & Novak column was biased, unfair, and determined to destroy the Carter presidency. They warned that the White House was not without resources with which to fight, and they meant to use them. But their threat was undermined by the evening network news blaring on the TV monitors, causing Powell and Jordan to interrupt themselves, or us, when there was something broadcast they wanted to catch.

Rowly was seething and just before seven o'clock stood up and said we had been there for an hour and had an appointment to keep. As we walked out of the White House, Rowly told me he never had been so humiliated.

Whatever Powell and Jordan had in mind, their effort to pressure us had one unintended consequence. Until then, Rowly had been pushing me and himself to find something positive to write about the new president. After the White House meeting, he gave up.

Carter was under fire from both Left and Right in his own party. The new Speaker, Thomas P. (Tip) O'Neill, suggested Carter was too conservative for congressional Democrats. In a conversation with Rowly and me, O'Neill made it clear he was not modeling his speakership after that of his fellow Massachusetts Democrat John McCormack who was virtually part of President Lyndon Johnson's staff. I concluded in the Evans & Novak column of May 21, 1977, that O'Neill "has surprisingly shown in four months the potential to be a great Speaker of the House" who is "fine tuned to the mood on the Hill" and will keep at "arm's length" from Carter. (The praise is ironic considering what O'Neill wrote about our relationship in his memoirs, about which I will report later.)

On the other end of the Democratic spectrum was the new senator from New York, Daniel Patrick Moynihan. Voting against confirmation of Carter's liberal nominee to be chief disarmament adviser, Moynihan told me that the president and his advisers were under the influence of "an appeasement psychology."

TREASURY SECRETARY W. Michael Blumenthal came from far outside Carter's inner circle, derided by Ham Jordan and disliked by the president. Blumenthal was a former Princeton faculty member who held several jobs in the Kennedy and Johnson administrations before going to the Detroit-based Bendix Corporation in 1967. In 1977 at age fifty-one, he was tapped by Carter's headhunters as a rare major corporation CEO who was a Democrat with government experience.

Blumenthal looked to me at first like a self-righteous liberal who had risen in the corporate world, but I was mistaken. He was likable and unpretentious enough to be one cabinet member who did not insist on having all meals in his office. He came to breakfast or lunch with me occasionally at the Hay Adams, where he learned he could trust me not to quote him by name.

Blumenthal related Carter's obsession with penny ante tax reform. He told of traveling to Paris for an International Monetary Fund meeting on August 6, 1977. He had billed the government for round-trip first-class commercial airfare to Europe to save the wear and tear of riding in cramped tourist class. I reported in the Evans & Novak column that business executives did the same thing and, for the sake of efficiency, Blumenthal felt they should continue to receive a tax deduction for first-class tickets. I continued:

> But influential aides at the White House strongly disagree. They support Sen. Edward Kennedy's long-standing proposal to permit tax deductions only of tourist-class fares. What's more important, President Carter feels the same way.
>
> Similar disagreements abound. Blumenthal is skeptical about other Kennedy-style proposals—such as crackdowns against expense-account business luncheons and interest deductions on vacation homes—that would cause irritation without generating much tax revenue.

Those were the petty tax changes Carter loved and that doomed any chances of a serious reform. Early in 1978, Blumenthal gave me a wonderful insight into the president. Rowly and I had signed a contract with Random House, publisher of *Nixon in the White House,* to do a similar book on Carter prior to the 1980 election. I had begun background interviews. One of the first was with Blumenthal, who told me this story (which never has been published because the book never was written):

Early in 1977, Blumenthal told Carter that he had prepared a reading list for him considering the president's desire for tax reform. "Oh, Mike," Carter responded, "I'm way ahead of you. I've started reading the Internal Revenue Code." It was as if somebody interested in automotive engineering had started by reading a mechanic's manual word for word. "Mr. President," said Blumenthal, "I really don't think that's the way to go about it." Carter flashed the frozen smile and steely gaze, saying: "But, Mike, *I* do, and *I* am the president." That summed up the Carter presidency.

JOHN CARBAUGH MIGHT have been the best source I ever had, and 1977 was the best year for what he gave me. Carbaugh was a "legislative assistant" on Senator Jesse Helms's government payroll but had precious little to do with legislation. Carbaugh, age thirty-one in 1977, knew everybody in the right wing of American politics, and had his hands on multiple clandestine operations. He ran a secret organization called the Madison Group (that met at Washington's luxurious Madison Hotel), consisting of conservatives who plotted initiatives in Congress and the executive branch. He could be found most mornings at breakfast in the Hay Adams dining room whispering to somebody. It was me about once a week. I don't think John considered me a true-believing conservative then, but he did view me as a reporter who relished an exclusive.

In early February of 1977, two weeks after Carter was inaugurated, Carbaugh showed up in our office on Pennsylvania Avenue to give me an accordion-style manila folder. Twenty-eight years later, I have the folder and its contents before me. It contains copies of documents found in the briefcase of the late Orlando Letelier.

The background of the folder goes back to September 4, 1970, when a minority of Chile's voters elected as their president Salvador Allende, a Marxist-Leninist aligned with the Soviet Union and Communist Cuba and antagonistic to U.S. interests. Allende's defense minister (and former foreign minister), fellow Marxist-Leninist Orlando Letelier, was imprisoned after Allende was murdered in a military coup on September 11, 1973. Released in 1974, Letelier came to Washington, where he had been Chile's ambassador at the start of the Allende regime. Letelier became a fellow at the leftist Institute for Policy Studies (IPS) in Washington and worked with Soviet and Cuban agents to try to restore the Left in Santiago.

On September 21, 1976, an auto carrying Letelier around Sheridan Circle on Washington's Embassy Row was demolished and its occupants killed by a car bomb. The FBI at length traced the crime to the secret police of Chile's military dictatorship and apprehended the bombers. District of Columbia police had recovered intact and turned over to the FBI Letelier's black Samsonite briefcase. Copies of its contents found its way into Carbaugh's hands via a route kept secret from me.

The handsome, dashing Letelier was a favorite of Washington's diplomatic circles for his charm, but not for keeping an orderly briefcase. It contained letters, memoranda, an address book, and notations of financial dealings. This collection showed an Orlando Letelier quite different from his self-constructed image in Washington elite circles as a liberal idealist committed to ending the military dictatorship in Chile and returning his country to democracy.

The briefcase revealed links between Letelier and the Soviet, East German, and Cuban intelligence services. It showed that Letelier and his colleagues had received material from Julian Rizo, a Castro spy whose cover was as first secretary with the Cuban delegation to the UN. Letelier's address book contained Rizo's telephone number as well as the private Havana number of Cuban Foreign Minister Raul Roa (whose correspondence with

Letelier was contained in the briefcase). Letelier, while nominally working for IPS, was receiving $1,000 a month ($3,557 in 2007 dollars) from the Cuban government.

A March 29, 1976, letter from Letelier to Cuba laid out the strategy for building support in Congress. In the Evans & Novak column of February 16, 1977, I quoted Letelier declaring that his group of Chilean exiles was creating an image of "an apolitical character, oriented exclusively to the problems of human rights."

> "The object is to mobilize the 'liberals' and other persons, who if they don't identify with us from an ideological point of view, are in it for what human rights reflects," he added. Letelier also expressed concern that the Chilean human rights committee not be linked to Havana "since you know how these 'liberals' are. It's possible that one of the sponsoring Congressmen might fear that they might be connected with Cuba, etc., and eventually stop giving his support to the committee."
>
> Letelier never mentions "liberals" without quotes around the word. Nor does he have any doubt where he stands. Closing that letter, he declared: "Perhaps some day, not far away, we also will be able to do what has been done in Cuba."

An example of that strategy was paying the way for an idealistic, liberal congressman from Massachusetts, Michael Harrington, to attend a conference in Mexico condemning the Chilean military regime. Briefcase documents show $544.26 in 1975 ($2,048 in 2007 money) listed as "Harrington fare," with $174.26 paid from the Cuban fund and the remaining $380 "received from Helsinki." I speculated, incorrectly, that this might have referred to a money drop in Finland's capital. I soon found the truth was even worse.

It is difficult to exaggerate the anger that column raised among Washington liberals. For them, Orlando Letelier was a hero in life and a martyr in death. A *Washington Post* article about him three days after his death began with the adjectives "warm," "urbane," "kind," and "civilized"—"a cosmic optimist." On the day my column was published in the *Post,* Letelier's lawyer called the newspaper to report that the actual black Samsonite briefcase was in his possession and he would show its contents to a representative of the newspaper.

The *Post* sent Lee Lescaze, one of the newspaper's top diplomatic correspondents, to the lawyer's office with a photographer to inspect the contents of the briefcase. I had spent more than a week perusing the documents and getting translations of the Spanish, which I could not read. Lescaze could not read Spanish either, but quickly wrote his analysis as a news story for the next day's paper, February 17 (with the contents mostly paraphrased rather than translated).

Lescaze disposed of both my column and a December 20 syndicated column by Jack Anderson based on more limited access to the documents (which also ran in the *Post*): "After going through all the contents of the briefcase, it appears that the columns have followed the darkest possible interpretation of the scanty material." Lescaze decided that the conclusion reached by both Anderson and me that the money sent from Havana by the wife of a Castroite secret police officer was Cuban government money was "possible but unproven." Just how personal this had become was suggested by Lescaze when he wrote that the leaked briefcase documents "damage Letelier's reputation" and "distress his friends and family."

On the next day, February 18, the *Post*'s editorial page editor, Phil Geyelin, allowed a thousand words on the op-ed page to leftist activist Saul Landau to rebut me. Landau, a colleague of Letelier's at IPS, asserted that "a campaign has been launched with the apparent purpose of smearing Letelier's reputation." He then proceeded to make the same points as Lescaze and quoted from his story while lecturing on the need to bring Letelier's killers to justice (which they were).

After facing this rebuttal from the newspaper that had printed the column in the first place, I thought it necessary to write a second column on the Letelier papers. I wanted to clear up the confusion about money "received from Helsinki" and put Landau's comments in perspective. I admitted that the "mail drop" speculation was wrong about the money for Harrington because the reference to "Helsinki" actually referred to the World Peace Council, a Soviet front based in Helsinki that awarded its 1976 "peace prize" to Soviet leader Leonid Brezhnev. As for Landau, I quoted from a Landau letter in the Letelier briefcase that nobody had mentioned up to this point. Landau wrote:

> I think that at age 40 the time has come to dedicate myself to narrower pursuits, namely, making propaganda for American socialism. . . . We cannot any longer just help out third world movements and revolutions, although obviously we shouldn't turn our back on them, but get down to the more difficult job of bringing the message home.

While "the Mike Harringtons are truly concerned with human rights," I concluded, "the Saul Landaus and the Orlando Leteliers use that slogan to further ideological activism. The undisputed need to bring Letelier's murderers to justice does not alter that political reality."

I was up early Monday to read that morning's *Post,* and was devastated to discover the Letelier II column was nowhere to be found. Since the time the first Evans & Novak column appeared on May 15, 1963, the *Post's* editors had spiked only three of our columns. In each instance, we had received a heads-up call from the *Post* that the column was not running the next day because of a space problem or because it duplicated another column—never, until now, because of displeasure with the column's content.

It was midafternoon before Phil Geyelin returned my call, and what followed was not pleasant. Geyelin told me he had spiked the column because of its content, adding he would have spiked the *first* Letelier column had it not escaped his attention. I started to explain additional material in the second column that justified my position and would interest the newspaper's readers. "No," Geyelin interrupted me, "I am not going to have you or anybody else dancing on Orlando Letelier's grave on my op-ed page." I had been a syndicated columnist for thirteen years, long enough to know there was no point in arguing with a client newspaper's editor—particularly the most important client newspaper.

I retell this story because the incident was so unusual in my long, friendly relationship with the *Washington Post.* Four editorial page editors have printed my column for more than forty years. Usually, I was the only columnist used who was neither a *Post* staffer nor was syndicated by that newspaper. Whatever professional success I have achieved would not have been possible without the incomparable window to Washington provided me by the *Post.*

Another newspaper that printed the first Letelier column but not the second was the *Boston Globe,* which assigned its ombudsman to analyze what we had written. He was Charles Whipple, the *Globe's* former editorial page editor who was an acquaintance of Rowly's and mine. Charlie did not contact either of us before he published a scathing report (headlined "Evans and Novak's McCarthyesque Smear"). He swallowed whole Saul Landau's arguments and accused us of a "smear job . . . that would have turned the late Sen. Joseph R. McCarthy green with envy." Whipple said we had "blackened the name" of Letelier, referring to the Marxist-Leninist revolutionary as a "respected" diplomat.

The second column, Whipple wrote, "appeared in many papers, including Rupert Murdoch's New York Post. It did not appear, however, in The Globe or The Washington Post, and for very good reasons, we think." To pile it on Whipple solicited a quote from Phil Geyelin, who said the spiked column "broke no new ground," was "scurrilous," and impugned the motives of Letelier, "who can't answer."

Our relationship with the *Boston Globe* never recovered from the Letelier papers. The *Globe*'s use of the Evans & Novak column diminished and remained infrequent until 1984, when Rupert Murdoch bought the Field Syndicate and transferred Evans & Novak to his *Boston Herald*. Thankfully, we stayed in the *Washington Post*. But there was further deterioration of Geyelin's attitude toward us.

If I had it to do all over again, would I have just ignored the file folder brought me by John Carbaugh and saved myself all these troubles? There are some columns I wish I had not written, but not these. The canonization of a Marxist-Leninist revolutionary by our colleagues in journalism was their problem, not ours. Nevertheless I felt more alienated after those events from the mainstream of Washington journalism.

NOWHERE WAS THE shift in policy from Nixon-Ford to Carter more abrupt than in southern Africa. Republican ambivalence toward ending white minority rule gave way to Democratic support for immediate empowerment of the black majority. The danger, as seen by Rowly and me as cold warriors, was Soviet domination of the continent.

Rowly had written several columns about the region and wanted to go to Africa for a firsthand report. But Evans had been doing most of the column's overseas traveling, and this was one I wanted to make. The reason I pushed to go to southern Africa, and the reason Rowly deferred to me, was personal.

The Jews of the late-nineteenth-century Russian Empire faced a bleak future, inducing many—like my grandparents—to go to America. A much smaller number, including relatives of both my mother's and my father's families, went to Africa. One of my mother's relatives founded Cape Town's premier department store. On my father's side, my grandfather's baby sister at age seventeen was sent to Southern Rhodesia for an arranged marriage with a Jewish landowner named Baron. Her son was to become a member of the Rhodesian Parliament.

Relatives in Cape Town from my mother's family greeted Geraldine and me with warm hospitality and held a big family dinner for us (to which they invited relatives from my father's side, who had left Rhodesia ahead of black power). It was thrilling to see on the wall in southern Africa the same family tree we had in our house.

As Jews, my relatives always had been liberal on the race question and opposed apartheid—segregation instituted in 1948 by the Afrikaaners and their ruling Nationalist Party. Now they viewed with alarm a black takeover in South Africa.

R. F. (Pik) Botha had just become foreign minister after a hitch as ambassador to Washington. Tall, handsome, and charismatic, Botha had cut quite a figure in the U.S. capital as the first South African diplomat to work the Washington press corps and go on the TV talk circuit. Botha laid out for me his plan to calm his country's turbulent racial waters. As a *verligte* (enlightened) Afrikaaner, he wanted to end apartheid gradually while giving nonwhites a slice of the economic pie and a piece of political power.

In his Foreign Ministry office, Botha—speaking as a longtime friend of America—told me of his frustration with Jimmy Carter's demand for immediate black majority rule: "We South Africans are profoundly concerned about the United States appearing to demand that change should be so fundamental that it might lead to our destruction as a people." Off the record, Botha told me he worried about the *verkrampte* (intractable) Afrikaaners reacting to Carter by doing what they wanted all along: going "into the laager"—forming a suicidal armed camp against the rest of the world.

Botha regarded me as sympathetic and talked Prime Minister John Vorster, who normally did not meet with foreign journalists, into seeing me. Botha told me he hoped Vorster, belying his gruff exterior, would be reasonable. But Vorster was barely civil when introduced to me. After I opened the interview by asking his comment on his apparently futile meeting with Vice President Walter Mondale in Vienna the previous month, Vorster exploded in his thick Afrikaaner accent: "Now that is a truly stupid question! I have answered that question many times, and it has appeared in the newspapers. Don't you read the newspapers? Didn't you prepare for this meeting? Are you totally uninformed? I am a very busy man, and I think it an insult for you to waste my time."

I kept my temper and tried to think of a question that would not trigger another outburst. Mercifully, Vorster ended his "interview" with me after twelve minutes. (He was forced out of office on corruption charges a year later.)

I wrote in an Evans & Novak column from Cape Town on June 24 that the "overriding problem" in South Africa was "how minority whites can share decision-making with majority non-whites short of political self destruction." I added:

> It is precisely that delicate question that the new U.S. policy, no longer viewing South Africa as an anti-Communist bulwark against Soviet penetration on the continent, considers irrelevant.

. . .

GERALDINE AND I arrived in Salisbury, Rhodesia, from Johannesburg late on a Friday afternoon at the height of happy hour in our hotel. Well-dressed white people of all ages with drinks in their hands spilled out of the cocktail lounge into the lobby. Everyone was talking as loudly as possible. I compared it to a New Year's Eve celebration just before midnight, except the gaiety seemed forced—even desperate.

If the end of white rule in South Africa was inevitable, in Rhodesia it was imminent. The colony's unilateral declaration of independence from Britain twelve years earlier had alienated the rest of the world. Every day more whites left this beautiful country (with nearly all my relatives gone). To the outside world, the white men who stayed were archreactionaries trying to maintain a privileged way of nineteenth-century colonial life. But I soon found Rhodesia was not what it seemed to the rest of the world.

I had arranged an interview with Prime Minister Ian Smith. He was maligned as an anachronism dedicated to a whites-only government in a black country, and the photos depicted a sour, crabbed reactionary at war with reality. But I took a liking to him and have kept in touch with him over three decades, long after he had relinquished power. A photo of us together at the prime minister's office in Salisbury still hangs in my office.

In contrast to the *verkrampte* Afrikaaner John Vorster, Ian Smith was polite, almost courtly. It was just the two of us seated in his modest governmental office as he answered my questions on the record, thoughtfully and logically. He saw himself as a lifelong patriot, first for the British Empire (as an RAF pilot in World War II) and then for little, beleaguered Rhodesia.

Smith knew the time had come for a black-led government in Salisbury. All he wanted was free elections and guaranteed property rights for white Rhodesians. That was too high a price for the Soviet-supported and supplied guerrilla leader Robert Mugabe. And if the black opposition did not agree, neither did the British government or the Carter administration.

There was a shooting war in the Rhodesian bush, and I wanted to get a feel of it beyond briefings in Salisbury. The Rhodesian military agreed to my request to interview officers on the Mozambique frontier where the war was in progress. "How am I going to get there?" I asked the Rhodesian colonel handling press relations, assuming that I would be driven overland by an escort officer (perhaps accompanied by an armed trooper). "Well, Mr. Novak," the colonel responded, "there are several reputable auto rental companies here in Salisbury. But I would advise you travel strictly by day. The roads are much safer by daylight."

I was being told to travel, alone and unarmed, through the Rhodesian countryside in the midst of a guerrilla war. I thought of begging off but decided not to generate stories about the cowardly American journalist. I did not disclose to Geraldine how dangerous I thought this was but arranged for her to fly to Victoria Falls for sightseeing on the day I set off in a rented Land Rover in search of war. (In two days on the frontier interviewing white farmers and military officers, I did not hear a shot fired in anger. But guerrillas blew up railroad tracks not far from Victoria Falls, where Geraldine was sightseeing.)

In an Evans & Novak column datelined Umtali Regional Military Headquarters, I was gloomy about saving this rich and beautiful country from "economic and political anarchy leading to oppression and possible Communist control." That latter fate was avoided only because the Soviet Union collapsed, which saved the African continent from coming under the Kremlin's domination. But Rhodesia did not avoid Mugabe's corrupt dictatorship. Ian Smith, suffering intense persecution, never left his homeland despite unrelenting pressure from the country's new rulers to do so.

MY LAST AFRICAN stop would be the annual summit of Africa's black leaders, held this year in Libreville, Gabon, on the continent's west coast. I was worn down after nearly a month in Africa. In Zaire's capital of Kinshasa I had foolishly removed my blazer and put it on the back of my chair in the hotel cocktail lounge. My wallet was soon lifted from the jacket's inside pocket, causing a fellow journalist to comment: "WAWA"—West Africa Wins Again. Arriving in Gabon, I learned my luggage was missing, meaning that now I not only was without credit cards and extra cash but also toiletries and all clothing except what I was wearing.

The State Department had informed our office that immigration controls had been relaxed in Gabon for the once-in-a-lifetime diplomatic conference there, and I would be admitted without a visa. In fact, Gabonese immigration officers were ready to jail me for the night because I had no documents. I was saved when, just before midnight, a young U.S. embassy official arrived for a routine airport check. He quickly cleared me through customs, let me spend the night at his apartment, gave me a change of underwear and socks, and told me what a rotten little dictatorship Gabon was under its petty tyrant, Omar Bongo.

As the FSO walked me to the embassy the next morning, I noticed Gabonese watching an excavation for a new presidential palace. "That's all they have to do," my guide told me. The laborers were all Caucasian— imported from Yugoslavia. Gabon produced enough oil to be a member of

OPEC and earned enough foreign capital to hire whites to do manual labor that the Gabonese disdained.

The hero of the summit was Uganda's murderous Idi Amin, who swaggered around the floor of the conference in full military regalia, wearing a sidearm and surrounded by bodyguards. I wrote in a column ("The Face of Black Africa") from Libreville:

> Not only was Amin cheered whenever he set foot into the conference center, but his comic-opera allegation of a Western plot to kill him and other African leaders drew sustained applause. Amin's colleagues said nothing about mass murder in Uganda. Nor would they say a word against him privately to reporters. . . .
>
> Therefore, a controlling principle in Africa: Human rights are violated only if a white man abuses a black man; a black man repressing or imprisoning another black man is worthy of no attention.

> I left Africa with the premonition of tragedy ahead.

IN AUGUST, John Carbaugh had something he said was much better than the Letelier material. But he did not want to be seen entering our Pennsylvania Avenue building (where the neighbors included *Newsweek,* the *Boston Globe,* the Newhouse newspapers, and the Johnson publications). Instead, he would meet me in front of our building, driving one of the eight red convertibles he owned (this one a Triumph TR-6). I took an unmarked envelope from him, and he sped away.

Once upstairs, I closed the door of my inner office and ripped open the envelope. It was a copy of an extract from a top secret document: PRM-10 (Presidential Review Memorandum), the Carter administration's strategic study. In three single-spaced pages it conceded one-third of the territory of West Germany in the event of a Soviet invasion. The invaders would be stopped at a line formed by the Weser and Lech rivers, only after the surrender of Saxony and most of Bavaria. The planning document continued: "If the Soviets persist in their attack, a U.S.-NATO conventional defeat in Central Europe is likely." This defeatism, of course, was to be kept secret from our NATO allies—especially West Germany.

PRM-10, prepared by liberal civilians brought into the Pentagon by Carter, said increased U.S. defense spending needed to forestall the bleak scenario would not be acceptable to the American public. Even if military outlays increased, the document said, it "may provoke adverse Soviet *and* allied reactions" and "might provoke a similar Soviet counter-buildup or even a preemptive attack" and therefore "might actually undermine deterrence." PRM-10's alternative:

> The U.S. might pursue arms-control initiatives more vigorously to obtain reductions in threats and opposing force level, thereby minimizing the risks of unilateral U.S. reductions. With respect to the Soviet Union, the U.S. might undertake a broad program of assistance to the U.S.S.R. on trade, credits, food, and technology, thereby "lowering political tensions and reducing the risks of war."

When the Evans & Novak column revealed PRM-10's outlook on August 3, 1977 ("Conceding Defeat in Europe"), the Carter team the same day amended the document to promise "ultimately to restore prewar boundaries"—without saying how. At the August 3 White House press briefing, Jody Powell derided "another in a series of 'Oh, my God, they're caving in to the Commies columns' by Evans and Novak."

Carter's German strategy was not the only stunning policy shift contained in PRM-10. A month later, Carbaugh gave me another extract from the document. It conceded the loss of Seoul in an invasion from North Korea, granting the communists their principal war goal. The top secret document stripped bare the consequences of Carter's decision (later reversed) to remove the U.S. 2nd Infantry Division from Korea. Another Evans & Novak column, on September 7, 1977, contained stunning news for the Republic of Korea:

> "Once the U.S. land forces are out of Korea," says PRM-10, "the U.S. has transformed its presence in Asia from a land-based posture to an off-shore position. This . . . provides the U.S. flexibility to determine at the time whether it should or should not get involved in a local war."
>
> The document goes on to reveal an unpublicized reason for removing the 2nd Division: to give Washington the choice of whether or not to intervene. With the troops gone, says PRM-10, "the risk of automatic involvement [which was a major factor in removing land forces from Korea] is minimized." . . .

Like many reporters, I have enjoyed letting the public know about things nobody else knows without worrying whether I have influenced policy. Nevertheless, my exposure of PRM-10 did change policy—in a direction I favored. It inhibited Jimmy Carter from adopting a strategy to write off one-third of West Germany and the capital of South Korea. It helped convince Carter that withdrawal of U.S. ground troops was a bad idea. That's a good couple of days work for one columnist.

Using his many autos, Carbaugh delivered to me highly classified defense documents for more than a year. Carbaugh, the cutoff man in intelligence lingo, never told me from whom he obtained these documents. Whoever he was, I believe he not only gave me great stories but also provided valuable service to the nation.

CHAPTER 27

Supply-Side and China

As 1978 BEGAN, the twelve-year relationship of Rowly and me with Channel 5 WTTG in Washington ended after protracted deterioration. Ed Turner, who had brought us to the station, was long gone. Turner's successors were reflexive liberals who had no use for Rowly and detested me.

But in 1977, we had signed a two-year deal with the RKO General group of television stations. Each month we interviewed three major newsmakers in their Washington offices on a single theme, followed by an Evans and Novak analysis. The programs attracted little attention—with a notable exception that would have enduring consequences. It was our February 1978 program, and the subject was corruption in government. Our principal guest was Thomas P. O'Neill, in his second year as Speaker of the House of Representatives. We filmed the interview February 14 in the speaker's private room just off the Capitol Rotunda.

In my introduction to the O'Neill interview, I said he "is not only the strongest figure in Congress today but may well end up as the most powerful speaker of his time, and that includes Sam Rayburn." Tip O'Neill, feisty and self-confident at age sixty-six, was handling our questions with ease until we brought up Bruce Caputo. He was a freshman Republican House member representing a New York polyglot district stretching from the Bronx into Westchester County. Intending to run against Senator Pat Moynihan in 1982, Caputo had attacked the Speaker's connection with the latest Washington scandal ("Koreagate"), involving influence-peddling charges against Korean wheeler-dealer Tongsun Park. As a member of the House Ethics Committee, Caputo leaked closed-door testimony that Park used O'Neill's majority leader's office (before he became Speaker) as a "hangout." When I noted Caputo's claim that there was a cover-up, O'Neill erupted into incoherence:

Well, of course, I haven't any confidence in him. I've never had a conversation with him. Apparently any fellow that has, and from what I understand, from what I've been told, has two employees on his payroll who check the sex life of his colleagues, check whether they're out cheating on their wife, whether they go on corporate planes. . . .

Now if he feels as though he wants to have his employees do that, and that's what I understand. Now does he have any respect for his fellow man? No. His fellow Congressmen? No. He's leaked everything, from what I can gather, that he had, and he's exaggerated. . . .

And he's trying to, he's trying to propel himself into higher public life. Now, to me, to me, unbelievable. It's a rare occasion that a man of the type of Caputo comes to the Congress of the United States.

For the only time in our brief RKO tenure, we made big news. It hit page one of the February 17 *Washington Post* with a 620-word piece by veteran congressional reporter Richard L. Lyons ("House Speaker Denounces Freshman N.Y. Republican"). Lyons called it an "extraordinary personal attack." O'Neill's advisers were appalled, but it took them four days to get the Speaker to go on the House floor on February 21 to make this brief speech:

On reflection, I feel that I should not have uttered the personal remarks which I made last week in an interview relating to a colleague in the House. When I am interviewed as Speaker, I have an official responsibility to be above the battle. I should not have challenged his motives, and I am sure it was unwise to have made references to conduct on his part where I am unwilling to substantiate or corroborate those charges.

It was a humiliating moment for a proud public figure. I think O'Neill blamed us for his reckless behavior. His attitude toward us, warm until then, chilled. He never again appeared on television with us, rejecting—without explaining why—many invitations from me to our CNN program in the 1980s. In time, he concocted an outright lie about us that was to alter relationships beyond the grave.

EVANS AND I had worked hard reporting the Byzantine politics of arms control during the Nixon-Ford administration, and we went into even more detail during the Carter administration. The struggle between "hards" and "softs" on arms control cut across party lines.

Richard Perle filled me in on all the intrigue. Early in December 1977, Richard gave me one bit of information that, though insignificant compared with much of what he told me, caused me more trouble than anything I had written until then.

Perle's tip concerned the newly elected leader of the Senate's Republican minority, Howard Henry Baker Jr. of Tennessee. Perle told me Baker was playing it both ways on Carter's SALT II by publicly condemning it while privately consulting an expert who favored it. I called Senator Baker, who confirmed the facts involved, and gave me a couple of quotes. This did not justify an Evans & Novak column, but with news hard to come by at year's end, I wrote a five-paragraph secondary item for Sunday, December 4, 1977. Considering how much trouble this caused us, I think it worthwhile to reproduce the item in full:

> Sen. Howard Baker, the never obvious Senate Republican leader, has a leading figure in the arms control lobby as a part-time consultant while hardening his own opposition to the SALT II treaty now nearing agreement.
>
> Baker alarmed conservative colleagues when Alton Frye, secretary of the Council on Foreign Relations, suddenly appeared as his adviser on strategic arms. Frye spread word that he had the ear of the possible 1980 Republican presidential nominee.
>
> That raised right-wing concern that Frye would eclipse the scholarly Dr. Fred Ikle, disarmament agency director of Nixon-Ford days who is also advising Baker. Those fears escalated when a hard-line SALT speech prepared for Baker was undelivered.
>
> Nevertheless, Baker told us that the neutrality he professes on the Panama Canal treaties does not apply to SALT. "I haven't got a neutral bone in my body on this issue," he said, adding that the Carter Administration may be "giving away the store." Baker talked of "many things I disagree with Alton on," especially Frye's contention that a three-year limitation on the U.S. cruise missile need not be permanent.
>
> Why, then, consult with Frye? Apart from being a fellow Tennessean, Baker told us: "I want to know what the other folks are thinking." That may be the source of Baker's strength—but also of the profound suspicions he always generates.

Rowly considered Alton Frye, a former RAND Corporation strategic analyst and U.S. Senate staffer, an amiable liberal lightweight. I had appeared with Frye on an arms control panel and had not been impressed. I had never exchanged a word in anger with him when the column of December 4 appeared.

Our five-paragraph item of December 4, 1977, though actually about Howard Baker, apparently broke Frye's zone of comfortable isolation by briefly making him a public figure. My conclusion is that something snapped, and we became his obsession. He was by trade a researcher, and threw himself into researching the journalistic product of Evans and Novak. By year's end, he had prepared a brief attacking our work product and sent it out to newspapers that published our column. None printed it. In the new year, he delved deeper into what we had written the last two years, and sent a second essay to our newspapers.

This time, Frye had one taker. It was the liberal paper in Frye's native city of Nashville, the *Tennessean* (which had published the Evans & Novak column from the beginning). On February 26, 1978 (my forty-seventh birthday), the *Tennessean* published a double-length op-ed piece by Frye under the title, "Evans, Novak: Reader Beware." It began dramatically:

> This is a citizen's arrest. Defendants: Rowland Evans and Robert Novak. Charge: chronic inaccuracy.
>
> Like petty vandalism, Evans and Novak's frequent mistakes in print are generally too minor to warrant the effort to prosecute and victims remain silent. Yet, collectively, their repeated errors are a clear and present danger to public misunderstanding.

Frye proceeded to dispute our columns dealing with national security, including those on the Sonnenfeldt Doctrine and PRM-10. Near the end of his screed, Frye finally got to our item about him. While calling his treatment "inconsequential" in comparison with our other transgressions, he denied everything that had been confirmed to us by Senator Baker.

"Having admired their early work together," wrote Frye, "I present this indictment more in sorrow than in anger" because of our "growing pattern of mistakes and distortions." He contended that while we "once enjoyed the esteem of journalists and politicians, they now elicit widespread contempt and misbelief."

In keeping with his policy that every attack must be answered, Rowly insisted on responding to Frye's essay even though only one newspaper actually published it. I disagreed, saying it would only spawn a second attack by Frye (which indeed it did). But I bowed to Evans's wishes. His response, which was printed in the *Tennessean,* refuted, point by point, Frye's allegations and concluded with an analysis of what Rowly and I thought this was all about:

> Frye did not see fit to write this essay until he was mentioned in our column. We were quickly informed that he immediately began asking people how best to launch an attack against Evans and Novak. He was able with remarkable speed to put together an attack on columns going back nearly two years. That raises certain implications.
>
> We know from firsthand reports that advocates of arms control in private strategy sessions often single out our columns as an obstacle to approval of a SALT II treaty. They feel, and we agree, that our columns present information and analysis of a kind found nowhere else today on a consistent basis. Consequently, with the Senate debate on SALT II looming, we are not surprised that there is a conscious effort to soften, reduce or eliminate our voice. . . .
>
> It is, of course, no coincidence that all the columns listed by Frye were of a piece: analytical accounts of information uncomfortable to advocates of a certain school of foreign policy. Is it too much to suggest that what Alton Frye objects to is information that does not fit his fancy, not our accuracy?

Frye's predictable response in a second essay (published in the *Tennessean* of April 2) expressed outrage that his veracity had been challenged for the "first time" in "two decades of writing and broadcasting." He argued that Evans & Novak's "real argument is not with me but with responsible authorities in the U.S. government." But Frye drew blood with this market analysis of the Evans & Novak column:

> The column seems to be in serious decline. Not only did the *Los Angeles Times* drop it some time ago; the *Los Angeles Herald-Examiner* has now suspended use in favor of the new column by Jules Witcover and Jack Germond. The *Atlanta Journal,* the *Dayton Journal Herald,* the *Kalamazoo Gazette* and the *New Orleans States-Item* no longer carry Evans and Novak at all.
>
> The *Minneapolis Star* and *Philadelphia Inquirer* indicate they now run the column quite infrequently, and *The Burlington Free Press* publishes it "less and less." When the *Long Island Press* failed, *Newsday* picked up its major features—with the notable exception of Evans and Novak.

Even *The Washington Post,* their principal outlet, has refused to run
Evans and Novak material in three instances, and has reduced its use
of the column.

Frye erred in his April 12 column that the *Washington Post* had recently
spiked three Evans & Novak columns. Only the second Letelier column
met that fate. But he was accurate when he said that the *Post* had "reduced
its use of the column." For years, Phil Geyelin had complained about our
weekend column because it was "too tabloid" for the *Post.* But it was our
most popular column with many newspapers. In 1978, Geyelin stopped
running the item column in the *Post.* The change came in the middle
of Alton Frye's campaign, when Geyelin had been discussing our work
with Frye.

Frye was premature reporting that the *New Orleans States-Item* had
dropped us; that did not happen for another three years. But he was accurate in saying we had been cancelled by the *Los Angeles Times, Atlanta Journal,* and the *Dayton Journal Herald.* Frye said the *Philadelphia Inquirer* and
the *Minneapolis Star* carried us "quite infrequently," but soon those two
newspapers cancelled the column outright.

That was not all. In a relatively limited amount of time, we were cancelled by the *Baltimore Sun, Miami Herald, Louisville Courier-Journal,
Cleveland Plain Dealer, Des Moines Register, St. Louis Post-Dispatch, Kansas
City Star, Denver Post, Portland Oregonian*—and later, Alton Frye's newspaper of choice, the *Nashville Tennessean.* That's a better client list than most
syndicated columnists ever enjoy.

Frye's campaign, I think, was a contributing cause for our shrinking list.
The primary cause was that the nation's newspaper editors were moving
Left, while our column was moving Right (though the campaign by Jewish
readers and advertisers also contributed). The stated reason for cancellation
given was usually what Frye contended: deterioration in quality. Yet I defy
anybody to compare our columns of the early sixties with those of the late
seventies and not conclude we had improved markedly.

In 1978, our television earnings—mainly from RKO—were minimal.
The column still provided more annual income for Rowly and me than any
other source, but the idea that syndicated newspaper columnists were rich
was absurd (particularly if two columnists were splitting the pot). A sweet-
heart contract with the Field Syndicate protected us from an income loss
from our shrinking newspaper client list, but it was now apparent we never
would significantly *increase* our income from the column above the present level of thirty thousand dollars each. We were unable to exceed fifteen

hundred subscribers for the *Evans-Novak Political Report,* which produced around ten thousand dollars a year for each of us. Our twice-a-year-political forums netted about ten thousand dollars each for us. W. Colston Leigh, our agent in New York, told me he just couldn't get one thousand dollars a lecture for me. I agreed to go on the Ben Franklin lecture circuit, where I joined inspirational speakers, comedians, and other theatrical performers getting $750 a pop. Rowly and I split evenly approximately twenty thousand dollars brought in by Leigh. This all added up to an annual income of around sixty thousand dollars (plus forty thousand dollars for two years from an online commentary windfall). That was way more money than most reporters made. But my earnings were frozen while the Jimmy Carter inflation rate was rising fast.

I was dipping into the separate *Evans-Novak Political Report* checking account for an occasional thousand dollars or so, which I took care to repay promptly. Sometimes that was not enough, and I would walk across Pennsylvania Avenue to my bank for an unsecured ninety-day note of ten thousand dollars. The interest rate in the Jimmy Carter economy was just under 20 percent, leading me to ask my bank vice president what the loan sharks were charging if this was her rate. Rowly enjoyed a much richer standard of living without seeming to be pressed for money. Such is the advantage of inherited wealth.

(I have to confess that in 1978, I was betting up to one thousand dollars a day on basketball, baseball, and football—a practice started in 1973 and continued for about twenty years. I never won much or lost much in any year, but taking these risks was exciting. I suppose I had a gambling problem to accompany my drinking problem.)

I worried less about my declining financial balance sheet than I was concerned at age forty-seven that my career was fading, having lost newspapers and my regular television gig. But two events intervened: the advent of supply side economics and the opening of Communist China. One event energized me personally and the other strengthened my fading reputation.

JIMMY CARTER'S FOOLISH nagging about trivial aspects of the Internal Revenue Code was dwarfed in importance by two parallel developments. First was the Kemp-Roth bill, which would cut individual income tax rates thirty percentage points over three years. On September 30, 1977, it became official party policy by vote of the Republican National Committee—marking the GOP's first serious move toward tax reduction since the 1920s. Second, a popular tax revolt was building in the states, most dramatically in

California where voters were poised to pass Proposition 13 reducing property taxes.

On the Saturday before the Prop. 13 referendum, I paid a visit to Palos Verdes, which I described in a column as an "opulent suburb of Los Angeles where a 37-year-old economist spins an economic doctrine that is radically transforming Republican theory and possibly American politics." Seldom would I be so clairvoyant, though the term "supply-side economics" was still unknown to me. The economist was Professor Arthur Laffer of the University of Southern California, a founding father of supply-side. I had intended to spend an hour with him but I stayed the rest of the day, an experience that changed my politics and my life.

When I visited Laffer in June 1978, it was hard for me to accept cutting taxes without commensurate spending reductions. In the 1976 presidential campaign, I had criticized both Ford and Carter for not demanding sacrifices by individual Americans—that is, income tax increases. But Laffer fascinated me. This is how I described him and his message in an Evans & Novak column:

> The notion of cutting taxes without cutting the budget is hard to take for many conventional Republicans, and so is Art Laffer himself. Spouting ideas a mile a minute and sipping wine on the patio of his $225,000 home in Palos Verdes on a sun-drenched afternoon while a big green macaw perches on his shoulder, he is no buttoned-down conservative economist.
>
> One nationally known Republican operative, meeting him for the first time, was put off "to find this young guy in a leisure suit and high heels." He was even more put off to find that non-politician Laffer was exuberantly putting forth the Kemp-Roth Bill as the modern Philosopher's Stone transmuting unelectable Republicans into officeholders.

This description enjoyed a rare protracted shelf life. As Laffer often complained to me, the image of him in a leisure suit with a parrot on his shoulder persisted. But beyond his colorful appearance, Laffer's theories enthralled me. The Laffer Curve indicated that lower tax rates would produce more revenue by accelerating the economy until the area of diminishing returns was reached, while higher tax rates in due course would produce less revenue. Although no reputable California politician (including Ronald Reagan) so far had publicly endorsed Prop. 13, Laffer thought it a terrific idea that would generate economic growth.

But it was Kemp-Roth that most excited Laffer. He told me of two principal missionaries spreading his gospel. One was Congressman Jack Kemp. The other was Jude Wanniski, who, as associate editor of the *Wall Street Journal,* wrote the paper's tax editorials. Laffer told me that if I was interested in what he was telling me, I would not fully appreciate it until I read Wanniski's new book, *The Way the World Works.*

No book other than *Witness* by Whittaker Chambers has so influenced my political thinking. Just as Chambers shaped my darkening view of the West's struggle for survival against the communist juggernaut, Wanniski pointed to the sunny uplands in the midst of Jimmy Carter's malaise—when low growth, double-digit interest rates, constant inflation, and high unemployment seemed a permanent part of American economics. With brilliant analogies, Wanniski explained how stupidities of government led to economic disaster—and election defeats. Laffer called it "the best book on economics ever written," but it also was a political book, with passages such as this one:

> [I]n November 1974 the Republicans, carrying the burden of Ford's [proposed 5 percent surtax,] lost three dozen seats in the House of Representatives. In the days immediately following the GOP debacle, White House Chief of Staff Donald Rumsfeld was persuaded by Laffer that the correct policy was tax reduction, not tax increase. It was for Rumsfeld's assistant, Richard Cheney, that Laffer drew his Curve for the first time on the back of a paper napkin in the Two Continents Restaurant a block from the White House. The stock market stopped its decline and began a serious advance in December 1974 with the first hints that Ford was turning on tax policy. And while the "tax cuts" announced by Ford in February were inefficiently designed by the administration's conservative Keynesians, it made a great deal of difference to the economy that there would be some movement down the Laffer Curve instead of a leap upwards.

If Chambers pointed only to ultimate defeat at the hands of the communists, Wanniski showed the way to prosperity and political success. Contacting Wanniski to discuss his political-economic model of the world, I made a new friend and found a new insight into the way the world works.

IN THE SUMMER of 1978, Ray Cline of the Center for Strategic and International Studies (CSIS) asked Rowly to participate in a conference in Seoul on U.S.-Korean relations, all expenses paid. Cline was a former CIA professional who, like many Agency officials past and present, was close to Rowly. My partner had no interest in making his first visit to Korea, but told Cline that I had reported from there several times and might be interested. I eagerly accepted the invitation—for an ulterior purpose. I wanted to get to China.

President Nixon's 1971 visit established mutual "liaison offices" in Peking* and Washington (a rung below formal diplomatic relations). The Chinese diplomats sent to Washington gave Rowly and me the Communist version of the royal treatment with invitations to receptions, lunches, and dinners. Our column beat a steady tattoo on the Soviet Union. The Chinese, at the height of their anti-Soviet frenzy, felt "the enemy of my enemy is my friend." Rowly did not appreciate Chinese food and always had a much fuller social schedule. Increasingly, I would show up at the Chinese events, while my partner passed.

Starting in 1976, the Chinese pressed me to visit their country. I wanted to go, but it was frightfully expensive and Rowly didn't think the story was worth me blowing half my expense budget. So Ray Cline's all-expense-paid trip to Korea opened the way for me to go.

The Chinese quickly gave me a visa. The founding fathers of Communist China—Mao Tse-tung and Chou En-lai—were dead. Their designated successor, Hua Kou-feng, was a mystery to the outside world. I applied for an interview with him without hope. I had been told by China experts in the U.S. government that I would be lucky to sit down with a fourth-level bureaucrat in the Foreign Ministry.

At this point, I had a chance encounter with Henry Kissinger. He had been Rowly's source, not mine, but he wanted to plant an idea with me. Cardinal Karol Wojtyla of Kraków, Poland, had just become Pope John Paul II, and Kissinger was concerned that a Polish prelate was so accustomed to making deals with the Communists that he would be subservient to the Soviet Union. This proved a spectacularly incorrect analysis, as I suspected at the time. But I used my momentary proximity with Henry to ask a favor. Could he get me an interview with Hua Kou-feng? Kissinger replied that he was not sure Hua was all that much in control of China, but said—without apparent conviction—he would do what he could for me. I think he might have been partially responsible for my subsequent good fortune.

* I am using transliterations in use at the time of these events, that is Peking instead of Beijing and Teng instead of Deng.

. . .

AFTER THE SEOUL conference, I would spend one day in Hong Kong—Thursday, November 23, 1978, Thanksgiving—before going on to China. I had asked for a China briefing at the U.S. Consulate in Hong Kong even though it was an American holiday, but Consul General Thomas Shoesmith said he had something better in mind. He and his key staffers would host me for dinner that evening at the Hong Kong Press Club, with some of the city's Western correspondents who had recently reported inside the PRC.

I learned that night about the "wall poster rebellion" in the Chinese capital. On Sunday, November 19, prodemocracy posters popped up across Peking. Their central theme, I was told, was support for the protesters at Tian An Men Square in the center of Peking who two and one-half years earlier had been arrested, stripped of their jobs, and in many cases imprisoned. The posters denounced leading Communists responsible for this.

How was this free expression possible in a Communist dictatorship? Everybody agreed one man got the credit for permitting it: Teng Hsiao-ping. Testifying to the inadequacy of my Washington briefings on China (including one by the CIA), I had never heard of him. These China experts told me Teng, only a vice premier, now ran the authoritarian government of China and had wrested power from Hua Kuo-feng (who became a figurehead). I said I had asked for an interview with Hua. That would be a waste of time, I was told, but I surely would not get to see him or anybody else in the upper strata of Chinese leadership. Not since Chou En-lai was interviewed by Scotty Reston in 1971 had a major figure submitted to a Western journalist's interview.

The consulate's China watchers filled me in on Teng. He was a junior member of the Mao-Chou generation of revolutionary leadership—at age seventy-four, seventeen years older than Hua. He had bourgeois tastes (chain-smoking cigarettes when not chewing tobacco, bridge, mah-jongg, multicourse banquets) that, combined with apostasy on many points of Marxism, contributed to accusations that he was a "capitalist roader." He had been purged from power as a vice premier in 1966 and again in 1975. But Teng had been a thirty-year-old political commissar on the fabled Long March of 1934, and the People's Liberation Army (PLA) remained his power source. His 1978 government base was the chairmanship of the government's PLA committee.

I CROSSED THE frontier into the PRC from Hong Kong Friday morning. I was met by a young Foreign Ministry worker (reading an English-language international edition of the *Reader's Digest*) who accompanied me on the train ride to the southern metropolis of Canton. It showed no signs of tumult, with the biggest excitement there being a chrysanthemum show. I left Canton for Peking by air that evening and was greeted in the capital by another Foreign Ministry official, this one older and less westernized, who assured me nothing at all was happening in Peking.

I was driven to the Min Zu Hotel, a dreary old place where I was told foreign journalists always were assigned. My guide walked me up to a threadbare hotel room and there informed me I would be on my own to explore the city for the weekend but advised me to be ready for "a very important interview" on Monday. Saving the best until last, he informed me there was "a possibility" I would be seeing Teng Hsiao-ping. I had not requested to see Teng, not even knowing his name when I left Washington. Like all the Chinese Communist leaders, he did not see Western journalists. So the regime had in mind some use for me, which I could not yet identify.

THE 1973 ARRANGEMENT did not permit permanent journalistic correspondents in each other's country, leaving that amenity for the establishment of full diplomatic relations. In November 1978, I was the only American journalist in this country of more than one billion souls. I had been informed that the brightest resident Western correspondent in China was a young Canadian: John Fraser of the *Toronto Globe and Mail.* I met him in his apartment on Saturday afternoon, and he told me that I had arrived at a time of breakneck change. Earlier that day, Fraser told me, he had gone to the Hsi Tan Wall where the posters were displayed. For the first time, he had been engaged in conversation by Chinese in the street, asking how democracy worked in the West.

Fraser, his wife, and I went to Hsi Tan on Sunday night. I had gone there Saturday and again on Sunday afternoon on my own, and since then the crowd had expanded from the hundreds to the thousands. It was a cold, wintry night with gusts of fierce wind creating clouds of dust in the gloomy, grassless area. After reading the posters, the Chinese—mostly young men—leaned against each other in little groups to debate political issues. I described what happened next in an article for *Look* magazine:

> Fraser approached one such assembly to ask a few questions in halting Mandarin. When he was able to convey that we were both journalists, a hundred Chinese pushed around us in a moment, with more moving double-time to join us. A young woman with a fair knowledge of English volunteered to be our interpreter, and a robust, leather-lunged man shouted her Chinese interpretations to the growing throng. They

pressed in on us, pushing and shoving. But soon the order of a disciplined society prevailed, and they formed themselves into rows—some kneeling and some standing, a few climbing into the trees for a better view—into a sort of a rough amphitheater around Fraser, his wife and me, with the gusts periodically blinding us all with dust.

The questions startled me. How do you criticize your leaders without being considered a traitor? How do you change governments without a revolution? Then Fraser mentioned that I might be seeing Teng the next day.

Suddenly, a lusty and prolonged cheer went up. That Teng was their man was indisputable. Suggestions for what I should say to Teng or what I should ask him were shouted. The encounter degenerated into chaos, but Fraser asked that their comments and questions be put in writing. Soon scraps of paper were passed forward to me, amid smiles and excitement.

At seven thirty Monday morning, my Foreign Ministry keeper informed me by phone that the interview with Teng was on. He instructed me to eat breakfast, then wait in my room. At nine fifty, a Shanghai-built sedan drove me the few blocks to the Great Hall of the People. The *Look* account continued:

Arriving just before 10 o'clock, I did not encounter the normal wait to see a head of government. Teng Hsiao-ping, a faintly quizzical look on his face, awaited me in the corridor.

As others had reported, Teng appeared much younger than his 74 years. His appearance and manner were not those of an old man, and he seemed a few inches taller than the 4-foot-11 listed in many press accounts. We entered a cavernous conference room and after a brief picture-taking session, sat down side by side—the usual cups for hot tea between us. Flanking on each side was a platoon of note-takers and government officials.

At the outset I told Teng I hoped to question him on China's domestic situation once we completed our discussion of international affairs. He nodded agreement but quickly added he preferred I not use the tape recorder I carried with me. A Chinese functionary then instructed me not to quote Teng directly though nothing was off the record (a peculiar formulation that I interpreted as "quotes without quotation marks"). To continue the *Look* article:

> Teng was everything I had been led to believe, and more. I had been informed that he was the one man in China today who could and would depart from boilerplate in public pronouncements. Despite his melancholy background of purges, he seemed buoyantly confident of his authority, seeking no prompting from official doctrine. Even in translation (which in short bursts interrupted his Chinese) the wit and dynamism was preserved. The vibrancy contrasted sharply with the listless recitation of official policy in press interviews given by contemporary world leaders. From the moment I began the interview by trying to assess the Chinese view of American will and strength, Teng was off on a *tour d'horizon* of world policy (punctuated by highly vocal use of a spittoon).

I got in all the questions I had when one of the Chinese officials gave the high sign. It was noon. I rose and asked Teng about his statement that he wanted to visit Washington "before I meet Karl Marx." A little wistfully, he replied that was his desire but he did not know whether it would be fulfilled. Then he looked at his wristwatch. "It's been two hours," Teng said in a tone of wonderment.

As promised, I called John Fraser following lunch to pass on Teng's answers to a couple of questions from the Hsi Tan crowd that I had addressed to the Chinese leader. Fraser wanted me to meet him and other Western correspondents at seven p.m. at the wall to relay those answers to the Chinese. I excused myself because I had committed myself to dinner with Chinese journalists whom Rowly and I had entertained for dinner at Evans's home the previous summer. After dinner, I finished writing the first of two Evans & Novak columns on the Teng interview and telexed it to the Field Newspaper Syndicate in Chicago.

I started by telling the world that Teng (described by me as "China's dominant figure today," a reality not yet widely understood) "heartily endorses free speech in wall posters now covering Peking even while disagreeing with some of their comments and considers it a return to the brief 'let a hundred flowers bloom' campaign two decades ago." I continued:

> Vice Premier Teng confirmed to us in an exclusive interview that the Communist Central Committee had been meeting here but denied a

purge of radical members. While also denying a de-Maoization campaign, he admitted the late Chairman Mao Tse-tung made a few mistakes. And Teng brushed off reports of a power struggle by him against his nominal superior, party chairman and Premier Hua Kuo-feng; he could have had the premiership last year if he wanted, Teng said.

On U.S. relations, Teng declared Taiwan could maintain its own non-Communist economic and social system under unification with the mainland—the furthest he has gone to ease a U.S. switch in diplomatic relations from Taiwan to Peking. This normalization of relations, said Teng, would do more for U.S. security than any number of SALT treaties with Moscow.

That summary contained big news that far surpassed my expectations. I concluded the column:

Teng acted like a man who needs nobody's approval to express opinions. But he also emphasized he wanted no more of the political turmoil that has plagued China's 20-year-old Communist regime. His stress was stability, not further purges or power grabs.

This tiny, feisty man who became a Communist with Chou En-lai in France a half century ago, is at his advanced age clearly in a hurry. His drive for a rational economic and political system and quest for an American alliance against Moscow represent the pulse of China today.

It was past one in the morning when I finished telexing the column, and I took a detour walking back to the hotel from the state cable office so that I passed the Hsi Tan Wall. I was puzzled to find hundreds of Chinese milling around at that very late hour, but there was no way for me to communicate with any of them.

Just as I fell asleep at my hotel, I was awakened by a telephone call from Jay Matthews, the *Washington Post* correspondent in Hong Kong. He asked what in the hell was going on in tightly controlled Peking. He was amazed to learn that I knew nothing about the bizarre events that Monday evening. Thousands had gathered at Hsi Tan Monday evening to hear Teng's answers—relayed by John Fraser—to the questions they had given me, and it turned into a full-scale political rally. When Fraser reported Teng telling me there was "nothing to be afraid of" in the wall posters advocating democracy, the crowd cheered wildly. When he told them Teng said he would evaluate himself as correct only 60 percent of the time, they murmured in approval of his modesty. After Fraser's briefing, the Chinese marched—seventy abreast—the two long blocks from Hsi Tan to Tian An Men Square, singing the "Internationale" and the Chinese anthem. The throng, approximately ten thousand, spent hours hearing impassioned oratory in behalf of democracy and freedom.

The Evans & Novak column was given major coverage all over the U.S. The *Washington Post* ran it over four columns on top of the November 28 op-ed page, headlined "An Interview with China's Teng Hsiao-ping" with a three-column photo of Chinese crowded together reading wall posters. But the big news that hit American front pages was an unauthorized political rally in Communist China.

A terrific story was taking place in the Chinese capital, where I was the only American reporter to cover it. The irony was that I could not stay in Peking, but was leaving early the next morning. I was not a free agent who could come and go as I pleased. I was an official guest of the Chinese government, which explained the red-carpet treatment bestowed on me (though, of course, the government billed me for everything).

Rowly and I had felt recent visits to China by American journalists were unproductive because they got bogged down in Peking talking to unresponsive bureaucrats rather than getting news in the vast Chinese countryside. With no global issue hotter in the late seventies than energy, I had decided in Washington to visit the Ta Ching oil fields in northeast China (formerly Manchuria) and spend as little time as possible in the national capital.

After completing my Tuesday schedule in the Manchurian metropolis of Harbin, I wrote a second column on my interview with Teng:

> Contending that the Soviet Union has surpassed U.S. naval strength in the Western Pacific and has established Asian footholds in Afghanistan and Vietnam, Communist China is pressing hard for not only diplomatic relations with Washington but also a strong Sino-American alliance against Moscow. . . .
>
> So anxious did [Teng] appear to form this alliance that he suggested retaining a special status for Taiwan and even recognized an important role for South Korea's anti-Communist government in Korean unification. . . .
>
> [A]n alliance aimed against the Kremlin is the best reason for normalization, say the Chinese Communists.

I should have been fascinated by the first visit by an American journalist to China's prized oil fields, but instead I was frustrated as I worried about the upshot to my own story in Peking that I was missing. When my train pulled into Peking at eleven a.m. Friday, I learned from diplomatic and journalistic sources what had happened during the three days I was gone. Tuesday and Wednesday nights, I wrote in the *Look* article:

> . . . saw rallies and speechmaking in Tian An Men Square, and word later circulated of sympathetic rallies in Shanghai and Nanking. Finally, five days after this remarkable train of events was set in motion at Hsi Tan, Teng decided things had gone far enough. The highly efficient Chinese political communications system—internal radio broadcasts to Communist Party units and circulars—instructed Chinese to stop demonstrating and discuss these problems in their party units instead. But there was no word of criticism. . . .

When I finally returned to Peking from Manchuria, the crowds at Hsi Tan were markedly different in character—less excited, more subdued. Many posters defending free speech remained, but others voiced the party line that workers should discuss these matters in their party units instead of in public. When I was interviewed at Hsi Tan on these events by the BBC [on Saturday], just one week after the excitement began, hundreds of Chinese pressed in—but nobody tried to speak to us.

The U.S. deputy chief of mission—J. Stapleton Roy, a career diplomat (and future ambassador to China)—had been trying to sit down with me ever since my interview with Teng, and we finally dined in an excellent Peking restaurant on Friday night. Roy wanted to confirm that Teng really used the word "alliance" in describing his desired relationship with the United States against the Soviet Union and that he was as reasonable as I described him in not regarding the Taiwan and Korea situations as impediments to full diplomatic relations between the two countries. I got the idea that the U.S. Liaison Office (USLO), not in close touch with China's rulers, was grateful for my input.

I believe Teng devoted two hours for me to send Washington the message that he wanted "normalization" quickly and did not have a high asking price. (Diplomatic relations were established the next year without new U.S. concessions on Taiwan or Korea.) But the wall poster upheaval accidentally coinciding with my visit required Teng to address the domestic balance of power.

Roy felt Teng not only permitted but inspired the wall poster campaign denouncing hard-liners in the government in order to solidify control over the bureaucracy. Teng's rivals in the regime were the same Maoists who had ordered the repression of the Tian An Men Square demonstration of April 5, 1976. But the wall posters soon went beyond Teng's desires by calling for democracy and denouncing Mao. Therefore, Teng in my interview made a lukewarm defense of Mao and rejected parliamentary democracy. When this did not slow down the demonstrations, Teng put an end to them while I was traveling around Manchuria.

But in my final column from China I came to a conclusion that I don't believe was shared by the USLO. I wrote that Teng's

ambitious modernization program . . . depends on those very students and workers who demonstrated for democracy last week to challenge the dead hand of the vast bureaucracy. For their part, the demonstrators don't want to provoke a comeback by the hard-liners being purged by Teng. Thus, that the demonstrators and Teng need each other is the best hope for cautious liberalization in China. . . .

Teng and the demonstrators made an effort to please each other. The orders to end the demonstrations were followed. However,

there is no evidence of any order to end contacts with foreigners. In answer to our repeated questions, well-placed Chinese officials refused to criticize either the demonstrations or the part in them played by Western newsmen; instead, they praised political involvement as conducive to "China's four modernizations." The demonstrators so praised are young, mostly students but many workers. . . .

The regime's call for election of workshop leaders and other cadres to shape up the bureaucracy created demand for democracy on top. While selecting plant superintendents, said one poster put up during the demonstrations, "we have no say about the people who run this country." For that sentiment to surface in China after a generation of developing Socialist Man under the world's tightest thought-control system is nothing less than a tribute to the human spirit.

That elegy has come in for criticism in view of the blood spilled in Tian An Men Square a decade later, but I believe my analysis was correct— except for one fatal error. My vision of China evolving peacefully toward democracy depended on a seventy-four-year-old man. After Teng, there was nobody who could command the loyalties of the students and workers while controlling the army and its leaders.

I thought then that Teng Hsiao-ping, though surely no democrat, was one of the few great men with whom I ever had come into contact. In 1989 he was officially retired but reputedly still in control and made the decision to use brutal force against the students and workers in Tian An Men Square. I cannot believe Teng, at the peak of his powers in 1978, would have given that signal. Perhaps he lived too long.

WITH MY CHINESE interlude completed, I needed to get to Las Vegas as soon as possible to satisfy my obsession. I don't mean gambling. The University of Maryland basketball team was playing the University of Nevada at Las Vegas on Saturday night. I could barely make it in time for the tip-off. Arriving in Tokyo from Peking for a layover, I telephoned the Maryland sports information director Jack Zane asking him to find me a game ticket and a hotel room. More than a quarter of a century later, Zane was still retelling my scramble from Peking to Las Vegas as the epitome of hoops mania.

CHAPTER 28

A Young Congressman from New York

WHEN I VOTED for Ronald Reagan in the 1976 Maryland primary, it not only signified a protest against Jerry Ford's failed presidency but also the belief that the old movie actor would be much better in the Oval Office. But he would be sixty-nine years old on February 6, 1980—surely too old to run for president.

I booked Reagan, making a visit to Washington, late in 1978 for our RKO television program. I considered Reagan at this point an elder states-man of the Republican Party, not its coming presidential candidate. We taped the interview at the Capitol Hill Club (the Republican watering hole two blocks from the Capitol), during which he was as smooth as ever. After we finished, Reagan sat down with Rowly and me to chat off the record. I asked whether he would even consider trying again for president in 1980, assuming he would say no. "Oh, boy," he replied, "I sure would like to." That took my breath away.

Through 1979, his age worried even supporters—such as Robert Walker, a thirty-six-year-old second-term congressman from Pennsylvania. Reagan agreed to address a congressional fund-raiser June 12, 1979, in Walker's home base of Lancaster. I decided to go there for the speech.

When I telephoned Walker for advance information about the event, he volunteered a concern about Reagan's age that I had heard with increasing frequency from Republicans. Walker told me he felt Reagan should pledge to serve only one term as president—and pledge it *now*. That, he said, would end speculation about a man entering his second presidential term well into his seventies. Walker said he was going to put this proposition straight to Reagan when he came to Lancaster.

Reagan turned Walker down. John Sears, Reagan's campaign manager for 1980 as he was in 1976, told me the disclaimer would only call attention to the candidate's age. I thought then that Bob Walker had a good idea. In retrospect, I believe the "age issue" was unimportant and the cover for something else—an unspoken, unadmitted reluctance to risk another Goldwater fiasco. This concern was conveyed to me, not for quotation, by prominent Republicans.

In the spring of 1979, I had a weekend speaking engagement in Nashville, and suggested to Geraldine that it might be fun for her to come along and take in the Grand Old Opry—a bit of country-western Americana that neither of us had experienced. Lamar Alexander was governor of Tennessee, and I called him to see if he could get us a couple of good tickets. He could, and invited Geraldine and me for dinner at the governor's mansion. Alexander came from the "liberal" wing of the Tennessee GOP, but he was not *that* liberal and in 1967 had cast his lot with Nixon. Now, Lamar suggested to me that Reagan's nomination might do the party great damage in Tennessee and around the country.

A few weeks later in Chicago, I was having coffee with Illinois governor James Thompson at his suite in the Ambassador Hotel and heard an identical analysis—though characteristically delivered more vehemently. "I'm afraid we wouldn't recover politically for a generation," Big Jim told me. (I remembered that doleful prognosis twenty-five years later when Thompson, commenting on Reagan's death, claimed that he had been Reagan's man in Illinois from the start.)

An Evans & Novak column suggested that "one reason for the intense interest in [Reagan's] age is the meager intellectual content of his current speeches." He was still working off the three-by-five index cards that he had used on the General Electric Company lecture circuit two decades earlier. That deficiency would be corrected by an odd course of events that began as a potential threat to Reagan's nomination.

FOR HIS FIRST five years in Congress after his 1970 election, Jack Kemp was just another upstate New York conservative. But in 1976, he met *Wall Street Journal* editorial writer Jude Wanniski, and the result of their collaboration was the Kemp-Roth tax reduction bill. After the Republican National Committee's unprecedented endorsement of the bill in 1977, Kemp became a party favorite. Having molded the former quarterback into political leader of the new supply-side movement, Wanniski now wanted to make him president of the United States.

John Sears was disturbed by James Jackson Kilpatrick's column of May 6, 1978. Writing that Reagan was "getting a little long in the tooth," the conservative columnist suggested Kemp should run. Longtime Reagan aide Pete Hannaford arranged a meeting with Kemp in the congressman's Washington office. As Hannaford told me the story late in May while driving along a California freeway on my way to an appointment with Reagan, Kemp knocked down Kilpatrick's proposal before Hannaford had a chance to open his mouth. He voluntarily pledged his support for Reagan and told Hannaford to disregard Kemp-for-president talk.

When I telephoned Wanniski to discuss this still unpublished development, Jude said he was appalled by what Kemp had done in backing Reagan. At the moment, however, I could not fully appreciate the extent of Wanniski's dismay. I was just getting to know one of the most unique characters I ever met. The genius level of his intelligence set Wanniski apart, but what really made him different was his obsessive nature.

On May 12, Wanniski lunched with Hannaford in Los Angeles and told him the situation changed by a development immediately after Kemp had pledged his support to Reagan. Kemp had telephoned Reagan and asked him to help the seemingly quixotic U.S. Senate campaign in New Jersey being waged by Jeff Bell, Reagan's young former aide. Bell, who was seen by Wanniski as one of his two most important supply-side acolytes along with Kemp, was running against veteran liberal Republican Senator Clifford Case in the New Jersey primary on June 8 (which Bell would win in an immense upset). Reagan, advised by Sears to play the party regular in anticipation of the 1980 race for the nomination, turned down Kemp.

Then, as Wanniski related it to me, he told Hannaford that Kemp's support for Reagan was predicated on Reagan accepting supply-side doctrine. But, Wanniski went on, Reagan broke the compact by refusing to help Bell. Next he applied the clincher to Hannaford: This was force majeure—an irresistible tide building behind Kemp that would sweep away trivial personal promises. It was a tortured argument that I doubted Kemp really bought into. But Wanniski exerted tremendous influence on Kemp, and the congressman found an excuse for reneging on his pledge—an exercise in which I played an inadvertent part.

Based on my conversation with Hannaford, I wrote a June 4 Sunday item reporting Kemp's declaration of loyalty to Reagan. "You have my word in blood," Hannaford quoted Kemp as saying, and I included that in my column. Wanniski now thought Kemp had another pretext for reneging on his promise to support Reagan, and he convinced Kemp. Kemp told the Reagan camp that his commitment to Reagan was strictly *private* and that when Hannaford leaked it to me, he no longer was bound to support Reagan. That was ridiculous, and Kemp kept his reneging secret for the time being.

In July 1978 at the Republican National Committee's meeting in Detroit,

I reported in an Evans & Novak column a "desire for a new Republican face, and the new face likely to have finished first in a secret ballot of [RNC] members was Kemp." As "a leader of the national tax revolt," I wrote, "non-candidate Kemp has surpassed a half dozen potential candidates in bringing a sense of excitement to all kinds of Republicans." Hearing the Kemp buzz in Detroit, longtime Reagan aide Lyn Nofziger assured me that Kemp had assured Reagan he supported him—a claim I included in my column from Detroit.

When Kemp decided to make public his decision to renege, it was leaked to me and first became known in our column of August 18. I wrote that Kemp "no longer feels bound to honor his commitment to support" Reagan and "may announce his own candidacy" in November. I later got to know Jack personally (better than I did most politicians), and in hindsight I don't believe there ever was a chance he would challenge Reagan for the 1980 nomination. While daring in advocating new concepts, Kemp was risk-averse about his own career. But in the summer of 1978, I took Kemp's self-professed presidential intentions seriously. Sears did as well. Indeed, Sears walked Reagan into the supply-side movement to nullify Kemp and prevent him from eating into Reagan's conservative base.

In his introduction to the second edition (1982) of *How the World Works,* Wanniski revealed that in the early summer of 1979, Kemp met Reagan in Los Angeles and talked supply-side doctrine with him for three hours. After that session, Kemp—for the second time—privately pledged his allegiance to Reagan. This time it stuck. The price of Kemp's endorsement was Reagan's initiation as a supply-sider. Kemp was about to be named national chairman of the Reagan campaign while Reagan sang the praises of Kemp and his tax policies.

In early October 1979, I picked up Reagan addressing a Maryland Republican fund-raising dinner in suburban Baltimore County. With a Hunt Valley, Maryland, dateline for an Evans & Novak column, I wrote:

> When Ronald Reagan told the Maryland Republican dinner here about tax-cutting ideas of "a young Congressman from New York, Jack Kemp," he signaled a campaign strategy change of potentially profound consequences.
>
> That morning at a Hopkinsville, Ky. rally, Reagan plugged Kemp. The night before at a black-tie, $500-a-plate dinner on a Kentucky horse farm, he did the same. The night before that, Reagan praised the Congressman (seated beside him) in a dinner in his Buffalo con-

stituency. Indeed, since summer's end, Jack Kemp has replaced the no-torious "welfare queen" of 1976 as a stock character in Reagan's stump oratory.

More important, pushing tax relief for blue-collar workers has replaced flogging welfare recipients. Alone among Republican presi-dential hopefuls, front-runner Reagan ardently pressed a huge across-the-board tax reduction. While the Reagan of early summer still played to Main Street merchants by castigating federal regulation, he now seeks to sway broader audiences away from Sen. Edward M. Kennedy [then the leading Democratic presidential prospect] by preaching economic hope through tax cuts instead of austerity through reduced growth.

No more did Reagan say in private that the country needed a good, deep recession to clean inflation out of the system. That set him apart from presidential hopefuls who were then thought the most formidable threats to him. John Connally, refusing to endorse Kemp-Roth, called a balanced budget the principal imperative. Howard Baker declared that Carter's new Secretary of the Treasury G. William Miller was correct when, at the World Bank meeting in Belgrade, he called for "austerity" by Americans. At Hunt Valley, I got time alone with Reagan before his speech and asked him about Miller's comments. Reagan replied: "He is voicing the old-fashioned eco-nomics that the choice is between inflation and recession."

Ronald Reagan was on a course that would profoundly affect U.S. poli-tics and policies for the next generation and beyond.

EVERYBODY THOUGHT Ted Kennedy was a sure winner for the Demo-cratic presidential nomination in 1980 because Carter looked like a sure loser. More than most reporters, Rowly and I knew just how bad a presi-dent Carter was because of the Carter book we intended for publication in the summer of 1980 prior to Carter's reelection campaign. In early 1979, we started doing in-depth interviews with former Carter aides that were only for the book, not our column, and definitely not for attribution. But that was a quarter of century ago, and I think the statute of limitations has run. What follows is just one sample of what we were told.

In a four-hour interview Carter's first Treasury secretary, W. Michael Blumenthal, said he never had encountered anybody in government or business like Carter. This was the portrait he painted of the president for Rowly and me:

I saw him in 1977 and 1978 with outside groups in various settings, and I always felt that he made a very good impression because he would ask questions and listen. But I realized after a while that it was a PR operation because he paid absolutely no attention to what they said. He wrote it down, but nothing would happen with it. After a while, you get a sense of it. This was his way of trying to impress people. . . .

He has a deep sense of inferiority, a very deep sense of inferiority. I discovered it when I began to realize that he confided in no one. Charlie [Chief Economic Adviser Charles Schultze] would have a weekly meeting with him, and he would come out and say to me that he had never worked for a man like that before. He never reacts. Occasionally, he would ask a question. He never debates. He never disagrees. . . .

He doesn't want strong people. He ruled out [John] Dunlop [for Secretary of Labor] and he ruled out George Ball [for Secretary of State]. He ruled out when he knew the people were strong, aggressive, confrontational personalities. He didn't know me from Adam. Had he known me, he would never have invited me in. . . .

He dislikes people who are very strong and successful. That is why he doesn't like major businessmen, bankers or people who run big labor unions. You have to watch him, and he is very uncomfortable with them. He has this outward sort of politeness and gives his little spiel, but his eyes glaze over and later on he frequently makes derogatory comments about them. He feels very put upon by these people, and it is essentially that he is afraid that they know more than he does. . . .

The danger of isolation is great, and flattery is a commodity in abundance. We had a few Cabinet meetings, and people were kissing his ass. I asked if he recognized it when it was subtle and indirect, and he responded that he could tell. I could see increasingly that flattery went very far with him—a person who does not recognize when he is being shamelessly flattered and who enjoys it. . . .

He briefs very quickly with sort of a veneer of knowledge and he can give back in an orderly fashion, but he doesn't retain it for very long. . . . I think the President when he came into office was a very inexperienced and poorly informed man.

I doubt there have been more searing indictments of a president's character by a close associate, untainted by ideological or partisan bias. Interviews such as this were so rich in material that Rowly and I were sure we had a book.

But we ended up returning the advance (which was a strain on my bank account). The reason was timing. With the book to be published in mid-1980 to coincide with the presidential campaign, Rowly and I thought Kennedy would defeat Carter in the primaries and clinch the nomination in advance of the convention.

ON JULY 17, 1979, Carter fired a third of his cabinet—the administration's most experienced, distinguished officials, including Jim Schlesinger (Energy) and Mike Blumenthal (Treasury). Immediately after the cabinet reconstruction, I asked pollster Pat Caddell (who had been helping us since Ollie Quayle died) to pick a New Hampshire ward that was a reliable barometer of statewide voting in that first primary state for a mini-poll. Caddell was not only Carter's pollster but also one of his key political advisers. Yet, although Evans and Novak barely paid him enough to cover the expenses of our mini-polls and nothing faintly comparable to what he received from Carter, Caddell always was straight with us.

Caddell selected ward 9 in Nashua just over the Massachusetts state line. On July 18, we interviewed sixty-two registered voters in ward 9 who had voted in 1976. The result was a six-to-one for Kennedy. Since news of the cabinet shakeup broke in the midst of our interviewing, Caddell suggested we repoll ward 9 by telephone. Sixty interviews showed the huge Kennedy margin slightly *higher*.

"The voice from the New Hampshire weathervane," I wrote in an Evans & Novak column, "sounds remarkably similar to Washington's conventional wisdom." How could Kennedy possibly lose ward 9? How could he possibly lose New Hampshire? How could he possibly lose the nomination?

SHORTLY AFTER OUR New Hampshire mini-poll was published late in July 1979, George Herbert Walker Bush made an appointment to see Rowly and me in our office. Nobody had heard much of Bush since the Democrats won in 1976.

A summer cloudburst preceded Bush's visit. He and an aide were soaking wet when they entered our little conference room. Bush said he wanted "my old friends, Rowly and Bob" to be among the first to know that he was running for president. I feared Rowly's response, and my fears were realized. "President of *what*, George?" a grinning Evans asked.

Bush rivaled past Democratic public servants such as Jimmy Byrnes and Averell Harriman in the number of offices held. But Bush had not been elected to anything except two terms as a congressman from Houston thirteen and eleven years earlier and had not run for anything since his second losing race for the Senate from Texas nine years earlier. The conventional wisdom was that George Bush had run his last race, his future public service depending on appointment by a Republican president.

Bush conceded to Rowly and me he was "an asterisk" in any poll of Republican candidates—signifying insufficient support for a percentage. But he said an effective grassroots organization in New Hampshire was being assembled for him by the redoubtable Hugh Gregg.

"I think we can surprise everyone in New Hampshire," Bush told us. "I'm going there several days a month. Why don't you come along sometime?" Rowly and I agreed privately it would be a waste of time. But Bush was the first presidential candidate ever to pay a visit to our office, and I took him up on his invitation.

At seven a.m. on Tuesday, July 31, 1979, I was standing with George Bush beside largely untraveled Route 115 in sparsely populated Coos County in New Hampshire's North Country. Bush, wearing running garb, was about to jog three miles down the highway. I was in coat and tie and not about to jog anywhere.

Another nonjogger standing by was Hugh Gregg. He had headed Reagan's near-miss campaign in the state's 1976 primary against President Ford and now had switched sides to lead Bush's state campaign. When as a *Wall Street Journal* reporter I paid my first reporting visit to New Hampshire in the autumn of 1959, he was the state's most dynamic Republican. He had been elected governor in 1952 (New Hampshire's youngest ever at age thirty-four), serving a single two-year term. After that, Gregg was the loser in seven consecutive New Hampshire elections as either a candidate or manager.

Hugh Gregg never acted like a loser and never was treated like one. On that Bush visit in 1979, Hughie drove his van at eighty-five miles per hour as he roared through winding back roads of New Hampshire's North Country and kept up a simultaneous nonstop political commentary on Bush's chances. Sensing my distress, he reassured me: "Don't worry, I just bought one of these." He pointed to a radar detector. It was not the police that worried me.

In New Hampshire, Bush trailed not only Reagan and John Connally but congressmen Phil Crane and John Anderson. It was obvious that day that nobody in New Hampshire knew him. But everybody knew the man at his side, Hughie Gregg, who was introducing Bush to the state.

I wrote in my Bush column from New Hampshire:

During the 24 hours that we followed Bush, it is doubtful he was seen by more than 100 registered Republican voters. Yet, he probably pinned down a half dozen local county leaders. That's retail politics, which could set the foundation for an upset transforming Republican politics in 1980.

Looking back at what I wrote, I am disappointed that my column ignored two issues with prolonged influence on American political life.

First, I suggested there was no difference between Reagan and Bush on economics, when Reagan in fact had endorsed Kemp-Roth and Bush had not. That issue was not raised with Bush in New Hampshire by me or by voters he saw on this trip. My supply-side epiphany had not yet become an obsession. Nor was it yet a Republican litmus test.

The second issue was abortion. Everywhere Bush went in New Hampshire those two days, he was followed by prolife demonstrators, quiet middle-aged women who let their placards do their talking. The first time I revealed their impact was in 1999 in my book *Completing the Revolution:*

> I was the only journalist traveling with him [Bush]. He said, almost to himself, "How am I going to get rid of these people? Are these people going to follow me around all year?" I said, "I'll bet they do, George." And when he responded, "How do I get rid of them?" I told him, "Change your position." He did. I'm certainly not saying that my advice did it, and I never thought he would take me seriously. But he wanted to be president, and that is what the party activists required of him.

AFTER KENNEDY ANNOUNCED his candidacy on November 7, 1979, I asked to see him before he set off for New Hampshire on his first campaign trip. Arriving at Kennedy's Senate office, I found his anterooms filled with Kennedy family political servitors who had played important roles in the presidential campaigns of his two brothers.

As I talked to the old Kennedy hands, I sensed absolute confidence in Teddy's election and a sense of relief. After Bobby's tragedy and Teddy's indecision, they felt the long-delayed Kennedy restoration was at hand and the interloper Carter would be gone. In my brief conversation with Kennedy that day, he was brisk and articulate—nothing like the man who stumbled incoherently through a November 6 interview with CBS's Roger Mudd. A national Gallup Poll taken immediately after Kennedy's announcement showed him leading Carter among Democrats by 56 percent to 36 percent.

But less than two weeks later on a reporting trip to New York City, I observed the Kennedy campaign coming apart. In a column datelined New York, November 21, I wrote:

The two weeks of stumbling following the shock of the interview "Teddy" on CBS have so debilitated Sen. Edward Kennedy's supposed political domination in New York that sharp-tongued Gov. Hugh Carey privately calls him a "plummeting star."

Kennedy's ineptitude on the network documentary, followed by incompetence and neglect in his campaign's early days, has transformed the political landscape here. Neither Carey nor Sen. Daniel Patrick Moynihan, seemingly sure Kennedy boosters, has endorsed him. While President Carter's operatives round up organization Democrats, Kennedy's men have offended both centrists and reformers.

New York was no exception. Gallup, whose poll in early November had Kennedy twenty percentage points ahead of Carter among Democrats nationally, in mid-December showed 48 percent for Carter against 40 percent for Kennedy.

As the Iranian hostage crisis dragged on, the American people rallied behind President Carter. Kennedy, in contrast, hurt himself by attacking the deposed government of the shah. Mostly, I think, as voters got a better look at Ted Kennedy, they found he was not a duplicate of his murdered brothers.

ROWLY HAD REPORTED from Tehran many times during the shah's reign, and was back there in April 1979 after the takeover by the mullahs. We had to try to get to Iran again in the midst of the hostage crisis, and I wanted to make this trip in December 1979. Rowly agreed, and we made a rough plan. I would start by going to Saudi Arabia, then Iraq, swing over to the Gulf states of Bahrain, Kuwait, and Oman, and wind up going to Ayatollah Khomeini's Iran.

But Iran's Revolutionary Council refused me a visa on the grounds we "had written the worst stuff about Iran of anybody." Making matters worse, Iraq had not come through with a visa for me. Tension between Iran and Iraq was the second biggest story in the region.

The remaining reason to go was the prospect that doors would be opened to me in Saudi Arabia that were closed to other American journalists. The mysterious oil kingdom, whose ambiguous relationship with Washington was key to much else in the region, was notoriously inhospitable to visiting reporters. But I had two assets.

One was the liberal Democratic activist Fred Dutton. The former JFK New Frontiersman (assistant secretary of state) and personal aide to George McGovern in the 1972 presidential campaign was improbably ending his

My two immigrant grandfathers. Jacob Sanders (left) dodged Czarist conscription and began life in America as a peddler in the Pennsylvania countryside. Ben Novak (right), a veteran of the Russian Imperial Army, worked on the production line in the John Deere company in Moline, Illinois.

My adoring mother, Jane Sanders Novak, with her dressed-up only son. A spoiled child, I was called "Little Baby Jesus" by some of my nine older female first cousins on my mother's side of the family.

My father, Maurice P. Novak, a chemical engineer, trying to explain to his technologically challenged son how a light meter works. The "ruins" behind us are what was left of an unfinished house next to ours, whose construction was halted during the Depression. Abandoned construction sites were favorite playgrounds for kids in Joliet, Illinois.

I am shown as a college junior with King, the St. Bernard mascot of my fraternity house at the University of Illinois, Alpha Epsilon Pi. The dog loved me, which could not be said for many of my fraternity brothers.

Second Lieutenant Robert D. Novak wearing a sidearm as Officer of the Day at Ft. Devens, Massachusetts. I missed being sent to combat in Korea, where the war was in progress, but while in uniform, I read Whittaker Chambers's *Witness,* a long step in my spiritual development.

At my work desk in the Omaha, Nebraska, bureau of the Associated Press in 1955, my first journalistic stop after the Army. My principal duty was rewriting the news for Nebraska radio stations, but it was a start.

Birch Bayh, the twenty-nine-year-old Democratic Minority Leader of the Indiana House of Representatives (and future U.S. senator), with the twenty-five-year-old reporter for the AP. Bayh is taking notes on my copy of tax plans by the huge Republican majority, information that had been denied to Bayh and the Democrats.

Geraldine and I leaving Vice President Lyndon B. Johnson's mansion in Washington after our wedding reception there on November 10, 1962, with LBJ behind us. Geraldine was one of LBJ's secretaries, but my relations with him went downhill from then on.

Rowland Evans Jr. and I in September 1964 in the second year of our thirty-year partnership. Two months earlier, we had moved into new offices at 1750 Pennsylvania Avenue, a block from the White House. My desk is hopelessly cluttered, its perpetual condition.

My first national TV appearance, on CBS's *Face the Nation* in 1963, interviewing Democratic senator Joseph Clark of Pennsylvania, with his back to the camera. CBS correspondents Charles Von Fremd and Paul Niven are the other panelists, left to right. I was scared to death.

Reading my first book, *The Agony of the GOP 1964*. While the book is incorrectly remembered as an attack on Barry Goldwater, in fact, it is an assault on feckless liberals and moderate Republicans.

As I drift rightward, I laugh it up with William F. Buckley at a Washington reception in 1970. In the background is a young George F. Will.

On my first visit to Indochina and my first reporting from a war front, I am shown here with Colonel Dien, commander of the 1st ARVN regiment. Like most of the South Vietnamese officers in his (and my age) bracket, he had fought with the French against his country's independence and relied heavily on U.S. support against the Communists.

Rowly and I meet with Gerald R. Ford early in his presidency, the first time I had been in the Oval Office. He had been a friendly source of mine since my arrival in Washington seventeen years earlier. But as president, Ford came to think much less favorably of me.

Rowly and I, eighteen years into our column, are not yet altered physically, as reflected in the 1963 *New York Herald-Tribune* poster shown behind us.

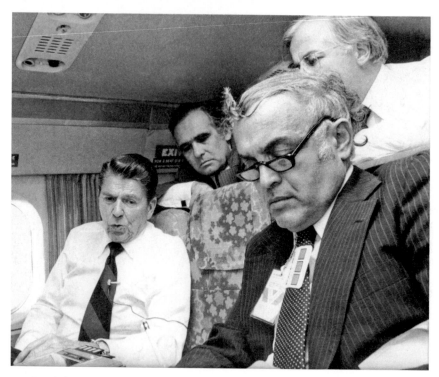

Candidate Ronald Reagan in 1980 spells out his foreign policy views to me. Two aides, Ed Gray and Richard V. Allen, listening in, stand behind us in the chartered plane. They never interrupted or offered additions and corrections.

I shake hands with the ruler of China, Teng Hsiao-ping, at the Great Hall of the People in Beijing in December 1978 before starting the most important and least expected interview of my career. Between us is the superb Chinese interpreter Yao Wei.

Talking to Jack Kemp, one of my all-time favorite and closest sources—perhaps too close for a proper relationship between reporter and politician.

With David Stockman at a dinner party at our suburban Maryland home. He was one of my best sources ever for most of 1981, when he was the Reagan administration budget director.

Another great source, Robert S. Strauss, talks to his fellow Texan Geraldine and me in the 1970s during his tenure as Democratic national chairman.

I am aboard a donkey after arriving at the Nicaraguan Contra camp in 1985. I reluctantly took my first and only trip riding a four-legged animal after I was told the alternative was walking the last seven miles to the insurgents' clandestine headquarters.

The donkey took me to visit the well-equipped Contras (on the left), backed by the Reagan White House. Earlier, I photographed a ragtag band of unauthorized Contras, led by the charismatic guerrilla leader Commandante Zero (his back to camera) at a secret camp inside Nicaragua.

President Reagan visits the third-anniversary celebration of *The McLaughlin Group* with its original members (left to right): Pat Buchanan, John McLaughlin, Mort Kondracke, Novak, and Jack Germond. All are smiling except my good friend, hopeless liberal Germond.

Vice President George H.W. Bush questions me and Andy Glass of the Cox newspapers about our just-completed trip to Poland to observe the struggle between Communism and freedom. By the time he ran for president, Bush was refusing to see me because I criticized him.

Bob Novack —
Best Wishes, [signature]

I am talking to then Russian President Boris Yeltsin (through the interpreter at his side), seated with Vice President Dan Quayle, at a dinner in Yeltsin's honor at the Kennedy Center in Washington. The White House and State Department boycotted the event, but Quayle showed up (inscribing the photo to "Bob Novack," validating that he was not first in his class in spelling).

Rowly and I tape Secretary of Defense Dick Cheney at the Pentagon for an *Evans & Novak* program on CNN in 1991. This was my first venture outside my home in three weeks after cancer surgery.

I am recognized along with District of Columbia Chief Judge Eugene Hamilton at halftime of the 1995 University of Illinois homecoming football game. In 1983 I received my bachelor's degree, thirty-one years late, after it was decided that physical education courses would provide me the additional credit hour I needed to graduate.

Four *Capital Gang* members—(left to right) Al Hunt, Novak, Margaret Carlson, and Mark Shields—on the floor of the 1996 Republican National Convention in San Diego. We were televised live on the floor following adjournment of every convention session of both political parties from 1988 through 2000, until the CNN brass in 2004 limited us to two afternoon appearances.

I appear as a caveman at the Gridiron Club's annual show, one of the least elaborate costumes I wore for a performance at the Washington journalists' club for more than two decades. After seeing me in that outfit, Geraldine imposed a rule for my future Gridiron appearances: "No more nipples!" On the left is Henry Trewhitt of the *Baltimore Sun,* whose nipples are prudently covered.

A U.S. Army videographer caught me in a free fall (tethered to a member of the Army's Golden Knights) in 2003 for CNN's *The Novak Zone.* We wanted to interview the Golden Knights, but the Army invited me to jump. Geraldine and my physician, Dr. Chuck Abrams, complained this was not proper for a seventy-two-year-old, out-of-shape journalist.

President Bill Clinton forces a smile as he greets me at a White House Christmas party. Except for the four hours I spent seated beside him at the 1998 Gridiron Club dinner, my only contact with Clinton as president were these brief holiday encounters.

President George W. Bush greets me at the White House for a confidential briefing the morning of his 2003 State of the Union Address prior to the U.S. invasion of Iraq. It was Bush's only confidential presidential briefing of conservative journalists to which I was invited. When my columns indicated that he had not convinced me, I received no more invitations.

The cake given me on June 20, 2004, marking my forty years on NBC's *Meet the Press* (244 appearances at that point). On my 236th appearance, I first encountered Joseph Wilson in the greenroom to begin a long and difficult episode for me.

Geraldine and I, our children and their spouses, and our seven grandchildren on the deck of our beach house at Fenwick Island, Delaware, on Labor Day weekend 2006.

career as a Washington lawyer with one client: the Kingdom of Saudi Arabia. The other asset was the conservative Arabist Harry Kern. A former *Newsweek* foreign news editor with fabulous contacts in the Arab world, he was now a consultant for what he reverentially referred to as "The Kingdom."

Thanks to Dutton and Kern, I had confirmed appointments with high-ranking Saudi officials who usually did not see journalists. They also gave me the officials' private telephone numbers.

Rowly and I decided the Saudi connection was worth making the long, expensive trip (though just barely). On Tuesday evening, December 4, I left New York on a Saudi Air red-eye flight to Riyadh, Saudi Arabia. I traveled first class as usual, and included in that cabin were a couple of gorgeous young Saudi women (accompanied by their husbands) with elaborate hairstyles and facial makeup, dressed to kill and adorned with jewelry. I awoke from a nap a half hour out of Riyadh to find the two women covered head to toe by burkas with eye slits. I was going to a country where much was hidden, but I didn't realize how much.

"RIYADH IS PROBABLY more difficult to adjust to than any place you've been to, including China and Africa," Rowly told me in a detailed memo preparing me for my first visit to a region he knew so well. The consensus among professional foreign correspondents was that in no other country was the government less cooperative to visiting journalists or was it harder to see government officials. I doubted the Saudis would be as unhelpful as government officials I had encountered in Cambodia, Zambia, Tanzania, Sandinista Nicaragua, or the Communist regimes in Czechoslovakia, Poland, and Romania. With doors opened for me by Fred Dutton and Harry Kern, I relished boasting when I returned to Washington that Saudi Arabia was no problem.

In fact, the kingdom proved a nightmare. My scheduled appointments must have been written in invisible ink, because government functionaries acted as though these dates never existed. As for private telephone numbers given me in confidence, all were out of date.

The trip was shaping up as an expensive fiasco. But when I arrived in Kuwait, I received a telegram from Washington with good news. Iraq had given me a visa.

I SHALL ALWAYS carry with me my first impressions of Baghdad under Saddam Hussein. Iraqi customs confiscated my Olympia portable typewriter because I had not made advance arrangements for its entry. In this totalitarian state a writing machine was a lethal weapon. It took twenty-four hours to get it back. The mandatory first stop in Baghdad for visiting foreign journalists was the Ministry of Information, where a wall-to-wall mural in a large waiting room depicted one scene after another of Arabs committing mayhem on British soldiers sixty years earlier.

I learned that I would have a private meeting with Tariq Aziz. He was then deputy prime minister and would be foreign minister in 1991 when Saddam invaded Kuwait, but his job title did not matter. A Christian who spoke flawless English, he was the dictator's mouthpiece in dealing with Americans from the secretary of state to major journalists. He was also a theoretician of the ruling Baathist Socialist Party. Because he spoke quietly and avoided harsh language, he was sometimes misinterpreted as a moderate. In fact, he never deviated from Saddam's brutal line.

Tariq Aziz, in seeing me the morning of December 14, had a message from Saddam: "We now have Arab 'solidarity,' but this is not Arab 'unity.' That will come when all the Arab states have similar political, economic and social systems." My Evans & Novak column continued:

> Since Iraq obviously will not copy Saudi Arabia and the Gulf emirates [ruled by royal families], Tariq Aziz wants them to be "similar" to Iraq. How? "By internal forces," he replied, quickly adding that Baathist Socialists in these countries will be helped by Baghdad.
>
> Baathist Socialism—revolutionary but anti-Communist, Islamic but radical—is backed by Iraq's 300,000-man, Soviet-equipped armed forces, now the area's strongest. Despite Iraq's "solidarity" with Arab neighbors, Baghdad is viewed with concern by the hereditary states. Kuwait, rich and weak, particularly worries about unsettled Iraqi border claims.

I added that Kuwait might well worry about "historical determinism" expressed by "one influential Iraqi" in describing the Gulf states, including Saudi Arabia as well as Kuwait: "These are weak regimes. They live on the surface of life. They are so rich. They cannot survive this way." The "influential Iraqi" was Tariq Aziz, who asked that I not attribute those words to him.

I can still hear those fateful words, spoken so softly, as they tumble down the corridors of history. Saddam was telling me through his mouthpiece he was going to take Kuwait and, after that, Saudi Arabia. All I could write about his words in conclusion was that "Iraq's hard-bitten leftist leaders are reaching for domination over the Persian Gulf's conservative oil monarchies."

CHAPTER 29

The Birth of CNN

Rowly and I had been without a television connection all through 1979 when that autumn we received a phone call from Ed Turner, our old patron at Channel 5 in Washington, that would alter my career and my life.

Ed informed us he had a job with a venture being launched by the eccentric Atlanta entrepreneur and yachtsman Ted Turner (no relation). It was to be an Atlanta-based all-news TV national cable network. Ed was vice president for news, and he asked us to join political figures and journalists he was signing up for the Cable News Network's start of broadcasting in 1980. Rowly and I had some sharp arguments over money with Ed back in the Metromedia days, and he informed us now sternly that his offer was nonnegotiable. Every commentator he signed would tape five commentaries a week and would be paid $10,000 ($25,000 in 2006 money) a year—and not a cent more. Rowly and I would split the commentaries and the money—$5,000 apiece. It was take it or leave it, and we took it: $5,000 was money I could use, and I was glad to be back on TV.

Cable was foreign to us. Major cities, Washington, D.C., included, were not yet wired for cable. I still thought of cable as a way to bring television to rural areas.

Ed Turner was the only CNN executive we knew, and the new venture was so unimportant to our world that neither Rowly nor I thought it necessary to make a special trip to Atlanta to get acquainted. But I was going to be in Atlanta the night of January 3, 1980, in my addiction to University of Maryland basketball, to watch the Terrapins play Georgia Tech, and I called ahead to see CNN brass that afternoon. I was given appointments with all its executives—including Ted Turner—at CNN's first headquarters, a run-down former Russian Jewish country club.

Robert Edward Turner was a hard-drinking, womanizing, southern playboy, age twenty-five in 1963 when his father committed suicide. Ted restored to health his father's Atlanta billboard company. In 1970 he took Channel 17, the humdrum UHF (ultra-high frequency) station WTBS in Atlanta, and turned it into the Turner Broadcasting System (TBS), the first national cable network. Turner operated at low overhead by running old movies, cartoons, and sports, seemingly a worshiper of the almighty dollar who couldn't care less about quality broadcasting.

That stereotype crumbled in 1979 when Turner conceived CNN. To raise capital, he sold a profitable UHF station in Charlotte, North Carolina. Turner told me he figured CNN would lose two million to two and one-half million dollars a month for the foreseeable future. "This could ruin me," he said. I asked why he was risking everything. "I've made a load of money by putting out a lot of bad movies and other crap [on WTBS]," he replied. "I think I owe the country something of value, and that's what I'm going to give it on CNN." He was true to his word so long as he maintained control of CNN.

TEDDY KENNEDY AND I both were in Iowa on January 7, 1980, two weeks before the caucuses. I stood a few feet from Teddy and his wife, Joan, seated side by side in Oskaloosa at the county courthouse to take "town meeting" questions. "Senator, I wonder if I might ask something about *Mrs.* Kennedy?" asked an elderly man. "What is *she* interested in?" The expression on the face of each Kennedy can be described as devastated. Joan opened her mouth after several seconds of silence. Just as she was about to speak, Teddy intervened: "Why, Joanie, you're into music, aren't you?" She nodded, but said nothing. Her husband mercifully called on another questioner. We all knew that Joan was an alcoholic, that Teddy had a severe drinking problem, and that the marriage was doomed. But nobody, myself included, wrote about those things. Political reporters then were less into psychodrama than their next-generation successors. At that poignant moment in Oskaloosa, I became certain Edward M. Kennedy would lose in the Iowa caucuses. I also was pretty sure he could not win the Democratic nomination. And I strongly suspected he never would be president of the United States.

GERALDINE PROBABLY always wondered why every four years I would leave her and the children for extended periods in snowy Iowa and New Hampshire. I don't believe I could have appreciated the gravity of Kennedy's dilemma in Iowa had I not seen his rural tour firsthand. Similarly, when I attended a Republican "candidates night" in Janesville, a small town in east central Iowa, I gained insights into the Republican presidential contest that I reported in an Evans & Novak column:

> The principal speaker . . . was George Bush. Sen. Howard Baker's daughter Cissy was present. So were campaign leaflets and posters for Bush, Baker, Connally, Crane and Dole. But there was no sign of Reagan—not a campaign button, not a poster, not a word—in Reagan's rural heartland.
>
> "This is what we've been complaining about for months," a local Reagan loyalist told us. "There is no visible Reagan campaign." That absence, when compared with Bush's painstakingly built organization, suggests Reagan could finish second to Bush at Republican precinct caucuses Jan. 21. Reagan's overwhelming grassroots popularity, counted on to negate Bush's organizational edge, has been undercut by the infrequency of his visits to Iowa, climaxed by his boycott of the Jan. 4 presidential debate.
>
> Since Reagan's campaign is based on invincibility and inevitability, losing Iowa would not be easily overcome. Thus, the cautious strategy of campaign manager John Sears undergoes an early critical test. If Dutch Reagan loses the state of his young manhood, the Sears strategy will be blamed.

My reporting from Iowa suggesting a Bush upset in Iowa put me ahead of my colleagues. My Iowa column on Monday, January 14, 1980, was a big story that the *Washington Post* put at the top of the op-ed page with this headline: "Reagan: Once Invincible, Now Invisible."

THE JANUARY 21 Iowa caucuses proved a disaster for Kennedy, with 71 percent for Carter and 26 percent for Teddy. Now Kennedy had to go to his home territory to make a comeback in New Hampshire. Six months earlier, my mini-poll in ward 9 of Nashua, New Hampshire (selected by pollster Pat Caddell as a barometer precinct), showed a six-to-one advantage for Kennedy over Carter. Two weeks after the Iowa caucuses, I went back to ward 9 to see how hard times affected Kennedy among his base voters: middle-income white-collar and skilled blue-collar in New England. Our interviews revealed a new world in ward 9: Carter two-to-one over Kennedy. I found little enthusiasm for Carter but sudden, almost irrational animosity toward Kennedy.

Carter defeated Kennedy easily in New Hampshire by eleven percentage points on February 26. If Kennedy could not win in New Hampshire, where could he win? Kennedy loyalists thought Illinois was still Kennedy country, where the March 18 primary would begin Teddy's comeback. I arrived in Chicago on March 10 and quickly found this was romantic nonsense. The curse of Chappaquiddick cut Kennedy as deeply among Chicago Democrats as it had in Iowa. Richard J. Daley was dead, and the Daley Machine was a shadow of its former self.

On March 18, Teddy suffered a humiliating defeat, losing the Illinois primary to Carter, two-to-one.

DESPITE SEARS'S BLUNDER in keeping Reagan's profile so low in Iowa, he barely lost the caucuses: Bush 31.6 percent, Reagan 29.5 percent. Although Reagan's Iowa defeat should not have surprised any reporter who really had worked the state, it was widely reported as an upset—magnifying its impact. Pollster Lou Harris showed that Reagan's national Republican margin over Bush of twenty-six points disappeared overnight after Iowa and that Reagan and Bush were now in a dead heat. In New Hampshire, Reagan's double-digit lead over Bush became a double-digit deficit.

Overjoyed by sudden good fortune, George Bush displayed a goofy side that would plague him the rest of his political career. Had the New Hampshire primary come just one week after the Iowa caucuses as it did two decades later, Bush likely would have won there and gone on to be nominated. But in 1980, New Hampshire would not vote until February 26, five weeks after Iowa. "I've got the 'Big Mo,' " an ebullient Bush shouted when he got to New Hampshire the day after Iowa, looking silly.

I was in Nashua early the next morning for a packed Chamber of Commerce breakfast. The grinning Bush seemed dazed by his new status as putative front-runner. I wrote in an Evans & Novak column that Bush had "reverted to the fence-straddling that has plagued moderate Republicans." I added:

> The breakfasting businessmen at Nashua came to be impressed and left disappointed by Bush's repetition, imprecision and refusal to take a hard position on issues ranging from child daycare to nuclear power.
>
> The room cooled when Bush declared he didn't know enough to have an opinion on the Seabrook, N.H. nuclear power plant. A consulting engineer from nearby Amherst told us before hearing the speech that he reduced the field to Reagan and Bush, but planned "to cement my choice for Bush today" because of "better experience

and more smarts." After the speech, the Yankee verdict: "Too much waffling. It's back to Reagan."

I had gotten ahead of the pack by forecasting Reagan's problems in Iowa, and now I tried to do the same with Bush's difficulties in New Hampshire, where the front-runner would have to cope with Jeff Bell.

REAGAN HAD A secret weapon. He was for tax cuts, and Bush was not. Reagan's treatment of the tax issue in New Hampshire is not reported in standard accounts of the 1980 campaign, and I did not learn the full story until after Reagan was elected president. But I am convinced that at this point, Jeffrey Bell saved the Reagan campaign and that the much maligned John Sears also should get credit.

Bell had no early connection with the 1980 Reagan campaign, but Sears reached out to him in December 1979 to produce supply-side spots for Reagan's presidential campaign similar to those used for Bell's own Senate campaign two years earlier. They would be narrated by Reagan himself just as Bell had narrated his 1978 ads. Three of them had Reagan on camera calling for tax cuts. In one thirty-second ad, Reagan invoked John F. Kennedy as a tax-cutter. A sixty-second spot concluded with Reagan saying: "If we put incentives back into society, everyone will gain. We have to move ahead. But we can't leave anyone behind."

This was Reagan's version of Bell's "Good Shepherd" ad promising not to "leave anyone behind." In 1980, that concept seemed downright un-Republican, and that was why it appealed so much to Sears. I believe these ads won the New Hampshire primary and, ultimately, the presidency for Reagan, but that was not apparent at the time.

The conventional wisdom was that the February 26 New Hampshire primary was won in a final debate in Nashua February 22. Jerry Carmen, a New Hampshire Republican leader running Reagan's campaign in the state, engineered a coup. Bush, stubbornly insisting on a one-on-one showdown, was maneuvered into being responsible for a two-man debate while Reagan came over as the good guy unsuccessfully trying to get the other four Republican candidates on the platform. In truth, thanks to the Bell tax cut ads, Reagan had passed Bush in the New Hampshire polls and was nearing a double-digit lead by February 22. In *The Reagan Revolution,* I wrote, "Bush was devoured in the debate, which once and for all underlined their differences on the tax question. Reagan flatly condemned Bush's acquiescence in the Carter budget's income tax increases, which Bush could not and did not deny."

· · ·

BY FEBRUARY 26, Reagan's victory in New Hampshire was not a surprise. What came as a shock was his landslide with 50 percent against Bush's 23 percent, a twenty-seven-point margin. The contest for the Republican nomination was over.

On the afternoon of the primary, Reagan surprised the political world by firing Sears, along with his deputies, Charlie Black and Jim Lake. Reagan's early fascination with Sears had changed to personal dislike. Reagan was repelled by the power play the past November when Sears, Black, and Lake forced out longtime Reagan aide Mike Deaver. Nevertheless Reagan wanted to win so badly that he stuck with Sears so long as he looked like a winner. The Iowa defeat doomed Sears, but Reagan could not fire him at that point in what would look like scapegoating.

Getting rid of Sears meant that Deaver, Lyn Nofziger, and Marty Anderson would return to the campaign after being expelled by Sears. Sears's nominal successor was sixty-seven-year-old William Casey, who as a young man during World War II ran secret agents in Europe and was to become President Reagan's director of Central Intelligence. Casey, assigned to clean up the fiscal and administrative mess left by Sears, had little to do with strategy. That would be handled by Ed Meese, returned from Sears-imposed obscurity and on the road every day by the candidate's side. John Sears had opened the Reagan door to the supply-siders. Would Ed Meese close it?

On Tuesday, April 15, 1980, I was following Reagan campaigning in Pennsylvania prior to the state's primary a week later. The Reagan entourage, press, and staff, was in the dining room of the Howard Johnson Hotel in Scranton for an early dinner prior to that evening's rally. Ed Meese motioned me over to sit with him at a table with other Reagan campaign staffers (and no other reporters).

This was the only time Meese approached me on the campaign trail, and I hoped he had called me over to give me a little news. Unfortunately, he had a question rather than an answer: "Do you think it's too late for Governor Reagan to give up on the tax cut?"

I assumed this was Meese's way of tipping me off about a radical change in Reagan's policy. It was not my business to be an unpaid adviser, but I had become dangerously committed on this issue and felt I must answer: "It's much too late, Ed. How can you abandon the centerpiece of your domestic policy?" Meese gave no indication whether he agreed with me.

Prominent Republicans still found it hard to swallow anything as radical as Kemp-Roth and pressed Reagan to reduce its scope, stretch it out, or do both. That opposition was reflected by Meese feeling out my reaction. The tax cut was toned down in the Reagan campaign at times, but never abandoned.

TED TURNER'S CABLE News Network went on the air at six p.m. Eastern time on Sunday, June 1, 1980. Ed Turner had explained to me that CNN could not afford full-time staffers anyone had heard of—with one exception: Daniel Schorr, a contentious veteran of twenty-three years with CBS was hired as CNN's chief Washington correspondent. Affordable, anonymous young men and women hired by the new network would put out the news product, but CNN needed recognizable faces in addition to Schorr for start-up promotions. That was the role played by commentators like Coretta Scott King, William Simon, Phyllis Schlafly, Joyce Brothers—and Evans and Novak.

I believe the plan was to let the commentators drift away once they had served their promotional purpose. Just about all left within a year, with the exception of Evans and Novak.

Rowly and I were saved by Ed Turner. He found an interviewing niche for us at CNN on a Saturday morning program *(Newsmaker Saturday)* hosted by Schorr. Sharing a one-hour interview every other Saturday was not much of a CNN role, but it was something.

AT NINE THIRTY a.m. on Monday, June 23, 1980, I had an appointment with Paul Weyrich in his Capitol Hill office—headquarters of a network of conservative activist organizations set up by Weyrich under the rubric of the "New Right." A former newspaper and radio-television reporter, Weyrich was founding president of the Heritage Foundation (which was to become the premier conservative think tank). Weyrich was more interested in action than thought and left Heritage to develop his interlocking network.

When I met him that June morning in 1980 for the first time, Weyrich was thirty-seven and a rising political power. Weyrich told me a major political development was being overlooked. Born-again Christians who supported Carter in 1976 were disillusioned and ready to back Reagan. Weyrich was mobilizing Evangelical preachers, seeking to deliver the South and Christian conservatives against native southerner and born-again Christian Jimmy Carter. Weyrich offered to take me south the next week to watch it happening.

On June 30, I went with Weyrich to the huge Forrest Hills Baptist Church in Decatur, Georgia. There, by invitation-only, were two hundred

Georgia preachers. I was the only reporter present. As leadoff speaker, Weyrich predicted President Carter would veto any school prayer bill passed by Congress. Dr. William W. Pennell, pastor of the host church, like most clergymen present had supported Carter in 1976. He assailed the president's foreign policy: "I've had about all the born-again diplomacy I can stand." That elicited laughter, applause, and shouts of "Amen, brother" from his fellow preachers.

In the Evans & Novak column of July 4 with an Atlanta dateline, I wrote:

> The preachers feel Carter has betrayed them on the social questions they care about most deeply, as stressed in the Atlanta conference: abortion, the Equal Rights Amendment, homosexuals (usually referred to as "queers" during the meeting) and school prayer. There was no talk about economics or taxes. While "socialism" was never mentioned, "humanism" was anathematized repeatedly. . . .
>
> Even before the Atlanta meeting, Georgia clergymen were passing out to parishioners a tract called "Ronald Reagan: A Man of Faith." In it, Reagan supports private Christian schools and school prayer while attacking abortion and homosexuality. "The time has come to turn to God and reassert our trust in Him for the healing of America," he says. That spells big problems for Carter among voters he cannot afford to lose.

This was a prescient column, perhaps my most important one in the seminal political year of 1980. Yet, none of my fellow political writers picked up on it. Inexplicably, through the whole year, I did not write another word about this development that was critical to finally breaking the Democratic Party's lock on the South.

WHEN THE 1980 national convention of the Republican Party began in Detroit on July 7, CNN was five weeks old and not ready for prime time. The consensus of delegates showed a mild vice-presidential preference for Bush, runner-up to Reagan in the primaries. Reagan aides spread the word that their candidate did not care for Bush. That raised hope among supply-siders that Reagan, who liked Kemp personally and as a tax-cutting ideologue, might pick his former intern.

But late Wednesday afternoon, July 16, word leaked out of Reagan's suite in the Detroit Plaza Hotel of the most startling development in my national convention experience since JFK's selection of LBJ in 1960. Principals of Reagan and former president Ford were in serious negotiations about a Reagan-Ford ticket, contemplating an expanded vice presidency for Ford as would befit a former president.

Interviewing Ford on the CBS evening news that Wednesday, Walter Cronkite asked whether Reagan could accept "something like a co-presidency." "That's something Governor Reagan really ought to consider," Ford replied. The evocative "co-presidency" exposed an unpleasant reality about the "dream ticket." If Ford were more than a vice president, Reagan would be less than a president.

Reporters covering the story (including me) were less interested in this dangerous equation than reporting whether Reagan and Ford really had a deal. My sources told me the Reagan-Ford ticket was a done deal, and I went on the air live to say this, as a CNN reporter interviewed me on the convention floor early Wednesday evening. Correspondents for the broadcast networks were saying the same thing. My home paper, the *Chicago Sun-Times,* got the story from its own reporters and put out an extra revealing the "dream ticket."

That evening, Tom Korologos pulled me aside on the convention floor. Korologos, a big-time Washington lobbyist and Republican insider, had been my source for years. "It's over," he whispered in my ear. "The deal fell through. It's going to be Bush. Trust me. It's over." Korologos, who had been helping coordinate the Reagan-Ford negotiations, had been one of my sources reporting the Ford vice presidency for CNN and maybe he thought he owed me a rapid heads-up that the news had changed.

I had a clear exclusive to beat the rest of the country. But how was I going to report it in real time on television? I was on the convention floor with CNN credentials, but I was only a commentator—electronically naked, without microphone or camera, lacking even the mobile telephone that was still rare in 1980. I rushed all over the floor seeking a CNN reporter. I finally found one, and my "scoop" immediately went on the air. Too late. The substitution of Bush for Ford had been revealed to the world a few minutes earlier by NBC floor reporter Chris Wallace, the thirty-two-year-old son of CBS superstar Mike Wallace. He was covering his first convention, and he had its biggest story.

ON THE CONVENTION floor Thursday night before Reagan delivered one of the best acceptance speeches in my experience, I talked to Lyn Nofziger. Three days earlier he had advised me that Kemp was a strong possibility to be picked. That had impressed me because Nofziger never was enthusiastic about Kemp. So I asked Lyn what had sunk Kemp. "It was that homosexual thing," he replied. "The governor finally said, 'We just can't do this to Jack.' " *That homosexual thing!* I could hardly believe it.

It went back to 1967, Reagan's first year as governor of California. The Virgin Islands hosted the National Governors Conference that autumn aboard the SS *Independence,* cruising in the Caribbean. (I was aboard, and I believe I was the first to call it the "Ship of Fools.") During the voyage, columnist Drew Pearson in Washington was about to reveal the existence of a homosexual ring in Reagan's office involving key aides.

Two of Reagan's top assistants resigned, and several other Republican political operatives were involved. None ever returned to politics. Pearson's column also mentioned "an athlete" in the homosexual ring, and the word was spread aboard the *Independence* that he was referring to Jack Kemp, then star quarterback for the Buffalo Bills. Neither I nor the other reporters aboard the ship ever had met Kemp. Nobody reported Kemp's name in public, but it repeatedly was whispered as the years went by and he became a nationally prominent Republican.

In 1978, the untraceable rumors became partly traceable for me. I learned that the usually noncombative Democratic National Chairman John White had told a reporter that there was no need to worry about the Kemp-Roth bill because Kemp was a homosexual. About the same time, Andy Glass (then a reporter for the Cox newspapers) told me Carter aide Hamilton Jordan had said not to consider Kemp a presidential prospect in 1980 because he was a "queer."

I wanted to report this rumormongering as reprehensible behavior, but I couldn't because of at least the possibility that the rumors were true. After eleven years, I finally had to find out for sure. I started by calling Lyn Nofziger, who in 1967 as a Reagan aide had leaked the homosexual scandal aboard the *Independence* as a preemptive strike against Drew Pearson's column. Now he told me he had no reason to think Kemp was a homosexual. He suggested I check with one member of the homosexual ring (let's call him "Jones") who after his exposure had disappeared from public view. Nofziger said he was sure "Jones" would tell me the truth—*if* I could find him. After weeks of searching, I located him in San Francisco, totally removed from politics. I had used "Jones" as a source before the scandal broke, and he agreed to see me.

Late in the summer of 1978, I met "Jones" for drinks at the cocktail lounge off the lobby of San Francisco's Fairmont Hotel. He was adamant that Kemp was not part of the homosexual group that reached into Reagan's office. His denial was all the more credible because "Jones" was a liberal Republican who did not like Kemp or his politics.

I still did not want to be the person who revealed to the world the slander against Kemp. Jude Wanniski solved this problem for me. Jude felt these rumors would dog Kemp all through his political career and block his path to the White House unless they were disposed of now. Kemp and his political high command thought it was madness to spread this calumny.

Wanniski, who never accepted advice from anybody, acted on his own. The occasion was an interview with him by *New York Times* reporter Martin Tolchin for an article about Kemp that Tolchin was writing for *Esquire*. Wanniski told Tolchin about the homosexual canard and urged him to look into it. In the *Esquire* of October 24, 1978, Tolchin quoted Kemp as saying: "There is absolutely not a shred of evidence. There is nothing, and there was nothing." Tolchin himself concluded: "Everyone who has looked into the case has come to the same conclusion."

Although Wanniski was satisfied, I thought Tolchin's verdict was a little ambiguous. I wanted to write a more definitive conclusion, plus the revelation of the White and Jordan slanders, once I pinned down one remaining allegation: a supposed police file relating to homosexual conduct by Kemp. The result was an Evans & Novak column of December 29, 1978, that named John White but at Andy Glass's request, referred to Hamilton Jordan only as a "White House aide":

When we checked the story with White, he seemed genuinely apologetic; he said he had heard the rumor from another newsman and was merely passing on what he had heard. The White House aide, informed later by the reporter [Glass] that there apparently was no substance to the story, asked the reporter to forget about it and to be certain not to disclose his identity. . . .

After considerable checking, we can now report that the rumor comes as close to being disprovable as any personal slander ever is. For example, contrary to one recurrent part of the rumor, there never was any police file on Kemp; he was not investigated.

One principal in the 1967 case ["Jones"] whom we tracked down with some difficulty to his new job and his new life said he never had known or been told of an illicit association between Kemp and those who resigned under a cloud. Indeed, the sole source of the rumor that has haunted Kemp's career for 11 years is the fact that he traveled, on an official basis, several times with one of the Reagan aides who later resigned. That, and nothing more, is the "case" against Kemp

With the Republican convention winding up Thursday night, we had one more full Evans & Novak column with a Detroit dateline (for Monday's newspapers). I wanted to write about the resurfacing of the homosexual issue; Rowly, wisely, talked me out of it.

PAT CADDELL had told me Carter would clinch the election once he got Reagan one-on-one in a televised presidential debate, without independent candidate John Anderson around to muddy the waters. Reagan finally agreed to a one-on-one debate in Cleveland on Tuesday, October 28, with Anderson excluded.

I had never before attended a presidential debate, in 1960 and 1976 watching on TV with the rest of America. But I wanted to be there for this late campaign event that might decide a close election. Rowly and I both went to Cleveland and got good, nonpress seats in the Cleveland Convention Center Music Hall.

From that vantage point, the debate looked to Rowly and me like a clear Reagan win on style, substance, and debating points. Compared to the composed Hollywood actor beside him, Carter was ill at ease. I counted the president reaching for his glass of water eleven times during a ninety-minute debate. Although neither candidate committed a blunder to compare with Ford's gaffe about Poland four years earlier, Carter came close when he pursued his theme that Reagan was a menace to world peace: "I had a discussion with my daughter Amy [age thirteen] the other day before I came here, to ask her what the most important issue was. She said she thought nuclear weaponry and the control of nuclear arms." That looked to me like Carter at his worst: weak and silly.

Polls later showed the debate was a disaster for Carter, with Reagan carrying undecided and independent voters, two to one. The election was over, though few people were ready to acknowledge it.

STU SPENCER, who in 1968 pledged to me he would do anything to keep Reagan from the Oval Office, in 1980 came aboard the Reagan campaign plane as senior adviser. Reagan, not a man to hold grudges, accepted Spencer without a second thought as the best director to finish shooting this movie. Spencer brought with him James Baker, who until now had always opposed Reagan. The third man in the front compartment of Reagan's chartered jet was Lyn Nofziger.

Late in the campaign, Spencer, Baker, and Nofziger, with the help of nominal campaign chairman Bill Casey, forced a change in super-cautious campaign tactics. On October 27, the day before the debate, weeks-old TV spots attacking Carter's credibility finally went on the air. On Thursday, October 30, two days after the debate, Reagan himself finally addressed Carter's competence from a New Orleans airport hangar. I was there and wrote about it in the last Evans & Novak column on the campaign (to be published on November 3, the day before the election):

> Recalling Carter's 1976 campaign promise of a government as good as the American people, Reagan told the New Orleans rally: "He only gave us a government as good as Jimmy Carter, and that isn't good enough."
>
> That and other applause-getting lines were brand new. Ken Khachigian, a 36-year-old California public relations man who once wrote speeches for Richard Nixon, months ago applied for a job with the Reagan campaign, which turned him down as too expensive. Three weeks ago, with Reagan's rhetoric and poll ratings sagging, it was decided no price was too high. Thus, Khachigian's prose became Reagan's rhetoric in New Orleans and across the country.
>
> Reagan's revived oratory coincided with post-debate good news . . . Reagan forging ahead in traditionally Democratic Louisiana and swing state Missouri and no worse than even in overwhelmingly Democratic Arkansas.

My November 3 column's dateline was Des Plaines, Illinois—a Chicago suburb where Reagan spoke to high school students on Friday, October 31. The Des Plaines youngsters clapped and yelled when Reagan promised: "Not just one 10 percent tax cut, not just two 10 percent tax cuts, but three 10 percent tax cuts—30 percent over three years." It was Kemp-Roth, and Reagan recited that chant the last two weeks in Khachigian's speeches. The connection of Reagan's emphasis on tax reduction to his late campaign surge was lost on reporters covering the Republican candidate.

One of them was Walter Isaacson, a twenty-eight-year-old *Time* correspondent. The former Rhodes scholar, in his second year with the magazine, was given the plum assignment of covering Reagan. On the campaign trail that last week, he introduced himself to me and started a conversation about Reagan's and my tax-cutting views. He said he believed I was the only journalist he knew who actually supported Kemp-Roth, which accurately reflected the political press corps' mind-set. "I just wonder if you could explain to me how you got there," he said. Walter sounded like a modern scientist encountering somebody who believed the earth was flat.

My Des Plaines column concluded with speculation that Reagan may have changed too late. Had it "started eight weeks earlier," I wrote, it might "have produced a GOP landslide." The *Washington Post*'s headline on the column: "It Could Have Been a Landslide." That column and headline subjected me to never-ending postelection chiding because it *was* a landslide.

REAGAN WON BY a commanding ten percentage points, with an electoral vote landslide, 489 to 49. Republicans gained twelve Senate seats, transforming a seventeen-seat deficit into a seven-seat advantage, unexpectedly giving Republicans control of a House of Congress for the first time since 1953–54. Republicans picked up thirty-three House seats, reducing the Democratic margin to fifty-one seats—amounting to control by the conservative coalition.

At long last this heralded realignment, impeded by Watergate, Vietnam, and Republican mindlessness, had arrived. Except for his own Georgia, Carter lost every southern state. The Senate's southern caucus was no longer solid (eleven Democrats, ten Republicans, one conservative independent). Southern Democrats still prevailed in the House, seventy-two to thirty-seven, but that was illusory because so many conservative Democrats would help Reagan.

Commenting for CNN on election night I thought I concealed my glee—but apparently not from Daniel Schorr. Making no effort to hide his discomfort with the election's outcome, Dan told me after midnight: "Well, with your people in power, it will be a little hard for you to be a critic, won't it." "Not a bit, Dan," I replied, and I meant it.

CHAPTER 30

The Reagan Revolution

J ACK KEMP HAD tipped me off to David Stockman, a thirty-four-year-old Congressman from Michigan, as a smart supply-sider. My first real contact with him was on October 24, 1980, when we both addressed a business convention in Chicago. We had coffee together, and I was attracted to his keen intelligence and warm personality. After the 1980 election, I used the Evans & Novak column to report his likely appointment as director of the Office of Management and Budget, a supply-sider who did not worship at the altar of the balanced budget.

More than five years later, Stockman misrepresented my support in his best-selling memoir *The Triumph of Politics.* These comments in 1986 should be measured against the fact that our relationship long since had deteriorated, that we had not exchanged a word since late 1981, and that Stockman had soured on the Reagan Revolution and supply-side ideology. In his book, he told of plotting with Jack Kemp immediately after the election toward what then seemed his improbable elevation to the cabinet.

> We [Stockman and Kemp] had lunch with Bob Novak. He's a brilliant, brooding reporter who is known around Washington as "the Prince of Darkness." Novak has a steeltrap mind and he knew our catechism cold. He wasn't like many of the other, self-righteous reporters who pretended they were objective but were really liberals.
>
> Novak's typewriter didn't even work in the objective mode. Everything which came out was pure bias—in behalf of the supply side. Naturally, I considered that first-class reporting. He was dealing in truth, not just news.
>
> Novak wrote a column saying there was a movement growing to put Stockman in at the Office of Management and Budget. At the time he wrote it, it was a movement of three or four, if you included

the minority of my staff that favored the idea. But after his column appeared, it did become a movement of sorts.

Stockman's account is nearly pure fiction. Jack Kemp, Dave Stockman, and Bob Novak *never* lunched together at any time—a fact corroborated by my records and those of Kemp's office.

This is the truth: Shortly after the election, Jude Wanniski phoned to inform me that he, Kemp, and the other supply-siders had decided to promote Stockman for OMB. I said I thought that was a good idea, and I went to work as a reporter to find out whether his nomination might happen, not to promote him. I called Stockman, who told me OMB was the one Reagan administration position he was interested in filling and that he was optimistic about his chances. I placed calls to two excellent sources on the Reagan transition team, who told me Stockman was indeed the leading candidate for OMB. The Stockman candidacy made its way through the bulky Reagan transition bureaucracy, and he entered the cabinet presumed to be the agent of those who wanted Reagan's presidency to be a revolution.

EDWIN MEESE III, the Reagan campaign's chief of staff and director of the presidential transition, was widely expected to become White House chief of staff. Nobody outside Reagan's inner circle, however, knew that on the day after the election, Reagan informed Meese that he would not get the top White House post. It would go to James A. Baker III, who had run George Bush's campaign against Reagan, while Meese would be named counselor to the president with cabinet rank. Meese was devastated but was a good Reagan soldier who stayed on.

On Sunday, January 11, 1981, Rowly and I flew to California for a sales meeting the next morning at our newspaper syndicate, now headquartered in Orange County, and Stu Spencer invited us for Sunday night dinner at his oceanfront home at Newport Beach. Spencer was in high spirits during a prolonged cocktail hour. He was on the inside with the president-elect, his opposition to Reagan's 1968 and 1976 presidential candidacies forgiven and probably forgotten.

How could Reagan reject his longtime faithful lieutenant and dedicated conservative Meese in favor off the ideologically androgynous Baker, who had vigorously opposed Reagan's nomination in 1976 and 1980? California conservatives blamed Spencer as Reagan's Rasputin. True, Spencer was a close friend and fishing companion of Baker and distant from Meese. But Stu told us Reagan was well aware of Meese's administrative shortcomings and on his own made the change.

Surprisingly, the supply-siders were delighted. Based on Meese's performance during the campaign and the transition, Jeff Bell and Jude Wanniski both told me Baker would be more aggressive in pressing for tax reduction and less inclined to capitulate to orthodox budget-balancers. I'm not sure Baker ever really understood the theoretical underpinnings of what Reagan was doing, but the tax cuts were passed under his watch without serious dilution—the most important economic legislation since the New Deal.

NEVER IN EIGHTEEN years as a columnist had I enjoyed such access to senior officials as I had at the start of the Reagan administration. My appointment book for the first few weeks of 1981 shows private sessions with Jim Baker, Ed Meese, Alexander Haig, Donald Regan, Caspar Weinberger, James Watt, Martin Anderson, Lyn Nofziger, Norman Ture, Paul Craig Roberts, and David Stockman.

Stockman was my best source. For most of a year, he might have been the best high-level source I ever had. By the time Reagan named the unknown young congressman to the OMB post on December 11, 1980, Stockman and I were on close terms. My appointment book shows me meeting with Stockman through the first nine months of 1981 more than with anybody else, on top of innumerable phone conversations.

Early in the Reagan administration, I dined with Stockman at Paul Young's restaurant in midtown Washington, a favorite hangout for congressmen and lobbyists. Dan Rostenkowski, a lieutenant in the Chicago Democratic political machine who had just become chairman of the House Ways and Means Committee, was at a nearby table with cronies. He came over and a debate over tax policy ensued between the hulking Rostenkowski and the slight Stockman, who a few weeks earlier had been a backbencher in the impotent Republican minority whom Rosty barely recognized. The chairman had no idea he was about to be rolled by a Republican–Southern Democratic coalition to pass Reagan's tax cuts.

Soon after Stockman took office, we started having breakfast every other Saturday, where Stockman could leak at length in the nearly deserted Hay Adams dining room. He played "Pilgrim" in *Pilgrim's Progress* as he described malefactors blocking the supply-side agenda—powerful Democrats in Congress and secret advocates, embedded within the Reagan administration, of a Nixon-Ford restoration.

One of Stockman's fiercest antagonists was Secretary of Transportation Drew Lewis. A millionaire business consultant (who later would head Union Pacific Railroad) and Pennsylvania Republican leader, Lewis turned

Transportation from a governmental backwater into an outpost for ideological warfare against the free marketeers.

On Friday, March 6, my supply-side sources at the Treasury Department passed on an internal memo for my edification but not publication. It reported efforts by Lewis to save the ailing automotive industry with a government "industrial policy" based on curtailing foreign imports. I immediately telephoned Stockman, who told me he had a lot to add to this story and we should get together as quickly as possible. We met over breakfast at the Hay Adams Saturday morning at nine a.m., later than usual. Normally a hearty breakfast eater, Stockman contented himself with coffee and orange juice as if he had already eaten (which, I would learn later, he had with left-wing journalist Bill Greider).

Stockman told me the kind of story I have loved to report for half a century. In 1979 President Carter named Charles Swinburne, a career civil servant, as deputy assistant secretary of Transportation for policy and international affairs. Seven days before Carter left office, the Transportation Department released Swinburne's report calling for reduced Japanese auto exports to benefit America's automotive industry. Stockman called it a "statist tract" uniting business, labor, and government in a corporate welfare bailout.

Stockman told me Lewis had retained Swinburne, disobeying Reagan's direct orders to cleanse his administration of officials from the "permanent government." Lewis went further and embraced the protectionist Swinburne report. "The bureaucracy has completely captured Drew Lewis," Stockman told me (a quote I attributed in our column to "one critical colleague"). That was not all the information Stockman imparted to me. In a Tuesday cabinet meeting that week, Lewis and his allies had so monopolized the thirty-five minutes allocated to the auto imports question that Stockman and Treasury Secretary Donald Regan had only two minutes to reply in opposition.

That Saturday I told Rowly this was such a hot story that we had to scrap our column for Monday, March 9, already sent to newspaper clients and to substitute this new one. In addition to the inside dope of inter-cabinet wrangling, our column made a serious point:

> Whereas Lewis sees reduced imports as bait for labor restraint, his opponents within the Administration think such collaboration between labor, business and government smacks more of Benito Mussolini than Ronald Reagan. They fear cracking down on Japanese imports may inhibit growing realization by trade unions that their own labor contracts contribute to non-competitiveness of U.S. industry.

Five years later in *The Triumph of Politics,* Stockman gave an inaccurate account. Describing himself in combat against Lewis, he claimed untruthfully he had initiated the column by calling me. He termed the Evans & Novak column "a kind of supply-side dartboard. You could use it to stick somebody in the forehead fast, if you had to."

Stockman's 1986 memoir said: "When he [Lewis] found out I was responsible for Novak's column [of March 8], he went into orbit." In return for Lewis promising not to fight his battles in the press, "I agreed not to have breakfast with the Prince of Darkness for a while." That agreement did not preclude frequent phone conversations between Stockman and me during which he did not shrink from continuing to criticize Lewis.

However, at the annual Gridiron dinner on March 28 (where Stockman delivered the Republican speech, thanks to me), the OMB director called me aside during the predinner head table reception. "Drew Lewis is really a terrific public servant," he said, contradicting everything he had told me up to that point. "Bob, you're really too hard on Drew. I wonder who's been downgrading him to you." I *felt* like saying, "Why, it was you, Dave." But I maintained stony-faced silence. I glimpsed Lewis eyeing us from the other side of the room. Stockman had staged a charade for Lewis's benefit.

The moratorium on Stockman-Novak breakfasts ended after one month. My appointments book shows an eight a.m. Saturday breakfast date with Stockman at the Hay Adams on April 11. I asked Stockman that morning about his struggles with the Republican Senate Budget Committee chairman, Pete Domenici, who was endangering the Reagan tax cut by insisting on a balanced budget. The next Evans & Novak column, assailing Domenici's "green eyeshade worship of the sacred balanced budget," was obviously the product of several sources. But in his memoir, Stockman bragged "I posted a message on the Bob Novak bulletin board."

Of course Stockman was using me, as I was using him. I hope he was astute enough to recognize that I recognized this mutual use. I was happy to get a column exclusively reporting important developments and one that helped an ideological cause that, it turned out, I believed in far more strongly than Stockman did.

AMONG THE NIXON-FORD obstructionists named to me by Stockman was David Gergen. He was only thirty-eight years old but seemed to have been around forever as a speechwriter for Nixon and Ford who managed to hang on in the Reagan White House. My image of the six-foot, six-inch Gergen had him hovering over shorter colleagues and bending down to whisper in their ears. Conservatives regarded him as amiable, intelligent, and an excellent writer but a courtier type whose agenda did not transcend his own personal advancement. Although Gergen was reputed to be a prodigious leaker, I had experienced no more contact with him than a handshake at occasional receptions.

So I was surprised late Monday afternoon, February 16, 1981, to get a telephone call from Gergen asking to see me first thing the next morning. He was seated in my little conference room at nine a.m. on Tuesday, and he did not come empty-handed. He opened his briefcase, and took out working papers for Reagan's historic tax reduction message to be delivered to Congress on Wednesday night. Reagan's actual message was leaking all over Washington, but Gergen gave me something none of my super-sources in the Reagan administration provided and what no other reporter had: the draft of material for the Reagan message that was *not* used. It gave me a terrific Evans & Novak column for Friday, February 20, that began:

> "Why this is just a supply-side primer," complained Murray Weidenbaum, chairman of the President's Council of Economic Advisers, on Friday the 13th, then rolled up his sleeves to rewrite totally the introduction to President Reagan's economic report that had been drafted by best-selling economics writer George Gilder.
>
> When Weidenbaum and the White House had finished, no trace of Gilder was left in the report—not even the words "supply side" describing the economic philosophy Reagan has adopted as his own. . . .
>
> [D]octrinal justification for tax reduction is put down by everybody in the White House, with the notable exception of Ronald Reagan.

Why would Gergen volunteer this information to a reporter he hardly knew and was not a natural ally? Surely he could not believe I was so naïve that I would consider him a sudden supply-side acolyte. Rather, I think Gergen, the ultimate Washington survivor, was working the source-or-target model with me. Gergen never really became my source, but he was not my target either—which I believe was his intent.

ON WEDNESDAY EVENING, March 12, 1981, Rowly and I flew to New Orleans to address a business convention the next day. A week earlier, the New Orleans States-Item cancelled the Evans & Novak column after having bought it for nearly eighteen years. I invited the editor of the States-Item to breakfast to try to keep the business even though my batting average for such efforts was about zero. I wanted Rowly—a better salesman than I— to join us but he refused, contending that it was a waste of time and that he would rather breakfast with Moon Landrieu, the former mayor of New Orleans.

Our column never got back into the New Orleans market, and the breakfast was unproductive. What made it worse was my glance at that morning's *Wall Street Journal* being read by a man at the table next to ours. My eyes still could make out the paper's old-fashioned banked headline on page one:

THE ODD COUPLE
EVANS, NOVAK STILL RILE
READERS AFTER 18 YEARS
OF RIGHT-WING PURITY

COLUMN GOES PAST REPORTING
TO PRESS STRIDENT VIEW,
PROMOTE JOBS FOR FRIENDS

We had been expecting the *Journal* piece by James M. Perry after he interviewed Rowly and me at length in our office on February 13. Jim Perry was one of Washington's best reporters who years later won the National Press Club's Fourth Estate Award for lifetime achievement in journalism. I had trouble concentrating during the next hour on a fruitless conversation with a boring editor, hardly able to conceal my impatience to read Perry's piece. It turned out to be a pretty nasty article from a previously friendly colleague who had lavished praise on our Johnson and Nixon books.

I thought it was a pedestrian effort by Perry, below his usual standard. He started with the cliche of "the slender, debonair" Evans and "the short, rumpled" Novak constituting "journalism's oddest couple." Contending we had "now become the most controversial and talked about columnists in town," Perry then addressed his basic argument:

What they have been doing . . . is try to hold the Reagan Administration's feet to the pure flame of their own increasingly strident brand of conservatism.

They seem to believe that the nation may not survive unless an undiluted supply-side economic program is developed at home and a tougher defense and foreign policy position to contain the Russians is put in place around the world. . . .

It's the old journalistic conundrum: Should reporters . . . actually come down out of the press box and take part in the game?

Perry quoted an unnamed "editor of a big-city daily who has dropped their column. 'They're out there on the field, blocking and tackling and telling the coach what plays to call. I don't need that kind of stuff in my newspaper.'" We were being criticized for what columnists do. The real complaint with us was that we were taking *conservative* positions. This complaint was widely voiced among our colleagues, including my good friend Jack Germond, who was about the only critic that Perry quoted by name. "They do seem to have gotten a little apoplectic," Germond said of us.

Perry gave me a chance to explain in print why we had become such a target. "We are running against the grain of the conventional wisdom within the journalistic community," I told him, adding this was particularly true of economic policy. Perry quoted me further: "Most journalists find it hard to abandon the viewpoints they have held for years. If supply-side economics works, it will be the death knell for much of the system this establishment has built up over the last 40 years."

Only two things about Perry's piece pleased me. One was mentioning that my fifteen-year-old daughter, Zelda, was a ball girl for the Washington Bullets basketball team. The other was a rare factual mistake by Perry. Rowly and I never revealed how much money we made to any interviewer, because we would be embarrassed by how much lower our earnings were than generally expected. Perry had tried to calculate our individual pieces of income and concluded that we each earned "in excess of $200,000 annually" (which would constitute more than $445,000 in 2007 money). Actually, our joint efforts were bringing in less than $80,000 each. I was delighted to have everybody—including my friends—think I was making big money. Nobody ever asked me about the accuracy of Perry's figure, and I never volunteered the truth.

IN 1981, IT had been nearly ten years since our last book, *Nixon in the White House*. It was my idea to attempt, immediately after the 1980 election, a quick Evans & Novak book on the coming Reagan administration. Our newly acquired agent, Esther Newberg (a former Democratic activist on her way to becoming a senior executive at International Creative Management) wanted it short enough to be delivered on time for publication early in the autumn of 1981. She got us a good contract with E. P. Dutton, with the book edited by the company's publisher, Jack Macrae. He was a rising star in the New York world of books and, like almost everybody in the business, was a liberal. I thought the very idea of *The Reagan Revolution* (the title was my idea) soured Macrae's stomach, but he was a professional who soldiered on. So did we, and the book was coming in on deadline.

We wanted a verbatim interview with President Reagan as the book's penultimate chapter, and I had called the president's press secretary, James Brady, early in March to request one. When Rowly and I walked into the Oval Office at four p.m. on March 23, we were surprised. Usually two or three senior aides are at any president's side for a private meeting, but Brady was the only other person. There was no sign of bulky White House recording equipment. Every on-the-record utterance of a president normally is transcribed for posterity, but only our own little office tape recorder retained Reagan's answers. Stranger still, after about five minutes, Brady glanced at his watch and left the room. We were alone with the president.

It was a sunny early spring afternoon, and Reagan's mood matched it. In the presidency for only two months, he "was obviously having the time of his life" (as I later wrote in the book's introduction to the interview). Reagan did not betray the turmoil in his official family centering around Secretary of State Alexander Haig, who was engaged in a power struggle with White House staffers headed by Jim Baker. Reagan was able to maintain a cheerful composure in the midst of internal strife.

The purpose of our interview for a book to be published six months later was to probe Reagan's philosophy and his personal outlook as to how revolutionary his administration would and should be. Rowly asked which philosophical thinkers and writers had influenced him the most. "Oh, boy, Rowly," Reagan replied. Fearful Reagan was at a loss, Rowly noted that President Carter "used to talk about Reinhold Niebuhr" and then mentioned, without a clear connection I thought, Adam Smith, Thomas Hobbes, and Spinoza. But those weren't Reagan's models, and he didn't need prompting. He was just collecting his thoughts.

Describing himself as a "voracious reader," Reagan cited nineteenth-century British free trade advocates John Bright and Richard Cobden and twentieth-century Austrian free market economists Ludwig von Mises and Friedrich von Hayek. He also said, "Bastiat has dominated my thinking so much." Bastiat? Rowly and I had to look him up. Claude-Frédéric Bastiat (1801–1850) was a French political economist who preached against protectionism and socialism. Later in the interview, Reagan talked about liberal clergymen who had been influenced by Reichenbach's advocacy of big government taking care of the poor. Reichenbach? That sent Rowly and me back to the reference books to look up Hans Reichenbach (1891–1953), a German philosopher who belonged to the Vienna Circle of legal positivists. Reagan was better read and better educated than we were.

Without benefit of his famous three-by-five index cards or any notes, Reagan cited from memory budget statistics dating back to Eisenhower (totally accurate, we found, after we checked). More important than demonstrating an actor's good memory was his personalized understanding of what supply-side economics was all about.

> Novak: *Why* are you so convinced, Mr. President, that your tax rate reduction will work as a means of reviving the economy?
>
> Reagan: 'Cause it always has. It did when Kennedy did it. It did in the time of Coolidge. Andrew Mellon [President Coolidge's Treasury Secretary] has written about the tax cuts and they worked. . . . I take my own personal experience in [motion] pictures. I was in that exceedingly high tax bracket after World War II, and I know what *I* did. I would be offered scripts of additional pictures and, once I had reached that bracket, I just turned 'em down. I wasn't going to go to work for six cents on the dollar.

He also had his own simplified cold war strategy, embracing a rationale that had eluded the other postwar presidents:

> I believe in trying to negotiate, certainly, a reduction in strategic arms, to reduce the threshold of danger. And there's never been anything like it in the world before, weapons that can literally destroy civilization. But to go to a table to bargain, you gotta have something to give. When you sit down opposite someone who has the superiority that could lead—if they continue this increase—toward the delivery someday of an ultimatum, what do you have to say to persuade them to reduce that strength? But, on the other hand, if you've embarked on a course of saying, "We're not going to let you have that superiority," strained as they are to provide. We know they can't provide consumer goods for their people. Now, there would be some *reason* for them to listen. Because we can say to them, "We can go one of two ways. We can both keep on straining in this direction [arms buildup], or we can mutually agree to some reductions in strength."

We had gone five minutes over our designated thirty-minute limit when Brady wandered back into the Oval Office and hand-signaled me that time was up. Rowly and I squeezed out another five minutes of q-and-a, ending with a Reagan joke, to make it a forty-minute interview.

One week to the day from our session in the White House, John Hinckley shot Brady and Reagan outside the Washington Hilton Hotel. A disabled Brady kept the title of press secretary through the Reagan presidency's eight years but never was able to perform the office's duties. I think Reagan missed Brady's relaxed style. Access to the president was sharply curtailed for all news media, and that included Rowly and me. Larry Speakes, the de facto press secretary, worked for Baker and treated Evans and me like the enemy. When we would write an inside dope column critical of Baker, Speakes would rip us in the morning briefing. Brady, I am sure, would have tried to work with us to get a better column next time.

Although Reagan's wounds were much less grievous than Brady's, I think that the president, as well as his press secretary, would never quite be the same after the shooting. Rowly and I caught him at his best on the afternoon of March 23. As outstanding as his performance was in changing America (and the world), it could have been even better were it not for John Hinckley.

THE FIRST EVANS & Novak column I wrote after returning from a reporting/family vacation trip to Europe in July 1981 belied Daniel Schorr's 1980 election night taunting of me as someone who could not criticize President Reagan. By July, I had criticized the new administration for betraying the Reagan Revolution's principles—but never Reagan himself. In my column of Friday, July 10, I crossed that line. Thereafter, many of the president's men viewed me as more of a critic than a supporter.

I received a telephone call on July 8 from William Gribbin, a junior White House aide. I met Bill the previous summer at the Republican convention in Detroit where he was editing the party platform. He was intense and very conservative. I think Bill learned to trust me, and that is why he called now to say he had something important. Unlike many leakers, Gribbin was not interested in currying favor with me or promoting himself. He was disturbed by the president's announcement the previous day, July 7, that he intended to nominate the nation's first female Supreme Court justice: fifty-one-year-old Sandra Day O'Connor, a former Republican majority leader of the Arizona State Senate who two years earlier had been appointed to the Arizona Court of Appeals by a Democratic governor. Gribbin and the Christian conservatives who had so vigorously supported Reagan for president considered O'Connor unacceptable because of her positions on abortion.

"Why Did He Choose Her?" was the *Washington Post's* headline on our column about O'Connor. The answer was contained in the document Gribbin gave me: a memo written to the attorney general of the United States by his thirty-five-year-old counselor, Kenneth W. Starr.

Gribbin told me that O'Connor's sponsor was Dave Gergen, who wanted a woman justice to give Reagan a foothold in the feminist movement and distance him from the social conservatives. The formal recommendation, echoing the White House staff, came from Attorney General William French Smith, Reagan's personal attorney and the weakest member of the cabinet.

Reagan telephoned Smith on Monday, July 6, when social conservatives erupted after O'Connor's selection leaked—the president's first inkling of how controversial this nomination would be. The president wanted a quick check on complaints that his first Supreme Court selection was proabortion. Smith did not have a clue and bucked the question over to young Ken Starr. On the next day, July 7, Starr handed his boss the two-and-a-half page memo that Gribbin supplied me on July 8. My column, published July 10, called Starr's memo "hurriedly prepared" and "error-filled," but added that it "convinced" Reagan to go through with the nomination.

Starr's investigation that cleared Judge O'Connor on abortion appeared to consist solely of a telephone interview with her, and she was less than truthful. O'Connor told Starr she could not remember how she voted on a 1979 Arizona legislative bill to legalize abortion. Starr did not look into records showing that Senator O'Connor was a co-sponsor of the measure and voted for it as it lost in committee.

Starr's memo concluded: "Judge O'Connor further indicated in response to my questions that she had never been a leader or outspoken advocate on behalf of either pro-life or abortion rights organizations. She knows well the Arizona leader of the right-to-life movement, a prominent female physician in Phoenix, and has never had any disputes or controversies with her." Starr was referring to Carolyn Gerster. I phoned Gerster, and learned that Starr had not called her. "I had an adversary position with Sandra O'Connor," Gerster told me, calling her "one of the most powerful proabortionists in the Senate." Gerster harbored an eleven-year-old grievance against O'Connor for burying an antiabortion proposal in the Senate Republican caucus. I wrote in the Evans & Novak column of July 10:

> [I]nnocence has departed for right-to-life activists. Dr. Gerster cannot forget a 45-minute meeting with Reagan in Rye, N.Y., on Jan. 17, 1980, in which candidate Reagan promised her that his first appointment to the Court would share their anti-abortion views. She chooses to believe that the President has been misled by advisers.
>
> But the more plausible explanation is that Reagan shares the view of Jim Baker and his other aides that the Moral Majority [the social

conservatives] is not vital to his political coalition. He has given that signal by ignoring its sensibilities in selecting Sandra O'Connor.

With this, I burned bridges to the White House, Baker, and maybe the president. Many Republican sources claimed I was overheated and that Sandra O'Connor would turn out fine on abortion. Indeed, Justice O'Connor was a clever politician who in her first years on the court seemed to be voting with conservatives. But before long, she evolved into the swing vote on a five-to-four divided court that nearly always swung left on social issues. In 1993, she voted with the majority upholding the *Roe v. Wade* decision legalizing abortion. From a conservative standpoint, O'Connor was not the worst choice ever by a Republican president for the Supreme Court, but she was pretty bad. Ronald Reagan, Jim Baker, and Ken Starr were wrong about her, and I was right.

ALTHOUGH I WAS no lapdog for Ronald Reagan, I applauded much in his presidency—far more than any other president in my twenty-four years in Washington. On July 29, 1981, the House passed the historic Reagan tax cut. I watched from the House Press Gallery, where one of my colleagues said sarcastically, "Well Novak, I guess this is a really big day for you." The tax bill followed passage of a Reagan-backed budget that curtailed the growth in government spending. I wrote in an Evans & Novak column published two days after the tax bill passed:

> The House vote capped the passage of Reagan's economic package in 200 days, a feat unmatched since Franklin Roosevelt's 100 days in 1933. It also was a unique personal triumph for Rep. Jack Kemp, who began his tax crusade seven years ago against bipartisan ridicule. But in addition, it revealed profound political misconceptions by the Democrats.

Those misconceptions were reflected in Speaker O'Neill's bitter closing speech to the House in which he called this "a great day for the aristocracy." I wrote: "To the very end, Tip O'Neill could not believe that the people really prefer lower taxes to bigger government." I recall that speech whenever I hear romantic nonsense about the Reagan-O'Neill "friendship" in a golden era of bipartisanship.

Five days after the tax bill passed, the Professional Air Traffic Controllers Organization (PATCO)—the only labor union that endorsed Reagan in 1980—broke their no-strike oath. Secretary of Transportation Lewis and

Attorney General Smith pleaded with Reagan to negotiate rather than risk national economic chaos. Reagan was adamant, as he made clear over live TV on Monday, August 7, from the White House Rose Garden, where (I wrote in an Evans & Novak column) he taught "the striking PATCO union a lesson they were learning the hard way."

> The lesson: when Ronald Reagan picks a target, he is as blunt and stubborn as a sledgehammer, despite his velvet glove of affability.
>
> Among the 13,000 striking controllers, learning that lesson will cause anguish, tears and probably tragedy after the excitement of early combat wears off . . . Reagan's sense of his own rectitude is the real guarantee against retreat.

I concluded that this performance was "likely to reverse the dangerous erosion of presidential power at a time the Western World has maximum need for a strong presidency." That final paragraph in my August 7 column generated widespread derision that I had lost all sense of perspective. In fact, it was understated. We now know that the impact of Reagan's resolve in the air controller strike reached into the heart of the Kremlin. A week later, after breakfast with me at the Hay Adams, Lyn Nofziger confided he was advising Reagan that he had made his point and now should let the air controllers go back to work. Reagan refused. He knew better than Nofziger, a hard conservative, that the benefits of his principled position would be lost if he pulled defeat from the jaws of victory.

The tax bill's passage and the air controller strike confirmed that this was no ordinary presidency. I had a selfish satisfaction. We had sent the final pages of *The Reagan Revolution* to the publisher in June, before these events took place. Our preview of the Reagan presidency was a gamble that it would not look ordinary when published in September. We won the bet.

THE EARLIEST REVIEW of *The Reagan Revolution,* the first Evans & Novak book in ten years, was delivered orally by Maurice P. Novak. My father tried to read everything that ever appeared under my byline. He did not like *The Reagan Revolution.*

"It's too uncritical. You're too soft on Reagan," he said. My father was a liberal Republican who just did not like Reagan, even though he had voted for him rather than endure four more years of Jimmy Carter. In contrast, my mother loved the book and felt Reagan was the best president of her long lifetime.

The split verdict by my parents predicted the verdict by reviewers in early September. This was the most ideological book written by Rowly and me. Admirers of Reagan liked the book. Nonadmirers did not.

James Fallows, the Washington editor of the *Atlantic Monthly* who had been a White House speechwriter for President Carter, was snide in the *New York Times Book Review.* He complained about our "near-total enthusiasm for the 'revolution' that they describe," adding: "I suspect (and here I display my own bias) that in future years that they will not look with pleasure on their explanations of how the President will be able to cut taxes and increase military spending without worrying about a budget deficit." (Twenty-four years later, I still "look with pleasure" at what I wrote.) I think Fallows's admitted bias was personal. As a Carter speechwriter, he had leaked me material, expressed unhappiness about the way I used it and then anguished that he had leaked against his better judgment.

I had no personal experience with Anthony Holden, an editor at *The Times* of London who was even more snide than Fallows in reviewing for the *Washington Post Book World.* Holden was particularly derisive of our interview with Reagan, calling the president "fundamentally inarticulate." Charles Kaiser produced the nastiest review in the *New Republic,* asserting that "no one has ever substituted sycophancy for skepticism more successfully" than we did and assailed our "determination to transform themselves from journalists into official publicists for their newest hero."

In plugging the Nixon book in 1971, I got a gracious reception from Phil Donahue on his new TV talk show, then based in Dayton, Ohio. Donahue, now rich, famous, and relocated to Chicago, greeted me in 1981 with abuse for being a Reagan patsy. He was obsessed by the official White House photograph on the book jacket showing me smiling at Reagan. "Whatever happened to the tough reporter Novak we used to know?" he asked.

On the other side Fred Barnes of the *Baltimore Sun* (a conservative and friend) took issue with Fallows in the *American Spectator* for writing "a snotty, barely serious critique." Edwin M. Yoder Jr., editorial page editor of the *Washington Star* (no conservative but also my friend) in the *Washington Journalism Review* called us "masters of the subcurrents of personal fealty and influence that stir beneath deceptively placid surfaces."

The content of *The Reagan Revolution* has enjoyed a long shelf life— cited frequently in books about Reagan, particularly its long sections on supply-side economics. But its sales were disappointing, perhaps suppressed by the unprecedented ideological defection of a key Reagan official that threatened to bring down Reagan's Revolution.

CHAPTER 31

A Near-Death Experience

On November 10, 1981, David Stockman celebrated his thirty-fifth birthday. That day, Democrat Gary Hart rose in the Senate to read into the record an advance copy of an article in December's *Atlantic:* "The Education of David Stockman" by the left-wing journalist William Greider (then a *Washington Post* assistant managing editor).

Greider's article dealt Reagan a devastating blow, based on eighteen tape-recorded conversations between Stockman and Greider during ten months of Saturday morning breakfasts at the Hay Adams (alternating with me every other Saturday). OMB Director Stockman pronounced supply-side tax cuts, whose virtues he had been proclaiming publicly, a fraud on the American public. It was as if Stalin, in the midst of the Bolshevik revolution, had repudiated Marxism.

There were early warning signs about Stockman beginning with a *Washington Post Magazine* article on February 8, 1981. Walter Shapiro, a staffer for the magazine who had been a Carter presidential speechwriter, painted Stockman as a small-town Midwest version of Sammy Glick. He portrayed Stockman's journey from anti-Vietnam student protester to live-in acolyte of Harvard professor Daniel Patrick Moynihan to liberal Republican aide and friend of Congressman John Anderson to supply-side congressman and ally of Jack Kemp. After Geraldine read Shapiro's article, she told me: "If this is true, he's a monster." I shrugged off Shapiro's piece to Geraldine, but I learned from it things about Stockman I had not known and that bothered me.

The Washington Gridiron Club president for 1981 was Ed O'Brien, the Washington correspondent of the *St. Louis Globe-Democrat* and a rare conservative in the capital's press corps. The Gridiron president picked speakers for the club's annual white-tie spring dinner, and O'Brien asked me for suggestions. I recommended Stockman, the most interesting member of the new administration, as the Republican speaker and his old mentor, Pat Moynihan, as the Democrat. Ed agreed, and at his request I called them. Both accepted.

Senator Moynihan was the hit at the ninety-fourth annual spring Gridiron dinner on March 28, 1981, at the Capital Hilton as he related his experiences with Stockman when he was a Harvard divinity student and guest in the Moynihan home:

> . . . Liz [Moynihan's wife] and I were assigned David Stockman. Fresh from Michigan State and the Students for a Democratic Society and Vietnam Summer.
>
> Dave was *everything* you could dream of as a mole. Corn fed and cowlicked, he was the best boob bait for conservatives ever to come out of the Middle West.
>
> The only trouble was he couldn't stop talking about the Viet Cong and American imperialism and the immorality of the Vietnam War. . . .
>
> Stockman is peerless. I have never known a man capable of such sustained self-hypnotic ideological fervor. One day he arrives at Harvard pressing the infallibility of Ho Chi Minh. Next thing you know he turns up in Washington proclaiming the immutability of the Laffer Curve.

"The Gridiron may singe, but it never burns" was the motto of the club's soft-core satire, and I thought Moynihan crossed the line. He was not kidding.

Even before Stockman was sworn in, Jude Wanniski had come to regard as the enemy the new budget chief he had helped select. Stockman was such a good source for me I was reluctant to write him off. But he quickly moved to another stage of his life's twisting political journey. Our eight a.m. breakfast on October 12, 1981, at the Hay Adams was the last of so many private contacts between Stockman and me.

In the *Atlantic* article, two vivid metaphors used by Stockman—"Trojan horse" and "trickle down"—seized the political community's attention. Greider wrote:

> "The hard part of the supply-side tax cut is dropping the top rate from 70 to 50 percent—the rest of it is a secondary matter," Stockman explained. . . . "I mean, Kemp-Roth was always a Trojan horse to bring down the top rate." . . .

"It's kind of hard to sell 'trickle down,'" he explained, "so the supply-side formula was the only way to get a tax policy that was really 'trickle down.' Supply-side is 'trickle-down' theory."

I was traveling with Jack Kemp in upstate New York (getting material for a *Reader's Digest* article about him) as this story broke on November 10. Kemp was a sunny optimist who wanted to think the best of everyone. When we arrived at Washington National Airport in early evening, Kemp called Stockman (celebrating at a Washington restaurant) to wish him a happy birthday. Then Kemp handed me the telephone: "Bob, say hello to Dave and wish him a happy birthday." After I did so, Stockman told me: "You must think I'm Judas. We've got to get together soon." We never did. That was the last conversation I ever had with David Stockman.

I assumed Stockman was finished, but he stayed on, incredibly, for three and one-half years until he resigned, of his own volition, on July 31, 1985. All that time, he was fighting the supply-siders and pushing for tax increases. His 1986 memoir, *The Triumph of Politics,* repudiated supply-side doctrine and the ideological foundations of Reagan's Republican Party. "By keeping Stockman on the job," I wrote in the Evans & Novak column of November 27, 1981, "they [Reagan and his closest aides] court divisiveness on economic policy."

I predicted to friends that Stockman would climax his life of twists and turns with a final metamorphosis to become a liberal Democrat. Instead, he went underground politically. His wife, Jennifer, became a leader in Republicans for Choice. I was told by a friend of Stockman that after 2000 he went on cable television to abjure his apostasy and return to faith in the supply-side gospel. It did not get much attention, because nobody cared about him any longer. My personal anger toward David Stockman because of his duplicitous conduct toward me has subsided, and I hope he finds whatever he is seeking.

JEFF BELL NOTED that after the *Atlantic* article, I quoted anonymous Stockman aides (it usually was his chief economist, Lawrence Kudlow) rather than Stockman himself. "Won't Dave return your calls?" Bell asked me. "I don't call him," I replied.

Why did I end nearly all contact with Stockman after the Greider article? (I use the word "nearly" because I twice requested, through channels, Stockman as a guest to be interviewed by Rowly and me on CNN. Stockman refused.)

I answered the question in the *New York Times Book Review* of June 22,

1986. In the May 11 issue, Michael Kinsley (then editor of the *New Republic*) had reviewed Stockman's *The Triumph of Politics* in which he repeated with obvious relish Stockman's distorted depiction of our relationship. Kinsley, my future liberal debating partner on CNN's *Crossfire,* was incensed that my conservative column was based on reporting (as Kinsley put it, "an ideological agenda masqueraded as factual reportage"). Through my book agent Esther Newberg, I got the *Book Review* to publish a long letter correcting Stockman that was a short essay on my dealings with the OMB director (the only time I ever have been published in that publication). I concluded:

> The reason I stopped seeking private chats [with Stockman] was not because we no longer agreed on what was best for the American economy. If, as a columnist, I was so arrogant as to see only public officials with whom I agreed, I would not be getting much news and, in truth, would see precious few people. Some of my oldest and most valuable news sources are people who disagree with me about virtually everything. Instead, I had simply come to the point where I could not tell when David was or was not telling the truth.

EARLY ON THE morning of Wednesday, January 13, 1982, Rowly and I flew up to New York's La Guardia Airport to be driven by limo to Nassau County, Long Island, to address a luncheon meeting of real estate agents. After we arrived on Long Island, a severe snowstorm cancelled all flights between New York and Washington. Now we had to take a train home, and we wanted to catch one early enough to attend a black-tie dinner in Washington that night honoring Lyn Nofziger. An abbreviated lecture performance was fine with me. I felt one of the bad colds I got every winter coming on but never bothered to see a doctor about or take any medicine for.

When Rowly and I arrived via limo at Penn Station in Manhattan, we encountered at the ticket window William Colby with his frozen, unrevealing expression. This was the man who as head of "pacification" in Vietnam had enraged liberals with the Phoenix program to murder Vietcong operatives and who as director of Central Intelligence had enraged the CIA's old hands by giving a hostile Congress the Agency's most treasured secrets ("the family jewels"). Colby's cold spymaster stare was intimidating but now suggested a confused man unaccustomed to finding his own way in a blizzard without help from aides.

Colby told us he just learned what I thought anybody would know: his plane ticket was useless at Penn Station. He was in a quandary because he did not carry money or credit cards. I was at the ticket window, and Rowly shouted: "Bob, buy Bill a ticket to Washington." I did, amid promises by the former spymaster that I would soon be repaid. When Colby excused himself to visit the washroom after we boarded the train, Rowly—ever the enthusiastic reporter—rubbed his hands in glee over the prospect of grilling Bill Colby on a long train ride through the snow to Washington.

Thanks to the storm, that trip took more than eight hours or nearly twice the normal duration. We all had drinks, and I put down two or three Scotch and waters. Little did I dream that these were the last Scotch and waters I would ever finish.

My impression is that Colby, Rowly, and I talked about Vietnam and the CIA the whole trip, and I have a vague recollection that Colby was philosophical rather than informative. But it is only vague. I kept nodding off, because now I was getting really sick. I felt feverish and about to pass out. (As I expected, Colby did not repay me for the train ticket. Those little details escape the attention of a DCI.)

We arrived in Washington around midnight, far too late for the Nofziger dinner (which had been cancelled anyway). It was surreal as huddled masses braved the continuing snowstorm outside Union Station, queuing for taxis. I had to wait more than a half hour in the snow, and I thought I would faint. I dozed most of the long ride into the Maryland suburbs in the storm.

I had not missed a day's work during nineteen years as a columnist, and I was not going to let a little cold keep me from meeting two of my best sources. I had a ten thirty a.m. Thursday meeting scheduled on Capitol Hill with Senator Scoop Jackson and a twelve thirty lunch at the Maison Blanche restaurant (would-be successor to Sans Souci) with Richard Perle, now an assistant secretary of Defense. So, rotten though I felt, I arose at six a.m. to drive the snow-covered roads into Washington. I found that the Jackson and Perle appointments had been cancelled because of the weather. I also found that, feverish, dizzy, and in pain from a nonstop headache, I could not concentrate enough for writing or reporting. For the first time, I could not finish the day because of illness and, in early afternoon, I drove back home to Maryland.

When Geraldine took my temperature and found it was 104 degrees, she called the doctor. He was Dr. George T. Economos, who became our physician twenty years earlier when I was in need of help for an asthma attack and the medical society gave me his name. Geraldine and I grew fond of George, a warm human being without the hauteur of many physicians. A

Greek immigrant with a mostly African-American patient list, Economos was no society doctor.

What bothered us were his diagnostic skills. "He's never cured us of anything," Geraldine would say. Her lack of confidence in George stemmed from a 1966 incident when Zelda was an infant. Eva, a pretty teenager from Sweden living with us as an au pair, was injured on the roller coaster at the Glen Echo amusement park outside Washington. Dr. Economos treated her, but after a couple of weeks her wound was not healing. We were terrified that this poor foreign girl in our care was dying of gangrene. We took her in to see George again, but he said after examining her he could do no more than continue the same ineffective medication. Geraldine, uncharacteristically assertive because of her concern about Eva, told him that simply wasn't good enough. "Well," Economos told Geraldine in his thick Greek accent, "I'm open to suggestion."

A very different George Economos was functioning the night of January 14, 1982, when, over the telephone, Geraldine described my symptoms—fading in and out of consciousness, headache, and very high fever. He said he better come right over. A house call! I had not experienced a doctor's house call since I was a little boy. Economos lived nearby. But the previous day's snowstorm had resumed, and it took him forty-five minutes to reach our home.

George found my fever had risen to 105 degrees. He told us he believed I had spinal meningitis. It was only his opinion, and he was not sure because he had never before encountered that dreaded disease. But if he was right, he felt we must quickly get me under expert care—the world-class neurology department at the George Washington University Hospital in Foggy Bottom. He said I should have an ambulance, but it could take hours to get one in this snowstorm. "That would be too late," Economos said. *Too late!* He thought I was about to die if I did not get attention quickly.

So George took me in his car. This was amazing in 1982. A doctor was making a night house call and then driving his gravely ill patient to a distant hospital—in the midst of a severe snowstorm. On the way to GW, George passed two perfectly good hospitals—Suburban and Sibley. But neither had the neurology department he felt was needed to save my life. What normally would be a thirty-minute journey took two hours, as I intermittently lapsed into a fitful nightmarish sleep.

The doctors at GW were ready when we arrived after eleven p.m. After bombarding me with questions about whether I knew where I worked and how many children I had (which I had trouble answering), the neurology team instituted an excruciatingly painful spinal tap. Dr. Economos's intuitive diagnosis was dead-on. I had spinal meningitis. George T. Economos had saved my life. No more did Geraldine and I kid about his diagnostic skills.

When I checked into the hospital that night, it was not certain that I would ever check out. Rowly came to see me the next day and played the macho combat marine, refusing to put on a hospital mask as everybody else wore in my room. He took my wife and children out to dinner Friday night, trying to reassure them everything would be all right. He later confided to me he thought I was going to die, a thought that entered my own mind.

I survived after a struggle of nearly two weeks in the hospital and another two weeks convalescence at home. I was not the same man I had been before January 10. The illness left me, permanently, a little deaf in my left ear. Tests showed I had suffered a small stroke—information I did not impart to anybody except Geraldine. Mostly I felt depleted, lacking the energy that had been more important than talent in propelling my journalistic career.

Our first social engagement after my convalescence was a dinner on February 26 hosted by Andy and Ellie Glass at their Northwest Washington home, celebrating my fifty-first birthday. At that point, I had not touched an alcoholic beverage in more than a month—my longest period of abstinence since I was sixteen years old. I eagerly anticipated my usual Scotch and water and made an occasion of breaking my alcoholic fast at the Glasses. But I gagged on my first sip, tried another sip and gagged again. I just could not get it down. I tried again a few days later, with the same result.

After downing countless thousands of them over thirty-four years, I had consumed my last Scotch and water. I learned to like vodka straight in small doses, enjoyed an occasional beer, and sometimes drank wine with meals. But my serious drinking days were over. If I had a drinking problem, it was gone. Spinal meningitis had applied a drastic remedy.

Not long after the Glass dinner, Geraldine and I dined with Jeff Bell at Montgomery County's Marriott Hotel—my first restaurant meal since my illness. Bell brought some Catholic literature for me. Jeff had converted to the Roman Catholic faith in 1978 (the year of his first Senate race in New Jersey), but this was his initial step toward proselytizing me. I have kidded Jeff that he must have figured I was near death and he had better try to convert me before it was too late. In fact, he thought my experience might move me closer to my God.

I thought Bell was wasting his time if he expected me to become a

Catholic. But I began wondering whether there was some purpose in my illness. Was it mere chance that Dr. Economos had saved my life? Was there a purpose that illness abruptly curtailed my drinking? Was a hidden hand changing my life? Would it bring a spiritual awakening?

ON SUNDAY, Valentine's Day, February 14, I was convalescing at home in the Maryland suburbs when John McLaughlin telephoned. He asked to come over to see me with Richard Moore, his old colleague from the Nixon White House and now his business partner.

Months earlier, McLaughlin called to say he had finally found a tentative sponsor for "our" program. What program? I had forgotten our 1974 conversation. He had asked me then to be a panelist on a more conservative version of *Agronsky and Company*. I said yes then, thinking it just another of the dozens of TV shows pitched to me and then abandoned.

McLaughlin had doggedly sought financial backing and snagged Dick Moore, a White House lawyer during Watergate, as a partner. In 1981, Moore was semiretired at age sixty-seven after a successful career as a television executive. Moore brought to the table three things McLaughlin lacked: money, broadcasting experience, and a warm and engaging personality. Everybody liked Dick Moore. Hardly anybody liked John McLaughlin.

Even with Moore's help, it is mind-boggling to think that McLaughlin contemplated putting together a major television program. His journalistic and political credentials were slender, and he was remembered in Washington, not at all fondly, as an unpleasant Nixon super-loyalist who still supported the disgraced president after the battle was lost. But persistence paid off. McLaughlin informed me that the Edison Electric Institute, a national association of shareholder-owned power companies, had agreed to bankroll the program if he produced an acceptable pilot.

With McLaughlin having spent eight years searching for sponsors, I was surprised how little thought he had given to who would join what became *The McLaughlin Group* other than him as moderator and me as a conservative panelist. He had no candidates to be my liberal counterpart, and requested my suggestion. I immediately proposed Jack Germond, who I said was feisty, funny, and much farther to the Left than he admitted. I'm not sure McLaughlin knew exactly who Germond was, but—without further search—he asked Germond to join us.

McLaughlin's interest in tilting his panel rightward had waned since 1974. He now was more interested in diversity and told me the other two seats on his panel must be filled by a woman and a black man. McLaughlin wanted thirty-four-year-old Judith Miller of the *New York Times*, who had joined the newspaper's Washington bureau five years earlier with her glittering journalistic reputation still in the future. The ex-Jesuit priest had an eye for the ladies, and I think John was smitten with Judy Miller's exotic beauty.

As for the black man, McLaughlin had no idea and asked me if I had any. I suggested C. Sumner (Chuck) Stone, a *Philadelphia Daily News* editor. I had known Stone since the early 1960s when, as editor of the *Chicago Defender,* he was helpful to me as I covered Chicago's civil rights conflicts. He was an odd choice as a non-Washington journalist for a Washington talk show, but he had worked for Congressman Adam Clayton Powell of Harlem (and was an excellent source for me). Chuck was good-looking, articulate, and experienced in TV with his own interview program in Philadelphia.

We shot a pilot at WETA, the public broadcasting station in Arlington. Although I never saw the tape, it did not feel like a good performance and I gather the technical quality of the station's production was poor. McLaughlin a week later said we had to shoot a second pilot, this one at the NBC studios in Northwest Washington. After the taping on December 15, I felt our performance was even worse the second time around.

The Christmas–New Year's holidays delayed progress on the show, and my illness stopped anything from being done because McLaughlin and Moore wanted me to see the second pilot. That's why they brought the videocassette to my home on Valentine's Day. Geraldine, our two children, and I viewed the thirty-minute tape in our family room. I was still groggy from my near fatal encounter with spinal meningitis, but not so groggy I could not tell that the performance I now watched was horrible.

There was dead silence when the tape concluded. McLaughlin turned to me and, in that stentorian tone that would become familiar to TV viewers nationwide, demanded: "Novak, what do you think?" Unwilling to deliver a death sentence, I answered passively: "I think we'll get better." Another silence followed. Then McLaughlin turned to my sixteen-year-old daughter with a demand for her opinion. Zelda was lovely, demure, and a little shy, much like her mother, and never had been encouraged by me to boldly express her opinions. But she was gaining in confidence and next year as a high school senior would be editor in chief of the student newspaper.

Zelda paused for a moment, then said softly: "I think it's pretty bad." "Well, young lady," McLaughlin thundered, "what would you do about it?" She quickly replied, raising her voice a little: "Get rid of the black guy and the woman!" McLaughlin responded with his trademark chortle, but Zelda was right and we all knew it. Judy Miller and Chuck Stone were fine journalists and engaging personalities, but poor fits for McLaughlin's show.

Miller lacked opinions, and Stone lacked knowledge. The program needed Washington generalists; Miller was a foreign affairs specialist and Stone was no longer a Washingtonian.

McLaughlin in the next week asked me about replacements. From the start, I thought that Pat Buchanan would be terrific, had not McLaughlin's yearnings for diversity gotten in the way. They had been comrades in the Nixon White House and were good friends. (Buchanan had declined an invitation to be best man at McLaughlin's wedding.) But McLaughlin resisted, noting Buchanan had his own TV programs—including the nightly *Crossfire* on CNN. "Wouldn't this downgrade our product?" McLaughlin asked me. John obviously feared that the better informed, more insightful Buchanan would eclipse him. I tried to reassure McLaughlin that adding Buchanan would be a sign of strength, and McLaughlin—somewhat reluctantly, I thought—finally agreed.

With McLaughlin, Buchanan, and Novak tipping the panel rightward, we obviously needed another liberal to join Germond. Mort Kondracke was strictly McLaughlin's idea, but I thought it was brilliant. Morton Kondracke was my fellow townsman from Joliet who as a recent high school graduate worked for me for two weeks in the late summer of 1954 when I filled in as sports editor of the *Joliet Herald-News.* By 1982, Kondracke had begun a slow shuffle to the middle of the road. But when McLaughlin put his panel together, he was a senior editor for the liberal *New Republic* and still far enough Left to represent ideological diversity for the panel. He was forty-six years old but looked much younger, a needed contrast to the program's grumpy old men.

Buchanan and Kondracke both accepted, and the five of us shot a third pilot at NBC on Thursday, May 20, 1982. This quintet worked, as the previous combination had not, and WRC Channel 4, NBC's owned-and-operated station in Washington, liked what we had done so much that they were going to run the tape at seven thirty p.m. on Saturday, May 22. What's more, the plans were for WRC to run us every Saturday night at that time (a half hour after *Agronsky and Company* on WDVM Channel 9).

Dick Moore got NBC to agree to tape the show every Friday at noon at its Washington studios and to carry the program on its owned-and-operated stations in New York, Los Angeles, and Cleveland as well as in Washington. Simultaneously, Moore had arranged for WTTW Channel 11 in Chicago, a prestigious public TV station, to carry the program and sponsor it for all Public Broadcasting outlets except for those in the four designated NBC cities. Edison Electric was providing commercial sponsorship and financing.

From the start, the capital's political mavens loved *The McLaughlin Group* as a substitute for *Agronsky and Company*, which had become predictable. Germond was no enthusiast about anything run by John McLaughlin. But after a month of programs, Jack noted to me (out of McLaughlin's hearing) that talk around town about the program was growing at an "exponential" rate.

In all fairness to a man I came to loath, McLaughlin's skillful performance as moderator had a lot to do with the program's instant popularity. This was neither the demagogic Nixon apologist of the past nor the autocratic TV shouter of the future. McLaughlin was innovative when not consumed by ego, and in the early stages of *The McLaughlin Group* his obnoxious personality was restrained by fear of failure. I think it galled John that each of his four colleagues on the panel, all younger, was better known than he was and knew more about both politics and broadcasting. At age fifty-five, he knew this was his last chance to become rich and famous.

THREE WEEKS AFTER being diagnosed with spinal meningitis, I concluded I was not going to die from the disease and wrote Rowly a two-and-a-half page memo thanking him for doing all the work during the past three weeks. The memo's tone indicated I was physically and psychologically spent, gloomy about my future at age fifty-one:

> . . . I well remember that each of us agreed [last summer] that we were working at the peak of productive capacity and could do no more. Now, some nine months later, I must *reduce* the level of my work.

The solution was to hire a full-time reporter. I had raised the idea with Rowly the previous summer and he expressed reluctance as he always did with any suggestion that would cost our partnership money—a TV set, a refrigerator, and then a color TV set. He finally accepted these expenditures, as he did now for a $16,000-a-year reporter ($35,000 in 2007 dollars).

We quickly agreed the reporter would be John Fund, who in 1981 as a University of California at Davis student was the best intern we ever had. He was well equipped to take off our backs the burden of writing the column for *The Star* and the special column we then wrote for weekly newspapers, plus legwork for our column. I called Fund in Davis, where I thought he was graduating in June. John informed me he still had a quarter to go but could come to work in September. I told him that was too late, that it was now or never: leave college without a degree, or permanently give up a chance to work for us. He left college. (John later picked up his degree. But

I believe his subsequent splendid career with the *Wall Street Journal* was made possible because Evans & Novak, not a UC Davis degree, was on his résumé.)

Although I stressed in my memo to Rowly that I needed to make more money as well as cut my workload, my financial situation was not nearly so desperate as I indicated. My new CNN annual salary was up to $15,000 ($31,400 in 2007 money), the McLaughlin payment began at $15,600 and my net income for 1982 from multiple sources totaled $138,000 (the equivalent of $289,000 in 2007 dollars). I wasn't rich, but I was getting by nicely.

MY ILLNESS HAD forced me to cancel a trip to Central America, which I considered a key battleground in the cold war but then was on the back burner in the Reagan White House. Nicaragua had joined Cuba as the second Communist state in the hemisphere, and a full-scale war against communist guerrillas was being waged in El Salvador. Low-level civil war persisted in Guatemala, and a leftist insurgency was in danger of sprouting in Honduras. But Ronald Reagan, the staunchest cold warrior to enter the Oval Office, had yet to heed these developments. That enabled State Department professionals to carry on the same passive policy they ran under Jimmy Carter.

I rescheduled my Central America trip, arriving in San Salvador on Sunday, May 16, for a ten-day journey through four countries. The winds were blowing rightward in embattled Salvador. To the State Department's dismay, voters had just expressed their frustration with vacillation in handling the Marxist insurrection by giving a dynamic new political party, the right-wing National Republican Alliance (ARENA), a majority in the National Assembly. ARENA was eager to tell its story to a conservative columnist from Washington and arranged an informal buffet supper at the home of a rich supporter to meet the party's leaders.

The host was Guillermo (Billy) Sol, an American-educated (Texas A&M 1952) landowner getting into politics for the first time. He was among Salvadoran businessmen who felt that the land reform policies of the former president, Christian Democrat Juan Napoleon Duarte, were wrecking the economy without stalling the communist guerrillas. Sol picked me up at the Hotel Camino Real. I was surprised he was driving his own auto without a bodyguard. When I mentioned this as we drove away from the hotel, he told me to look behind us. We were trailed by a truck-load of heavily armed men. Sol had reason to be cautious. His arm was in a cast because of gunshot wounds—fired, he said, by Duarte's Christian Democrats rather than Communists.

The National Assembly was in session that night to water down Duarte's land reform, which looked to me a lot like the old Bolshevik model but was uncritically applauded by the U.S. State Department. Arriving late at Billy Sol's spacious home were ARENA's leading assemblymen, who had just passed their bill. They were headed by the newly elected Assembly president: Roberto D'Aubuisson, a thirty-eight-year-old former major in the army's secret service. To read the U.S. and European press, he was the most notorious figure in the hemisphere—accused of leading death squads and called a "pathological killer."

D'Aubuisson was small, dark, and intense. Taking off his jacket in Billy Sol's living room, he revealed an automatic pistol stuck in his belt. I wrote in an Evans & Novak column of May 24 that D'Aubuisson sounds more like Ronald Reagan, whom he "greatly admires, than a Latin American *caudillo* as he talks about free-market economics."

I did not know the truth about D'Aubuisson's past, but I liked him and what he said about the present—describing him as El Salvador's "most charismatic" political figure. He was devastated that the United States was supporting land reform and other leftist economic programs ruining the country's economy. His theme was that Ronald Reagan could not possibly be consciously pursuing this disastrous agenda. In my column, I pointed up the irony of Reagan's representatives defending "confiscation or collectivization of private property against exponents of a free market economy." In fact, it would be ARENA and D'Aubuisson, not Duarte, who would lead El Salvador to victory over the Communists.

The U.S. diplomats I met in Central America were earnest professionals, but almost all seemed oblivious to the Sandinista regime establishing the first Marxist-Leninist state on the American mainland. The exception was the U.S. ambassador to Honduras: John Negroponte, a forty-two-year-old Foreign Service officer on his first ambassadorial assignment. During a one-on-one dinner at his residence in Tegucigalpa, Negroponte stressed the need to stop the Communists in Salvador and get rid of them in Nicaragua. "Alone among senior U.S. diplomats I met in Central America, Negroponte perceives the potential trail of fallen dominoes triggered by Nicaragua," I wrote in the *American Spectator*.

My faithful source John Carbaugh at that time was covering Central America for Senator Jesse Helms and was invaluable to me in putting me in touch with sources throughout this trip. In the lobby of the Hotel Maya in Tegucigalpa, I met and conversed with two men whom I never would have been able to contact had it not been for Carbaugh. Dressed in blue jeans and polo shirts, they were former officers of dictator Anastasio Somoza's

National Guard and leaders of the anti-Sandinista guerrillas (the future Contras), located in a secret location in Honduras. They told me their ranks expanded with new volunteers after each new cross-border raid into Nicaragua. But they admitted being in desperate need of arms and trainers from the United States.

In Managua, I lunched with Adolfo Calero, the Coca-Cola bottler there who I was told would have a lot to say if I gained his confidence. He was a big, good-natured man who picked me up in his Mercedes to take me to an elegant little restaurant. Like other private citizens I met in Managua, he described Sandinista Nicaragua as a Communist police state. Swearing me to secrecy, he described himself as part of the anti-Sandinista underground. (He soon left Managua to become the Contra civilian leader in Washington.)

"I think your Ambassador is too soft," Calero told me, referring to the boyish-looking new U.S. envoy in Managua, Anthony C. Quainton. "I would say your diplomacy is very meek." In his second ambassadorial posting at age forty-one, Quainton was a rising star in the Foreign Service. He would not publicly label Nicaragua's Sandinistas a Communist regime—a ridiculous position he reiterated to me privately over drinks at his residence.

I concluded in the *American Spectator* that "the role of the United States in Central America seems confused, contradictory, committed to no overriding strategy." But the Reagan Revolution would reassert itself in Central America before long.

ON FRIDAY, May 28, 1982, General Alexander Haig was forced out as secretary of state. Haig was less than a true-believing Reaganaut. A protégé of Henry Kissinger, he overrode Reagan's own wishes as he more vigorously pursued détente with Moscow. But the Evans & Novak column treated Haig more gently than other apostates, protected frankly as a longtime source of Rowly's. On the day Haig fell, Rowly had just completed a European reporting trip and was taking a little vacation time with Katherine at an English country inn. That meant I would write the column for Monday, May 31, and it would not be nearly as understanding of Haig as it would have been had Evans been in Washington.

In that May 31 column, I noted that the dismissal of Richard V. Allen as national security adviser had not been, as generally interpreted, "a coup for Haig, cementing his vicarship." Instead, it sealed his fate. Allen's successor was William Clark, Reagan's close friend and first chief of staff as governor, who "would not tolerate Haig's insistence on overriding everybody— including the president himself—on policy questions." Haig's final mistake was setting himself against Reagan's hard-line opposition to the proposed Soviet natural gas pipeline to western Europe.

The Evans & Novak column had lost a source, but Reagan had gained a secretary of state in George Shultz who would not interfere with his winning the cold war.

THE MAY 31 *Newsweek* described what was purported to be the president's rage ("Ronald Reagan, mad as hell, was not going to take it anymore," the story began) over the "steady drumbeat of criticism from the Republican right, much of it aimed at chief of staff James A. Baker III." *Newsweek* reported:

> The critics find outlets not only in New Right publications . . . but also in the Evans and Novak column, which some Reagan aides call "Errors and No-facts." Not long ago the President himself, incensed by an Evans and Novak column accusing Baker of sniping at Secretary of State Alexander Haig, dashed off a note—unsent—calling the columnists' sources "liars—repeat—liars." Some Reagan advisers suspect Evans and Novak of giving space to anti-Baker sentiment to help derail a possible 1984 Presidential bid by [Vice President] Bush in favor of Rep. Jack Kemp, if Reagan does not run again.

The authors of the story listed by *Newsweek* were two strong liberals: White House reporter Eleanor Clift, my future colleague on *The McLaughlin Group,* and deputy Washington bureau chief James Doyle, my old source in the Watergate special prosecutor's team. They might seem odd as protectors of Ronald Reagan from his vilifiers, but they were being fed by Jimmy Baker.

Nobody in my long experience was more skillful in manipulating reporters than Baker, who devoted the equivalent of one full working day each week to massaging the important news media. Eleanor Clift and other newsmagazine reporters came by at week's end for a Baker "feeding." Baker boosted the president's cause, but his primary concern was protecting Jimmy Baker. *Newsweek*'s hit job was Baker's retaliation for our criticism of him though he couched this in terms of the president, not himself, denouncing us. The remarks in *Newsweek* did not sound much like Reagan, who never in our meetings ever uttered a word critical of me. It sounded like Baker, and that did not bother me.

But it bothered Bob McCandless, my former target who had become not only a source but a friend. He insisted I could not, as a leading conservative columnist, afford to be called a purveyor of lies by the president. He urged me to go to Baker in the White House and inform him that attack and counterattack between us should not continue. In effect, McCandless was urging a mutual nonaggression pact, which I considered a lapse in journalistic ethics. Still I pondered what McCandless proposed, and after a week asked Baker for an appointment.

I was uneasy about my mission when I entered Baker's White House office at eleven a.m., Friday, June 11, 1982, with nobody else present. After small talk I told Baker I did not appreciate his smearing me to newsmagazine reporters. He neither denied nor defended his conduct. "Jim," I said, "I don't think any column has been more supportive of the president on the issues—tax policy and the cold war—than ours. I don't think we deserve the treatment you've given us."

Baker, after a moment's silence, said something I never shall forget: "Bob, we appreciate your support of the president. But you have been very unfair to me." There was nothing wrong in the literal meaning of what Baker said. But I interpreted him as really telling me: "It's all very well for you to be in the bag for Reagan, but I'm interested in what you do for *me*."

After our conversation on June 11, Baker and I treated each other differently. He stopped dumping on me in conversations with other reporters. The column was still zinging Baker on occasion (on July 9 I wrote that Baker and Stockman had foisted on Reagan "a policy of austerity in the teeth of a recession."). But my hits on Baker were less frequent and not nearly so punishing. In the early autumn of 1982, I hardly mentioned him and, halfway through a column of October 4, wrote: "Baker, stigmatized as a liberal mole but actually a traditional conservative, has industriously mended his fences on the right."

Had Baker changed? Had I merely reassessed his posture? Or had I backed off in a tacit version of the mutual nonaggression pact McCandless suggested? The last possibility was no way for an independent journalist to act. It bothered me in 1982 and still troubles me today.

I WAS SCHEDULED to address a business group in Atlanta on Thursday, August 19, 1982, and I called Ed Turner at CNN headquarters to make a date for dinner on August 18. I wanted to review my future, if any, with CNN as the cable network began its third year. As I expected, the daily commentaries for Rowly and me had run their course. All that was left for us was alternating, every other week, on the *Newsmaker Saturday* interview program hosted by Daniel Schorr.

Turner made a dinner reservation at Bones, a steak house on the outskirts of Atlanta, for what I had hoped would be a confidential chat. Consequently, I was disconcerted to see Ed walk in with Burt Reinhardt, president of CNN. Reinhardt had been a cold fish in dealings with me. An old news service executive (UP Movietone News), he concentrated on pinching pennies.

Over dinner, Reinhardt and Ed Turner indicated they were not pleased with *Press Box,* a half-hour weekend discussion program. Indeed, Ed asked Reinhardt, "What would you think, Burt, if we put back together the 'Evans and Novak' interview show I had at Metromedia to replace 'Press Box'?"

I was ecstatic to have my own interview program again, and thought Rowly would be as well. But when I telephoned him the next morning, he expressed concern we would be pushed into live Saturday broadcasts. I was too insensitive to realize that at age sixty-one and with no money worries, my partner had started the long, slow glide to retirement. He did not want a new TV show to interfere with weekends at his farm in Rappahanock County, Virginia, where he would ride his horse and enjoy bibulous dinners with the neighboring country squires.

We were told we could tape the show Friday except under extraordinary circumstances. Rowly could still ride his horse Saturdays. CNN in those days was short of programming, so *Evans and Novak* would be broadcast for the first time at seven p.m. on Saturday and then be repeated three more times over the weekend.

We got Ed Meese as the guest for our first program to be taped at ten a.m. on Thursday, September 9, 1982. We made a little news when Meese predicted Reagan would seek a second term in 1984, the first time anybody that close to the president had said so. Our little show was off on a twenty-year run—an eternity in television.

CHAPTER 32

The Slowest Realignment in American History

I N THE 1982 midterm election, Democrats gained twenty-six seats in the House, wiping out the operational control of the House that had passed Reagan's tax and budget measures in 1981. The Republicans maintained their eight-seat margin in the Senate. My *Evans-Novak Political Report* forecast had overestimated Republican losses—thirty-four in the House and two in the Senate. That reflected my opinion of the way the White House ran the campaign.

Michael Deaver's schedule for Reagan was calibrated entirely to the president's own political needs and not to help the party's candidates. I was aboard Reagan's press plane his last two days of 1982 campaigning (in the Rocky Mountain West). In an Evans & Novak column datelined Las Vegas, I wrote that Reagan's political operation "could find no other states where he was welcome and where [his aides] would risk sending him." I continued:

> Failing all year to devise a campaign strategy, the President's men did not even focus the Great Communicator for [the last] week's finale (a failing that explains why a major election-eve address was ruled out). Instead, speechwriters patched bits and pieces of old Reagan oratory into a pastiche of warmed-over sloganeering.
>
> The dispirited trek hit bottom when Air Force One arrived in Las Vegas. The President was rushed to the Convention Center where a surrealistic scene awaited him: a hurriedly arranged, late-afternoon rally entertained by Robert Goulet and Wayne Newton, with performers in tuxedos and revealing black evening gowns. . . .
>
> The yearlong exercise by senior aide Mike Deaver to protect the President at all costs put Reagan in the mountain states and the inside newspaper pages for the campaign's last week. If President Nixon was

reviled for his final outrageous burst of midterm campaigning in 1970,
President Reagan a dozen years later was ignored.

Wayne Newton crooning and showgirls prancing symbolized to me the
political folly of backing away from the Reagan Revolution. The 1981 passage of the Reagan tax cut was a huge political triumph, but the bill was
back-loaded to delay its impact. Worse yet, David Stockman and Bob Dole
convinced Reagan to go along with "budget-balancing" tax increases the
following year. Late in 1982, Reagan drew the line against further tax hikes.
But it was too late to avert double-digit unemployment that assured Republican losses in the midterms.

My postelection Evans & Novak column was ridiculed because I put forward as Republican models two candidates who were defeated on November
2 ("Learning From 2 Losers," was the *Washington Post* headline). Multimillionaire businessmen running for governor in their first and only bids for
public office—Lewis Lehrman in New York and Richard Headlee in Michigan—had winnowed down to single-digits the landslide leads by heavily
favored Democrats (Mario Cuomo and James Blanchard). "While the President was urging Americans to stay the course, Lehrman and Headlee took a
hard right-populist turn: cut taxes to induce prosperity." I continued:

> Nothing important has happened in the White House this year with-
> out Jim Baker's approval. He is neither a visionary nor ideologue, but
> a practical man accustomed to dealing with today's, not tomorrow's,
> problems. Nevertheless, the demonstrated popular appeal of two
> right-wing visionaries dismissed as hopeless cases conceivably could
> influence him at this turning point for the Reagan presidency.

Indeed, after the 1982 elections, Dave Stockman and Bob Dole lost
Chief of Staff Baker as a dependable tax-raising ally. Whether Baker was
reading tea leaves from November 2 or interpreting a stiffer spine from Reagan, he abandoned the tax increasers. Ronald Reagan had agreed to his last
tax hike.

AT THREE P.M. on November 1, 1982, Geraldine and I were in a Capitol
Hill real estate office to close the sale of the house at 1 Terrace Court N.E.
behind the Supreme Court that we had bought just before we were married
in 1962.

We lived at Terrace Court for only a year and a half but kept the little
row house as a rental property. Now we were selling it for $75,000 (a gain of

$57,500) and I would turn the proceeds over to Richard Gilder, a man I had met only a few weeks earlier. It would guarantee financial security for me and my family, and the immediate cause was a critical decision by Paul Volcker.

Volcker was appointed chairman of the Federal Reserve by two presidents—Jimmy Carter and Ronald Reagan—each of whom preferred someone else but was pressured by economic advisers and the financial establishment to name a "sound" moneyman. I wrote more about monetary policy than any Washington political columnist, and most of it was critical of Volcker's tight money policies. Volcker's critics included not only supply-side Republicans but also easy-money Democrats, who formed a momentary alliance.

Within the administration and in Congress, there was strong sentiment for Reagan to drop Volcker when his term as chairman ended in 1983. But in October 1982 just before the midterm elections, the Fed announced it was no longer targeting the M1 money supply aggregate. Volcker was abandoning Milton Friedman's monetarist theories, and that meant the central bank was easing. It won Volcker reappointment by Reagan.

The stock market boomed. Jude Wanniski told me I could take it to the bank. He also gave me the name of the banker: Dick Gilder. A handsome, debonair New Yorker who lived on Fifth Avenue, Gilder was a multimillionaire in 1982 and would make millions more in the coming bull market. He would become a buyer of American historical documents and a prominent philanthropist (who donated seventeen million dollars in 1993 for a bridle path in New York's Central Park). An early supply-sider he was a selective contributor to the right kind of Republican candidate. Gilder in 1999 founded the Club for Growth to funnel campaign funds into ideologically connected primary elections.

But what was relevant about Gilder for me was that he was a world-class stock picker. I was fifty-two years old and had owned hardly any common stock when I decided that Volcker's policy reversal, plus Reagan's tax cut, made this the moment to invest the full $75,000. I met Gilder at the Gilder Gagnon offices in Manhattan, and he agreed to manage my money though it was below his normal minimum. Gilder's rule: He would invest for me without discussion or permission. He did not buy stocks on the Dow-Jones Industrial Index but invested in new companies with great ideas—Federal Express, to begin with for me. I had been netting $6,200 a year in rental income from the Terrace Court property, but before long Gilder had doubled my $75,000—and that was just the start. If you are not a rock star, NBA player, or drug trafficker, it is hard to get rich without investment income.

That's what Dick Gilder did for me (with assists from Paul Volcker and Ronald Reagan).

TEDDY KENNEDY'S announcement after the 1982 elections that he would not run for president in 1984 disappointed the romantics yearning for Camelot II. But it cheered Democratic realists who saw Kennedy as the probable nominee but certain to lose big against Reagan in the general election. The Democratic problem was that with Teddy out, probable nominee Fritz Mondale was no less liberal and appeared just as sure a landslide loser in November.

The only apparent hope to guide the Democrats back to the center looked like Senator John Glenn. Actually, the heroic marine aviator and astronaut did not dissent from the liberal dogma of Kennedy and Mondale. I doubt Glenn ever gave much thought to public policy until he became a national celebrity and was embraced by the Kennedys. He swallowed whole the liberal agenda, but he just did not *seem* like a liberal.

Greg Schneiders, who had gotten into politics in 1976 as Jimmy Carter's body man and now supported Glenn, told me over lunch at the Palm that the senator's listless candidacy would be energized by a new movie, *The Right Stuff,* based on Tom Wolfe's best-selling book about the Apollo 7 astronauts—especially Glenn.

That did not happen. Glenn was widely derided by political reporters as boring and less than bright. Still, I had not totally given up on Glenn, and I followed him to Florida just before Christmas 1983. Glenn's strategists saw Florida with its military and aerospace infrastructure as receptive to the old astronaut's appeal. But instead of sticking to "values" as planned, he harped on a budget deficit he promised to narrow with a massive tax increase. During a press conference in Boca Raton, I asked Glenn why he would not raise taxes high enough to completely erase the budget deficit. When Glenn replied that would wreck the economy, I asked him how he knew just how much of a tax increase would not hurt. He mumbled unresponsively as tax increasers always did when I asked that question.

Alone with the candidate for a brief chat, Glenn told me he had something he wanted to discuss, strictly off the record. The issue of gays in the military had arisen, and the marine colonel jet pilot stressed to me he was absolutely against it. "Bob, I can tell you, this is absolutely destructive of morale and discipline," he said. While I detected his handlers programming the candidate to appeal to a conservative columnist, I had no doubt of John Glenn's sincerity. That might have been the worst news for him. The homosexual lobby was gaining strength among Democrats, and an antigay candidate was going nowhere in the party. That day in Florida convinced me that if anybody was going to stop Mondale for the nomination, it was not going to be John Glenn.

I thought Mondale's nomination was so certain that I skipped my quadrennial expedition to Iowa. Mondale scored a lopsided victory there, winning 45 percent of the vote against a humiliated Glenn's 5 percent. Senator Gary Hart of Colorado, the 1972 George McGovern campaign manager, finished an unexpected second with 16 percent—and was declared the "winner" by the news media!

Reporters thought Mondale pedestrian, a certain loser to Reagan, and he was no fun to cover. With Hart in hot pursuit of Mondale, he suddenly became the second coming of JFK. Except for movie star good looks and reckless personal behavior, Jack Kennedy and Gary Hart had little in common. Whatever his faults, JFK was interesting in private and inspiring in public. I found Hart dull in personal conversation and unable to stir an audience.

Not long after his Iowa "triumph," Hart came to New Hampshire with his first speech, on the environment, scheduled at a landfill outside Manchester. Much of the national press corps was there to hear him.

On the edge of the crowd was Pat Caddell. As a twenty-two-year-old fresh out of Harvard, Caddell had polled for McGovern's presidential campaign in 1972 and then formed his own polling company (whose smallest, most irregular client was Evans & Novak). By the time Caddell backed Jimmy Carter for president, he was also a key political strategist—a role he played throughout the Carter presidency.

At the New Hampshire landfill, Caddell told me Hart was accepting his advice: to depict Mondale as part of the "old politics" and asked me whether the state's Democratic leaders still thought Mondale was going to win New Hampshire. When I replied that they did, Caddell told me: "They have no idea. Believe me, Hart will win here." Trusting shrewd political analysts such as Caddell often put me ahead of the pack in predicting political outcomes. This time I flinched. In my February 27 column the day before the primary, the best I could do was a super-cautious forecast that Hart "could well pass Glenn, surpass 20 percent and keep Mondale below 30 percent."

Just as Caddell predicted, Hart won New Hampshire—easily, with 39 percent to Mondale's 27 percent. He soared ahead of Mondale in the polls nationally and in states to be contested on "Super Tuesday." When Hart ran away with the Florida primary that day, it meant the Illinois primary on March 20 was critical for Mondale. The old Democratic machine was not what it used to be but was enough to provide Mondale a 41 percent to 35 percent victory, surprising everyone and halting Hart's momentum. Mondale would lose to Hart in Ohio and California, but he won many more primaries than he lost after Illinois. The Illinois primary really ended Hart's improbable challenge. Sooner or later, voters had to take a good look at Hart and seek a reason to vote for him other than the fact that he was not Mondale. That's what they started doing in Illinois.

ON FEBRUARY 28, 1984, New Hampshire primary day, I received a telephone call from Sol Levine. He was producer of CNN's *Crossfire* and wanted me to appear on that night's program as conservative co-host, substituting for Pat Buchanan. It was my *Crossfire* debut, but supposedly only a one-shot appearance. I had no idea this would begin a major part of my life for twenty-one years.

Crossfire in 1984 was CNN's hottest program. Its origins dated back to 1977 when two combatants from the 1972 presidential campaign—Pat Buchanan (a Nixon speechwriter) and Frank Mankiewicz (McGovern's campaign director)—put together a three-minute daily syndicated radio mini-debate called *Confrontation*. Mankiewicz soon took a better job as head of National Public Radio and was replaced by Tom Braden, his collaborator in a double-byline syndicated column marketed (without success) as a liberal version of Evans & Novak. Mankiewicz might have been a match for Buchanan, but not Braden, too slow of thought to handle the ferocious and quick-witted lifelong Washingtonian.

Buchanan and Braden soon became an established team on both talk radio and television. With Ed Turner as midwife, *Crossfire* was born June 25, 1982, as a nightly half-hour right-versus-left interview program.

With no cable television in Washington, I had never seen the program when Levine called me. If I had, I would have known it was an interview show in name only. The hosts' "questions" were declarations concluded by question marks, and the guests responded with their own speeches. After watching *Crossfire* a few times, it seemed to me the program should be called *The Buchanan Show*. Buchanan dominated Braden so thoroughly he reminded me of the Harlem Globetrotters of my youth, then the world's best basketball team, as they toyed with their touring partners, the all-white and all-losing Washington Generals.

Buchanan was forty-three, twenty years Braden's junior, when *Crossfire* was launched. Braden and his glamorous wife, Joan, traveled the same dinner circuit frequented by Rowly and Kay Evans. From afar, Tom had seemed to me as glamorous as his wife. He had spent years in CIA secret operations, had owned a daily newspaper in Oceanside, California, bankrolled by Nelson Rockefeller (Joan's great and good friend), and once ran for lieutenant governor of California. His white-shoe pals regarded him as the salt of the earth. But he was rude and unpleasant to me, whether he looked down on me as a commoner or was demonstrating contempt for all conservatives.

I was an inadequate stand-in for Buchanan that night. I was an experienced television interviewer, but questions on *Crossfire* were designed to elicit not information but conflict—and entertainment. It took me a while to figure it out.

THE DEMOCRATS FINALLY figured it out in 1984 that, for five presidential elections starting in 1964, the party holding the least contentious national convention won in November. Walter Mondale's campaign was determined that the July convention in San Francisco would escape the acrimony that marked the party's conventions in losing years. Indeed, it was the first Democratic gathering completely free of internal strife since 1940. It was also more peaceable than the contentious Republican convention in Dallas the next month.

But Mondale's fate would be sealed by two decisions he made in San Francisco. One was the selection of his vice presidential running mate. The other was his promise to raise taxes if elected. Each was regarded within the Mondale inner circle as a coup. Each was a catastrophe.

Arriving in San Francisco late on Wednesday, July 11, the week before the convention, I went to my room in the San Francisco Hilton and hit the telephone in quest of sources. The only one I could get on the line was David Rubinstein, a former humble Carter White House staffer and future fabulously rich founding partner of the Carlyle Group investment bankers.

Now, in San Francisco, Rubinstein was helping the Mondale campaign. He told me Mondale had made his decision for vice president and would announce the next day, July 12, that it was Congresswoman Geraldine Ferraro. He said I better move fast if I wanted CNN to be first with the news. Although I assured CNN producers my source was gold-plated, they said they needed confirmation from a second source. By the time they got it, the news was out on other networks. Four years earlier, CNN had blown my scoop that George Bush would be Ronald Reagan's running mate.

Ferraro was included on Mondale's vice presidential short list, but I had not taken her seriously because of her slender résumé. Gerry Ferraro was unknown to the public when she appeared on CNN's *Evans and Novak* before the convention in her role of platform chairman. This was her first contact with Mort Kondracke, substituting for Rowly on that program, and he was impressed. Mort, trying hard to see the best in the Democrats, in our postinterview commentary said: "I thought that was a terrific performance. . . . I had always feared . . . that having a woman in the vice presidential slot would become the issue of the campaign rather than Ronald Reagan's record and I think she could sort of put that issue to rest."

I did not add something I thought too subjective and personal for TV commentary. Her performance on *Evans and Novak* reinforced my impression of her reached after covering her during platform committee meetings: a fast-talking, wise-cracking bottle blonde, New Yorker to the core. She was the first Democrat on a national ticket with a distinctive New York accent since Al Smith, and I wondered whether she would do any better than he had in the hinterland. She also struck me as arrogant. But after I got to know and like her as co-host on *Crossfire* eight years later, I came to believe this appearance of arrogance masked insecurity. If she worried about being overmatched on *Crossfire,* what must she have thought about being thrown into a frightening new world in 1984?

In our telephone conversation the night of July 11, Rubinstein was ebullient, viewing Ferraro as a masterstroke. Mondale's chaotic vice presidential selection process, Rubinstein added, had narrowly averted disaster. The logical choice was Senator Lloyd Bentsen of Texas to try to save part of the South, but Mondale advisers wanted a more daring selection. They needed a woman. Rubinstein told me Mondale was "enchanted" by his preconvention interview with Mayor Dianne Feinstein of San Francisco. Based on national experience, her résumé was even skimpier than Ferraro's. "Enchanting" she was, however: statuesque, elegant, with a melodious voice. In the Evans & Novak column written on Wednesday, July 12, I said:

> As late as Tuesday night, Feinstein was Mondale's first choice, but nobody saluted that flag. . . .
>
> [T]he Feinstein trial balloon was sinking quickly. Did Mondale really want a thrice-married, once-divorced Jewish woman who had made unavoidable political accommodations with the San Francisco homosexual community and who lacked experience above the municipal level?

But I did not disclose the real reason Feinstein was dumped. Rubinstein told me the background check found that Feinstein's fabulously rich husband, international investment banker Richard Blum, would not pass muster. "I'm so glad we really checked carefully this time," said Rubinstein, referring to the catastrophic failure of due diligence on Tom Eagleton's mental health record in 1972. But there was no thorough check of Ferraro and her New York real estate developer husband, John Zaccaro. Mondale's aides did not even know that Ferraro had failed to include her husband's income in her congressional financial disclosure. The Republicans did not overlook it, and Reagan campaign manager Ed Rollins had the Democrats off balance right up to Labor Day by raising questions about the ethics of Geraldine and John Zaccaro.

For San Francisco in mid-July, Democrats (and many journalists) shared Rubinstein's optimism that the first woman on a national ticket would widen the gender gap enough to elect Mondale. One poll during the convention even showed Mondale passing Reagan in the popular vote. I didn't take that seriously. I suspected there were women who would not appreciate Gerry Ferraro's style and that some from an older generation would not want any woman on the ticket. Holding that view was Jane Sanders Novak. After the convention she phoned to tell me her favorite niece, Lucille, had told her how thrilled she was by a woman vice president. "Well," my mother said, "it makes me sick."

What would be the campaign's climactic moment came on the convention's last night with the presidential nominee's acceptance speech. In the CNN booth a couple of hours before the speech, I read through Mondale's prepared text, which struck me as uninspired—until I came upon this line: "Mr. Reagan will raise taxes, and so will I. He won't tell you. I just did." It was sheer madness that Mondale thought a promise to raise taxes would win votes.

I underlined this historic line in Mondale's speech, and went on the convention floor to see Dan Rostenkowski. The chairman of the House Ways and Means Committee was seated in the front row of the Illinois delegation. I handed him the underlined passage, and his physical reaction was more eloquent than anything he might have said. Rosty slumped his big body in his chair, cast his eyes up to heaven, and contorted his expressive Polish face in a look of pain. Whatever faint chance Mondale had was lost in San Francisco.

WHEN REPUBLICANS GATHERED in Dallas in August 1984, temperatures exceeded one hundred degrees. I was staying at the decrepit Dallas Hilton and there were no convention floor votes or debates. Yet, it was an extraordinary political event for me. The Reagan Revolution went forward at Dallas without the approval of Ronald Reagan—or at least that of Chief of Staff James Baker.

It was a revolution of rank-and-file conservative delegates led by House Minority Whip Trent Lott, an ardent Reaganite. Jim Baker had committed a rare tactical error in letting supply-sider Lott become platform chairman. Baker assumed that Lott, as a party man, would follow White House orders. Instead, Lott packed the platform committee leadership with his allies.

Lott vetoed Richard Darman as White House liaison to the platform committee. Darman, Baker's policy aide, was a co-conspirator with David Stockman (incredibly, still the OMB director) in pushing for tax increases. With Darman forced to watch the convention on TV from Martha's Vineyard (a playground for rich liberal Democrats), Baker talked Drew Lewis, now CEO of Warner Amex Cable Communications, into taking the thankless liaison task.

Lott and Jack Kemp wanted—and got—an economic plank that endorsed the gold standard, a flat tax, and doubling the personal tax exemption—all opposed by Lewis on behalf of the White House. What Baker and Stockman back in Washington really wanted in the platform was "wiggle room" for the president to raise taxes as a "last resort." Baker should have known that "wiggle room" language would validate Mondale's prediction of a Reagan tax increase. Lott prevailed, saving Reagan from his own staff. I reported the conclusion of the previous week's fight from Dallas on August 20, the first day of the convention:

> The moment of truth for the 1984 Republican National Convention came when the White House agent on the platform, Drew Lewis, was rebuffed by Rep. Tom Loeffler of Texas [Chief Deputy Minority Whip of the House and Lott's deputy in the platform fight].
>
> Lewis asked Loeffler not to press his platform amendment removing the White House-requested "wiggle room" for President Reagan to raise taxes next year. "The President won't like this," said Lewis. "You mean Dick Darman won't like it," the Congressman snapped back. . . .
>
> Ronald Reagan himself seemed remote and shadowy. . . . Lott, Kemp and their allies said they were acting in accordance with the President's "true wishes."

MEG GREENFIELD, editorial page editor of the *Washington Post*, invited a group of politicians and journalists (including me and Geraldine) for a preconvention dinner party at Ruth's Chris Steakhouse in Dallas on Wednesday, August 15. Drew Lewis, who had been making no progress with Lott and Kemp (also at the dinner), was out of sorts that night. He was not going to bring up the tax issue over dinner, but he got going on abortion.

Lewis was unhappy personally with the platform plank that was even more prolife than the 1980 version and contained no exemptions for rape, incest, and the life of the mother. He had quite a bit to drink and launched a diatribe about the religious right taking over the Republican Party. I said the Christians were essential to Republicans becoming the majority party and more important than proabortion country club Republicans.

Lewis abruptly turned to Geraldine, whom he had never met before. "Now, Mrs. Novak," he said. "Surely you favor exemptions for rape, incest and the life of the mother, don't you?" Geraldine detested political debate, and I'm sure she would rather have been anywhere else. But she was asked a direct question and answered it: "No, I don't." "You are not in favor of *any* exemptions?" Lewis persisted. "No." "Not even for the life of the mother?" "No," she insisted. A moment of silence followed, before an embarrassed Lewis told my wife: "Well, that's your opinion, and stick to it." Lewis had no idea that my wife was a prolife activist doing volunteer work for the National Right to Life Committee. I could not have been more proud of her courageous stand taken with a couple dozen pairs of eyes fixed on her.

I thought the little exchange between Drew Lewis and Geraldine Novak epitomized the debate in Dallas and, indeed, within the Republican Party. Drew symbolized corporate executives, lawyers, lobbyists, and campaign consultants who were trying to plane down the new Republican Party's rough edges. Geraldine typified new Republicans who were loyal to Reagan but not to Reagan's aides. She had come to Washington twenty-four years earlier as a born-and-bred Texas Democrat, a twenty-three-year-old secretary on Lyndon B. Johnson's staff. She had changed her registration to Republican mainly because of abortion. If the Republican Party abandoned her on this issue, I knew she would abandon the Republican Party. I'm not sure that Drew Lewis fully understood that.

THE RUNNING STATE-by-state count of electoral votes I kept for the *Evans-Novak Political Report* showed Geraldine Ferraro had helped Mondale not at all. After the Democratic convention, I had Reagan leading Mondale 504 to 34 in electoral votes. After the Republican convention a month later, I had Mondale winning only Minnesota and the District of Columbia, losing 525 to 13.

I was on the press plane for Reagan's first major post–Labor Day campaigning on September 12 in upstate New York. The *Washington Post* used my headline for the September 15 column from Buffalo: "Mush From The Gipper." Reagan campaign manager Ed Rollins was the anonymous source who told me to expect a campaign "diet of pure mush" from Reagan, fitting the syrupy TV advertising campaign of Reagan's "Morning in America." Why cut up Mondale or offer new programs with the polling too good to be believed?

On Sunday, October 7, in Louisville, Kentucky, when the candidates met in the first of two debates, I found it difficult to concentrate on presidential politics. The Chicago Cubs, the baseball team of my childhood, appeared headed for their first National League pennant since 1945. The Cubs led two games to none over the San Diego Padres in the best-of-five League championship series and needed only to win that afternoon. I watched the game on TV from a Louisville hotel bar, and saw the Cubs kick away the game. I had a premonition the Cubs would lose the next two games and lose the pennant once more. They did. I had a further premonition that Dutch Reagan, the old Cubs radio broadcaster, would lose that night's debate. He did.

My account in the *Evans-Novak Political Report* described the Louisville event as the "most one-sided televised Presidential Debate since they began in 1960"—a clear victory for Mondale. I continued:

[T]he Debate was so *devastating* for the President (who appeared overtrained, overstatisticed, overloaded and overtired) because it showed him *stumbling and ineffective,* raising the *age issue* that the Democrats wanted to raise but could not on their own.

In the postdebate spin room where candidates' advocates now held forth, Jim Baker claimed Reagan had won. But not even that consummate spinmaster could pull that off. Outside the spin room, Reaganites whom I talked to that night were bitter about debate preparation. Senator Paul Laxalt, general chairman of the Republican Party, blamed Dick Darman for his incessant drilling of the president in debate rehearsals. Laxalt told me Nancy Reagan blamed Darman's boss, Jim Baker.

I stand by my assessment of the debate in the *ENPR.* Where I went wrong was my evaluation of its impact. Suggesting that the debate "*could* actually turn the Presidential contest into a *horse race,*" I added that a Reagan landslide "now seems considerably less certain than it appeared before." This was the worst kind of inside-the-Beltway analysis that assumed the overwhelming opinion of American voters could be overturned by one poor debate performance.

Louisville temporarily cut Reagan's popular vote lead from ten to six points, but U.S. presidents are not elected by popular votes. After the first debate, I checked carefully to detect any change in my projected electoral vote. I found a little slippage by Reagan in New York and California but nowhere else, and he led in those states. The *ENPR* still had Mondale carrying only Minnesota and D.C.

I went to the second presidential debate on October 21 in Kansas City, where Mondale needed a clear victory. He did not come close. Following my practice of traveling with a candidate in the campaign's closing days, I joined Reagan on November 1 on a swing through Illinois, Massachusetts, and New York. I wrote in a column from Rochester, New York, that Reagan's basic speech was "no longer the mushy confection of six weeks ago, thanks to a sustained assault on Mondale's tax increase." Furthermore, TV advertising had switched from "Morning in America" to hard comparisons between tax-cutting "Reaganomics" and tax-increasing "Mondaleconomics."

Nevertheless, I sniped at the Reagan campaign for the familiar failure by a Republican president to campaign for his party's congressional candidates. The cautious hand of Jimmy Baker was still evident. I concluded from Rochester: "While Fritz Mondale was riding to defeat aboard a ghost ship of Democratic totems, Ronald Reagan was marching to victory with a hollow strategy seeking no true mandate."

MY FORECASTS IN the *Evans-Novak Political Report* were accurate. Ever since the Republican convention, I had Mondale carrying only Minnesota and D.C.—exactly how it turned out. I also was exactly right with a two-seat Republican loss in the Senate but still keeping GOP control of that chamber. I underestimated the Republican gain in the House at eight seats, while it actually was fifteen—still well short of the twenty-six seats lost in 1982. Republicans missed the thirty- to thirty-two-seat gain needed to execute a back-room deal with conservative Southern Democrats to oust Tip O'Neill and achieve coalition control of the House.

However, the Democratic share of the white vote hit an all-time low, with the party losing four seats in Texas and three in North Carolina. The slowest realignment in American political history was accelerating slightly.

CHAPTER 33

"I'll Try Ollie North"

W HEN I HEARD Nancy Reagan was blaming Jim Baker for Ronald Reagan's poor performance in the 1984 Louisville debate, I figured there would be a new White House chief of staff in 1985. Actually, Baker had had enough as ringmaster of the Reagan circus. What nobody could imagine was that Baker would go to the Treasury to replace Donald Regan, who would come over to the White House in place of Baker. The swap was cooked up by Baker and Regan, then accepted by the president.

Reporters were shocked that a passive Reagan would let two subordinates exchange senior positions in the government, demonstrating to them that the president was an empty suit of clothes. I thought I understood Reagan better than they did, thanks in part to *The Films of Ronald Reagan* by Tony Thomas (1980), an obscure book about his Hollywood career. Each chapter was devoted to one of Reagan's fifty-two motion pictures over twenty years, with a variety of different directors. So Ronnie was accustomed to seeing an unfamiliar face in the director's chair the first morning of shooting a new movie. What difference did it make whether Baker or Regan was the White House director?

But I did not fully appreciate how Reagan's leadership transcended maneuvers between his lieutenants. Viewed from too close, the second term was marred by Don Regan's ineptitude and looked like a failure. Viewed from a distance, the second term was seen making the Reagan presidency a historic success—winning the cold war, presiding over sustained economic growth, and invigorating the American people. I came to understand that the presidency is a leadership position that has very little to do with management.

SOON AFTER THE great Baker-Regan swap, a second surprise had far-reaching personal implications for me. At noon on Friday, February 1, 1985,

as *The McLaughlin Group* gathered at the NBC studios for our weekly taping, we learned it would be Pat Buchanan's last broadcast. He was returning
to the White House for the first time in a decade, now as communications
director. Buchanan was rich by a journalist's standards, thanks to his TV,
radio, syndicated newspaper column, and lecture income—annually over
$400,000 (in 2007 money, around $752,000), according to his government
disclosure form. Why would he give that up for a staff job? "Bob, this is our
time," Pat told me. "Our time has come, and I have to be with the chief."

That convinced me that Pat Buchanan's journalism was a temporary expedient, not a life's work as it was for me. It explained Pat's position on *The
McLaughlin Group* in support of Reagan's first-term backtrack for higher
taxes, leaving me as the only panel member in opposition. "I'm a party
man," Buchanan told me off camera, in explaining his pro-tax position.

The reason Buchanan had not joined "my chief" earlier was that he had
not been asked. And he never would have if Jim Baker had remained. It was
Don Regan's most daring move when he took over. Buchanan was put in
charge of what Reagan considered the strike force of his White House: the
speechwriters. They were militantly, eloquently conservative in a White
House whose staff was otherwise surprisingly nonideological. For Reagan's
first term, they had been supervised—and suppressed—by Baker's hit man,
Dick Darman. Now, in 1985, Darman was with Baker at Treasury as deputy
secretary.

Freed of Baker and Darman, President Reagan used conservative
speechwriters to flourish as the Great Communicator when he told Mikhail
Gorbachev to "tear down this wall!" and preached freedom at Moscow State
University. Baker and Darman never appreciated what a weapon the spoken word could be for a president. Buchanan did, and so did Ronald Reagan. That helps explain why Reagan was the first truly successful president
since Franklin Roosevelt.

BUCHANAN'S DEPARTURE TOOK CNN management by surprise. The
network was able to catch its breath Monday, February 4, 1985, Buchanan's
first day at the White House, because it had in the can a taped *Crossfire* program with regulars Buchanan and Braden. It made sense to run the tape as
Monday night's broadcast—to everybody except Dan Schorr. He had a fit
over Buchanan being on CNN's air when he already had become a member
of Ronald Reagan's staff. Schorr's fits were commonplace at CNN, but this
time he vented his displeasure in public. It was a fatal mistake for Schorr's
desire to continue with CNN beyond his contract's expiration in mid-1985.
It gave Ed Turner a pretext for getting rid of him.

Schorr was renowned as the last of "Murrow's Boys"—CBS newsmen hired by the legendary Edward R. Murrow. Schorr was in the CBS tradition that threw out objectivity and broadcast a resolutely leftish work product. Ted Turner, who had signed Schorr to a personal service contract, was grateful to him for giving the cable network needed credibility at the start. But after Schorr's outburst over Buchanan, Ed Turner convinced CNN president Bert Reinhardt and Ted Turner that Schorr was so prone to publicly criticizing the network that he had to go. Ed Turner was a conservative Republican who did not want CNN to become a cable version of CBS News with Dan Schorr impersonating Ed Murrow.

ON MONDAY, FEBRUARY 11, Ed Turner called from Atlanta and said that, "for the time being," I would do most *Crossfire* shows. But, Ed stressed, I was not the "permanent" replacement for Buchanan because that had yet to be determined. I interpreted that to mean CNN considered me the best they could find for now but were searching for something better. I did not see anything wrong with agreeing to this temporary arrangement, with one caveat. I had been going on *Crossfire* under terms of my general contract with CNN that now paid me twenty-five thousand dollars a year. I needed a little something extra. Turner offered two hundred dollars a program. That was only half the rate paid Braden, but I accepted it as a "temp."

Some temp. After Buchanan left, I was on *Crossfire* 109 times in 1985, all but the first three at the $200 rate. That yielded me an extra $21,200 ($39,900 in 2007 cash), nearly doubling what CNN had been paying me. That was not much by big-time TV standards but extra money I could use with a daughter in college and a son in private school.

I cannot say I ever thoroughly enjoyed being on *Crossfire* in the way I did on *Evans and Novak* and *The McLaughlin Group*. Doing *Crossfire* was more difficult. I often had to perform on *Crossfire* more as a political advocate than a journalist.

But *Crossfire* did change me. My deepening conservatism was based mainly on anticommunist foreign policy and supply-side economics. But now, because of *Crossfire,* I found myself engaged on issues I seldom wrote about: capital punishment, gay rights, abortion, and gun control. I was never asked to take any position I opposed, but the process had the effect of hardening my positions. I was ever more becoming a right-wing ideologue.

ROWLY SCHEDULED A meeting on May 14, 1985, about Nicaragua at the Metropolitan Club with John Carbaugh and Mad Dog Sullivan. Carbaugh, my longtime super-source, by 1985 had left Senator Jesse Helms's staff to

open a lucrative international consultancy. But Carbaugh was still performing international missions for Helms and worked closely with the most colorful member of the senator's colorful staff: David (Mad Dog) Sullivan, an
alumnus of the Marine Corps and CIA.

Sullivan, Carbaugh, Rowly, and I were gathered around a table in the
Metropolitan Club's library. Mad Dog had just returned from visiting a
maverick band of Contras in Nicaragua commanded by Eden Pastora, the
most famous Sandinista guerrilla fighter against the Somoza dictatorship
under the nom de guerre of Commandante Zero. He had turned against
the Sandinistas and entered an unlikely alliance with Jesse Helms, opposing
both the Marxist-Leninist dictatorship in Managua and the Republican administration in Washington. The U.S. government, concentrating efforts
on the main force of Contras, was not giving Pastora a dime.

The CIA had poisoned the water against Pastora, according to Sullivan
and Carbaugh, wasting a vital manpower source under an experienced
guerrilla leader. Sullivan pulled out photographs he had just taken in Pastora's camp, showing armed young men ready for battle. There was Mad
Dog, a .45 pistol on his hip, arm-in-arm with Commandante Zero. Sullivan
said these people were ready to wreak havoc with the Sandinistas if we
would supply them more arms.

Sullivan and Carbaugh said a Pastora supporter had made available an
old C-47 transport plane, which put Sullivan in the insurgent camp. It
would be available to me, I was told, if I wanted to go.

I would go—with one stipulation. I could not go to Nicaragua to report
on Commandante Zero's ragtag band without also visiting the main force
of Contras. But with Congress cutting off aid to the Contras, the freedom
fighters did not want reporters poking around. Pat Buchanan at the White
House and Adolfo Calero, now the Contras' man in Washington, each
failed to get permission for me.

"I'll try Ollie North," Rowly told me. "Who is Ollie North?" I asked.
Rowly said North was a marine lieutenant colonel assigned to the White
House to handle Nicaraguan affairs. North and I got together at a reception
in a downtown Washington hotel, where we chatted about what I wanted
to do in Nicaragua.

"Well, enjoy yourself down there, and call me afterwards to tell me
your observations," North said. I suggested it was not that easy to gain access to the Contras. "Mr. Novak, don't worry about it," he said. "We'll call
you tomorrow." True to North's word, his staff worked out the details of
the trip the next day. I learned then who was running the U.S. show in
Nicaragua.

· · ·

ON SATURDAY MORNING, May 25, 1985, the creaky old C-47 loaned to
Pastora landed on a makeshift landing strip at the camp of the Democratic
Revolutionary Alliance (ARDE). Pastora had four hundred soldiers—
several without rifles, some barefoot—lined up to greet me. I began an
Evans & Novak column, datelined the San Juan River, Nicaragua.

> Eden Pastora, fabled and much maligned guerilla leader, is operating
> on the Nicaraguan side of this river where his impoverished men are
> daily fighting and dying against Nicaragua's Marxist forces.
>
> Those facts are based on our personal observations, contradicting
> accusations that Pastora is a pure propagandist based in Costa Rica—
> perhaps in collusion with his former Sandinista comrades.

I found the famous Commandante Zero, who became a national hero
when he led the storming of the National Palace in Managua in 1978 to
begin Anastasio Somoza's downfall, to be charismatic and engaging. We
stayed up late Saturday night talking about ARDE's plight. He was bitter
about CIA specialists on Nicaragua ("the geniuses from Harvard") and told
me: "If we had gotten as much money from the CIA as the FDN [the main
force of Contras], we would be in Managua today." He said: "The CIA is
fooling the President of the United States. I would like to see the President
so that I could say to him, 'These people are lying to you, Mr. Reagan.' "
When I expressed surprise at a picture of Augusto Sandino over his
bunk, Pastora told me the regime in Managua misrepresented itself as "Sandinista" and should be called "Communist." He added: "Sandino was never
a Communist. He was a nationalist—like Senator Helms." The catalyst for
the improbable alliance of Jesse Helms and Commandante Zero was revealed to me Saturday after dinner with a short-wave radio call from Deborah DeMoss, another of Helms's fascinating staffers. After saying hello to
me, she engaged Pastora in a conversation in Spanish for an hour.
Deborah DeMoss was a lovely, committed young woman from a rich
Republican family. She had her hands on all aspects of Helms's Central
American policy and was able to charm the toughest warriors. In El Salvador, she worked closely with Roberto D'Aubuisson. She brought Helms
and Pastora together, explaining them to each other as fellow "nationalists."
I could not attest to the accuracy of the briefing by Pastora's high command, claiming that seven thousand of his guerrillas occupied ten thousand
square kilometers inside Nicaragua. But one thing was certain: The FDN
charge that ARDE never left the Costa Rican capital of San José and did not

fight was demonstrably false. Late Sunday afternoon, I witnessed the arrival of a motorboat containing casualties from a skirmish that afternoon fifty kilometers away: two dead ARDE guerrillas, and their twenty-nine-year-old platoon leader, still alive but dying from a gunshot wound in the belly.

When I arrived, Pastora apologized for catching him at a bad time for food. We would have to skip lunch, but he hoped for provisions coming in by boat. Unaccustomed to missing meals, I was ravenous when we sat down for Saturday night dinner. It featured roasted meat in plentiful supply. As I retired for the evening listening in the distance to Commandante Zero conversing with Deborah DeMoss, I wondered about what I had eaten. I had seen no food supply arriving, but then it occurred to me. Monkeys! The jungle was filled with wild monkeys, and they surely were my Saturday night dinner.

I spent Sunday night at a San José hotel, where I enjoyed a badly needed shower and a good meal. But the next morning, my stomach was queasy, and I decided it was prudent to skip breakfast. Tuesday morning in the Honduran capital of Tegucigalpa, Ollie North delivered as promised. The FDN picked me up in a four-wheel drive vehicle for a three-hour trip through the mountains to the Contra encampment inside Honduras. By now, I was feeling miserable from what I believed was the delayed effect of Commandante Zero's monkeys. When we stopped for lunch, I made the mistake of trying to eat—and lost everything.

I next learned that the last miles to the Contra camp would be covered by donkey. I told my FDN guides that I had never ridden a donkey (or a horse, for that matter) and was not about to start at age fifty-three with my stomach in an uproar. "Then you'll have to walk, Mr. Novak," I was told, "and the distance is seven miles through the mountains." I rode the donkey.

In contrast to Pastora's forces, every man in the FDN had shoes and a rifle. I wrote in an Evans & Novak column (datelined On the Nicaraguan-Honduran Border):

> Operating nearly 200 miles from the border, guerillas last week cut the road leading to Bluefields on the Atlantic (temporarily capturing two towns).
>
> This is cause for the visibly high morale we found at the base camp. Here was no band of revanchist Somosista thugs. Some 800 guerillas passed in review before FDN political leader Indalendo Rodriguez, former president of Nicaragua's Catholic University and son of an associate of Johnny Sandino himself. "I was anti-Somoza from childhood," he told us.

I was a guest at an elaborate dinner for Rodriguez with barbecued meat (not monkey) that I dared not touch. I had a long talk with Commandante Enrique Bermudez, the FDN's military leader, who claimed seventeen thousand troops under his command, with only four thousand in Honduras. The rest, he said, were inside Nicaragua fighting the enemy.

Bermudez, though lacking Eden Pastora's charisma, seemed more credible. While his troops were better equipped than Pastora's, they still suffered from the cutoff of U.S. funds nearly a year earlier and were financed by private money sources who kept the revolution alive with weapons bought on the open market (including Soviet AK-47 rifles and SAM-7 ground-to-air missiles).

Both Pastora and Bermudez, both ARDE and FDN, heartened me. Here in Nicaragua were people fighting for their freedom while the Democrats in Congress were doing their best to save a brutal Communist dictatorship. I concluded in the column that "the survival of the Contras is indisputable." What I never expected was that the effort by patriotic Americans to aid that survival would nearly bring down Ronald Reagan.

ON THIS LATEST visit to Central America, I stopped in El Salvador for another look—my third in the last four years—at how the government there was coping with Communist insurrection.

In the capital of San Salvador, I interviewed the minister of defense, General Carlos Vides Casanova. He told me U.S. aid and trainers had so improved the army that victory was inevitable, but he added that a long battle against FMLN guerrillas was in store.

My plan was to see for myself how the government was coping with the old guerrilla stronghold of Chalatenango Province in northern Salvador. In September 1984, the esteemed Colonel Sigfredo Ochoa had been given command of the 4th Infantry Brigade at El Paraiso in Chalatenango. Nine months before Ochoa got there, guerrillas had overrun brigade headquarters and occupied it briefly. On the day he arrived, 50 percent of the province was under FMLN control. Now, less than nine months later, the colonel had restored government control to all but the fringes of Chalatenango. He was the man of action I needed to see.

On the night before this planned sojourn, I was guest of honor at a large buffet dinner in the palatial home of Alfredo Cristiani. He was the thirty-eight-year-old son of one of El Salvador's richest families. Like other Salvadoran businessmen, Fredy Cristiani saw his personal interests and the nation's economy being crushed between two competing leftist dogmas:

Communists and Christian Democrats. Consequently, they created and bankrolled Major Roberto D'Aubuisson's ARENA.

I had met both D'Aubuisson and Cristiani on my first visit to Salvador in 1982 at Billy Sol's house. D'Aubuisson was a dynamic figure, under global leftist assault as a killer. Cristiani was a slight, nice-looking young man, who had graduated from Georgetown University in Washington and spoke flawless English (and, unlike D'Aubuisson, did not carry a gun). But he seemed obscured by D'Aubuisson.

I had followed D'Aubuisson into rural El Salvador in his 1984 campaign that came close enough to electing him president of the country that professional diplomats at the U.S. State Department were terrified. My column was the only favorable comment on his campaign in any major American newspaper, and I gave him a global platform with a thirty-minute CNN interview on the campaign trail with each of us in khaki jungle garb. At Cristiani's house a year later, D'Aubuisson embraced me as a brother.

After dinner that night, I was called to the telephone. It was the embassy's press officer telling me he had been ordered to cancel our scheduled motor trip to El Paraiso because it was too dangerous. I shouted over the phone that it was outrageous to cancel the trip after ten o'clock at night, too late to make new travel arrangements for my last day in the country.

Cristiani asked the source of the trouble after overhearing the uproar, and I told him. Cristiani then offered to fly me in his own helicopter. We took off at dawn the next morning, just Fredy at the controls and me. When we reached El Paraiso, a squad of soldiers carrying rifles was on the ground waving us away. "Don't they know we're coming?" asked Cristiani. "Yes," I said, "but not by helicopter." Fortunately, nobody shot us down. With Fredy as my interpreter, I explained who I was and that I had an appointment with Colonel Ochoa.

The colonel showed me his troops, and they looked vastly superior to the undisciplined soldiers I observed two years earlier. Ochoa was grateful that all his soldiers now had M-16 rifles, but he said he needed grenade launchers, trucks, radios, and helicopters. He added: "So long as the Sandinistas rule Nicaragua, this war [in Salvador] may last another twenty years."

It all fit together, as Ronald Reagan understood far better than the Foreign Service professionals now that he was fully engaged in the problem. Nicaragua's Marxist-Leninist dictatorship was a cancer infecting its neighbors.

I am a pessimist by nature, which is why I have spent my life as a journalist instead of trying to be a leader, which requires optimism. I didn't really believe the Nicaraguan Contras could force the Sandinistas to capitulate, as they did. I wasn't sure ARENA could win an election in El Salvador. What I never dreamed was that four years later the ARENA candidate elected president would be Alfredo Cristiani.

FOR ITS FIRST fifteen years, the Evans & Novak column was litigation free. That streak ended on May 4, 1978, with the publication of our column on the appointment of Bertell Ollman, a tenured professor at New York University, as head of the University of Maryland's Department of Politics and Government. Ollman would be the first avowed Marxist to head the political science department at a major public university.

My May 4 column said Ollman's "candid writings avow his desire to the use the classroom as an instrument for preparing what he calls 'the revolution.' " Ollman twice had finished sixteenth and last among all candidates in unsuccessful candidacies for the council of the American Political Science Association after campaigning "to promote the study of Marxism." In his principal scholarly work published in 1971, he wrote that the "present youth rebellion," by "helping to change the workers of tomorrow," would help produce "a socialist revolution."

To buttress our claim that Ollman was a Marxist hack, we quoted a "political scientist in a major Eastern university, whose scholarship and reputation as a liberal are well known" as saying "Ollman has no status within the profession, but is a pure and simple activist." Would he say that publicly? "Not a chance of it. Our academic culture does not permit the raising of such questions."

Identity of that professor has been concealed for twenty-seven years, and keeping it secret caused me anxiety and threatened disaster. The reasons for concealment have long since disappeared. The source was Professor Jeane Kirkpatrick of Georgetown University. The use of "he" was an effort to limit attempts to discover her identity. As for calling her a "liberal," she was then a Hubert Humphrey Democrat whose rapid journey into the Reagan administration and the Republican Party was still in the future.

The decision to hire Ollman was reversed by the university president, John Toll. Ollman blamed the Evans & Novak column, and filed a six-million-dollar libel suit against us. Although Ollman's attorneys had cited the column as it appeared in the *Washington Post*, they filed suit not against the *Post* but against Rowland Evans and Robert Novak (thus the name of the case, *Ollman v. Evans*). The *Post* had deep pockets; Evans & Novak did not.

Rowly arranged lunch at the Metropolitan Club for us with the in-house legal counsel of the *Washington Post*. I fantasized that he might offer to defend us on the *Post*'s dime. No such luck. It was not the *Post*'s problem. The lawyer politely suggested that Rowly and I might avoid debilitating litigation by settling with Ollman out of court.

After lunch, Rowly and I agreed that a settlement ought to be our last resort. That would require a statement we indeed had libeled the Marxist professor and an apology—a humiliating surrender that was Ollman's goal. Our only hope for financing our legal resistance—a frail one—was our flagship newspaper, the *Chicago Sun-Times*.

In a telephone call to *Sun-Times* editor in chief Jim Hoge in Chicago, I acknowledged that the newspaper was not a party to the libel suit. But noting that Rowly and I had been employees of the paper since 1966, I expressed hope that the *Sun-Times* could help us. Hoge did more than just help. He generously assigned the newspaper's lawyers, the prestigious Chicago firm of Isham, Lincoln & Beale (the Lincoln was Robert Todd Lincoln, eldest son of President Abraham Lincoln) to defend us—fully paid for by the *Sun-Times*. A. Daniel Feldman, a crack litigator and experienced libel lawyer, took the case.

In September 1979, a federal district judge in Washington threw out the suit. Ollman appealed, and it took four more years for a three-judge panel of the U.S. Court of Appeals for the District of Columbia to overrule the district court and set the case for trial. The appellate court agreed with Ollman's lawyers that the anonymous quote about Ollman having "no status in our profession" was libelous if not attributed to a real person. If I had just made up the quote, it would constitute "actual malice." Our attorney, Dan Feldman, told me it was imperative that we identify the source if we went to trial. I told him I would not do it unilaterally.

Soon after the libel suit was filed in 1979, I explained my predicament to Jeane Kirkpatrick and asked her if I could reveal her name if necessary. Her silence on the phone was not reassuring, after which she said she would get back to me. A few days later Kirkpatrick's lawyer told me she could not release me from my pledge of anonymity because it might endanger the job of her husband, Evron Kirkpatrick, executive director of the American Political Science Association. When the 1983 decision by the appellate judges had made the quote all-important, I renewed my request through her attorney. Her husband's job security was no longer at issue because he had retired in 1980. She now was U.S. ambassador to the United Nations and a conservative icon, presumably no longer threatened by "our academic culture." Nevertheless her answer was still no, this time without explanation. I thought her attitude selfish and arrogant.

In 1983, Feldman told me I would have an agonizing choice when the suit came to trial. I could break my reporter's unwritten oath and reveal Kirkpatrick's identity, or I could lose the suit with a jury likely to go well beyond six million dollars in punitive damages. Given Kirkpatrick's intransigence, Feldman said our only fragile hope was an appeal to the D.C. Court of Appeals for a rehearing to prevent a trial—a tactic that succeeded very rarely, he told us.

But the judges on the prestigious D.C. Circuit thought that the suit raised important questions about freedom of expression by a columnist, as distinct from a reporter, and on October 7, 1983, ordered a rehearing.

The hearing was set for March 6, 1984, but on January 10 came unexpected news. Rupert Murdoch had purchased the *Chicago Sun-Times* from the Field family. Rowly and I had several handshake agreements with the newspaper not included in our written contract. The most important of these was assuming legal costs of the Ollman case, which I calculated by now at more than a hundred thousand dollars and counting. Would the new *Sun-Times* owner pick up the tab?

I had not seen Murdoch since eight years earlier when Rowly and I pitched him on keeping our column in the *New York Post.* Shortly after the announcement of the *Sun-Times* purchase, I made an appointment to see Murdoch at the old *Post* building. I hurried through the noncontract benefits provided us by the *Sun-Times,* ending with the open-ended commitment to Isham, Lincoln & Beale for defending the libel suit. Before I could make my impassioned plea for help, the publishing king interrupted me: "Oh, that's no problem. Consider it done." I think Rupert had more important things to do that morning, but it was an extremely generous act. Other people I have worked for would not have done that.

On December 7, 1984, the D.C. Court of Appeals reversed the three-judge panel by a six-to-five vote and again threw out Ollman's suit. The alignment on the court ran counter to normal expectations, which would have liberal Democratic judges supporting a journalist's expression of opinion and conservative Republican judges preserving what was left of libel law. Judge Ruth Bader Ginsburg, a future Supreme Court justice, was the only liberal who opted for press freedom by ruling in favor of Evans and Novak. Judge Antonin Scalia, also a future Supreme Court justice, was the only conservative who ruled against us. In his dissent, Scalia, who took a constricted view of First Amendment press freedom, called our column "a coolly crafted libel."

The majority opinion was written by Judge Kenneth W. Starr, the future special prosecutor. Starr might have recalled that three years earlier I had whacked him for his recommendation (as a Justice Department lawyer) of

Sandra Day O'Connor for the Supreme Court. Readers of the Evans & Novak column, Starr wrote in his opinion, expect "strong statements, sometimes phrased in a polemical manner that would hardly be considered balanced or fair elsewhere in the newspaper." Judge Robert Bork's concurring opinion asserted Starr had not "adequately demonstrated that all of the allegedly libelous statements at issue here can be immunized as expressions of opinion." Not for the first time, Bork led all his colleagues in eloquence.

Ollman appealed to the Supreme Court. In early May 1985, Dan Feldman called me from Chicago with bad news. The high court's two most conservative members, Chief Justice Warren Burger and Justice William Rehnquist, had agreed to accept the appeal. Feldman opined that with the chief on board, the two additional justices needed for the high court to accept the case surely would be found. Once the Supreme Court agreed to hear the case, Feldman went on, it almost surely would reverse the D.C. decision and order a trial, with all the expense, pain, and danger that involved.

But surprisingly, no other justice ever joined Burger and Rehnquist. On May 28, 1985, while I was in Central America, the Supreme Court announced it was rejecting the appeal in *Ollman v. Evans*. The legal nightmare finally was over after seven years.

In the *New York Times* of December 10, 1984, three days after the D.C. Circuit ruled, left-wing columnist Anthony Lewis—who had never evidenced affection for Bob Bork or me—wrote in praise of the D.C. Circuit's decision and especially Bork's concurrence. Tony Lewis stood alone. Liberal mainstream journalists ignored this landmark decision expanding their own freedoms. They seemed more interested in protecting a Marxist professor. Maybe some were rooting for Novak to get his comeuppance.

AT AGE FIFTY-FOUR I had been so engrossed in my work that I had paid little attention to my children. Zelda was a nineteen-year-old Kenyon College student who surprised me in the spring of 1985 by saying she loved Ernest Hemingway's *The Sun Also Rises* and especially the episodes at Pamplona in Spain, with "the running of the bulls" and death in the afternoon at the bull ring. I had fallen in love with the same episodes in the same novel at the same age. But to me as a college sophomore, Hemingway's profiles of the "lost generation" in the twenties were a world away. I never would have dreamed of asking my loving but staid parents to go to Pamplona on vacation. But that's what Zelda wanted of me, and that's what she got.

We went to Pamplona for the Festival of San Fermin, which ran for ten days beginning July 8, 1985. San Fermin had not been a secret since Hemingway wrote about it, and thousands of teenagers from all over Europe now descended on the town. Many, camping out in the park, were astounded to find Zelda and Alexander staying at the pricey Hotel Tres Reyes with a room of their own.

Every night our children left us for dancing and drinking (the Spanish were not bothered by underage alcohol consumption). Geraldine, concerned about her children in a foreign city, would try to stay up until they came in, but she never made it before falling asleep. One morning, Geraldine awoke early and found the children's bedroom empty. She was terrified, but they soon arrived from all-night revels.

Alexander, at age sixteen, had decided he would run with the bulls down the main street of Pamplona early each morning. Geraldine was opposed, but I talked her into letting him do it. Several runners each day were gored and hospitalized. But I figured Alexander, unlike me a good athlete with quick reflexes, could stay out of harm's way. He became more daring as the week went on, dodging around the bulls in the final stage of the spectacle when the bulls and amateur toreros all were inside the bull ring, until he was nicked on the arm by a hoof (earning a scar to show the girls back home in Maryland). Geraldine called it the worst vacation of her life, not knowing whether to worry more about her son running with the bulls or both her children's late-night adventures with the youth of Europe. I enjoyed it because it showed our children could adapt to exotic new situations and that Alexander was brave and adventurous. The sadness for me was that I had not become better acquainted with them, a regret my frenetic life had left so little time for my children.

I RETURNED FROM Spain on July 17, 1985, to find Ronald Reagan convalescing from two blows. On Saturday, July 13, surgeons at Bethesda Naval Hospital outside Washington removed a large tumor from the colon of the seventy-four-year-old president. While the surgery was in progress, Reagan also was cut by the Republican majority leader of the Senate. It led to one of the unique TV experiences of my life.

The new majority leader, starting in 1985, was Robert J. Dole, a former national chairman of the Republican Party, its nominee for vice president in 1976, chairman of the Senate Finance Committee, and a serious candidate for president in 1988. Dole's rigid mind-set favored the "old-time religion" of deficit reduction even if it meant higher taxes. As Finance chairman, he had collaborated with Jim Baker and David Stockman in passing tax increases during Reagan's first term that lessened the impact of the Kemp-Roth cuts. But immediately after Reagan's reelection, I wrote that Baker was bailing out of tax increases for the second term and Stockman was "on a solo flight" in his fifth (and last) year as OMB director. That also isolated Dole as an old-time religionist.

Blocked from further tax increases by the White House under newly installed chief of staff Don Regan, revenue-enhancer Dole moved to reduce cost of living allowances on multiple federal programs—including Social Security. Democrats could not believe their good fortune for the 1986 midterm elections as Dole carried this politically poisonous package through the Senate by a single vote.

Unfortunately for Dole, Reagan followed Jack Kemp's advice and reneged on accepting the Dole plan—dooming the Social Security cuts. As Reagan went into the hospital, the Saturday newspapers on September 13 reported the majority leader's extraordinary attack on the president. Dole accused Reagan of "surrendering to the deficit" and lashed out at Don Regan, Secretary of Defense Caspar Weinberger, and unnamed House Republicans (meaning Kemp).

Crossfire executive producer Randy Douthit was frantic to book Dole and got him for Thursday, July 18, my first full day back from Spain. When *Crossfire* was cancelled in 2005 and I was asked to suggest memorable programs for valedictory presentations, I selected that Dole interview. CNN's archives in Atlanta were in deplorable condition, and the tape could not be found in time for the closing programs. But in preparation for this book, my staff located a tape at the Dole Institute of Politics in Lawrence, Kansas.

In my mind's eye, I thought of Dole and me shouting at and constantly interrupting each other. That failure of memory, I believe, is testimony to the decline of *Crossfire,* where shouting and interruptions over time became commonplace.

In 1985, Dole and I spoke in modulated tones and seldom interrupted each other. The primitive set at Wisconsin Avenue had Dole, Braden, and me seated in upright chairs at close quarters. The eerie quality of the tape is enhanced by how good Dole and I looked. The tape is stunning because of what Dole and I actually said to each other.

> Novak: Senator, you said you don't want to quarrel with Republicans. But I was just going through the clips of the last couple weeks—
> Dole: Probably yours.
> Novak: No, I was just going through the news story clips, Senator. And I found you attacking—
> Dole: I didn't know you read news stories.
> Novak: I sure do.
> Dole: I thought all you read was Evans and Novak.

Novak: Well, I *write* Evans and Novak. I *read* the news stories, sir. And I was reading that you were attacking the Republicans in the House. You were attacking the President for surrendering to the deficit. . . . You were attacking Don Regan. You were attacking Caspar Weinberger . . . for giving you wrong information.

Dole: He *did* give us wrong information. That's not an attack. That's credibility. . . .

Novak: You think that's productive in the Republican Party? To go day after day after day—

Dole: I don't know. You do a lot of it. You attack me in every column.

Novak: I'm not a Republican. I'm a journalist. . . .

Dole: You're an advocate. You're not a journalist. . . .

Novak: Do you think that it's productive in the Republican Party to attack the President?

Dole: I think that it's productive that people understand where we come from. . . . But you don't want me to succeed. . . .

Novak: Oh, I want you to. I want you to be strong.

Dole: You're against me. Every time you come out with a column, it's "Bob Dole is a bad guy" and "he's always doing somebody in." So, we start off: you're an antagonist.

Novak: That's not true.

Dole: You wouldn't give me a break if I hung the moon. You'd write something bad about me. . . .

Novak: We wrote an article in *Reader's Digest* that predicted—

Dole: You accused me of bribery.

Novak: No, we didn't. We predicted that you were going to be the strongest Majority Leader since Lyndon Johnson. . . . Do you think that maybe we went overboard for you? Because I don't see that you've done that much in the Senate. . . .

Dole: Well that's how much attention you pay. I think we've done quite a bit in the Senate. . . . We passed, I think, a terrific deficit reduction package. . . .

Novak: But it's not going anywhere.

Never before had I been spoken to that way by a United States senator. Nor had I ever before spoken that way to a United States senator. The postinterview dialogue between the co-hosts (an Ed Turner touch that internally at CNN was called the "yip-yap") was unusually harsh, sounding like a conversation between two men who did not like each other much (which was the truth). Braden could not even bear to call me by my first name that night.

> Braden: I was glad to see the Senator go after you, Novak. I really was. Because he's one of the few leaders in the Republican Party who is not an ideological, rigid kind of man.
>
> Novak: What his problem is is that he's got left-wingers like you who like what he's doing.

Crossfire executive producer Douthit was beside himself with joy over what he considered *Crossfire* at its best. Dole came in to do the program twice more within the next five months with me as co-host, but Douthit was sorely disappointed. Dole was, as usual on TV, colorless and uncommunicative.

The circumstances of his July 18 flameout could not be replicated. Dole was a bitter man who stored up grievances against many people—including me—that he normally kept under control. He felt Jack Kemp and Don Regan had conspired to get the president to betray him, and viewed me somehow as a co-conspirator. Apart from Dole's obsession with the deficit in the midst of the longest economic recovery in American history, I submit his temperament was unsuited for high political leadership, much less the presidency.

I AM SOMETIMES asked who was most qualified to be president and did not make it. A clear contender would be Daniel Patrick Moynihan. He was an effective public servant, an inspired innovator, and an eloquent orator. But he had serious problems, the most important of which was that he never figured out where he belonged politically—as witness his service in Richard Nixon's cabinet as a Kennedy Democrat.

In 1977, the new senator had an all-star staff of conservatives: Elliott Abrams, Charles Horner, Checker Finn, and Eric Breindel. Moynihan might have been a one-term senator had not a young Democratic political operative named Tim Russert arrived from Buffalo to become his press secretary. Russert gently edged Moynihan leftward, and the conservative all-stars left his staff—and ultimately the Democratic Party—one by one. Moynihan survived for a twenty-four-year Senate career, but the liberals who ran the Democratic Party distrusted him and barred him from presidential consideration.

Pat's other problem was that he drank too much. Still, he was able to perform remarkably while under the influence. A classic example came September 19, 1985, when Moynihan was a guest on *Crossfire*. We were taping the show early because I was invited to a stag dinner that night at the Madison Hotel honoring television executive Frank Shakespeare, about to leave the country to become U.S. ambassador to Portugal. Moynihan told me he was going to the same event for his old Nixon White House colleague Shakespeare, and he suggested we have a drink or two after the taping. I could not keep up with Pat drinking in my best days, and now I could hardly drink at all. I begged off his invitation without fibbing because I had to get back to my office and finish editing a column with Rowly.

Knowing Moynihan's destination after *Crossfire,* I was not surprised when the senator did not show up at the Madison. Well after dinner was finished and halfway through speeches honoring Shakespeare, Moynihan staggered in about as drunk as I had ever seen him. My table was closest to the door, and he walked over to it. Pat said nothing but picked up the wineglass of Ed Meese, now attorney general of the United States, and drained it as Meese looked on in astonishment.

This being a well-organized Republican-style event, the speakers were lined up and their speeches prepared in advance. Moynihan was not on the list. But as he stood drinking Meese's wine, Pat quietly waited for the current speaker to finish his remarks. Without permission or introduction, he then delivered his own oration. He described each of Frank Shakespeare's sterling qualities by quoting an appropriate line from William Shakespeare—and then staggered out. To prepare this clever Shakespeare-on-Shakespeare rendition and commit it to memory and then deliver it flawlessly would have been remarkable for someone sober. To do so (albeit with thickened tongue) despite depredations of alcohol was truly amazing. What an intellect! What a performer! What a waste!

CHAPTER 34

The Last Days of Reagan

PAT BUCHANAN, as White House communications director, was trying to put Reagan in closer touch with ideologically sympathetic journalists by inviting them for lunch at the White House. Each luncheon would include three journalists, the president, Don Regan, and Buchanan for an hour-long off-the-record conversation.

It was my turn on February 18, 1986. The story of the day was the struggle of Ferdinand Marcos to survive as president of the Philippines. The P.I. vote held February 6 was tainted by fraud so massive that Marcos's defense minister and senior army commander both defected to challenger Corazon Aquino. On February 15, Reagan declared Aquino the winner

At the White House lunch, Reagan signaled that the U.S. government had ended support for the corrupt despot and was seeking ways to get him out of the country and avert civil war. I saw Don Regan cast a worried glance at the president, as if admonishing the president for divulging too much. At that point, Reagan asked: "Have you ever heard of the Philippine Scouts?" Without waiting for a reply, he declared he had always wanted to make a movie of these Filipinos who fought for the United States against the Japanese invaders, first as scouts and later as guerrillas. As Reagan verbally sketched out his imaginary screenplay, precious time was ticking away. But who could tell the president of the United States to knock it off?

In one other peculiar exchange during the lunch, I asked Reagan: "What ever happened to the gold standard? I thought you supported it." "Well," the president began and then paused (a ploy he frequently used to collect his thoughts), "I *still* do support the gold standard, but—" At that point, Reagan was interrupted by his chief of staff. "Now, Mr. President," said Don Regan, "we don't want to get bogged down talking about the gold standard." "You see?" the president said to me, with palms uplifted in mock futility. "They just won't let me have my way."

After we left the White House and were on the Pennsylvania Avenue sidewalk, one of the other journalist guests pulled me aside. It was Arnaud deBorchgrave, editor of the *Washington Times* and a conservative admirer of Reagan. "What in the world was all that about the Philippine Scouts?" asked deBorchgrave, suggesting the president had gone around the bend. I urged Arnaud not to worry, because this was Reagan's way of getting us off the scent of his still unrevealed decision to move Marcos out of the Philippines.

That Reagan was more clever—and more devious—than most people imagined also was signaled by how he handled my question about the gold standard. The supply-side movement's hopes to regularize global financial arrangements by going back to gold had foundered against the financial establishment's opposition. It would have been a hopeless undertaking, and the best thing Reagan could do was pose as an undefiled pure believer and helplessly blame his all-powerful chief of staff for frustrating him.

IN THE Evans & Novak column of March 17, 1986, I pierced the veil of secrecy enveloping the Federal Reserve Board, America's central bank. I revealed that the announced unanimous vote by which the Fed had cut the discount rate was preceded a week earlier by a secret vote of four to three for the same result. I also reported the startling fact that the seemingly all-powerful Fed chairman Paul Volcker was on the losing side.

Don Regan at the White House and Preston Martin, the conservative Republican named by Reagan as Fed vice chairman, had been furious at Volcker (while silent publicly) for keeping money tight, I wrote, "to wring out the last drop of inflation despite unused capacity and sluggish economic growth." Volcker was arrogant and shortsighted, for he had lost his majority on February 7 when two new Reagan-appointed governors took their seats. "What was surprising," I wrote, "was that master bureaucrat Volcker did not turn around and lead the new majority but instead opposed the four Reagan appointees." Thus, the secret four-to-three vote on February 27 to ease money. My conclusion in the column:

> The backstage revolt at the Fed shows how President Reagan's two newly appointed governors have changed the central bank. Volcker, the Fed's most masterful leader ever, is now a lame duck whose tight anti-inflation attitudes can be outvoted by his new board. The Volcker era is ending.

Volcker had dropped his mask of imperturbability at the prospect of this humiliation. His colleagues never had seen him so upset. He pleaded with them to keep the decision secret, wait for the impending interest rate cut by the German Bundesbank and then vote unanimously for the cut, as if in reaction to the Germans. The plan was strictly a device to save face for Paul Volcker. It worked until the Evans & Novak column was published March 17.

That column, I am sure, generated yawns from most readers. Even Rowly was less than excited. But in the global financial community, this was the greatest scoop of my career. It was devastating for Paul Volcker. While he would serve out his final term as chairman until the summer of 1987, his domination was over. As in *The Wizard of Oz,* the curtain had been pulled back and revealed not the masterful central banker but an uncertain bureaucrat.

How could Evans & Novak, who only sporadically wrote about the central bank, uncover a story that eluded publications such as the *Wall Street Journal, New York Times,* and *Washington Post,* all of which had excellent financial reporters covering the Fed?

For years, I had been seeking a personal relationship with at least one Federal Reserve governor. I finally succeeded in the early eighties with Vice Chairman Martin, who became my occasional luncheon companion. I was even closer to one of the two new Reagan appointees to the Fed: Manuel Johnson, a supply-sider who as an assistant secretary had been my best source at Treasury. But neither Martin nor Johnson leaked this story to me.

On Friday, March 14, at nine a.m. while seated at the office computer (we had reluctantly abandoned typewriters in 1979), I received a telephone call from Alfred Kingon, the fifty-six-year-old secretary of the cabinet. He had spent ten years as editor in chief of *Financial World* when in 1981, he came to Washington as an assistant secretary at the Treasury. He was one of four aides taken by Regan from Treasury to the White House when he became chief of staff. They all were slight of stature, pale, and ostentatiously subservient to their overbearing chief. Holdovers at the White House wickedly labeled them the "Mice." I cultivated all the Mice and was most successful with Kingon. In telephone conversations and lunches, I found him insightful though unwilling to leak any information to me that Don Regan would not approve.

The March 14 call lasted no more than five minutes. A nervous Kingon pressed me not to reveal my source. All that remained to write a column for Monday was for me to confirm what Kingon told me by calling Preston Martin and Manley Johnson. Though sworn to keep the secrets of the temple, they could not deny the accuracy of Kingon's report.

Kingon had not interpreted his facts for me. He figured that as a sophisticated reporter, I would understand the significance of the story and the significance of Kingon's call (which, of course, I did not put in the column). Don Regan felt that Volcker had cut him out when he was at Treasury and instead worked with Jim Baker at the White House. I was sure Regan could not tolerate Volcker having foolishly allowed himself to be outvoted at the Fed and then keeping secret the chairman's humiliation. I cannot imagine Kingon leaking this information without his boss's approval or even inspiration.

Journalists like to give the impression they develop exclusive stories through exhaustive investigation and research. Most such scoops, I believe, come on a single leak such as Al Kingon gave me. Kingon called me partly because he knew I had criticized Volcker's tight money policy. As a columnist, I could comment on this development as a straight news reporter could not. In addition, I was a columnist whom Kingon knew. That is why Rowly and I spent so much time with sources who produced scant hard news. Rowly and I did not get much column material out of many meals we separately scheduled with Al Kingon. But when he had a big story to leak, he thought of us.

WITH CNN'S LAMP still in the window for Buchanan in 1986, there was no designated replacement for *Crossfire*. But I was the undesignated substitute, appearing on 166 programs for the second year of Buchanan's absence. The most memorable of them for me came on July 11 with an interview that rivaled in nasty intensity the Dole program a year earlier. I think it widened the already considerable gap between me and Tom Braden. The reason was the guest, Robert Strange McNamara.

Of many political personalities I have disliked during a half century in Washington, I would place McNamara on top. From my first interview with him as secretary of defense when the Evans & Novak column started in 1963, I regarded him as overbearing and hypocritical.

McNamara had been moving left to expiate his role as architect of the Vietnam catastrophe. By the summer of 1986, I thought he had gone much too far in appeasing the Kremlin by advocating that the U.S. pledge no first-use of nuclear weapons, even if the Soviets invaded Europe. This was unprecedented for a former secretary of defense, and McNamara compounded the outrage by quoting Reagan out of context to make it appear that the president had the same position.

The reason McNamara came on *Crossfire* on July 11, 1986 (as he had on previous programs with us), was a personal request from Braden. I knew they both traveled the Georgetown party circuit, but I thought there was something odd about the self-professed friendship between the two dissimilar men, McNamara hyperactive and Braden lethargic—how odd, I was not to realize for more than a year.

The July 11 program started with an intense though still civil debate between McNamara and me over U.S. strategy. What I said next prompted McNamara, for the only time in my experience, to start shouting:

Novak: Mr. McNamara, you are a very clever man, and you're giving a lot of people the idea that you and Ronald Reagan are in the same boat on this issue, and you know you're not. And we can agree that there is a big difference between his concept of the Strategic Defense Initiative and yours. . . . I don't want to say something behind your back that I wouldn't say to your face. . . . [W]hen distinguished Americans such as you and [Carter disarmament chief] Paul Warnke are defending the Soviet position and saying that these are good offers and the American president is at fault for not responding to them. I really feel I have never seen anything with former Cabinet members in my time in Washington taking that position in regard to a Soviet-U.S. negotiating stance. And I just question whether or not you are performing an invaluable service, inadvertently—

McNamara: Mr. Novak, let me say something to *your* face. I deeply resent the implication. You're implying I'm a Communist.

Novak: I did not imply—

McNamara: You sure as hell *did*. And I deeply resent it. And you're absolutely wrong to present it. And you're absolutely wrong in stating my beliefs. I am not taking issue with the President. . . . Will he respond to the Soviets? I think he will respond. I hope he does. I have respect for our President. Maybe you don't, but I do.

Novak: I have a lot of respect for him. I have respect for *you*.

McNamara: Well, I hope you do, but it doesn't sound like it.

Novak: I am not questioning your patriotism.

McNamara: Well, it sure as hell sounds like it. You were implying I'm a Communist. I don't like that at all. . . .

Novak: I'm questioning your judgment, which is different from questioning your patriotism.

McNamara: Novak, let me go back. You were implying I'm a Communist. I don't like that at all.

Novak: Now that's—

McNamara: You shut up for a moment and let me talk.

Novak: Well, that's rude.

McNamara: It *is* rude, and its rudeness is deserved. . . .

Novak: Mr. McNamara, you are advocating that he [Reagan] go into extension of the ABM [Anti-Ballistic Missile] treaty.

McNamara: Absolutely.

Novak: Which would undoubtedly, downstream, reduce our ability to have a Strategic Defense Initiative and put us again at the mercy of the Soviet strategic superiority.

McNamara: Mr. Novak, [Reagan] senior military adviser Paul Nitze has recommended exactly the same thing. . . . Nitze's not a Communist and neither am I!

Novak: I never said you were. I said it four times. I said your judgment is bad and I think you are performing a disservice to the country.

McNamara: A service for the Soviets. That is absurd.

That ended the interview. During the commercial break, McNamara told me he never would appear with me again and might well boycott all CNN programs—then stormed out of the studio. Braden acted as if personally wounded. "You have insulted our guest and humiliated me," he said in the few seconds prior to our postinterview analysis. The temperature of our never-warm personal relationship dropped significantly and permanently after the McNamara program. However, Braden had been even more detached than usual during my rancorous dialogue with McNamara. The passivity continued during the yip-yap, with Braden saying to me: "Maybe I'll leave it to you. Do you think you handled the guest correctly? Were you kind? Were you insulting?"

(The possible source of what I viewed as Braden's ambivalence toward McNamara was suggested on September 8, 1987, in the Style section of the *Washington Post* when staff writer Charles Trueheart disclosed a "zesty" book proposal by Tom Braden's glamorous wife, Joan. In it, she revealed her longtime "romantic" relationship with McNamara, including travels with him throughout the world. Joan Braden was quoted by Trueheart as saying Tom "encourages" her travel with McNamara, adding: "He never asks me what goes on." I was told Joan's relationship with McNamara was common knowledge in Washington social circles, but those were circles I did not frequent. By the time the *Post* story ran, Buchanan had returned to *Crossfire* and I was no longer on the program regularly. I was glad I was not sitting next to Tom Braden on the set the night of September 8, 1987.)

ON OCTOBER 5, 1986, in Nicaragua, Sandinistas shot down a C-123 transport plane carrying supplies for the Contras. One crew member survived and was taken prisoner by the Sandinistas, the first appearance of a long shadow cast over the final two years of the Reagan administration. The prisoner was Eugene Hassenfus, a former U.S. Marine who as an American soldier of fortune had worked for the CIA in Vietnam as a "kicker" (kicking supplies off transport planes). Now he was performing the same function in the Nicaraguan resupply effort under the supervision of Marine Lieutenant Colonel Oliver North at the National Security Council. This was a covert government operation violating various Boland amendments passed by Congress to prohibit U.S. government help for the Contras.

Prisoner Hassenfus told the Sandinistas he was working for the CIA, just as he had in Vietnam. But the CIA denied having anything to do with Hassenfus, and President Reagan contended the pilot was working for "private groups and private citizens that have been trying to help the Contras." That story was gripping the capital on Friday, October 10, at two fifteen p.m. when Elliott Abrams came to the CNN bureau to tape *Evans and Novak* (to be broadcast the next day). It was to be one of the most consequential of our weekly programs over twenty years.

Abrams was the neoconservative prototype: Democrat, Jewish, New Yorker, son-in-law of neocon pathfinder Norman Podhoretz, fierce anti-communist and cold warrior, intrepid supporter of Israel. Like his close friend Bill Kristol, Abrams was a quick-witted graduate of Harvard College (and went on to Harvard Law School). At age twenty-seven in 1977, Abrams joined the Senate staff of neocon Democrat Pat Moynihan. When Moynihan moved into the Democratic Party's liberal womb, Abrams went the other direction and became a Republican.

In 1981, President Reagan named Abrams, at age thirty-two, as the youngest assistant secretary of State in the nation's history and a key supporter of the Contras. Abrams was my source, and I liked him personally. His answer to Rowly's opening question in the October 10 taping would haunt him for years:

> Evans: Mr. Secretary, can you give me categorical assurance that Hassenfus was not under the control, the guidance, the direction, or what have you, of anybody connected with the American government?
>
> Abrams: Absolutely. That would be illegal. We are barred from doing that, and we are not doing it. This was not in any sense a U.S. government operation. None.

After I took up the questioning, Abrams reiterated that Hassenfus was not working for the government. He expressed a desire "to repeat that categorical assurance that he was not." I persisted:

Novak: Now when you give "categorical assurances," we're not playing word games that are so common in Washington? You're not talking about the NSC, or something else?

Abrams: I am not playing games.

Novak: National Security Council?

Abrams: No government agencies. None.

Abrams's answers were so "categorical"—and so incorrect—that they became the basis for efforts to paint Contra support as a sinister conspiracy and ultimately to impeach or indict Ronald Reagan. I know of no statute that prohibits lying, intentionally or not, to a journalist. Yet, when it became clear that the Contra resupply was being run out of the White House, what Abrams told us was seized on by enemies of Reagan and the Contras. The leftist writer Theodore Draper, in his anti-Contra book *A Very Thin Line,* upbraided Abrams for the "temerity" of his performance on our program. If Abrams were to escape criminal conviction, wrote Draper, "it is hard to see why anyone should have been punished for misbehavior in the Iran-Contra affair."

Independent Counsel Lawrence Walsh, an octogenarian retired federal judge, agreed. What Abrams said on our program was used by Walsh to hound him into a plea bargain on charges of misleading Congress. He failed to wring from him information incriminating Walsh's real prey, Ronald Reagan.

Abrams's foes regarded Rowly and me as feckless victims of the conspiracy, who did not bother to question him closely. On the contrary, *Evans and Novak* was an adversarial program—and never more so than on the October 10 taping. We pressed Abrams hard, but he would not budge on his insistence. It led me to conclude in our postinterview, on-camera conversation: "You know, I've seen a lot of cover-ups in this town, Rowland, and we both may end up with egg on our face before this is over, if this is all an elaborate lie. But this doesn't look like a cover-up, and it doesn't because there is no equivocation."

We did get egg on our face, but I am still convinced Abrams was not lying to us that Friday afternoon. He just did not know the truth.

THE FINAL MIDTERM election campaign of an eight-year presidency can be a dreary business, and 1986 fit that description. In the preelection issue of the *Evans-Novak Political Report,* I began:

In the final weeks of the campaign, President *Ronald Reagan* failed to nationalize the campaign on any issue other than himself. What little trend has appeared in recent weeks looks to be *Democratic,* but *not* enough to promise a real sweep.

In the *ENPR,* I predicted a Democratic gain of three seats in the House and three in the Senate. The actual gains for the Democrats on November 6, 1986, were five seats in the House and eight in the Senate.

The difference between prediction and results was insignificant in the House. The eighty-one seat Democratic edge continued the same magnitude of Republican deficiency prevailing since the 1982 midterm elections. But missing the Senate outcome by five seats was a disaster for me as well as the Republicans. A three-seat Democratic gain would have meant a fifty-fifty balance in the Senate, enabling Vice President Bush to cast the deciding vote and maintain Republican control of the upper chamber for the full eight Reagan years. An eight-seat gain meant a fifty-four to forty-six edge for the Democrats—ending six years of Republican control. My only defense was that nobody else—including my Democratic sources—saw the takeover coming. The consequences were far-reaching, the most immediate being the defeat of Robert Bork for confirmation to the Supreme Court. That blocked a conservative majority on the Supreme Court, and saved *Roe v. Wade* for the abortion lobby.

Since Democrats still enjoyed an overwhelming advantage in the House of Representatives, I wondered what had happened to political realignment. A partial answer was that realignment was blocked by the South's lingering attachment to its ancestral party. In the states of the old Confederacy, the 1986 election for the House still returned eighty-two Democrats against forty-two Republicans. But realignment was not dead—just moving very slowly.

POLITICAL FOLKLORE HAS attributed the poor Republican performance in the 1986 midterms to the revelation of the Iran-Contra scandal. In truth, the disclosure came twenty-one days *after* the election. For the covert arms sales to Iran's revolutionary regime and the diversion of their proceeds to the Contras, Ollie North was immediately fired from the National Security Council staff and his boss, Rear Admiral John Poindexter, resigned as NSC director. Firing North and handing him and Poindexter over to the inquisition was a brutal act of political disloyalty urged on President Reagan by Don Regan and by an even more influential presidential adviser, Nancy Reagan. If Don Regan thought he saved himself by throwing North and Poindexter overboard, he was wrong. He too was on Nancy Reagan's purge list, and was gone on February 27, 1987.

On Thursday, February 26 (my fifty-sixth birthday), I flew to Boca Raton, Florida, for the annual conference that Rowly and I put on with Jude Wanniski. Early Friday morning at Boca Raton, a White House source called to advise that Reagan's third chief of staff would be Howard Baker and would be announced that afternoon. As Senate majority leader, Baker had made no secret of his displeasure with Reagan initiatives from tax cuts to the Contras. Since leaving the Senate at the end of 1984, he had spent scarcely two years cashing in as a seven-figure lawyer-lobbyist. He was coming back, out of duty to a thankless job.

On Friday afternoon in my Boca Raton hotel room, I wrote an Evans & Novak column for Monday contending that Howard Baker succeeding Don Regan "means respectability rather than renewal of the Reagan Revolution is the goal of the President's final two years." This was the column's last paragraph:

> [W]hatever happened to Secretary of Education William Bennett, pushed by the New Right as a chief of staff who might revive the Reagan Revolution? "Too contentious," said one insider, adding that Bennett would cause trouble on the Hill. The First Lady and her friends were seeking succor in Congress, not a new agenda.

Hand-wringing by me and other conservatives meant we still did not understand Reagan. He was a successful president because of tunnel vision that kept his gaze on big goals. Chiefs of staff came and went just as directors did in his Hollywood days, and Reagan did not care much about them.

Reagan's implacable calm in the face of adversity was demonstrated early in January 1987 when Rowly attended the last in a series of intimate lunches with the president arranged for conservative journalists by Pat Buchanan. After a full hour over lunch with the president, Evans—in typical Rowly style—sidled over to him for a private word. "Mr. President," he asked, "how in the world do you keep so cool when all hell is breaking loose?" Reagan smiled, cocked his head, and, as he often did, answered the question by telling a joke. "Rowly," he replied, "did you ever hear the story about the two psychiatrists?"

Two psychiatrists, one old and one young, traveled to and from work together each day. The young psychiatrist finished each day bedraggled and disheveled, with a mournful look on his face. The old psychiatrist, on the other hand, finished each day as chipper and bright as he had started it. The young psychiatrist finally asked, "Doctor, how do you look so good after a full day of hearing endless stories of woe and sadness from your patients?" The old psychiatrist answered: "Doctor, it's simple. I don't listen." Reagan added to Evans: "Neither do I."

ON THE EVENING of Friday, January 2, 1987, Maurice Pall Novak died at the age of eighty-five at Suburban Hospital in Bethesda, Maryland. My parents had lived in the Washington suburb of Rockville, Maryland, since 1982. After the death in 1981 of Sarah, my mother's only sister and her last sibling still living in Joliet, Geraldine suggested that there was nothing anymore to keep my parents in Joliet, and they should join us in Washington to be near their beloved Zelda and Alexander.

In my eulogy, I described my father's story as "a quintessentially American story—specifically a story of Jewish-American immigrants and their values." I praised his "keen insightful mind" but said "what set Maurice Novak apart were his personal virtues. They were old-fashioned virtues, seen ever less frequently in a fragmented society: loyalty, devotion to duty, morality, love of friend and family." I concluded by turning from eulogist to only son.

> I am so grateful for the way he taught me to enjoy sports and follow current events, for his advice, his patience and his support in hard times, his tolerance of my shortcomings. What estimable qualities I have resemble my father's; my defects clearly were not derived from him.

A few days after the funeral, I received my first telephone call in many years from Katherine Graham. My mother had met the proprietor of the *Washington Post* during a reception at the Graham mansion many years earlier. Jane Sanders Novak was awed by no one and felt she could charm anybody. So Mrs. Novak sat down and had a very nice conversation with Mrs. Graham. Now, with the publisher the only person in authority at the *Post* whom my mother knew, she had sent her a text of my eulogy with the suggestion that it might be nice if the *Post* printed it. Clearly embarrassed, one of the most powerful women in America told me: "Bob, it is a lovely eulogy, but it really isn't—" I interrupted her: "Kay, please don't give it a moment's thought." I thanked her for the compliment, told her how much our family appreciated the report on my father's death published at the top of the Sunday *Post*'s obituary page, and assured her I would explain to my mother that Mrs. Graham liked the eulogy even if it had no place in the newspaper.

. . .

IN THE SPRING of 1987 not long after Howard Baker's appointment as White House chief of staff, I walked out of the Capital Hilton Hotel after lunch and found the billionaire founder of CNN standing alone on the 16th Street sidewalk. Ted Turner said he had a date with Howard Baker in forty-five minutes, with nothing to do until then. I suggested he take the ten-minute walk with me to my office at 1750 Pennsylvania Avenue, take a look at our office, and then stroll over to the White House, a block away at 1600 Pennsylvania.

This would be my first extended personal conversation with Turner since my pre-CNN employment chat with him in Atlanta seven years earlier. Turner had been a guest on *Crossfire* from Moscow in 1986, where he was attending the first Goodwill Games international athletic competition that he arranged. When I pressed him during the interview about getting too close to the Soviets, Ted snapped back in his raspy Georgia accent: "Remember, this is *my* network." Subsequent efforts to book him as a guest on *Evans and Novak* all failed.

As we walked across Lafayette Square on the way to my office, Turner said: "I can't understand, Novak, why you're in favor of all-out nuclear war." He then launched a defense of the Kremlin's arms control policies and lauded the people's paradise in Cuba. I tried to argue back, but it was tough getting a word in edgewise with Ted Turner. When we reached my thirteenth-floor office, I introduced him to a young woman in the Evans & Novak outer office whose main job was handling the phone calls. Turner looked her in the eye and asked: "How do you feel working for a man who is in favor of a nuclear holocaust?"

The woman looked at Ted as though he were mad, and to a certain extent he was. I think it is easier for madmen to be creative entrepreneurs and visionaries, and that's what Turner was. He made CNN a wonder of the world of communications, and the network was never the same after he left.

THOMAS P. O'NEILL Jr. left Congress at the end of 1986 and a year later published his memoir of ten years as Speaker of the House, thirty-four years in Congress, and sixty years in elective politics. A brief passage in *Man of the House* about Rowly and me constituted the worst lie about us ever committed to print by a public figure. O'Neill claimed that after he had been elected House majority leader in 1973,

> Evans and Novak came to my office [and] had the gall to offer me a
> deal. If I kept them informed as to what was happening in Congress

and the White House, they would see to it that they would help smooth the way for me to be the next speaker. I was ashamed to be in their company, and I kicked them right out of my office.

Rowly and I agreed that such a blatant untruth must be answered immediately, and I did so in the column of September 14, 1987:

In a combined 70 years of reporting in Washington, neither of us has offered anybody such a deal or been kicked out of anybody's office. We did visit O'Neill when he became leader (as we similarly visited Jim Wright years later). When we expressed hope we could see him occasionally, O'Neill smiled assent.

Indeed, after that meeting, we enjoyed an amiable relationship with O'Neill for many years. When he encountered me, he would cuff me on the head (which I took as a sign of affection, though I disliked it). As indicated earlier in this book, the Evans & Novak column praised Tip extravagantly after his election as Speaker in January 1977.

On March 18, 1977, he addressed the closed-door semiannual Evans and Novak Political Forum. In February 1978, we interviewed him on television for our RKO General series. That was the interview in which he made wild charges against Republican congressman Bruce Caputo for which he underwent the humiliation of a public apology on the House floor.

The bad taste left with O'Neill by that interview (his fault, not ours) may have been why he spurned further invitations from us for the remaining eight years of his congressional tenure, but he never offered an explanation. When the lie appeared in *Man of the House,* I called the former O'Neill aide with whom I had the most experience. He said he had not come to work for the Speaker until six years after the fictitious 1973 incident but added that Tip talked about it frequently. That was O'Neill's "reason"—not previously conveyed to me—for spurning my invitations. In the September 14, 1987, column, I quoted the aide as saying: "I think that if you gave the Speaker sodium pentothal, he would tell the same story." I did not use the aide's name, but it was Chris Matthews. (In a 1989 *Crossfire* guest appearance, Matthews implied that he was present in O'Neill's office that day. That ended for me what until then had been a cordial relationship.)

I was not the only victim of lies in O'Neill's memoir, but the other victims were dead and could not defend themselves. Reviewers of *Man of the House* made no effort to check out O'Neill's fantasies. That included Bill Safire, the former New York press agent and Nixon publicist who gushed in his *New York Times* column about O'Neill's "disarming frankness" and "practical political reasoning." Fawning book reviews fit the general news media attitude toward O'Neill, who became a lovable national icon after his retirement in 1987 (and even more so after his death in 1994). The news media made over the mean-spirited O'Neill who was a big government ideologue, soft on Communist penetration of the Western Hemisphere, and a Boston machine politician who was brutal to such enemies in the House Democratic Caucus as Phil Burton and Tony Coelho. My regret is that, like many colleagues, I was deceived by his Irish charm into writing too many admiring columns about him.

THE SEPTEMBER 25, 1987, issue of *USA Today* carried CNN talk show host Larry King's breezy, Walter Winchell–style column that captured my attention because of one single-sentence item: "I'll bet you that Pat Buchanan comes back to Crossfire on CNN." That's all he wrote, but it spoke volumes to me.

I knew Larry would not write that sentence without having been informed by somebody in authority at CNN. So why did CNN tell Larry King and not me, the person Buchanan would be replacing? It was just the CNN way, in good times (which was 1987) and in bad (which would come later). At CNN, people were discharged and transferred without notice. When King's item aroused press interest, *Crossfire* producer Sol Levine told reporters that CNN over the last two years just had not been able to find anybody who filled the program's need as Pat Buchanan did. So much for me.

Pat had resigned from the White House on March 1, 1987, just two days after the man who had hired him, Don Regan, had been forced out. However, Buchanan would have been gone even if Regan had stayed.

After the dreary election of 1986, Howard Phillips and other right-wingers began pressing Buchanan to run for president in 1988. I wrote in an Evans & Novak column published Friday, January 16, that Buchanan "has all but decided to run for president." But I was then unaware of a meeting in Buchanan's big suburban Virginia home two evenings earlier when a wide assortment of conservatives gathered to plan Buchanan's campaign. It was thought Pat was ready to flash the green light that night, but things did not go as expected, as I wrote in a column published January 21:

It was not a happy evening. Supporters ready to get the campaign rolling were disturbed by a lack of organization and the presence of conservatives who preferred [Jack] Kemp to Buchanan (notably Tom

Winter and Allan Ryskind of Human Events). What bothered them most was their prospective champion's newly apparent indecision.

By the following Monday morning, Buchanan had decided not to run and let the world know it. I talked to Pat on the phone that morning, and he relayed to me his apprehension about splitting conservative forces so that George Bush or Bob Dole was nominated. He told me that if a conservative (presumably Kemp) were elected, Pat Buchanan would get the credit; if not, maybe 1992 would be Pat's time.

I asked Buchanan if that meant he was going to stay in the White House. "No, Bob," he replied. "I can't do that now. I've been to the mountaintop, and I cannot go back down." I did not realize at the time that Pat's "mountaintop"—running for president—in his mind forever barred him from future government service, in the White House, in the cabinet, in Congress (either House or Senate). But he felt a calling to be president.

BUCHANAN WAS WRITING a new book and did not return to *Crossfire* until Monday, October 26, 1987. I had become more comfortable on *Crossfire* and sometimes even missed being on the program, but the reduction in income from CNN did not hurt me.

Art Buchwald had guided me in 1986 to the Washington Speaker's Bureau, my third lecture agency. They produced $100,000 of income for me in 1987, a year where my taxable income was $440,000 ($784,000 in 2007 dollars). I could not believe I was making that much money, because I sure did not feel rich. Being a millionaire did not mean what it once did, but my net worth—thanks to riding the Reagan stock market with Richard Gilder—was more than a million dollars. I no longer had to take out emergency bank loans, but I was still the same driven, obstreperous newspaper reporter looking for news and looking for trouble.

AT NOON ON September 15, 1987, at Aspen, Colorado, I debated Carl Rowan, my fellow *Chicago Sun-Times* columnist, before executives and customers of Quaker Oats. Secretary of Defense Frank Carlucci also was speaking at the event. A Quaker Oats official noted to Carlucci that in our debate, Novak would be pro-Reagan and Rowan would be anti-Reagan. Carlucci snorted: "Well, if we have to rely on Novak, we're in a hell of a shape."

Reading my columns for the last two years of the Reagan administration, I can understand Carlucci's exasperation. I found little good to say about the administration, whose natural fatigue in its seventh and eighth years running the government was intensified by Iran-Contra.

But as in the story of the two psychiatrists, I doubt Reagan paid much attention to our column. He saw himself winning the cold war, energizing the U.S. economy, and transforming the American political balance of power. The Lilliputian maneuvers I dwelled on in the column did not bother him. He knew better than his critics the power of his rhetoric. On May 31, 1988, amidst the hand-wringing, Reagan went to the Soviet Union to deliver a speech at Moscow State University that seized the world's attention by extolling "the power of economic freedom."

CHAPTER 35

Blowup

A S MANEUVERING FOR the Republican presidential nomination got under way in early 1987, Don Devine, a prominent conservative and key adviser to Bob Dole, laid out for me a strategy to nominate his candidate as the real conservative. Devine advised Dole to support Reagan tax cuts but to draw the line against Jack Kemp by also stressing the reduction of budget deficits. Laboring under the delusion that Dole and I were both conservatives who could get along if only forced to spend time together, Devine invited me on a two-day trip with the candidate to New Hampshire on Sunday and Monday, February 15 and 16, 1987.

I arrived at Washington National Airport Sunday morning and climbed aboard a twin-engine private plane that would carry Dole north. The senator looked distraught when he spotted me. Either Devine had not told him I was coming, or Dole had not fully prepared himself for me.

We had no real conversations during my two days with the senator, the longest period I ever would be in close proximity to him. But overhearing him talk to Devine, to other aides, and over the phone, I gained an insight into Bob Dole (that I did not write about because I thought it would violate his hospitality). I never heard Dole utter a word about beliefs, policy, or strategy. He was into details. Who would be attending his events in New Hampshire and later that week in the Midwest? Who would greet him when he arrived? What was the stage configuration for a future rally? I cannot imagine such questions from Ronald Reagan, the old movie actor who trusted his directors. Dole was a hopeless micromanager, inappropriate for a presidential candidate and indeed for a president.

Still, Dole was following Devine's instructions. I wrote in an Evans & Novak column datelined Keene, New Hampshire: "Dole frequently refers to himself as a 'conservative' or 'spokesman for the Right.' Refuting his pro-tax reputation, he pledges to keep the low rates set by last year's tax reform and puts 'economic growth' first among deficit-reducers." But Dole also returned to his Social Security benefits cut that President Reagan torpedoed in 1985 on Kemp's advice. My column continued:

> . . . Dole does not sound like a movement conservative. He still throws around the rhetoric of Republican moderation: "problem-solving," "pragmatism," "sensitivity." To one adviser [it was Devine], the searing experience of being impaled by the news media in his disastrous [1976] run for vice president has made him "talk less conservative than he is."
>
> He certainly talks differently from the way he did before Devine came aboard in 1985. His formerly biting wit is invariably turned against himself, making him seem funny and humble at the same time. The former champion of Washington's meanness derby is now into niceness. He resists the professional legislator's impulse to list bills instead of talk issues.

I doubted Devine's advice would stick, and it did not. Less than four months later at the biennial Midwestern Republican conference in Des Moines, I described Dole as "sounding like more of a moderate than Bush" when asked to describe his vision for America: "Open opportunity for all, a world free and peaceful, an end to the nuclear nightmare, breakthroughs in health and education, science and the environment." I wrote that this vision was "congenial to liberal Republicans of the 1950s and similar to what today's Democrats say."

If Don Devine did not know he had failed to bring Dole and me together, my column of September 4 should have convinced him. I used government records to show that Secretary of Transportation Elizabeth Dole was traveling the country at government expense (especially into presidential primary states) delivering unstinted praise for her husband. I was told that the senator was furious, at me and at the vice president's office for leaking the information to me. He was right about the source. Lee Atwater, Bush's crafty young campaign director, had slipped me the documents.

IN EARLY 1987, the conventional wisdom was that the Democratic nomination for president had been locked up by Gary Hart. I had never been impressed with Hart as a candidate when I went to Shenandoah in southwest Iowa on Wednesday, April 29, 1987, to watch him campaign among Democratic caucus-goers in rock-ribbed Republican Page County. The handful of super-liberal Democratic activists who ran the party there did not seem impressed either. I wrote in a column that local Democrats would not commit to him, making Hart a "shaky" front-runner.

I got home from Iowa on Thursday, May 1, and wrote my Hart column with a Shenandoah dateline for publication Monday. Hart's schedule listed no weekend campaign activity that would affect what I wrote, with Friday and Saturday designated as "Washington: Private Time." It turned out not so private. The *Miami Herald,* enticed by his fervent denials of philandering, reported a good-looking young woman named Donna Rice "spent Friday night and most of Saturday" with Hart at his Washington town house. Such was the lack of fervor for his candidacy that he was out of the race five days later.

That left eight little-known candidates (including Congresswoman Patricia Schroeder) competing for the Democratic nomination: "Snow White and the Seven Dwarfs." I went to Houston for their first debate, a dull affair. I remember best a postdebate encounter in a steamy little press room. I was writing a special report for the *Chicago Sun-Times,* when I felt a presence behind me reading my laptop copy over my shoulder. I turned and looked into the smiling face of somebody with whom I had not exchanged a word in seventeen years: Albert Gore Sr.

"Senator," I said, "can I help you?" "Yes," he replied, "by not writing anything bad about my son." His son was thirty-nine-year-old Senator Albert Gore Jr. ("Al" while the father was "Albert"), one of the "Seven Dwarfs" and a very dark horse for the 1988 nomination. I wondered how it would be to have a father (turning eighty in December) who thought the country made a terrible mistake in passing him over for president in 1960 and desperately wanted his son to redeem that error.

Gore was so lackluster in the Houston debate that I did not mention him, pro or con, in either my report to the *Sun-Times* or in the Evans & Novak column that followed. I wrote that the governor of Massachusetts, the "earnest, forceful" Michael Dukakis, "starred" at the event.

I dropped in to watch the Seven Dwarfs again on July 28 and 29, 1987, at the Democratic Governors Association (DGA) conference at Mackinac Island, Michigan.

My trip to Mackinac provided my third extended personal encounter with Bill Clinton, the first being a lunch with the governor of Arkansas at the 1985 Governors Conference in Boise and the second a chance meeting aboard an airliner in early July 1987.

In that second encounter, Governor Clinton suddenly plopped down next to me in the first-class section and volunteered, "You probably wonder, Bob, why I'm not running for president." The word had spread through political circles that Bill did not want national exposure of his history of philandering and neither did Hillary for the sake of what was considered a tenuous marriage. Clinton explained to me that he and Hillary thought Chelsea was too young in 1988 to be deprived of her parents in a presidential campaign. "And, Hillary and I have really overcome our difficulties," he said, reassuring a near total stranger.

At Mackinac, Clinton greeted me like a long-lost brother and filled me in on his assessment of presidential candidates who had appeared in closed session before the governors. His colleagues loved Clinton because he had so much of what they and the presidential candidates lacked: charisma. After drinking a little and talking a lot late into the night at Wednesday's closing dinner, I was up early Thursday to catch a six thirty a.m. Northwest regional flight to Detroit to connect with an eight forty-five flight to Washington. I would arrive at eleven fifteen a.m., in time for a two p.m. taping at CNN with Attorney General Meese for the *Evans and Novak* program.

When I arrived at the little island airport at six a.m., I was informed the flight to Detroit—the only one that morning—had been cancelled because of a mechanical problem. There was no way now I could get back for the Meese interview. "I'm screwed! Absolutely screwed!" I shouted, stamping my feet and uttering a string of expletives. The few people in the small airport waiting room stared at me, and I recognized one of them. It was Bill Clinton.

"What's the problem?" Clinton asked. When I explained, Clinton said: "That's not a problem." He was flying back to Little Rock, he told me, but would be happy to give me a ride to Detroit. "But won't that take you out of your way?" I asked. "Yes, it would," he said, "but I would like to help you." I should not have done it, but it was the only way I could get to Washington for my TV date. The plane appeared to be a corporate jet from an Arkansas company, loaned to the governor for his use.

The flight to Detroit took only half an hour, and Clinton talked to me all the way. He expressed concern that his party was listing too far to the Left, and he came across as just the kind of moderate Democrat I might like. The column I wrote under a Mackinac Island dateline contained this paragraph:

Had Gov. Bill Clinton of Arkansas last month entered the race as expected instead of bowing out as he did, he could have been the DGA candidate. [Michigan Gov.] Blanchard was ready to back him, as were Montana's Gov. Ted Schwinden and probably Kentucky's Gov.

Martha Layne Collins, perhaps setting off a parade. Clinton is what the governors want: attractive, Southern, moderately liberal, non-confrontational.

Would I have written this if Clinton had not given me a badly needed ride to Detroit? Of course I would. At least that's what I told myself.

My column from Mackinac Island said Dukakis once again performed best of all the presidential candidates. Dukakis, I wrote, "typifies today's Democratic governors: earnest, intelligent, well informed, hard working, humorless, moderate in tone, a little boring" and was "well-liked" by his colleagues But he was not endorsed by them because they—Clinton included—thought him to be a loser in November.

MY PARTING OF the ways with John McLaughlin was preordained by the events of Friday, February 5, 1988, but the ground had been prepared long before that. *The McLaughlin Group* was in its sixth year, and the time when he would call me the night before a taping to seek my advice on topics or would ask me to drive him to a cut-rate auto mechanic's garage were years in the past.

With the success of his television career (including a weekly interview show, *McLaughlin: One on One*), John's hauteur was overpowering. Replacing his balky old car was a staff-chauffeured limo (copied after Bill Buckley's). McLaughlin now hosted elegant dinner parties (that I report strictly by hearsay). His growing staff was instructed to address and refer to him as "Dr. McLaughlin."

A former intern of mine, an ardent conservative and ambitious journalist looking for work (whom I shall call Jim), had two job offers: one from *Rotor and Wing,* a magazine about helicopters; the other to work for McLaughlin. Asked for my advice, I urged him to stay away from McLaughlin. Placing a quest for excitement over prudence, Jim went to work for McLaughlin and soon was performing the most menial tasks. When McLaughlin returned to Washington from out of town, Jim was stationed at the airport arrival gate. Upon spotting McLaughlin, he would notify a colleague driving the limo via mobile phone: "The eagle has landed! The eagle has landed!" Jim then would carry McLaughlin's bags to curbside where the alerted limo would be waiting, not a moment having been lost for the founder and CEO of Oliver Productions.

Jim was a testy young man, and, as I expected, did not last three months before he quit. That was the rule, not the exception. The only permanent aide was producer Allyson Kennedy, a pleasant young woman who some-how stuck it out. By 1988, McLaughlin communicated off camera with panel members only through phone calls from Ally Kennedy.

Tension on the *Group* was palpable between the panelists and our com-mon enemy, McLaughlin. Germond and I often made fun of him to his face during taping breaks. During one long intermission while technicians got ready for the PBS segment, I propounded a question I thought might annoy the former Jesuit priest: "John, now that you have broken your vows of poverty and chastity, I ask you what is more important to you, money or sex?" McLaughlin guffawed and answered promptly: "Money! Money, all the way!"

McLaughlin's arrogance was most intense in road performances of the *Group* where we would simulate our program for conventions or corporate meetings. Each panelist would get $2,500 per road show, while McLaughlin would pocket the balance, from $10,000 to $15,000. Germond threatened not to appear at these events unless McLaughlin showed him a full account-ing for every occasion. McLaughlin refused, and Germond took himself off the out-of-town trips. For all my newfound wealth, I could not turn down $2,500 a show. Besides, I had enough troubles with McLaughlin, and I was not ready to break with him.

McLaughlin's introductions to each TV segment got longer and longer. I told him he was seeking a point where he could do the whole program by himself and the panelists would be irrelevant. At the same time, he com-plained (always through his staff) that I was talking too much and assigned staffers to count the words uttered by each panelist. At one point he hired Tammy Haddad, one of Washington's most talented TV professionals (sometime producer of *Crossfire, Larry King Live,* and *Hardball*). She was forced to give me my word counts and convey Dr. McLaughlin's instruc-tions that I talk less. Tammy did not last long.

Ally Kennedy once told me Dr. McLaughlin felt I was the only *Group* member who had the intellect to make it in the Jesuits. I am sure she passed on that piece of flattery at John's direction. But increasingly, he was insult-ing to me and the other panelists. When Germond and I were inducted into the Washington Journalism Hall of Fame on the same night in 1987, McLaughlin declined an invitation but in an attempt at humor sent a graceless message that since he had saved the declining careers of Germond and Novak, we had him to thank for being honored.

Executive producer Richard Moore, an old Hollywood hand, told me there were many people in show business who hated each other but collaborated for years. "I just want to be an honest broker," Dick told me, "and I want to make sure you get along well enough to keep you together." No honest broker, Dick Moore was a hired gun for McLaughlin just as he had been for Nixon.

THE CRITICAL EXPLOSION came during the taping of February 5, 1988. Since it involved a confrontation between McLaughlin and me, let a third party tell the story. This is Germond's account in his memoir (*Fat Man in the Middle Seat*):

> During a segment on the [presidential] primary campaign, Novak accused McLaughlin of being opportunistic in trying to butter up someone in the Dukakis campaign he might need later on. It was an accusation we frequently made against McLaughlin and one that we knew was accurate. Usually he laughed them off. But this time, for reasons that never were made clear, was different. When we broke for a commercial, McLaughlin started screaming imprecations at Novak at the top of his lungs. His face was red, and the cords in his neck turned white.
>
> Novak tried to reply, but he was more startled than angry and McLaughlin wouldn't listen. He grew more and more offensive, suggesting finally that if Novak didn't like the way he ran the show, he could take a hike.
>
> I finally told him to cool down, turned to Novak, and said, "If you want to walk out on this son of a bitch, I'll go with you." Novak shook his head, and by the time the commercial break ended a minute or so later, McLaughlin had regained control of himself. We finished the taping somewhat awkwardly.

During the last commercial break, McLaughlin stared at me malevolently and intoned, almost chanting, "Vile. Vile. Just vile." I knew then I had not heard the last of this incident.

Five days later, I received a call at home from Ally Kennedy. Dr. McLaughlin had decided it would be best for me not to be on this week's program, she told me (adding that I would receive the full six-hundred-dollar program fee that my contract stipulated I received anytime McLaughlin cancelled my appearance). I asked Ally whether McLaughlin would talk to me on the phone. She said she was sure that he would not but suggested I might want to get in touch with Dick Moore. I failed to reach

Moore before leaving for the airport, and figured I would try again from Columbus, Ohio, where I was making a luncheon speech to the American Society of Travel Agents.

McLaughlin had sent a message. Solely because of personal pique, he was willing to remove me from the program that would analyze the Iowa caucuses held earlier that week even though I had been there reporting the event and presumably had insights. McLaughlin was willing to risk permanently losing the panel's most visible member in order to demonstrate his total control.

From my hotel room in Columbus, I got Dick Moore on the phone in Washington. I told him it was insulting and counterproductive for John to remove me from the post-Iowa program. I warned Moore that if I was pulled off this program, I probably would have to resign from the *Group*. With his trademark stutter, Dick told me not to do anything hasty and said he would get back to me. Moore called within half an hour and told me John was adamant about keeping me off this week's program. I then told him I was quitting, and he could consider this my formal resignation. Once I hung up the phone, I wondered whether I *had* been too hasty. But Moore called me again within another half hour. He told me McLaughlin had thought better of it and I was back on this week's program, provided I still wanted to be there. I said I did.

McLaughlin conducted the February 12 taping without incident, though we had nothing to say to each other off camera. That also was true of the February 19 session, when I had a lot to comment about that week's New Hampshire primary that I had covered. But on Monday, February 22, McLaughlin dropped the other shoe. Dick Moore told me that with the Iowa and New Hampshire competition finished, John wanted to go in a different direction and that I would be off the program for the taping of February 26 (which happened to be my fifty-seventh birthday). Moore was no longer the friendly intermediary, and momentarily he had shed his stutter. He also informed me that I would not receive my six-hundred-dollar cancellation fee for this program or any other program from which I was pulled. When I protested this violation of my contract, Moore was strictly McLaughlin's hard-nosed lawyer: "Bob, you don't *have* a contract. Remember, on February 11 over the phone, you quit and said this was a formal resignation."

I had unwittingly furthered McLaughlin's grand design. It was not merely that he wanted to keep me on the hook every week, not knowing whether I would be on the panel until a few days before the taping. Every panelist would be given the same treatment. Nobody would have a regular spot on the program. Inadvertently, by my hasty "resignation" I had enabled McLaughlin to cancel me for any program without paying a cancellation fee, and he wrote the same leeway into future contracts with other panelists. McLaughlin seemed to have concluded that this program was his and he did not need anybody's help. If he could risk my quitting, he could risk losing the rest of them. Ultimately he did lose most, and *The McLaughlin Group* suffered.

After receiving Moore's call on February 22, I made one more effort to settle my differences with McLaughlin. I wanted to sit down with him and ask whether he wanted me to leave the program. If he did, I would go quickly. If he wanted me to stay, he had to restore the terms of my original contract.

His secretary told me he would be out of town all week. McLaughlin was going to Dallas early for a road show on Wednesday afternoon, February 24, with *The McLaughlin Group,* appearing before the National Roofing Contractors Association. I was flying to Dallas for the event late Tuesday night. As was frequently the case in the McLaughlin operation, we were staying in different places in Dallas—John at a luxury hotel, the rest of us at a commercial hotel. (Sometimes at airports, a limousine picked up McLaughlin while the rest of us traveled in a van.) I said I would be happy to go to McLaughlin's hotel for breakfast, lunch, or a cup of coffee on Wednesday at any time before our two thirty p.m. appearance.

I soon received a call saying Dr. McLaughlin would be busy all day Wednesday preparing for the event. What's more, he would be out of touch the rest of the week—and, indeed, for the foreseeable future. In short, McLaughlin would *never* see me.

I knew my days with *The McLaughlin Group* were numbered. I sat down at my computer when I returned to my office Thursday and drafted a memo to Ed Turner at CNN suggesting a talk show to compete against McLaughlin.

WHILE I WAS wrestling with John McLaughlin, George Bush and Michael Dukakis were sewing up the presidential nominations.

Although managers for Bush and Dole felt the prize would go to the candidate who convinced primary voters that he was the bona fide Republican, neither was a conservative. The conservative candidates, quite different from each other, were Jack Kemp, televangelist Pat Robertson, and former Delaware governor Pierre du Pont, who like Bush started as a liberal Republican but unlike Bush was now a sincere conservative. None could get the traction to contend against Bush and Dole.

Dole won the Iowa caucuses, thanks in large part to backing from Senator Chuck Grassley, leader of the state party's conservative wing. Bush, who for four years had been marching majestically to the nomination, was staggered. He did not have the five weeks before New Hampshire that Reagan used in 1980 to recover from Iowa. The 1988 New Hampshire primary came in eight days, on February 16. Dole looked like the winner in New Hampshire and probably the nominee, if only he could come over as conservative as he had done in Iowa. But in New Hampshire there was no "conservative" to vouch for him, no Chuck Grassley. It was up to Bob Dole, and he did not, indeed, *could* not, play the conservative. That was shown in the final week when du Pont challenged Dole—still leading then—to take a no-tax-increase pledge. He would not.

I spent the night of February 16 at studios set up by CNN in a Manchester office building, dashing back and forth between commentaries for CNN and writing a report for the first edition of Wednesday's *Chicago Sun-Times* on Bush's comeback victory. It was after one a.m. before I got back to the no-frills Hampton Inn outside Manchester assigned me by CNN. I was up before five o'clock to write a postelection column that I wanted wrapped up before I left no later than twelve thirty to drive to Boston to catch a three thirty flight to Washington. At about seven a.m. I received a telephone call from John H. Sununu, the governor of New Hampshire.

I had first met Sununu in Washington a few weeks after the 1980 presidential election at the annual black-tie dinner of the American Enterprise Institute. He told me he was a conservative, a former member of the state legislature and the head of his own engineering firm for twenty years. He wanted to be Reagan's secretary of Energy. The AEI dinner was loaded with conservative aspirants for high federal office, but Sununu was so pushy in urging my help that I checked him out with a Reagan transition team source. Not a chance, I was told quickly and with vehemence. Sununu was described as a loser who had lost several bids for statewide office in New Hampshire.

Two years later in 1982, Sununu arose from the chaos of New Hampshire Republican politics to be elected governor—helped by endorsement from the *Manchester Union-Leader* as the most conservative candidate. As the 1988 presidential primary approached, Sununu in his third two-year term attached himself to Bush. He had been a feisty governor with multiple enemies and there were anticipatory rumbles at Bush campaign headquarters making Sununu the scapegoat for Bush's impending loss in New Hampshire that would probably give the nomination to Dole.

But Bush won and Sununu's victory call to me Wednesday morning was an effort to make sure I got the story right and gave credit where it belonged. I remember being annoyed by this interruption from a self-serving politician as I sat at the tiny desk in my cramped motel room pounding on my laptop trying to meet my deadline. I inferred three basic messages from Sununu: First, Bush's win was a spectacular resurrection from death's door. Second, John Sununu had a lot to do with this triumph. Third, George Bush was a lot more conservative than I imagined. I incorporated part of Sununu's analysis in my postelection Evans & Novak column. After calling Bush's win "a triumph of organization and tactics," I wrote:

> On Friday morning just four days before the polls opened, the Vice President was a loser. It was then that campaign manager Lee Atwater and media consultant Roger Ailes decided on a negative commercial branding Dole as a straddler and a taxer.
>
> While Bush spread-eagled Boston television, Dole was silent. He had no time to prepare commercials, even to say that all of Dole's tax-increasing bills had been supported as administration measures by the Vice President. . . .
>
> Dole captured the most liberal, anti-Reagan precincts even after consciously wooing the Reaganite vote. His base was the upscale, ex-urban areas near the Massachusetts state line that had voted for George Bush and Howard Baker in 1980. Had Dole expanded beyond this base into conservative backwoods Republicans, he would today be hailed as the prospective nominee.

This column was published Friday, February 19, and I had breakfast that morning at the Army and Navy Club with David Keene, just beginning a long tenure as chairman of the American Conservative Union. Keene and his sidekick Don Devine had been tireless in trying to push Dole into the conservative void. He told me over breakfast that he agreed with my column's point that morning that there was still such a void to be filled.

Keene disclosed that the Dole campaign had been unable to get an anti-tax ad on television in the closing hours when Bush was making his comeback. To Keene that represented the ineffectiveness of Bill Brock, who had resigned as secretary of labor the previous autumn to run Dole's campaign.

After our breakfast, I later learned, Keene was phoned by a disconsolate Dole who invited him aboard his campaign plane as he headed west for primaries in South Dakota and Minnesota. Devine also was brought aboard, and the candidate's spirits revived when the son of the Great Plains won in those two midwestern states against minimal Bush effort. I reported over

CNN that Keene and Devine had taken over the campaign from the plane, cancelling Dole's plans to go south and instead keeping the candidate in the Midwest and adding a new stop in Oklahoma. After my report, Brock issued an ultimatum to Dole: Fire Keene and Devine, or fire me. Dole could not at this late date lose Brock and thus dismantle his national campaign. Keene and Devine were literally removed from the campaign plane, taking with them whatever frail chance remained for Dole to win the Republican nomination as the conservative candidate.

TEDDY KENNEDY in 1986 slipped into law new regulations barring ownership of both a newspaper and a TV station in the same city, the purpose being to require Rupert Murdoch to sell the *Boston Herald* (which had taken the Evans & Novak column from the *Globe* on Murdoch's orders after he purchased the Field Syndicate). Murdoch also had to sell the *Sun-Times,* but publisher Robert E. Page arranged a purchase by a New York leveraged buyout group that retained him in that post.

I suggested to Page the paper might throw a party to celebrate the twenty-fifth birthday on May 15, 1988, of Evans & Novak. I was thinking of a cocktail party at the National Press Club, but Bob wanted something grander. We ended up in the main ballroom of the Willard, which had been made over into a luxury hotel. I just got in under the wire to take advantage of Page's generosity, because he was eased out of the *Sun-Times* in August.

The Evans & Novak celebration was grand indeed, not only because of the sumptuous buffet and open bar in the glorious new ballroom but also because of our one thousand invited guests—senators and congressmen, cabinet members and foreign ambassadors, many of whose limousines were lined up on Pennsylvania Avenue outside the Willard.

All living presidents, past and present, sent messages except Jimmy Carter (who my sources told me vehemently refused to do so). The "Dear Bob" letter from my old adversary Nixon concluded: "One of the best ways to learn what's going on in politics is reading Evans and Novak. One of the best things about being retired from politics is not having to return their calls." (Of course, he never returned them.)

Three people we asked to speak—Art Buchwald, Bob Strauss, and *Washington Post* publisher Donald Graham—roasted us, but with the flame turned down. A view of us after twenty-five years by the liberal establishment appeared on page one of the *Washington Post* Style section the morning after the party. The *Post*'s Marjorie Williams wrote a long piece about us illustrated by a huge photograph of us. She chronicled old complaints about our alleged lack of ethics and accuracy but conceded—as did Reagan and Nixon in their congratulatory letters—that we broke exclusive stories.

When Marjorie Williams visited our offices at 1750 Pennsylvania ("beyond messy, way past disheveled, inching toward foul"), she met me for the first time. I think she represented a younger generation of liberal Washington journalists who regarded me with fear and loathing as a mean-spirited reactionary. I am a "surprise," she wrote, who "comes across in person as almost diffident" and somebody who "smiles easily and talks more softly than his partner." But she also wrote, in comparing me to Rowly: "Novak is not only the one with the higher profile; he is also the one who, from the beginning, had a stronger ideology, and perhaps a stronger will to use the column to bring about change."

Williams's overall assessment:

Evans and Novak have practiced a form of journalism unlike anyone else's—fact-based and ax-grinding at once, simultaneously far ranging and arcane. Deliberately melding their styles and even their ideologies, they have broken news and possibly careers. They are alone among journalistic partnerships—in their methods, their longevity, their passions.

That assessment, the entire Williams piece and the whole celebration, taken together, indicated to me that Evans and Novak had survived two decades of assault from the Left that was launched, following early praise for the column, when it was realized we were not liberals after all.

WHEN I ARRIVED in Atlanta on July 13, 1988, the week before the Democratic National Convention there, the presidential nomination had been locked up by Michael Dukakis for months.

On Saturday evening, July 16, in a reception at the Carter Center, Rowly and I waited in a long receiving line to shake hands with Jimmy Carter. Rowly told me he planned to ask the former president why he had refused to send a message of congratulations to our twenty-fifth-anniversary celebration. I implored Rowly not to, but there was no way to dissuade him when he was determined. "Oh, Rowly," responded Jimmy, all smiles, "your invitation must have got lost. I would have been happy to send you a note." I had been reassured by a Carter intimate that Jimmy had given strict instructions not to acknowledge Evans and Novak in any way. Nearly eight years after leaving office, Jimmy Carter was still lying about matters large and small.

On Sunday night, July 17, Meg Greenfield of the *Washington Post* hosted her customary preconvention dinner party. I had a long talk with Bill Clinton and again found him engaging and insightful. The governor of Arkansas confided he was apprehensive about fulfilling his only convention duty: the nominating address for Dukakis on Wednesday night. In fact, Clinton delivered one of the longest and worst speeches in convention history, unable to come to an ending until convention managers pulled the plug. It now occurred to me he might be too undisciplined and self-indulgent, not realizing that his reservoirs of charm and energy overrode his liabilities.

Dukakis made a bold overture to the white South by naming Senator Lloyd Bentsen as his vice presidential running mate. Bentsen was not the southern conservative he once was, particularly not since his 1976 run for the Democratic presidential nomination. Still, he was a moderate tax-cutter, well thought of in the corporate world.

The great hope for Bentsen was that he would energize the old boy network in Texas to bring back that state's big cache of electoral votes from the Republicans. In Atlanta, I encountered my Texas friend George Christian, Lyndon Johnson's last White House press secretary who had become one of Austin's big-time lobbyists and was not much of a Democrat anymore. But Bentsen had called on Christian to come to Atlanta to help out. Christian complied, attending his first Democratic national convention since LBJ's nomination in 1964. "It's like a college reunion," Christian told me, referring to the conservative Texans rejoining the national party.

To keep these old boys loyal, Dukakis had to prevent black activist Jesse Jackson—his last remaining primary opponent—from taking over the convention. He tried, but failed. Word seeped out that Jackson was being bought off with money, additional members and staffers at the Democratic National Committee, and joint Dukakis-Jackson campaign appearances. I noted in an Evans & Novak column that Jackson's "triumphal address" to the convention Tuesday night mentioned Dukakis "only in passing."

I was on the convention floor after the Wednesday night balloting when Bill Daley spotted me and suggested we hit a nearby hotel for a drink. I incorporated in an Evans & Novak column what he told me that night of his "concern about the mood conveyed by Atlanta." Without quoting him by name, I continued:

"For those who watched television," one Midwestern Democratic operative [Bill Daley] told us, "what they saw looked like a black party." That troubled Democrats who are anything but racists. The depletion of Dukakis's lead, according to polls released during the convention, is attributable to the Jackson factor.

William M. Daley was no racist, and there was no more loyal Democrat. The son of a former mayor of Chicago and the brother of a future mayor, he was not one of the white Chicago Democrats defecting from their ancestral party. But Daley feared the disastrous candidacies of George McGovern, Fritz Mondale, and now Mike Dukakis posed a bleak future for traditional Democrats.

A FEW MONTHS before the Republican convention in New Orleans, press secretary Pete Teeley told me Bush had turned down my most recent request for an interview. Teeley was my good friend and all year had tried to bring his candidate and me closer together. Now Pete informed me: "Bush says he is giving up trying to get along with you. He's tired of getting whacked by you." The vice president was terminating a twenty-one-year relationship that began when George and Barbara Bush hosted Geraldine and me for dinner at the Houston Country Club in the summer of 1967.

Unlike Nixon, however, Bush never ordered his subordinates to stay away from me. One of them was Bush's coolly ruthless campaign manager Lee Atwater. I first met Atwater at the 1980 Republican convention in Detroit when he was twenty-nine years old, introduced by his fellow South Carolinian and mentor John Carbaugh. Atwater, who seemed several steps below Carbaugh in intellect, was deferential to John. But since 1980, Atwater had ascended the greasy pole rapidly to become first a senior political aide at the Reagan White House and now Bush's campaign manager.

The Republican convention was two weeks away when Atwater phoned to pitch me, unsuccessfully, an anti-Dukakis rumor that turned out to be false. I took the opportunity to ask Atwater about the one piece of unsettled Republican business going into the convention: selection of a vice presidential candidate. The consensus was that Bush's choice was between Dole and Kemp. Although a month earlier Dole had seemed inevitable, Bush resented the harsh things Dole had said about him during the primaries. Conservatives were pressing for Kemp, but Bush told some he felt the former football star was "too light." Actually, Bush aides told me he dreaded the prospect of a President Bush being second-guessed every day by a Vice President Kemp. Atwater, claiming he was just "speculating," told me there was a way out for Bush. He gave me the name of a running mate who would replicate the vigor and conservative backing Kemp would bring to the ticket without carrying with him Kemp's difficult personality.

Was Atwater trying to give me one of the great exclusives of my career? Or was he really just "speculating"? For once I erred on the side of caution—and thereby missed one of my biggest scoops.

I was writing a column that Monday, for publication on Wednesday, August 3, about the Republican condition in advance of the national convention. I threw in Atwater's tip in the last paragraph, after briefly talking about the vice presidential selection:

> The newest serious possibility is Sen. Dan Quayle, a 41-year-old moderate conservative from Indiana with a growing reputation in national security. Why an unknown? "We get Kemp without Kemp," responds a Bush operative.

The "Bush operative," was Lee Atwater. It is now clear he was trying to hand me a huge story and I was too stupid to accept the gift.

I WAS SITTING in for Pat Buchanan doing *Crossfire* on August 19, 1988, in what developed into an unpleasant incident with a long tail. The guest on the Left was Chris Matthews, former aide to Speaker Tip O'Neill who had been hired by the *San Francisco Examiner* with the title of Washington bureau chief (actually a columnist) as his entry into the riches of television.

Matthews had tried out as a substitute for Tom Braden as a left-wing co-host on *Crossfire,* and had not performed well. The future cocksure TV personality was tentative then. But now in 1988 he was developing his combative *Hardball* style in pounding away against Dan Quayle. It irritated me because Matthews on the attack adopted the manner of the hired political gun he used to be, while posing as a newspaperman. That was why I said to Matthews: "When I first met you, you were a paid flack for Tip O'Neill."

That was not nice to say, but it was the truth. It wasn't the kind of truth Matthews wanted to hear, as he launched his new career. He is an emotional man, and he reacted emotionally: "The reason you keep bringing up Tip O'Neill's name is because he would never give [you] an interview and he threw you out of his office and you can't get over it." I was stunned. This was a reference to the imaginary incident in Speaker O'Neill's 1987 memoir that was supposed to have occurred in 1973, six years before Matthews went to work for him. "That is a lie, like a lot of other things that come from you, Mr. Matthews," I said. Contending I had tried for years to get into O'Neill's office, Matthews said: "I was there."

The "I was there" comment could only be interpreted by a viewer as meaning that he "was there" when I was thrown out by the speaker. That was a flat-out lie on national television and ended any relationship between us. Matthews's only public comment on this I know of came in the media critic Howard Kurtz's 1996 book *Hot Air,* that included this remarkable paragraph:

> Matthews says he knew nothing of the original incident but that O'Neill repeatedly cited it to him in refusing to appear on Novak's CNN show. "I was always a great source for Bob," he says. "I liked the guy. But he decided he doesn't like me. Tip O'Neill was too big for them to take on, so I guess he decided to focus on me. I was playing defense for my old boss, who I'm loyal to."

Matthews was never a "great source" for me. As for O'Neill being "too big for them to take on," the Evans & Novak column had called the former Speaker a liar in 1987 after his book was published. Finally, I take "playing defense" to mean he was not telling the truth on *Crossfire.*

I ARRIVED IN Los Angeles on Thursday, October 13, 1988, to cover the second and final Bush-Dukakis debate. Their encounter at UCLA could prove important for the presidential election, but I had my mind on something else. I was at a hotel on the UCLA campus in Westwood in time for a scheduled eleven thirty conference call to put the final touches on the debut of *The Capital Gang* on CNN just two days away. The gestation period had been six and one-half months, which in television is short for putting a new show on the air and much faster than the old broadcast networks ever could do.

I had decided I must leave *The McLaughlin Group* when John McLaughlin stiffed me in Dallas on February 24, but long before that I had been mulling over what kind of talk show I would run if I had the chance. I put it down on paper on Monday, February 29, in my confidential memo to Ed Turner at CNN in Atlanta.

I proposed a program called *Novak's Washington* (following the pattern of *The McLaughlin Group* and *Agronsky and Company*). I would be the moderator and write the scripts setting up each segment. The regular panelists, if they agreed, would be Pat Buchanan, Al Hunt, and Mark Shields (though I had not yet breathed a word to any of them). Shields was fifty-one, Buchanan was forty-nine, Hunt was forty-six, and I was the senior citizen at fifty-seven. The fifth panelist would be a rotating nonjournalist newsmaker—a member of Congress, a White House staffer, a cabinet member, a governor, or political leader. We would alternate between Democratic and Republican guest panelists. Since the regular panelists would be split half and half ideologically (Hunt and Shields on the Left, Buchanan and Novak on the Right), rotating outside guests meant the ideological balance would alternate, liberal or conservative, three to two.

The political celebrity guest was one new twist setting this program apart from *The McLaughlin Group* and *Agronsky and Company* (which that year became *Inside Washington with Gordon Peterson* after Martin Agronsky retired). The other difference was that we would be aired live on Saturday night. The older programs, taped on Friday afternoons for Saturday night broadcast, missed news occurring Friday night or during the day Saturday. I proposed we broadcast at seven p.m. Eastern time, the same time as *Inside Washington* and a half hour ahead of *McLaughlin.*

Ed called me three weeks later to say the idea had cleared the CNN bureaucracy. I met for breakfast in the downstairs grill at the Army and Navy Club at eight a.m. on March 23 with Ed Turner and Randy Douthit, who was the executive producer for *Crossfire* and *Larry King Live* and would play the same role on the new program. Turner over the years had prodded me to leave McLaughlin and do this kind of program for CNN. As usual, he was my big booster and backer at CNN.

Turner liked my two innovations and was delighted by my proposed panel (if I could get them). Turner drew the line, however, at *Novak's Washington,* saying: "I think one CNN program with your name on it is enough" (referring to *Evans and Novak*). That was wise because my tenure as moderator would be brief. My next step was to sign up my panelists, and there were problems with each of them.

I first learned of Albert R. Hunt antagonizing conservatives when he was a young *Wall Street Journal* reporter covering the House Ways and Means Committee on my old beat. I had written him off as a liberal stiff from Washington's Cleveland Park leftist enclave until I met him on the campaign during the seventies. I had dinner with him and found him an engaging companion who loved two of the things I did: sports and politics.

Hunt and I had developed a personal relationship, exchanging insults and wisecracks in a framework of ideological debate. It sometimes got out of hand as it did one night at a small 1981 dinner party in the sumptuous Watergate apartment of Bob McCandless. The guest of honor was Chuck Grassley, an Iowa farmer just elected to the Senate. This was before spinal meningitis permanently curtailed my alcohol intake, and I had too much to drink that night. So did Hunt and we engaged in a profane shouting debate over tax policy, as our wives and the new senator looked on in horror.

I observed Hunt throwing a temper tantrum in the lobby of the dilapidated Dallas Hilton hotel at the 1984 Republican convention when he could not get into his locked room, exhibiting what reporters who worked for him say they experienced frequently. Although many of them hated Hunt, he was a terrific newspaperman who I thought put out the best product in Washington after he became the *Journal*'s bureau chief in 1982 at age forty.

Al was the Washington personage near the level of Scotty Reston and Arthur Krock that Barney Kilgore, founder of the modern *Wall Street Journal*, had craved as his bureau chief. He also had become a poised TV performer as a regular panelist on PBS's *Washington Week in Review* but quit when he was named bureau chief, to show his big, fractious staff how committed he was to the newspaper. I felt Al loved being on TV, and I hoped he was ready to terminate his sabbatical after five years.

I picked Hunt under false premises to fill what I conceived as a *slightly* left-of-center slot. For years, I had kidded Al about being a limousine liberal. While we were in Illinois covering the 1980 campaign, I needled him about his criticism of America and asked him to name his favorite country. Playing along with me, he replied: "East Germany!" That came back to haunt him as I passed on to dumbfounded interviewers doing articles on Hunt that he had told me his favorite country was the Stalinist dictatorship. In truth, however, I underestimated how reflexive a liberal Hunt was, which made for a livelier program.

The hardest choice for me was Mark Shields as the panel's left-wing populist. Our relations had become relatively civil since our 1971 drunken shouting match in Bob McCandless's living room, helped along because I no longer drank much and Shields did not drink at all. There was a cultural-ideological edge to our relationship rooted in class warfare and mutual accusations of hypocrisy. But I hesitated putting Shields on the panel because I was bothered by picking him over Jack Germond, an old friend whose company I dearly enjoyed. Jack wanted to be sprung from *The McLaughlin Group*, was staying there only because he did not want to give up the money and would have joined my new group in a second. Furthermore Germond was well known and good on television.

But Shields was the very best. In 1979 at the age of forty-two, he had made a midlife change ending his career as a Democratic political consultant. Meg Greenfield hired him as an editorial writer for the *Washington Post*, where he had to take typing lessons. That role did not work out, but Shields became a syndicated columnist, a much-acclaimed PBS commentator, and one of the most popular speakers on the lecture circuit. I had debated Mark in many venues, and I was lucky if I could hold my own. This was not a matter of my picking the person I liked best, but selecting the one I thought would do the most for the new program.

I wanted to make my offer to Mark in person, and it took a month before we could get together on Friday, April 22. I worried whether Shields would sign on to a new project with somebody whom he did not care for all that much, and he did not seem enthusiastic in that first discussion.

Patrick J. Buchanan had neither Hunt's problem of going back on television nor Shields's lack of affinity for me, but I thought he might be the least likely of the three to come aboard. Only Pat of *The McLaughlin Group* panelists enjoyed a good relationship with John McLaughlin. I thought he might think twice before leaving with me and delivering a double blow to his old Nixon White House comrade. To my surprise, Buchanan quickly said yes on the phone. I guessed that Hunt and Shields, who were close friends, conferred together. They soon called me back, separately, to accept. As much as print journalists profess disdain for television, I found few say no when offered the exposure and money that TV provides.

I now had my panel, but Ed Turner and Randy Douthit were busy getting ready for the national political conventions. Nothing more could be done until late August. The strictest secrecy had to be maintained because I did not want McLaughlin to know, and I cannot even find in my confidential schedule the taping date for our first pilot. I am fairly sure it was the last week of August. I decided to simplify it by not bringing in an outside panelist for this first test run.

Unlike the first *McLaughlin* pilot in 1981 when I knew even during the taping that it was a bomb, I felt pretty good about this effort—until I viewed the tape. It was awful. Feeling there was something basically wrong, I sought the opinion of David Smick, formerly Jack Kemp's chief of staff who had become a multimillionaire financial consultant after losing a race for Congress in Maryland. Smick's only television experience was as a fellow panelist with me on *Money and Politics,* an excellent Washington TV talk show that was cancelled after a couple of years. But he was one of the smartest people I knew, and I valued his judgment. After viewing the pilot, Smick had no trouble locating the problem: It was Bob Novak.

Smick told me that not only was I a poor moderator but that role robbed the program of the abrasive commentaries that were my trademark on *The McLaughlin Group.* I soon concluded that Pat Buchanan should be the moderator, and he agreed to give it a try.

We taped the second pilot on Saturday, September 10. This time I invited an outside guest: Robert Strauss, whom we swore to secrecy. As I expected, Buchanan was an excellent moderator, and the second pilot was terrific. I was exuberant as Geraldine and I took Bob and Helen Strauss to a celebratory dinner at the Jockey Club. Never shy about his own abilities, Strauss raised doubt that we could find outside guests matching his breadth of knowledge. We managed.

I once referred publicly to my relationship with John McLaughlin as "a bad marriage," and now I felt like a man sneaking out on his shrewish wife for another woman. On October 6 CNN announced the creation of *The Capital Gang* with its first broadcast on Saturday, October 14. It took everyone by surprise, including McLaughlin. CNN's official announcement listed Randy Douthit as senior executive producer and me as just another panelist. But I was much more than that. Calling it *The Capital Gang* was my idea. So was each panelist ending the program with an "outrage of the week." The outside guest on the inaugural program—Thomas Foley, the House majority leader—was my decision, as was just about every outside guest over the next seventeen years.

I was doing the executive producer's job, working all week on arrangements for the program, and coming in at eleven thirty a.m. Saturday for a seven p.m. live broadcast. Douthit designated me as co-executive producer. As such, I suggested to Ed Turner that $100,000 sounded right as my payment for the program. Ed said that was too much and came back with $60,000 (about $102,000 in 2007 money), which is what I wanted in the first place.

The story in the October 7 *Washington Post* by staff writer Carla Hall began by saying Novak, "the strident-hard-edged conservative who never talks in less than a raised voice on 'The McLaughlin Group,' is leaving his chair on the popular television show and starting his own." One line in the *Post* story brought me up short. It said that Buchanan "will continue to accept invitations" to *The McLaughlin Group*. When I asked Pat about that it turned out he was going to be a McLaughlin regular. I had assumed that Buchanan was leaving McLaughlin along with me. He now said he had intended all along to do both programs, and I took him at his word. Would I have accepted Pat if I knew he was sticking with McLaughlin? I don't know. Let's just say it would have been *The Capital Gang*'s loss if we did not start with Pat Buchanan as our moderator.

The first *Capital Gang* program jumped 37 percent over CNN's September average and led all of CNN's Saturday night shows, setting a pattern persisting to the end. Randy Douthit placing the panelists cheek-by-jowl created a more conversational atmosphere than was the case on *The McLaughlin Group*, where panelists were seated distant from each other and tended to shout their positions. Substantively, we could not lose with the main topic on the *Gang*'s debut: The first round knockout in Thursday night's final presidential debate.

NOBODY NEEDED TO wait to determine the winner of the Bush-Dukakis debate at UCLA. CNN anchorman Bernard Shaw, moderating the debate, began by asking Dukakis: "Governor, if Kitty Dukakis were raped and murdered, would you favor an irrevocable death penalty?" Dukakis responded with perhaps the single worst answer I have heard in a half century of political debates. "No, I don't, Bernard," Dukakis replied without a trace of emotion. Cold and precise, he added there are "better and more effective ways to deter violent crime," before launching into a wonkish discussion on liberal ways to do just that.

Two nights later on the first *Capital Gang*, our first outside guest, Majority Leader Foley, was blunt in saying what his candidate should have done: "I think that if he [Dukakis] had said something about human emotions: 'I would get the guy and kill him right on the spot. He would never have left the house alive.' " That answer confirmed my shaky belief that politicians could contribute on a journalists' talk show. Foley got the point that this was not about the pros and cons of capital punishment but a liberal candidate for president looking bizarrely uncaring.

Bush had erased a seventeen-point deficit. On the eve of the UCLA debate, the *Evans-Novak Political Report* had Bush leading in the Electoral College, 391 to 147. My final forecast had it 447 to 91. When it ended 426 to 112, we had picked forty-eight of fifty states correctly. The Bentsen ploy did not move Texas. New York was the only major state carried by the Democrats.

Although this was the third straight Electoral College landslide for the Republican Party, GOP celebration was restrained. My *ENPR* forecasts, which I was still making myself, were on the nose. I predicted the Democrats would gain one seat in the House and two in the Senate. It ended up a two-seat gain in the House and one seat in the Senate. That meant comfortable Democratic margins: eighty-two seats in the House and nine in the Senate. Realignment still seemed a distant dream.

The post-Reagan Republican Party was uninspired, and Bush did not have a clue as to what was wrong. He did not realize he won big because he was blessed with a Democratic opponent who could not have beaten anybody.

CHAPTER 36

Believing Their Own Spin

As it became clear late in the 1988 campaign that George Bush would be elected comfortably but saddled with big Democratic majorities in Congress, he reverted to his liberal Republican roots. I traveled with him going into the campaign's final weekend and found he had abandoned what was left of the Reagan Revolution: no support for the Contras or the Strategic Defense Initiative, no mention of conservative social issues, no supply-side departures. I described one saving grace in the last paragraph of the Evans & Novak column running November 7, 1988, the day before the election:

> The sharp exception to the impression of George Bush coasting on a centrist track in the final days is his insistence he will not raise taxes. "I don't want to raise your taxes, and I won't do it," he tells his rallies. Even if Wall Street and the media don't believe him, it is the one piece of beef in a bland campaign-ending stew.

Contrary to a future misreading of history, Bush did not make the no-new-taxes pledge just once at the New Orleans convention by reciting speechwriter Peggy Noonan's "read my lips" rhetoric. He repeated that pledge throughout the campaign. Nevertheless only the truly naïve (such as I) took him at his word. Al Hunt bet me a new vest (I had become a daily vest wearer when I became a regular TV performer in the early eighties) that Bush would break his word his first year in office.

It was announced shortly after the election that the Bush transition would be handled by Bob Teeter, Bush's pollster and political adviser, and Craig Fuller, Vice President Bush's chief of staff who was supposed to fill the same post for him as president. Everybody had expected John Sununu, just finishing six years as governor of New Hampshire, to head the transition and then head back home. I've never been smart enough to report by deduction, but this looked to me like a signal Sununu was going to be chief of staff.

I had not talked to Sununu since his triumphal telephone call the morning after the New Hampshire primary. But when I called him on Friday, November 11, he became a source. Yes, he said, it was a done deal but I could not quote him and had to pin my column on the deduction that his not heading the transition cleared the way for him to be chief of staff. I hurriedly rushed in a lead item for the Sunday column of November 13: "The strong belief inside the Bush transition group is, despite no confirmation from the president-elect, that Gov. John Sununu of New Hampshire will be named to the key post of White House chief of staff."

The official announcement was made the next Thursday. Fuller was devastated and declined Bush's offers of other high positions (at age thirty-seven, his government service ending permanently). Sununu told me that his appointment destroyed any notion of Jimmy Baker being a deputy president as secretary of state—which I reported in an Evans & Novak column Friday morning, without attributing it to Sununu.

The accession of John Sununu shocked liberal Washington. He was Lebanese and Roman Catholic, anything but a Bushie High WASP. Nor did he fit Bush's ideology. Sununu was pro-Contra, antiabortion, pro-nuclear power, antitax increase. I wrote:

> Bush makes his own decisions—and keeps them secret. Associates believe he decided on Sununu three weeks ago, but whispered not a word to anybody—not even Fuller, his solitary companion in months of crisscrossing the continent. . . .
>
> [L]ong knives out for Sununu cut him up as a hayseed and zealot. In fact, he is about as familiar with Washington as Baker was eight years ago and has rare experience as a governor dealing with legislators. He is known for adhering in principle without losing his composure, though his adversaries sometimes lose theirs.

John Sununu and I were pleased with each other—for now, anyway. Shortly after this puffy column ran (which proved demonstrably wrong about Sununu never losing his composure), I visited Sununu at Bush transition headquarters in an old office building up Connecticut Avenue. He told me he saw a nucleus of four conservatives driving policy: Sununu, Vice President Quayle, Jack Kemp, and William Bennett. He said Bennett was going to fill the new post of drug czar and a place would be found for Kemp.

· · ·

NAMING SUNUNU WAS a sign the Bush administration might not be as bad as I expected. Another sign came during a black-tie dinner at the Omni Shoreham Hotel to honor Jack Kemp, sponsored by the Heritage Foundation. I reported in the column:

> [T]here is a tendency in the Bush camp to write off as crackpots Republicans who sound like Ronald Reagan. Accordingly, when the cream of the American Right assembled in black tie Dec. 1 to honor Kemp, the words of Bush and Baker were startling. They praised the originator of supply-side tax cuts for inspiring the Reagan Revolution. Days later conservatives were still talking about Secretary of State-designate Baker's confession of faith in the supply side.

That faith was fine, but it was not a guarantee Bush would stick to his no-tax-increase pledge. It was not even a guarantee Kemp would join the cabinet.

My sources close to Bush said he could not stand the thought of having Kemp around spouting conservative rhetoric. But how much would he have to hear from Kemp if he were secretary of Housing and Urban Development (HUD), which is the job Bush gave him?

Not that his restricted HUD jurisdiction limited Kemp. Early during the Bush administration, I showed up at HUD for an appointment with him. He was late as usual. After fifteen minutes, about six people walked out Kemp's inner office. I recognized two of them: William Schneider and Michelle van Cleave, both hard-line foreign policy and defense analysts. "Who were you meeting with?" I asked. Kemp chuckled, then said: "Oh, that was my national security team."

ONE LOW-LEVEL BUSH administration appointee was of personal interest to me. Immediately after the collapse of the Kemp presidential campaign (where she did opposition research), my daughter Zelda accepted an offer to be research director of the 1988 campaign for the U.S. senator from Maryland by Assistant Secretary of State Alan Keyes. The offer came from Bill Kristol, who had been Keyes's graduate school roommate at Harvard and now was his campaign manager.

On June 23, 1986, I had met Bill at one of the Kenyon College seminars I had been attending for years. He was a young University of Pennsylvania professor who as recently as 1976 was a college student campaigning for Democrats Pat Moynihan and Scoop Jackson. Now, he said, he was an undiluted Republican. I had brought sixteen-year-old Zelda, a high school junior, to Kenyon as part of her college tour (she fell in love with Kenyon, applied for early admission, and was accepted). Kristol, Zelda, and I had several meals together, beginning a relationship that would play a large part in my daughter's early career and would develop what I thought was a lasting friendship between Bill and me.

A flamboyant, right-wing African-American Republican, Keyes had no chance in Democratic Maryland. But the campaign was great fun for Zelda. After Keyes's inevitable defeat, Zelda planned to apply for graduate school in political science at Boston College. But Bill Kristol intervened. He was joining Vice President Quayle's staff, and soon would head it (and help turn the vice president's office into a center of conservative intrigue in the Bush administration). Kristol asked Zelda to join him, and she took about a minute to abandon plans for graduate school.

Zelda was assigned to Quayle's political office, and she helped write his political briefing books for trips. She got to travel with the vice president occasionally, including a trip to El Salvador for the inauguration of President Alfredo Cristiani, my intrepid helicopter pilot of a few years earlier.

It was a fabulous experience for a twenty-three-year-old just out of college, but I don't believe Zelda was all that comfortable working with uptight Republicans. She would, I was sure, find a good life outside politics.

THE BUSH TRANSITION did not interfere with our annual Christmas sojourn with Geraldine's family in Texas, and I drove to Austin in search of column material. The talk there was less about the new president from Texas than his son, George W. Bush.

George W. had run for Congress from West Texas and lost at age thirty-two in 1978, disappeared from politics for eight years as a less-than-successful oilman in Midland, and then moved with his family to Washington in 1986 to work full-time on his father's presidential campaign. I was introduced to him by Bush's press secretary Pete Teeley, and I took both of them to dinner at the Army and Navy Club. George W. was quite pleasant and the most conservative Bush I had met (I had covered his liberal grandfather, Senator Prescott Bush of Connecticut, three decades earlier). At first glance, however, the grandson did not overwhelm anybody. I could hardly envision W. running for governor of Texas.

Yet, that was the buzz in Austin during the 1988 Christmas season. I dropped in to see the sharp-tongued Texas State Treasurer Ann Richards, the smart money pick as the next Democratic nominee for governor. She had skewered President Bush in her Democratic keynote address at the Atlanta convention, and now she was getting ready for his son. She told me in her Texas singsong: "I don't know George Bush Jr., I don't know where he lives, and I don't know what he does." But soon she would. While it was decided in the Bush camp that 1990 was too early for W. to make his move, he would defeat Governor Richards for reelection in 1994.

I wrote in the Evans & Novak column of December 30, 1988, that W. was "traveling Texas and boning up on the oddly configured state government." Two of his father's political managers, Lee Atwater and Charlie Black, were making calls into Texas asking operatives there to show W. around. I noted that a young political consultant in Texas named Karl Rove was "helping out." This must have been the first time George W. Bush's and Karl Rove's names ever were linked in a national political column. Indeed, I think it was the first such column that speculated on George W. Bush as a candidate for major political office.

GEORGE H. W. BUSH'S presidency began with an illustration of his impotence facing huge Democratic majorities in both House and Senate. Capitol Hill Democrats were frustrated facing four more years of a Republican president (twenty out of twenty-four years, with the four lone Democratic years marred by somebody they did not consider one of their own, Jimmy Carter). Democrats mobilized against the nomination of former senator John Tower as secretary of defense, accusing their erstwhile colleague of alcohol abuse, womanizing, and improper relations with defense contractors. The Senate rejected Tower, fifty-three to forty-seven, on March 9, 1989.

The next day was a Friday, and Rowly and I had a ten a.m. taping at CNN for *Evans and Novak* with Dick Cheney. He had enjoyed a spectacular career since I first met him in 1969 as Don Rumsfeld's aide. Richard B. Cheney had become Ford's White House chief of staff at age thirty-four. Two years after leaving the White House, he was elected to Congress from Wyoming and quickly moved into the House party leadership and then minority whip, second ranking in the party hierarchy. I considered Cheney a natural leader, likely the first Republican Speaker of the House since 1954, and maybe future presidential timber. He was still only forty-eight years old when he sat down that morning for our interview.

But Cheney was distracted, seemingly fearful of disclosing something— especially when we asked about Tower's successor. The reason was that President Bush early that morning had asked him to become his secretary of defense and swore him to secrecy until it was announced later that afternoon.

Of course, the tape was worthless and had to be discarded. We scrambled to find a substitute for broadcast time at noon Saturday (coming up with Tom Foley, then House majority leader—bailing us out not for the last time). I was furious at Cheney. He should have cancelled the taping and explained later, but I am sure his mind was spinning from the unexpected turn of events. I felt Dick Cheney owed me one, and he paid it back before long.

THE FALL OF John Tower set off a chain of events exerting a lasting impact on American politics. It propelled Cheney on a path that would make him one of the nation's most powerful figures. It revitalized the long frozen political realignment by bringing a unique political figure off the backbenches of Congress.

After the 1988 election younger Republican members of Congress looked at the eighty-four seat Democratic margin in the House and blamed Bob Michel's passive leadership. I described in a column the sixty-six-year-old Michel, starting his thirty-third year in Congress, as "the prototypical Old Bull" and a "hail-fellow-well-met from Peoria, Ill." Junior Republican members complained Michel was enjoying life in perpetual minority status, playing golf with Tip O'Neill and breaking into song at the Capitol Hill Club. Cheney as party whip was seen by the Old Bulls as a link to the Young Turks—partisan and conservative but flexible enough to have been Jerry Ford's top aide. Michel was devastated when Cheney was suddenly pulled into the Pentagon.

Even worse news for Michel was that Newt Gingrich was running for whip. With eight years in the House under his belt at age forty-five, Gingrich was not the young Rockefeller Republican I had met in the late sixties. The former history professor had adopted Robert A. Taft's maxim that the business of the opposition is to oppose, and his opposition now was to bring down Jim Wright as Speaker on ethics charges. Michel and the Old Bulls were appalled.

In February 1989, I asked Newt privately what he hoped to get out of incessantly pounding Speaker Wright, which I thought only antagonized Democrats and divided Republicans. "No," Gingrich replied. "Jim Wright is gone. He is finished. He'll be out of there before you know it." I was impressed by the force you never saw in the Old Bulls.

Nobody saw it in Michel's candidate for whip: Edward Madigan, a fellow Illinoisian whom Michel had named chief deputy whip. In an Evans & Novak column that ran March 22 (the day House Republicans were to vote on Cheney's successor), I described Madigan as "a backroom deal maker unknown to the outside world. Representing a downstate district adjoining the Minority Leader's, he is Michel without the charisma."

The morning that column ran I had a date with a congressman at the Republicans-only Capitol Hill Club. As I waited in the first-floor lobby, I came face to face with somebody I had never met. "So I'm 'Michel without the charisma,' " he snarled at me. It was Ed Madigan.

That day, Madigan—and Michel—were defeated ignominiously. Gingrich won, eighty-seven to eighty-five, in the most important intraparty congressional vote in my time in Washington. The House never would be the same again though Michel would hang around as leader at Gingrich's sufferance for another four years. President Bush gave Madigan a graceful exit from Congress by appointing him secretary of agriculture.

Congressman Vin Weber of Minnesota, one of the shrewdest strategists in politics, was Gingrich's campaign manager and convinced me Newt could win when hardly anyone gave him a chance. Although the news media, Democrats, and a lot of Republicans were blind to it, a Republican House of Representatives was in sight.

THE CONVENTIONAL WISDOM in Washington in the spring of 1989 was that Gingrich's accession to the leadership saved Jim Wright on the grounds that Democrats never would give the Republican firebrand the satisfaction of overthrowing the speaker. I tended to agree, but I suddenly changed my mind, as reflected in the Evans & Novak column of April 25:

> A Democratic House member went home for last week's recess ready to support Speaker Jim Wright's fight to survive, but was quickly transformed to a probable anti-Wright vote not by angry constituents but by a 279-page beige government paperback.
>
> Studying the report on Wright by the House Ethics Committee outside counsel, Richard J. Phelan, stunned the Congressman. As a lawyer, he had accepted at face value the private briefing by Wright's attorney assuring the Speaker's Democratic colleagues that no House rule had been broken, much less any law. But reading Phelan's report on the long plane ride home to the West Coast obliterated this Congressman's previous forecast of a bare 20 Democrats who could vote against Wright on the floor.

My source was no backbencher and no maverick. It was Robert T. Matsui of California, a party regular who kept out of trouble by holding his tongue. He was one of my very best sources, whose identity can be revealed now because he died all too young at age sixty-three on January 1, 2005.

Matsui was a hardworking, low-profile congressman whom I met in 1981 at one of the big dinner parties hosted by Bob McCandless, then a lobbyist for Transamerica. I found him not only well-informed and insightful but also gentle, a quality not common to politicians. He became a super-source for me, though he never was quoted in the column. When sometimes I would ask to attribute an inoffensive quote to him, Matsui would protest, "Oh no, Bob, nothing like that. No, no." For fifteen years, he gave me an invaluable window into the House Democratic caucus. We had breakfast or lunch two or three times a year, always in the Members Dining Room of the House in full view of his colleagues. Nobody ever suspected our arrangement, partly because we often were seen on CNN debating each other.

Matsui did not leak to me out of self-protection. Nor did he seem to have political or ideological motives. He just seemed to want me to get it straight. I think that was Matsui's motive on Monday, April 23, 1989, when he telephoned to say his previous statements to me that there would not be twenty Democrats against Wright were mistaken. It was because of reading the Phelan Report flying back to Sacramento.

If the Speaker had lost Bob Matsui, Jim Wright was gone. I did suggest in the column that Wright's fate was undeserved. There were "far more blatant offenders" in the ranks of Congress, I wrote, contending that "the Speaker's obsession with an extra bundle of bucks here and there is widely reflected in the House."

ON FRIDAY, APRIL 28, 1989, Dick Cheney paid us back for the wasted March 10 interview. He crossed the Potomac to the CNN studios near Union Station for a taped *Evans and Novak* interview to be broadcast the next day. That trip was part of Cheney's expiation. Usually we traveled to the Pentagon to tape a secretary of defense.

In his opening question, Rowly asked Cheney whether he thought Soviet president Mikhail Gorbachev's "peace offensive" would result in Congress forcing major troop withdrawals from NATO. Cheney said it would be a terrible mistake to withdraw *"until we know that Gorbachev is for real."* I followed up by asking what he really thought of the Soviet leader. He then made more news than any single answer in the program's twenty-year history:

I think you have to distinguish between what [Gorbachev is] trying to do and whether or not he's actually going to be able to do it. And I think the bottom line is that if I had to guess today, I would guess that he would ultimately fail. That is to say, that he will not be able to re-form the Soviet economy to turn it into an efficient, modern society. And that when that happens, he's likely to be replaced by somebody who will be far more hostile than he's been in terms of his attitude towards the West.

Cheney had said all that needed to be said, but Rowly pressed him for more and the defense secretary complied:

> Cheney: My personal view is that the task that [Gorbachev] set for himself of trying to fundamentally reform the Soviet system is inca-pable of occurring. I don't think you can take a system, run it for seventy years as a Communist dictatorship, stamp out all of the spirit of initiative and entrepreneurship in that society and then overnight or even within a short period of time, say, a few years, come back and create an efficient economy. And I have yet to see any evidence of any improvement in the economic performance of the Soviet Union.
>
> Evans: But you think the likelihood, if that happens and he fails, is that he would be displaced, not that he would change his own policy?
>
> Cheney: It could be either one. He could modify his policies and have to accommodate to a more conservative line. He could conceiv-ably be replaced. The point is we don't know. . . .
>
> Evans: When is this going to happen?
>
> Cheney: Nobody can make that prediction, and nobody can pre-dict what will come afterwards. We do know that for forty years, the Soviet Union has been governed by men whose interests were not ours. They've invaded Hungary, Czechoslovakia, ruled with an iron hand. Now we've had a brief period of time with a man who appears to be more of a realist and pursuing policies friendlier to the West. We don't know whether that's a permanent change that's going to last or whether it's a temporary aberration. And as long as there's a possibility it's an aberration, we have to be careful.

In our postinterview commentary, Evans said: "That was the most can-did, forthright observation or, say, criticism of what's going on in the Soviet Union, and I don't think anybody in this administration . . . or, in Europe, has said it so forthrightly, that he thinks Gorbachev can't make it." I noted that Cheney "really said what he thinks. He's going to have to watch that." That afternoon, by chance, I had a private interview, one-on-one, with

James Baker in the ornate little room on the seventh floor of the State Department that the secretary of state uses on such occasions. Baker spoke without an aide present, the only secretary of state ever to do so with me. I was questioning him on the record for a *Reader's Digest* profile of him.

After Baker and I finished and I turned off my tape recorder, I played Bertrans de Born and stirred up strife by telling him: "Dick Cheney told me this morning that he thought Gorbachev would fail." Baker maintained his customary cool. "It was off the record, I suppose," he said. "No," I replied, "*on* the record." "Really?" Baker said, displaying a trace of anxiety. "Yeah," I went on, "it's on *television*. On CNN tomorrow noon." *"Really!"* Baker said, now fully animated.

I am certain Baker's next step was to call President Bush. Cheney's *Evans and Novak* interview was big news worldwide. Bush asserted he did not agree with his secretary of defense, making clear Cheney spoke only for himself.

Cheney was right about Gorbachev failing but wrong about being replaced by somebody worse. I think Cheney's primary motive was to cut off liberals who wanted to use Gorbachev as an excuse to reduce defense spending. But beyond that, I think he was upset—as I was—by Bush and Baker doting on Gorbachev. I think he also realized that Gorbachev's goal was to preserve the Soviet Union as a Communist state, and that in the end was not compatible with U.S. interests.

AT AGE FIFTY-EIGHT in my twenty-sixth year as a columnist, I never had been to the Soviet Union and never had traveled abroad with a senior U.S. official. I corrected both those deficiencies in May 1989.

Reporting my *Reader's Digest* profile of James Baker as the new secretary of state, I accompanied him on his first mission to Moscow. Baker's two-day visit was concluded by a six-hour meeting with Gorbachev on Thursday, May 11, 1989. We reporters had been briefed going to Moscow on Baker's strategy. He wanted to take the emphasis off arms control issues that the Soviets for two decades had used to divide the West. Baker would shift emphasis to questions that divided the two superpowers and did not cast the Soviets in such a favorable light.

But in their last meeting, Baker was ambushed. Gorbachev started by proposing negotiations on short-range missiles that he knew Baker must reject, to the consternation of European NATO allies. Then Gorbachev informed Baker he would unilaterally reduce the Soviet short-range force by five hundred missiles. He won a "gentleman's agreement" from Baker promising not to disclose these details at the televised press conference concluding two days in Moscow. When Baker's plane was airborne, Soviet Foreign Minister Eduard Shevardnadze forgot the "gentleman's agreement" by announcing the warhead cuts and chiding Baker for a "very negative position" that "seriously concerns us."

Baker knew he had been taken to the cleaners. On the plane ride Thursday evening from Moscow to Brussels (where he would brief NATO members the next day), Baker three times came to the rear of the plane to explain himself to reporters. I had started the column aboard the secretary's plane, and it was early enough thanks to the time gained traveling westward for me to finish the column in Brussels and still make Friday morning's newspapers. While experienced State Department beat reporters were hemmed in by dictates of straight news to relate all aspects of a detailed story, I was the only columnist on the plane and could tell what really happened. Friday's column (under a Moscow dateline) began:

> Having come here for the first time determined to change the subject from arms control, Secretary of State James A. Baker III found himself rolled by the new master of international politics.
>
> Mikhail Gorbachev . . . pulled yet another of his "unilateral" arms cuts that enable him to pose as the world's leading crusader for peace while the United States is seen as being the warmonger.
>
> Baker is one of the foxiest of inside operators dealing with Congress and in American politics. But he is a new boy in the global high-stakes game, and Gorbachev left him sprawled in the dust. . . .
>
> Once again, the Soviets have done precisely what Baker sought to avoid here: exploited arms control to further undermine Western unity and make the Americans seem the aggressor.

Of all the barbs I directed at Baker, I think this was one that got farthest under his hide (especially the title, "Gorbachev Rolls Baker"). Six years later in his memoir, *The Politics of Diplomacy* (1995), Baker sniffed that my column played into "another of [Gorbachev's] public relations coups."

I DON'T BELIEVE CNN management intended to be cruel to longtime employees. It was simply insensitivity, which reached a new low on Monday evening, November 25, 1989. It was eight p.m., and Tom Braden had just finished another *Crossfire*. Executive producer Randy Douthit told Braden that it was all over, that his contract was not being extended.

At age seventy-one, Braden was cut loose after eight years without warning, without explanation, and without public announcement. Word leaked out, and the next day CNN issued a bloodless statement: "We exercised our contractual option to end the relationship between CNN and Tom Braden." But a *Washington Times* reporter got hold of Douthit, who expressed (not for attribution) what he really thought. Braden had been ill, frequently stuttered, could not remember names, and was not always lucid. "A lifetime of hard living finally caught up with him." That ended Tom Braden's journalistic career and, indeed, his public life.

Mark Green, a New York City Democratic politician, long had been Braden's heir apparent. Green would come down from Manhattan and take a room for two weeks at the Holiday Inn on Wisconsin Avenue near the old CNN bureau while Braden was on vacation. The CNN brass wanted Green as Braden's permanent replacement, but Buchanan did not and he had the clout to make his veto stick. The second choice was *New Republic* editor Michael Kinsley, who was agreeable to Buchanan.

Green was devastated. An ambitious Democratic politician, Green had been the party's nominee for the U.S. Senate from New York in 1986. Nevertheless, he was willing to give up politics and move to Washington to become Buchanan's sparring partner. (In 2001, Green won the Democratic nomination for mayor of New York, and he told me he would have Pat Buchanan to thank for becoming the leader of the nation's largest city. Alas, Green lost to newly anointed Republican Michael Bloomberg in the general election.)

A U.S.-SOVIET SUMMIT was hurriedly arranged on the Mediterranean island of Malta on December 2–4 as a "get-acquainted" session between Bush and Gorbachev.

The news from Malta was not that exciting, but Bush's debut on the world scene met my worst expectations. The catchword in official briefings for this summit had been "linkage"—getting Gorbachev to end financial support for the Communist insurrection in El Salvador in return for magnanimous U.S. positions on arms control and trade liberalization. In fact, I wrote from the Maltese capital of Valletta, "there was no linkage between Soviet good conduct in Bush's backyard and his [Bush's] proposals that exceeded expectations of everyone—including the Kremlin."

My biggest insight on this trip came the day after the Malta summit on Monday, December 5, at NATO headquarters in Brussels, where Bush had gone to brief his allies on the Gorbachev meeting. CNN's State Department correspondent Ralph Begleiter invited me to his interview with Baker. Begleiter asked the secretary of state about a prediction from Bonn by U.S. ambassador Vernon Walters that Germany would be unified within

five years. Baker replied coldly that what Walters said certainly did not constitute U.S. policy.

Dick Walters was a charming and colorful seventy-two-year-old survivor in the great game of global politics who (as an army general) was an
interpreter and troubleshooter for U.S. presidents when Jimmy Baker was
a lawyer in Houston. He had served worldwide for the U.S. government,
including stints as ambassador to the United Nations and deputy CIA
director.

Baker's putdown of Walters was so abrupt that I got him aside after the
taping to ask about it. Going off the record, Baker said this really endangered relations with the Soviet Union and that Walters was way out of line.
Baker said much the same thing in his State Department memoir six years
later. With the Berlin Wall down and all the Iron Curtain countries in
peaceful revolution in 1989, Baker—and the Bush administration—were
behind the curve. Baker had been correct in saying Walters's prediction was
wrong. Instead of five years, it was less than one year. Germany was unified
on October 3, 1990.

ONE MORNING EARLY in 1990, Rowly came into the office with a block-
buster announcement delivered matter-of-fact. He would be sixty-nine
years old in March, he said, and he planned to retire. Really retire, by giving up the column, the television program, the newsletter, the lectures, the
forum—the whole works. I had suspected something like this when Rowly
started letting me make reporting trips to the Soviet Union and cover international summits (Helsinki after Malta).

I considered Rowly the preeminent reporter of the cold war, putting the
Evans & Novak column far ahead of the pack in reporting the rollback of
communism in Poland, Czechoslovakia, and East Germany. Now he apparently was ready to call it a career.

When? Rowly was vague, suggesting not too soon but by the end of the
year. Total retirement would double my workload, and I could not handle
it by myself. I needed a new partner, and Fred Barnes seemed to me the
only candidate. He was compatible with me personally and ideologically
and one of Washington's best reporters. I was on the phone with him the
next day with my proposal of partnership, which I figured would bring him
over $100,000 a year to start with (plus whatever he made from lectures and
The McLaughlin Group where he had replaced me). Fred seemed stunned
and said he would get back to me.

Weeks passed without my hearing from either Rowly or Fred. After
more than two months, I told Evans I surely was not anxious for him to

leave but needed a little firmer departure date so that I could begin the complicated procedure of putting a new operation in place. Rowly looked at me as though I had just asked him his plans for flying to Mars. "Oh," he said, "I'm not retiring. Not at all. I was never serious about that."

Fortunately, I thought, I had not heard from Barnes, which I interpreted as meaning he was not interested. A few days after Rowly's nonretirement statement, Fred called to say that yes, he would be happy to be my partner. I told him Evans had just changed his mind and was not retiring. I felt like a fool.

THE LONG ARMED struggle against the Marxist-Leninist regime in Nicaragua established by the Sandinistas had succeeded. There was no victory parade in the streets of Managua, but the first Communist dictatorship on the American mainland agreed to elections on February 25, 1990—forced by the Contras. That was the good news. The bad news was that the Sandinistas were heavily favored to win at the ballot box what they could not secure by the sword. The Sandinistas were better organized and much better financed than the loosely organized opposition coalition of fourteen feuding political parties.

Allen Weinstein, who ran the Center for Democracy in Washington, urged me to spend a few days observing the campaign. I would go on my own dime, but Weinstein's organization would make sure I had access to *both* sides—marking the first time in many trips to Nicaragua that the Sandinistas opened their doors to me.

I arrived in Matagalpa, eighty-four miles northwest of Managua, on Saturday morning, February 10, in time for a massive rally. The opposition presidential candidate—Violeta Chamorro, proprietor of the famous liberal newspaper *La Prensa*—was hobbled by a broken leg and arrived seated in an open jeep, riding down the streets of Matagalpa amid the crowd's cheers.

The first person I recognized in Matagalpa that day was Ambrose Evans-Pritchard, a Washington correspondent for the *Sunday Telegraph* of London. He was derided by the Washington press corps as a right-wing sensationalist, but I considered him a great reporter. When I asked him how the election campaign was going, his answer was unequivocal: "The Sandinistas are going to lose." When I expressed skepticism, Evans-Pritchard told me not to take his word for it but go out and do my own reporting. "Go talk to ordinary people," he advised.

I took that advice, the result of which was an Evans & Novak column a few days later, under a Matagalpa dateline that began:

The tableau of 40,000 Nicaraguans in the town square to hear opposition presidential candidate Violeta Chamorro bolstered claims that an honest vote count Feb. 25 will end 10 years of Sandinista revolution.

Campesinos arriving here from the countryside on foot and on horseback, under scrutiny of the Sandinista police, confirm that fear has been conquered in the face of government intimidation. If the people dare attend open rallies, they surely can muster the courage to vote in the country's first free and competitive election.

I was climbing onto a limb about an election in a foreign country. Evans-Pritchard and I were the only foreign reporters in Nicaragua who predicted a Sandinista defeat. A Communist victory was taken for granted not only in the American news media but in Jimmy Baker's State Department, which secretly planned postelection peace overtures to the Sandinistas.

I could not have had a better fifty-ninth birthday present in Washington on Monday, February 26, when it was announced on early morning TV that Violeta Chamorro had unseated the Marxist-Leninist Daniel Ortega as president of Nicaragua. American network correspondents in Managua and anchors in New York and Washington acted as if they had lost a loved one.

Nobody seemed more dismayed than Jimmy Carter, who had headed the international election observers. He had inveighed against the Contras for years and during the Nicaraguan election far exceeded his authority by lecturing opposition parties to cut ties with the armed resistance. On television on February 26, Carter could not hide his bitter disappointment. While demanding demobilization of the Contras, he advised Chamorro not to be too aggressive in claiming victory for fear of riling up the Sandinistas. I thought Jimmy Carter was just as poor a former president as he was a sitting president.

ON THE EVENING of June 26, 1990, I was at the Marriott Hotel in Warsaw on a reporting trip to Eastern Europe and the Soviet Union (accompanied by Geraldine). I was watching CNN when it reported President Bush had just abandoned his no new taxes pledge. I turned to Geraldine and said: "Well, now we have a one-term president."

It had taken a year and a half for Bush to break his word, much longer than many predicted. (The delay in the president's betrayal won for me a handsome red vest from Brooks Brothers, the prize in my bet with Al Hunt over whether Bush would raise taxes his first year as president. I have worn the vest every Christmas season since then.) In my heart, I knew the tax

battle was lost the moment Bush named Dick Darman as his budget director. It was only a matter of time.

Richard G. Darman was a malevolent influence on Republican policy
for a dozen years. I referred to him as "the mysterious Mr. Darman" early in
the Reagan administration, seeing him as Baker's sinister lieutenant. Always
wary of each other, we lunched together frequently and Darman accepted
invitations from me to *Evans and Novak* and *Capital Gang* on CNN, the
Evans-Novak Political Forum and the annual Wanniski conference. Personally I think he enjoyed my company as I did his. Professionally, he understood the kind of news I wanted, and would drop morsels for me that
always benefited *his* agenda. Only Darman knew the exact parameters of
that agenda.

I did not know who Dick Darman was and I doubted he was sure himself. Neither conservative nor a supply-sider and not much of a Republican,
he was the administration's most influential domestic policymaker. Cultur-
ally, he was Ivy League (Harvard) and Protestant (Episcopalian). He had
seemed as High WASP as his mentor Baker until a profile in the *Washington Times* of May 18, 1989, reported that Darman had a Jewish grandfather
(Arthur Darman), a fact Dick protested would be "exceedingly improper"
to report. I was offended by the *Times* going back two generations for Darman's "Jewish problem," and I told Darman I considered it a reversion to
Nazi-style racial purity standards. For once, Darman did not have a quick
reply and seemed not to want to pursue the subject. He failed to inform
me, as I later learned, that the newspaper did not have to go back two generations because Dick himself had been bar mitzvahed, just as I had.

Darman was pursuing the same anti-supply-side goals at OMB in the
Bush administration that David Stockman had pressed during the Reagan
administration. But while Stockman transformed himself from my source
to my target, erstwhile target Darman became my source. I was suspicious
but reported Darman's self-description of working for the two supply-side
goals of the Bush administration: no tax increase and a capital gains tax cut.
I believe he wanted to keep me from sniping at him while he made a tax increase unavoidable for Bush. As for his supporting a capital gains cut, he
shed few tears when the Democrats killed it.

I had thought Sununu, measurably more conservative than any of Reagan's four presidential chiefs of staff, would be a counterweight to Darman.
Instead, Darman charmed him as he had George Bush. I gained an insight
into the Darman-Sununu relationship in the late summer of 1990 when I
was reporting for a *Reader's Digest* profile of Sununu. Sununu figured I was

a friendly reporter so that transparency was the way to go. He gave me access to things reporters don't see, including one cabinet-level meeting on clean air legislation. With Sununu at one end of the long table and Darman at the other, they dominated the proceedings—taking turns tossing their colleagues around like a professional wrestling tag team. They were the two smartest people in the room, and they knew it. They were also wise guys, each prone to show off mental agility.

Sununu seemed now to be so firm an ally of Darman that he would not resist him as tax increase details were pinned down. Once Bush announced that he was breaking his word, the partisan overpowered the ideologue in John. For a year and a half, Sununu had been the voice on the inside arguing against a tax increase. But once Bush broke, Sununu was a total tax increaser. I wrote in a column: "One presidential aide compares Sununu's labor for Darman's budget deal to Col. Nicholson's obsession with building the bridge on the River Kwai demanded by his Japanese captors—a good man captivated by an evil project."

As House minority whip, Gingrich participated in the bipartisan budget summit at Andrews Air Force Base outside Washington. He was outraged by the veto given Democratic leaders there and was the summit's sole dissenter from the tax increase deal. Gingrich and Sununu once had conferred daily. Now they did not speak to each other. Gingrich was persona non grata at the Bush White House.

So was I. After avoiding me for weeks, Darman agreed in October 1990 to meet me for lunch at the Army and Navy Club—*if* we limited our conversation to what *he* wanted to talk about. It turned out he did not want to talk about much, making for an unproductive lunch. He finally broke the silence with a revelation: My "hero," Newt Gingrich, was not an active participant in the budget talks but was silent, doodling on the pad in front of him. What's more, Darman had a copy of Gingrich's doodles for me. Darman's implicit challenge to me was that if I was a real reporter, I would write the truth about Gingrich. I thought this silly, and I ignored it.

JANE SANDERS NOVAK died in her apartment's bedroom in Maryland on August 10, 1990. Seven months earlier, I arranged a ninetieth birthday party at our house where people who knew her best described what a wonderful person she was. She had been diagnosed with inoperable pancreatic cancer in November 1989, but was able to live a full life until the week before her death. She told me she did not want a Jewish religious service (which she had requested for my father three years earlier). We held the memorial service in our living room, mainly a rerun of the birthday party. I delivered the eulogy, and Geraldine and the children did the readings, including excerpts from Scripture.

My mother was the first person in her family to attend college (one year at Joliet Junior College), at a time when my father's two sisters did not get beyond eighth grade. She worked for nine years as a private secretary, an unusual occupation for girls from immigrant families in the 1920s. But her attitude about relations between the genders belonged to the nineteenth century. She felt she was on earth to serve the men in her life (my father and me), and she expected us to take care of her. My father's financial condition was a little precarious after retirement, but my mother had a cavalier attitude about bank balances. The nurse we had hired after my father's stroke became a forty-hour-a-week employee, staying on to take care of my mother for the rest of her life. My mother asked me once or twice whether my father's estate was sufficient to pay for her nurse and all the other expenses. I told her it was, though in fact my mother's meager widow's inheritance had run out long before that.

My mother had bestowed her ample supply of affection on my first wife, and she was devastated when our brief marriage collapsed. She told me she never again would reach out to another wife of mine (*if* there were another wife, which she indicated might not be that good of an idea). But withholding of love was impossible for Jane Novak. She came to love Geraldine, who took care of her in the final years as if she were her own mother.

As a spoiled only child, I was the principal object of my mother's uncritical affection. I could do almost no wrong (though in later years, my mother took me to task whenever she thought I was being too harsh with her adored grandchildren). She was really angry only when somebody was mean to her dear son, as during a surprise party for Geraldine at Columbia Country Club outside Washington to mark her graduation, with honors in economics, from the University of Maryland in 1981. Bob McCandless was one of the speakers I had selected to say a few words. McCandless made it a roast of me. Turning to Geraldine's mother, who had come up from Texas for the graduation, Bob said: "She had hoped for Geraldine to marry somebody who was both gentle and gentile, but she got neither." After the meal, my mother—all five-feet-one of her—walked up to the hulking McCandless with a few choice words: "I *hate* you! I *hate* you!" she said. But hatred was not Jane Novak's style, and McCandless became her friend.

My children returned their grandmother's love, and Zelda in 1996 named her first child Jane Sanders Caldwell. Every time I look at this vivacious, loving little girl I see my mother.

. . .

ON AN EARLY September morning in 1990, I was in the downstairs grill at the Army and Navy Club when I spotted a newly familiar face seated alone for breakfast a dozen feet from me. It was Judge David Souter, President Bush's nominee for the Supreme Court.

Should I ignore him and not disturb his privacy? No, I could not resist the opportunity. When I introduced myself, Souter responded with a look of terror. He had been stashed away in a room at the club by his sponsor and fellow New Hampshireman, Senator Warren Rudman, and probably had been told this was a place where nobody would bother him as he prepared for confirmation hearings. Now, he might be thinking, I am confronted by this right-wing columnist who has been so critical of my nomination.

In July, when Bush named Souter to replace the ultra-liberal Justice William Brennan, I sensed something was wrong but did not guess how wrong. The Evans & Novak column of July 25 two days after his nomination suggests I was confused, but so was the White House. "Bush's lawyers assured him that Souter was dependably conservative," I wrote, "but, new to the federal [appeals] bench and Yankee-reticent in revealing his sentiments, he had few footprints and none at all on the abortion question." My suggestion was that Bush "chose the sure path to confirmation" in naming Souter.

The column implied that the issue was his confirmation "gamesmanship," not his ideological mind-set. In his memoir (*Combat: Twelve Years in the U.S. Senate*), Rudman said he always knew that Souter supported *Roe v. Wade*—and so did George Bush, despite the president's professed desire to overturn the abortion decision. "I suspected," Rudman wrote, "that the President was less concerned with how his nominee eventually voted on *Roe* than that he/she would be nominated without a fight."

With Souter's liberalism extending beyond abortion, he emerged as a soft-spoken replica of William Brennan. He was the least revocable of George Bush's many blunders as president. Sununu, who as governor of New Hampshire had named Souter to the state Supreme Court, years later admitted to me he had erred in pushing Souter for the Supreme Court of the United States. But Rudman would be delighted by Souter's record on the high court. In the late 1990s I spotted Rudman and Souter lunching together at the Army and Navy Club, obviously having a good time. Warren Rudman was one of few Republicans who could still smile about David Souter.

MIDTERM ELECTION CAMPAIGNING by a president is usually awkward and seldom effective, but George H. W. Bush's effort in 1990 was just about the worst I ever had seen. I got on the presidential press plane for two days the last week of the campaign in Florida, Massachusetts, and Ohio.

Bush would begin his basic rally speech with the banal Republican pep talk he had been perfecting over thirty-five years. Next, he would launch a defense of the budget deal that Republicans detested, evoking mainly pained looks from listeners. Finally, he would announce he was about to "shift gears" away from partisan oratory and issue a call to war that was meant to be stirring but wasn't. From the moment in August when Saddam Hussein sent Iraq's troops conquering and occupying Kuwait, Bush was determined to roll them back by U.S. force. "In Massachusetts Thursday," I wrote the last week of the campaign, "[Bush] got out of control in claiming that Saddam has surpassed Hitler in brutality. His set speech . . . left $50-a-ticket listeners passive and unresponsive—surely not eager for combat in the desert."

In Ohio, with Air Force One filled, a portly politician was given a seat in the front row of the crowded press plane. A couple of network correspondents, enjoying themselves drinking Stoli as the day ended, were not pleased by the presence of this intruder and were rude to him. They covered the White House, not national politics, and did not recognize the man. But I knew him, and he provided the lead of my preelection column under a Cincinnati dateline:

> President Bush had just tried again to rev up both Republican spirits and the national mood for war, when an important party leader here asked a question echoed by GOP colleagues across the country.
>
> As Air Force One left Cincinnati for its next destination Friday, the Ohio Republican mused: "I wonder whether the President was here to help us or help himself."
>
> Then, in effect answering his own question, he told us: "If I had my druthers, I would have preferred he not come."

The unnamed pol was Bob Bennett, who had been named Ohio Republican state chairman in 1988 but whom I had known for years as an astute party pro who was candid with me. Political reporting means talking to the Bob Bennetts of the world.

Starting from a low base, the Republicans got lower on November 6, 1990, with a net loss of one seat in the Senate and eight in the House. (In the *Evans-Novak Political Report,* I forecast the Republicans losing one seat in the Senate and thirteen in the House.) The huge Democratic majorities now were twelve in the Senate and an even one hundred in the House.

Twenty years earlier after tasting defeat in the 1970 midterm elections and fearing defeat for reelection in 1972, Richard Nixon sat his political brain trust down to devise a new game plan. "There is no such wisdom in the Bush White House," I wrote in my postelection column, "where the spin doctors believe their own spinning." Senior aides expressed their delight with the elections, pointing out that moderate Pete Wilson had been reelected governor of California and that Democratic gains in the House had been kept below double digits. John Sununu, who had entered the White House as a breath of conservative fresh air, blamed the defeat on Newt Gingrich and other Republican foes of the Bush budget sellout. I had no doubt that the Bush team counted on a military victory in Iraq to save reelection in 1992.

CHAPTER 37

Yeltsin Up, Bush Down

ON JANUARY 16, 1991, I was filling in on *Crossfire* when we were interrupted by the beginning of the U.S. bombing of Iraq. It was an event that would cast a long shadow on Iraq, the United States, the Bush family, and Evans and Novak.

The crisis began August 2, 1990, when Saddam Hussein sent 100,000 troops into defenseless Kuwait. Rowly and I, who had been consistent cold war hawks, opposed the military option in Iraq. We felt a bloody war with unforeseeable consequences could be avoided by negotiating with Saddam. On *Capital Gang* Al Hunt called me "Neville Novak" (recalling the appeasing British Prime Minister Neville Chamberlain).

Having reached the political mountaintop against all odds, Bush seemed to me an unhappy president. He could not come to grips with the prevailing Republican opinion on taxes, abortion, racial quotas, and other social and economic issues. Saddam's invasion of Kuwait enabled Bush to conceive of himself as confronting a barbaric global threat, not a mere Arab land-grabber.

The bombing launched January 16 was followed by the land war beginning February 23 that ended victoriously in three days. I was delighted and surprised by this swift success of U.S. arms. But in sixty-three Evans & Novak columns on the crisis after Iraq's invasion, the overwhelming preponderance written by Rowly, our message was that military intervention was unnecessary and dangerous.

We were wrong about the danger, and I told Rowly we should do a column that, if not exactly a mea culpa, explained the error of our ways. Rowly did not believe we ever needed to explain a change in direction or analyze a failure in our judgment. I insisted that it was necessary in this case, and Rowly told me to draft a difficult column—in effect, apologizing for what he mostly had written. Our column of March 8, 1991 ("On Being Wrong") began by stating "two miscalculations that deserve explanation":

First, we overestimated Saddam Hussein's powers of resistance and underestimated the effectiveness of high-tech American arms. Second, we overestimated the dangers of negative reaction by the Arab "street," which turned out to be surprisingly subdued.

Now the war has been won with minimum expenditure of time, fortune and blood. Questions remain, however, about the President's procedures in sending the nation into the Gulf War, the necessary diplomatic tradeoffs and the overriding reason for war. To be wrong about the outcome of the war, we believe, is not necessarily to be wrong about the necessity of going to war.

I wrote about "one conservative House GOP leader who was haunted by visions of body bags" and who confessed to me he would have voted against the war resolution if he had had a free choice. "Luckily for his political future," I wrote, "party discipline bound him." Since his political future is behind him, I now can identify him as Vin Weber—one of the brightest men I ever knew in politics. After the military victory in the desert, Weber rejoiced that Bush had been correct. My column continued:

We come far closer to that judgment than to left-wing critics of the President who see no vindication in victory . . . But we do continue to question the means chosen by Bush to go to war: mobilization and deployment 8,000 miles away of an immense military force without a single vote of Congress; then—at the very flash point—the rush on Congress to approve it. Under such procedures, it is hard to imagine any bar on any president against waging war in the future that he says is required to correct gross injustice.

The prophetic quality of those words chills me.

ON THURSDAY, FEBRUARY 7, 1991, I was in Moscow scheduled for a multipurpose interview that afternoon with Boris Yeltsin in his office as president of the Russian Republic. The bill for the trip to Russia was being paid by the *Reader's Digest* for an article on Yeltsin. The first part of the interview would be taped and then edited for broadcast as a half-hour *Evans and Novak* on CNN. Finally, I would draw on the interview's raw material for an Evans & Novak column. Thus, I planned a journalistic trifecta.

To schedule a Yeltsin interview represented the triumph of hope over experience. Seven months earlier, I was scheduled to tape Yeltsin for an *Evans and Novak* program. I was in Moscow that summer of 1990 for the Soviet Communist Party's Congress where Gorbachev was trying desperately to save the party, communism, and the Soviet Union.

Except for Dick Cheney, the Bush administration—led by Jim Baker—stubbornly supported Gorbachev. Young intellectual reformers had embraced Yeltsin as their best hope to lead the Russian people to a nonsocialist, nonimperial state. That seemed daring after Yeltsin's reported drinking bouts on 1989 visits to the United States and Western Europe. I wrote in the Evans & Novak column of Friday, July 6, 1990, under a Moscow dateline:

> A reputation for instability persists because of incidents such as one here last weekend. Yeltsin was personally committed to do a televised interview with us to be broadcast internationally over CNN, but, without warning, failed to show. When aides cited vague "health" reasons and called his appearance "a physical impossibility," the worst suspicions were aroused.

When I arrived back in Moscow in February 1991, Yeltsin as president of the Russian Republic was locked in a power struggle with Soviet president Gorbachev. State Department and CIA experts convinced Bush that Gorbachev was the hope for peace between the nuclear superpowers while Yeltsin could inadvertently trigger a holocaust. Yeltsin had resigned from the Communist Party while Gorbachev kept trying to "humanize" Lenin's inhuman creation. Yeltsin gave almost no interviews. The *Reader's Digest,* then still conservative with a strong anticommunist tilt, wanted the truth about him. Against my better judgment, I sought another meeting with Yeltsin.

Reporting in Moscow, Leningrad, and the Georgian capital of Tbilisi before the Yeltsin interview, I became convinced the only hope for democracy was, with all his faults, Yeltsin. In Tbilisi, the reformer Valerian Avadze—who had just resigned his membership in the Communist Party after twenty-four years—took me to a Sunday anticommunist rally where speakers thundered denunciations of Gorbachev for the slaughter of civilian protesters. Avadze and other Georgia democrats he arranged for me to meet all expressed disappointment in Bush for not speaking out against Gorbachev's massacre. An economist, Avadze told me: "For the last seventy-three years, these so-called socialists have made this rich country very poor. Only the Communists can do this." I wrote in an Evans & Novak column:

> Such sentiments are shared by [the] Georgian government, which is functioning independently of the Kremlin. The government building

in Tbilisi flies the flag of the Kingdom of Georgia [and] is adorned by a poster commemorating the April 9 killings. . . .

No Soviet flags are to be seen in Tbilisi. Statues of Lenin have been torn down. Georgia's native son, Josef Stalin, is in disgrace, the Stalin museum at his birthplace closed. Serge Ordzhonikidze, the Georgian Bolshevik who led Red Army troops into Georgia to annex it to the Soviet Union in 1919, is referred to in Tbilisi as "the traitor."

To the Georgians, Gorbachev turned down his chance for federation last year, and now this republic will go its own way.

In one busy Sunday, I had learned what the Bush administration refused to accept. Georgia was finished with the Soviet Union, just as the Soviet Union itself was finished.

THE MEETING WITH Yeltsin went on as scheduled Tuesday, two days later. Yeltsin was gracious, enthusiastic—and sober—during the two hours he spent with me. He seemed anxious to impart his own thoughts after a lifetime of parroting the Communist line. Yeltsin was blunt in the interview for CNN:

The Communist Party does have real power today, and it is on the offensive today. . . . The KGB [is] a monster. It's a mammoth state within a state. . . . [Gorbachev] is striving after one-man power, and gradually he is getting it. Autocracy . . . It's high time Mr. Bush and Mr. Baker finally saw the processes that are under way in the Soviet Union, saw them more deeply and more clearly. . . . I think the time is coming [for me] to establish a contact with the U.S. President. . . . Gorbachev, [Prime Minister] Pavlov and the others, and the entire administrative system . . . will have to collapse. . . . First of all, I am a non-party man. Secondly, if from the entire spectrum of parties internationally, one were to choose one, I would choose the position of a social democrat.

After the camera went off, Yeltsin talked in a more conversational tone. In an Evans & Novak column, I reported that he raised the danger of civil war but only if the Russian Army supported Gorbachev's decrees. "On the whole," he told me, "I don't think the military will fight against the people. The KGB? Maybe some of its divisions." On a personal note Yeltsin related that his chauffeur-driven car had been in four crashes that year, hospitalizing him once with serious injuries. He added: "Every time I have to think: Was that really an accident?"

"Few major political leaders have moved so far, so quickly, so late in life, as Boris Yeltsin," I wrote in the *Reader's Digest* article, the third part of my trifecta:

> . . . Yeltsin has emerged as a firm proponent of a market economy. In a country where symbolism is important, Yeltsin probably crossed the Rubicon when he removed Lenin's picture from his office wall. "There is now just a nail," he told us in his typically irreverent manner.

I concluded, as was common in my *Reader's Digest* articles, with an editorial note:

> Is Yeltsin for real? During our interview he remarked that President Bush was too close to Gorbachev: "All reliance on just one person," Yeltsin says, "is mistaken." That's good advice. As long as Yeltsin's actions live up to his words, it is he—and not Gorbachev—who deserves Western support.

Bush and Baker did not take Yeltsin's and my advice and stuck with Gorbachev. Cheney had been right in forecasting the Communist coup attempted that summer of 1991, but he was wrong in thinking it would succeed. Yeltsin was right in predicting the army would stand with the people instead of the Communists, but he made that come true as president of the Russian Republic. I was right in saying Yeltsin was for real.

AT THREE P.M., Tuesday, June 4, 1991, I received a call from Chuck Abrams that disrupted my life. Dr. George T. Economos, who had saved my life with his brilliant diagnosis of spinal meningitis in 1982, had retired. His practice was taken over by Dr. Charles Abrams, a much less humble man than Economos but a brilliant physician whose diagnostic skills were to keep me alive. In his June 1991 call, he informed me that my PSA was alarmingly elevated. *PSA?* I could think only of the defunct Pacific Southwest Airlines. Abrams explained to me that PSA stood for prostate-synthesis antigen, and it was a new blood measurement to detect possible prostate cancer. He then informed me I almost certainly had cancer.

Cancer! It is a terrifying word. Geraldine was her usual stoic self, but other associates—Rowly included—reacted as though I already had passed from the realm of the living. Elizabeth Baker, the warm-hearted producer of *Capital Gang,* burst into tears. Bob McCandless insisted that I go to Baltimore to see the world's greatest prostate surgeon: Dr. Patrick Walsh of the Johns Hopkins University.

He had devised a new surgical protastectomy that he had performed on McCandless's brother and would later perform on Bob himself. In years to come, a small army of prominent Washingtonians would go under Pat Walsh's knife. Walsh told me the choice was mine whether I wanted to use surgery or radiation, but he made clear he thought surgery was the surest course to save me. After our conversation, I felt for the first time that I would survive.

Because I had to draw my own blood for transfusions in four installments over a month, it was not until July 16—forty-three days later—that Dr. Walsh operated on me in Baltimore. My full schedule during that interval included a banquet at the Kennedy Center in honor of Boris Yeltsin, who greeted me warmly. Vice President Quayle was there and was impressed by Yeltsin though it was not Bush administration policy to be impressed and the dinner was boycotted by the State Department. (A photograph was taken of Yeltsin, Quayle, and me that the vice president—much abused for a celebrated spelling error—inscribed to me as "Bob Novack.")

The operation was a success. I remained at Johns Hopkins the rest of the week, then recuperated at home for another two weeks. My first cautious foray into work was an *Evans and Novak* taping at the Pentagon with Dick Cheney on Thursday, August 5. I was shaky and had to sit on a pillow. I was fifty-nine years old, and I don't think I ever fully recovered. I was thinking more of mortality, my soul, and the life beyond.

ON JUNE 27, 1991, Geraldine and I were invited to dinner at the vice president's mansion on Massachusetts Avenue—the only journalist at the large outdoor event. I remained on George Bush's social and political blacklist throughout his presidency, but I regularly was invited by Dan Quayle. I attributed that not to my twenty-five-year-old daughter Zelda being on his political staff but to Quayle's chief of staff, Bill Kristol, then my good friend.

During predinner cocktails, I was summoned by John Sununu to a poolside conversation. I am sure he was not happy with my sniping at him over the president's budget sellout. Unlike his boss, however, the White House chief of staff regarded me a friendly conservative in a sea of liberal media foes. Sununu felt I would share his opinion about the successor to Supreme Court Justice Thurgood Marshall, who had just retired at age eighty-two. Sununu stressed to me, though not for quotation, that Bush was not going to chance the replacement of Marshall, an African-American liberal, with another "stealth" candidate like David Souter, lacking an ideological paper trail. This time the president would name a solid conservative.

Although he claimed nothing final was set, Sununu indicated the person who best met these specifications: Clarence Thomas, a forty-three-year-old African-American named less than two years earlier to the U.S. Circuit Court of Appeals for the District of Columbia for his first judicial experience. Sununu said the decision could come any day.

The vice president's party was on Thursday night, and the next column I would be able to write was for the following Monday morning, July 1. Reflecting what Sununu had told me, I hinted strongly in the Monday column that Judge Thomas would be named to the Supreme Court. Sununu had told me the White House believes "the prospect is for an Armageddon in the Senate that will exceed in fervor" the 1987 rejection of Robert Bork. I wrote: "Bush strategists believe liberals would like to punish conservative Thomas for straying from their own 'politically correct' standard for black thinking. . . . [T]he President's men last week concluded that Clarence Thomas might face the toughest confirmation fight."

On July 1, the day my column ran, President Bush nominated Judge Thomas for the Supreme Court. It truly was Armageddon that followed. The ferocity of the attack on Thomas—centering around unsubstantiated sexual harassment charges made by the nominee's former associate Anita Hill—was intended to force him to quit. Instead Thomas accused his adversaries of staging "a high-tech lynching for uppity blacks." The fifty-two to forty-eight Senate confirmation vote on October 15 produced a bitter Clarence Thomas who was unlike the open, good-natured man he was preceding his nomination. He became socially reclusive, at war with the liberal Washington establishment that had treated him so brutally.

(As a justice, Thomas routinely ignored invitations to the annual white-tie dinner of the Washington Gridiron Club. As one of the club's few conservative members, I was delegated in 1997 to seek a response from him. Returning my call, he said he considered members of the Washington news media the enemy and would not attend their dinner. He would, however, accept *my* personal invitation. So Geraldine and I hosted Justice Thomas and his charming wife, Virginia, for dinner at the 701 Restaurant on Pennsylvania Avenue in the building next to our apartment.)

At the June 27, 1991, dinner at the vice president's home, Sununu told me he considered Thomas a sure vote to roll back *Roe v. Wade*—but not a *necessary* vote. Still in denial about David Souter, Sununu insisted that his fellow New Hampshireman provided the necessary fifth antiabortion vote.

Souter was a liberal vote on abortion as on everything else, and Thomas was only the fourth vote. Justice Anthony Kennedy, the replacement for Robert Bork who had been called more conservative than Bork when Reagan nominated him, was entranced by liberal law guru Lawrence Tribe (as I described in a column) into voting to reaffirm abortion rights. The issue appeared settled, and the prolife lobby had lost.

WHEN PAT BUCHANAN was talked out of being a presidential candidate in 1988 to give Jack Kemp a free path, I knew he still had the bug and would run sooner or later. I did not think it would be as soon as 1992 against an incumbent Republican president until I heard reports in November 1991 that he would do just that. I phoned Pat on November 13 to check it out. No dissembler, Buchanan said he would announce his candidacy against Bush in a few weeks. "It is wide open for a conservative voice in New Hampshire," he told me.

I reported this in an Evans & Novak column on November 15, asserting Buchanan would likely get 35 to 40 percent in New Hampshire against Bush, promising "dire consequences for the President." Buchanan won 37 percent, and Bush never recovered from that humiliation.

I liked Buchanan personally, and I had come to dislike Bush. But Buchanan's conservatism had evolved into something quite different from mine. While Pat shared my misgivings about U.S. military adventurism, I did not share his "new nationalism" laid out as he announced his candidacy in Concord, New Hampshire. The state was on the cutting edge of a new recession, and Buchanan proposed fighting it with trade protectionism.

Following Buchanan to New Hampshire for his announcement, I was impressed as he campaigned in economically depressed Manchester. The Bush brain trust had been writing off Buchanan as a replica of Congressman John Ashbrook of Ohio, who challenged Nixon in 1972. Though beloved in the conservative movement, Ashbrook never dented New Hampshire. I wrote in the Evans & Novak column:

> How different Buchanan is from Ashbrook could be seen as he walked the Elm Street Mall in Manchester, previously uncrowded for Christmas shopping. He needed to introduce himself to few store clerks or shoppers, who volunteered their [economic] distress. On the street, drivers honked and waved in approval.

Buchanan, a private person never known as a glad-hander, proved an unexpectedly eager hand-shaker. . . .

Many attending his first day appearances said they were unemployed or underemployed.

Every time Buchanan made a move in or out of television there were ramifications for me—in this instance complicated because Pat Buchanan was returning to politics as John Sununu was getting out.

SUNUNU'S THIRD AND last year as White House chief of staff was troublesome. The High WASPs, friends of Israel, and prochoice Republicans all were in full chase against the conservative Lebanese-American, and he made life easy for them with abrasiveness and contempt for his conservative base of support.

The incident that finally did him in was trivial. In June 1990, a hostile White House staffer leaked that Sununu took a chauffeured government limousine from Washington to New York to purchase rare stamps. "Sununu has tromped on so many toes the past two and one-half years," I wrote in a column, "that any petty indiscretion is widely welcomed. He can count on vengeful associates to disclose details of a day off in Manhattan. Even conservatives who ought to be in his cheering section are muted." The long good-bye lasted five months. George W. Bush, who sometimes did his father's dirty work, finally publicly designated Sununu a political liability as the president's popularity was tanking for other reasons. The son was delivering a death sentence, and Sununu was sacked a week later, on December 3, 1990, as Buchanan prepared to announce his candidacy.

Sununu's fall was an improbable godsend for Michael Kinsley. When it became obvious Buchanan again was leaving *Crossfire*, Kinsley—no fan of Novak—suggested John Sununu as Pat's replacement. The CNN brass jumped at the prospect of a name at least as big as Buchanan's, and Sununu eagerly seized on a way to ease his humiliation over being fired by the president. CNN rejected me after seven years' experience on the program to hire a fired politician with zero experience in TV.

Sununu left the White House determined to make real money for the first time. He became a Washington lobbyist, a former White House chief of staff who could open doors for clients paying top dollar. An ebullient Sununu told me that in his first year out of government he made more money than he had in all the previous years of his life combined and that in his second year he again surpassed his previous total combined income, the first year as lobbyist included. That suggested a long client list, which Sununu kept secret.

CNN could gloss over ethical considerations, but television pros Ed Turner and Randy Douthit were interested in quality they were not getting from Sununu. A TV neophyte, he never showed much interest in polishing his on-camera skills. The overriding problem was that Sununu substituted a half-smile wisecrack for Buchanan's robust debating style that I tried to approximate. Combining Sununu's sarcasm with Kinsley's heavy emphasis on irony resulted in the impression of two smart alecks who did not care that much about what they professed to be debating. It was the beginning of *Crossfire*'s long decline.

TO A LESSER degree, Buchanan's departure also hurt *Capital Gang*. Al Hunt agreed to my suggestion that he replace Buchanan as moderator. Though he never matched Pat's flair, Al did an excellent job.

Filling the panelist's seat left open by Hunt's move to moderator was more complicated and exerted a lasting, not entirely satisfactory, impact. I believed we needed a conservative woman, and I had one in mind even before Buchanan left. A year earlier in December 1990, I received a telephone call from Mona Charen that I thought was a little forward but caused me to admire her for that very reason. I knew she had been a young editorial assistant at *National Review,* hired by the Reagan White House for the right-wing speechwriters' enclave, then left to join Jack Kemp's presidential campaign. For the past three years, she had been engaged in the long, hard climb to establish a syndicated column. Now, she told me over the phone, she wanted to break into television and asked my "advice" (which I interpreted as meaning "help").

Over lunch at the Army and Navy Club on Friday, December 14, 1990, Mona gave me the full charm treatment, which I surmised was not her natural mode. We had a good time, yielding a flirty little postlunch note from her to me saying, "I had so much fun it had to be immoral." I thought she might do well in TV: attractive, articulate, and very conservative. I told her I knew of no immediate opportunity but promised to keep her in mind.

A year later in December 1991, I phoned Charen to ask whether she wanted to go on *Capital Gang*. She reacted with surprise, elation, and profuse gratitude. I had opened a door into the world of television that might have stayed closed otherwise. But gratitude in Washington is not forever, particularly with Mona Charen.

I immediately perceived a problem between Mona and Al Hunt. My intuition told me that Mona was too abrasive a conservative woman for him. My solution to stave off a real train wreck was to put *two* women on *The Capital Gang* panel, a liberal alternating with Charen. I picked somebody who was sure to delight Hunt and Shields: Margaret Warner, chief diplomatic correspondent for *Newsweek*. An attractive young woman, she was just about the nicest person I ever met who also was an accomplished journalist. She had TV talk show experience, performing well on PBS's *Washington Week in Review.* Margaret also had worked with Hunt as a *Wall Street Journal* reporter before going to *Newsweek* and had recently married John Reilly, a partner in one of Washington's top law firms and a longtime Democratic operative. Reilly and Warner constituted a Washington power couple who ran in the same social circles as Al Hunt and his TV journalist wife, Judy Woodruff. By constructing a package deal with two women, I thought I cleverly had made it impossible for Hunt to reject Mona Charen.

Too clever by half, I'm afraid. I had inadvertently built into *The Capital Gang* an ideological imbalance that never would be corrected. When Buchanan was moderator the three-to-two ideological advantage alternated between Left and Right depending on whether the outside guest was a Republican or Democrat. The unintended consequence of splitting the seat between Charen and Warner meant the liberals *always* would have a three-to-two advantage. When we had a Republican outside guest, Warner would be on. When we had a Democratic outside guest, Charen would be on.

I make so much of this because for the next fifteen years, I was pounded by conservatives about the liberals who ran CNN foisting an ideological imbalance on me. I told them disingenuously that I was tough enough to take on two liberals. But the problem I had created bothered me even though I could not solve it.

DURING A COMMERCIAL break in the *Evans and Novak* CNN interview with Senator Daniel Patrick Moynihan on May 10, 1991, he asked me what I was doing about the Market Square project. "Nothing," I said. "Oh, oh, that will never do," Moynihan said. "No, you and Geraldine must go over to see Liz [his wife]—*immediately*. I'll arrange it."

Pat Moynihan, chairman of the Pennsylvania Avenue Project, was father of the famous street's revitalization. He was transforming a dreary thoroughfare, which mixed run-down commercial buildings with great public structures, into what the designer of Washington, Pierre L'Enfant, meant to be the Great Avenue of the Republic. Kann's department store in the avenue's 700 and 800 blocks was torn down and replaced by two magnificent buildings constructed by the Trammell Crow developers of Dallas. In a city limited to thirteen-story buildings that could not overshadow the capital's public structures, 701 and 801 Pennsylvania Avenue were multiuse—shops, offices, and apartments. The complex was called Market Square, though the city's marketplace that had been across the street was torn down during the Depression to make way for the National Archives.

With both of our children having finished college, Geraldine and I considered moving back to the city. At the urging of Liz and Pat Moynihan, who were the first to move into Market Square, Geraldine and I decided to splurge and buy a $600,000 ($892,000 in 2007 money) condo with a wide, fifty-five-foot long terrace overlooking Pennsylvania Avenue. We moved there in February 1992, leaving our large home in the Maryland suburbs after twenty-four years.

ON THE EVENING of Wednesday, January 8, 1992, I was seated at a sushi bar on the Ginza in Tokyo with my friend and colleague, the Japanese television journalist Yoshiki Hidaka. Called to the telephone by a beeper, Hidaka returned in an alarmed state. "Your president has collapsed at the dinner," he told me. I was in Tokyo to cover Bush's visit to Japan, and that night the president was a guest at a state dinner in the prime minister's official residence. "He has been rushed to the hospital," Hidaka continued. "He may be dying."

I hurried out of the restaurant to Hidaka's waiting car, which rushed us to the Okura Hotel where CNN and other U.S. media entities covering the presidential visit were located. Bush had collapsed at the banquet table and had vomited over his host, the prime minister, but he had not gone to a hospital and had been put to bed with stomach flu. The embarrassing incident symbolized the most feckless foreign mission by an American leader in my experience, feeding my suspicions that Bush was a one-term president.

As the military victory against Iraq faded from public memory, Bush was in deepening trouble. The economy was going south, with a Republican administration having repeated Herbert Hoover's mistake of raising taxes when it should have been cutting them. Democrats led by House Majority Leader Dick Gephardt, Republicans led by Secretary of Commerce Robert Mosbacher, and corporations led by the Detroit automakers all blamed Japan for America's woes. I was on the *Meet the Press* panel on December 28 when Mosbacher announced that the president had accepted his plan to bring along eighteen American corporate leaders on a scheduled presidential trip to Japan.

After the state dinner and the presidential swoon, I wrote this for an Evans & Novak column:

The presence of the business leaders, most of them pleading for protection, doomed this trip. . . . Japanese officials were astonished that a state visit years in the planning suddenly had turned into a trade mission they see as designed to appease the President's protectionist critics.

"We cannot believe how insensitive your President is," one well-placed Japanese official told us. The presence in the official entourage of Chrysler's Lee Iacocca, corporate America's leading Japan-basher, was considered a gratuitous insult.

ON WEDNESDAY, JANUARY 15, 1992, one week after he collapsed in Tokyo, President Bush was in New Hampshire. So was I, and it was memorable because I became absolutely convinced that day that George H. W. Bush would be a one-term president.

Governor Judd Gregg was Bush's state chairman, as his father Hugh had been in 1980. He finally convinced the White House that it was essential for the president to go to a state where Pat Buchanan was campaigning as savior of the unemployed suffering from a severe recession that Buchanan blamed on Bush's tax increase. I was told Gregg wanted Bush to tell the voters of New Hampshire that "Barbara and I care," adding he was not a candidate who had "just discovered New Hampshire for the first time"— meaning that Pat Buchanan and Bill Clinton were. That was simple, but George Bush could mess up the simplest script. I reported in the column:

> Bush on Wednesday did not encounter the New Hampshire of desperate men and women Buchanan has rubbed shoulders with during his campaign visits. In six stops, the President's schedule encased him in a sealed environment. He spoke at three of the state's rare prosperous companies, facing audiences whose composition was not left to chance.

My column did not mention what I thought was Bush's real problem. He seemed goofy, using Bush-speak at the Exeter Town Hall: "Message: I care." Addressing Liberty insurance employees, Bush told them not to worry about his well-being with these words: "Don't cry for me, Argentina!"

A MONTH AFTER Bush's horrific day in New Hampshire, I was in the state again covering Bill Clinton, now the prohibitive favorite for the 1992 Democratic nomination. A routine campaign slog for the governor of Arkansas became anything but routine when the *Wall Street Journal* on

Thursday, February 6, 1992, published a story by Washington reporter Jeffrey Birnbaum about Clinton's avoidance of military service as a twenty-three-year-old in 1969.

When Clinton entered the lobby of the Tara Hotel in Nashua that Thursday morning, he was surrounded by reporters asking about the *Journal* report. Clinton had made a long-term commitment to enroll in the University of Arkansas law school and join the Air Force ROTC, protecting him from the draft. After it was announced on September 19, 1969, that President Nixon was ending the draft, Clinton pulled out of his ROTC commitment (and never enrolled in the university). In the reporters' scrum in the Nashua hotel lobby, I managed to get in the question that I considered critical. Clinton had said he had dropped out of ROTC because his conscience, aroused by the death of friends in the war, dictated that he make himself eligible for the draft. So I asked: Was he aware of the September 19 announcement ending the draft before he dropped out of his ROTC commitment? His answer astounded me: "I didn't know that." I was not the only reporter astounded, as I wrote in an Evans & Novak column under a Nashua dateline:

> The denial generated stares of incredulity by reporters in the same age bracket as the 45-year-old Clinton. They would never forget how the Sept. 19 announcement of President Richard Nixon's decision set off wild campus parties across America. It seems improbable these glad tidings could have escaped Clinton, then at Oxford on a Rhodes scholarship and apparently immersed in maneuvers to escape military service.
>
> These maneuvers are now described by Clinton as neither "wrong" nor "illegal." True, they were routinely engaged in by other well-educated young men of the late '60s averse to fighting and dying in the Vietnam War they hated. So the question goes not to Clinton's martial ardor but to his credibility and character.

Questions of "credibility and character" were underscored that Thursday evening when reporters again cornered the candidate with questions about draft evasion. His set answer was that this was a "stale" story rejected by Arkansas voters in six elections. But Clinton went on to explain that he had joined the University of Arkansas ROTC and "stayed a couple of months" before his conscience impelled him to make himself draft eligible. This was an outright lie. Clinton never served one minute in the ROTC, much less "a couple of months." It occurred to me that this talented, charismatic man would say anything if he thought his listeners did not know the difference.

I was not an original member of Hillary Clinton's "vast right-wing conspiracy" determined to destroy her husband. When in late 1991 Clinton's enemies in Arkansas put out stories of his serial womanizing, I questioned their propriety for a presidential campaign. I was even put in the position of the pro-Clinton host on one *Crossfire*. That may explain my experience in Chicago on Saturday, November 23, 1991, at the national meeting of Democratic state chairmen. I was chatting with Bill Daley at a Friday night reception in the new Comiskey Park when we were joined by an attractive woman who looked vaguely familiar but whom I did not recognize. She came over as friendly to Daley and even friendlier to me, telling me how much she appreciated me in print and on TV. Only after she had moved on as she worked the crowd did I realize it was Hillary Rodham Clinton.

The campaign against Bill Clinton as a womanizer picked up the week of January 13, 1992, when the *Star* supermarket tabloid accused him of an affair with the state employee and sometime nightclub singer Gennifer Flowers. The story then seeped into the mainstream press and TV. On January 19, during a two-hour televised debate of Democratic candidates in Manchester, New Hampshire, moderator Cokie Roberts of National Public Radio asked Clinton about the accusations of marital infidelity. Clinton accused Arkansas Republicans of spreading "a pack of lies," adding: "The American people are sick and tired of that kind of politics."

James Carville was a campaign consultant who had been neither particularly prominent nor successful until Clinton hired him in 1991, opening Carville's door to fame and fortune. He struck me as a loudmouth interested mainly in manipulating me and other reporters. But I sought him out at WMUR-TV in Manchester, site of the Sunday night presidential debate. Furious about Cokie Roberts's question, Carville told me Clinton would give his response at a rally of supporters that very night. Carville suggested I come to the rally and said he would try to arrange a brief word for me with the candidate.

My word with Clinton was brief indeed, during which he repeated what he said at the rally. I was impressed by his speech and described what I called "Clinton's emotional appearance" in the last paragraph of an Evans & Novak column about the debate:

Flanked by his wife, Hillary, and their 11-year-old daughter, Chelsea, Clinton declared: "We can be one country again." His appeal for na-

tional unity was certainly more uplifting than the programmatic pre-
scriptions sounded by all five debaters Sunday night. Clinton could be
hard to catch.

Early the next day, Monday morning, I telephoned Carville asking to
see him for help on a column I was writing for Wednesday's newspapers.
Apparently not wanting to be seen with me anywhere we would be noted,
he said he would meet me at a little diner whose doors I had never entered
during thirty-three years of covering politics in New Hampshire.

That yielded a memorable half hour, during which I hardly got in a
word. Dressed in his trademark skintight blue jeans and white T-shirt, the
rail-thin "Ragin' Cajun" had lots to say in his high-pitched Louisiana accent. What concerned him was Cokie Roberts and "self-righteous" mainstream journalists who would imitate her, spreading "salacious" rumors
from the supermarket tabloid press throughout the country. Carville told
me (in a quote I attributed to "one bitter Clinton adviser"): "The media
don't *like* this sort of thing. They *love* it."

Carville's harangue to me in the Manchester diner was delivered to
many other journalists. But he knew they shared my view that Clinton's
dalliance with Gennifer Flowers and however many other women was not
grounds for political inquiry. Beyond that, I had not seen the press corps so
excited by a presidential candidate since John F. Kennedy forty-two years
earlier. They did not want Clinton brought down by the tabloid press.

In the two weeks after Carville lectured me over coffee, he did his work
well. During that time, a reporter asked about the sexual allegations only
once, on January 26, and the questioner was shouted down by voters' chants
of "We don't care!" Even though Clinton was inundated by questions about
the draft on February 6, I still thought he was assured of the nomination
against an unimpressive field. But he had lost me because, first, he had lost
credibility in handling the draft question, and, second, because of what he
was saying on the campaign stump. I wrote from New Hampshire:

> The aura of moderate conservatism [Clinton] exhibited heading the
> Democratic Leadership Council vanished in New Hampshire's
> snows. Having pinned down the state's conservative French-Canadian
> vote, he has moved left. . . . An 11-page prepared speech to a "town
> meeting" held at Phillips Exeter Academy was politically correct
> down to the last detail: pro-choice, anti-nuclear power, pro-gun con-
> trol, anti-right-to-work law, pro-strike replacement law, anti-global
> warming.

My relationship with Bill Clinton changed. My columns grew more critical, analyzing in depth his equivocation and obfuscation on issues ranging from abortion to the Gulf War.

As I was covering Clinton campaigning in the New York primary, the *New York Post*'s editorial page editor Eric Breindel invited me to sit in on an interview with the candidate at the newspaper. Clinton looked surprised, not pleasantly so, to see me there. When I was called upon for a question, I asked whether Clinton as president would employ a racial quota system in government hiring. "Oh, that's a typical Novak question," Clinton replied. "You can't trap me on that."

I WAS MAKING a routine election year visit to California and paying a routine visit to State Attorney General Daniel F. Lungren in Sacramento on Thursday, April 29, 1992. But that day was not routine. Lungren and I were talking politics when a staffer walked in and announced that a mostly white jury in Los Angeles had acquitted all four LAPD officers charged with the beating of Rodney King. "Oh, no!" Lungren said reflexively. Adding that he feared the worst of what would happen in Los Angeles, Lungren suggested he better get to work and terminated our meeting.

The rioting started Thursday in LA but early Friday morning I flew from Sacramento to Los Angeles to fulfill appointments there. Joe Cerrell called me at the hotel to cancel our scheduled dinner that night. With the mob two blocks away from his Los Angeles home, Cerrell asked me: "If the Feds can save Kuwait, why can't they defend LA?"

That night I wrote the Evans & Novak column datelined LA:

Systematic burning was engineered by the city's pernicious gangs, which suspended their vicious civil war to unite in en masse arson. Football great Jim Brown, who has close relations with gangs, correctly says they are a mystery to black politicians. But to believe that the riots were politically inspired, it is necessary to accept Brown's dubious premise that the gangs have a programmatic agenda. Targeting Korean shop owners smacks more of racism than program.

The looters who followed were even less political. Families of all colors who streamed into stores to steal confirmed Prof. Edward Banfield's judgment in the '60s that rioters were after "fun and profit." The holiday mood heightened Thursday after it became clear the LAPD would not arrest, much less shoot. Few looters even pretended they were carrying away sofas to avenge Rodney King.

Nevertheless, rioters were given revolutionary status by such black politicians as State Sen. Diane Watson and City Councilman Mark Ridley-Thomas. They wandered from one television channel to another deploring what the King verdict had brought, but they were not seen on the streets imploring the mob to go home.

Even worse than Watson and Ridley-Thomas was an old *Nightline* debating adversary of mine from the 1988 Atlanta convention, Congresswoman Maxine Waters. She took issue with her fellow African-American Democrat, Los Angeles Mayor Tom Bradley, for calling the rioters "criminals" and "gangsters." Waters insisted on calling the chaos in LA an "insurrection," as did outrageous press reports. I think my column performed a service. "No Insurrection in Los Angeles," said the *Washington Post* headline.

BY THE SPRING of 1992, my personal presidential election choice seemed to me as difficult as choosing between Carter and Ford sixteen years earlier. I could not vote for Clinton, but this time there was a genuine third party alternative: Texas billionaire Ross Perot. When I flew to Dallas on May 6, 1992, to interview Perot, I thought I actually might vote for him. Perot had become the first independent candidate ever to pass the Republican and Democratic candidates in presidential polls.

"Perot sounds like a Republican, touting private over government solutions," I wrote, adding: "He also rejects redistribution of income via the tax system, which is inherent in the Clinton tax policy. In response to the Los Angeles riots, he supports zero capital gains taxes in the inner city and wants a greater role for organized religion in instilling ethical values among disadvantaged youth."

I found it hard to fall in love with any presidential candidate (even John F. Kennedy and Ronald Reagan, both of whom I liked personally) because, as a reporter, I observed them at close range. The May 6 interview with Perot served that purpose and incidentally guaranteed my eventual, reluctant vote for Bush. I began the Evans & Novak column based on that meeting:

After concluding a 90-minute interview in his modest 17th-floor North Dallas office, Ross Perot stopped us at the door to confide his dream: a one-on-one debate with President Bush, with no questions from journalists and nobody else interfering.

But what about the third man in the presidential race, Bill Clinton? Perot sloughed off our question. The putative Democratic nominee just isn't on the mind of the Texas billionaire as he prepares his independent candidacy. He sees the election as Ross Perot vs. George Bush. . . .

[H]e makes clear he does not consider Bush much of a president. . . . Perot told us he believes he is hurting Bush more than Clinton, basing that opinion on polls showing him ahead in three big Sunbelt states dear to Republican hearts: California, Texas and Florida.

By the same token, Perot traces hostile probing by the news media to inspiration from the Bush camp, not Clinton. Bush "started the character assassination as soon as I got ahead of him in Texas," he told us.

Perot hired a campaign team headed by two famous professionals: Hamilton Jordan, mastermind of Jimmy Carter's climb to the presidency, and Ed Rollins, campaign manager of Ronald Reagan's landslide reelection. I took a six thirty a.m. flight to Dallas on July 1 to spend a day at ground zero of the Perot campaign. In an Evans & Novak column, I reported that the North Dallas headquarters was "a Potemkin Village," adding:

Large and vastly more opulent than any campaign office we have seen, it is filled with people who seem to have no useful function and a multiplicity of sophisticated computers that the political pros have no idea how to use.

Even today, there is no speechwriter, no advertising team and no readiness to send a message. With less than four months to go before the election, there is no Perot campaign as normally conceived.

What makes matters worse is that Perot has been his own campaign manager, not a good idea for any candidate but potentially disastrous for a novice in politics.

That night I took Rollins and his California associate, Sacramento-based campaign consultant Sal Russo, to dinner at Brennan's. Rollins and Russo were not happy campers. The two Republicans were reluctant to disclose too much, but they signaled that Ross Perot was hard to work for. They did not realize that they would be out the door in just fourteen days.

On July 14, with the Democratic convention in session at New York's Madison Square Garden, Perot abruptly ended his candidacy. I got Rollins on the telephone, and this time he opened up. I reported from New York:

One of the political operatives [Rollins] hired to transform Ross Perot's petition drive into a real presidential campaign after two frustrating weeks on that job, decided on a bold approach that only proved he and the other professional handlers were laboring under a profound misunderstanding.

The adviser asked Perot whether he had ever heard of Madonna. When he replied that of course he had, the political pro then said: "Ross, she's a multimillion-dollar star. But she doesn't schedule her own event. She doesn't rent the bus. She doesn't book the hall and get the band. She doesn't write the script. She hires people to do all these things, and she just performs."

The obvious message to Perot: Let us handle the details, and you concentrate on being the candidate. When Perot did not disagree, the adviser believed he had made his point. In fact, he had not. But the bigger misunderstanding was the assumption that the only problem afflicting the embryonic campaign was the tycoon's propensity to micromanage. Beyond insisting on details, Perot was loath to dip into his $3 billion net worth to finance his candidacy.

The shocked politicians, after two turbulent months in Dallas, now sadly conclude that Perot didn't really mean it when he said he would spend $100 million of his own money. In one private conversation two months ago, he even hinted that the figure might go as high as $200 million or $300 million. If indeed Perot never intended to spend that kind of money, his presidential venture was a hoax.

Rollins told me Perot did not fire the esteemed TV ad maker Hal Riney because he disliked the spots, as was widely reported. "He loved them," said Rollins, "but he hated the cost." Riney's work cost $100,000 for each ad, and Perot said he could find a friend who would do them for $2,500 apiece. "But the number that really appealed to Perot was not 2,500," I wrote, "but zero." Perot wanted "free" television made possible by scheduling himself.

Perot later got back into the race, without Rollins and without any promises to spend his own money. But the glitter was gone, and his clear purpose now was not to elect himself but to beat George Bush. That was what he always had in mind.

SIMULTANEOUS WITH THE news on July 15 that Perot was dropping out came new polls showing a twenty-percentage point lead by Clinton over Bush. James Baker, who had achieved legendary status as a campaign manager despite a losing record in elections dating back to 1976, was looked upon as the cavalry riding to the rescue when he resigned as secretary of state to take over the Bush campaign. When he failed to affect the outcome,

Baker typically let it be known that he came in too late to help. It also was leaked that he had tried and failed to get Bush to dump Quayle, though in fact the vice president was not a campaign issue one way or another. The real problem was Bush, who could not even bring himself to criticize Clinton's draft evasion, as urged by his advisers.

THE 1992 ELECTION forecasts in the *Evans-Novak Political Report* (which still represented my personal forecasting) were right on the nose. I predicted Clinton defeating Bush in the electoral vote 372 to 166; the actual outcome was 374 to 164. I predicted a net gain of one Republican seat in the Senate; the actual outcome was no change, maintaining a fourteen-seat Democratic margin. In the House, I predicted a gain of six Republican seats; the actual Republican gain was eight seats, but the Democratic margin in the House was still eighty-three seats. Was this reverse realignment, back toward solid, perpetual Democratic control of the government?

CHAPTER 38

Clinton = Republican Tsunami

THE 1993 SWEARING-IN of Bill Clinton was the first presidential inauguration after Geraldine and I moved from the suburbs to our Pennsylvania Avenue condo in downtown Washington, where our long terrace would provide a splendid view of the Inaugural parade route. We moved our quadrennial Inaugural party from an evening in the suburbs to a midday brunch, where my guests could watch the parade while sipping Bloody Marys on the terrace.

As the Clintons' limousine passed our building, CNN anchor Bernard Shaw commented on the air in jest that the new president had better watch out because he was passing Bob Novak's apartment. With the possible exceptions of John F. Kennedy and Ronald Reagan, no president had entered the Oval Office with a warm feeling toward me. But on January 20, 1993, I perceived unmatched hostility from the White House. I would have liked to write something nice about Clinton. That proved impossible. Clinton was a man of the Left who disguised himself as a man of the center. His opening agenda was higher taxes, socialized medicine, and homosexual rights. Combining this with his personal misadventures meant the nineties would prove a dreadful decade for Democrats.

During the Clinton transition, the Democratic Party was being suffocated by the demands of racial and ethnic quotas—my question Clinton had refused to answer during his campaign interview at the *New York Post.* Clinton reneged on his offer to Bill Daley to become secretary of Transportation because he needed a Hispanic in the cabinet. The only Hispanic immediately available was Federico Pena, who just had completed eight unexceptional years as mayor of Denver. The only available place for him was Transportation. Pena's political importance did not extend beyond his surname, Clinton hardly knew him, and Pena knew nothing about transportation.

Daley was well known to the president-elect and had been instrumental in carrying Illinois as his state chairman. But Clinton correctly surmised that when he rejected Daley in favor of Pena, the son and brother of Chicago mayors was too much of a Democratic loyalist to protest publicly. Daley's private analysis was included (without attribution to him) in my Evans & Novak column of January 4, 1993:

> [Daley's] rebuff shows how lightly Clinton seems to value the "Reagan Democrats" now that the election returns are in. The Cabinet contains no traditional urban Catholic typified by the Daley organization. Bill Daley has been an intrepid warrior in preventing a hemorrhage of whites from his ancestral party in Chicago.

Clinton's diversity plan also called for the first female attorney general of the United States. He was turned down by sixty-four-year-old Judge Patricia Wald of the U.S. Circuit Court for the District of Columbia. Clinton subsequently nominated two young female lawyers unqualified to be attorney general. Both had to withdraw because they had not paid Social Security taxes for their nannies. Clinton, in a temper tantrum, demanded a woman who did not have and never would have any children and, therefore, no nanny. That peculiar standard for an attorney general produced Janet Reno, district attorney of Dade County (Miami), Florida. She was fifty-four years old, six-feet-two, homely, unmarried, and self-described as "an awkward old maid."

Unsubstantiated rumors that Reno was a lesbian led to a compensatory deluge of praise for a woman nobody knew. The plaudits poured in from New York's *Daily News,* the *New York Times, New York Post, Boston Globe, St. Louis Post-Dispatch,* Mark Shields, Nina Totenberg, Al Hunt, Margaret Warner, Charles Krauthammer, Morton Kondracke, and Les Gelb, plus many more. Reno critics in Miami could not have cared less about her sexual preferences, but they were stunned that this woman of minimal talents was to be attorney general of the United States. I believe Clinton put a lower premium on talent in his cabinet-making than any predecessor in my experience.

CLINTON'S MALFEASANCE IN naming an incompetent Janet Reno to run the Justice Department was mitigated slightly for me when I realized she was not in charge. That task was assigned to the man Clinton identified as his closest friend: Webster Hubbell, a partner with Hillary Rodham Clinton in Little Rock's Rose Law Firm. Hubbell preceded Reno at Justice as associate attorney general, the department's third-ranking position. Justice sources told me Clinton demanded that prospective nominees for attorney general permit Hubbell to make all "political" decisions. Judge Wald refused, but Reno agreed.

Hubbell slowed down federal prosecution of veteran Democratic congressmen Dan Rostenkowski and Harold Ford and issued an unprecedented order for the resignation of all U.S. attorneys. He derailed temporarily a federal investigation of the Clintons' investment in the Whitewater development. After the government's fiery destruction of the Branch Davidian complex near Waco, Texas, it was Hubbell—not Reno—who conferred with President Clinton.

Webb Hubbell did not understand how reporters in Washington functioned. "He yearned for the closed world of Little Rock," I wrote in the June 1994 issue of the *American Spectator,* "where secrets were secrets and the lines between politics and business were fuzzy." In the same article, I wrote:

> In Washington, [Hubbell] is viewed, however dimly, as a slightly sinister figure who represents the unfortunate Clinton conjunction between personal affairs and government. In Little Rock, he is remembered fondly as a prototypical good old boy—football player, country clubber, regular fellow, distinguished citizen. On a visit to the Arkansas capital, we could find nobody—friend or foe—who would speak harshly of Webb Hubbell. Nothing better typifies the difficulty of transplanting to Washington this special culture.

The transplant failed. In 1994, Hubbell was convicted of federal mail fraud and tax evasion and sentenced to twenty-one months in federal prison. Clinton was responsible for his ruin, but Hubbell never said a word critical of the president.

(The visit to the Arkansas capital to report on Hubbell was made not by Robert Novak but by Zelda Novak. When my daughter's boss, Vice President Dan Quayle, was defeated for reelection, I asked her to fill a vacant reporter's job in my office. She came to work in mid-1993, after interning at the *Northern Virginia Sun* through Stan Evans's National Journalism Center. Her duties for me included ghostwriting an international column distributed by Japan's Kyodo news service and producing and writing for a weekly program I did for the conservative National Empowerment Television cable network.

Like other reporters, she found Clinton-dominated Little Rock gothic and intimidating. She provided about half the reporting and writing for the *American Spectator* article, which was signed "By Robert D. Novak and

Zelda Novak." Zelda at age twenty-eight was a relatively late-starting but talented journalist, and I fantasized about her becoming my column-writing partner before I quit. In October 1994, she married Christopher Caldwell, a brilliant journalist then with the *American Spectator,* and she left my employ to have her first baby, Jane, in 1996. I hoped she might return someday. But three babies later I'm still waiting.)

ON FEBRUARY 25, 1993, the day before my sixty-second birthday, Geraldine and I arose before dawn to fly to Champaign, Illinois, to visit my alma mater, the University of Illinois, for the ninth straight year. It would be different from the previous eight years because this year I would become a graduate—unexpectedly and forty-one years late.

I had kept my distance from the university my first thirty-three years as an alumnus. Solicited for capital campaigns, I had contributed small amounts. I am afraid my last year at the university, nearly being expelled and failing to graduate, may have cooled my ardor for my alma mater. My attitude improved in 1985 when I received an unexpected letter from Professor George Scouffas, who had cleaned up my writing more than any news editor ever did. He was up for the university's award for excellence in undergraduate teaching (he got it), and was soliciting former students for recommendations. I was flattered that he called me despite my senior-year academic flameout.

After writing a heartfelt endorsement, I suggested I would like to see him. The university rolled out the red carpet, including luncheon with Scouffas, an interview on the university radio station, a visit to the *Daily Illini,* and dinner with the chancellor. The visit reminded me how much the university had meant to my family, what a wonderful education it had given me, and how much fun I had there as a student. I wanted to repay the university, and in 1991, I endowed in perpetuity the Robert D. Novak Scholarship in nonfiction writing. The winner of competition administered by the Department of English gets five thousand dollars in senior tuition assistance.

From then on, my annual visit centered around meeting the year's Novak scholar. On my 1993 trip, I also visited with Dr. Larry R. Faulkner, dean of the College of Liberal Arts and Sciences (and soon to become president of the University of Texas). "I've got a surprise for you," Faulkner said and handed me a black hard-covered folder. Inside was a University of Illinois diploma, dated January 15, 1993, making me a bachelor of arts in Liberal Arts and Sciences.

In the chaos of my senior year, I had fallen one hour short of the 120 hours needed for a degree in 1952. I figured I would go through the rest of my life without a college degree, listed as "student 1948–52" in *Who's Who in America.*

Faulkner explained I had taken four mandatory courses in physical education my first two years in college when they were noncredit. But if taken in 1993, I would have received a one-hour credit for each. The real question is whether anybody would have found the loophole for my degree if I had not achieved some prominence and become a generous donor.

THE PARTNERSHIP OF Rowland Evans and Robert Novak in writing "Inside Report," the longest-lasting double byline column in American journalistic history, came to an end on May 15, 1993—our thirtieth anniversary.

After Rowly's false alarm in 1990, I asked him to give me a six-month notice in writing of his real retirement so I could reorganize our enterprises. On March 21, 1992, he handed me a full-page memo that said "Reddy [nickname of his redheaded wife, Kay] and I have decided to make the end of the year the goal"—ending the column between November 1992 and February 1993. He asked me to keep "this plan entirely confidential," meaning he did not want me to go back to Fred Barnes.

As I read the memo thirteen years later, I find it no more comprehensible than I did in 1993. Rowly and I were very different people. Senator Phil Gramm, retiring from the Senate at the end of 2002, sat down that year for a farewell interview with me. When I finished Gramm asked me why I, then aged seventy-one, did not retire. I replied: "Phil, I don't hunt, I seldom fish, I don't golf, I don't play cards anymore, I no longer gamble, I don't drink much and I don't chase women. What would I do if I retired?" Gramm replied: "Bob, you better not retire." In contrast Rowly belonged to a regular poker group, played squash nearly every day and tennis once a week in season, rode horses at his country place, went skiing out West every winter, and went camping summers in Maine.

Yet Rowly's 1992 memo, written when he was seventy, cited these pastimes as the reason to retire: "I find that the unusually high exertion level over weekends [horseback riding mainly], which I could not give up without heavy costs to psyche and *joie de vivre,* results in a kind of tiredness I did not have to cope with five or more years ago." He was saying that he was ending regular reporting duties because it interfered with his athletic activity—a sentiment difficult to understand for anybody as nonathletic as I was.

Rowly agreed with me it would be a bad idea for him to retire simultaneously with a change of government in Washington probable after the 1992 election. We mutually decided to make it an even thirty years for the Evans & Novak column by ending it in May 1993.

At the time of Rowly's false alarm resignation in 1990, he indicated he was withdrawing from everything—which is why I solicited Fred Barnes as a partner. Now, though Evans was three years older, he proposed something entirely different. He would continue to appear with me each week on CNN's *Evans and Novak,* collaborate with me on three or four *Reader's Digest* articles a year, help arrange and co-host our twice yearly Evans-Novak Political Forum, and help produce a report for a Japanese think tank that we put out thirty-six times a year. Rowly earlier had drastically curtailed his time on the lecture circuit and had not helped out much lately for the *Evans-Novak Political Report* (which we had sold to Tom Phillips's publishing conglomerate).

So the only real change was leaving the double byline column, and even that was not ended totally. Rowly's memo told me he wanted to "keep my hand in" reporting and making overseas trips, requiring him to write a column once every three or four weeks under the Evans & Novak double byline (for which I would compensate him). I considered this arrangement awkward, and I was unenthusiastic because it wrecked my hopes of gaining access to Rowly's fabulous national security sources. But I agreed because of everything Rowly had brought to our extraordinary partnership.

In 1990, I had sought a partner because I could not continue all our activities by myself. In 1993, Rowly was retaining such a role that there would not be enough work—or income—for a new partner. When word got out that Rowly was retiring, a procession of would-be partners—most represented by surrogates—found its way to me. I will not embarrass anybody by revealing names, except to say Fred Barnes definitely was not among them.

On April 15, 1993, Rowly and I scheduled lunch with Meg Greenfield, as was her preference, at the Hay Adams. At age sixty-two, Meg was one of the most accomplished women in American journalism and also had become a grande dame of Washington. I was scared to death—frightened that Meg Greenfield would drop the column from the *Post* now that Rowly was retiring.

Actually, I knew Meg before Rowly did. She came to Washington in 1962 as a thirty-one-year-old correspondent for the *Reporter,* a wonderful magazine that I moonlighted for as a *Wall Street Journal* staffer. I thought we liked each other and that a warm relationship survived over the years. I had a particularly good time at the 1976 Republican convention in Kansas City with Phil Geyelin, the *Post*'s editorial page editor and Meg Greenfield, who was promoted to be his deputy in 1970. Geyelin and Greenfield did not know that many Republicans. So Maureen Reagan, her boyfriend of the moment, and I escorted them on a tour of Republican parties the three nights preceding the convention. In 1979, Greenfield abruptly was promoted to replace Geyelin, and relations for Rowly and me with the *Post* editorial page improved sharply.

Meg in 1980 started hosting dinner parties the week before each political convention, a couple of which I have mentioned in this book. I valued these events as not only entertaining but also valuable to me as a reporter. Consequently, in the summer of 1992, I noted to Rowly that I had not received an invitation to her party at that year's first convention, the Democrats in New York City. Rowly paused, then said: "Bob, she didn't invite you because she doesn't like you." If anybody knew this, it would be Rowly. He was one of Meg's best friends, and she adored Rowly. She regularly hosted Rowly and Kay at her Bainbridge Island, Washington, home on Puget Sound.

If I obsessed about learning about everybody in Washington who did not like me, I would be a wreck. But hearing that about the editor at the most important newspaper that ran the column was reason for obsession. I belatedly realized Meg had greeted me coldly in recent years when we met socially. I never knew why. I long had been a boogeyman to the Left, but Meg Greenfield did not take directions from the Left.

Rowly and I decided that in advance of the April 15, 1993, lunch, he would alert Meg to his retirement plans to avoid an explosion at the Hay Adams. "She was not pleased," Rowly told me following the alert. Over lunch, I told Meg how much we appreciated the *Post*'s regular use of us for thirty years. She was coldly unresponsive. Then per our plans that Rowly would do most of the talking, he said I planned to cut the full column from three times to twice a week, from Monday-Wednesday-Friday to Monday-Thursday. (Rowly did not mention the Sunday item column, which the *Post* had not run for twenty years.) "Well," Meg said, "I'm not so sure I want to anchor all our columnists for a set day of the week. Maybe they ought to compete with each other on a day-by-day basis."

I left the hotel in physical pain. Being anchored in the *Washington Post* had been essential for our column. I feared I would be wiped out having to compete with *Post* staffers for the op-ed page twice a week. "Don't worry," Rowly told me. "Meg was just pulling your chain a little. If she was going to spike the column, she would have said so." Rowly proved correct.

Rowly had asked Meg to keep his retirement quiet until it was announced, but I heard he was dropping hints about it on the dinner party circuit. The word got to the *Washington Post* media reporter Howard Kurtz, who broke the story April 29. Kurtz dredged up a lot of old cliches, such as the "Prince of Darkness" versus "the picture of urban gentility" and the "Errors and No Facts" label, and used a snide quote from Michael Kinsley, who never had a good word for me. Kurtz's conclusion: "The Evans and Novak column is a Washington institution—relentlessly conservative, frequently breathless, often consumed by political arcana—but required reading for insiders, particularly during Republican administrations." Considering things written about me since then, I guess Kurtz could have done worse.

I still had not pinned down new arrangements with the syndicate. The old syndicate that had handled our column starting in 1963 was part of the Field properties that, along with the *Chicago Sun-Times,* were sold to Rupert Murdoch in 1984, with the Field News Syndicate renamed the News America Syndicate. When Teddy Kennedy's legislation forced Murdoch to sell the *Sun-Times* in 1986, he sold the syndicate to Hearst, which renamed it the North America Syndicate. Three years later, we signed with Creators Syndicate, located in ground-floor offices near Los Angeles International Airport. Creators's founder, Rick Newcombe, was a Chicagoan, the son of a *Sun-Times* executive, a former newsman himself, and a conservative Republican. It was a perfect fit.

Now, four years later in early May 1993, Newcombe was taking me out to dinner at the 72nd Main Street restaurant in Venice, California. Rick agreed to reducing the column's frequency by one (so long as it was not my Sunday item column, our most popular offering for many newspapers). He surprised me pleasantly by saying that despite the reduction in the number of columns, I would receive the full $100,000 that Rowly and I previously had split.

The last regular Evans & Novak column was published May 14, 1993. I suggested to Rowly that the final column take an overview of thirty years' collaboration, but he wanted no valedictory since there would be occasional future E&N columns.

There was no better company at work or at play than Rowly Evans, and I missed the nonstop political bull sessions and even the frequent disputes. But life had just gotten simpler for me. The processing time for each column was reduced by about two hours, and I could make decisions without hashing them out with Rowly. As of May 17, 1993, at age sixty-two, I was flying solo for the first time in my life.

ON JULY 24, 1993, Margaret Warner was a panelist on *The Capital Gang* for the last time. She was leaving *Newsweek* to become the replacement on PBS for her friend Judy Woodruff, who was moving to CNN. Margaret was just slightly Left of Center, her moderation diluting the left-wing dominance on the program that had been built in ever since Pat Buchanan left.

My first choice to replace Warner was Maureen Dowd, then a forty-one-year-old *New York Times* reporter in Washington. A year away from getting her own column in the *Times,* she was not yet that well known and without TV experience. But I knew her from the campaign trail and found her witty and irreverent, and she had an unusual voice and an exotic beauty. Ideologically, I did not think then she was any more liberal than Margaret Warner, and maybe a little less so. I thought she would be a star.

Consequently, I was disappointed when Dowd told me over the telephone she was not at all interested in television. I talked her into breakfast on August 19, 1993, at the Army and Navy Club, where she told me she had had one bad experience on TV and did not want to try again. I implored her to think it over, and said I would call her in a day or two. When I did, I suggested she try just one *Capital Gang* and see how it works out— "You know," I said, "a one-night stand." "Oh," said Maureen, "if you're really talking about a one-night stand, I might be interested." I told her to get serious, but she made it clear the answer was no.

In her memoir-collection *(Anyone Can Grow Up),* Margaret Carlson mourned, tongue in cheek, that she was my second choice for *Capital Gang.* Actually Margaret was my *third* choice. My second choice was *Newsweek* correspondent Eleanor Clift, who had come on *The McLaughlin Group* as a substitute while I was still on the program and was now a regular. She made no pretense at moderation and would have moved the *Gang's* orientation still farther Left. But Clift had become a proven performer on *McLaughlin.* I also admired her as a tough New Yorker and a single mother who had worked her way up from Atlanta's *Newsweek* bureau secretary to become one of the magazine's top Washington reporters. Finally, I was small-minded enough that I savored taking away one of John McLaughlin's stars.

Eleanor and I met in my office at 1750 Pennsylvania Avenue on the thirteenth floor, one floor above the *Newsweek* bureau. She seemed concerned at trading a regular weekly slot on *McLaughlin* for alternating on the *Gang* with Mona Charen. I assured her she would be on much more often than half the time (substituting when Shields or Hunt could not make it), that her overall income actually would increase at CNN, and that she would have additional opportunities at CNN (for which I had authorization from executive producer Rick Davis). She told me she would let me know in a day or so, and I thought we had her. But Eleanor stayed with *McLaughlin.*

That left Margaret Carlson of *Time,* whose friends were lobbying me. I did not know her well, and being the frequent (albeit platonic) escort of Michael Kinsley did not recommend her to me. She was a woman who was "cute" into late middle age, and seemed to me higher on charm than talent.

But among the substitutes who tried out after Warner left, Carlson was the best, and she became a member of *Capital Gang* on October 9, 1993.

Margaret Carlson's ideology, though leavened with wit, sent the *Gang's* political balance farther Left. But her chemistry on the panel was excellent. I have concluded I was lucky to be turned down by Maureen Dowd. She became a famous columnist and author and lost her television phobia to go on the air occasionally. As I watched her on a *Meet the Press* roundtable in September 2005, she seemed brittle while recycling her *Times* columns. I don't believe she could have participated in the bantering give-and-take the way Margaret Carlson did during twelve splendid years. I was fortunate to get Margaret.

LATE IN SEPTEMBER 1993, James Carville and his partner Paul Begala were running the off-year reelection campaign in New Jersey of Governor Jim Florio. "Florio is a cold, unlovable professional politician who has spent his life running for office and owns neither home nor automobile," I would write. In his first year as governor, he broke his 1989 campaign pledges and raised taxes by $2.8 billion. Anti-Florio anger revived a somnolent New Jersey Republican Party, which took control of the legislature in the 1991 elections (including two assemblymen whose campaigns were managed by my son, Alex). As for reelection in 1993, the governor should have been dead.

But Florio was far from dead. In September, a *New York Times* poll put him twenty percentage points ahead of his Republican opponent, Christine Todd Whitman, whose highest public office had been as Somerset County freeholder. On the morning the *Times* ran its poll, Carville called me to gloat. "It's the end of supply-side, Novak," he yelled. "It's all finished." Carville hated the Reagan tax cuts and desperately wanted to prove them politically untenable. His laboratory was New Jersey, where Christie Whitman was running on a tax cut crafted for her by supply-siders Steve Forbes and Larry Kudlow. Carville had pounded her with negative advertising that, I later wrote, put her "on the defensive over assault rifles, drunk drivers, and welfare while painting her as part of the uncaring rich." Carville was euphoric to show that Jim Florio—or Bill Clinton—could raise taxes in his first year in office, confident the voters would forget about it by reelection time in the fourth year if the "Ragin' Cajun" was around to change the subject. If Carville had not rung my bell with his boasting telephone call, I doubt I would have gone to New Jersey to report directly on the campaign.

After spending half a day with Whitman, I described her as "warm, a little fuzzy and a millionaire heiress" who, thanks mainly to Carville's ridicule, regarded the Forbes-Kudlow tax plan as a burden rather than her salvation.

"It's the right thing to do," she told me bravely. After covering her first debate with Florio on October 7, 1993, I wrote in an Evans & Novak column: "Whitman could not fire the tax pistol. Indeed, she seemed embarrassed by the weapon." She looked like a loser to me.

I began to change my mind shortly after the debate when I sat down with peripatetic campaign consultant Ed Rollins, brought in at the end of September to try to save Whitman. The rap on Rollins in political circles was that he told the ugly truth to reporters about his candidates, which made him a reporter's dream. He described Whitman to me as an upper-class airhead surrounded by Republican hacks who pushed her away from the Forbes-Kudlow tax cut. But Ed was a tough little guy, and he told me he would make Christie swallow the tax cut if he had to force it down her throat.

Also in trouble was George Allen, the Republican candidate in Virginia, the only state other than New Jersey with the governorship at stake in 1993. He was trailing the Democratic candidate, Virginia's attorney general Mary Sue Terry, by more than twenty percentage points. Campaign consultant Bob Squier, one of my best Democratic sources, was working for Terry and called her a perfect candidate. Allen, at age forty-two, had served briefly in the Virginia legislature and Congress, but was best known as the son of the former Washington Redskins football coach George Allen.

I was ignoring this seemingly one-sided contest when I received a phone call from an acquaintance I made as a University of Maryland athletics booster. It was Russ Potts, director of the university's athletic promotions in the seventies who I was amazed to learn was now Virginia State Senator H. Russell Potts Jr. He was later to abandon the GOP to make a quixotic independent run for governor in 2005. But in 1993 he was a loyal Republican who asked if he could bring George Allen in to meet me. Allen was more impressive than I expected—calm and confident despite a double-digit deficit. "I guarantee you I'll beat Mary Sue," he told me. "No problem."

The third major Republican candidate running that November was Rudolph Giuliani in his second try for mayor of New York. Four years earlier, he barely lost to Democrat David Dinkins, who became the city's first African-American mayor. Dinkins had brought a new level of incompetence to City Hall, and he was an even worse campaigner than he was a mayor. I began my premayoral election column on Monday, November 1, under a New York dateline, with this sentence: "Nearly every politician in this city not on Mayor David Dinkins's payroll says Republican candidate Rudolph Giuliani will be elected tomorrow." My friend Bob Shrum was on the Dinkins payroll, and he had assured me over dinner that Dinkins would be reelected.

The rap on Shrum, just the opposite of the complaint with Ed Rollins, was that he fell in love with every politician who hired him. Over dinner in Manhattan on October 28, Shrum claimed Giuliani had made a fatal error putting the "urban terrorist" label on blacks who had killed a housing policeman. Giuliani's promise the final week of the campaign to arrest more drug dealers, Shrum said, would swing Jewish liberals and Hispanics back to Dinkins. I did not buy it. I thought Shrum was misreading New York as Democrats were misreading the whole country.

NOVEMBER 2, 1993, was unusually predictive of the future. The off-year elections were swept by Republicans, winning previously Democratic-held offices for governors of New Jersey and Virginia and for mayor of New York. Earlier that year on April 10, Republican multimillionaire Richard Riordan was elected mayor of Los Angeles, ending long Democratic occupancy of that office.

The Republican National Committee exulted over this four-for-four takeover, but the Republican quality of the victory actually was diluted. When I visited Riordan in his first year as mayor, he began our conversation by showing me a campaign-type pin saying "R.I.N.O." That meant "Republican in Name Only," and the jovial Riordan told me that was exactly what he was. In New York, Giuliani was not much more of a Republican. I had written of him:

> Giuliani is no conservative and hardly a Republican (starting out as a George McGovern Democrat). He has switched from pro-life to pro-choice on abortion and courts homosexuals with gay rights advocacy. He has rejected term limits, private school choice and an end to New York's rent controls.

Christie Whitman in New Jersey was at best a Bush Republican. Of the four winners, only George Allen seemed to be a Reagan Republican, and that was in conservative Virginia. Consequently, Democrats wrote off the 1993 results as wholly without national political consequence.

Notwithstanding the nature of the Republican winners, however, the 1993 results comprised terrible news for the Democrats, as I wrote in my postelection column of November 4. The best and the brightest of Democratic strategists—Bob Squier in Virginia, James Carville in New Jersey, and Bob Shrum in New York City—had lost to "Republican candidates ranging from lackluster to just above adequate and who convey little vision."

The reasons, I concluded, were that the Democrats were on the wrong side of taxes, gun rights, the religious Right, bloc voting, and negative TV ads. Whitman won in New Jersey because Ed Rollins hounded her into plugging away for her tax cut "in the face of ferocious news media disapproval." While Democrats linked Allen to Pat Robertson in Virginia, the Christian Coalition "was instrumental in Allen's victory." Even though 97 percent of the black vote backed Dinkins in New York and Hispanics were much more supportive of him than expected, the massive white turnout for Giuliani showed "a Democratic image as special pleader for minorities is counterproductive." The merciless negative television spots against Giuliani, Allen, and especially Whitman were insufficient because "no positive image for Dinkins, Terry or Florio ever emerged."

Bill Daley in Chicago was a loyal Democrat who also was astute and realistic. I quoted him (identified as a "well-placed Democratic leader") assessing the 1993 results:

> I'm afraid the Reagan coalition is forming again after we took it apart last year [1992] because we don't know what we're doing. Our people in Congress, and, I'm afraid in the White House, don't have a clue. We have to look more conservative.

ON APRIL 22, 1994, Richard M. Nixon died at age eighty-one. I thought he was a poor president and a bad man who inflicted grave damage on his party and his country. In my column of May 6, I wrote about what was the only true link between Nixon and me:

> Amid the deluge of words following his death, there was only passing mention of the seminal event in Richard Nixon's half-century political career: the Hiss case.
>
> Had it not been for the young Congressman from Southern California, Alger Hiss likely would have dodged exposure as a Soviet espionage agent. That exposure afforded Nixon a rapid escape from obscurity onto the national stage. Moreover, the case froze Nixon forever as the enemy of the Left and the champion of the Right, no matter how much he later deviated from those stereotypes.
>
> In fact, Nixon was no conservative in either his domestic or his foreign policy. Both his inability to appease the implacable hostility of liberals and the steadfast loyalty to him by conservatives can be traced to his anti-Communist image forged by that long-ago struggle.

In that column, I did not dwell on my nonrelationship with Nixon during his long retirement. When Nixon started granting interviews to selected journalists during the 1980s, I contacted Roger Stone, the Republican political operative and my frequent source who was helping out the former president in arranging the press contacts. He failed to get me in. "Nixon still thinks you're a Rockefeller Republican," Stone explained.

Accordingly, I was surprised to receive in the mail a personal note from Nixon dated July 2, 1990. He told me he had discovered he was without his copy of *Witness* by Whittaker Chambers. Nixon purchased the book's 1987 edition, published by Regnery and containing an introduction by me (in which I said Nixon performed an indispensable service in exposing the liberal icon Hiss as a Soviet agent). Nixon wrote to me: "The highest compliment I can pay is that it reads like Chambers."

I presumed that the letter was Nixon's way of opening the channels of communications between us that had closed many years earlier. But when I asked Stone to try again in 1990, he returned with the response that Nixon still considered me a Rockefeller Republican.

ON JULY 14, 1994, my internist, Dr. Charles Abrams, administered my annual physical examination. On July 18, I received a telephone message from Abrams informing me that X-rays revealed a spot on my right lung that could be my second bout with cancer. Abrams found the spot on an X-ray from two years earlier too small to be spotted even by his eagle eye. So it looked like a slowly growing cancer. That was a confirmed on July 27 by an MRI.

On Friday, July 29, Geraldine and I drove to Johns Hopkins University Hospital in Baltimore, where my prostate cancer had been removed in 1991. The brilliant prostate surgeon Pat Walsh did not do lungs, but he recommended highly the Hopkins specialists. After examining the charts, a bright young doctor laid out a daunting schedule. I would be opened up for biopsy. If the growth was malignant as expected, a date would be set for removing most or all of one lung. That anticipated a long hospital stay and weeks of recuperation. As Geraldine and I drove back from Baltimore, I did not experience the same fear that had overwhelmed me when I was diagnosed with prostate cancer three years earlier. This time I was just depressed by the long ordeal awaiting me. I wondered why I had to undergo two operations—one for the biopsy and one for the surgery.

On Saturday night, we drove to our new getaway home: a large oceanfront place at Fenwick Island, Delaware, that we had bought the year before. In a state of depression Sunday night, I called Bob McCandless in

Washington. It was he who in 1991 had steered me to Pat Walsh at Hopkins, and now he steered me toward Dr. Donald Morton, head of the John Wayne Cancer Institute in Santa Monica (who had provided health care for TransAmerica, McCandless's client).

McCandless faxed me a forty-page file on Morton's life and times—awards, triumphs, and controversy. His life's work was developing a vaccine for deadly melanoma, but he also was a world-class cancer surgeon. I telephoned him from the beach Monday morning LA time. He knew my name and said he agreed with my politics. (So did Dr. Walsh. A conservative patient must be pleased with conservative surgeons who have your life in their hands.) Without criticizing the Hopkins doctors, Morton said he preferred a procedure that would not be as onerous for me. He told me to catch a plane to Los Angeles that very night and be in his office at nine o'clock the next morning.

A big, athletic-looking man of fifty-nine, Morton was the son of a West Virginia coal miner and a nurse and still had the Mountaineer State in his voice. He was decisive bordering on arrogant, as any great surgeon should be. After new tests, Morton declared I had a small cancer on my right lung that should be removed forthwith. Was it because of my chain smoking that I ended in 1963? Morton did not know and did not care. There was no need for a biopsy, he said. Nor was there any reason to remove much of the lung. He would enter through my back, do a quick test to make sure that the growth was malignant, and then clip off the tumor without removing the lung. If all went well, Morton said, he would have me out of the hospital in three days and back home in Washington within a week. I cannot exaggerate how much this new prospect lifted my spirits. We set surgery for seven days later, Monday, August 10.

Geraldine and I took a noon flight on Sunday, August 9, to Los Angeles and checked into the Century Plaza where we had stayed many times over thirty-nine years. We scheduled dinner that night with Joe and Lee Cerrell, and for sentimental reasons I selected Trader Vic's at the Beverly Hilton. That was the site in 1959 of the first of my many dinners with Joe and Lee. I suggested this would be a fitting place for what could be my last supper.

Monday, Morton operated at midday and I woke up in the early evening in excruciating pain. But the operation was a great success, and Morton was as good as his word. I was released from the hospital Thursday morning, worked on columns from my hotel room Thursday and Friday, went to the movies (*Clear and Present Danger*) Thursday night, had dinner at a Mexican restaurant with the Cerrells Friday night, flew back to Washington Sunday, and was at work in my office Monday, August 14, one week after surgery. People could not believe it when I told them, and I hardly could myself.

With brilliant diagnosis and superb execution having saved my life for the third time, I was the last person to criticize health care in America. People asked why I would fly three thousand miles across the continent when there were so many great surgeons on the East Coast. The answer is I wanted the top care available. My freedom to pick the best doctor I could find brought home the danger to me—and all Americans—posed by the Clintons' plans for government-managed health care.

I pondered how I had survived spinal meningitis, prostate cancer, and lung cancer. Was it just good luck, or was it providential? Was I just meant to live a little longer for some unknown reason?

IN THE WEEK before the 1994 midterm elections, I was traveling with House Minority Whip Newt Gingrich in preparation for a *Reader's Digest* profile of him. On the afternoon of Tuesday, October 25, with a two-hour hole in his schedule after meeting in Midwest City, Oklahoma, with editors of the *Midwest City Sun,* Gingrich asked for use of the newspaper's conference room for a private staff meeting—no outsiders, no local politicians, no Novak. "Last minute campaign planning?" I asked Gingrich. "No, that's all wrapped up," Gingrich replied dismissively. "We're planning the transition." That would be the transition for the U.S. House of Representatives from Democratic to Republican rule for the first time in forty years.

The conventional wisdom was that there was no chance of Republicans winning the House. I believe I was the only Washington journalist predicting a Republican takeover. In the September 7 issue of the *Evans-Novak Political Report,* I projected a thirty-seat Republican gain, much higher than the consensus. On October 4, I raised the number to thirty-five. On October 18 (seven days before my Oklahoma conversation with Gingrich) I saw a forty-seat gain—just enough to take control. On November 1 (seven days before the election), I raised the number to forty-five and predicted a takeover in the Senate with a gain of five seats. On CNN's *Capital Gang* on November 5, I made the same prediction. As usual, my forecasts were based on seat-by-seat analysis, very cautious with a bias toward retaining the status quo.

A major reason Democrats could not recapture the House for the next decade was they had no inkling of what happened in 1994. They could not imagine how they lost so badly in a rising economy, with no war and no pending national crisis.

Clinton thought a big-government, universal care solution to health care would carry the Democrats. No decision was more feckless than his delegation to Hillary of this issue. Even so his bill nearly passed. Top Congressional Republicans were so frightened of being blamed for killing health care that they wanted desperately to cut a deal with Clinton that would have saved him. Pat Moynihan told me in the early summer of 1994 that at a Senate Finance Committee hearing, Senate Minority Leader Bob Dole passed this note to Chairman Moynihan: "Is it time yet?" That is, is it time to get together for a bipartisan health care plan? Moynihan did not reply. He had been treated badly by the Clintons and was not anxious to bail out the president.

Two people saved the Republicans from themselves. Hillary Rodham Clinton, in her intransigence and arrogance, spurned Democratic dealmakers and insisted on her own grandiose health care plan. The other savior was Bill Kristol, who after Clinton's victory in 1992 formed the Project for the Republican Future. From his small office came a torrent of paper that convinced Republican leaders to avoid a deal.

That summer I asked Paul Begala what the consequences would be if the Republicans prevented any health care bill from passing. "We'll just beat the Republicans like a bad piece of meat," said Begala, reverting to lingo from his Texas homeland. Indeed, he told me, Republicans would suffer for their sin for fifty years. I think that's what Paul told Clinton, and I think it is what Clinton believed. They could not have been more wrong. "Hillarycare" was an albatross around the necks of Democratic candidates.

THE ELECTION OF November 8, 1994, was one of the most important I ever reported and not because I predicted the outcome. By gaining fifty-one seats in the House and five in the Senate, the Republicans commanded only relatively modest margins in each chamber (twenty-five in the House, four in the Senate). But they had changed the face of Congress for a dozen years.

Behind the numbers, the slaughter of famous Democrats in 1994 claimed Governor Mario Cuomo of New York, Senator Jim Sasser of Tennessee (poised to become senate majority leader), Speaker Tom Foley, House Ways and Means chairman Dan Rostenkowski, and Jack Brooks, the LBJ crony from Texas whose high-handed chairmanship of the House Judiciary Committee typified forty years of one-party rule.

This finally was the realigning election I had awaited for a generation. For the first time Republicans won a majority of House seats in the eleven states of the old Confederacy, leading sixty-four to sixty-one with a pickup of sixteen seats in the region—a margin that would expand in years to come. The South would be as "solid" for Republicans as it once was for Democrats, compensating for losses elsewhere to keep control of the House.

CHAPTER 39

"Will Success Spoil Newt Gingrich?"

B OB DOLE'S RETURN as Senate majority leader for the first time in eight years surprised him as much as it did the Washington press corps, and he had no plans for real change. But the prospect of Newt Gingrich as the first Republican speaker of the House since stodgy old Joe Martin forty years earlier was cause for excitement. Bob Michel would not be part of a Republican majority in the House. Unable to stave off Gingrich's promised challenge, Michel at age seventy-one did not seek reelection in 1994. Now, to the mortification of Democrats, Gingrich would be third in line of presidential succession.

At that point, I do not think any journalist was closer to Gingrich. I was on the telephone to him 1994 election night, November 8, and talked to him several times in the flush of victory Wednesday. I wanted him to do *Evans and Novak* as his first postelection TV interview show. Done. I booked him live on CNN at twelve thirty p.m. Saturday. I needed another long session with him immediately for my *Reader's Digest* article. Done. He gave me two hours starting at nine forty-five a.m. Friday at the House minority whip's office on the second floor of the Capitol.

The "transition" meeting at Midwest City, Oklahoma, in October, from which I had been excluded, concerned matters more important than new draperies in the Speaker's office. Gingrich had it all figured out, and now he told me about it. He said Dick Armey of Texas would be elected House majority leader without opposition in his ninth year of Congress. That was not surprising. Totally unexpected were Gingrich's plans to control committee chairmanships—something no Speaker had attempted for sixty or seventy years. As a professor of American history, Gingrich was looking into the past when the Speaker was much more powerful than even the most successful recent Democrats in that office, Sam Rayburn and Tip O'Neill.

Gingrich's models were two long-ago Republican speakers, Thomas Brackett Reed and Uncle Joe Cannon—known historically as Czar Reed and Czar Cannon.

With seniority theoretically inviolable for both parties in the House, Gingrich would simply violate it case-by-case. The Appropriations chairmanship would go to Bob Livingston of Louisiana, jumped by Gingrich over four committee members with more seniority. Henry Hyde of Illinois would give up a leadership position and jump one notch in seniority to become Judiciary Committee chairman.

Only in the secret balloting for House majority whip, the third-ranking leadership post, was Gingrich not in complete control. I had assumed the job would go to Gingrich's lieutenant, Bob Walker of Pennsylvania, who would defeat Tom DeLay of Texas with Gingrich's help. But Newt said that though he personally would vote for Walker, he would not campaign for him. I interpreted that as meaning Gingrich thought he could not beat DeLay and did not want to alienate him.

Gingrich talked to me mainly about process that morning, but the process was intended to enact far-reaching reforms proposed by his Contract with America: taxes, Social Security, budget, welfare, and torts. It was an exciting prospect, and I would have unparalleled access that would enable me to write the definitive book on the historic 104th Congress.

I contacted my agent Esther Newberg, who came up with three bids. I settled on The Free Press, a division of Simon & Schuster, whose offer was the high bid of $155,000. Esther told me I would be fortunate to have as my editor Adam Bellow, son of the famed novelist Saul Bellow and a rare conservative in publishing.

Bellow was enthusiastic about the project, something not always true of editors assigned me by big publishing houses. I would start sending him chapters as the legislative product of the 104th Congress began to emerge late in 1995, and I would finish right after the 1996 election.

WHEN THREE DAYS after his 1994 election triumph Gingrich laid out to me his plans to rule the House of Representatives, he did not reveal his collateral design to amass a personal fortune and do it quickly. The desire of politicians without inherited wealth to become powerful *and* rich has been documented through the centuries although I believe it intensified in the 1960s. As politicians dealt with fabulously rich benefactors benefiting from their legislative decisions, they yearned for their share of the gold.

Gingrich wanted too much, too soon. Ironically, he shared the desires of Jim Wright, whose clumsy implementation of those desires enabled Gingrich to drive him out of the Speaker's chair. Actually, Wright's scheme of having organized labor buy bulk copies of his paperback memoir—a booklet more than a book—was penny ante compared to what Gingrich attempted.

Gingrich had barely been installed as Speaker when it was learned he had signed a $4.5 million book contract with HarperCollins, part of Rupert Murdoch's publishing empire. House Democrats saw an opportunity to do to Gingrich what Gingrich had done to Wright. Since Gingrich's book could not generate sufficient royalties to come close to covering a $4.5 million advance, this looked like a subsidy from a conservative publisher to a conservative politician. I believed Gingrich when he said he did not know HarperCollins was owned by Murdoch, and I believed Murdoch when he said he knew nothing about the contract. Although I admired both Murdoch and Gingrich, this deal still did not pass the smell test. Gingrich quickly came to the same conclusion, gave up the $4.5 million advance, and said he would make do with the return on royalties from actual sales.

That was not good enough for the Democrats. Senator Christopher Dodd, newly installed general chairman of the Democratic Party, on CBS's *Face the Nation* Sunday, January 15, 1995, advised Gingrich "to cut the deal immediately, take nothing, move away from it." The next day, I was on the telephone with the new House majority leader Dick Armey and asked him what he thought about Dodd's advice. "It might be the best thing to do," Armey told me. I wrote down his answer, word for word, on the yellow legal pad on my desk. I asked: Was that on the record? It was, Armey replied. He said the HarperCollins contract was a distraction the Speaker should eliminate, and I agreed.

I thought that showed extraordinary candor by Gingrich's deputy, in keeping with what I then thought of as the essential Dick Armey. My first contact with Armey came the Sunday night before the 1984 election when, traveling with Vice President George Bush, I was in Denton, Texas, for a rally. As I sat in the press section awaiting Bush's speech, my attention was aroused by a preliminary speaker calling for radical tax reform and dramatic reduction of the federal government.

It was Richard Armey, professor of Economics at North Texas State University in Denton, who would be elected two days later in an upset. I met him as a first-year congressman early in 1985 when Armey asked me to lunch. He had won unusual publicity and the displeasure of his party's elders by sleeping on his office sofa and showering in the House gym.

He soon acquired conventional lodging and advanced faster than anybody in the Class of 1984. After eight years in the House, he was elected—with Gingrich's sponsorship—chairman of the House Republican Conference by ousting Michel ally Jerry Lewis of California. While I admired Gingrich, I considered him a political adventurer who might return to his liberal Republican roots. In contrast, I trusted Armey as a true believer.

My column of Thursday, January 19, 1995, about the Gingrich book deal used Armey's quote ("It might be the best thing to do") given me in our Monday phone conversation. Armey was asked about it at a press conference that day, and said he had been "misunderstood" by me. That meant I misquoted him.

A reporter does not issue statements saying he has been maligned by a politician. I could write a column calling Armey a liar, but that would make me a crybaby and burn my bridge to the majority leader. I could call Armey on the phone and express my displeasure, but that would serve no purpose other than to poison our relationship.

By a lucky twist of fate, Armey was scheduled to be at CNN to do the *Evans and Novak* program live two days later on Saturday. I carefully crafted what I would ask on the air:

> Novak: About a week ago, sir, in a telephone conversation that you and I had, I mentioned that Senator Chris Dodd, the new Democratic General Chairman, suggested that the Speaker should cancel his book contract. And you said to me it might be the best thing to do. Do you no longer feel that way?
>
> Armey: No, in fact, when we had that exchange, that was the first I had the question put to me. It is my nature almost always, if somebody says, "Dick, let's go have a cup of coffee," my natural reaction to it is it might be a good idea. But you prompted me to think this through and I think to this point the fact is this is not the right thing for the Speaker to do. He has something to say to America. The book can be very important to the American people. It ought to be written. And he's perfectly entitled to have a legitimate contract in the writing of that book.

It was an artful answer, not one that could have come from the blunt, right-wing college professor who had entered the House ten years earlier. My faith in term limits has grown firm as the concept has lost support. I believe few members of Congress improve with seniority, and Dick Armey was no exception. He proved a good source for years to come, but I never really trusted him after the Gingrich book incident.

. . .

MONA CHAREN AND *The Capital Gang* were not a marriage made in heaven. The wonder was that the arrangement lasted from December 1991 until April 1995. She was articulate and attractive, but the chemistry with the male panelists was never there. Al Hunt could not stand her. Mark Shields did not like her either, but I think he could have learned to live with her had it not been for Al.

The relationship hit bottom early, at the 1992 Democratic National Convention in New York. Starting that year and continuing until 2004, the *Gang* went on CNN from the floor every night of each convention after the last gavel. Mona Charen and Margaret Warner alternated in 1992, and the first night Mona was on in New York she assailed Hillary Clinton, quoting from an *American Spectator* article criticizing her association with left-wing children's advocacy groups. Hunt went ballistic on live national television. He was sensitive about "kids," detested the *Spectator,* and now took off on Mona. While harsh words between the other *Gang* members often took place off-camera, that was not true of Mona and Al. Just about all the unpleasantness between them occurred on-camera for the world to see. There was very little interchange between them when the red eye was off. Mona could be a charmer, and I hoped she would use her feminine wiles on Al. But I think she disliked Al as much as he disliked her, and she was a proud woman who would not kowtow to him.

I told Al and Mark they better learn to live with Mona because she was going to be with us forever. But that was not good enough for Mona. After a *Gang* program one Saturday night in January 1995, I was walking toward my car in the CNN garage when Mona came up to me and let me have it. She felt I had conspired with Hunt and Shields, joining them as they ganged up on her and said she deeply resented my not siding with her. Not about to debate in a garage, I simply muttered some apologies.

While I thought Mona was unfair in her characterization of me, I could understand her frustration. I was less tolerant, however, when she carried her complaints about me to the CNN brass in Atlanta. The next week our executive producer Rick Davis told me Mona had complained directly to CNN president Tom Johnson about Novak's support of Hunt and Shields in their persecution of her.

It was not a smart move by Mona. I likened her complaint to Johnson to her joining the mob falsely accusing Pat Buchanan of anti-Semitism after he had been her benefactor in the Reagan White House. I did not complain to Mona but decided she had to go, which happened quickly.

Capital Gang was such a success that Atlanta was putting on a Sunday night knockoff, *Capital Gang Sunday,* with a different panel. I proposed Mona Charen as a regular on the Sunday night show, arguing she was now an experienced TV personality who would help the Sunday program while improving the chemistry of the Saturday show by leaving it. Tom Johnson agreed but only on the condition that it was acceptable to Mona. At first she was reluctant to leave a solid program with a future for a new show with uncertain prospects (and which, indeed, enjoyed a short life). She finally agreed, perhaps because she would be getting more money as an every-week participant but also would be entering a more pleasant environment.

Rick Davis's choice as the conservative woman to replace Mona was Josette Shiner, managing editor of the *Washington Times.* She was intelligent, beautiful, and dignified—perhaps too dignified for *Capital Gang.* While I was sure she could get along with Al and Mark, I did not think her the right fit. I convinced Davis we should audition on-air several conservative women, including Josette.

No decision had been made when I addressed a *National Review* event on Saturday night, June 3, in Washington. John O'Sullivan, the magazine's editor, told me Kate O'Beirne would make a fabulous *Capital Gang* panelist. I had never met her prior to that evening, but I had seen her a few times on television and thought she was impressive: tall, blond, New-Yorker feisty, and exceptionally well informed. My problem was that now she was at the Heritage Foundation and had never been a journalist, which I had made a prerequisite for *Capital Gang.* No problem, said O'Sullivan, because she was joining *National Review* as chief Washington correspondent.

Kate auditioned on the *Gang* for the first time on June 24, and she was dynamite. My decision was quickly made. Kate O'Beirne was a tremendous asset to the program, no less conservative than Mona but better informed and able to charm the socks off Hunt. I think Boston Irish Shields was less susceptible to the charms of an Irish lass from New York, and Kate always felt Mark resented a tough conservative woman. But Kate radically improved the program.

In covering 1996 primary elections on-site in Iowa and New Hampshire, we used both women—Margaret Carlson and Kate O'Beirne—without an outside guest. It worked so well that I started scheduling all five *Gang* members about half the time. The two women were opposite in both appearance and ideology: short, liberal Margaret and tall, conservative Kate. But they became friends, bonding together against the three male chauvinists they had to confront.

We now had the best quintet since our original gang, though it almost had broken up in 1994. Mark told me then he was getting sick of the program and wanted to leave. I don't think he ever got over losing *Inside Washington,* the excellent PBS interview program he moderated (doomed because it lacked a Washington outlet). To keep Mark on *Capital Gang,* I suggested he might be interested in moderating. He was interested, provided Hunt would agree to be displaced. Al loved moderating the program, and he was good at it. But he took a bullet for the team to keep the *Gang* and CNN's top weekend program intact another eleven years.

THE *READER'S DIGEST* profile of Speaker Gingrich that I had been working on since October appeared in the April 1995 issue under the title "Will Success Spoil Newt Gingrich?" I am sure it was not what Newt had in mind when he gave me so much of his valuable time.

The Gingrich profile and other *Reader's Digest* articles still came out under the Evans & Novak byline as they had since we started writing for the world's largest circulation magazine in 1981. Rowly and I were listed on the masthead as "Roving Editors," producing four articles a year. The *Digest* was the most heavily edited publication we ever wrote for, but William Schulz, a conservative who ran the *Digest's* Washington office, was the best editor I ever encountered and always improved my copy.

Schulz had less to do with the final nature of the Gingrich article than another conservative, Kenneth Tomlinson. A former newspaper reporter and longtime *Reader's Digest* staffer, Tomlinson had headed the Voice of America in 1982–84 during the Reagan administration and returned to the magazine as managing editor, to become editor in chief in 1989 at age forty-five. Ken was much more intimately involved in what I wrote than his predecessors, always in a positive way.

Even before Gingrich was sworn in as speaker, Tomlinson expressed to me misgivings about him. He urged me not to go overboard on Newt, and I was having second thoughts myself, starting with the aborted $4.5 million book contract.

Gingrich put the House on a backbreaking schedule to pass elements of the Contract with America that were mainly procedural. Was this revolution merely cosmetic? I thought Newt sometimes got entangled in the trivial, as in renaming the House's standing committees.

On Monday, December 5, 1994, nearly a month before the new Republican Congress was sworn in, I was addressing right-wing congressional staffers, activists, and lobbyists, giving an optimistic preview of the Gingrich Revolution when I got this question from the audience: "What would you say, Mr. Novak, if I were to tell you that half the Democratic professional staffers on the House Appropriations Committee are being retained by the Republicans?" "I would say it was an outrage," I replied.

It was all too true. In addition to 35 Appropriations staff members allocated to the Democratic minority, I learned that 50 out of the 119 staff slots allocated to the Republicans were actually holdovers. The rationale, I wrote in a December 15 column, was that "numbers-crunching skills, needed by the committee are claimed to be too arduous for the available Republican talent pool." I explained:

> The incoming chairman [Bob Livingston] argued that only experts can perform an arcane procedure called "cross-walking"—making the federal budget and appropriations bills conform. He pleaded that he should not abandon an "institutional memory" and promised that ideological and partisan Democratic staffers would be fired.
>
> This is viewed as nonsense by well-informed Republicans. . . . They contend there is a wealth of outside talent to perform rudimentary clerical tasks.
>
> The test will be whether the appropriators end their long complicity in dipping into the public treasury and instead fight each other in the great struggle for the role of government.

They did not. I saw Livingston on February 6, 1995, in preparation for my book on the 104th Congress. I had never met the new Appropriations chairman, whom I had regarded as a southern conservative closely allied with Gingrich. I sat down in front of his big desk in the chairman's office just off the House floor and was startled to see behind that desk a large portrait of a man who looked like the late Silvio O. Conte, a very liberal Republican from Pittsfield, Massachusetts. Conte was the rapidly disappearing archetypal New England Republican, who posed so little threat to the Democrats that seven of the sixteen times he was reelected he had no opposition (and was the last Republican elected from that district). A new chairman gets to pick the portraits for his office, and I thought this southern conservative's choice was strange.

"Is that Sil Conte?" I asked Livingston. "Yes," he replied. "Sil was my mentor. He told me everything I know about appropriations." Now I realized Bob Livingston was less a Republican or a conservative than he was an appropriator, as was Conte. House Appropriations Committee members constituted a band of brothers who crossed party and ideological lines in dictating how much, where, and what would be spent by the government.

I had thought Gingrich reached four rungs down the seniority ladder for Livingston to get a conservative reformer ending this buddy system of appropriators, but that was not it at all. I now realized that Gingrich was not trying to break this closed circle but merely trying to get a younger, more competent appropriator than the old-timers ahead of Livingston in seniority. Livingston was keeping the Democratic staffers because he was an appropriator at heart.

Four days after seeing Livingston, I came to total agreement with Ken Tomlinson that we had better hedge our bets about Gingrich in the *Reader's Digest* article. On that day, February 10, I breakfasted with Gingrich in the House Members Dining Room. He already had ceased to be the exuberant visionary who had so excited me after his 1994 election triumph. He seemed less tired than just plain bored with the workaday world of legislation.

I noted speculation about Gingrich for president in 1996, expecting a routine denial. Instead, Newt said: "Well, wouldn't you say that I had accomplished everything here [in the House] that I could?" I first thought he might be joking. But he wasn't. Nothing substantive had been accomplished in the 104th Congress—no tax reform, no expenditure reform, no welfare reform, no tort reform. Yet Gingrich was ready to move on, his attention span apparently exceeded.

So I began "Will Success Spoil Newt Gingrich?" by asking whether he really could "radically reform the House of Representatives and dismantle 'the liberal welfare state'?" I replied with the theme of the *Digest* article:

> Gingrich clearly has the vision, energy and intellect to do so. But he also has exhibited an overweening ego that many fear may be his Achilles' heel—compromising on his ability to deliver on the promises he made to Americans who want a smaller, less intrusive federal government.

I don't think that was what Newt expected to be written about him for the more than fifty million readers of the *Reader's Digest*, but he never said a word about the article to me. Although I continued to enjoy access to him, coolness entered our relationship. It would grow cooler still, as my disappointment mounted.

EARLY ON THE evening of Friday, June 23, 1995, Rick Davis dropped in to see me at the little office at CNN Washington that the right-wing *Crossfire* hosts used. I was substituting on that night's program for John Sununu. John had shared the conservative host's chair with Pat Buchanan starting early in 1993 when Pat returned to the program for a second time following his 1992 run for president. But Buchanan had left *Crossfire* for the third time early in 1995 for another presidential campaign. So Sununu was doing nearly all the shows again.

Davis, the executive producer of *Crossfire* as well as my weekend shows, had a proposition. Would I go on *Crossfire* as a regular co-host, sharing the right-wing chair evenly with Sununu? Rick gave me some baloney about *Crossfire* wanting me more often. But the real reason was that big-time lobbyist Sununu was not happy doing the show five nights a week, and I was the only experienced person who could step in immediately.

A few years earlier I would have eagerly accepted Rick's offer, but now I was not sure. I told Davis I was unnaturally busy at age sixty-four and I doubted I wanted anything else on my full plate. He replied that *Crossfire* would enable me to turn down physically exhausting out-of-town lectures with an increased CNN salary making up the difference. I told Rick I'd think it over, and he replied he needed an answer by Monday.

Geraldine did not want me to do it. She never had cared much for *Crossfire,* and it was not my favorite activity either. So why did I call Davis and say yes? For one thing, I had trouble turning down money. But my decision had more to do with ego than greed. *Crossfire* was the premier program of CNN at the time when the network was still riding high on the wave of its Gulf War triumph. My new hitch on *Crossfire* began Monday, July 3, 1995.

In addition to Buchanan, Michael Kinsley also was leaving. Kinsley was a talented journalist who changed jobs frequently and always had his eyes open for something better. Six years at *Crossfire* was a long time for him, on a program he never really enjoyed. But the money was good and nothing better beckoned until 1995, when Microsoft's billionaire founder Bill Gates started *Slate* as an online magazine and recruited Kinsley.

With Kinsley gone, I thought Davis might conduct a thorough search for a left-wing version of Pat Buchanan. Instead, he quickly selected somebody who was unqualified and unsuited for the role but was the most famous person ever to become a regular on a CNN program: Geraldine Ferraro.

CNN was jubilant it had signed a former vice presidential nominee. Like Sununu Ferraro was a political celebrity with no television skills and no apparent desire to acquire them. Unlike Sununu, Ferraro shied away from heated debate and was surprisingly unfamiliar with issues.

As a reporter, I had regarded Ferraro as a typical know-it-all New York pol. As her colleague and combatant on television, I saw Gerry as motherly and vulnerable, and became quite fond of her. I don't think she really liked the program, and she didn't need the money. She was doing it for exposure prior to a political comeback. CNN executives understood they were being used, but they did not care. After leaving *Crossfire* she was mauled in the 1998 New York Democratic senatorial primary by Congressman Chuck Schumer, who was smarter, tougher, and better organized but definitely not as nice as Gerry Ferraro. I seldom show much compassion for professional politicians, but I did feel sorry for her.

However feckless was Rick Davis's selection of Ferraro, he did not commit the ultimate sin of putting her on *Crossfire* full-time. Ferraro against Sununu and Novak five nights a week would have been a bloodbath. From the start, Davis scheduled her for only half the shows. The liberal seat on the other programs was filled by a wide variety of liberal auditioners in a process spread over several weeks, with Robert F. Kennedy Jr. clearly the worst. Kennedy was a leftist lawyer who was at sea on any issue other than the environment, and he wisely took himself out of consideration after two disastrous performances.

I told Davis my emphatic choice of the auditioners was Bob Shrum and not merely because he had become my friend. He had been a champion collegiate debater at Georgetown University, and I ended up second best to him all too many times when we confronted each other on TV.

Had he joined *Crossfire,* Shrum would have gotten out of the campaign consulting business and devoted himself to the nonpolitical clients of his highly profitable firm. I think he felt it time to turn the page in his career, which would have saved him the frustration of the 2000 and 2004 presidential campaigns he ran for Al Gore and John Kerry.

CNN's choice was not Shrum but Bill Press, a liberal political activist from California who had been an aide to Governor Jerry Brown and later was Democratic state chairman. Rick Davis did not quite come right out and say it, but I inferred the reason was mainly cosmetic. Press was tall and good-looking with a full head of luxuriant white hair. Shrum was chubby, less than handsome, and balding. However, previous *Crossfire* hosts certainly had not been selected on the basis of their looks.

I don't know exactly what CNN executives expected from Bill Press, but they were dissatisfied with him from the start and always seemed to be looking for a replacement. I thought Press was quite good even if he was not up to Shrum's standard, and he became the first liberal *Crossfire* host with whom I had any kind of social relationship off-camera (going out to dinner with our wives occasionally in Washington and at the shore). I got along with both Press and Ferraro much better than I had with Braden or Kinsley.

JOHN SUNUNU POSSESSED an extraordinary propensity to infuriate people. Many people who encountered him in politics and government told me how tempted they were to smash this short, plump, grinning antagonist. Mark Shields came close one time.

In 1994, Shields, Sununu, and I were nearing the end of a three-cornered debate in Minneapolis. Shields had launched his familiar attack on Republican tax policies. I had heard this spiel so often from Mark that I pretty well tuned him out. But John typically wanted the last word, beginning his rebuttal of Shields's statistics with an old cliché: "Figures don't lie, but liars can figure." Shortly thereafter, Shields, Sununu, and I were on our feet acknowledging the audience's applause when I saw Mark grab Sununu tightly by the arm, and whisper something in Sununu's ear. John turned chalky white. When I asked Shields what he said to Sununu, he replied: "I told him: 'John, you're a fucking asshole.' " Mark Shields and John Sununu never again shared the same lecture platform.

During the 1996 Democratic National Convention in Chicago, I appreciated Mark's aggravation with Sununu. Monday, August 26, the first night of the convention was Geraldine Ferraro's sixty-first birthday. Her pals in the labor movement were throwing a bash for her at the Field Museum after the convention adjourned for the night, with hundreds of convention delegates invited. It actually was a kickoff for Gerry's 1998 Senate bid, but her new colleagues on *Crossfire* were expected to attend.

The party's principal host was the notorious Arthur Coia, head of the mob-controlled Laborers International Union of North America. I had been pounding the Clinton administration for coddling Coia, whose links to organized crime were exposed a few weeks before the convention in congressional hearings. I felt uncomfortable wining and dining at Arthur Coia's table, and I feared I would be exposed as a hypocrite by the opposition *Chicago Tribune.* I told Rick Davis I couldn't go, and he just shrugged. But Sununu insisted that for me not to go would insult Gerry. After all, John said, if *he* were going, why couldn't I? Reluctantly I agreed to attend.

Arriving a little late at the Field Museum, I was surprised to find Sununu was not there yet. I was told John had other appointments and had been slowed by heavy traffic. Coia was followed by photographers, and I kept out of his way. Finally, it was time to sing "Happy Birthday," and Bill

Press literally manhandled me onto a raised platform. Still no Sununu. I had no alternative but to shake hands with a beaming Coia who embraced me as cameras clicked. Sununu never arrived.

I was relieved the next morning to find neither the *Tribune* nor any other publication thought Coia's bear hug of me newsworthy enough to publish. But I was still furious. Later that day, when I confronted Sununu and asked where the hell he had been, he protested he could not be held responsible for Chicago traffic. But he was flashing that sarcastic smile I had come to know and that I interpreted as saying, "Well, Novak, I really put one over on you." I felt like belting him.

LATE ON THE afternoon of July 27, 1995, Speaker Gingrich spent three hours behind closed doors at the House Ethics Committee answering nuisance allegations by House Democratic leaders in their campaign of retribution for Jim Wright. He went straight from there to La Brasserie restaurant on Capitol Hill where he was a guest at a dinner of the Saturday Evening Club, which was not a club and never met on Saturday night. R. Emmett Tyrrell, editor of the *American Spectator*, had purloined the Saturday Club label from the gathering presided over long ago by H. L. Mencken. Tyrrell from time to time would invite twenty or so people, mostly male conservative journalists, to sit at a long table at La Brasserie for an elegant French meal and discussion with a guest who almost always was a conservative politician (though Tyrrell once got the left-wing novelist Norman Mailer).

I was a regular at these dinners, and they generally were lively, cordial affairs. But not the night of July 27. I had concluded that the Gingrich Revolution after six months was losing its vigor, and my column that morning zeroed in on Newt's failure to attack racial quotas. Exhausted from his encounter with the ethics police, Gingrich had no sooner taken his seat than he took off on me about the column. David Brock, then still a supposed conservative working for the *Spectator*, was there and later described Gingrich "flying into a red-faced, table-pounding rage" at me. My version of what happened, in a column published shortly after the dinner, was less graphic. I wrote that Gingrich "erupted in anger at the dinner table," continuing:

His voice rising, the Speaker pointed to journalists at the table and said they were acting like, well, like journalists. He was "infuriated," he said, by my column on affirmative action and asserted that I was wrong in saying his book, "To Renew America," does not touch the subject. He cited a two-page chapter on "Individual Versus Group Rights" (that never mentioned affirmative action or quotas or proposed a specific solution). . . .

He does fear alienating such blacks as his Georgia Congressional colleague and fighter for civil rights in the '60s, Rep. John Lewis, and warned against instilling apprehension about "resegregation."

Gingrich idolized Lewis as a hero of the civil rights struggle. He never seemed that comfortable as a right-wing radical and was regressing to his Rockefeller Republican roots after less than seven months as Speaker. Ironically, Lewis had only contempt for Gingrich. The deeper irony was Newt committing what as a backbencher he had told me were mistakes made by Dewey and Eisenhower in abandoning the Republican base. In the column, I described Newt's attitude as "nobody can be to the right of me and be respectable."

Gingrich's growing alienation from his right-wing base was so dramatically demonstrated that night that my vague fears hardened about my book contract with The Free Press. For all its sound and fury, the Gingrich Congress was not about to produce the legislative output that was the book's premise. By the late summer of 1996 my premonitions were realized. The 104th was a do-nothing Congress, as far as landmark conservative legislation was concerned. I informed Adam Bellow that we had no book. (I fulfilled my contract with *Completing the Revolution: A Vision for Victory in 2000*—which contained unheeded advice for the Republicans.)

ON THE MORNING of Thursday, August 8, 1996, in San Diego the week before the Republican National Convention, I was seated in the little wooden building devoted to CNN's weekend shows that was part of the network's sprawling complex adjoining the convention center.

My friend and tipster, lobbyist Rick Hohlt, tracked me down to relate this unlikely news: Bob Dole had selected his longtime adversary Jack Kemp as his vice presidential running mate. That was by far the biggest story Rick ever had given me—if it were true. I could not reach Kemp or anybody else to confirm it. A lot of my sources were en route to San Diego or there already and hard to reach.

Just then somebody on the other side of the room yelled out, "Novak! Bob Dole on the phone!" I was sure it was a gag. Dole had last placed an unsolicited telephone call to me in 1988 (to complain about a column). It had been weeks since Dole had clinched the presidential nomination, and not a week went by that I did not complain, in print or on the air, what a bad idea his candidacy was for the Grand Old Party.

I'm sure Dole thought I hated him, but I just thought he was a poor candidate. I admired him as a fighter, not only for overcoming his terrible war wounds but in his determination to become president. The 1996 campaign was Dole's fourth for national office and surely his last try for the White House.

Dole had almost lost the nomination against a weak field. Heavily favored in the Iowa caucuses, Dole lost more ground the more he campaigned and barely finished ahead of Pat Buchanan. Dole never had learned how to campaign in New Hampshire and looked stiff and uncomfortable— particularly compared with Buchanan's flamboyant style, carried over from his surprise New Hampshire showing in 1992.

When it looked as though Buchanan was going to win New Hampshire, Dole voters started to peel off to support Lamar Alexander (former governor of Tennessee, former U.S. Secretary of Education) to stop Pat. Alexander, a protégé of Howard Baker, may have been a little too moderate for what the Republican Party had become by 1996 (and for me as well, though I liked him immensely on a personal basis). Nevertheless, I felt that if Alexander could win New Hampshire, he could sweep the remaining Republican primaries and then would be the kind of candidate who could beat Clinton.

In response, the well-financed Dole campaign unleashed a vicious TV blitz unfairly attacking Alexander's record in Tennessee, in particular a tax increase (truly ironic for Dole). Alexander, with neither the time nor money to respond, started slipping. That enabled Buchanan to win, with Dole barely surviving by finishing second ahead of Alexander (who was now out of the running).

Mark Shields and I agreed this was a golden opportunity for Buchanan to become the Republican nominee for president. Arizona was next, and Buchanan had a legitimate chance to win there and then withstand the monolithic assault on him to keep him from being nominated. However, Pat had to sidestep gently toward the center, less on substance than on rhetoric. Instead, he reinforced his right-wing populist image, campaigning in Arizona with a black cowboy hat and holding a shotgun over his head. It was almost as though he did not want to be the nominee for president.

I picked up Buchanan and Dole campaigning in Phoenix the day before the primary. Don Devine, Dole's long-suffering conservative guru, told me their overnight poll tracking showed it would be hard to beat Steve Forbes and the heavy money he had poured into Arizona. If Dole finished third behind Forbes and Buchanan, Devine mournfully told me, that might finish him off. Would Forbes, campaigning as a supply-sider, then be in the driver's seat?

Malcolm S. Forbes Jr., eldest son of the publishing tycoon, was as unlikely a presidential candidate as I ever have seen. More conservative in ideology and certainly lifestyle than his flamboyant father, Steve was shy and lacking in charisma. I think his friend and fellow Jerseyite Jude Wanniski was instrumental in talking him into the race. (Typically, when Forbes did run, his political managers found Jude so obnoxious that they locked him out of the campaign.) In early 1995, Wanniski talked me into putting Forbes on an *Evans and Novak* broadcast, despite misgivings by CNN producers. It produced more news than our program usually did, with the AP running a long story when Forbes used *Evans and Novak* to break the news that he might well run for president.

Forbes won Arizona with Dole a narrow second-place finisher over Buchanan. That appeared to leave the Republican presidential race in utter confusion, but not for long. After losing Delaware (where Forbes spent heavily and won) on February 27, Dole on Tuesday, March 5, swept eight out of eight primaries. How was that possible? Don Devine, a shrewd political analyst, described it as "Dole, Incorporated." I defined that in a column describing Dole's recovery:

That is the entire Republican Party, plus allied corporate moguls, Washington lawyers and lobbyists, uniting in righteous indignation to repel outsiders—and reform. The Grand Old Party, which like the British Tories, has many of the characteristics of a private club, controlled its own nomination.

With no real campaign conducted in those eight states, Dole won on reputation and a heavy TV ad purchase. The rule of thumb was that Dole won primaries only when he did not campaign and nobody campaigned against him, and that was not a good omen for November.

Dole's performance on platform deliberations in San Diego the week before the convention was dreadful. While he once had been considered a faithful foe of abortion, I believe his corporate backers (egged on by their wives) and his staffers urged him to provide wiggle room on the issue. Dole, disregarding the importance of religious conservatives in the Republican Party of 1996, tried to amend the platform to promise "tolerance" for prochoice Republicans. Congressman Henry Hyde, the platform committee chairman and a hero of the prolife movement, told me over breakfast the morning of the first platform deliberations in San Diego that he would oppose Dole to the end. Dole yielded only after Vin Weber, the convention's policy chairman, told him that the nominee could force his position on the party but it would provoke Armageddon on the convention floor and poison his campaign.

IT WAS DOLE on the phone, all right. He got right to business, informing me he was down to his last three picks for vice president. "What would you think if I named Jack Kemp?" he asked. It was a politician's way of leaking to me that he had in fact picked Kemp.

Dole indicated to me the announcement was imminent, making it impossible for me to write a special exclusive column for Friday newspapers. The telephone conversation lasted no more than five minutes, and I rushed to the CNN studio in its convention complex. I was on the air live within ten minutes broadcasting the news to the world. Although Matt Drudge later claimed he was the first to report the Kemp selection, his Web site was not widely read in 1996. Rightly or wrongly, I got credit for the scoop.

The Kemp selection was the biggest exclusive I ever gave CNN. The network's executives, led by Ed Turner, showered me with congratulations. But I detected a little resentment from some of the network's reporters, who did not like an outside commentator breaking news.

(That resentment may have increased when on Monday I had another exclusive for CNN: Pat Buchanan would endorse Dole instead of launching an independent candidacy, as his supporters wanted. I also got this news from the primary source: Buchanan told me over dinner Sunday night. With all of CNN's huge news staff, I had the only two major news beats at a convention that was shy on hard news.)

"Surpassing even John F. Kennedy's selection of Lyndon B. Johnson in 1960," I wrote in my column, "Dole's choice of Kemp is the most startling development in any of 19 national political conventions I have covered." It was more startling than the LBJ selection, because Johnson was Senate majority leader and one of his party's most powerful figures while Kemp was considered a political dead man. For the first time since 1972, Kemp had been omitted from the speaking schedule at a Republican national convention.

Why, then, did Dole pick Kemp? Because he was shrewd enough to know the convention and indeed the party needed a lift. Kemp might have been persona non grata to the party's insiders, but he was immensely popular among the delegates. Roaming the convention floor, I found Kemp's selection energized the convention. I think Dole showed how much he wanted to be elected by picking as his running mate a man he disliked and whose ideology he disdained.

But why would Dole leak the story to me considering his personal distaste for me? Because he knew I was close to Kemp, would be thrilled by his selection, and that I might even put in a kind word for Dole. He was right. In my column running the first day of the convention, I noted that Dole's closest aides all argued against Kemp, then added: "Outside Dole's inner circle, Kemp's selection was exhilarating—not merely because it rehabilitated the successor of Barry Goldwater and Ronald Reagan but because of what it revealed about Dole's largeness of spirit."

MY COLUMN THAT ran August 26, the first day of the 1996 Democratic convention, contained this truly remarkable sentence: "Even more than Bill Clinton's party, this—at least temporarily—is now Dick Morris's party." It was remarkable for two reasons. First, Morris was a professional political consultant who was not even a Democrat. Second, hardly more than forty-eight hours after publication of this column, he was out of the Clinton campaign and out of Democratic politics, presumably forever.

I was the first reporter to report Morris had returned to Clinton's political circle and was working full-time out of the White House. I wrote it on April 15, 1995, to lead off the weekend column of shorts. I checked some of my old New York Democratic sources to find they remembered Morris as a left-wing activist in the reform movement twenty-five years earlier. However, they said Morris was no ideologue but a scoundrel who did not believe in anything. Indeed, most of his recent clients were Republicans and he was close to Trent Lott. But his most famous client, dating back to 1977, was William Jefferson Clinton.

I had been told Morris was inaccessible to journalists. In fact, I reached him easily, beginning my most productive relationship with any Clinton aide. He put everything off the record, but his insights were invaluable. I took Morris to lunch at the Army and Navy Club, and soon he was inviting me to his permanent suite (No. 205) at the Jefferson Hotel for room service meals. (This was the same suite where he entertained the prostitute who proved his downfall.) He appeared on our Evans-Novak Political Forum on April 12, 1996.

Morris was careful never to criticize Clinton in conversations with me. But during many such talks, I perceived a fascinating tension between him and the president. For all his claims of being a "New Democrat," Clinton was an old-fashioned Democrat who loved big, intrusive government financed by higher taxes and delighted in playing class-warfare politics. Morris had been a counterpoint to these self-destructive leftist tendencies by Clinton for two decades, enjoying remarkable success because his client liked winning elections even more than he liked left-wing policies.

That explained Clinton's new tolerance for tax cuts and enthusiasm for a balanced budget, but the most spectacular Morris policy success was the president's signature on the Republican welfare reform bill against the wishes of his entire White House staff and congressional Democratic leadership. Democrats were less than happy as they gathered in Chicago to nominate their first president to be reelected since Franklin Roosevelt. The delegates hated, as I wrote from Chicago, that the Democratic Party "is now Dick Morris's 'party.' "

I did not know then, and neither did Morris, that the *Star* (along with its sister publication in the Murdoch empire, the *New York Post*) was poised to publish an exposé of his yearlong dalliance with a prostitute. Clinton, with so much personal baggage of his own, immediately cut Morris loose. Without Morris, Clinton's campaign drifted into conventional liberalism and his lead dropped into single digits. But there was no way he could lose to Bob Dole.

AN EXUBERANT Jack Kemp was delighted to be back in the game. But I thought Jack now lacked the focus necessary for a serious national candidate. Nowhere was this more obvious than in St. Petersburg, Florida, on the evening of October 14 when Kemp debated Vice President Al Gore. Kemp, one of the most effective political stump speakers in my long experience, was a notoriously poor debater. My column on the St. Petersburg debate began:

> Six hours before Jack Kemp faced the largest television audience of his life to debate Al Gore, his aides felt he looked terrified. Their impression was confirmed by what he told them: "My mind is mush. I don't think at this point I can even explain our own economic program."
>
> Kemp thought he had been overbriefed. Advisers grumbled he had not taken the briefing seriously enough. Whatever the cause, however, there is no argument that he lost the debate to Vice President Gore.

It is testimony to the triviality of politics that Kemp's staff was less distressed by the fact that he lost that debate than my accurate rendition of his predebate complaint. (I tried in 2005 to get the source to permit me to identify him, but he declined because of the ferocious outrage that the disclosure would bring even ten years after the event.)

· · ·

DURING THE 1996 presidential campaign, I frequently wrote about the Clinton scandals—illegal foreign contributions, shady Arkansas land transactions, illicit payoffs. These stories were not all that interesting then, and are downright boring a decade later. The Clinton administration's unsavory nature did not bother most Democrats, but there were exceptions. One was my friend Bob McCandless.

If I had to pick any Democrat least likely to defect to the Republicans, it would be Robert C. McCandless. Born and bred a left-wing populist in Hobart, Oklahoma, he was a true blue Democrat. At age fifty-nine in 1996 he never had voted for a Republican for any office. But McCandless was idealistic, a strange quality for a Washington lobbyist that had cost him heavily in the past. When at age twenty-nine he took over the 1968 Humphrey presidential campaign, it ended his marriage. When in 1973 he helped represent Nixon aide John Dean against the president, he was dismissed from his law firm. But his idealism was most personally self-destructive when McCandless was announced as the head of Democrats for Dole. Bob was to learn that the Republicans would show him no gratitude and the Democrats no forgiveness.

I don't believe McCandless accepted any of the Dole agenda. But he admired Dole, his longtime neighbor in the Watergate. To make sure I would not get it wrong, lawyer McCandless gave me an explanation written in longhand on a yellow legal pad. Dole was a man, he said, "whose word is his bond, who knows right from wrong." As much as McCandless liked Dole, he disliked Clinton. McCandless gave me an exclusive to announce his move in advance in newspapers of September 12, and I quoted from his legal brief prepared for me:

> I have always believed and still believe in the party of FDR, JFK and LBJ. I still believe that the people who are left behind need the help of the central government to get their feet on the first rung of the ladder. . . .
>
> I do not believe what President Clinton says. I do not think he has a compass of ideals, morale and directions for this country. I think his North Star is determined by public relations polls. . . .
>
> I am not interested in nor would I accept any kind of White House or administration job. I remain a Democrat, and if we can defeat Clinton, I want to help rebuild the Democratic Party to be protectors and the encouragers of the underclass.

Dole complimented McCandless. "Nice column," he said. "But when is he going to write a nice one about me?" Not anytime soon.

CLINTON'S FINAL WINNING margin was in single digits (8.4 percentage points). Clinton recorded an Electoral College landslide, 379 to 159—seventeen fewer votes for Clinton than the *Evans-Novak Political Report* forecast.

Democratic leaders who had regarded the Republican sweep of 1994 as an aberration, akin to 1946, were bitterly disappointed. Democrats gained only ten seats in the House, leaving a thirty-seat Republican majority. (The *ENPR* predicted a Democratic gain of thirteen seats.) In the Senate, Democrats *lost* two seats, raising the Republican edge to ten seats (the *ENPR* prediction was right on the nose). For the first time since 1928, Republicans had carried Congress in two consecutive elections. Realignment was a reality.

CHAPTER 40

Conversion

IN EARLY JANUARY 1997, my CNN executive producer Rick Davis asked me into his spacious office. His face was even more mournful than customary, and he appeared uncomfortable. I liked Davis, and I was fond of his lovely wife and two cute little daughters. I think he liked me. Yet, we could not become true friends because of the role he played. Like many business executives, he brought to the table no particular talents. Rick prospered because he was tall, nice looking, and well groomed with a winning personality, and worked very hard. My problem with Rick was that, like other people climbing the CNN corporate ladder, he was most interested in pleasing the corporate suits in Atlanta. As friendly as Rick was to me, when it came to the choice between "the company" and me (or any of his colleagues), "the company" always came first.

That was what was involved when Rick called me into his office. He informed me that Pat Buchanan, having concluded his second presidential campaign in 1996, was coming back to *Crossfire*—the third such return after a political sojourn. Buchanan would split conservative host time with John Sununu, with Novak the odd man out.

"Rick," I asked, "can you really say that John did as good a job as I did?" Of course, he could not. Instead, he said something so blatant that I wrote it down immediately: "It would look bad politically if CNN dropped Sununu." I had no idea CNN was in politics. Buchanan told me he urged Davis to drop Sununu and keep me, but it was no use.

I had two CNN contracts then, both expiring in the spring of 1997. One paid me $62,400 a year for *Capital Gang,* and the other $95,000 for *Evans and Novak* and other programs for a combined $157,400. However, my 1099 form for 1996 showed $360,000 from CNN! The difference came from my splitting *Crossfire* right-wing host duties with Sununu while Buchanan was running his 1996 presidential campaign.

With Buchanan returning Davis came back with a new compensation package that added up to $207,500 a year—more money than I had ever anticipated from TV, but still a pay cut of $152,500 from 1996. It would not put me in the poorhouse. I was then making a combined $250,000 from other journalistic sources, but a pay cut of this magnitude was a vote of no confidence from CNN. I told Davis I might have to look elsewhere.

Davis passed my warning on to Atlanta. Ed Turner, my longtime benefactor and Davis's boss, scheduled an eight thirty a.m. breakfast on February 10, 1997, at the ritzy Four Seasons Hotel, where he always stayed in Washington. After hearing my varied complaints about CNN, on the spot, he proposed increasing my package from $205,700 to $225,000. That $20,000 bump meant my pay cut would be $130,000. I decided to test the market with a couple of telephone calls.

One was to Tim Russert, NBC's Washington bureau chief and *Meet the Press* moderator. Tim sounded excited when I told him I was thinking of leaving CNN and asked him whether there might be anything at NBC or its cable network, CNBC. He got back to me quickly to report no interest by NBC News president Andrew Lack.

My other call was to Eric Breindel, who had just moved up in Rupert Murdoch's publishing empire from editorial page editor of the *New York Post* to executive vice president of News Corporation in charge of strategic planning. Breindel was an original neoconservative, who in 1977 joined the Senate office of his former Harvard professor, Daniel Patrick Moynihan. I first met him when he joined the *New York Post* in 1986. We became good friends, and my column never had a stronger supporter in the newspaper business. (Tragically, he died from liver failure in 1998 at age forty-two.) When I called Breindel in early March 1997 to ask whether there might be a place for me at Rupert Murdoch's new Fox cable network competing with CNN, he answered enthusiastically in the affirmative.

At four fifteen p.m. on March 4, 1997, I entered the Manhattan office of Roger Ailes, CEO of the new Fox News Channel and a former Republican political operative. I first met Roger in the mid-seventies and we had an amiable relationship. In 1993, Ailes became head of CNBC and made the struggling cable network watchable and profitable. In 1996, Murdoch tapped Ailes to do the same thing with his new network challenging CNN.

"Are you sure you really are willing to leave the mighty CNN for our little network?" Ailes asked soon after I sat down. He was not being sarcastic. CNN in 1997 was far ahead of Fox in prestige and profits. Because of CNN's huge lead in ratings and Fox's trouble getting on major cable systems, I would be seen by far fewer people if I changed networks.

Ailes then raised an issue I had not expected. He said he would like me to reproduce *Capital Gang* at Fox and asked whether I could bring Al Hunt and Mark Shields with me. Al and Mark were not that happy with CNN. After being pledged to secrecy when I called them separately, each indicated a willingness to go where I went.

Finally, Ailes got down to money, asking how much I wanted. I said I could not leave CNN for less than $300,000 (not mentioning that I received $360,000 the past year or that the highest CNN offer on the table was $225,000). "That's a little rich for our blood," he said. Ailes said he would confer with "my people" and be back with an offer in two weeks. He said there would be no counteroffer if CNN bettered it because he did not want a bidding war. I said I did not either, and I did not envision CNN as a possible bidder considering what had transpired so far.

On April 10, Ailes submitted his offer to my lawyer, Les Hyman. My $300,000 was no longer "too rich" for Fox's blood, because it offered me $380,000, going up to $405,000 the second year and $430,000 the third. It also contained "fringes" that I had not requested: health and life insurance, and four weeks' vacation. For all that, I would be executive producer of a "panel program (similar to *Capital Gang*)" including Hunt and Shields, I would appear on a weekend half-hour interview show that looked like *Evans and Novak* without Evans and with Fox's Brit Hume occasionally joining me, "frequent" on-air reporting, commentary, and analyses, and twelve appearances a year on Fox's Sunday talk show (hosted by Tony Snow).

Hyman informed me of something in my CNN contract that I had signed but not read in its entirety. I was required to submit to CNN any competitive offer, which CNN then had twenty-one days to match or surpass. Since Fox was abjuring a bidding war, CNN could keep me by matching its offer. I was sure it would not.

On the very last day of the twenty-one-day clock, CNN came through with an offer that took my breath away. Its first-year offer of $292,000 was still $88,000 short of Fox's, but its second year of $418,000, third year of $442,000 and fourth year at $462,000 significantly surpassed Fox. It was at least a matching offer, and the bidding was over thanks to previously stipulated ground rules. I was staying at CNN.

The reason for CNN's big jump from the first to the second year was that it had to pencil in a big pay cut when they moved me off *Crossfire*. In adhering to its pay-for-work policy, CNN decided they had to bring me back to *Crossfire* and drop John Sununu. CNN could have put me on *Crossfire* immediately by buying out Sununu's contract, but instead it waited until the contract expired. That means I did not resume my duties as a

Crossfire regular, one hundred times a year, until May 11, 1998. Under the CNN system, I fell a little short in the first year with the difference made up the next year.

I do not retell the details of these negotiations to demean Rick Davis, who is a decent man. It was the cultural climate of CNN that led executives to find ways to protect themselves from mistakes rather than seek creative initiatives. I believe that mind-set caused Rick to lowball me in order to win plaudits from Atlanta when he could have had me signing for half the money CNN finally paid, without my ever approaching Fox. I also think this climate contributed to CNN's long, slow decline relative to Fox.

The one loose end that had to be tied up was sweetening the pot for Hunt and Shields now that they, too, were staying at CNN. Keeping to CNN's policy of matching pay with work, it was decided that Al and Mark would be added to *Evans and Novak* which was given the unwieldy new name of *Evans, Novak, Hunt and Shields*. I believe CNN felt that Rowly at age seventy-six had lost a step, and was phasing him out. He would be on the program only once a month. I would be on every program, with Hunt and Shields alternating on the other programs. Rowly did not like this arrangement, and neither did I.

My subsequent eight years at CNN were productive, and I am grateful to CNN for its confidence in me. In all candor, however, I feel I would have been treated with more respect at Fox and would have been better off there. But because of the fine print in my contract, I had no choice.

ON THE MORNING of Wednesday, July 16, 1997, a phone call alerted me to a story in that day's edition of *The Hill*, one of two competing newspapers covering Congress.

Written by a young reporter named Sandy Hume, it was perhaps the greatest exposé of behind-the-scenes Capitol Hill machinations that I had seen in half a century of Congress-watching.

Hume reported that long-simmering discontent within the big, unruly Class of 1994 had reached critical mass when Speaker Gingrich continued his leftward lurch by abandoning efforts to defund the National Endowment for the Arts. The ringleader in a plot to oust Gingrich as Speaker was a second-term member who until then had not received much attention: Lindsey Graham, a forty-two-year-old trial lawyer from Seneca, South Carolina.

Majority Whip Tom DeLay, third-ranking in the leadership, contacted Graham. DeLay then brought three other members of the leadership into the cabal: Majority Leader Dick Armey, Conference Chairman John

Boehner, and Bill Paxon, who held an appointive leadership position created by Gingrich. They met July 8 and 9 and hammered out details of a coup under which Armey would become speaker, Paxon would replace Armey as majority leader, and Gingrich would be toast.

DeLay reported back to the rebels. But Tom Coburn, a forty-nine-year-old practicing obstetrician from Muskogee, Oklahoma, one of the really hard edges in the Class of 1994, told him the rebels did not want Armey as speaker. Their choice was Paxon, in his ninth year representing his upstate New York district, though he was only forty-three years old. Stunned by this development, DeLay left the room to report back to his fellow leaders, and Coburn commented ruefully: "I think I made a big mistake." On July 10, knowing now he would not become Speaker, Armey told his colleagues in the leadership that it would be "immoral" to proceed against the Speaker and then notified Gingrich's office of the plot. That ended the coup, and its planners could only hope it was kept secret.

It was secret until Sandy Hume's July 16 story. What *The Hill* reported was news to most House Republicans. I wrote in my column of July 20:

> At Wednesday's [July 16] closed-door meeting of the House Republican Conference, Armey denied complicity. An outraged Lindsey Graham crashed through rows of chairs toward a floor microphone but was restrained by colleagues. Graham . . . told friends he was considering resigning from Congress then and there. . . .
>
> Once the coup plot was publicized, Gingrich's advisers told him that a head must be severed. It had to be Paxon's, the only member of the leadership appointed by the Speaker rather than elected by the Conference. At a leadership meeting, Paxon volunteered to quit. "I'll take it," said Armey.

Paxon, the rising Republican star on Capitol Hill, was finished in congressional politics. More significantly, the failed coup spelled the end of visionary aspirations that the Republican landslide of 1994 would bring true reform to Capitol Hill.

I wrote that Republican spin-doctors were claiming that Gingrich's colleagues in the leadership had not been plotting a coup but "were just trying to warn him." I added: "But after extensive checking of sources, I am convinced that Hume's reporting was 100 percent correct."

Sandy's father, Brit Hume, the Washington managing editor of Fox News, told me that his son viewed my column with so much pride that he posted it on his wall. After my column ran Sandy made an appointment to see me in my office. A delightful young man, he expressed the opinion that if I had not substantiated his reporting, the perfidy of the House Republican leadership never would have been known. I replied that someone else would have supported Sandy's reportage if I did not, but I added the failed coup never would have come to light if it had not been for him and *The Hill.* Sandy told me he always had admired my reporting, but I told the twenty-five-year-old reporter it was I who admired him for getting a story that none of the old pros, including me, even suspected.

A year later, Sandy Hume committed suicide. The circumstances of this tragedy were none of my business, but I was devastated. While I was not in the practice of mentoring young journalists (not many sought me out), I knew Sandy was something special. At age twenty-six, he had been on his way professionally, nominated for a Pulitzer Prize, wooed by *U.S. News,* and going to work for Fox News. I did not like wakes and usually went only when a very close friend or relative died. Yet I was drawn to Gawler's Funeral Home for Sandy's. When I spoke to Brit at the viewing, I could not keep my voice from breaking, and my eyes were filled with tears.

MY OBSESSION WITH University of Maryland basketball by 1998 had developed to a point where I tried to attend every game, home and away. My routine for road games was to take a commercial flight from Washington the afternoon of the game, and Coach Gary Williams would let me fly back on the team's chartered flight so that I could put in a full day's work the next day.

On January 21, 1998, I took a three p.m. flight from Washington to Atlanta, arriving in plenty of time for that night's nine o'clock game between Georgia Tech and Maryland. But when I landed in Atlanta and called my office in Washington, I learned that the world had turned upside down with reports of a sexual affair between Bill Clinton and former intern Monica Lewinsky. I was told CNN wanted me to come to its main studios in Atlanta immediately to comment on something about which I knew nothing. I admitted on the air I never had heard of Monica Lewinsky and then suggested that we all should avoid indicting or impeaching the president of the United States on unsubstantiated rumors.

On *Capital Gang* Saturday night, I was less censorious about the president than his staunch supporter Al Hunt, who suggested it was a matter of time before Clinton left office. "I think that is premature," I contended, adding: "I don't think you can impeach a president on the basis that he lied about having sex, [and] I don't believe that this president is about to resign." Nearly a month later on February 15, I was still cautious when I appeared on *Meet the Press.* I said: "[H]e cannot be impeached, in my opinion, and won't be impeached by a Republican majority. It has to be bipartisan. The Democrats are solidly with him right now, and so I think it's going to be very unlikely that that happens."

Beginning in 1991 with the rumors about Clinton's sexual infidelity spread by enemies in Arkansas, I had been on record against traveling this road. But did I pull any punches on the Lewinsky affair because I was president of the Gridiron Club that year and did not want to frighten Clinton away from sitting next to me at the club's annual dinner? I hope not.

I SPENT FOUR hours seated next to Bill Clinton on Saturday night, March 21, 1998, after not having exchanged more than a word or two with him since the 1992 preconvention campaign. The president of the Gridiron Club of Washington by tradition had the head table seat next to the president of the United States at the organization's spring dinner.

There was an archaic quality about the Gridiron that was part of its addictive charm for members. Prestige journalists such as Al Hunt might say the club provided a moment in the sun for the bureau chiefs of provincial newspapers, but even Hunt grew fascinated with the oddity of the club when he became its president—as did I. The club's spring dinner was one of only two Washington functions (the other being a charity ball) to require white tie and tails.

I was admitted to the club in 1979, and it took me two decades to become president in 1998. The Gridiron operated under laws of term limits (one year only for president) and seniority. Active or inactive, members inexorably climbed the seniority ladder. There were no contested elections. Some presidents devoted full-time to the club, but I could not and still fulfill my journalistic responsibilities. So I delegated like mad to the talented producers of the annual show.

However, I used my dictatorial powers to make sure the Gridiron lived up to its philosophy of singeing but never burning just in case Clinton came to the dinner. The smart money was that in the middle of the Lewinsky scandal, Clinton would not show up to be satirized by smart-aleck journalists, sitting at Novak's side no less.

We did not get a clear response from the White House, and I killed anything in the show that would humiliate Clinton, including a wickedly clever parody of "Thank Heaven for Little Girls." This was one of those magic Gridiron songs where the entire audience was sure to burst into applause and laughter as they heard the first words. I would have loved it if I were not facing the prospect of being seated next to Clinton. Alan Cromley, retired bureau chief of *The Daily Oklahoman* of Oklahoma City and one of the Gridiron's all-time great songwriters, pleaded in vain with me to reinstate "Little Girls." It was a decision I did not regret when we received word that the president would attend the dinner.

IF AGREEING TO spend four hours with me was Bill Clinton at his most open-minded, the 1998 Gridiron Dinner exhibited Hillary Rodham Clinton at her worst. I had spent weeks trying to get her to be the Democratic speaker. Her staffers stalled me until finally I insisted on a yes or no, and they said no. I talked the White House chief of staff, Erskine Bowles, into speaking. White House staffers later told me any chance I had of getting Mrs. Clinton as Democratic speaker vanished when they learned whom I had secured as the Republican speaker: Newt Gingrich.

An hour before the dinner, the Gridiron Club office in the Capitol Hilton was asked by the First Lady's press aide when Speaker Gingrich was scheduled to give his speech. While the president appeared only five minutes late for the dinner's seven p.m. start (punctual for him), we received word from the White House that Mrs. Clinton was unavoidably detained but would be along as soon as possible, so we should start without her.

Shortly after Gingrich finished his speech, the White House called saying Mrs. Clinton was on her way to the hotel. In keeping with Gridiron tradition, Geraldine as the wife of the club president was dispatched to meet Hillary and escort her to the head table.

Poor Geraldine! She hated politics, avoiding debate and confrontation. But beneath her calm, Geraldine cared deeply about issues. The born-and-bred Texas Democrat long ago had switched her party registration to Republican. Geraldine detested the Clintons, and now she had to be Hillary's hostess. Geraldine did not care for the Gridiron, and I am sure she got through this ordeal only because she knew it was her first and last Gridiron spring dinner.

This was the presenatorial Hillary who did what she wanted and did not conceal her hardness. There never had been anything like the First Lady's politically purposeful tardiness in the 113-year history of the Gridiron Club. Her husband, however, delivered the best speech of the night.

"So how was *your* week?" asked Clinton, guaranteeing an opening wave of laughter following seven more days in which he was hounded by the Monica Lewinsky scandal. "Please withhold the subpoenas until all the jokes have been told. I offer my remarks with this caveat: They were a whole lot funnier before the lawyers got ahold of them."

People asked me what Bill Clinton and I had to talk about for four hours. Well, it wasn't really four hours. Clinton spent one hour with me and three with the man on his right: Conrad Black, the Canadian CEO of Hollinger International, Inc., the owner of the *Chicago Sun-Times*. Traditionally at the Gridiron, the seat to the right of the president of the United States goes to the publisher of the Gridiron Club president's newspaper. But the publisher of the *Sun-Times,* another Canadian named David Radler, was Black's *junior* partner in the Hollinger publishing empire, and so the place of honor next to Clinton went to Black. (Within six years, Black and Radler would have lost all their newspapers and faced prison sentences for fraud.)

Conrad Black was somewhere to my Right ideologically and had been far more enthusiastic than I in seeing Clinton's personal peccadilloes investigated and reported by the *American Spectator.* Black was a good friend of *Spectator* editor (and Clinton nemesis) Bob Tyrrell and a financial supporter of the right-wing magazine, which in 1993 bestowed its highest annual award on Black. So I could not figure why Clinton seemed much more at ease talking to Black than to me.

Only later did I learn that Clinton and Black had a common hero: Franklin D. Roosevelt (who was no hero of mine). Five years hence, Black published a massive (1,360-page) biography called *Franklin Delano Roosevelt: Champion of Freedom.* That night, these two strong, complicated men enjoyed themselves talking about another, strong complicated man. Beyond that, I think Clinton and Black liked each other because they both were intelligent, reckless, charismatic risk-takers. I simply was not in their class.

I did get a rare hour with Clinton, albeit chopped up in pieces. I had made clear in my column and on TV that I found almost nothing to applaud in Clinton's five years as president. So Clinton and I talked about a common interest—college basketball. He dispatched a Secret Service agent to give us periodic reports of that night's University of Arkansas Razorbacks game. He chuckled at skits making fun of him, not knowing that they had been toned down on my orders.

In one skit, Gridiron Club member Deborah Howell played a prostitute. Howell, the Washington bureau chief of the Newhouse newspapers, was a mature woman who normally would not attract Bill Clinton's attention. The head table was on the other side of the large ballroom from the stage, and so we could not see the performers in great detail. But Clinton could see Deborah's nice set of legs shown off in her hooker's costume. He pointed toward her and asked me almost reflexively: "Now, *who* is *that* woman?" In the midst of the Monica turmoil, Clinton was instinctively attracted by a woman with beautiful legs.

I did raise one serious matter with the president, and I wrote about it in my column:

I was not about to pose embarrassing questions, and the President did not lecture me on the error of my right-wing extremism. But late in the evening . . . I told him that young people whom I often address are surprised and angry when they discover the havoc wrought by FICA [tax deductions] on their first paychecks.

Had he read Sen. Daniel Patrick Moynihan's Harvard speech of March 16? The Senator proposed to cut the payroll tax by one-sixth from 12.4 percent to 10.4 percent (returning $800 billion to Americans over the next decade) as part of a plan to save Social Security.

The President did not even seem familiar with Moynihan's latest plan but remembered that in 1989, the Senator had proposed payroll tax cuts. . . . [T]he President told me he is repelled by the regressive nature of the tax, which is hardest on lower-wage workers and takes more money from 80 percent of American taxpayers than the progressive income tax. . . .

Bill Clinton could make all the difference. But Democratic skeptics caution not to make too much of what the President, charming and congenial, says in the midst of a festive evening.

The skeptics were correct. Clinton never said another word about payroll taxes.

FOR MOST PRESIDENTS of the Gridiron Club, the spring dinner affords rare exposure in the Washington spotlight for hardworking journalists who labor in lifelong anonymity. Even for somebody with the TV omnipresence that I had achieved by 1996, it was a special weekend. It began Friday night with a sit-down dinner in my honor at the Army and Navy Club for 126 guests, mostly Gridiron members and their spouses, co-hosted by Conrad Black and Tom Johnson. Starting Friday night and extending through Sunday night, Geraldine and I stayed in the Capitol Hilton's presidential suite.

The long Gridiron dinner, concluding around eleven fifteen p.m. Saturday, was not the end of the evening. Postdinner receptions continued well into Sunday morning, though as I grew older I went home shortly after midnight. But as club president staying overnight in the hotel, I planned to be around until the last dog was buried. I was sixty-seven years old, and had cut back my drinking ever since spinal meningitis fourteen years earlier. But I drank a little more on Gridiron nights, and I certainly would have more than my usual one drink the night I was president. At Friday night's dinner, I enjoyed two predinner vodkas, quite a bit of wine with dinner, and a glass of port afterward. On Saturday night, I had two vodkas before the dinner, followed by a generous intake of wine at dinner, and then the closing champagne.

I was in high spirits following the dinner and, as usual, I started off the rest of the evening by going to the Hearst reception, where I guzzled another vodka. I was receiving congratulations on an excellent Gridiron night, when suddenly I was assaulted by nausea and dizziness.

I staggered to the hotel men's room and barely made it to a toilet stall before I vomited all over my white ruffled shirt. I then fainted, falling heavily against the toilet. The next thing I knew, my son-in-law, the journalist Christopher Caldwell, was bending over me. I was conscious now, though still dizzy and suffering from what I thought was a sore leg resulting from my fall. Fire department paramedics were called to the scene, but I adamantly refused to be taken to a hospital. Instead, I insisted on going to my hotel suite. Incredibly, amid the Gridiron hubbub, my misfortune attracted no attention.

I awoke Sunday morning to discover my "sore leg" in fact was a damaged ankle (I thought it must be sprained) that hurt so much I did not think I could walk. Geraldine got me a cane, and I showed up with it, limping badly, at the Sunday brunch for Gridiron members at the Mayflower Hotel sponsored by General Motors. Reporters are normally the most inquisitive of people, but hardly anybody noticed. Nor did I get much reaction at the Capitol Hilton Sunday night when I presided onstage over the rerun of the skits and repeated my "speech in the dark," cane in hand. Not a word appeared in gossip columns or in the *Washington Post* account of Gridiron weekend, which usually chronicled mishaps and embarrassments.

When belatedly I got medical attention on Monday, I learned that my ankle was broken. Dr. Chuck Abrams, who twice had saved me from cancer, put me through a battery of tests and found no evidence of heart trouble or any other serious malady. He suggested that I now had a low tolerance for alcohol and had too much to drink on Gridiron weekend. I should have taken his advice more seriously than I did.

Eight months later in November 1998, I was in New Orleans for a post-midterm election Republican gathering and was attending a party at the home of Julia Reed, the *Vogue* and *Newsweek* writer and daughter of my old friend, Mississippi Republican leader Clarke Reed. I was seated with the anti-tax activist Grover Norquist, who was orating to me when again I got that dizzy and nauseated feeling, simultaneously vomiting and fainting. Once again, I refused to go to a hospital and showed up for a lunch date with Julia the next day.

In June 2003, I collapsed at the outdoor reception in Greenville, Mississippi, celebrating Julia Reed's wedding. I was taken to the hospital but refused to stay overnight. The word had circulated among wedding guests that I was near death, and I created a stir when I showed up at the Sunday brunch concluding the gala wedding weekend.

I went to Dr. Abrams for a thorough examination, and he found nothing wrong with me as a seventy-two-year-old man except for high blood pressure and high cholesterol that were kept under control by medication. Abrams's prescription: I must further reduce my drinking, no more than one a night and perhaps limited to three a week. Being old is hell.

AT ST. PATRICK'S Church in downtown Washington a few blocks from our apartment on May 20, 1998, a Roman Catholic mass starting at six thirty p.m. marked a milestone in my life. In the ritual lasting until after eight o'clock, I was baptized as a Christian and confirmed as a Catholic at age sixty-seven.

A sizable congregation assembled at St. Patrick's, the oldest church in the Federal City. It was diverse, including many non-Catholics such as Rowly and his wife Kay (practicing Episcopalians), CNN colleagues, and fellow University of Maryland sports fanatics. A few politicians were headed by two Catholic friends, Democratic Senator Daniel Patrick Moynihan and Republican Congressman Henry Hyde. Senator Rick Santorum of Pennsylvania, a conservative Republican, called me and asked to come to the mass. I did not know him well, but he was a daily Catholic communicant and I welcomed him. After the mass, we all adjourned to my apartment for a festive reception and buffet dinner.

Most people who heard about my conversion were curious, but a few were nasty—especially fallen-away Catholics who somehow resented me entering a church they had left. That probably included Kitty Kelley, the notorious pop biographer who encountered me at a large reception. Describing herself as having been "raised Catholic" (a euphemism used by hostile lapsed Catholics), Kelley demanded of me: "What in the world made you become Catholic?" For the first time, I replied: "The Holy Spirit."

I heard nothing from my many Jewish relatives, most of whom had come to Washington in 1994 for Zelda's wedding. But I ran into Cherie, a favorite cousin, at a political reception in Los Angeles that autumn. Although she lived in California, we had remained in frequent contact and I had flown out to San Francisco the year before for her daughter's wedding. No sooner had we embraced at the Los Angeles reception than she repeated pretty much what Kitty Kelley said: "Bobby, what possessed you to become a Catholic?" I gave the "Holy Spirit" answer, and Cherie shot back: "What do you think your mother would think of this?" "I guess she's rejoicing in Heaven," I said. I refrained from adding, as I contemplated saying, "with Jesus at her side." Even without that flourish, my answer did not sit well with Cherie. Since then I have seen her only once, at a family wedding (Jewish) in Illinois.

IN THE YEARS since my 1998 conversion, I have gradually doled out some of my story, but what follows is the fullest account.

Although I abandoned my adolescent pretensions at agnosticism when I prayed as a young army officer that I would handle myself bravely if I went to war in Korea, I still flinched at religious ritual. My first marriage in Indianapolis in September 1957 had been planned at a Unitarian church. My father-in-law to be, a devout Presbyterian, at the eleventh hour insisted that his pastor deliver a blessing at the ceremony. I refused to allow it. A tough lawyer and hard-shelled Republican, he said that killed his bankrolling of a big church wedding and lavish reception. So be it, I replied, ignoring my fiancée's pleas for compromise. I felt the Unitarian ceremony represented enough compromise by me, and I maintained the deal to which I had agreed had been broken.

The invited wedding guests were uninvited. We were married in the Unitarian church sacristy, with only our immediate families present. With my new father-in-law and me barely speaking, the marriage was off to a rocky start. From the distance of half a century, it is hard for me to understand why at age twenty-six I was so adamant against the introduction of Christianity in our wedding. Including it might have helped our marriage.

In the marriage's early months, we occasionally attended Unitarian services in Washington. We soon decided to sleep in Sunday mornings rather than endure an experience we both found uninspiring. I now believe the reason was the absence of God.

In trying to cope with my depression when my wife left me in 1958, after several weeks I unilaterally ended my visits to a psychiatrist and walked unannounced into the study of Reverend Russell C. Stroup, pastor of the Georgetown Presbyterian Church near my apartment. He bucked me up a little and suggested I might want to attend Sunday services. I did for a while, and it helped, even though the Christian ritual made me feel out of place. Four years later, I returned to Georgetown Presbyterian and asked Reverend Stroup to perform the wedding ceremony for Geraldine and me. It was short, beautiful, and essentially non-Christian.

Geraldine had grown up in a devoutly Methodist family in rural Texas, but she was nearly as uninspired by her church's ritual as I was by Jewish services and had no desire to return to her religious roots. In the early days of our marriage in 1963, we occasionally attended an Episcopal church on Capitol Hill. But soon after Zelda was christened there in 1965, we ceased attendance. I often have said I was repelled by the pastor's political (liberal) sermons, but in retrospect I believe I really was uncomfortable with the Christian liturgy. Except for weddings and funerals, I did not attend a religious service for another thirty years. I left everything in child raising to Geraldine, and that included religion. She sometimes took Zelda and Alexander to Protestant Sunday school in the Maryland suburbs. But they were uncomfortable as outsiders who did not know the other children, and Geraldine discontinued the practice.

I think Geraldine and I both were experiencing spiritual hunger, but only she recognized it. We never talked politics with each other, and I was one of the last to know that she had become an antiabortion activist by the 1990s. She started going out Sunday mornings in quest of a church in suburban Maryland that accommodated her prolife beliefs and provided spiritual sustenance—without success.

When we moved into downtown Washington in 1992, Geraldine walked the few blocks to St. Patrick's to attend Catholic mass. She told me she really liked it, and asked whether I would like to go with her. I did and, in contrast to my previous Christian church experiences, I was moved by the ritual.

One reason I was more comfortable there was the presence of Father Peter Vaghi. As an active Republican lawyer and adviser to Senator Pete Domenici before he became a priest, Vaghi had been a source for the Evans & Novak column. He was much closer to Rowly, to whom he broke the news over lunch at the Metropolitan Club that he was entering a Catholic seminary in a late vocation. "Peter," an alarmed Episcopalian Evans warned his friend and source, "that will ruin your career!" Vaghi greeted me warmly when he first spotted me at St. Patrick's attending mass with Geraldine.

Another reason for my comfort level with Catholic liturgy was Father C. John McCloskey. A decade after Jeff Bell handed me the Catholic reading matter following my recovery from spinal meningitis in 1982, he introduced me to Father C. John. We began a series of breakfasts, lunches, and dinners spread over two decades. Father C. John, a politically and theologically conservative Opus Dei priest, was a world-class proselytizer. He brought the abortion doctor Bernard Nathanson, New York gubernatorial candidate Lewis Lehrman, and the Wall Street economist Lawrence Kudlow into the church, and now he was working on me.

I was a tough nut to crack, but McCloskey never faltered. He was a fascinating table companion, and sometimes whole meals would go by without a mention of theology. At one Army and Navy Club lunch, I mentioned the homily delivered the previous Sunday by Peter Vaghi (now a monsignor and St. Patrick's pastor) deploring young Catholics who thought the Communion wafer only symbolized the body of Christ when in fact it *is* the body of Christ. "How can anybody believe that?" I asked Father John. "It comes from the mystery of Holy Communion," he told me. I realized then how much I must believe that if I ever was to become a Catholic.

Monsignor Vaghi and Father McCloskey surely helped, but now as a Catholic I feel that they were part of a divine plan which led me to embrace this church. Could Geraldine's quest for a church, Peter Vaghi's presence, and C. John McCloskey proselytizing all be coincidental? Or did they reflect the hand of the Holy Spirit? My realization that the latter was the case was brought home by a spiritual event at highly secular Syracuse University.

On October 22, 1996, I came to Syracuse to deliver the annual Flowers Lecture, partially financed by the conservative Young America Foundation and sponsored by the College Republicans. Standard procedure for college lectures is a prespeech dinner for the speaker, hosted by the sponsoring student committee. There was one woman on the College Republicans committee, seated across the table from me. She was striking looking, wearing a gold cross on her neck.

What happened next may be distorted in my memory and shaped by the religious mysteries that I see entwined in this episode. Without mentioning the cross, I was impelled to ask the woman a question that normally I would not consider posing. Was she a Catholic? I thought she answered yes and then asked me whether I was one. "No," I replied, "but my wife and I have been going to mass every Sunday for about four years." "Do you plan to join the church?" she asked. I answered: "No, not at the present time."

Then the young woman looked at me and said evenly: "Mr. Novak, life is short, but eternity is forever." I was so shaken by what she said that I could barely get through the rest of the dinner and my speech that night. Sometime during the short night before rising to catch a seven a.m. flight back to Washington, I became convinced that the Holy Spirit was speaking through this Syracuse student.

I did not seek the name of the woman. But in writing this book in 2005, I asked my staff to try to find it. The only woman we could identify at the dinner was named Barbara Plonisch. When we located her, she said she could not recall any such exchange with me. An e-mail response from Barbara P. Edmunds (her married name) began: "Well, I am Russian Orthodox Christian, not Catholic. I do wear a small gold cross. I don't think I'm the one you're looking for. Although I can't help but think that I may have made such a comment."

That ambiguous response from Mrs. Edmunds would have left me in a quandary had she not also sent along by e-mail a recent photo of her with her husband and infant son. It was she! I could not forget that distinctive face, even though she now was nine years older. That she had forgotten what she said to me only confirmed my belief that the Holy Spirit was speaking through her.

Back in Washington, I suggested to Geraldine that the time had come for both of us to enter the church. I believe Geraldine had been ready for some time and was waiting for me. Geraldine joined RCIA (Rite of Christian Initiation for Adults) at St. Patrick's, a process under which a small group of initiates takes instruction in the faith and then is confirmed on Easter Sunday.

The semipublic nature of RCIA was not for me, and Monsignor Vaghi agreed to give me private instruction. I would read assigned sections of the Catholic Catechism, and meet Vaghi early in the evening each week at St. Patrick's. He told me our dialogue went deeper into the mysteries of the faith than most cradle Catholics experience.

The special May 20, 1998, mass for my baptism and confirmation at St. Patrick's was celebrated by Monsignor Vaghi with Father McCloskey as a co-celebrant. The godparents that I selected both were younger than I: Jeff Bell (himself a convert) and Kate O'Beirne. I chose as my patron saint the martyred Thomas More, who beneath his robes as chancellor of England wore the hairshirt of a Christian ascetic.

At our apartment after the mass, Pat Moynihan said to Al Hunt: "Well, Novak is now a Catholic. The question is: When will he become a Christian?" Behind the laughter was the serious inquiry of whether my conversion would change me. Liberals wanted me now to favor redistribution of income and oppose capital punishment, but those changes were not to happen. I do know my new faith has given me a source of strength in coping with an old age that was to be anything but serene.

REPUBLICANS NEVER RECOVERED from the government shutdown of 1995, which Clinton successfully blamed on Gingrich. Now in October 1998, I wrote that House Speaker Gingrich would give Clinton anything to avoid another presidential veto shutting down the government. Gingrich passed the Clinton budget with only 30 percent of Republicans voting for it, and far more Democrats than Republicans in support. That was a dangerous posture that former history professor Gingrich years before told me always meant disaster for a party leader.

On the morning of October 15, 1998, when my anti-Gingrich column ("GOP Surrender") was published, I was in Los Angeles at the Century Plaza Hotel. At five thirty a.m. California time, my office patched through a call from the Speaker of the House.

Gingrich shouted his displeasure with that morning's column: "Everything in it is wrong!" He demanded a column by me correcting my alleged errors, but he did not inform me that he already had sent client newspapers a letter critiquing the column. Gingrich's outburst yielded not a corrective column but another critical one, which ran a week later on October 22 and included this:

> Gingrich initiated his first telephone call to me since the last week of December 1996, when he was on the brink of losing the Speakership and convincingly pleaded his ethics case. Last Thursday, Gingrich told me that I had accomplished the impossible by getting everything wrong except critical quotes from the Speaker's old friend, Jack Kemp, which he said would have meant more "if he was elected Vice President." Claiming I ignored Republican "victories," Gingrich in his letter to newspapers accused me of "an exercise in disinformation, rumor and outright falsehoods" of which "the White House would be proud."

"In reality, I made no errors," I wrote, then disposed of Gingrich's complaints, one by one. The October 22 column included a zinger that was harsher than anything in my previous column. It accused Gingrich of "a mindless tactical incompetence that invites defeat." My long-standing relationship with Newt had gone up and down over his four years as Speaker, but I think it came to an end with our exchange in October. I regretted it, but I was sure Newt would not be on the national stage much longer.

THE *EVANS-NOVAK POLITICAL Report* predicted Republican gains in the 1998 midterm elections of eight seats in the House and four in the Senate. In fact, the ten-seat Republican margin in the Senate was unchanged. In the House, the Republicans *lost* five seats, a thirteen-seat variance from my prediction. Journalistically, that was not acceptable.

Gingrich had promised Republican gains in the House, a losing result for Clinton that would have been normal for a president in his second midterm election. I could try to correct myself for 2000, but it was too late for Gingrich. He resigned from Congress three days after the election, recognizing he could not be reelected Speaker because he had alienated the conservative base in the House. I wrote in my column this appreciation of Gingrich's four years as speaker.

> The former college history professor envisioned something never before attempted in American history: reshaping the Republican Party, and indeed the nation itself, from the House of Representatives. In reaching for that unachievable goal, Gingrich failed as a legislator or even as a party leader unifying a slender House majority.

> Lost in the Republican confusion was the fact that Republicans had controlled Congress for the third straight election despite an indifferent record on Capitol Hill. Call it realignment.

CHAPTER 41

The Rise of George W. Bush

O N Sunday afternoon, January 10, 1999, Geraldine and I were leaving Cole Field House on the University of Maryland campus after the Terrapins defeated North Carolina State University in basketball. I was not paying much attention when I slipped on ice from a recent storm and fell heavily. The pain was terrific. I tried to stand up, but I could not and knew something was broken. I was operated on at Sibley Hospital in Washington early Monday evening and had a pin inserted in my hip.

A broken hip is no fun, particularly for a man a few weeks shy of his sixty-eighth birthday. I progressed from wheelchair to walker to cane, with mandatory physical therapy that I hated. I did not miss a column and was back on my rigorous CNN schedule after less than two weeks.

After recovering from my broken hip, I made the largest charitable commitment of my life. It dated back to April 27, 1996, when I was at the Four Seasons Hotel in Chicago addressing a breakfast meeting of the President's Council of the University of Illinois Foundation, consisting of generous alumni. I told them how my interest in my alma mater had revived and how I had established the Robert D. Novak scholarship in nonfiction writing four years earlier. I continued:

> Shortly after my scholarship was announced, two Illinois students interning in Washington contacted me. They described themselves as conservatives and asked—rather unpleasantly—how in the world could I, as a conservative journalist, contribute to a corrupt left-wing [university] administration. Their manners could have been improved, but I understood where they were coming from, even if I disagreed with their final diagnosis and prescription.

I then quoted Pat Buchanan at the 1992 Republican National Convention describing "a cultural war . . . for the soul of America." I agreed, asserting that I wanted to stop the retreat of traditional values on the college campus:

> I vividly remember my first class at the university, a 9 a.m. Tuesday lecture at Gregory Hall on the History of Civilization—Western civilization, really. It was a golden moment for a 17-year-old boy from Joliet, leading to four years of exploration in the riches of our heritage: Plato, Aristotle, Chaucer, Castiglione, Machiavelli, Shakespeare, Milton, John Donne, Hawthorne, Melville, T.S. Eliot—dead white men all. How barren would be my life without that background?

Next I invoked as "a witness for liberal education from nearly five hundred years ago" my future patron saint: Sir Thomas More. I described him as a "courageous advocate of individual freedom and God-given free will against unlimited governmental power—going to the executioner's block in defense of his ideals and in opposition to tyranny. He crusaded for an international fraternity of Christians to end aggressive war, and founded it on the bedrock of liberal education."

I concluded that while I could not "dictate policy positions to the faculty," I could help position the University of Illinois "as a bastion of traditional academic values in the cultural war." I then offered my proposal:

> Within my limited means, I would hope to influence the future of the University by helping in the years to come to endow a chair. . . . My hope for the University of Illinois is that for as long as can be imagined into the future, young men and women can on a bright early autumn morning attend a lecture on Western civilization as I did as a seventeen-year-old from Joliet and have their eyes opened to the riches of our great tradition of learning and virtue. That, I contend, is winning one very important great cultural war.

For me to propose a Chair of Western Civilization and Culture in those conservative terms was, in retrospect, audacious. I did not know whether I could afford endowing a chair at a great university. I did not even know how much it would cost. I did not know whether the University of Illinois wanted a chair endowed by a right-wing columnist to study the works of dead white men. After all, Princeton had recently spurned such a bequest from a much more prestigious alumnus than I.

Finally, conservative friends to whom I revealed my intentions told me I was taking a terrible risk with a left-wing public university. Surely after I was dead and perhaps even while I was still alive, these skeptics warned, my chair would be filled by an exponent of racial and gender diversity. If I was determined to part with my money this way, they said, I would be better off endowing a chair at right-wing Hillsdale College. My response was that Hillsdale did not need my chair, but Illinois surely did.

The university graciously accepted my offer, informing me it would cost me $1.25 million. The proposal for the chair was drafted by Jesse Delia, dean of the university's College of Liberal Arts and Sciences. He knew exactly what I wanted. Jesse was no conservative, but he understood my conservatism. This is his description:

> It is desired and expected that the holder of the Chair shall contribute directly to academic work in his or her academic discipline and to the broader goals for the College of Liberal Arts and Sciences as it relates to sustaining understanding of the central values and traditions of Western civilization and culture.
>
> These values and traditions concern the great themes of individualism and human dignity, the primacy of freedom, equality, liberty and democratic choice in political life; the rights of individuals to hold and create property as foundational to economic life; the centrality of personal expression and an unfettered press in a free society; the openness of inquiry and the pursuit of knowledge as goods in themselves; the enduring significance of Judeo-Christian concepts and religious practices; and the importance of personal relationships and the family as the foundational elements of social life.

We reached this point with glacial speed, which was about to get slower still. Two and a half years passed after I had made my proposal in Chicago without any progress in pinning down financing.

But I had a plan when I went to New York City on Monday, November 30, 1998, to attend the annual black-tie dinner at the Metropolitan Club hosted by Conrad Black, CEO of Hollinger International, Inc. (owner of my home newspaper, the *Chicago Sun-Times*). I made a predinner appointment with Black in his Manhattan office for five thirty p.m. He was a big, handsome guy with all the charisma his sidekick F. David Radler, publisher of the *Sun-Times*, lacked. I figured that if I made my proposition to Black one-on-one, he might give me a quick yes.

I proposed a *"Chicago Sun-Times*–Robert D. Novak Chair of Western

Civilization and Culture" at the University of Illinois to be financed fifty-fifty—$625,000 by Novak, $625,000 by Hollinger. I tried to sell Black, a conservative and an intellectual, on the idea he would be taking action to preserve the Western tradition. I also pitched him as a businessman who could see the benefit of his Chicago newspaper getting more involved with the state's great public university. In retrospect, I think Black was more into his own ego than focused ideology or even business. It drove him three years later to give up Canadian citizenship and sell his Canadian newspapers to achieve his heart's desire of becoming an English baron: Lord Black of Crossharbour.

Nevertheless, Black's first reaction was positive: "That sounds terrific! Let's do it!" He asked me to put the deal in writing and mail it off to him. But my letter with the details Conrad had requested went unanswered. So did a second letter. So were my phone calls to Black. My fourth call was returned by a Black aide who asked what I wanted. When I told him, he said Mr. Black was in London and he would contact him. More silence followed. I then called the aide, who said that Mr. Black wanted me to know this was a Chicago matter and that Mr. Radler was in charge of everything in Chicago. So if I wanted Hollinger to help in funding the chair, I had better see the thoroughly unlikable Mr. Radler.

Arranging that ate up more than four months. It was May 1999 before I was seated in Radler's large office on the seventh floor of the Sun-Times Building in Chicago. While Conrad Black was Right of center politically, I found nothing conservative about David Radler. I believe he fancied using the *Sun-Times* to make himself a kingmaker in Chicago Democratic politics, which my sources in the party there found laughable. In any conversation, Radler quickly would get on my back about Israel. He was a fervent Zionist and thought it his duty to lecture me on the subject, though my column published in his newspaper seldom dealt with Israel now that Rowly had retired. I got right to the point with my sales pitch for the *Sun-Times* to share the project with me at a cost of $625,000.

"Not a chance," Radler replied. When I asked him why, he explained: "This is a Chicago paper. We don't have much connection with a downstate university." I was infuriated by the ignorance of this Canadian interloper. The University of Illinois was a beloved institution all over the state, including the Chicago metropolitan area. I pointed out that a majority of the university's students came from the newspaper's circulation area. "Well," he countered, "we never contribute to projects like this anyway." That surprised me, I told Radler, because Conrad Black had said yes in New York the previous November. Flashing his only smile of the meeting, Radler declared: "Conrad says yes to everybody. He can't say no. That's what he has me for. I can say no."

While they were giving me the runaround on $625,000 (to be paid over several years), Black and Radler were looting a half billion dollars from the *Sun-Times* and their other newspapers. In September 2005 at age sixty-three, F. David Radler was sentenced to two and one-half years in federal prison for fraud. That was about half the stretch Radler would have had to serve if he had not become a witness for the prosecution against Lord Black of Crossharbour, who at age sixty was indicted by a federal grand jury in November 2005, was convicted, and in 2007 was sentenced to six and a half years. For once, Radler could not just say no.

When I left Radler's office in April 1999, I had decided to fund the chair by myself. I could do it, thanks to an American economy made vibrant by tax cuts and to the stock selections of Richard Gilder. It was a blessing. Think how embarrassed both the University of Illinois and I would have been had my partners in the chair been exposed as thieves. Instead I look to the Novak chair (filled by Professor Jon Solomon, a renowned classicist who was formally invested on April 20, 2006) as a perpetual contribution that will outlive me and anything I have written.

GOVERNOR GEORGE W. BUSH of Texas was the front-runner for the 2000 Republican presidential nomination when he was scheduled to go to Iowa State University in Ames for the quadrennial presidential straw poll on August 14, 1999. I had been trying to get him on *Evans and Novak* ever since his election as governor in 1994, but strategist Karl Rove said it was not time for him to do "national" interviews. Now, however, Rove said Bush would tape the program (which had become *Evans, Novak, Hunt & Shields*) in Iowa that weekend, the first national TV show he had done.

My role was a tiny element in the intricate design laid out in the early nineties by Rove for moving George W. Bush, a failed businessman and a failed politician, into the governor's mansion in 1994 and the White House in 2000. Bush was made available to me anytime I came to Texas during that decade. I took Rove's overtures not as an effort to establish a buddy-buddy relationship between George W. and me (which I am sure neither of us desired), but an attempt to avert a repetition of my hostility toward his father.

I met with Bush after his 1994 election and wrote that he "does not sound much like his father as he voices the Gingrichite rhetoric of the '90s." In 1997, I described him as "what Republicans want for president in 2000: non-Washington, Southern, on good terms with both the Country Club and the Religious Right, not mean-sounding or overly partisan and a robust 51-year-old family man."

In June 1998, I reported how Republican operative Ron Kaufman, a devoted supporter of the elder Bush, sent a fund-raising letter for the governor's reelection campaign urging contributors to "send an important signal about the strength of the Bush network." I wrote in a column:

Alarm bells went off nationwide. . . . [D]oes the bright, likable and conservative younger Bush carry the unwanted baggage of politicians and advisers associated with his father's dreadful campaign of 1992?

According to sources, Kaufman was scolded by someone close to the Governor for suggesting a family cabal.

Insiders could guess that the "source" and the "scolder" were the same person: Karl Rove. Indeed, Rove let me know that the boarding party had been repelled and that Kaufman and the rest of the Bush Senior entourage would not be on the son's ship.

Unsubstantiated rumors of past cocaine use by Bush dominated political news in early August 1999. I was at our summer place at Fenwick Island. In phone conversations, Rove stressed two points. First, Bush never would answer *any* question about cocaine, no matter how many ways the issue was broached. Second, sooner or later, reporters would get sick of these nonanswers and stop asking them.

We taped the interview Saturday morning, August 14, 1999, in a suite CNN rented at the Marriott Hotel in Des Moines. Rowly, who had never met Bush, said after the interview he was favorably impressed. So was I, as I indicated in the column:

Contradicting claims by Steve Forbes [running second in Iowa] that he hides his views or doesn't have any, Bush was responsive in detailing his position on more than a dozen issues—with a surprise or two.

He proposed rolling back President Clinton's 1993 tax increases (something that the Republican Congress has never attempted). He promised to act if China attacks Taiwan. He said he would end, not mend, the present affirmative action system. He liked being called the nation's most anti-abortion governor, and praised the National Rifle Association.

Such newsy discussion took up the first twenty minutes of the interview's twenty-two-minute airtime. But none of it made the weekend news and talk shows. That was because of what happened in the last two minutes of the interview when Rowly asked a carefully framed question about "possible past use of hard drugs." Bush, apparently thinking he had dodged the bullet with the interview nearly over, looked a little surprised before he answered:

> Bush: When I first got going in this campaign, I started hearing about these ridiculous rumors. I made up my mind in this point of time not to chase every single rumor that had been floated about me. . . .
>
> I'm going to tell you something. It's time for some politician to stand up and say enough is enough of this. The game of trying to force me to prove a negative and to chase down unsubstantiated, ugly rumors has got to end. And so, therefore, I'm going to end it.
>
> Evans: This is the only rumor. There's not a lot of rumors swirling about you. And this is the only [one] . . . Are you never going to answer that question?
>
> Bush: Let me tell you something. It's not the only rumor. The minute you answer one question, they float another rumor. I know how the game works. I saw it firsthand. And I ain't playing. . . . And the process needs to be cleaned up. . . .
>
> What I did twenty-five to thirty years ago is—is—I'm not just going to inventory.

Uncommunicative though Bush's remarks were, they were the only thing he had said about cocaine and were all over weekend television (while his substantive remarks in our interview were ignored). I was told Bush staffers felt I had betrayed Rove by asking the cocaine question. Of course, I had made no such commitment, and Rove never complained.

My continued good relations with Rove were demonstrated during our Texas Christmas trip of 1999, which was the last of its kind for Geraldine and me. Her mother died on December 15, 2000, ending nearly four decades of holiday visits to Geraldine's family. In 1999, with Bush's presidential campaign in full blast, I asked to see Rove in Austin. He not only gave me an office visit, but arranged a dinner party for Geraldine and me at his home attended by Bush's full campaign team. It's hard to extract much news from an event like that, but I thought Karl made the point that he wanted me to feel I was highly regarded by the Bush operation.

LATE ON TUESDAY night, February 24, 2000, I was in the CNN bureau in a strip mall office on the outskirts of Detroit when I was called upon to deliver an instant analysis of John McCain's stunning victory over George W. Bush in the Michigan primary. I went on the air to say this was a golden opportunity for McCain to wrest the presidential nomination away from the anointed Bush. It had been an improbable journey for McCain, who had begun trailing Dan Quayle, Steve Forbes, Elizabeth Dole, and Pat Buchanan among Bush's challengers in the polls.

McCain outlasted them all and was Bush's last remaining serious challenger when he was interviewed by Mark Shields and me on *Evans, Novak, Hunt & Shields* on January 15, 2000, from Des Moines. McCain was there for a debate in which he turned to Bush and declared: "Your tax plan has 36 percent of it going to the richest 1 percent in America." I pressed him in our subsequent TV interview, evoking this reply: "When there's a growing gap . . . between the haves and have-nots in America . . . now is the time to give the break to middle-class Americans." What he said at the debate and in our interview was Democratic class-warfare rhetoric, which is why his Republican candidacy appealed so much to Mark Shields and Al Hunt.

During the interview, McCain said: "I think that Mr. Novak's insults that he's hurled at me all these years have kept me awake many nights." That was sarcasm with a twinkle in his eye, reflecting the peculiar relationship we had. When I came in late once to a packed town meeting rally in New Hampshire, McCain spotted me and yelled: "Ah, there in the back is the Prince of Darkness!" Reporters liked McCain, and I was no exception, though I was troubled by his playing to applause from Hunt and Shields.

Independents in New Hampshire could vote in either primary, and in 2000 they selected the Republican ballot to vote for McCain. His landslide win thrust him ahead of Bush in polls taken all over the country, even in conservative South Carolina where the next primary test came on February 19. An unusually fierce Karl Rove appeared on *Evans, Novak, Hunt & Shields* on February 5 and promised: "We're not going to allow Senator McCain to do what he did to us in New Hampshire." His rough campaign against McCain defeated the senator in South Carolina, leading to Michigan three days later on February 22.

In the absence of a Democratic primary in Michigan, the Democratic-Independent turnout for the Republican primary was a stunning 51 percent, enabling McCain to edge out Bush while winning only one-third of Republican voters. Making calls to Republicans around the country from that Detroit strip mall, I found McCain's second primary win was eroding support for Bush.

The big test would be the Republicans-only primary in Virginia on February 29, one week after Michigan. Polls showed Bush's big lead in Virginia had turned into a dead heat. If McCain could win Virginia, he might be on the way to one of the great surprises in American political history. But McCain squandered the opportunity.

In Virginia Beach the night before the election, he delivered a jeremiad against two leaders of the Christian Right who happened to be Virginians. By calling Pat Robertson and Jerry Falwell "agents of intolerance" and warning his party against "pandering to the outer reaches of American politics," he symbolically declared war on the engine of majority status for Republicans. McCain lost Virginia—and any hope for the nomination—by following the advice of his friend, former senator Warren Rudman, who detested religious conservatives. I wrote then and I believe now that the hot-tempered senator acted out of rage, incensed by the religious Right's campaign that lost him South Carolina.

BILL CLINTON WAS not wild about Gridiron Club dinners and bagged his final one (the second time in eight years) on March 25, 2000. Vice President Al Gore would substitute, giving the presidential speech in the year he would be the Democratic nominee for president.

I learned the Gore operation had waited until the last minute to put his speech together when I received a telephone call from my friend Bob Shrum, Gore's media specialist, on the Wednesday before the Saturday night dinner. Shrum asked me to participate in a "good-natured" gag video to be inserted in Gore's speech. I would be videotaped as a reporter asking questions of George W. Bush. A clip of Bush would have him answering every question with one word: "General." That was the answer he gave when a local TV interviewer in Boston asked him the name of the President of Pakistan and he did not know it.

Why would I lend myself to such a stunt, intended to make Bush look dumb? Shrum could not have been surprised when I responded that Gore would have to pay a price. Not since 1988 preconvention activity had Gore gone on television with me, ignoring my repeated requests. I could understand why. I had been pounding Gore for years. But now for me to help out the vice president, he would have to submit to a half-hour interview on *Evans, Novak, Hunt & Shields*. While Shrum agreed immediately, I said *his* word was not enough. I wanted to hear it from Al Gore himself before I fulfilled my part of the bargain.

Early that evening, the vice president phoned me at my apartment. We had not exchanged a word for many years, but he was cordial as he thanked me for agreeing to help him. I reminded him politely of his commitment to follow that favor promptly with a TV interview. Gore said he understood and agreed, without equivocation. On Thursday, I taped the questions at CNN. My participation in Gore's stunt shocked some Gridiron guests, though it was one of the evening's entertainment high points.

I called Shrum the next week, seeking a firm date for the interview. It was the first of many such conversations extending for weeks and then months. Finally, in August, a contrite Shrum gave up. Gore simply would not schedule the TV interview.

Bill Daley had just been named Gore's national campaign chairman, and I telephoned him at his Nashville headquarters in mid-August. I felt that unless we got this done before Labor Day, any chance of it happening would disappear. Raised in Chicago politics where commitments were taken seriously, Daley seemed appalled when I told him about Gore's conduct. He sounded as though he thought he could fix it. But when he called back, Bill said it was no deal. However, he quickly asked, would I settle for a print interview for the column or the *Sun-Times*? It was not what I was promised, I said, but I would take it. Daley soon called again with more bad news. Gore would not do that either. He would do nothing for me. "I thought a deal was a deal," I told Daley. "So did I," he replied.

Would my treatment of Gore over the next two and one-half months have been any softer if he had kept his word? I hope not, but who knows? Al Gore demonstrated that he was even more of a phony than I had thought.

THE 2000 PRESIDENTIAL campaign was the eleventh and probably last where I hooked up with a candidate in its final days. I got aboard Bush's plane the Thursday night before the election and spent all day Friday following him, ending up in Morgantown, West Virginia. A visit to a state with few electoral votes that usually went Democratic was unusual. But this was not your father's West Virginia, and Karl Rove was not kidding when he said this would be a very close election (where Bush in fact needed West Virginia to be elected). What I never expected was being on hand for a "November Surprise" by the Democrats.

With no more than five percent of the electorate undecided, Bush's tax cuts and smaller government were going over better with the undecided middle than Gore's gun control and prescription drug subsidies. I had expected a late missile launch by Gore. But by my November 1–2 visit to the Bush campaign, I thought it might be too late.

I should have known it's never too late for a "roorback" (a smear on a candidate so close to election day that it's impossible to rebut effectively). It came the Thursday before the election. In Portland, Maine, a "civic-minded" judge had tipped off an "enterprising" lawyer about a long-hidden, twenty-four-year-old arrest of George W. The thirty-year-old Bush, in 1976 a heavy drinker, was arrested for a drunken driving violation in Maine where he was staying at his father's Kennebunkport house. Reporters covering his campaign could not conceal their elation.

Working on the road with a cell phone on Friday, I had a tough time finding what was behind the story. I couldn't get Karl Rove in Austin, and other sources pleaded ignorance. Then, for the only time in forty years on the campaign trail, I received serious help from a competitor.

Carl Cameron of Fox News was thirty years younger than I and one of the nation's best young political reporters. He tipped me off to what really happened and provided the names of the cast of characters. That enabled me to place calls to Maine and elsewhere over that weekend, and have a well-reported column for Monday, the day before the election. Carl knew, of course, that I was a commentator for CNN, Fox's hated rival, in addition to being a newspaper columnist. But I guess he figured it was important that his not be the only report demonstrating that the real duplicity in this story rested with Gore. Besides, he would have broadcast the story before I commented on CNN's *Capital Gang* Saturday night. This is what I wrote in Monday's column:

> Portland, Maine, lawyer Tom Connolly, who attracted only 13 percent of the vote as the [Democratic] party's 1998 nominee for Governor, is renowned as a character who wears his long-billed fishing cap into court.
>
> It was Connolly who leaked Bush's 1976 Maine arrest record after supposedly being tipped about it by an unnamed "political official" whom everybody in politics knows is Portland Probate Judge Billy Childs. Connolly and Childs are political compatriots and proteges of Joe Brennan, the state's last Democratic governor. . . .
>
> Maine sources say Childs . . . dug up Bush's court record some four months ago. Its impact would long ago have faded had it been released then. Five days before the election could be another matter.

I am convinced the DUI revelation cut into a rising Bush tide, costing him a popular vote majority and nearly giving Gore the presidency. While Gore's campaign denied complicity, I suggested in my November 6 column that it was inconceivable that the vice president's political operatives were unaware of what Judge Childs had in his hands for four months. The campaign's Maine connections were manifold. Press secretary Chris Lehane was born and raised in Kennebunkport, and his sister was a partner with a

Democratic law firm in Portland. Connolly was a Gore delegate to the 2000 national convention.

The Bush camp's argument that Gore's roorback had no impact on the outcome was a postelection attempt to evade responsibility for a stupendous tactical blunder. Rove, Karen Hughes, and the other Bush insiders all knew of the drunken driving arrest but bet that the Democrats would never discover it. It reflected an ominous tendency by the Bush inner circle toward secrecy and deception.

IN FORECASTING 2000, the *Evans-Novak Political Report* was right on the nose in the House with a two-seat Republican loss, reducing the GOP majority to eleven seats. The *ENPR*'s Senate projection of a one-seat Republican loss was further off the mark, compared with a loss of four Republican seats that narrowed the GOP margin to what turned out be a perishable one-seat margin. The Electoral College projections, made by me and my reporter Mike Catanzaro, seemed way off by projecting a 308 to 230 Bush victory while Bush in fact won by 271 to 266 after the Florida dispute was settled. Actually, we only missed three states—incorrectly putting Michigan, Wisconsin, and Delaware in the Bush column.

Michigan, along with Pennsylvania and Florida, constituted the "Trifecta" of 2000. If either Bush or Gore won all three states, he would be president. I attended a luncheon at The Palm hosted every Election Day for a group of conservative journalists and Republican strategists by Bill Schulz of *Reader's Digest*. As we left the restaurant and walked onto 19th Street, I observed my *Crossfire* adversary Bill Press and a few other liberals, after eating at the restaurant, whooping it up on the sidewalk as they scrutinized sheets of paper. They were reading exit polls, supposedly secret until the voting was finished, that showed Gore sweeping the Trifecta and winning the presidency.

Press and I went on *Crossfire* from CNN's Washington studios at seven thirty p.m. Eastern time, before the polls had closed in key states. That meant we were not supposed to say a word about the exit polls indicating a Gore victory. Press was so excited he could barely contain himself on the air without telling all he knew.

The Florida voting was just ending when *Crossfire* finished at eight p.m. The Voter News Service (VNS), the combine that made election night decisions for the networks and the AP, immediately awarded Florida to Gore on the basis of exit polls. This was ominous for Bush, inasmuch as Florida was considered the most likely Trifecta state to go Republican. At nine p.m., VNS awarded the other two Trifecta states, Pennsylvania and Michigan, to Gore. It looked like an early evening.

But at that point, my Republican sources—Karl Rove included—told me in phone calls that the raw vote numbers pouring in from Florida showed the state's exit polls were wrong and that VNS's award of the state to Gore had been premature. It took VNS experts an hour to agree, retracting their Florida call at ten thirteen p.m. and saying the presidential election was too close to call. It was midnight, and nobody knew who had been elected. At two sixteen a.m., the Fox News Channel called Florida—and the presidency—for Bush. The other networks quickly followed, and at two thirty, Gore conceded in a phone call to Bush.

I was wired with a microphone and earpiece to comment on Bush's victory. I did so around three a.m., but the latest Florida vote count showed Bush's lead there diminishing quickly. As Gore retracted his concession, the networks retracted their victory call and when a voter recount mandated by Florida kicked in, I was asked to stay wired to comment from time to time. I remained in that seat, making several commentaries, until five a.m., when I was told to go home.

I caught a couple hours of sleep at my apartment before going to my office to work on a column for Thursday morning and an edition of the *ENPR*. I figured we surely would know who won by noon. I could not conceive what was coming.

CHAPTER 42

Death of a Partner

On Friday, November 10, 2000, three days after the deadlocked presidential election, Senator Robert Bennett of Utah called me. "Bob, they're stealing the election in Florida!" the normally cool Bennett told me in a near shout. "They're going to count Gore in! And we're not doing anything about it!" The Democratic plot, he said, was focused on heavily Democratic Broward County (Fort Lauderdale). Bennett pleaded with me to report what was happening there, and (after working the phones) I wrote this for Monday's newspapers:

> [Broward County] last week soon became the focus for turning apparent [Gore] defeat into glorious victory. Thousands of Broward voters, presumably Democratic senior citizens, did not apply enough pressure on the punch card to record the vote.
>
> Broward is one of the four [Florida] counties where a hand count has been requested by Gore, not merely to check accuracy of the two previous mechanical tallies but to validate ballots that previously were called spoiled. In effect, Broward's all-Democratic reviewing committee would determine that these voters had meant to vote for the Vice President but had been unable to do so. Vote canvassers openly talked about divining the intent of voters.

This strategy kept the 2000 presidential election in dispute until December 12 when a five-to-four decision by the U.S. Supreme Court ended the contest in Florida. Bennett had been right in his analysis but wrong in his fears that the Republicans would not fight. Big Republican legal guns were brought to the fray.

Entering the White House as a minority and disputed president was not the way George W. Bush wanted to take office. I wrote that Bush was unprepared for the "partisan opposition that will be nothing like the malleable Democrats [he dealt with] in Austin."

ON JANUARY 24, 2001, four days after the inauguration, I was sitting in the White House Mess for lunch. I was the guest of Karl Rove along with two other conservative journalists, Paul Gigot of the *Wall Street Journal* and Kate O'Beirne of the *National Review.* It was my second visit ever to the mess and would be my last. We were not supposed to be there.

My first visit to the mess came twenty-eight years earlier, when I was invited by James D. Hodgson, a Nixon secretary of labor. I understood that journalists were forbidden to enter the sacred premises of the mess, but who was I to spoil an obscure cabinet member's pleasure at inviting a columnist? Across the uncrowded dining room. H. R. Haldeman fixed an evil eye on me. The dictatorial White House chief of staff was several places above a mere cabinet member in Nixon's pecking order, and I was told he gave Hodgson a dressing-down.

Now, in 2001, I was sure the no-journalists rule was still in force. I noticed Lawrence Lindsey, Bush's National Economic Council director and an old Washington hand, looking at us suspiciously from across the mess. Lindsey knew the rules but was in no position to pull a Haldeman and rebuke Rove. In the 2001 power structure, Rove was on top. Karl later told me that he was informed—politely, I am certain—he had broken the rules.

In recalling that pleasant lunch five years later, Kate O'Beirne told me she felt Rove had invited us to show how much things had changed at the White House. I also felt Rove was telling us that Kate, Gigot, and I, as conservatives, were regarded as something special in this White House even if we did not always follow the Bush line.

Indeed in forty-four years as a Washington reporter, I never had better access to a White House as I did to start the George W. Bush administration. Karl Rove was a grade A-plus source. While he did not dispense state secrets, confidential political plans, or salacious gossip, Rove always returned my phone calls. He knew everything, and while he did not tell me all that he knew, he never lied or misled me and often steered me away from a bad tip.

Geraldine and I were guests of the Roves at a small dinner party in his Washington home, and he came to breakfast at my apartment. He was a regular speaker at the Evans-Novak Political Forum, and always attended my annual dinner party at the Army and Navy Club the night before the spring Gridiron dinner. We shared an interest in American political history, agreeing on a preference for William McKinley over Theodore Roosevelt.

When our relationship ended abruptly and completely for three years because of the CIA leak case, I missed him as a fascinating conversationalist as well as my best Bush administration source.

What did Rove get out of this relationship besides the dubious pleasure of my company? Not puff jobs. Nor was I a pushover for the administration. From the start, it was clear I would applaud what I liked (tax cuts) and criticize what I did not (a larger federal role in education, the prescription drug boondoggle). What you did not find in my columns was criticism of Karl Rove. I don't believe I would have found much to criticize him about even if he had not been a source, but reporters—much less columnists—do not attack their sources. The relatively mild criticism of him in my column appeared after he cut me off in the autumn of 2003.

AT TEN MINUTES before eight on Friday morning, February 23, 2001, I appeared at the secretary of the treasury's office for breakfast with the newly installed secretary Paul O'Neill. I was surprised to see David Broder in the outer office. Had I gotten the date wrong? No, O'Neill had invited *both* Broder and me for breakfast. I suppose somebody urged the new secretary to get acquainted with these two old columnists, and he figured it would save time if he got that chore out of the way in one instead of two breakfasts.

The next hour bolstered my belief that Alcoa CEO Paul O'Neill was the biggest personnel mistake of George W. Bush's young presidency. That he was the wrong man in the wrong job was apparent at his confirmation hearing when he said he supported Bush's tax reduction plan "not because it is a major component to drive the economy, but because it won't hurt."

How could somebody so far removed from Bush's economic strategy end up as his nominal chief economic spokesman? The answer goes back to the Nixon administration. When Don Rumsfeld, thirty-seven, resigned from Congress in 1969 to run Nixon's antipoverty program, with Dick Cheney, twenty-eight, as his chief of staff, they were assigned O'Neill, thirty-three, as their career civil servant. They were three smart, ambitious young men who got along well and stayed together under President Ford. Thirty years later, Vice-President Cheney brought both of his former sidekicks into George W. Bush's cabinet. Immediately after Bush announced O'Neill's selection, I asked Cheney whether he had picked O'Neill just for old-times' sake. I incorporated his answer in my column of January 4:

Cheney wanted to avoid continuing Republican appointments to the Treasury of successful financiers and corporation executives who were useless in Washington. Cheney's model for a Republican Treasury Secretary was James A. Baker III, no master of finance and no ideologue but an ace of bureaucratic politics. He was able to argue that O'Neill was not identified closely with Bush economic policies but wasn't aligned against them either (at least not lately).

A wizened Paul O'Neill was no dashing Jimmy Baker. But I was anxious to observe the private demeanor that so charmed Cheney.

The food fed guests by cabinet members has been largely pedestrian ever since the puritanical Jimmy Carter set a standard of parsimony. But O'Neill's Treasury breakfast was a new low. The orange juice, toast, and a meager fruit cup appalled a bacon-and-eggs guy like me and might have provoked a riot in any respectable prison.

The secretary's verbal sustenance, which is what I was after at the Treasury, was none too nourishing either. O'Neill told us what most interested him was worker safety. *Worker safety?* What did the secretary of the treasury have to do with worker safety? He worried about it especially at this historic Treasury building.

O'Neill next turned to another issue for which he did not have responsibility and was not on the Bush agenda: national health care. He outlined health policies he had instituted at Alcoa. I then asked O'Neill about Bush tax cuts. He was inarticulate and seemed uninterested. When I tried to engage him in global monetary policy, he was even less engaged.

O'Neill's body language and facial expression indicated he was not overjoyed to be spending valuable time across the table from Broder and me. Promptly at nine a.m., he arose, grateful that his purgatory was over. My suspicions that Bush had made a disastrous nomination were reinforced by O'Neill's utter failure to represent Bush's economic views. Incredibly Bush kept O'Neill on for two years before he sacked him. This was not a president who found it easy to admit a mistake.

ON FRIDAY AFTERNOON, March 23, 2001, I was backstage at the Capitol Hilton's ballroom participating in the dress rehearsal for the Gridiron Club's spring show the next night when my cell phone rang. Rowly Evans had just died.

Rowly was seventy-nine years old, young to go in his long-lived family. I never dreamed I would outlive him. In contrast to my multiple ailments, I don't think he had a sick day until he was diagnosed with cancer in the summer of 2000. Even then, his oncologist said Rowly acted like no cancer patient he ever had seen. A month before his death, he insisted on hosting my seventieth birthday party at his home as he had my sixtieth. He was his charming self, going from table to table with a word for everyone. Most people there did not realize he was sick. Two weeks before he died, he was playing squash, appearing on television, and climbing the mountain at his farm in Culpepper, Virginia (and closing a deal to buy the part of the mountain he did not own). When he entered the hospital with two days to live, he interrupted his doctor's grim prognosis to ask whether he could preside with me over the Evans-Novak Political Forum the next week.

As the guests offered me condolences at the Saturday night Gridiron dinner, many asked whether Rowly's funeral would be in the massive National Cathedral where memorial services were held for prominent Americans. Rowland Evans Jr. was a great figure in Washington, a survivor of the upper-class Protestant ascendancy, and one who had made a name in his own right. But when Katherine Evans phoned me at my apartment Sunday morning, she told me Rowly had dictated funeral plans that precluded a mob scene at the National Cathedral. He wanted his funeral at Christ Episcopal Church, where he attended services across O Street from his house in Georgetown, with burial in the church's small graveyard.

Kay Evans told me Rowly wanted a sermon by the church's pastor and just two eulogists: his wife and me. "But I'm not going to do it," Kay went on to say. "That leaves you. I've got some suggestions for you." When Katherine Winton Evans had that resolute tone in her voice, there was no use arguing. I was a long way from being Rowly's best friend. But we were not just business partners, much more like brothers, with all the ambiguities of such a relationship. Some brother: I don't think we really liked as much as we loved each other. Perhaps that's why he picked me for his eulogy instead of a pal from the Georgetown social circuit or the Metropolitan Club.

I was nervous the morning of March 28, 2001, drinking coffee at the Evans house as I waited to walk across the street for the eleven a.m. service. The small church was packed with Rowly's friends and sources, including current officials and lots of former ones: cabinet members, senators, CIA directors, generals, ambassadors.

Kay said she did not want a tearjerker and urged me to tell some Rowly stories that she proceeded to give me. I took her advice and added some anecdotes of my own. But I'm afraid I brought out some handkerchiefs with this:

He was a happy warrior, a delight at any dinner party, playing the piano, stirring up trouble. But beneath these high spirits burned the heart of a patriot—the Yale freshman who stood in line on December 8, 1941, to enlist in the Marine Corps, exchanging the privileged life he had always known for combat in the Solomon Islands.

Seated in the first pew below me was General James Jones, commandant of the Marine Corps, who had brought along a marine color guard to present Kay with a flag honoring her marine husband. Jones, in marine dress blues, was tall, handsome, and tough. When I read the line about the Yale freshman giving up the privileged life to go into combat, I saw the general wipe an errant tear from his eye. I almost lost it. My voice broke on the next line before I regained control.

While the obituary's headline in the *New York Times* calling him a "conservative" may have been accurate, I said, "I can think of words more descriptive of the whole man than conservative: reporter, patriot, mentor, competitor, even—and here using a description by his wife of fifty-one years—rascal." The title I put on my Thursday column about him was "Rowland Evans, Reporter." In both the column and the eulogy, I noted Rowly's brilliant reporting on Soviet arms control cheating, the fall of communism in Eastern Europe, and the Israeli attack on the U.S.S. *Liberty* and its cover-up by the U.S. government. These were high points in the history of the Evans & Novak column in which I played little part.

During the reception at the Evans home, I was asked for a text of my eulogy by several people—including Henry A. Kissinger, who said it was excellent. It was the only compliment I ever got from Henry, who was a buddy of Rowly's and not mine.

A mutual friend asked me whether Kay would cooperate in holding a memorial service at the Metropolitan Club where his old buddies could also eulogize him. She told me to say thanks but no thanks, because we'd already had our memorial service. In recent years, I have attended several memorial services for journalists held in private clubs, with absolutely no mention of God or a hereafter and an endless procession of silly anecdotes about the departed. I know Rowly would have hated it if we had done that to him.

ON TUESDAY MORNING, September 11, 2001, I had breakfast at the U.S. Senators Dining Room in the Capitol with Republican senator George Voinovich of Ohio; his press secretary, Scott Milburn; and my reporter, Mike Catanzaro. Voinovich did most of the talking. I think it was about excessive government spending, but it all has been erased from my memory.

As I walked to my car after breakfast, an elderly police officer recognized me. It was about nine fifteen, and he said that two planes had crashed into the World Trade Center in New York. "It looks like terrorism," he said.

Midway through my writing a quick analytical piece that the *Sun-Times* had requested from Chicago for an "extra," I received word that our entire 1700 block of Pennsylvania Avenue, one block from the White House, was being evacuated. Everybody else in my office left, but I stayed to finish my work. I thought evacuation was a typical bureaucratic overreaction.

Having e-mailed my "extra" piece to Chicago, I had started work on my regular column for Thursday when two policemen entered my office. Addressing me by name, they informed me that everybody else had left the building and that they were prepared to remove me forcibly if I did not depart voluntarily. When I asked for five minutes to pack my book bag, they offered one minute and no more.

Out of the building and on the street, I found the garage where my car was parked had been closed and was guarded by police. That meant I had to walk twelve city blocks to my apartment to finish my Thursday column. I made my way through a crowded mass of government and other office workers who had poured into the streets, creating gridlock as cars inched toward home. It was a scene out of a disaster movie, down to the haunted looks on the faces of fleeing Washingtonians.

In my column published two days after the disaster, I warned that the expected U.S. attack on Afghanistan would be interpreted as "launching a holy war against Islam." I correctly predicted "strong sentiment in Congress for hitting somebody, somewhere who has unsavory terrorist credentials even if not connected with Tuesday's attack." The column's last two paragraphs were its most contentious elements:

> Perhaps the biggest difference with Pearl Harbor is the cause of the conflict. Bush's eloquent call for unity talked of the need to "defend freedom." Unlike Nazi Germany's and Imperial Japan's drive for a new world order, however, the hatred toward the U.S. by the terrorists is an extension of its hatred of Israel rather than world dominion. . . .
>
> Stratfor.com, the private intelligence company, reported Tuesday: "The big winner today, intentionally or not, is the state of Israel." Whatever distance Bush wanted between U.S. and Israeli policy, it was eliminated by terror. The spectacle on television of Palestinian youths and mothers dancing in the streets of East Jerusalem over the slaughter of Americans will not soon be forgotten. The United States and Israel are brought even closer in a way that cannot improve long-term policy objectives.

In reading my words four years after 9/11, I found nothing disreputable and nothing requiring an apology. But what I wrote generated instant outrage from the neoconservatives led by Norman Podhoretz, editor at large of *Commentary* magazine. In a letter to the *New York Post* published Friday (the day after my column ran), Podhoretz expressed his "disgust" with what I wrote, which he called "shamefully perverse." He asserted that I had a "vitriolic" attitude and an "animus" regarding Israel. He said I favored the "disappearance of Israel" and might welcome "repeated—and worse—attacks than the one we suffered on Sept. 11." All this was based on the two paragraphs above.

By this time in my long career, nothing said about me should have surprised me. But Podhoretz's venom did. I had first met him at a Kenyon College conference three decades earlier when he was making his spectacular journey from left-wing man of letters to right-wing man of politics. We always disagreed about Israel, but there was so much on which we agreed. I thought, too, that we enjoyed each other's company.

Podhoretz was not alone in his rancor. What he wrote alarmed me as thousands of vituperative letters and e-mails from pro-Israel sympathizers over four decades had not. Podhoretz was no dentist from Long Island but one of America's most prominent journalists and a practiced controversialist. I had stepped over the line in suggesting America's catastrophe benefited Israel. His outrageous claim that I welcomed a terrorist attack on America began a neocon campaign against me.

ON THE SUNDAY after 9/11, I was in the CNN bureau when I encountered my old friend Richard Perle, who had ceased to be a major source for me with the end of the cold war. While we had collaborated as cold warriors confronting the arms controllers, we now disagreed on many aspects of foreign policy.

Rumsfeld had named Perle chairman of the Defense Policy Board, a previously somnolent advisory group that the new secretary of defense was packing with aggressive neoconservatives. I detected satisfaction that the carnage of September 11 had unleashed the American giant to do things Perle felt should have been done long ago. When I asked him what was next, he said military action was necessary and it should be unilateral—without the allies that constrained Desert Storm a decade earlier. "Not even the British?" I asked. "Not even the British," he replied. I commented that Secretary of State Colin Powell would not like that. "Colin would make a good secretary of HHS or HUD," Perle said evenly. "But he never should be permitted to have anything to do with national security."

I continued our dialogue by telephoning Perle on Monday. I began by assuming the first U.S. military response would be aerial bombardment of Taliban forces in Afghanistan. "Not necessarily," Perle replied. "There aren't that many interesting targets in Afghanistan." Well, I asked, where were there "interesting" targets? Richard did not hesitate to say it would be Iraq.

Perle was not alone in downgrading Colin Powell. William Kristol wrote in the September 25 *Washington Post* that General Powell, as chairman of the Joint Chiefs in 1991, "did his best to persuade President Bush not to wage that war against Saddam" but that the senior Bush "overrode Powell's resistance." Kristol's open letter to George W. Bush urging a wider war (signed by Richard V. Allen, Jeane Kirkpatrick, William J. Bennett, and Vin Weber, among others) was a slap at Powell.

On September 28, I received a telephone call at my CNN office from Ron Kaufman, the longtime Republican National Committeeman from Massachusetts and one of the senior George Bush's political associates who had been denied admission to George W.'s 2000 campaign by Karl Rove. I think Ron suspected I was more on Karl's side than his, but I'm sure Kaufman thought I was sympathetic to Powell slowing the march to war.

In the eight months his son had been president, George Herbert Walker Bush kept out of policy disputes involving the administration. But now Kaufman relayed to me that the former president had told him over the phone he was "incredulous" and "upset" over Kristol's attack on Powell. Referring to Kristol's article, Kaufman quoted Bush-41 as saying, "That is totally wrong. Powell never tried to talk me out of attacking Iraq." Kaufman said the former president wanted to talk to me about this on the telephone. It would have been my first conversation with him in fourteen years, and it would have been the first time Bush-41 had talked to any reporter about this new division in Republican ranks.

But it did not happen. I believe the senior Bush thought better of letting it all hang out with me. However, Kaufman agreed to let me quote the former president on what he said the elder Bush had told him. I put this in my column of October 4 as well as this telling line: "According to close associates . . . the President [George W.] did not share his father's rage over Kristol's Sept. 25 essay." Not one month had passed since the terrorist attack, and the internal debate over Iraq was frozen into a contentious form that would not soon change.

THE NIGHT OF April 1, 2002, was momentous for me. First, the Maryland Terrapins won the national collegiate basketball championship. Second, *Crossfire* underwent a radical face-lift.

For five proceeding years, *Crossfire* had suffered because of hosts leaving, left and right, for political pursuits. When Geraldine Ferraro departed in 1997 for her ill-fated Senate campaign in New York, CNN decided not to replace her. Bill Press would handle the entire liberal hosting indefinitely.

In 1999, Pat Buchanan left *Crossfire* for the fourth time and for his third presidential candidacy (ending up as the Reform Party nominee). Jennifer Zeidman, the latest *Crossfire* executive producer, dropped by my office at CNN. Would I go full-time as conservative host, as Press was doing on the Left? My answer was no. That did not surprise Jennifer, who said she had a choice to replace Buchanan that she wanted to run by me.

It was Mary Matalin, a onetime beautician who had become one of the Republican Party's premier staffers. Mary was a working-class Chicago girl and reminded me of the tough, sexy girls of Eastern European origin who were my schoolmates in Joliet. I liked her, and she had been a great guest for me on *Evans and Novak* and *Crossfire*.

When Geraldine and I went to the Georgetown home of Bob Shrum and Mary Louise Oates on January 8, 1991, for a dinner honoring Congressman Dick Gephardt, I was surprised to find Mary Matalin there with James Carville. They seemed a little distant from each other, which became understandable when I later learned this amounted to a blind date. In her joint account with Carville of the 2000 campaign *(All's Fair)*, Mary wrote: "I could think of plenty of ways to spend an evening rather than talking things over with Dick Gephardt, but I loved Bob Novak. There was really no reason to meet this Carville guy but I said yes because Novak is always good for a few yucks." I always felt I was present at the creation of a happy marriage and a lucrative business partnership where lectures made them rich.

Mary worked harder than any other *Crossfire* host, coming in early and devouring research material that Buchanan and I glanced over and Sununu ignored. I told Jennifer that Mary was a terrific choice, but I never mentioned one downside: Mary was no conservative. Not even close. Not only was she prochoice on abortion and pro–gay rights, she did not have much interest in conservative doctrine. What interested her was Republicans winning elections. She had spent her adult life as a Republican functionary, and the idea of dissenting from the party line was foreign to her. That changed the tone of *Crossfire*'s conservative hosts. Nobody could be sure where Buchanan, Novak, or even Sununu was going, which created the atmosphere of a train wreck in waiting. Mary brought predictability and order.

Matalin soon started sitting in on Bush 2000 campaign strategy sessions. Although she got approval from CNN, I thought privately it was a bad idea. Though nobody pretended that *Crossfire* hosts were objective, the idea of a television commentator opining on a strategy that he had devised bothered me. I was not surprised after Bush was elected in 2000 that Mary thanked me for my help and told me she was leaving *Crossfire* to be counselor to Vice President Cheney.

Mary Matalin's departure focused CNN on what to do about *Crossfire* in the context of the network's overall problems. Fox had passed CNN and was increasing its lead. Demographically CNN was a general disaster and programs like *Crossfire* and *Capital Gang* were specific disasters. Younger viewers, supposedly more likely to respond to commercials and beloved of the twenty- and thirty-something advertising buyers, did not watch these programs. *Crossfire* was going from thirty minutes to a full hour, as *Capital Gang* had earlier. Now was the time for changing the program, particularly with its top producer's slot open with Jennifer Zeidman marrying and transferring to New York.

I suggested as the new executive producer Sam Feist, a former intern who had rapidly climbed the CNN staircase (including a spell producing *Evans and Novak*). I don't know whether my recommendation counted, but Feist got the job. One evening in the late autumn of 2000, Sam called me into his office and revealed his plans. Bill Press was being dumped. He would be replaced by James Carville (once a week) and Carville's sidekick, Paul Begala (four times). Atlanta did not want to bring Pat Buchanan back for a fourth time. Replacing Matalin would be Tucker Carlson, a young journalist who already had a fat CNN contract. I asked where that left me. Feist replied there always would be a place for Bob Novak on *Crossfire*.

The Carville-Begala team was intended to rev up excitement and attract a more youthful audience. But the key to this plan was Tucker Carlson, younger looking than his thirty-two years with a winning smile and a trademark bow tie. While he had been a terrific writer for *Policy Review* and the *Weekly Standard,* I was not impressed by him on television, especially when he teamed up on CNN with Bill Press during the 2000 campaign in a fatuous late-night political talk show called *The Spin Room.*

Feist asked me what I thought of the new lineup. I told him I felt bad about Press, whom I liked and with whom I worked well. But I could tell that Carville-Begala was locked in, and Press was history. The problem I raised was whether CNN wanted four white men on *Crossfire* in the twenty-first century. I suggested Bay Buchanan, Pat's sister and a conservative activist in her own right. She often had filled in as a *Crossfire* host. When Sam asked me whom she should replace, I said it would have to be Tucker Carlson. I said while I was a conservative and Matalin was a Republican, Carlson did not seem to be either (I was right about his not being a

Republican, but I was wrong about his not being a conservative). Feist nodded, but my argument was going nowhere.

Just before the new lineup went on the air, Tucker asked me for a long talk. Over breakfast at the Army and Navy Club, he told me he needed tips from an old hand at *Crossfire*. I knew that was bull. I thought Tucker had heard I did not consider him conservative enough, and now was trying to ingratiate himself with me. In response to Tucker's request for advice, I told him it was best for the conservative host on *Crossfire* to be a conservative. He responded that I could not imagine how conservative he really was.

What Carlson really thought of me then was made clear by a brief description in his 2003 mini-memoir, *Politicians, Partisans and Parasites:* "Bob Novak, a seventy-year-old columnist who had been doing the show on and off since the early 1980s." He made clear he resented Congressman Tom DeLay and me libeling him as "too liberal to represent the Right on the air."

My belief that Carville, Begala, and Carlson were not good fits for *Crossfire* was irrelevant because this was not the old *Crossfire*. Feist's strategy to attract younger viewers included a bells-and-whistles makeover of the show. Interviews were much shorter while film clips, graphics, and sound bites were added. The biggest physical change was moving *Crossfire*'s venue from the CNN studios near Capitol Hill to the 250-seat Jack Morton Auditorium at George Washington University in Washington's Foggy Bottom. I thought the spirit of *Crossfire,* with camera close-ups of public figures under intense interrogation, was radically altered by a student audience hooting and hollering. Although the producers claimed they tried hard to balance the audience between Left and Right, they failed utterly. Democrats always were in the majority, often overwhelmingly so.

The new *Crossfire* was louder, shriller, and less substantive. As I had feared, there was a disconnect between hosts on the Left and on the Right. Carville and Begala were Democratic Party activists. Neither Carlson nor I had any connection with the Republican Party (and I had become a registered Democrat so that I could vote for local public officials in the one-party District of Columbia). Carville and Begala were enthusiastic Bush-bashers, attacking him as a fraudulently elected president. Carlson was an unreconstructed McCainiac who did not like Bush. That left me as Bush's defender, a position for which I was not suited psychologically or professionally.

Personally I enjoyed the company of Carville and Begala much more than I had Braden and Kinsley, and I liked having a drink and talking politics and sports with Carville when we were together on the lecture circuit. But being with them on the air was no pleasure. They treated *Crossfire* as political warfare. I could predict and, indeed, recite their nightly rants against George W. Bush.

Their unabashed partisanship was, I think, one reason *Crossfire* no longer attracted top-grade Republican guests. However, we were not getting the best Democratic guests either. *Crossfire* no longer was a program where politicians could have a long say. While a senator or House member could get to the CNN studios from the Capitol in five minutes, the crosstown drive to GW consumed half an hour or more. A busy political figure would have to spend at least an hour and a half for a twelve-minute interview that probably had to be shared with somebody on the opposite side. Sam Feist had given up a lot in search of higher ratings and improved demographics that he never got.

CNN TELEVISED its 2002 election night coverage from Atlanta, and the four hosts of *Crossfire* were brought down from Washington. Sam Feist produced the coverage and wanted *Crossfire* to play a major part for the first time in this, the twelfth national election since the network was launched. Paula Zahn, a former broadcast network star and now a CNN anchor, was the rose inserted to moderate the four *Crossfire* thorns. We went on the air once or twice every hour through the night.

This was my first sustained exposure to Paula, who was a beautiful and charming woman. But she knew nothing about politics, and her moderating the *Crossfire* blackguards was ridiculous. Carville and Begala never made any pretense at being political journalists, and all they knew came from Democratic operatives. Tucker Carlson was a phrasemaker and essayist, not well informed about individual races. I was the only member of the *Crossfire* team who had done substantial political reporting that year.

But this was show business. The CNN high command wanted *Crossfire* to put on a show, and so we did. Carville and Begala were devastated as bad news for Democrats poured in. Late in the evening, Carville put a wastebasket over his head to hide his shame. It was hilarious and made the morning newspapers. CNN was delighted. It wasn't journalism, and nobody pretended it was.

Because they were not journalists, Carville and Begala came to Atlanta genuinely expecting Democratic victories. But signals of a disastrous Democratic night came early, from voters not far from us in Atlanta. I began my Thursday morning column:

Shortly after 9 o'clock Tuesday night, election returns from Gwinnett County, Ga. (30 miles northeast of Atlanta), pointed to a national Republican triumph and to trouble for Democrats far into the future. The result validates President Bush's aggressive political strategy and signifies the collapse of the Democratic Southern remnant. These returns showed Republicans running well in Gwinnett, which is usually carried by GOP candidates for president but not for state office. The entire state of Georgia itself has been a stubborn holdout from Republican domination of Southern politics.

The signal from Gwinnett meant Representative Saxby Chambliss was going to oust Senator Max Cleland. That returned Senate control to the GOP, which had lost it briefly with the defection of liberal Republican Jim Jeffords, but it was not the only Democratic disaster from this state. Georgia was the only state which had not elected a Republican governor in the twentieth century. Governor Roy Barnes, a moderate Democrat with ambitions to follow the road taken by Jimmy Carter and Bill Clinton to the White House, was so sure of 2002 reelection to a second term that on Monday night he dawdled at a CNN reception in Atlanta rather than go about his election eve rounds. Barnes was defeated along with Cleland. So was Georgia House Speaker Tom Murphy, the nation's senior state legislator with forty-two years' service. Georgia was the last piece in the Deep South's realignment.

By 2002, I had delegated heavy-duty reporting on congressional races to my excellent reporter, Tim Carney. Thanks to Carney, the *Evans-Novak Political Report* was never more accurate. In the Senate, we hit the results on the nose: a gain of two Senate seats, giving back the majority to Republicans, fifty-one to forty-nine. In the House we predicted a Republican increase of seven seats, one more than the actual gain of six that extended the Republican majority to twenty-five seats. For the fifth straight election, Republicans had won a majority in both houses of Congress.

CHAPTER 43

Attacking Iraq and Attacking Novak

THE *NOVAK, HUNT and Shields* program of Saturday, November 9, 2002, featured Representative John E. Sununu of New Hampshire, son of the former governor and White House chief of staff. His election to the U.S. Senate four days earlier clinched, early in the evening, the return to a GOP Senate majority. This was the last program of what had started twenty years earlier as *Evans and Novak.*

I got the bad news a month earlier in a telephone call from Walter Isaacson, CEO of CNN. When I first met Isaacson on the 1980 Reagan presidential campaign plane as a twenty-eight-year-old reporter for *Time* magazine, he struck me as the reflexive liberal typical among journalists of his generation. But he was a smart, charming New Orleanian whose company I enjoyed and someone, I was sure, who was destined for big things. He would become a best-selling biographer (of Henry Kissinger and Benjamin Franklin), managing editor of *Time* in 1995 at age forty-three, and in 2001 Time-Warner's choice to head CNN.

Why pull the plug on *Novak, Hunt and Shields,* that was being cancelled as of November 9? Its ratings were decent, the budget was low, and guests were high caliber. It was the only national program of its kind anywhere on Saturday, so that we often got a good play in Sunday morning newspapers. I asked Isaacson in 2005 in preparation for this book why the program was axed, and he replied that the suits in Atlanta had been after us for a long time and that he repeatedly had saved *Novak, Hunt and Shields* (and *Capital Gang* as well). These weekly programs, he said, just did not fit the network's advertising game plan. That did not make sense to me. After all, didn't the network have to run *something* on the weekend? I think the problem was that the Atlanta executives, unlike Isaacson, did not like politics and probably never watched our programs.

Isaacson softened the blow for me by saying I would be given a new CNN vehicle in which I would conduct a seven-minute, one-on-one weekly interview. Walter asked me to come up with a name. I offered *The Novak Zone.*

The show debuted November 23, 2002, with an interview of Don Rumsfeld (he was in Brussels, I was in Washington) that could be described, charitably, as leaden. The inaugural *Zone* was so bad, in fact, it convinced me that fitting conventional newsmakers, who had been given twenty minutes on *Novak, Hunt and Shields,* into a seven-minute hole would not work. I decided to seek offbeat guests, many who had nothing to do with politics, whom we would tape at interesting locations away from the CNN studios. All guests and I would be eye-to-eye, never separated at remote locations as I was with Rumsfeld.

With those requirements, the *Zone* would need more time for preparation than I could spare. Bob Kovach came to the rescue. He was the producer of *Capital Gang* and had produced *Novak, Hunt and Shields.* Kovach was an ethnic from Cleveland who went to Catholic school from first grade through college, working for a network whose executive ranks were dominated by Jews in an industry where WASPs and Ivy Leaguers prospered. He reminded me of a lot of guys I grew up with in Joliet.

The Novak Zone energized Kovach. He did guest booking, site selection, question preparation, and technical production. He supplied most of the ideas as we taped the *Zone* at Ford's Theater, Oriole Park at Camden Yards, the Kennedy Center, the World War II Memorial, the former presidential yacht *Sequoia,* RFK Stadium, FedEx Field, Arlington Cemetery, and assorted museums and galleries. The guests included opera superstar Placido Domingo, baseball greats Cal Ripken and Frank Robinson, Hollywood actors Robert Duvall and Suzanne Farrell, cyclist Lance Armstrong, broadcaster Tom Brokaw, and composer-pianist Marvin Hamlisch (who wrote a ditty called *The Novak Zone,* which he played and sang to conclude our interview at the Kennedy Center).

Kovach used me as a participant as well as interviewer on some *Zone* programs. At the U.S. Naval Academy, I steered a training boat down the Severn River. At the Kennedy Center Opera House, I was a supernumerary in white tie and tails in *La Traviata,* cuddling a prostitute in the bordello scene.

My signature piece on *The Novak Zone* came in the summer of 2003 when Kovach sought an interview with the U.S. Army Golden Knights parachute jump team. Their public information officer told Kovach that they would be delighted, then asked: Would Mr. Novak like to jump with us? I had fantasized about jumping out of airplanes as I had fantasized about many things, but I thought such an adventure was far behind me at age seventy-two.

Afraid to be exposed as the coward I was, I agreed to jump when the Golden Knights came to Andrews Air Force Base outside Washington for an annual air show. I did not mention it to Geraldine until after the fact. When I visited Dr. Abrams for my annual physical soon after the jump, he asked why a seventy-two-year-old with multiple infirmities did not ask his doctor's permission. "Because you would have said no," I answered. He replied that was quite correct.

The army's prejump briefing for me at Andrews featured a video in which an officer sternly advised that the waiver I was about to sign relieved the U.S. government of any liability for injury or death even if the army was clearly negligent. That was not reassuring, but I did not explore in my own mind the possibility of backing out until I was flying over the drop zone. It was just like the movies with paratroopers seated on long benches on either side of the plane. But my fellow jumpers all were about fifty years younger than I. Then the jump master announced that Mr. Novak would be jumping first. It seemed like the last mile as I walked to a huge opening in the side of the plane. Although my army partner was attached to me as we jumped in tandem, it was up to me to screw up the courage to actually leap out the door. The jump was followed by a free fall during which I was instructed to maneuver acrobatically while scared stiff. Only then did my parachute open. People invariably asked me if the landing was tough, but it was a piece of cake compared with jumping out of the plane into free fall.

The jump took a lot out of an unathletic old man. I simply could not stand up after I landed, and we had to do the post-jump interview with me on the ground. I had a one-word answer—"No!"—when asked whether I would ever jump again. The interview was recorded for *The Novak Zone,* as was the actual jump (taped by an army cameraman who jumped at the same time).

My jumping tape was repeated on *Crossfire, Capital Gang,* and other CNN programs and got some press attention as well. Tucker Carlson, who until then had not joined my fan club, left a flattering message on my voice mail informing me how "cool" it was to have performed this stunt. The same adjective was used by Jane Sanders Caldwell, my mother's namesake and the eldest of my seven grandchildren. "You're cool, Grandpa!" exclaimed Jane, aged seven.

Except for the parachute jump, CNN brass ignored the program. The

Zone was aired at eleven forty a.m. Saturdays, not the choice time Walter Isaacson originally promised. I often suggested that the seven-minute program be used several times on the all-news, twenty-four-hour network during a slow news weekend, just as undistinguished news packages were repeated. Nobody rejected my requests. They just ignored them, as well as my pleas to include *The Novak Zone* among the plethora of promotional spots mandated for each CNN program. I believe Isaacson was a supporter of my programs and me but he was busy, overwhelmed as a print journalist trying to revive a cable network losing its competitive struggle with Fox. *The Novak Zone* went off the air in July 2005 after a vigorous life of a little more than two and one-half years.

GEORGE W. BUSH was to deliver his third State of the Union address on Tuesday, January 28, 2003. The day before the speech I and four other conservative journalists were invited to the White House for a special briefing. The briefer—whose words could be attributed only to a mysterious "senior administration official"—was none other than George W. Bush.

Of the five journalists, four were hawks on Iraq, and I was a dove. After U.S. military strikes on Afghanistan began on Sunday, October 8, 2001, I hurriedly wrote a substitute column for the next morning reporting "a strong viewpoint inside the Pentagon that the second target—after Afghanistan—has to be Iraq. Even the most hawkish officials privately admit that no evidence links Baghdad to the Sept. 11 attacks, but they want to conclude the unfinished task of a decade ago anyway." I predicted quick military victory in Afghanistan, after which Bush "will have an open mandate to press on against Saddam Hussein. That temptation will test Bush's prudence and wisdom."

More than a year later, I wrote in the column published Monday, January 27, 2003—the day of my White House briefing—that "prospects for war are . . . probable but not inevitable." I described unnamed critics as "apprehensive about the diplomatic fallout . . . of the Anglo-Americans going it alone."

I suspected I was included with the hawkish journalists because the White House wanted to send me a message. At the briefing, the president described himself as undecided "on whether or not to use troops, because this issue can be resolved peacefully." After a few minutes, he repeated himself and may have been referring to my column that morning: "Novak thinks I have made up my mind on troops. I want to make it clear. I haven't made up my mind on troops." Yet, in the next breath, Bush implied eventually he would send those troops against Saddam Hussein: "This speech is the beginning of a series of speeches. . . . One of these days there will be an 'Iraq-only' speech."

In my Thursday column, I quoted the "senior administration official" at length, turning his first person into third person when referring to the president. I thought any knowledgeable reader would know that I actually was quoting Bush, showing how futile were the White House ground rules. Not so. After the column was published, I asked two politicians and two journalists to identify the "senior administration official." None named Bush, and I certainly did not identify him. The White House cover was effective, though its purpose eluded me.

If including me in the presidential briefing was to convince me Bush had not really made up his mind, it failed. I did not want to make an overt accusation that the president was deceptive, but my Thursday column gave that impression nonetheless:

> Emotionally and eloquently, George W. Bush in his second State of the Union sounded like a war president. Yet hours before the address, the White House at the highest level [that was Bush himself] stressed that the President had made no final decision on using U.S. arms to remove Saddam Hussein from power. . . .
>
> That can be interpreted in two ways. One is that the President, in sending America's military might to the Persian Gulf, has made war inevitable and will declare it in a forthcoming second speech to the nation. The alternative interpretation is that Bush still feels Hussein can be forced from power short of war, unlikely though that seems. . . .
>
> [T]he President holds out the possibility of a peaceful solution. How? Clearly, he has no faith in the [weapons] inspection process. That leaves only removal of Saddam Hussein by internal forces in Baghdad. If not, the next Bush speech will end any doubts about his being a war president.

Going to war is entering a dark tunnel with unknown perils and potential calamities ahead, and I was sure Bush had decided to make that journey. My interpretation did not suit the White House. I was invited to no more private briefings, and that was the last I saw of George W. Bush except for Christmas party handshakes.

THE IRAQ-ONLY BUSH speech was delivered over live television from the Red Room of the White House on March 17, 2003. His ultimatum to Saddam Hussein: Get out of Iraq in forty-eight hours or U.S. military forces will come in. I knew the Bush administration and perhaps the country never would be the same. I listened to Bush in a state of shock, stemming not from the president's speech but from a cover story in *National Review* published that day.

The timing could not have been better for the magazine. "Unpatriotic Conservatives: A War Against America" was written by the Canadian journalist David Frum, who had resigned as a presidential speechwriter to write a memoir of his thirteen months at the White House. Frum began by declaring that "some of the leading figures" in what he called the "movement" against the war on terror "call themselves 'conservatives.' " He continued:

> These conservatives are relatively few in number, but their ambitions are large. They aspire to reinvent conservative ideology: to junk the 50-year-old conservative commitment to defend American interests and values throughout the world—the commitment that inspired the founding of this magazine—in favor of a fearful policy ignoring threats and appeasing enemies. . . .
>
> You may know the names of these antiwar conservatives. Some are famous: Patrick Buchanan and Robert Novak. Others are not: Llewellyn Rockwell, Samuel Francis, Thomas Fleming, Scott McConnell, Justin Raimondo, Joe Sobran, Charley Reese, Jude Wanniski, Eric Margolis and Taki Theodoracopulos.

Frum had put me in strange company. Buchanan and Wanniski were the only people mentioned who were my friends though I was an acquaintance of McConnell, who once had edited my copy at the *New York Post*. I had never heard of Raimondo, Reese, or Margolis. I knew of Taki but thought of him as a millionaire jet-setter and clever essayist. I had met Francis and Sobran once or twice and never had met Rockwell and Fleming at all; I considered those four to be ideological extremists whose views I did not embrace. A couple of members of this assemblage—and I am not talking about Buchanan—embraced anti-Semitic views that I abhorred.

I thought Frum's tendentious attack on "paleoconservatives" unworthy of *National Review*. His conclusion was most poisonous in assailing antiwar conservatives (including me): "They are thinking about defeat, and wishing for it, and they will take pleasure if it happens. They began by hating the neo-conservatives. They came to hate their party and this president. They have finished by hating their country."

Frum identified me as a "paleo," which must have been a shock to the real "paleos," considering my support of free trade, a global economy, and liberal immigration. From his immense research, Frum managed to extract only three citations to document my paleo credentials. He first cited a December 26, 2002, column in which I stated the Hezbollah organization's terror campaign was focused against Israel, not the United States as Bush administration officials suggested it was. He next turned to my September 17, 2001, column quoting congressional sources as saying the CIA was incapable of finding Osama bin Laden (which turned out to be true). Finally and predictably, he cited my September 13, 2001, column, which had so enraged Norman Podhoretz. That comprised slim evidence for stigmatizing me as somebody who wanted his country to lose in war.

Frum had been after Buchanan for years, attempting to drive him from the acceptable political mainstream by unfairly imprinting an anti-Semitic brand on him. Frum's attitude toward me was more complicated. We had patched up a stormy beginning, accepting mutual invitations to social occasions. While serving as a member of the *American Spectator*'s governing board, I had defended, unsuccessfully, Conrad Black's attempt to make Frum editor of the magazine. When Frum became a Bush speechwriter in March 2001, I called to invite him for lunch. He told me that all press contacts had to be cleared with higher authority and that ruled out lunch.

The White House rules eased enough so that Frum agreed to lunch with me at the Oval Room restaurant on September 19, 2001, shortly after the terrorist attacks. I had hoped I would leave the table with something usable for the column. But I did not know Frum was saving the good stuff for his memoir, which also was kept secret from the president and his White House colleagues. During a pleasant lunch, he dispensed no news and few insights. Toward the end, however, he told me he was restless as low man on the Bush speechwriting totem pole, was discouraged when he saw his prose discarded and admitted he missed his days as a newspaperman. I thought Frum was signaling he was not long for the White House, but that was not exactly a scoop.

The lunch was so unproductive that I did not contact Frum again or even think about him for the next four months. While friends were having dinner with me shortly after Bush's 2002 State of the Union address, they told me of an e-mail they had received from Frum's wife, Danielle. She had sent that same e-mail to so many people that it leaked out before I could write about it. But I called White House sources for a new angle on the story, and it made the lead item of my Sunday column of February 10, 2002. The best way to describe this bizarre incident is to repeat the whole three-paragraph item:

> Presidential speechwriter David Frum, embarrassed by his wife's bragging to friends that he authorized the "axis of evil" phrase in President Bush's State of the Union address, did not exactly write these words.
>
> According to White House sources, Frum proposed "axis of hate" to describe Iraq, Iran and North Korea. Chief speechwriter Michael Gerson changed "hate" to "evil," these aides said. Frum's wife, Danielle Crittenden, sent e-mails to friends saying, "my husband is responsible for the phrase" and expressing "hope you'll indulge my wifely pride."
>
> High-level presidential aides said Frum was not in trouble. But self-identification of language by a presidential ghost is strictly forbidden. "I'd be mortified if I were him," said one aide. Another staffer described Frum as "very embarrassed."

Two weeks later on February 26 (my seventy-first birthday), I got a tip from the White House that Frum had just resigned. The news would not hold for my column, and I broke the story on CNN's *Inside Politics* that day. While I reported there was "suspicion he's been kicked out," I quoted both Frum and presidential aides as saying the move was voluntary. Implausibly Frum declared publicly that I had libeled him and claimed he savored a libel suit to "finance my children's education" (ridiculous but also disingenuous because Frum was a man of inherited wealth who lived in a Washington mansion).

I reviewed Frum's *The Right Man* in the *American Conservative,* a new magazine co-founded by Pat Buchanan, Scott McConnell, and Taki. I suggested Frum had gone to work at the White House for the express purpose of writing this best seller. "For much of this book," I wrote, "Frum seems disengaged from Bush's policies." I said that "an aide just off the payroll and hungry for fame might be expected to 'kiss and tell,' but the truth is that Frum did precious little kissing there to tell about." His memoir, I contended, "becomes a brief for [Prime Minister Ariel] Sharon's Israeli policy."

The *National Review* article in March was payback time for Frum, but I suspected from the start that his article conveyed more than merely one man's pique. On an impulse, I put in a call to my friend Bill Kristol, who as editor of the *Weekly Standard* and a Fox commentator was the most authentic voice of the neoconservatives. When I asked Bill what he thought of

Frum's article, he replied he had heard nothing about it. I found that hard to believe, coming from somebody who prided himself on knowing everything before anybody else. I asked him to look into it, and he said he would call me right back. He never did.

In fact, March 17, 2003, marked the last telephone conversation between Bill Kristol and me. For years, we had been constant telephone communicants and frequent companions for lunch (which also came to an end). Bill had supplied a steady stream of news tips to me, even after he crossed over from newsmaker to journalist. No more. Sometimes silence is more eloquent than anything that can be said. In due time, Kristol would vocally demonstrate the change in our relationship.

Frum's article drew a dividing line in the conservative movement. David Keene, chairman of the American Conservative Union, was no less an advocate of the Iraqi intervention than was Kristol. But after the Frum article, Keene defended me and wrote that I had been "opposing the nation's enemies before Frum was even born." Keene said I was wrong about Iraq. "But to suggest, as does Frum," he continued, "that his disagreement with Bush's Iraq policy stems from a hatred of the President and the country is scandalously and irresponsibly absurd."

What do you do when a supposedly responsible journalist of David Frum's stature prints hateful lies about you? I wrote a column published on March 24, a week after the attack on Iraq and Frum's article:

> I feel constrained to identify myself as a Korean War-vintage Army officer (non-combat) who has always supported our troops and prayed for their success during many wars. This war is no exception.
>
> Dealing with statements about me even so calumnious as Frum's might seem petty in time of war. But broader issues are at stake. Frum represents a body of conservative opinion that wants to delegitimize criticism from the Right of policy that has led to war against Iraq.

I noted in the column that Frum could not "find anything I ever have said to indicate hatred toward George W. Bush, much less my country." Frum's citations of me asserting that U.S. policy was too closely bound to Israel's led me to write: "Implicitly, William F. Buckley's prestigious and influential magazine is saying, that is unacceptable criticism from a conservative."

That was the only mention in my March 24 column of *National Review,* and I said not a word to anyone of what I felt. But it was burning a hole in my heart. While I did not care what anybody as disreputable as Frum said of me, *National Review*'s complicity deeply grieved me. This was Bill Buckley's vehicle that created the modern conservative movement. I had been reading the magazine since its inception in 1955, had been writing for it for more than thirty years and (with Geraldine) had traveled on two of its fund-raising cruises. But on the second cruise (to New England and Canada) just a month after the 9/11 attacks, I felt like odd man out with *National Review* staffers who sharply disagreed with my hesitancy to go to war against Islam.

Not everybody connected with *National Review* approved of the Frum article. Neal Freeman, long an important figure in the conservative movement and a close associate of Buckley, was a member of the magazine's board of directors and unsuccessfully sought a public apology to me from *NR*. Bill Buckley himself sent me a nice e-mail: "You have to know how deeply I admire you. I've said it often enough in public." He added: "We disagree on the animating spirit and strategic analysis in the matter of Gulf Storm 2, which has nothing to do with my public estimate of you as a great conservative figure." That was closer to an apology than anything else from the magazine's staff even though he said he agreed with Frum's "larger points."

I heard that Buckley and Rich Lowry, the thirty-one-year-old editor of *National Review,* had tried but failed to amend Frum's article to separate me from the paleos. That was credible in the case of Buckley, who no longer micromanaged *National Review.* But I cannot imagine Lowry did not have the power to do anything he desired with the article. Unlike Buckley, Lowry sent me no commendation after publishing the Frum attack. I appeared with Buckley on a panel in the afternoon at *National Review*'s fiftieth anniversary celebration in 2005, but Lowry said nothing to me there or at the dinner that evening. Although there were no more articles in the magazine attacking me, *NR* staffers sniped at me via *National Review Online.*

I think the prevailing attitude at *National Review* was reflected in a column by William Rusher, the magazine's retired publisher. Unlike Buckley he did not separate me from the paleos, who he said had "started this fight" by claiming the neoconservatives had "hijacked the conservative movement." Frum's article, Rusher continued, "signals a firm alliance of the original [Buckleyite] conservatives and the neoconservatives against so-called paleoconservatism." Rusher rejoiced that "this will make it a lot harder for such TV shows as 'The McLaughlin Group' and 'The Capital Gang' to peddle Buchanan and Novak, respectively, as representative generic conservatives on their panels. They are no such thing." Rusher was reading us out of the conservative movement, with an implicit comment of "good riddance!"

As the *NR* Washington bureau chief, Kate O'Beirne must have known well in advance about the cover story. Kate was my Catholic godmother and I thought my friend. But I knew she disapproved mightily about my reluctance to go to war. On the Saturday night after Frum's attack on me was published, before we went on the air for *Capital Gang* I asked Kate what she thought of Frum's article. "Oh, Bob," she said in her best New York theatrical style, "it's so hard when two friends are fighting each other." I cannot imagine an answer more distressing to me than to put me on the same level with a cheat and a liar. I never again raised the issue with Kate, for the sake of our professional relationship.

Neal Freeman was the only person at the magazine that I know of who publicly defended my position. He argued that I "had made a plausible case [on Iraq] and a wholly responsible contribution to the public conversation. The historical record has now confirmed that judgment" (as he wrote in the June 2006 issue of the *American Spectator*).

Freeman sought a brief apology for Frum's article from *National Review.* Instead, after some weeks, the magazine published a mixed collection of comments about me. "The impression created by the 'collection,' " Freeman wrote in 2006, "was that Novak was a controversial and deeply divisive figure within the community. The reality was that he was, after only WFB [William F. Buckley] himself, the most admired and influential conservative journalist in the country."

Frum continues to write regularly for *National Review Online,* while Freeman left the magazine's board when Buckley withdrew as the magazine's proprietor. My three decades of writing book reviews, articles, and even cover stories for *National Review* came to an abrupt, unannounced conclusion.

THE PARACHUTE JUMP was my most publicized venture into the realm of Walter Mitty, but not the most difficult. I spent three days, April 9–11, 2003, at the Sebring, Florida, International Speedway trying to learn to drive racing cars.

I always loved driving cars fast. To start my junior year in college, my father bought me a used '47 Mercury convertible, the first of eighteen convertibles I drove over a span of sixty years. In 1961, I bought a Corvette for $5,000 (about $34,000 in 2007 money), when my *Wall Street Journal* salary was $10,000 a year. The subsequent years were filled with fender benders and many, many speeding tickets. As an adult in Washington, my driver's license was suspended twice for exceeding the point limit for speeding, and I had to join sullen teenagers in driver's education class each time.

Although both my skills and my prudence as a driver were questionable, I long had fantasized about racing autos and once thought about driving my Corvette in amateur sport car races. But at age seventy-one thoughts of such competition were in the distant past when on July 18, 2002, Geraldine and I attended a black-tie spina bifida charity dinner at the Hyatt Regency Hotel in Washington sponsored by Al Hunt and Judy Woodruff. The fund-raiser was held in conjunction with the first annual D.C. Grand Prix that coming weekend with world-class Formula One drivers competing on a course around RFK Stadium. A preliminary event would match celebrity drivers, including the actor William Shatner. One item on the live auction was a guaranteed spot in the second annual D.C. Grand Prix celebrity race, preceded by instruction at Sebring. I got caught up in a bidding contest with another nut, and won the prize for five thousand dollars, as Geraldine looked on in exasperation.

Washington, D.C., being Washington, D.C., the second annual Grand Prix never took place because citizens living near RFK Stadium objected to the roar of racing engines. I said I still wanted to get something for my five grand and insisted on taking my driver's course even though now I would not be driving in a race.

At Sebring in April 2003, I was more than twenty-five years older than the next oldest student in the class of a dozen men and fifty-four years older than one of them. I also was, without argument, the worst driver in the class. I asked an instructor whether I was the worst driver he had ever taught. "No," he said, "William Shatner was worse."

But I improved. By the afternoon of the second day, all of us were driving solo on the raceway without an instructor in the second seat. To get through the three-and-one-half-mile Sebring raceway and its seventeen turns, I had to learn how to shift the six gears up and down. It was hard work just to drive one lap. In poor physical shape, I was exhausted at the end of the day after circling the track twenty times or more. Nobody could tell me race-car drivers were not athletes.

MAY 15, 2003, marked the fortieth anniversary of my column, an eternity for a column to endure. In four decades, I had collected enemies like barnacles and the conclusion of my May 15 column was a little defensive:

> [T]his column has been called, before and after Evans retired, red-baiter, Arabist, Communist China (and U.S. corporate) apologist, labor-baiter, homophobe, warmonger, isolationist—and most recently, unpatriotic conservative. All these are base canards, but they

reflect the tensions of our era. The truth is that in every 650-word column, we were reporters.

I had alerted the *Sun-Times* about the coming milestone, but nothing was laid on as the weeks went by. Finally, I was told publisher David Radler had such a busy schedule that he could not come to Washington to host a party until June 18. A reception and sit-down dinner at the Army and Navy Club did not compare with the gala twenty-fifth anniversary party at the Willard hosted by the *Sun-Times*'s previous publisher Bob Page. But it was a nice affair, well attended by the political and journalistic communities.

The party could have been held on the actual anniversary date of May 15, however, because David Radler did not show. Part of the lavish lifestyle enjoyed by Radler at the expense of the *Sun-Times* while gutting the paper's newsgathering capabilities was his private executive jet. Radler had a habit of delaying until the last minute before heading for the airport. He was told June 18 that bad weather was coming to Chicago and he ought to get an early start, but he delayed until it was too late. I did not miss him, and I don't think he was desperately unhappy to miss me.

Karl Rove was there, as he regularly accepted my invitations. He pinned on one of the large campaign-style buttons proclaiming "I'm a source not a target" that were distributed at the party and was photographed, wearing the button, with me. That produced a picture I am sure he would have preferred never to have been taken but was published repeatedly after the CIA leak story broke.

The speakers that evening mostly poked fun at me, and they included Fred Hiatt, one of the five editorial page editors of the *Washington Post* for whom I have written. But Fred made one serious remark. He revealed that when he took over the *Post*'s editorial page in 2000 at age forty-five, he wondered whether it was worth continuing to publish this old right-wing columnist. After reading the column more closely, Hiatt said, he found it was worthwhile because it was based on reporting and always contained something new. I thought it was just about the nicest professional compliment ever paid me. I soon would be entering a stage of my long career where compliments would be in short supply.

CHAPTER 44

The Plame Affair II

My "mission to Niger" column that ran Monday, July 14, 2003, caused no immediate stir. I had not considered the revelation of Valerie Plame Wilson's CIA connection to be a major story, and it attracted no special attention at first—except from a mild-mannered Joseph C. Wilson IV.

Wilson called me Monday morning, exhibiting none of the rage toward me he was to manifest over television and on the lecture circuit in coming years. Our Monday telephone conversation—my second and last with Wilson—was cordial. He said he was calling because he was puzzled that my column attributed my information to "two senior Administration officials" while he said I had indicated in my conversation with him the previous Thursday that I had a CIA source. I did not remember saying that, but I guessed it was possible. I said: "If I said that, I misspoke." It came out differently in Wilson's 2004 memoir, *The Politics of Truth,* which quoted me as saying: "I misspoke the first time we talked."

In the book, Wilson said "I had many questions for Novak," but he listed only one and he did not actually ask it: "What did the inclusion of Valerie's name add to his article?" Had he asked that question, I would have replied that it was incidental to divulging that she was a CIA employee who suggested his mission to Niger. In *The Politics of Truth,* he said he told me the reason for "my call [to Novak] was to question his sources." I can only assume he was interested in making sure the Bush administration and not the CIA was at fault before he began his attack, although he could hardly assume otherwise on the basis of reading my column.

Wilson's memoir does not mention the only other point he brought up in our brief Monday morning conversation. He told me his wife did not use her maiden name, so that I had made a mistake in referring to her as Valerie Plame. He did not ask where I got the name. If he had, I would have answered, truthfully, that he had given me the name via the entry he provided *Who's Who in America.*

Two days later, on Wednesday, July 16, I received a clearer indication of what was ahead when David Corn, Washington correspondent for *The Nation,* phoned. After Geraldine Ferraro left *Crossfire* in 1997 to run for the Senate and Bill Press was the remaining permanent left-wing host, Corn became Press's regular substitute. He was a fierce combatant who situated himself on the far left wing in keeping with *The Nation*'s ideology, but I enjoyed sparring with him and liked him better than many of my permanent *Crossfire* dueling mates.

Because I thought we had an amiable relationship, I was shaken by Corn's accusative opening of his call to me July 16: "What in the world were you thinking of when you outed a CIA agent?" He told me my column was an outrage that violated the Intelligence Identities Protection Act. I thought Corn's indignation strange, considering his and *The Nation*'s ideological orientation. The far Left never had been interested in protecting intelligence assets and had opposed the 1982 legislation enacted in response to leftists publicly identifying CIA secret agents. On Thursday, July 17, one day after Corn contacted me, he telephoned Wilson, according to Wilson's book, "to alert me [that] what Novak had done, or at least what the person who had leaked Valerie's name to him had done, was possibly a crime" because it violated the 1982 act.

Wilson surely was misrepresenting Corn in quoting him nearly a year later as suggesting I might have committed a crime. Writing in *The Nation* of August 4, Corn said of the federal law: "Journalists are mostly protected. Thus, Novak need not worry." Wilson's failure to make such a distinction contributed to years of demands, blogged on the Internet, that I be imprisoned without trial. Actually, anybody who had read the Intelligence Identities Protection Act should have known that my sources need not worry either. Many hurdles would have to be cleared for them to be liable, and this case failed on the lowest hurdle—the exposure of a covert agent. Valerie Wilson failed to meet the qualification that she had been assigned outside the United States during the previous five years.

Nevertheless, Corn in his column (just as he advised Wilson) speculated that senior government officials did "break the law in order to strike at a Bush Administration critic and intimidate others." Corn also began laying down the heavy rhetoric that was to be so much a part of this case: "The Wilson smear was a thuggish act, a sign that with this gang, politics trumps national security."

The only other journalist who contacted me soon after the column's publication was someone I did not know: Timothy M. Phelps, the Washington bureau chief of the Long Island newspaper *Newsday*. I had not been on the phone with him more than a few minutes before I realized Phelps was not a friendly questioner.

I was not sufficiently on my guard in talking either to Corn, whom I then thought of as a friendly acquaintance, or to Phelps, whom I regarded as a journalistic colleague. I made one regrettable comment to each that came back to haunt me. I told Corn: "I figured if they gave it to me, they'd give it to others." That was my blanket explanation over the years for printing leaked information, but it was inappropriate in this instance. Much worse was what I told Phelps, which he quoted in the twelfth paragraph of a seventeen-paragraph story in the July 22 issue of *Newsday:* "I didn't dig it out, it was given to me. They [the sources] thought it was significant, they gave me the name and I used it."

My *Newsday* quote was reprinted endlessly for years to come, as was Phelps's introductory statement to what I said: "Novak, in an interview, said his sources had come to him with the information." I said no such thing. As I have related in chapter one, nobody came to me with this information. I sought out the two administration sources as well as the CIA source. It was shoddy journalism on Phelps's part, a faulty interpretation of what I actually said that was inexcusable for a senior newspaper reporter.

The *New York Times* and the *Washington Post* ignored the story for the time being. Nobody in the nation's capital read *Newsday*. Hardly anybody paid any attention to *The Nation*. I thought I could forget about the column. Oh, if only that were true.

ON SATURDAY NIGHT, September 27, 2003, I returned home about eight twenty p.m. after the usual live hour-long broadcast of *Capital Gang* on CNN to find I had been called by *Washington Post* reporter Mike Allen, who covered the White House. When I returned the call, Allen told me the *Post* was running a story in Sunday's paper that the Justice Department was investigating the CIA leak contained in my column two and one-half months earlier.

Judging from what Allen used in his story, the only interest in questioning me was my conversation with the CIA's public affairs officer, Bill Harlow. Allen recorded faithfully (in the twenty-first paragraph of the long Sunday article) my explanation to him of why I did not grant a CIA request to refrain from mentioning Mrs. Wilson in my column, a request made to me at the end of a conversation with Harlow about the mission to Niger:

"They said it's doubtful she'll ever again have a foreign assignment," he [Novak] said. "They said if her name was printed, it might be difficult if she was traveling abroad, and they said they would prefer I didn't use her name. It was a very weak request. If it was put on a stronger basis, I would have considered it."

I arose at six a.m. Sunday, September 28, fearing the worst from the *Post* account. The fear was well-founded. The page one story by Mike Allen and Dana Priest, who covered the CIA, reported accurately the hard news of the Justice Department investigation. But the sensational material came in the form of quotes from somebody identified as "a senior Administration official":

> Yesterday, a senior Administration official said that before Novak's column ran, two top White House officials called at least six Washington journalists and disclosed the identity and occupation of Wilson's wife. . . .
>
> "Clearly, it was meant purely and simply for revenge," the senior official said of the alleged leak.
>
> Sources familiar with the conversations said the leakers were seeking to undercut Wilson's credibility. They alleged that Wilson, who was not a CIA employee, was selected for the Niger mission partly because his wife had recommended him. Wilson said in an interview yesterday that a reporter had told him that the leaker said, "The real issue is Wilson and his wife."
>
> A source said reporters quoted a leaker as describing Wilson's wife as "fair game." The official would not name the leakers for the record and would not name the journalists. . . .
>
> Asked about the motive describing the leaks, the senior official said the leaks were "wrong and a huge miscalculation, because they were irrelevant and did nothing to diminish Wilson's credibility."

A close reading made clear that this remarkable account hinges on a single anonymous source. That makes it a reckless piece of journalism that would never be confirmed in the years ahead. Instead, the amazing account of the leak being shopped to at least six journalists faded and then disappeared from future retellings of the story.

Preposterous as talk of six contacted journalists seemed, it paled in comparison to such a confession from a "senior" official in an administration that prided itself on tight-lipped loyalty. On Monday, I called one of my best Bush sources to ask for an explanation of these quotes. I half expected him to brush them off as imaginary, but he did not. Instead he named Adam Levine, a middle-level White House press aide who, he said, he was sure had said those things. He advised me Levine would be gone before long, and that prophecy proved accurate. I decided it was not prudent for me to launch a personal inquiry to confirm the identity of a confidential *Washington Post* source. I am using his name now only because he virtually revealed his role in *Hubris,* the 2006 book by Michael Isikoff and David Corn.

Levine, a former television journalist (who once worked for Chris Matthews), seemed out of place in the Bush White House. Appearing to be neither Republican nor conservative, he was much freer with information than his colleagues when I tried to use him as a source. But I found the tidbits he delivered were mostly irrelevant and self-serving, and I stopped contacting him.

In the *Post*'s follow-up story on Monday under a single byline, Allen quoted the source—who suddenly had become a mere administration "aide" without the "senior" adjective, accurately describing Levine—as saying "the two White House officials had cold-called at least six Washington journalists and identified Wilson's wife." Allen reported that "more specific details about the controversy emerged yesterday" in a Wilson telephone interview in which he said "four reporters from three television networks called him in July" and said White House officials had urged them to go public with his wife's identity. If these accounts were accurate, why did these multiple reporters never appear in the subsequent multimillion-dollar federal investigation that went to court to get testimony from a newspaper reporter who was sentenced to jail and from a magazine reporter who nearly was?

I have no interest in critiquing the work product of colleagues except as it affected me personally. But the Sunday and Monday accounts in the *Post* gave the impression that two White House aides were "cold-calling" reporters without success until they came to me. The truth, as related in chapter one, is that I initiated contact with my two sources.

The further damage done by the Allen-Priest story was contained in the account of the CIA request not to use Mrs. Wilson's name:

> When Novak told a CIA spokesman he was going to write a column about Wilson's wife, the spokesman urged him not to print her name "for security reasons," according to one CIA official. Intelligence officials said they believed Novak understood there were reasons other than Plame's personal security not to use her name, even though the CIA has declined to confirm she was undercover.

Not even thinly disguised, the source for this paragraph was clearly Bill Harlow. While I hate to use the l-word, it was a lie to say that "security reasons" were cited. But it was not immediately clear to me why Harlow would do this.

The clue to this puzzle was contained in Allen's Monday story that reported "CIA officials approached the Justice Department about a possible investigation within a week" of my column's publication on July 14. He did not note that such CIA leak reports to Justice number around fifty a year, or about one a week. The letter from Director of Central Intelligence (DCI) George Tenet formally asking Justice to launch the investigation, Allen wrote, "was delivered more recently." But why the delay?

Unexplored in Allen's story were the tensions at Langley. CIA officials, unhappy with President Bush and his policy, were demanding that Tenet take action. It seems obvious to me that Harlow wanted to get off the hook for letting me go with the story and consequently fabricated statements to me that he never made.

Finally, the Allen-Priest story contained this claim, obviously made by Dana Priest's CIA sources: "After the column ran, the CIA began a damage assessment of whether any foreign contacts Plame had made over the years could be in danger. The assessment continues, sources said." Only later did I learn that Mrs. Wilson had not been stationed abroad in over five years and had not been engaged in covert operations since she was outed by the Soviet agent and traitor Aldrich Ames. Claiming that my column necessitated a damage assessment, therefore, was disingenuous at best.

It was one thing to be attacked frontally by Joe Wilson and sniped at in *The Nation* and *Newsday*. It was much more serious to be misrepresented in the *Washington Post*, the paper to which I owed so much. Those misrepresentations became the perceived truth about me.

AFTER READING Mike Allen's follow-up story on Monday, September 29, I called my attorney, Les Hyman. He told me that I needed representation from his partner in the Swidler Berlin law firm, James Hamilton. I had never met Hamilton, but he was known to me as a Clinton lawyer and prominent backstage figure in national Democratic politics. Hamilton advised me to be quiet and ignore news media calls. I said I would shut up after writing a column and making some obligatory television appearances.

On Tuesday, I began that column by saying "I had thought I never again would write" about Joseph Wilson's wife. But I protested that "my role and the role of the Bush White House have been distorted and need explanation." I proceeded to explain:

To protect my own integrity and credibility, I would like to stress three points. First, I did not receive a planned leak. Second, the CIA never warned me that the disclosure of Wilson's wife working at the Agency would endanger her or anybody else. Third, it was not much of a secret.

The current Justice investigation stems from a routine, mandated probe of all CIA leaks, but it follows weeks of agitation. Wilson, after telling me in July that he would say nothing about his wife, has made his investigation of the leak his life's work.

Valerie Wilson's identity, I continued, was given to me in an "offhand revelation" by a senior official "who is no partisan gunslinger." I noted that the conservative commentator Clifford May, writing in *National Review Online,* said he had been told of Mrs. Wilson's CIA identity by a non-government official and added that it was common knowledge. I also quoted an unofficial CIA source as saying she was an analyst and not in covert operations. "I regret," I wrote, "that I referred to her in my column as an 'operative,' a word I have lavished on hack politicians for more than 40 years." I regretted it because it gave the false impression that she was working as an undercover agent, which she was not.

My first TV appearance of the week was on Monday's *Crossfire,* where I said: "I have been beleaguered by television networks around the world, but I am reserving my say for 'Crossfire.'" After I delivered an abbreviated version of my column, liberal co-host Paul Begala claimed "a serious crime" had been committed by my leaker and expressed hope that "that person does a long stretch in a federal prison." Begala was an unabashed Democratic partisan and he signaled a line of attack that would be repeated relentlessly.

I had hoped my comments on *Crossfire* would satisfy my CNN obligations, but I was told I also must be interviewed by Wolf Blitzer on his nightly program. Wolf first came to my attention as longtime (1973–89) Washington correspondent for the *Jerusalem Post* only because he was one of many younger journalists befriended by Rowly Evans. He was occasionally used on CNN as an expert on the Mideast, and was hired by CNN as Pentagon correspondent in 1990. His prominence in covering the 1991 Gulf War propelled him upward at the network. When Wolf came aboard at CNN, I learned that we were brothers in the Jewish fraternity Alpha Epsilon Pi (he at the State University of New York, Buffalo). We each addressed AEPi's national convention in Washington one year, and we occasionally exchanged the fraternity's secret handshake.

Blitzer was a soft interviewer who seldom pressed on-air guests. Given that background and our personal relationship, I was surprised to hear Blitzer on Monday voice the canard that the White House had shopped the Valerie Plame story around to six journalists before finding one who would swallow it—me. But I assumed Wolf had just been reading what some harassed CNN staffer had put together hurriedly.

Blitzer on Tuesday evening launched an interrogation of me that was far more confrontational than his handling of big-time politicians. Blitzer took off on my statement that the CIA had informed me that Mrs. Wilson never would have another foreign assignment.

> Blitzer: The notion . . . that she would never be able to have a foreign assignment—shouldn't that alone have been enough to give you pause?
>
> Novak: Oh, no. Let's read what I said, Wolf. That's not what I said.
>
> Blitzer: This is in today's column.
>
> Novak: Yes. Read what *I* said.
>
> Blitzer: "He asked me not to use her name saying she probably never again will be given a foreign assignment."
>
> Novak: Yes . . . whether I wrote anything or not, he said she would never be given a foreign assignment. That was a fact that she had moved on to a different phase of her career. It was not because of anything I was writing.

Wolf moved on to the much-quoted *Newsday* account on July 22:

> Blitzer: The [*Newsday*] reporters said this: "Novak, in an interview, said his sources had come to him with the information."
>
> Novak: Now, these reporters made a bad mistake. They said they came to me with the information. I never told them that. And that's not in quotes, is it?
>
> Blitzer: That's not in quotes.
>
> Novak: So, then, they made that up. . . . You have to be very careful, Wolf, because . . . they're saying they came to me. They did *not* come to me. There are people putting out stories that the White House was trying to find a pawn to put out this information. They went through six people—
>
> Blitzer: —to smear Joe Wilson.
>
> Novak: And finally came to me. That's not true. As I have told you in detail . . . nobody came to me.

Blitzer: Other reporters are suggesting that they got these calls, and they didn't do anything.

Novak: I don't know if they did or not. But . . . I resented it when you said the other day, I really resented it, when you said they went to six people and finally found Novak. That's just not the truth. Nobody came to me with this story. I was reporting on Joe Wilson.

Blitzer: That was your initiative?

Novak: Entirely.

Wolf had one more dart for me.

Blitzer: Had you known that this information, releasing the name, could have endangered her and her colleagues, you would never have reported this?

Novak: *Had* I known. You're saying it *would* have endangered her and her colleagues. I still don't know that to this day. I will tell you this. If a CIA official said, "You are endangering the life of Mrs. Wilson and her colleagues," I never would have printed it.

I concluded by saying "the idea that this was some kind of carefully arranged plot to destroy this woman and her husband, as far as I am concerned, was nonsense." I left the set furious at my colleague and fraternity brother but did not continue the debate off-camera. I had been alerted to the kind of treatment I would receive on the network where I had become a trademark and had worked for a quarter century.

Of the dozens of interview requests that week, I had one in addition to Wolf Blitzer's that I felt obliged to accept. It was from Tim Russert on that Sunday's *Meet the Press*. I had been a semiregular on the NBC program for nearly forty years, and Tim as producer-moderator had even increased the frequency of my appearances. I felt I owed it to him.

Russert informed me in advance that I would be preceded on the program by Joseph C. Wilson IV. When Wilson had appeared on *Meet the Press* on July 6 and triggered my fateful column of July 14, he was blessed with a softball interview by NBC's Andrea Mitchell. On October 5 Wilson found that Tim Russert was no Andrea Mitchell. Russert's tough style was based not on spewing harsh rhetoric but on marshaling devastating facts. He read in full a statement by DCI George Tenet. Contrary to the impression given by Wilson, Tenet said that he never had sanctioned the mission to Niger and that the resulting oral report by Wilson was inconclusive. Wilson danced, responding in bureaucratese: "He [Tenet] would not have approved of it. This is the sort of thing that would have gone from a briefer down to the operational level. The decision would have been taken at the operational level. The results would have been reported back. . . . It never promised to be the definitive report."

Wilson faced a tougher question when Russert played the videotape of an August 21 speech by Wilson in the state of Washington:

> Well, I don't think we're going to let this drop. At the end of the day, it's of keen interest to me to see whether or not we can get Karl Rove frog-marched out of the White House in handcuffs. And trust me. When I use that name, I measure my words.

Under pressure from Russert, Wilson backtracked quickly on his accusation of Rove: "I don't know if he leaked it. I don't know if he authorized it." But, he said, "I have every confidence" that Rove pushed the story ("gave it legs") after the Novak column ran.

Russert next turned to the political orientation of Wilson, who had been claiming he was a nonpolitical former diplomat until Bush drove him into the arms of the Democrats.

My lawyers had urged me to stop writing about Joe and Valerie, but I could not resist following up a tip from a friendly Republican lawyer who regarded Wilson as a fraud. I was advised to take a good look at the Federal Election Commission (FEC) records of Mrs. Wilson's contributions in the 2000 election. The contributions of Joe had been widely scrutinized, but Valerie's had been ignored. I examined them and got a lead item for my Sunday column (available for Washington readers in the *New York Post*):

> On the same day in 1999 that retired diplomat Joseph Wilson returned $1,000 he contributed to Democratic presidential [candidate] Al Gore a month earlier because it exceeded the federal limit, his CIA-employee wife gave $1,000 to Gore using a fictitious identification for herself.

"Valerie E. Wilson" identified herself in the federal report as an "analyst" with "Brewster-Jennings & Associates." There was no Brewster-Jennings & Associates, and there never had been. Brewster Jennings was a famous oil tycoon of the previous generation who had died in 1968. He never had a firm in his own name but was president of Socony-Vacuum. Brewster-Jennings & Associates was no dummy corporation to shield Mrs. Wilson as a covert agent because she was not involved in clandestine activities. Instead, each day she went to CIA headquarters in Langley where she worked on arms proliferation. Some wag had given her the bogus Brewster-Jennings's corporate name.

The thousand-dollar contribution in Valerie's name, intended to cover Joe's illegally excessive contribution, was made on April 22, 1999. That made a lie of Wilson's assertion in *The Politics of Truth* that his Gore contribution was made after he claimed to be disgusted with Bush's tactics in the 2000 South Carolina primary campaign. In my October 5, 2003, column item, I did not mention (because I then did not know) that Wilson not only gave Gore money but also joined his foreign policy advisory group.

Given this background, Wilson's answers to Russert's questions were disingenuous. Asked whether he considered himself a Democrat, he said: "I certainly do now." Asked whether he would work to defeat Bush for reelection, he replied, "Yes, I certainly will" because his administration was "the antithesis of everything he campaigned on in the run-up to the first election." That glossed over the fact that he had worked against Bush in that first election, was employed by the Clinton administration, and for years had contributed mostly to Democratic candidates.

Wilson's last lie on the program was that a publisher had sought him out to write his memoir. In the fact-filled little item about Wilson in my column that Sunday morning, I reported: "In July, when he revealed himself an author of a report commissioned by the CIA, Wilson sought a book agent. After being turned down by a prominent agent, he has now found one." Contrary to what Wilson said in his book, my source was the prominent agent.

Russert's interview of me necessarily went over much the same ground as Blitzer had five days earlier. But Tim, known for searing interrogation, was far more civil in questioning an old colleague than Wolf. I thought the *Meet the Press* interview generated less heat but more light in getting my side of the story.

ON THE MORNING of Wednesday, October 1, the day my second Valerie Wilson column was published, the CIA leak case was leading the nation's newspapers and network news programs. I was walking in downtown Washington when my cell phone rang with one of the most peculiar calls I received in a half century in journalism.

The caller was lobbyist and former White House chief of staff Ken Duberstein, who happened to be on the street in New York and called my office from his cell phone (which was patched through to my cell). I name him because the incident was reported by Isikoff and Corn in *Hubris*. Duberstein was a political adviser to Richard Armitage and indicated he was calling me on the deputy secretary of state's behalf. Since we both were on cell phones, he did not mention Armitage by name but referred to him in a cryptic way that he knew I would decipher.

He said Armitage "wondered whether he had inadvertently given me some information" in the CIA leak case and that he wanted to check with me to see whether that indeed was the case. Armitage had a mind like a steel trap, and it was inconceivable that he would not have remembered what he told me. I surmised that Duberstein's use of the word "inadvertently" was to reinforce with me what I had said on CNN that week: that this was not a planned disclosure by the Bush administration. I figured Duberstein's question did not demand an answer, and I replied that my lawyers had told me to keep quiet about the case.

Next Duberstein told me Armitage was considering resigning from the government because of what he had divulged to me. "Oh, I wouldn't do that," I blurted out. Whether he kept his government post or not was none of my business, but I reacted reflexively against unintentionally forcing him out of office. It occurred to me only later that Armitage did not consider resigning after Valerie's name appeared in my column—only after the CIA referred the case to the Justice Department for investigation. His later statement, that he did not really think he was the source until I identified him on October 1 as "no partisan gunslinger," defies belief.

It was two and one-half years before it was revealed that Armitage, soon after Duberstein's conversation with me, identified himself to the Justice Department but apparently not to the White House and certainly not to the public. He did not resign.

A FEW DAYS after my conversation with Duberstein, I sat in the large, elegant conference room of the Swidler Berlin law firm at the Washington Harbour, overlooking the Potomac River on the edge of Georgetown. Seated across the huge table from me were my old lawyer Les Hyman, my new lawyer Jim Hamilton, and their young associate Kevin Amer, who was taking notes.

This case would cost me more than $160,000 in legal fees, a larger drain on my bank account than any previous legal representation. I realized I could not count on much help from the *Chicago Sun-Times* with F. David Radler as publisher grasping the purse strings (though John Cruickshank, who succeeded the disgraced Radler, generously paid for $30,000 of my legal bills).

Les Hyman had been my attorney for three decades and was a personal friend. Jim Hamilton's words of advice were valued by his clients—including the Democratic Party. Hamilton had led the vice presidential searches for candidates Bill Clinton and Al Gore, and he had vetted judicial nominees in the Clinton administration. He had kept out of the headlines while representing famous Democrats, and he would keep out of the headlines representing a right-wing columnist.

Shortly after it became known that the CIA had sent the case to the Justice Department, the FBI requested an interview with me. Hamilton suggested I comply with the request but not publicly disclose my compliance. That differed from advice given to reporters by *New York Times* and *Time* lawyers that ended in protracted legal proceedings and one jail sentence. Hamilton told me I had no legal grounds for noncooperation so that resistance in the courts probably would fail while financially devastating me. I told Jim I would not reveal my sources under any conditions. Hamilton said he understood that and advised me to keep their identity secret from him and his associates.

At two thirty p.m. on Tuesday, October 7, 2003, I was seated in the Swidler Berlin conference room for my first government interrogation about the case. My lawyers were at my side and across the table was FBI Inspector Jack Eckenrode, accompanied by two agents. Eckenrode was friendly, informing me that we occasionally attended mass together at St. Patrick's Catholic Church in downtown Washington.

Eckenrode's two-hour interrogation was thorough but polite and less inquisitorial than Wolf Blitzer or even Tim Russert had been. I said I would not give up the names of my sources, and the inspector did not press me for them. I did not realize that Eckenrode already had been told by Armitage that he was the source.

To THE STREAM of reporters asking to interview me, I declined even to get on the phone (pleading advice of counsel). Being journalists, most wrote about me anyway.

One would-be interviewer I brushed off was a *Baltimore Sun* reporter I had never met named David Folkenflik. He rushed out a long piece about me in the October 3, 2003, *Sun* with a lead paragraph packing a lot of misinformation into a small space: "In the privacy of his Pennsylvania Avenue penthouse, Robert D. Novak must be loving this." Our apartment, on the tenth floor of a thirteen-story building, was not a penthouse. Since this reporter had never exchanged a word with me, he had no idea whether I was "loving this." In fact, I hated the whole mess. Folkenflik's long piece was typical of what was being written about me by journalistic colleagues. He repeated the stupid quote I had given to *Newsday* instead of using a complete and cogent explanation from me that I made that week in my column and on television.

But the *Baltimore Sun* article represented a pretense of balance by mainstream journalism. The new element in communications was blogging on the Internet, and the attacks on me there knew no restraint. I was daily accused of treason and denounced in the most obscene terms, with personal threats against me and my family—even my grandchildren. Thousands of e-mails were far worse than the negative letters I used to receive. This is a typical example:

> You are the worst kind of traitor. I hope your children get cancer and die on your birthday, you faggot. It would be even better if you became depressed and killed yourself on your birthday. Do the country a favor and get in a fucking horrible accident or something. Just make sure everyone related to you is involved. Remember, God hates fags!

I think Joe Wilson was primarily responsible for encouraging this torrent of abuse. In his 2004 memoir, Wilson wrote of me: "To this day, I ask myself how his colleagues continue to tolerate him in their presence. Around Washington his critics call him Bob 'No Fact' for his sloppy tabloid-gossip articles that often stray far from the truth. Having long since prostituted himself to the Right as its uncritical shill, he offers little original thought." On the lecture circuit, Wilson lost all dignity in publicly using the vulgar epithet that I had applied to him in private. Most of this did not get published, but a student reporter recorded Wilson in a 2004 lecture at Northeastern University in Boston calling me an "asshole" and talking about throwing me out a second-story window.

THE BROTHERS AND sisters of the journalism fraternity normally band together when one of their own is hounded by the government demanding disclosure of sources. But not in my case. In the *Wall Street Journal*, editorial writer William McGurn bemoaned the lack of support by fellow journalists for my protection of sources. The reason was that in this case my sources were officials in the hated Bush administration who had given me information concerning a vocal critic of that administration. The blood of ideological solidarity was stronger than the water of journalistic togetherness.

The rationale for my fellow journalists abandoning me was contained in a February 6, 2004, op-ed in the *New York Times* by Geneva Overholser, a liberal high priestess of journalism. She was a former member of the *New*

York Times editorial board, former editor of the *Des Moines Register,* and former ombudsman of the *Washington Post.* Now a professor at the University of Missouri School of Journalism, she took upon herself the task of explaining why the admonition "never burn a source" (which she called "a cardinal rule of journalism") did not apply to Robert Novak.

My column about Wilson's mission to Niger, she wrote, had "turned a time-honored use of confidentiality—protecting a whistleblower from government retribution—on its head, delivering government retribution to the whistleblower instead." She had swallowed whole Joe Wilson's dubious claim to being a whistleblower. Alleging "ethical lapses" on my part, she declared "journalists should call upon Mr. Novak to acknowledge his abuse of confidentiality and reveal his sources himself."

I met Overholser for the first time a year after her op-ed piece. It was about eleven thirty p.m. on Saturday, March 12, 2005, at the Capitol Hilton, shortly after the annual white-tie dinner of the Gridiron Club had ended, as after-dinner drinking began. I was having a drink at the Hearst reception when a woman approached at a rapid pace. She had the crazed look with which I had become familiar in encountering cranks angry with me.

"I am Geneva Overholser," she said without offering her hand. "Oh," I said, "you're the famous Geneva Overholser who's been writing all these nasty things about me." I was trying to lighten up the encounter in the breezy Washington style that can take the menace out of confrontations between antagonists, but Overholser was having none of it. Her eyes blazing, she said: "I don't see how you can stand to see yourself in the mirror in the morning. You're a disgrace to journalism." I thought of something to say that she would resent. Her husband, a Washington newspaper bureau chief, had just been admitted into the Gridiron Club. "Geneva," I said, "I don't think your husband would approve of you talking that way to a fellow Gridironer." Hardly anything could better antagonize a liberated woman. "That's just the kind of thing you would say," she said, then stalked off.

Journalists of Overholser's stripe despised me for being a conservative. Support or opposition for me in the CIA leak case usually was a function of ideology. Conservatives, in and out of journalism, tended to back me up. But there were exceptions, including one notable one.

Shortly after the case exploded the first week of October 2003, I was in my office with C-SPAN turned on. An interview with Bill Kristol caught my attention when he was asked what he thought about my role in the CIA leak case. "Well," Kristol said, "Novak is a friend—[pause]—an acquaintance." An *acquaintance*? I could see Bill's agile mind working a mile a minute, first calling me a friend and quickly deciding he better downgrade our relationship of seventeen years standing. We not only had been social friends, but he had been a super-source for me before he became a full-time journalist as editor of the *Weekly Standard*. Hardly a week had gone by that I had not talked at length to Bill. But after I called him on March 17, 2003, to ask what he thought of David Frum's attack on me in the *National Review* and he never called back as promised, we did not speak to each other.

Now, in Kristol's interview on C-SPAN, I could hardly believe what I heard. Kristol called my conduct in the CIA leak case "reprehensible." He was the first conservative I know of to align himself with Joe Wilson, who took note of it. In *The Politics of Truth*, Wilson wrote: "Americans of all political professions, from William Kristol to Hillary Clinton, have expressed their outrage at what has happened to me and proffered their support." I would think Bill would feel uncomfortable twinned with Hillary as Joe Wilson's bedfellow. He was the sole conservative supporter cited in Wilson's 496-page memoir, which lavished praise on the left-wing antiwar Moveon.org and even used two pages of the book to publish its "open letter" to President Bush opposing the appropriations bill to finance the war. Kristol was a neoconservative leader advocating a war policy that Wilson abhorred and denounced.

Why did Kristol align himself with Wilson against me? I cannot say for sure, because Bill and I no longer discussed this or anything else. But I believe it had nothing to do with Joe and Valerie Wilson. Kristol echoed the extreme neoconservative position of Norman Podhoretz that found my position on the Middle East intolerable. For Bill, that trumped considerations of longtime friendship.

UNTIL DECEMBER 30, 2003, I had harbored hopes the CIA leak case could be settled expeditiously. My friend, Republican lawyer Victoria Toensing, privately in conversations with me and publicly in op-ed articles, made a convincing argument that nobody in this case had violated the Intelligence Identities Protection Act. As chief counsel of the Senate Intelligence Committee in 1982, Toensing helped draft the legislation that was enacted in the wake of the potentially fatal outing by leftist activists of America's secret agents.

Consequently, the way was open for Rich Armitage to identify himself as my source without fear of self-incrimination as a criminal defendant. What I did not know is that he already had identified himself to the Justice Department. My hopes for a judicious but relatively speedy settlement were dashed on December 30 when Attorney General John Ashcroft recused himself in what he called "an abundance of caution." He handed the case to

Deputy Attorney General James Comey, who in turn named as special counsel Patrick Fitzgerald, the U.S. attorney in Chicago. Unlike most federal district attorneys, Fitzgerald was a nonpolitical career prosecutor (a New Yorker) put in the Chicago post by the maverick Republican one-term senator Peter Fitzgerald (no relation). Pat Fitzgerald was politically untouchable, a modern Elliott Ness. People familiar with him told me to count on an investigation that was fair, thorough, and very long. For better or for worse, President Bush had lost control of how the case would be handled.

Fitzgerald immediately notified my attorneys that he wanted to interview me personally. He had a new twist that was worrisome for me and all other journalists involved. Fitzgerald had collected waivers, intended to relieve journalists of confidentiality restraints, signed by every Bush administration senior official who might have leaked information about Valerie Wilson. I did not consider that these blanket waivers relieved me from my vows of confidentiality (and neither did other journalists).

I faced a dilemma. Recent court decisions had indicated no inclination by the federal judiciary to recognize journalistic immunity. Jim Hamilton told me that carrying the case all the way to the Supreme Court would be expensive, futile, and damaging to press freedoms by strengthening case law against the reporter's privilege. On the other hand, I felt I could not give up the names of sources under any conditions. I had declared vaingloriously on national TV that such a surrender would mean the end of my reporter's career.

An appointment was set for Fitzgerald to come into the Swidler Berlin law offices to interview me on Wednesday, January 14, 2004. Fitzgerald wanted me to keep quiet about this and so did Hamilton. Nobody knew about my talking to the FBI back in October, and now nobody would know about my talking to the special prosecutor.

I met with Jim Hamilton and his young associate, Kevin Amer, at Swidler Berlin at one thirty p.m., January 12. Hamilton had news that changed everything. Although the special counsel had obtained confidentiality waivers from just about every administration official who could possibly have been my source, Fitzgerald told Hamilton he would be coming to his office with waivers signed by only two officials: Richard Armitage and Karl Rove.

What Hamilton told me constituted a shock too severe for a seventy-one-year-old man. I tried to stay calm as I said to my lawyers: "They have succeeded in identifying my sources."

I agreed with Hamilton that I had no choice other than cooperating with Fitzgerald when I faced him two days hence. I would name Armitage and Rove since Fitzgerald already knew them. But I told Hamilton I would not go into all details of my conversation with Armitage or my confidential interviews with other sources.

Pat Fitzgerald, accompanied by lawyers and the FBI team, entered the Swidler Berlin conference room at ten a.m. He was polite, and the interview was businesslike. Fitzgerald arrived not with just two waivers, but a third one. It was signed by the CIA's Bill Harlow (who subsequently would give other reporters an account of his conversation with me, relieving me from any restrictions on public disclosure).

Two hours of questioning by Fitzgerald covered the same territory as my FBI interrogation. The big difference was that now I was mentioning real names as my three sources. I drew the line at questions that delved into details of confidential discussions with the sources that did not directly concern the CIA leak. The special prosecutor did not press me to cross that line.

A month later I was subpoenaed to testify before the grand jury impaneled for this case. I dreaded this experience because of the many years that I had observed grand juries, with witnesses running a gauntlet of reporters, photographers, and TV cameramen on their way to and from the closed-door grand jury chamber. But Hamilton told me Fitzgerald assured him that he would protect my privacy. Jim thought that was a benefit in repayment for our being cooperative with the prosecutor.

Early on the afternoon of February 25, 2004, I drove to 3000 K Street (the Washington Harbour complex) and took the elevator to Suite 300, the Swidler Berlin law firm. At one thirty p.m. I entered an FBI sedan containing Inspector Eckenrode to be driven twenty blocks to the federal courthouse in downtown Washington, a couple of blocks from my apartment. The car entered a garage in the courthouse and I was hurried into a private elevator to be taken to a sequestered section of the courthouse that was journalist-free.

I was disappointed when I entered the inner sanctum of the grand jury. It was not nearly as nice as the building's trial courtrooms, where I had been several times as a journalist and once as a libel suit defendant. It looked like a shabby classroom, with grand jurors sprawled in their seats. Most seemed dressed for a day off at home, instead of a federal judicial proceeding. A couple were dozing, and many did not seem to be paying attention.

I wanted to read to the grand jury a statement I had written explaining why I, as a journalist, was before them disclosing confidential sources. Hamilton obtained Fitzgerald's permission. My statement—read after I took the oath—started by saying how uncomfortable I was being there. I explained that the special counsel already had discovered the identity of my sources, and it was pointless to pursue what my attorney had predicted would be a losing trip to the Supreme Court. The questioning, mostly by Fitzgerald, retraced my previous testimony in the law offices. It was not hard, because I told the truth as I remembered it. I mentioned in passing that the next day, February 26, would be my seventy-third birthday. When after two hours I finished testifying, the grand jury foreman wished me a happy birthday, and several grand jurors followed suit. It was nice to experience a little civility in a place where my very presence was a dark secret.

The federal courthouse in Washington is normally a wind tunnel of gossip and rumors, blowing straight onto the printed page and the TV screen. But not this time. Nobody knew that I even talked to the FBI, much less that I was cooperating and testifying before the grand jury. Pat Fitzgerald ran an extraordinarily tight ship (in contrast to leaky Independent Counsel offices I had covered over many years), Jim Hamilton was the tightest-lipped lawyer I ever saw, and I was not talking.

As months passed without leaks, Novak-bashers were enraged and expressed that rage on the Internet and in newspaper columns (including Bill Safire's) across the country. Why was Novak not subpoenaed? Was Novak being given special treatment? Why was Novak getting off so easy? Journalists speculated in print or on the air that the prosecutors had decided to leave me alone or that I was taking the Fifth Amendment or that I had negotiated a plea bargain with Fitzgerald.

AFTER MY GRAND jury testimony, I rushed to the Capitol Hilton Hotel for that evening's rehearsal of the Gridiron Club show for March 6. I had the juiciest part during twenty-six years in the club.

I loved showing off in gaudily costumed Gridiron skits. I could not sing or dance, I had neither the talent nor patience for writing parodies (I wrote but three all these years, and only one made the show) and I never helped produce a skit. But I had a loud speaking voice, and I was a big ham. Mostly, I was valuable as one of the club's most recognizable members, thanks to television. The celebrity-studded audience would cheer when I suddenly appeared onstage dressed as Jesse Jackson, John McCain, a gorilla, or in drag (though Geraldine objected to my caveman's costume in one of my first shows that exposed one breast. "No more nipples!" my wife told me.).

My 2004 Gridiron assignment was not only my biggest ever, but I was permitted to actually *sing,* not merely talk the song's words as the producers made me do the last time I was given a singing role. I was to come onstage dressed in formal afternoon wear, including gray gloves and top hat. That was the Gridiron's burlesque notion of a diplomat—Joseph C. Wilson IV being portrayed by Robert D. Novak.

To the strains of "Once I Had a Secret Love," I sang:

> *Novak had a secret source,*
> *Who lived within the great White House.*
> *And one day his secret source*
> *Told him about my darling spouse.*
> *So, he outed a girl spy*
> *The way Princes of Darkness do.*
> *Cross the right wing you may try.*
> *Bob Novak's coming after you.*
> *Now John Ashcroft's asking who and how,*
> *Could be headed for the old hoosegow.*
> *And now his game is hem and haw.*
> *'Cause Bob Novak's source is hiding from the law.*

When the audience at each of the three presentations—the Friday afternoon dress rehearsal, the Saturday night dinner, and the Sunday night reprise—realized it was I playing Joe Wilson, there were audible gasps (mixed with hissing Sunday night, which usually was the most liberal audience). I am sure many people who to my face congratulated me on my nerve muttered behind my back that the old boy had taken leave of his senses. My lawyers were not happy. Why did I do it? Because I could not give up what might be my last such theatrical opportunity. More seriously, I delighted in showing my contempt for a trivial incident that had been exaggerated into a scandal by the Left and its outriders in the news media.

MY SATIRICAL SONG at the Gridiron dinner, contrary to an AP report, did not constitute "comment" about the CIA leak. Following advice of my lawyers, I had written and said nothing about the case since October 2003. But in July 2004, I broke that silence of eight and one-half months because of two intertwined events. The first was a report by the Senate Intelligence Committee that effectively demolished the fabric of Joseph Wilson's lies. The second was inattention to this report by the news media.

Senator Pat Roberts, an ex-marine officer from Dodge City, Kansas, was an old-fashioned midwestern Republican who had become the Intelligence Committee chairman. I occasionally talked to him and in 2003 asked what he knew about Wilson's mission to Niger. I assumed he was just putting me off when he told me his Intelligence Committee was working on the case. I found how wrong I was the first week of July when Roberts's committee released a report it had been preparing for a year.

The report demolished the insistence by Wilson, the CIA's Harlow, and Democrats in Congress that Armitage was wrong when he told me that Wilson's CIA-employee wife had inspired his mission to Niger. The report said: "Interviews and documents provided to the Committee indicate that his wife, a CPD [CIA Counter Proliferation Division] employee suggested his name for the trip." The report also revealed that Plame wrote an internal CIA memo saying: "My husband has good relations with both the PM [prime minister] and the former Minister of Mines [of Niger] (not to mention lots of French contacts), both of whom could possibly shed light on this sort of activity." The report quoted a State Department analyst as telling the Intelligence Committee that an interagency meeting in 2002 was "apparently convened by [Wilson's] wife who had the idea to dispatch [him] to use his contacts to sort out the Iraq-Niger issue."

Thus, the Roberts committee's documentary and oral evidence proved that Wilson's wife had suggested his mission to Niger. The committee's Democratic minority did not challenge any of the evidence, though it abstained on the Republican majority's conclusions.

The report concluded that the burden of Wilson's claims "had no basis in fact." I thought Pat Roberts had put a dagger through Joe Wilson's heart, but the Intelligence Committee report received little attention in the news media—almost no page-one play in major newspapers and nothing on television, including the cable networks that had highlighted Wilson's every utterance. I felt constrained to break my silence and write about the Roberts report in my column of July 15, 2004, "because it has received scant coverage except in the Washington Post, Knight-Ridder newspapers, the New York Times (briefly and belatedly) and a few other media outlets."

At the time the Intelligence Committee report was released just before the Fourth of July holiday, Wilson appeared to have transformed himself from an obscure former diplomat into a national celebrity and a left-wing cause célèbre. He was much in evidence on Senator John Kerry's presidential campaign. As Kerry clinched the nomination, I am sure Wilson anticipated addressing the Democratic National Convention in Boston.

Pat Roberts's report deflated Wilson, even if it did not wind up on newspaper front pages or network television news. Wilson disappeared from the Kerry campaign and was nowhere to be seen at the Democratic convention late in July. He was confined for the time being to far-left precincts of cable TV, blogs, and the lecture circuit. However, I assumed that did not end my problems, and I was right.

CHAPTER 45

Farewell to CNN

B Y LATE 2003, the hottest prospect to become George W. Bush's
Democratic challenger was Dr. Howard Dean, the former governor of Vermont who became the first presidential candidate to harness the Internet
for agit-prop, fund-raising, and organizing. I wrote column after column
exposing Dean's radical, erratic foibles and wondering how the world's oldest political party could walk off the cliff with him.

As I arrived at the Des Moines airport on January 7, I ran into one of the
nation's best political reporters who had spent weeks in the state. "Dean's
got Iowa locked up," he said. "It looks like he's got the nomination locked
up, too, doesn't it?" I shrugged, saying I really had not yet been on the
ground in Iowa. What I didn't say was that my instinct told me that Dean
had peaked and was on his way down. Instinct sometimes trumps shoe-
leather reporting.

Beyond instinct, I had the advice of Bob Shrum, the Kerry campaign's
strategist. Bob said reporters were underestimating Kerry and I should give
him a close look. I was no more entranced than I had been when I first met
Kerry thirty years earlier as a radical Vietnam Veteran Against the War. His
greatest asset now was that he could appeal to liberal voters growing disenchanted with Dean. Kerry won Iowa with Dean third, and roared into New
Hampshire to win there and sweep nearly all the other primaries.

ON MAY 8, 2004, I received my third honorary degree: doctor of hu-
mane letters, from the University of St. Francis in Joliet, Illinois. My previous two honorary doctorates were from Kenyon College in 1987 and the
University of Illinois in 1998. I was too much of a right-winger for most of
America's institutions. Those that did honor me had a special connection.

Both of our children graduated from Kenyon as political science majors,
and I had attended public affairs seminars at the Ohio college dating back

thirty years. Zelda received her degree on the same day I was honored. The *Mount Vernon* [Ohio] *News* published a photo showing me, a smiling, applauding father in academic robes as his daughter crossed the stage, diploma in hand. Zelda later said it was just like me to horn in on her big moment.

St. Francis was honoring a hometown Joliet boy who was a Catholic convert. I began my commencement address by noting that long ago whenever I passed the then all-women's College of St. Francis, I "always took a good look at it. For a young Jewish boy, it was a place of mystery. I wondered: What went on with those Catholic girls?" That generated nervous twitters from the assembled clergy. Then I got serious:

> I encountered considerable criticism when I delivered the commencement address at my alma mater, the University of Illinois a few years ago. I offered this advice to the graduates then, which I now repeat to you: *Always love your country—but never trust your government!*
>
> That should not be misunderstood. I certainly am not advocating civil disobedience, much less insurrection or rebellion. What I *am* advocating is to not expect too much from government and be wary of its power, even the power of a democratic government in a free country.
>
> Ours is one of the mildest, most benevolent governments in the world. But it too has the power to take your wealth and forfeit your life. So, follow the teaching of St. Francis in being generous as a private citizen but be wary of the power of government. A government that can give you everything can take everything away.

The first time I advised young people to love their country but not trust their government was in 1995 at a Bullis School graduation in Potomac, Maryland, where I was the board of trustees vice president. After the ceremony when I was taking off my academic robe, a grim harridan approached me, identified herself as a George Washington University faculty member, and told me that comments such as mine had just led to the Oklahoma City bombing.

Three years later, I came in for criticism by employing the same formulation at the University of Illinois commencement. Because the 17,456 seating capacity of Assembly Hall was not large enough for all the graduates and guests, I had to deliver my address to two commencement ceremonies. The first group, mainly students from the College of Liberal Arts and Sciences, reacted tepidly to my advice. The second group, from the Commerce and Engineering schools, cheered lustily.

Six years later at St Francis, I again delivered my commencement address twice, in a much smaller auditorium—first to graduate students and then to undergraduates. The graduate students received my injunction in deadly silence. The undergrads cheered and clapped. I hoped that did not mean that too much education was to be avoided.

The Thomas More College of Liberal Arts, a small conservative school in Merrimack, New Hampshire, scheduled me for a commencement speech and honorary degree in May 2006. I tried to speak in the spirit of my patron saint, Saint Thomas More, when he was visited in prison by his successor as chancellor of England, the egregious Thomas Cromwell. More was offered a return to his previous high office if he would only submit to King Henry VIII. He replied that he no longer wished to exist in the world of power, telling Cromwell: "My whole study shall be upon the passion of Christ." Addressing the graduates, I recalled those words and added my admonition about never trusting their government, to universal acclaim at this small college.

AS HE BEGAN his acceptance speech at the 2004 Democratic National Convention in Boston, the nominee snapped off a military salute: "I am John Kerry, and I am reporting for duty!"

My intuition was that Kerry was making a mistake playing the military card, but I did not realize how much he delivered himself into Republican hands until the Democratic convention was nearly finished. I was on the last *Crossfire* show from Boston on Thursday, July 29, when I broke a story. Greg Mueller, a right-wing publicist, tipped me about a forthcoming TV ad by some of Kerry's fellow Vietnam War swift boat veterans challenging his war record. Carville and Begala scoffed on the air, but I thought I detected unease on their part.

There was a further development I did not mention on the July 29 *Crossfire*. The conservative publishing house Regnery was about to publish *Unfit for Command*, a scathing deconstruction of Kerry's war record co-authored by John O'Neill, Kerry's fellow swift boat skipper and longtime critic. Like most Regnery books, *Unfit for Command* was not widely reviewed. But thanks to promotion on talk radio and discussion on the Internet, the book's sales forced repeated new printings that propelled it to the top of the best-seller lists.

A fellow swift boat veteran had turned up in Iowa before the caucuses to tell a story of how Lieutenant Kerry saved his life in Vietnam, and two of Kerry's enlisted crew members also vouched for his heroism. But Kerry's fellow naval officers who contributed to O'Neill's book insisted that the presidential candidate's war record was spurious, and there was documentation to support them. I contacted these critics, including a former naval medical officer who told me that he treated the wound suffered by Kerry for the first of his three Purple Hearts and that it was "only a scratch." The doctor added that enlisted men had described John Forbes Kerry vowing he would "come out of the war as the next JFK."

Cable television's combative talk shows were anxious to air this debate. Instead of putting on the former enlisted men in Kerry's crew who claimed firsthand experience of the long-ago incidents, the Kerry campaign used as its spokesman the Washington lawyer Lanny Davis. Davis did not really know the details and had not even looked at *Unfit for Command* when he went on TV and began making factual errors.

Davis had read the book by the time he confronted John O'Neill on *Crossfire* on August 12, with me as the conservative host. I always had liked Lanny but in a column of August 16, I wrote: "Bill Clinton's calm advocate had become a shouter for Kerry who accused critics of being liars." That was an understatement. On *Crossfire* Davis interrupted O'Neill with screaming denunciations. After the show, I apologized to O'Neill for this experience and Davis apologized to me for going over the line.

Lawyer Davis tried to reduce conflicting testimony down to a simple issue: credibility. He insisted nobody who actually was in a boat with Kerry when he was wounded ever joined the veterans attacking his war record. In *Unfit for Command*, O'Neill asserted that Lieutenant William Schachte (who would retire as a rear admiral) was aboard a small Boston whaler with Kerry on Kerry's first combat mission on December 2, 1968. Repeating on *Crossfire* what he wrote in the book, O'Neill said Schachte "witnessed Kerry, with an M-79 [grenade launcher], fire it and wound himself." O'Neill could barely get out those words before Davis interrupted him, yelling: "That was a false statement!"

Davis was relying on the memories of two enlisted men who appeared with Kerry on the podium at the Democratic National Convention. They said there was no other officer aboard the boat thirty-five years earlier. They repeated that when I phoned them, but neither knew whether there was enemy fire or how Kerry was wounded.

Since Davis was basing Kerry's overall credibility on whether Schachte was aboard the Boston whaler, I thought it imperative to get hold of the admiral. After some difficulty, I contacted him at his home in Charleston, South Carolina, on Thursday, August 26, the week before the Republican National Convention convened in New York. Schachte told me he was politically independent, had not been contacted by the Bush campaign or any

Republican organization, and did not want to get involved. But after watching Lanny Davis's tirade on *Crossfire,* he told me, he had to speak out.

The admiral described to me Kerry's first taste of combat in the early morning of December 2, 1968, when the Boston whaler (he called it a "skimmer") operated close to the Mekong River shore in a technique that Schachte had designed. Schachte said that Kerry's M-16 rifle jammed and the new officer picked up an M-79 grenade launcher. "I heard a 'thunk,' " he said. "There was no fire from the enemy. Kerry nicked himself with an M-79. Kerry requested a Purple Heart."

But was Schachte really aboard Kerry's boat? "I was absolutely in the skimmer," he told me. It "was not possible," he said, for Kerry to have been the only officer aboard the Boston whaler on his first combat mission. I phoned two other officers, one of them Schachte's commander, who both said Schachte always was aboard the skimmer on such missions. The commanding officer said he had told Kerry to "forget it" when he asked for a Purple Heart, and the other officer said Schachte had told him the wound was not enemy-inflicted. All this I reported in a "bonus" column for Friday, August 27.

During this period, I learned the Kerry campaign was furious at me and was preparing a counterattack. Instead of rebutting what I had said or written, Kerry agents started leaking to reporters the fact that my son Alex worked for Regnery. I counted the days before I would hear from Jacques Steinberg, who covered the media for the *New York Times.*

The call from Steinberg came August 27, the day my interview with Admiral Schachte ran in the *New York Post.* Steinberg indicated he was planning a big takeout on me and had many questions that included one about my son. The question about Alex turned out to be all he wrote about me— a 153-word item in his "MediaTalk" column on Monday, August 30. Noting that I had commended *Unfit for Command* and John O'Neill, Steinberg wrote: "Unmentioned in Mr. Novak's columns and television appearances, however, is a personal connection he has to the book: his son, Alex Novak, is director of marketing for its publisher, the conservative publishing house Regnery. In a telephone interview, Robert Novak said he saw no need to disclose this link. 'I don't think it's relevant,' he said."

A few days later I was called by the *Washington Post*'s Fred Hiatt, who gently suggested I might want to disclose that link in one of my columns that ran in the *Post.* On September 6, this ran as a footnote to my column:

In response to queries by readers: My son, Alex Novak, is director of marketing for Regnery Publishing Inc., publisher of "Unfit for Command." He is 36 years old and has been employed at Regnery for six years, since receiving his MBA from the University of Maryland. He has had no connection with my reporting about "Unfit for Command," a best-selling book dealing with Sen. Kerry's war record whose news value is obvious. I plan to continue to pursue this story as developments warrant.

NEW YORK WAS a strange place for a Republican convention in 2004. The anti-Republican, anti-Bush animus created what I described in the column as the most "unpleasant" atmosphere I had seen at any national political convention (worse than the Chicago Democratic convention of 1968). On the streets of Manhattan, delegates (and reporters who were mistaken for delegates) were called "Nazis," "fascists," and worse. I got special treatment, as I wrote in a postconvention column:

> Many demonstrators recognized me from my TV appearances and condemned me as a "traitor" because of the CIA leak case, some suggesting I should kill myself. I had to resort to using a security escort to move a short distance to fulfill commitments for CNN.

Anytime I set foot on the streets of the city, I encountered abusive and obscene shouts. But it did not begin in New York.

Outdoors in the freezing cold at Cedar Rapids, Iowa, Paul Begala and I were waiting to do *Crossfire* live when a plump, smiley, forty-something Iowa matron approached Begala to tell him how much she liked *Crossfire*. She told him she would like to meet me, and Paul obliged. When I extended my arm to shake hands, she withheld hers and said: "You're a traitor—a traitor! You should be in prison!"

When the Democratic candidates and *Crossfire* moved from Iowa to New Hampshire, an unemployed anti-Bush activist named Brad Carr was there to stalk me. As Begala and I were shooting *Crossfire* at the Merrimack Diner in Manchester on primary day, January 27, Carr positioned himself behind the camera, repeatedly shouting "traitor" and "scumbag"—two of the Left's favorite epithets for me. He followed me out of the diner as the *Crossfire* crew walked toward the CNN bus. Screaming obscenities, he then gave me a hard shove. Infuriated I turned and half swung, half shoved back. At age fifty-four, he was eighteen years my junior and a good deal stockier. But in the scuffle, he went down.

Anti-Bush bloggers on the Internet made this the day's big story, eclipsing Kerry's New Hampshire victory. Takebackthemedia.com headlined:

"Bob Novak assaults man in New Hampshire! Contact CNN and tell them you don't like it!" I thought the little incident had escaped mainstream news media attention until I got a call a week later from the *Washington Post* gossip columnist Richard Leiby saying that Carr might file assault charges against me if I did not apologize. I replied: "I'm sorry it happened—if that's an apology." Carr did not press charges, but I never thought he would.

It was not just anonymous hecklers who gave me trouble about the CIA leak case when I was on the road. I was attending a *New York Times* party the weekend before the Democratic convention in Boston when I found myself in close proximity to John McLaughlin. I had not talked to McLaughlin for many years, but John put his face close to mine, and without a single word of salutation, asked: "Who was your source on Valerie Plame?" I put my mouth to his ear and said: "Fuck you!" McLaughlin issued his familiar cackle as I walked away.

I HAD TRIMMED my political travel in 2000, and now in 2004 at age seventy-three, I planned to cut back more. However, what happened on the early morning of September 31 demolished even limited travel plans.

I was in Coral Gables, Florida, on Thursday, September 30, for the first Bush-Kerry debate at the University of Miami. Bush, not much of a debater at his best, was at his worst at Coral Gables. It was past eleven o'clock when I got back to the Hyatt Regency, and I intended to go straight to my room to start my column for Monday's newspapers. But the Republican pollster Frank Luntz, in the lobby cocktail lounge, gave me the high sign. Luntz told me he had fascinating results from his debate focus groups. I sat down for my first drink of the day and learned Bush may have done even worse than I believed. Luntz's ordinary voters were turned off by the Bush smirk and his complaining that the presidency was such "hard work."

I got to my room exhausted, shortly before midnight, anticipating a short night. I had agreed to be a panelist discussing the 2004 campaign the next day at the annual conference in Aspen, Colorado, put on by Forstman Little, the New York investment banking firm. Teddy Forstman was sending a private jet to fly me to Colorado, with a limo picking me up at the Hyatt Regency at six a.m. for a seven o'clock takeoff. I caught a little sleep before getting up early to begin my column. I answered a three thirty a.m. wakeup call, and began the column under a Coral Gables dateline:

Depression among Democrats had reached new depths when the presidential candidates faced off Thursday night at the University of

Miami. An hour and a half later, they were elated that John Kerry's candidacy had been saved. But none of the Democratic candidate's shortcomings had been corrected.

Rather, the rise in Democratic spirits can be attributed to George W. Bush's defects in the first presidential debate. His stylistic deficiencies as a candidate in 2000, it turns out, have not been remedied. He was anything but relentless in exploiting his opponent's multiple weaknesses.

The gap in performance here between Bush and Kerry hardly seemed wide enough to reverse the popular tide that had been flowing in the President's direction. Nevertheless, it was enough to still the exuberant optimism in Republican ranks. With two more debates and a month to go before the election, Bush has serious problems to solve.

By five a.m., I had written about half the 690-word column, and went into the spacious bathroom of my deluxe bedroom to shave and then take my usual long shower. It was just before five thirty when I emerged from the shower, sopping wet, and fell on the wet tile floor.

The pain was intense, and I knew from past experience that I had broken my hip—the right one this time. The shower, where I had fallen, was at the far end of the long bathroom. To my horror, I discovered there was no phone in the bathroom, unusual for a luxury hotel. My cell phone was far away in the bedroom.

Wracked with pain, I decided my only course was to crawl naked and crippled to the bedside phone. That entailed inching my way down the entire length of the bathroom, then turning when I arrived in the bedroom to crawl the same distance to the phone. Fire department paramedics, summoned by the hotel and arriving quickly, expressed astonishment that I (meaning an old guy like me) could have made that journey.

The emergency room at Doctors Hospital was empty and the hospital staff could not have been more efficient or more courteous. Dr. Jack Cooper, one of South Florida's top orthopedic surgeons, recommended a hip replacement but waited to perform the operation until Geraldine could fly down from Washington. I had been through three cancer surgeries, spinal meningitis and multiple broken bones. But never before had I experienced such agony as I did at Coral Gables. Complications abounded, including a blood clot in my leg. But Dr. Cooper and the other physicians were terrific.

Groggy as I was, I still had my Monday column to wrap up. That meant I had to finish the column on Saturday writing on my laptop from my hospital bed the day after surgery. I found it hard to write without typos, and I repeatedly dozed off. It took me more than four hours to write the final 350 words of the column. The final version read no worse than usual, concluding: "Can a front-runner really lose the election because of poor debating skills? He might if the debate exposes the candidate's basic flaws. That's why Bush supporters are worried about the town hall debate Friday in St. Louis." (Bush did well enough in that debate and the third debate at Mesa, Arizona, to remove oratorical skills as a major factor in the election.)

On Friday, October 15, one week after my surgery, a flying ambulance transported me to Washington's Dulles airport. It was a small jet in which Geraldine, a paramedic, and a nurse crowded in around my stretcher. An ambulance took me to the George Washington University Hospital, where I would spend another week before I could go home.

Being in a hospital bed did not keep me from making calls to political sources and writing my three-a-week column. CNN executive producer Sam Feist had me join the network's analysts, via telephone, after the Friday night presidential debate. It was my first night at GW, and I felt lousy. After the debate, I had to undergo a complete blood transfusion that kept me awake much of the night.

The high point of my stay at GW came when Zelda brought me a tape of one of my favorite movies, *The Leopard* (1962) starring Burt Lancaster. She rented the much superior Italian-language version (with subtitles) instead of the English dub. It is a neglected masterpiece, perhaps because of its conservative theme. Its hero is a nineteenth-century Sicilian nobleman who deplores the affectations of the risorgimento's bourgeois politicians and liberal reformers. It rings true to me after observing firsthand a half century of sophistry.

BY ELECTION DAY 2004 on November 2, I was still wheelchair-bound but had recovered sufficiently to go to New York (by chauffeur-driven sedan) to join my three *Crossfire* cohorts on CNN's coverage that night. It was a close election, but careful tracking of the electoral vote by the *Evans-Novak Political Report* never had Bush behind—even after his horrid performance at Coral Gables. Yet, the other three *Crossfire* hosts all publicly predicted a Kerry win. Carville and Begala, of course, did so as a matter of theology. But Tucker Carlson, I believe, was a hard-core McCain backer who just did not like Bush. I don't think he ever broke down the 2004 campaign state by state but delivered his gut opinion that Bush was a loser.

When Geraldine and I arrived at the CNN studios in the Time-Warner building, a celebration was in place. Early exit polls suggested a Kerry landslide, reversing Bush's 2000 wins in Ohio and Florida—in Ohio by a huge margin. CNN staffers were ecstatic. I got Bob Shrum on the phone, and he was in a state of delight. Knowing I had to rehash the election for Thursday's newspapers, Bob was only too happy to list the mistakes by Bush and Karl Rove that led to their demise.

But, as in 2002, the exit polls were wrong. The *Evans-Novak Political Report,* in contrast, was as close to being perfect as it ever had been. *ENPR*'s heavy lifting for 2004 was done by Tim Carney, maybe my best political reporter since I began hiring them in 1982. We were wrong on only two out of fifty states, calling it 276 to 262 in electoral votes compared to the actual outcome of 286 to 252. We missed only one out of thirty-seven Senate races, forecasting a Republican gain of three seats instead of the actual four. Out of 430 contested House seats, we missed two that cancelled each other out so that the *ENPR* was right on the three-seat Republican pickup.

How could we be so right and the Democrats so wrong? They could not blame exit polls, because Democrats had been predicting victory for weeks. I gave my explanation in my Thursday column, written on deadline in my New York hotel room Wednesday morning after a long election night:

> Rove was correct and Democrats guessed wrong in guessing the American mood. A symptom was Democratic belief that former Rep. Tom Coburn of Oklahoma and Rep. Jim DeMint in South Carolina were just too conservative to defeat moderate Democrats for the Senate. In fact, each won easily.
>
> The electorate is simply too conservative for the Democrats, as shown by the defeat of Senate Minority Leader Tom Daschle in South Dakota. The formula of taking the straight liberal line in Washington and talking conservative at home does not work when a Democrat's every move becomes visible as a member of the leadership.

The gradual political realignment, which I had been watching for four decades and writing about in this memoir almost from the beginning, reached its apex on election day, November 2, 2004. Not only did President Bush carry all eleven states of the old Confederacy, but eighteen of the region's twenty-two senators now were Republicans after the gain of previously Democratic-held seats in Georgia, Louisiana, North Carolina, and South Carolina. "Domination of Congress by the GOP now enters its second decade," I wrote, "with Democrats largely restricted to enclaves on both coasts and some Midwestern industrial states."

I did not write, however, that all realignment comes to an end and begins to erode when the majority party runs out of things to say. I felt that time was fast approaching.

GEORGE W. BUSH was off to a slow start in his second term. He chose not to reconstruct his cabinet, did not order a quick withdrawal from Iraq to let the Iraqis sort out their own problems, and did not put flesh on the bare bones of his Social Security and tax reform initiatives. In contrast, Jonathan Klein, the new president of CNN/US (announced on November 22, 2004), moved quickly to effect dramatic change.

Former CBS executive Jon Klein was well known in the Manhattan-Hollywood TV world, but I had never heard of him. I would come to regard Klein as less interested in politics and government than any other major news executive I had known. But he was familiar with the *Crossfire* of Friday, October 15, 2004, which turned out to be one of the most influential broadcasts in the program's twenty-three-year history. The producers booked a single guest: Jon Stewart, host of *The Daily Show,* a popular program on the cable network Comedy Central.

Stewart was the first comedian to be on *Crossfire* except for entertainers like Mark Russell brought in for holiday programs. While Russell was a good-natured tweaker of Republicans and Democrats, Stewart was a left-wing ideologue obsessed with demeaning President Bush. A secondary target for Stewart was *Crossfire* in general and me in particular because of the CIA leak case.

If I was Stewart's principal *Crossfire* target, why wasn't I—instead of Tucker Carlson—the conservative host questioning him October 15? First, at the hour when Stewart sat across from Begala and Carlson at George Washington University's Morton Auditorium, I was a couple blocks away in a bed at GW Hospital awaiting a blood transfusion. Second, I am sure the producers knew that I never would have appeared on the program with Stewart and would have vigorously argued against scheduling him. I thought booking Stewart constituted a cheap grab for ratings, a mind-set hastening the decline of *Crossfire.*

Smart as he is, Tucker Carlson never anticipated he was walking into an ambush. Stewart took Carlson and Begala to the cleaners, telling them to "stop, stop, stop hurting America" and pleading for more "civilized discourse" on television's political programs. "You are partisan—what do you call it?—hacks," he told my colleagues.

The morning papers of January 6, 2005, reported Klein announcing cancellation of *Crossfire* at an undetermined time in the near future (it would be June 1). It was not just that Klein axed *Crossfire* unexpectedly but what he said in doing so. In talking to the nation's writers covering the news media, he repeatedly quoted and endorsed Jon Stewart's criticism of what had been CNN's longest-standing daily feature that still attracted relatively high ratings even though it had been withdrawn from prime time. "I agree wholeheartedly with Jon Stewart's overall premise," Klein said, adding he was opposed to "head-butting debate" and referred to *Crossfire* as "a bunch of guys screaming at each other." He broke the old rule that a TV executive does not denigrate his own product—even after he has cancelled it.

At the same time, Klein revealed that Tucker Carlson was leaving and gave the impression that he was being fired ("We just determined there was not a role here in the way Tucker wanted his career to go."). Actually I can testify that Carlson had become very unhappy. He had wanted to leave the previous April but had been prevailed on to stay through the 2004 elections and now had cut a deal with MSNBC for his own program. Reversing the old saw, CNN seemed to be saying to Tucker: "You can't quit! You're fired!" Most newspaper accounts suggested that Carlson had been sacked, except for the *Washington Post*'s Howard Kurtz, who concluded correctly: "Carlson's defection was a coup for MSNBC."

Kurtz's January 6 account contained additional news that no one else had: "The network also plans to end *Capital Gang*, the long-running Saturday night panel show created by Novak, later this year" (June 25, as it turned out). That was an even bigger surprise to everybody, including me, than the *Crossfire* cancellation. The program's rating still led all CNN weekend programs, and was one of the network's rare presentations that was competitive with high-flying Fox in its time slot. *Capital Gang* never had been accused, as *Crossfire* was, of being a shout program. It was popular in Washington. So why kill it? The answer was that Jon Klein just did not like politics. *Inside Politics,* also quite popular in Washington, was scheduled for the axe after its moderator, Judy Woodruff, left CNN.

Klein talked publicly about getting CNN into "roll up your sleeves story-telling" and said CNN on-air personalities should have more of the Bronx in them. I had no idea what he was talking about, and I doubt Klein knew exactly what he wanted beyond an end to political talk on his network. When the left-wing editorial voice of the *New York Times* praised Klein for siding with a comedian against *Crossfire*, there was no stopping him. Whenever asked, he would talk publicly about rebuilding CNN through deconstruction of its political shows.

"It's gotten to the point," I told Klein on February 17, "where I am embarrassed being associated with CNN." That was hyperbole, but I also regarded it as my tacit letter of resignation from the network I had served for a quarter century if Klein chose to accept it that way. It didn't worry me. Donald Regan used to talk about "f-u money"—about having enough money in the bank that you could say "f-u" to your boss and walk out. I believe Regan, in terms of 2005, would be talking about upward of fifty million dollars. While I was not even faintly close to that category, as a journalist I had accumulated—to my surprise, at age seventy-four—a net worth in the high single-digit millions. I did not need the job.

But Klein did not respond by firing me or even rebuking me. "We venerate you for all you have done for us," he told me with a straight face. Actually, the end of my CNN tenure was in sight.

The next time I heard from Klein came one morning the next month with a call placed to my cell phone. In my previous meetings, the CNN president's voice had been calm and friendly. Now he sounded frantic. "Why would you do this?" he asked. "It is wrong to attack the company's decisions in public." He was talking about a quote attributed to me in "What About Novak?" a forthcoming *Vanity Fair* profile by David Margolick. I replied that I had not yet seen the magazine and could not even remember what I told my interviewer. That was the absolute truth, but I think Klein was incredulous as he quickly terminated the conversation.

What had I told Margolick, a hostile left-wing journalist who had interviewed me in my office? When I located a copy of *Vanity Fair,* I found this paragraph:

> He [Novak] faults CNN president Jonathan Klein for endorsing Jon Stewart's criticism of Crossfire, which helped kill the show. "I thought it was stupid, and that's on the record," he says. . . . He ridicules CNN's folly in canceling what he insists are two highly rated programs.

That's all there was that had so antagonized Klein. The message was that he was more interested in his public image than anything else.

As I have made clear in this memoir, my attitude toward *Crossfire* always had been ambivalent. My affection for *Capital Gang,* on the other hand, was unequivocal and unconditional. I think its regular viewers were disconsolate, evidenced by thousands of e-mails protesting the cancellation.

After the program's demise was decreed, I called the Fox News Channel chief Roger Ailes to see if he had any interest in *Capital Gang.* He had been eager for the program eight years earlier when he nearly outbid CNN for my services, but not now. He explained politely that Fox, which had come from far behind against CNN in 1997 ratings to enjoy a widening lead in 2005, had a set program schedule that he did not want to alter. I next asked my *Gang* colleagues whether they wanted me to try to find a home else-where for the program, and they said they did not.

CNN wanted to do a big Washington farewell party for us, but my col-leagues had a sour taste and declined. Instead, Al Hunt put on a terrific party at his and his wife Judy Woodruff's large home in the Cleveland Park section of Washington. Many of the big-name *Capital Gang* guests at-tended. They included the guest for our pilot, Ambassador Robert S. Strauss, and the guest at our first program, former Speaker Thomas Foley. They included CNN staffers, headed by producer Deborah Nelson—all of whom worked so hard for *Capital Gang.* They did not include any CNN executives from Washington, Atlanta, or New York.

WITH THE DEMISE of *Crossfire* and *Capital Gang,* I was down to one reg-ularly scheduled CNN program, the seven-minute *The Novak Zone,* which would be cancelled at the end of July. My other duty was to come in a cou-ple of afternoons each week and be paired off with a liberal in what CNN billed as the *Strategy Session.*

Notwithstanding Klein's attitude toward *Crossfire,* CNN was wedded to the Right-versus-Left format for commentators and was not going to let me appear alone. I objected to the *Strategy Session* rubric for my duel with lib-erals. I was a reporter and an analyst, not a political strategist. It was ex-plained to me that the *Strategy Session* graphics had already been prepared. At least, I asked, could I be excused from appearing opposite Carville or Be-gala, who indeed were Democratic strategists? They would try, I was told.

With annual escalators, my yearly pay from CNN had reached $625,000 (my largest single source of income). That was not out of line in the world of cable television considering the workload I was carrying before the cancellation of *Crossfire, Capital Gang,* and *The Novak Zone.* But after they were all gone, I was overpaid.

When Klein appeared before the Television Critics Association in Bev-erly Hills, California, on July 17, the very first question was: "Why does Robert Novak continue to be employed by CNN?" He answered "It would be awfully presumptuous of us to take steps against a guy and his career based on second, third, fourth-handed reporting." What that meant I have no idea. When Klein called me "one of the most outstanding political re-porters this country has ever known," I felt like the baseball manager who gets a vote of confidence from the owner just before he is fired.

ON AUGUST 4, 2005, I made what had become an increasingly rare ap-pearance on CNN. The network had decided not to put me on any day when there was the slightest morsel of news about the CIA leak case since I would not answer any questions about it. That meant a majority of my *Strategy Session* appearances were cancelled.

The news of August 4 was leak-free, so I was scheduled to go on CNN. The problem was that I was paired with James Carville. Producers explained that Carville was the only person available August 4, and against my better judgment, I agreed to go ahead.

I was told that Ed Henry, CNN's young congressional correspondent, was anchoring that afternoon and would end the session by asking me just one question about the leak case based on my July 27 column: Did I really get Valerie Plame's name from *Who's Who in America*? I had revealed this fact many times dating back to 2003, and I figured there was no harm in revealing it once again.

As Carville and I waited to go on the air, I told him that I had heard his friend, the sports columnist Tony Kornheiser, comment on the radio that I was always sucking up to George W. Bush. I enjoyed Kornheiser's wit, but he was a reflexive liberal who knew nothing about politics. When I asked Carville to set Kornheiser straight about me, James replied: "Well, hasn't he got that right?" Carville, of course, was well aware of my frequent criticism of Bush. As wild as he was on camera, James usually was civilized in private conversation. If he was playing the Ragin' Cajun *off*-camera this day, I should have been prepared for the worst.

It came near the end of our segment when Carville rejoiced over news that the controversial congresswoman Katherine Harris now appeared assured of the Republican nomination for the U.S. Senate in Florida. Carville launched an abusive, sarcastic attack on her. "Don't be too sure she's going to lose," I said. As I tried to offer my theory that antiestablishment Republicans often do better than expected, Carville interrupted, in his high-pitched Louisiana accent, to claim I was trying to curry favor with the editorial page of the *Wall Street Journal*. I had been under the impression that James was not supposed to launch these tirades under the new *Strategy Session* format. "Just let me finish what I'm going to say, James," I said. "Please, I know you hate to hear me, but you have—" Before I could finish that, a shouting Carville overrode what I had to say. "He's got to show these right-wingers that he's got backbone," Carville yelled. "Show them you're tough." Two and one-half years of coping with Carville's ad hominem attacks welled up in me. "Well, I think that's bullshit," I said. "And I hate that. Just let it go." I removed my microphone and stalked off the set.

At the end of the segment, Henry said: "I'm sorry as well that Bob Novak obviously left the set a little early. I had told him in advance that we were going to ask him about the CIA leak case." I could not believe that he was suggesting I left the set to avoid being asked about *Who's Who*. A few minutes later, I asked Henry why in the world he would say that about me on the air. "What else was I to think?" he asked. I had been dubious when the obsequious Henry told me how thrilled he was to work with an old pro like me, and now my suspicions were confirmed that he was a duplicitous phony.

I apologized immediately to CNN management, but the network's public statement called my conduct "unacceptable." Klein defended Carville's comments as appropriate, and the word was put out that I was off CNN air indefinitely. I did not think I had committed a hanging offense. Mark Shields in the past had twice used the same obscenity I employed, once on *Crossfire* and once on *Capital Gang*, without comment by management. Klein's favorite TV critic, Jon Stewart, used much worse language in describing me. Indeed, I received a lot of favorable comment from conservatives who commented how pleased they were that I had finally told Carville how obnoxious he was.

I heard nothing from CNN until Klein called me about a week later. He was none too friendly, suggesting I take off the rest of August, adding we would regroup after Labor Day. I knew it was over. My outburst had taken CNN off the hook, and now it could get rid of me without fear of looking bad for firing their house conservative. Actually, it was a blessing for both CNN and me, and I felt an immediate sense of relief.

I did not hear again from Jon Klein until late September, and he did not waste time in our phone conversation. "We are not going to renew your contract next year," he told me. The truth was that CNN did not want me to work for it anymore, and I did not want to work for CNN anymore. CNN offered me a generous termination settlement that was not required under my contract, but stipulated that the details be kept secret. I agreed not to "intentionally disparage" CNN, and I believe I have adhered to that agreement.

Sam Feist had always promised that my departure from CNN would be a soft landing and scheduled an extended appearance for me Friday, December 30, on *The Situation Room* (the new afternoon program). But first there was one more incident connected with the leak case, thanks to my big mouth.

ON TUESDAY, DECEMBER 13, 2005, I traveled to Raleigh, North Carolina, to deliver my biennial luncheon speech to the John Locke Foundation, a conservative think tank. These appearances had been uneventful, and not a word I uttered had appeared in print. That may be why I threw caution to the winds on the very last question of the q-and-a period following my speech.

The question dealt with the leak case, the first mention of it during my appearance in Raleigh. I declared: "I'm confident the President knows who the source is. I'd be amazed if he doesn't. So, I say: 'Don't bug me. Don't bug Bob Woodward [who recently had said he also had been told of Valerie Wilson's identity]. Bug the President as to whether he should reveal who the source is.'" I added that my own role in the case had "snowballed out of proportion" thanks to a "campaign by the Left." I also charged "extremely bad management of the issue by the White House. Once you give an issue to a special protector, you lose control [over] it."

To my embarrassment, everything I said was reported in the *Raleigh News and Observer* the next morning. The story went all over the country, with the White House spokesman pressed for comment. Democrats called on Bush to reveal the name of the leaker.

As luck would have it, Geraldine and I were scheduled to be at the White House for a Christmas party for the media the next evening, December 15. Geraldine thought it might be better to just not show up, but I wanted to go. I had been cut off all the White House briefing lists since the CIA leak case broke, and the Christmas parties were my sole contact with the president. When Geraldine went through the receiving line at White House Christmas parties, Bush always gave her a jocular greeting noting that she was from Hillsboro (not far from his ranch). This time he called her "the Hillsboro Flash." As for what I said in Raleigh, he told me: "You put me on the spot." "I'm sorry, Mr. President," I replied. "Don't worry about it," he said.

On my CNN farewell appearance, Wolf Blitzer asked me about my comments in Raleigh. "I didn't think there were any reporters there," I said, adding: "That was really a dumb thing to say." Wolf pressed me on this, then trotted out the same tired old questions on the leak case that evoked the same tired old nonanswers from me. Sam Feist had told me the case would be mentioned only briefly in the introduction of what would be a retrospective of my twenty-five years at CNN, and I half believed him. In fact, Blitzer was nearly as adversarial as he had been the last time.

Bruce Morton, an old hand in TV and a real artist (who also was to join Judy Woodruff and me going out the door of CNN), did a beautiful package on me that included this:

He has a nickname, the Prince of Darkness, and likes to cause trouble and stir up strife, he said once . . . In public, at any rate, they take no prisoners. . . . His game is hardball. Since he's nicknamed a prince, I thought about saying goodbye in Shakespeare's phrase, "Good night, sweet prince." But, then, I thought, no, Bob would object to sweet, and he would be right.

I had a final thought myself after Wolf finished questioning me:

I want to thank CNN for making this network available to me for twenty-five years. Never censored me once—ever. And I said some outrageous things. . . . I think I worked hard for CNN, but it was a wonderful opportunity, and I want to thank them.

I wanted to finish a quarter of a century on a positive note, and so did CNN—especially Jim Walton, who was Jon Klein's boss as head of the CNN Group. He called me in December to propose a CNN farewell party, inviting top officials and politicians. I thanked him but felt I had to tell him that I was going to Fox News Channel, CNN's bitter competitor, as a contributor. Walton seemed to be taken aback by that, as if he thought I was leaving TV as well as CNN. I said I would prefer a party limited to the people who had worked with me at CNN starting in 1980: executives, broadcasters, producers, directors, cameramen, and makeup artists. I wanted no celebrities. This, I stressed, was not a retirement party.

The party was held January 26, 2006, at Charlie Palmer's Steakhouse, a swish lobbyist hangout at the end of Pennsylvania Avenue near Capitol Hill. Jim Walton came up from Atlanta for the event, bringing greetings from Ted Turner and Tom Johnson and extravagant praise (calling me a CNN "icon"). Jonathan Klein did not come down from New York, and sent no message. I think we both agreed that was appropriate.

IN JULY, Special Counsel Fitzgerald finally gave Jim Hamilton the green light. He was through with me, and I could speak out on the CIA leak case. I promptly wrote a column revealing everything but the identity of Richard Armitage as my primary source. That did not happen until he was clearly identified in *Hubris,* the anti-Bush screed by journalists Michael Isikoff and David Corn. Armitage then belatedly identified himself.

I was exonerated, as signaled by a remarkable *Washington Post* editorial that suggested Joe Wilson was "the person most responsible for the end of

Ms. Plame's CIA career." It concluded: "[Wilson] diverted responsibility from himself and his false charges by claiming that President Bush's closest aides had engaged in an illegal conspiracy. It's unfortunate that so many people took him seriously."

I had to write one more column about the case, on September 14, because of Armitage's false account of his answer to me when I asked why the CIA sent Wilson to Niger: "I don't know, but I think his wife worked out there." I related what he really told me ("His wife works at CIA, and she suggested that he be sent to Niger." "His wife works at CIA?" I asked. "Yeah, in counterproliferation."). I concluded: "Armitage's silence for . . . 2½ years caused intense pain for his colleagues in government and enabled partisan Democrats in Congress to falsely accuse Rove of being my primary source. . . . Armitage's tardy self-disclosure is tainted because it is deceptive."

On September 19, I received a telephone call from Karl Rove to volunteer some information about a column he heard I was about to write. That broke a three-year absence of substantive conversation between us that had been imposed by Rove's lawyers. I doubted that our intimacy ever could be restored, but his unsolicited call confirmed that the case was closed.

THE BEST EFFORTS of the White House and the Republican leadership were unable to prevent the 2006 midterm elections from being a referendum on an unpopular war and an unpopular president. The day before the election, I reported in the column that the outcome would be "either bad or very bad" for Republicans. More specifically, the *Evans-Novak Political Report* forecast (based mainly on the work of my reporter, David Freddoso) the Democrats gaining twenty House seats, losing control there for the first time in twelve years, and five Senate seats, one short of a majority.

It was worse than that for Republicans, giving up control of both houses (with loss of thirty seats in the House and six in the Senate). The Republicans looked dead in New York, Pennsylvania, Ohio, Illinois, Michigan, New Jersey, and California. They seemed to be healthy only in the states of the old Confederacy. The national electoral map looked like the mirror image of what it was in the 1920s, when Democrats were confined to the Solid South. The long, slow realignment of the past thirty-eight years had finally run its course. At age seventy-five I was still around to report a new phase of American political history.

CHAPTER 46

A Stirrer-up of Strife

IN THE IMAGE of Bertrans de Born, I have been a stirrer up of strife—
for half a century. But I was not merely causing trouble for trouble's sake.
Nor was I only interested in getting the news first. Over more than half a
century, I had become an advocate of small government, low taxes, individual economic freedom, civil liberties, defense preparedness, restraint in foreign policy, free trade, and against reliance on politicians.

As my children, Alexander and Zelda, hosted my seventy-fifth black-tie
birthday celebration on February 26, 2006, at the Stephen Decatur House,
I was no more a congenial figure than I had been as a scrappy young reporter for the Associated Press. Thanks to the CIA leak case, I came over as
more disreputable than ever.

Few honors had been bestowed on me, and I expected none at the end
of my career. In 2001, I did receive the National Press Club's Fourth Estate
Award for lifetime achievement in journalism. Walter Cronkite of CBS
News won the first award in 1973, setting the model for people who usually
are so honored. In thirty-three years through 2006, the only conservative
other than I to win the award was my patron, Vermont Connecticut Royster of the *Wall Street Journal,* in 1978. The only reason I won, I believe, is
that some of my pals from the Gridiron Club were on the Press Club committee and cooked the books. That's the way Washington works.

I am grateful for a lot more than journalism awards. As a husband, father, and grandfather, I feel blessed to have become a Catholic communicant, even so late in life. At this writing a growth on my kidney is probably
cancerous but is not getting larger and is the object of close observation.
That would be my fourth cancer. The third cancer, on a kidney, was discovered by the great cancer doctor Dr. Donald Morton at the John Wayne
Cancer Institute in Santa Monica, California, and was removed at the Johns
Hopkins Hospital in Baltimore by a brilliant young surgeon, Dr. Stephen

Solomon, on December 23, 2003. I was back in Washington that night for a Christmas party at our apartment attended by my seven grandchildren. Modern medicine is amazing. Beyond the wonders of medicine, I believe that my escape from so many serious illnesses shows the Lord has a purpose for me, and I hope I am trying to fulfill it.

Memoirists often are explicit in reporting their skimpy salaries in their early years and become reticent when monetary success comes. Breaking that pattern, I will disclose that my adjusted gross income for 2004 reached a high of $1.2 million. That may be less than some people thought I was making, but it was vastly more money than an old newspaperman could conceive.

I made a lot less than that in 2006. My profile for Fox News was much smaller than it had been at CNN, but I was treated with respect and permitted to deliver commentaries by myself without debating left-wing counterparts. The CIA leak case did not keep me off the air there as it had at CNN. I also became a TV commentator for Bloomberg News, working with old CNN colleagues Margaret Carlson and Al Hunt. My workload was diminished to a level appropriate for a seventy-five-year-old. I had more time for my column, which several readers actually told me had improved after I left CNN.

I am grateful for much more than material success. I am grateful for my family, my faith, my country, and having so much fun at the only trade in which I could imagine succeeding. I'd like to think that I emulated Bertrans de Born in stirring up strife but not in wreaking havoc, so that I will avoid an eternity in purgatory with my head in my hand. At least I hope so.

AUTHOR'S NOTE

In this memoir of my half century of Washington journalism, I have tried to combine three elements: my personal experiences as a columnist and commentator, my interactions with the famous and powerful, and the nation's political developments over those fifty years (including the historic political realignment). That's a lot of ground to cover, and my original manuscript would have translated into a fourteen hundred-page book.

Writing a reporter's memoir raises the question of revealing sources who are still alive. I requested the sources for some of my most important and controversial stories to permit me to use their names. Their responses were mixed, and I have heeded the wishes of those who wanted their identity kept secret. I have revealed the names of other living sources without asking permission because I felt that the material divulged was not that sensitive or that so much time had passed that no great damage would be done.

My assistants, Stefanie Hohn and later Christina Holder, performed research for me beginning in 2003. My reporters, Timothy Carney and later David Freddoso, edited the first drafts of chapters. The journalist Christopher Caldwell, my son-in-law, cut down the early chapters and set a pattern for me to follow in making my first reduction. The major editing to get the book to publishable size was performed by William Schulz, who had edited my *Reader's Digest* articles for many years.

Esther Newberg, my longtime agent, convinced me that a full-scale memoir was preferable to a collection of my writings plus explanations. Jed Donahue, my editor at Crown Forum, has been patient, enthusiastic, and helpful. My officer manager, Kathleen Connolly, and my wife, Geraldine Williams Novak, provided me invaluable support in a process that required nearly four years.

ROBERT D. NOVAK
Washington, D.C.
March 2007

INDEX